SOURCES FOR THE HISTORY

OF

BRITISH INDIA

IN THE SEVENTEENTH CENTURY

BY

SHAFAAT AHMAD KHAN

Litt.D., F.R.Hist.S.

UNIVERSITY PROFESSOR OF MODERN INDIAN HISTORY, ALLAHABAD
MEMBER OF THE UNITED PROVINCES LEGISLATIVE COUNCIL
AUTHOR OF *The East India Trade in the Seventeenth Century*

CURZON PRESS : LONDON
ROWMAN AND LITTLEFIELD : TOTOWA

First published 1926
New impression 1975

Curzon Press Ltd : London and Dublin
and
Rowman and Littlefield : Totowa : N.J.

ISBN
UK 0 7007 0047 1
US 0 87471 562 8

Library of Congress
Cataloguing in Publication
CD1042.A2K47 1974 016.95403 74-8129

Printed in Great Britain by
Lewis Reprints Ltd., London and Tonbridge

SOURCES FOR THE HISTORY OF BRITISH INDIA IN THE SEVENTEENTH CENTURY

ALLAHABAD UNIVERSITY STUDIES IN HISTORY

Issued Under The Direction Of

SHAFAAT AHMAD KHAN, Litt.D.,

University Professor of Modern Indian History

VOLUME IV

SOURCES FOR THE HISTORY OF BRITISH INDIA IN THE SEVENTEENTH CENTURY

BY

SHAFAAT AHMAD KHAN

PREFACE

THIS book is neither a catalogue of libraries and record offices, nor is it a selection of transcripts from the English and Indian archives. The object of the undertaking is twofold: in the first place, it aims at supplying a critical analysis of essential data for the study of seventeenth century British India; in the second place, it aims at bringing within one purview all the materials lying scattered in various record offices in England.

I started my enquiries into the history of the East India trade in the seventeenth century about ten years ago, and after six years of work in the Public Record Office, the India Office Library and Record Department, the British Museum and other English libraries, collected a voluminous amount of material.

I gave an account of the rich and varied data preserved in some of the leading British archives in a series of lectures delivered in the University of London, King's College, in 1920. It took me about three years to sort, rearrange, classify, and make substantial additions to the material collected, and now, after eight years of uninterrupted work, I present the results of my researches to the public.

The book has involved an amount of time and anxiety that can be felt only by those who have gone through the same ordeal. The deciphering of a single manuscript has sometimes cost me several weeks, and I was more than once tempted to give up the project in despair. It would have been a comparatively easy task to have copied the contents of the catalogues of various record offices and libraries mentioned in the book; but, as explained above, that was not the object of my enquiry. Every important document has been subjected to a close and careful scrutiny, and references have been given to printed works that throw further light on the matter.

The work is chiefly occupied with the *manuscript* materials for the study of seventeenth century British India, and deals mainly with the records preserved in the British archives. I have, however, appended a section on the records in India. This portion is, I fear, incomplete; but owing to the supply of abundant information on the contents of record offices in India, I have not deemed it necessary to mention all the documents on the subject that are preserved here.

I am a firm believer in what has been called the 'Archive Method'. I believe that before a person takes up his pen to write history, he should subject his data to the severe test of scientific analysis. I am convinced that the data must be carefully sifted and their contents subjected to a searching critical analysis. The historical method that has been so successfully developed in Paris, and in London, must, I am convinced, be followed in India if we are to free our works on history from the narrow, communal, religious and racial viii

bias. I have been trying to inculcate this ideal among my own students in the University of Allahabad, and the work done by students of this Department has won recognition at the hands of scholars of world-wide reputation. The maxim of the Allahabad School may be summed up thus : ' Do not write a line of history until you have mastered all the material on the subject and freed your mind from all prejudices, be they prejudices of theory or prejudices of race or religion.' This is the ideal at which we aim, and which we will strive to carry out with all our energy.

It is a pleasure to render my hearty thanks to the numerous friends who have helped me in various ways. My thanks are especially due to Professor F. J. C. Hearnshaw of King's College, University of London, whose kindness and courtesy are no less remarkable than his ripe scholarship, and varied experience ; to Sir William Foster, Registrar and Superintendent of Records, India Office, who is the greatest living authority on the records preserved in the India Office ; to the officers in charge of records at Bombay, Calcutta and Madras, for providing facilities for consultation of records in their archives ; to Miss L. M. Anstey for her active interest and constant help ; and to Mr. Gurty Venkat Rao, M.A., LL.B., sometime Research Scholar, History Department, for correcting the proofs. Lastly, I must thank the Oxford University Press and the printers for their help in the printing and publication of this book. It was exceedingly difficult to get a work of this kind produced in India.

UNITED PROVINCES LEGISLATIVE COUNCIL, SHAFAAT AHMAD KHAN
KAISARBAGH, LUCKNOW
18th December, 1925

CONTENTS

DOCUMENTS IN THE BRITISH MUSEUM

BRITISH MUSEUM

1600-1727. **Collections for a History of the India Company by James Pulham.** *Add. MS. 24934, 285 fols.*

This MS. contains copies as follows :

f. 1-3. 22 Sept., 1599. List of the Adventurers.

f. 4-11. 24 Sept., 1599. Minutes of the first General Court, and sketch of the building where it was held.

f. 12-66. Sept.-Dec., 1600. Extracts regarding the first voyage of the Company, equipment of ships, commissions to captains, various directions, etc.

f. 67-76. Copy of the First Charter and letter of Queen Elizabeth.

f. 77-189. 1603-74. Extracts and notes from Court Minutes.

f. 190-95. 1648-1726. Illustrations of the old East India House and later buildings.

f. 196-208. 1675-99. Extracts and notes from Court Minutes.

f. 209-19. 1724-27. Ditto.

f. 220-85. 1601-3. Further notes and references to Court Minutes and other sources regarding the formation of the Company.

The above are all late copies, and are useful only as a guide to the Court Minutes preserved at the India Office.

1600. **Privilege or Charter for the English Merchants trading to the East Indies, by Queen Elizabeth.** *Harl. MS. 306 (2), fols. 18-24.*

A copy of ' A Priviledge for fifteen yeares granted by her majestie to certain adventurers for the discoverie of the trade for the East Indies ', dated 31 December, 1600. Taken from *Purchas his Pilgrimes*, Part I, 1625, and printed as a separate pamphlet, of which the B.M. press mark is 679. h. 11.

1600. **Rules for the establishment of the East India Company, and privileges granted by Queen Elizabeth for fifteen years.** *Add. MS. 30567, fols. 200a-206a.*

Forty-one articles. This is a French translation of Harl. MS. 306 (2), fols. 18-24, for which see above.

1600-1703. **Exports to India.** *Add. MS. 13816, 153 fols.*

Tabulated account of exports to India. Small notebook. The gross amount of merchandise and bullion is given for the following years—1600, 1617, 1652-54, 1655-56, 1657, 1658-60, 1663, 1671-74, 1698-1703. The remainder of the volume deals with exports and imports, weights and measures, etc., of the eighteenth century. An important MS.

1600-1759. **Chronological Table of Events in the History of British India.** *Add. MS. 29209, fols. 517-32.*

This is an abridgment of Bruce's *Annals*. The 'table' begins in 1581 with the Turkey Company's first trading venture to India. The entries for the seventeenth century occupy 9 folios or 14 pages.

17th century (early). **Fragment.**

Cotton MS. Ch. III, No. 13, fols. 9-9a.

Fragment of a letter, without signature, regarding difficulties of trade at 'Lugho' and Banda. Addressed 'Worll'.

(?) 17th century (early). **Reasons for and against permission for trading with the Indies.**

Cotton MS. Vesp. C. XII, fols. 401-2.

For : Freedom of trade advantageous. The King of Spain must be induced to 'proceed more frankly'. A league of friendship and trade to the Indies with Spain would promote amity. *Against :* Free traffic never has been granted. It might prove offensive to Spain.

The writing is crabbed and extremely difficult to decipher. It is one of the earliest manuscripts on the East India Trade, and is important for the history of the first phase of the Company.

(?) 17th century (early). **Short notes concerning the Molucca Islands and the Dutch East India Company.**

Cotton MS. Otho E. VIII, fol. 241.

These notes, which are brief and sketchy, contain the names of some islands and other unimportant notes not relevant to British India.

(?) 17th century (early). **Advice concerning traffic in the East Indies.**

Cotton MS. Otho E. VIII, fol. 61.

A fragment only. Partially burnt.

1604. **Some considerations offered by the Adventurers in a voyage to the East Indies by the Cape of Good Hope, to be attended to in the Treaty with Spain.**

Cotton MS. Vesp. C. XIII, fols. 23-23a.

1604, July. **Reasons for the trade into the East and West Indies by the merchants of England. Gathered for the treaty between England and Spain.**

Cotton MS. Vesp. C. XIII, fols. 47-50a.

The MS. is signed 'Robert Cotton'.

(?) 1606 or 1607. **Petition of the East India Company.**

Harl. MS. 160, fol. 228.

Petition of the East India Company to the Lords of the Privy Council against Sir Edward Michelbourne's interference with their trade at Bantam and the seizure of their people and goods.

1607-8.
14 July,
1607—22
June, 1608.

Voyage to the East Indies.

Cotton MS. Titus B.
VIII, fols. 252-79.

Anthony Marlow's account of a voyage to the East Indies in the *Hector*, of London. The beginning is missing, but the voyage is said to have begun 12 March, 1606-7. The MS. begins in the middle of a sentence, and Anthony Marlow adds a certificate giving the date of the commencement of the voyage.

1607/8-1617. Journal of John Jourdain.

Sloane MS. 858, 118
fols.

A JOURNALL kept by JOHN JOURDAIN in a voiage for the EAST INDIES sett fourth by the Honourable Companie of Merchants trading to the same, in Anno 1607 [1608], in two good shipps, namely the ASSENTION and UNION. Wherein goeth Generall Alexander Sharpleigh, and Vice-Admirall Captaine Richard Rolls ; Maister, Phillipp Grove. The which voiage God blesse and prosper. Began att the Downes neere SANDWICH the 23th of March, Anno 1607 [1608]. With an addition of all my travails after the casting awaie of the Assention untill Anno 1617 of any worthy the writtinge.—JOHN JOURDAIN.

This valuable MS. has been fully edited by Mr. William Foster, C.I.E., and published by the Hakluyt Society, Second Series, No. XVI, London, 1905. It is amply illustrated by contemporary documents, and contains a learned introduction and bibliography.

1609-10.

Instructions given by Thomas Steevens, accountant to the East India Company, to John Lancellot, purser of the *Trades Increase*, and the purser of the *Peppercorn*, and ' *Littel Shelinge* ' respecting their accounts.

Cotton MS. Ch. III,
No. 13, fols. 1-4.

Contains specimens of accounts for the guidance of those concerned.

1609-10.
30 Dec.,
1609—9 Feb.,
1609-10.

Memoranda of the launch and fitting of the two East India ships *Peppercorn* and *Trades Increase*, by the captain of the former.

Egerton MS. 2100,
fols. 37-37a.

There is also a modern transcript of this MS. in the same collection (Egerton 2100), fols. 35-35a.

1610,
20 July.

Agreement of the Governor and Company of merchants of London trading to the East Indies to assign a share of profits to one of the Adventurers.

Add. MS. 18849, fol.
1.

The agreement is on a printed form with seal.

1611.

An account of the escape of Sir Henry Middleton from Mocha, 11 May, 1611, and of his subsequent voyage and proceedings: addressed to Lord Chichester, Deputy of Ireland.

Cotton MS. Otho E.
VIII, 244 fols.

He eventually reached his ship, the *Trades Increase*. Details of arrangements made with the '*Bashaw*'. His journey to England, via Socotra, Surat, the Cape, Madagascar, is also described.

1611,   **Certain notes gathered at Mocha.**   *Cotton MS. Ch. III*
Dec.,   *13.*

These notes are very fragmentary and include a few relating to India.

1611-44.   **Correspondence of factors in the**   *Egerton MS.* *2086,*
                 East Indies, merchants and sea-   *149 fols.*
                 captains, with Sir Thomas Smyth
                 and Sir Maurice Abbott, Gover-
                 nors, and the Committee of the
                 E.I. Co., and others, with bills of
                 lading and other papers, original
                 and copies.

Many of the papers have suffered from damp and are imperfect.

Some of the letters in this MS. have been printed by Mr. William Foster in his *Letters Received by the E.I. Co.*, and others have been abstracted by him in his *English Factories*. Where such is the case, only the date, writer and addressee are given, with a reference to the printed or abstracted version, *English Factories* being distinguished, for the sake of brevity, as *E.F.*

f. 4-4a.   March, 1611-12.   Statement by John Sayes, aboard the *Clove* in Socotra, to the Company, giving an account of the voyage of the *Clove, Hector* and *Thomas*, which sailed from the Downs, 18 April, 1611.   At Socotra they found letters from Sir Henry Middleton. Details of the method of barter at Socotra are given.   [Damaged and portions illegible.]

f. 6-8.   27 Jan., 1612-13.   Bills of lading at Bantam for goods in the *Seloman* for the third voyage.   Richd. Petty, master; Robt. Ward, Cape merchant; Edwd. Blythman, purser.

f. 9.   19 Feb., 1612-13.   Benjamin Greene, at 'Poola Pensem', to Sir Henry Mid[dleton] with the East India [fleet], accompanying 24 bags of 'Mohor' money.   [Damaged and partly illegible.]

f. 10-11a.   9 Nov., 1613.   N. Withington, at Ahmadabad, to Sir Thos. Smyth, Governor of the E.I. Company, per the *James*.

There is an abstract of the above letter on p. 298 of *Letters Received*, Vol. III.

f. 12-12a.   20 Dec., 1613.   James I's commission to Christopher Newport and Joseph Salbank, of the *Expedition*, in which ship the ambassador for Persia is to sail.

f. 13.   19 Dec., 1613.   General letter of King James I, sent by Captain Newport of the *Expedition*, to all rulers of countries which the *Expedition* may visit, requesting that courtesy may be shown to his subjects.

f. 14-15.   21 March, 1614-15.   Sir Maurice Abbott, Governor, and the Committee of the East India Company, to William Hoare, merchant in India, in reply to a letter received by the *Dolphin*.   They approve of the design to send Captain Weddell and the *Dragon* to Gombroom (Bandar Abbas), if it can be safely accomplished.   They remark on the action of the factors at Surat in selecting an agent for Persia, etc. [Slightly damaged.]

f. 16.   29 Jan., 1615-16.   Thos. Sprake, *en route* to Burhanpur, to Geo. Barkley, Cape merchant, at Surat.   He gives an account of customs demanded and refused, and of an altercation with a party of Rajputs demanding it.

f. 17-17a.   15 May, 1616.   Memorandum for Geo. [?D]avidge and John [?] Farye.   Instructions from [the President of Surat] for opening up a trade at Cambay.   A present to be made to the Governor.   Remarks on saleable commodities.

f. 17.   1616.   Instructions to [?] for a voyage from Siam to Cambay.

f. 18-19a.   [1616].   John Browne, at Patani, to the chief of the factory at Jambi.   Reports the death of Robert Larkin and the want of experienced assistants.   Dilates on the difficulties of the relations between the English and Dutch.

f. 20-20a.   1616.   Edward Connock and Thos. Barker [in Persia] to the President and Council at Surat, per the *James*, reporting their kindly reception by 'Zulphecan Sultan, the new presentt Governor'.

Only about a third of the document exists, the rest being torn away.

f. 24-24a.   7 April, 1616.   Nicholas Ufflete, in Jakatra, to [?] concerning trade, price of commodities, etc.   He describes an altercation with the Dutch, who had placed the colours of the Prince of Orange above those of the English on one of their ships.

The writing is difficult to decipher.

f. 26-28a.   15 April, 1617.   Nathaniel Courthope and Thos. Spurway, at Pularoon, to the Chief at Bantam.   Printed in Foster's *Letters Rceeived*, Vol. V, p. 345.

f. 30-30a.   9 July, 1617.   Nathaniel Salmon, of the *New Year's Gift*, to the Company, per the *Charles*.   Printed in Foster's *Letters Received*, Vol. VI, pp. 290-92.

f. 32.   15 Nov., 1617.   N. Ufflett, at Jacatra, to Geo. Ball, at Bantam. Printed in Foster's *Letters Received*, Vol. VI, pp. 307-8.

f. 33-33a.   29 Dec., 1617.   Edward Connock and Francis Upton, at Jask, to Geo. Ball, at Bantam.   Report on goods saleable, at Jask, and on the advisability of supplying that place from Surat.

About half of the document is torn away.

f. 34, 34, 36a.   15 Jan., 1617-18.   Edwd. Connock, etc., at Jask, to the Company.   They give an account of the settlement of trade at Jask.

Part of the document is torn away.

f. 38.   12 March, 1617-18.   Capt. Andrew Shilling, at Swally, to the Company.   Abstracted in Foster's *English Factories*, 1618-21, p. 28.

f. 40-41.   10 May, 1618.   N. Ufflett, at Jacatra, to Geo. Ball.   Notes on trade.   Report of the arrival of a Dutch ship and of hostilities between the Dutch and Portuguese fleets.

f. 42-43.   Feb.-June, 1618.   Robert Freeman, at the Cape, to Robert Bateman, London.   Gives a brief account of his voyage to the Cape and of events during his sojourn there.

f. 44.   29 June, 1618.   Nathl. Courthope, at 'Meylarky' to Capt. 'Cassarian David' at Pulowai.   He boasts that he will hold the place against the Dutch and will defy their pretensions.

f. 45-46.   9 Dec., 1618.   W. Methwold, at Masulipatam, to Sir Thos. Roe, at Surat (*E.F.*, pp. 49-50).

f. 47.   14 Dec., 1618.   Sir Thomas Roe [at Surat] to [John Browne, at Ahmadabad] (*E.F.*, p. 50).   [Badly damaged.]

f. 49.   10 Dec., 1618.   [Sir Thos. Roe] at Surat, to Capt. Bonner (*E.F.*, p. 50).   [Much damaged.]

f. 50.   17 Dec., 1618.   [Sir Thos. Roe] at Surat, to Edward Heynes [at Cambay (*E.F.*, p. 50).   [Much damaged.]

f. 51.   14 Nov., 1619.   Wm. Bedom, at 'Tecoo', to Giles Bedom, his father.   Remarks on the hostile relations between the English and the Dutch, the taking of four English ships by the Dutch and the seizure of three Dutch ships and a castle on the Coromandel Coast by the English.

f. 52-53.   7 July, 1620.   [John Hayward] at Succadana, to [?]   Gives an account of the rebuilding and settlement of the factory and the murder of Mr. Cockayne, at Pulo Banco, and sends news of a reported agreement between the English and the Dutch.   [Much damaged.]

f. 53-56.   15 August, 1620.   [John Hayward] at Succadana, to Richard Fursland [? at Bantam].   Gives an account of the factory at Succadana and of the goods required, as also a present for the Queen. Supplies an interesting account of Jambi and reports that the arrival of Dutch ships there is not acceptable to the King of Jambi.   [Much damaged.]

f. 59.   13 April, 1620.   E. Heynes, at Surat, to J. Bangham, at Ahmadabad.   With autograph signature (*E.F.*, pp. 188-89).

f. 60.   16 July, 1620.   A badly mutilated letter from Richard Cocks at Firando (Hirado), Japan.   [Three parts missing.]

f. 62.   25 June, 1620.   Humphrey Fitzherb [ert] to Capt. [?] Pring, from the Cape of Good Hope.   Reports on the health of the wife and children of the captain.

f. 63-63a.   11 Oct., 1620.   Richard Cocks, at Hirado, to [?].   Report on trade.   Butter presented to him by the Master of the *Bull*, etc.

f. 65, 67 and 68.   14 and 20 Oct., and 15 Nov., 1620.   John Fardoe, on board the *Gift*, to Capt. Humphrey Fitzherbert, Chief Commr. for the Company.   He has been charged with theft, imprisoned and fettered.   Demands a public trial.

f. 70-73.   28 [? 1621].   Capt. Humphrey Fitzherbert, aboard the *Royal Exchange*, in [?] to [? the President of Bantam].   Reports the seizure of Lantore by the Dutch, their attempt to surprise Pularoon, and their overbearing attitude towards the native inhabitants, whom they have compelled to deliver up their arms and rase the walls of their town.   Mr. Harris, the English Governor, refused to support the 'blacks' against the Dutch, who had 2,600 trained soldiers, 14 great ships, 80 prows, etc.   Peace was concluded after an exchange of prisoners.   The Dutch forced the native inhabitants to dismount the English guns at Pularoon.   The loss of the island is attributed to the cowardice of Mr. Harris.   The English still hold the castle on the little island.   [Damaged.]

f. 79-82.   24 Jan., 1621-22.   The factors, at Ruhestek, Persia to [? the Company].   R. Jefferies is defended against charges made against him by E. Monox.   Report on trade.   The advantage of Isfahan as a silk mart.   They are suffering from lack of goods from Surat. An interesting and important document.

f. 83-83a.   8 March, 1621-22.   T. Rastell, etc., at Surat, to [the factors at Ahmadabad].   Abstracted in *English Factories*, 1622-23, p. 56.

f. 84-85.   17 March, 1621-22.   Ditto to the President and Council at Batavia.   Abstracted in ditto, pp. 64-65.

f. 85.   11 March, 1621-22.   Ditto to J. Beversham, at Swally.   Ditto, pp. 63-64.

f. 85-85a.   16 March, 1621-22.   Ditto to J. Johnson, at Swally.   Ditto, p. 64.

f. 85a.   16 March, 1621-22.   Ditto to Ruy Freire, at Swally .(in Italian).   Ditto p. 64.

f. 86.   18 March, 1621-22.   Ditto to J. Salbank, at Swally.   Ditto, p. 67.

f. 86a.   18 March, 1621-22.   Ditto to J. Beversham, at Swally.   Ditto, p. 67.

f. 87-87a.   18 March, 1622-23.   Wm. Butler and G. Bruey, on board the *Roebuck*, in Saldanha Bay, to the Company.   They give an account of the difficulties and dangers of the voyage.   They were forced to put into Saldanha Bay for water and provisions.   They send news of the *Lesser James*, and of the loss of the *Trial*.   They are now about to sail for Jacatra.

f. 89.   6 June, 1623.   Capt. J. Bickell to the commander of the English homeward-bound [ships], on the *Hart*, in Saldanha Bay.   Gives an account of the voyage.   They fell in with a Dutch fleet, off the Lizard, and were in much danger, but escaped.   News of a peace concluded between England and Holland.

f. 104-5a.   ᶜ13 April, 1626.   The Governor and Committee of the E.I. Company to the Governor and Council of Batavia.   They report the safe arrival of various ships, acknowledge the receipt of letters, give instructions for negotiations with the Dutch, etc., etc.,

f. 107-8.   8 Jan., 1627-8.   Jas. Slade, Master of the *Blessing*, at Swally, to the Company.   Abstracted in Foster's *E.F.*, 1624-29, pp. 215-17.

f. 109-9a.   1 August, 1628.   Wm. Burton, at [? Isfahan], to [?].   Muhammad Ali Beg intends sending an ambassador to the King of England in 1628.   Report on trade.   [Beginning missing.   Damaged.]

f. 110.   [? April, 1629].   Mirza Muhammad, a merchant of Surat, to the Company.   Abstracted in *E.F.*, p. 325.

f. 112-13.   1 August, 1632.   The commanders of Capt. Weddell's fleet to the Company, dated from St. Augustine's Bay, Madagascar.   Abstracted in *E.F.*, 1630-33, pp. 222-24.

f. 114-14a.   5 Jan., 1635-36.   W. Methwold, &c., at Surat, to the factors at Baroda.   Abstracted in *E.F.*, 1634-36, pp. 149-50.

f. 115-16a.   5 Jan. 1635-36.   Ditto to the factors in Persia.   Ditto, p. 150.   [First part missing.]

f. 116.   15 Jan., 1635-36.   Ditto to the factors at Baroda.   Ditto, p. 154.   [First part missing.]

f. 116-17.   15 Jan., 1635-36.   Ditto to the factors at Ahmadabad.   Ditto, pp. 153-54.

f. 117-17a.   15 Jan., 1635-36.   Ditto to Capt. Brown, in the *William* [at Swally].   Ditto, p. 154.

f. 117a-18.   18 Jan., 1635-36.   Ditto to ditto.   Ditto, p. 155.

f. 118-19a.   [29 Jan., 1635-36].   [Ditto] to the E. I. Company.   Ditto, pp. 159-60.   [End and date missing.]

f. 120-22.   11 Jan., 1635-36.   [Ditto] to the factors at Ahmadabad.   Ditto, pp. 150-51.

f. 122-22a.   11 Jan., 1635-36.   Ditto to the factors at Baroda.   Ditto, p. 151.

f. 122a-24a.   15 Jan., 1635-36.   Ditto to the factors at Tatta.   Ditto, pp. 152-53.

f. 125-25a.   [? 1635-36].   [Ditto] to the factors at Ahmadabad.   State that disappointment in obtaining goods will delay the sailing of the *Discovery*.   Report of what goods provided.   The Portuguese are leaving Cambay.   [End missing.]

f. 126.   14 Sept., 1636.   Ditto to the factors at Ahmadabad.   Abstracted
    in *E.F.*, p. 291   [First part missing.]

f. 126-26a.   14 Sept., 1636.   Ditto to the factors at Baroda.   Ditto,
    p. 291.

f. 127-27a.   19 Sept., 1636.   Ditto to John Drake, at the Court of the
    Mogul.   Ditto, pp. 293-94.

f. 128-30.   20 Sept., and P.S. of 29 Sept., 1636.   Ditto to [the factors at
    Masulipatam].   Ditto, pp. 294-95.

f. 130.   21 Sept., 1636.   Ditto to the factors at Ahmadabad.   Ditto,
    p. 298.

f. 130-31.   22 Sept., 1636.   Ditto to ditto.   Ditto, p. 298.

f. 131-31a.   22 Sept., 1636.   Ditto to the factors, at Baroda.   Ditto,
    p. 298.

f. 131a-32.   26 Sept., 1636.   Ditto to ditto.   Ditto, pp. 298-99.

f. 132-33.   27 Sept., 1636.   Ditto to John Drake, at the Court of the
    Mogul.   Ditto, p. 299.

f. 134.   28 Aug., 1637.   R. Cartwright, at Masulipatam, to the President
    and Council at Bantam.   Abstracted in *E.F.*, 1637-41, pp. 25-26.

f. 135.   27 July, 1638.   Capt. Swanly and P. Mundy, in the *Sun*, to Capt.
    Minors.   Ditto, p. 81.   Printed in *Travels of Peter Mundy*, ed.
    Temple, Vol. III, Part II, pp. 379-80.

f. 137.   28 July., 1638.   Protest by the above against Capt. Minors and
    his Council.   Ditto, p. 81.   Printed as above, pp. 381-82.

f. 145.   28 July, 1638.   Capt. Wm. Minors, in St. Augustine's Bay,
    Madagascar, to the Company.   Ditto, pp. 81-82.

f. 139-40.   29 July, 1638.   A. Cogan, aboard the *Discovery*, to the
    Company.   Ditto, pp. 82-83.

f. 141.   29 July, 1638.   T. Wheeler, in the *Discovery*, to the Company.
    Ditto, p. 83.

f. 143.   29 July, 1638.   Capt. Wm. Minors, in the *Discovery*, to the
    Company.   Ditto, pp. 81-82.

f. 144.   29 July, 1638.   Ditto to [?].   Ditto, p. 82.

f. 147.   17 June, 1644.   T. Gee and T. Wotton at sea, near Dartmouth,
    to the Company.   Abstracted in *E.F.* 1642-45, p. 183.

1611-12, 11 Jan.	**Letter from John Crayford and Francis Kelly at 'Suckadano,' dealing with details regarding trade.**	*Cotton MS. Ch. III, No. 13, fol. 5.*

1612, 27 May.	**Instructions for the Coast of Coromandel.**	*Cotton MS. Ch. III, No. 13, fols. 5a-6.*

These are dated at Bantam and are signed by Peter Floris, etc.   They contain
names of various Indian piece-goods, their length and price.

1612, 4 Oct.	**Minutes of the East India and Turkey merchants' complaints before the Lords of the Council.**	*Landsdowne MS. 160. No. 36, fol. 144.*

Reasons why the trade with Turkey is more profitable than that with the East
Indies and Persia.

Reasons offered by the Persian ambassador for trading direct with the Persian
Gulf rather than by way of Turkey.   A suggestion that the Persian monarch shall take
kerseys (English woollen cloth) and return silk in exchange ' at a double valewe '.

1613,   **Papers concerning the trade to**   *Cotton MS. Galba*
5 April.   **India.**   *E.I. fols. 371-76a.*

Two Latin documents and a third with an English translation on the subject of trade with India, said to have been sent to the Commissioners for the Indies. The translation deals with a controversy between England and Holland concerning trade.

1613,   **Nicholas Downton's account of his**   *Cotton MS. Otho E.*
30 Sept.   **voyage in the** *Peppercorn* **in the**   *VIII, fols. 244-47a.*
            East Indies under the command
            of Sir Henry Middleton, address-
            ed to Lord Chichester, Deputy of
            Ireland.

The beginning of this MS. appears to be missing and the top of each sheet is burnt off. The first sheet seems to have been reversed, fol. 244a containing matter of prior date to that on fol. 244. The dates, so far as can be ascertained, run from 23 July, 1610, to 30 September, 1613. The narrative includes an account of Sir Henry Middleton's imprisonment at Mocha and his escape thence (11 May, 1611), with his subsequent relation with the 'Bashaw'. The places touched at include the Cape, Madagascar, Aden, Mocha, Socotra, Surat, Sumatra and Java. The ship was at St. Helena in June, 1613, and off Ushant in the August following.

See above in the same collection (*Cotton MS. Otho E. VIII*, fols. 1-244) for a full account of these incidents, under date 1611.

(?) 1614.   **Letter from [Robert] Bell to Sir**   *Stowe MS. 174, fol.*
            Thomas Edmondes, Ambassador   *367-67a*
            in Paris.

Complaint by the company of merchants of England trading to the East Indies that ships are being prepared in England and France for unlicensed voyages to India, to the prejudice of their trade. They request that an embargo may be put on persons and ships harbouring such a design in France.

1614/15-   **Walter Peyton's second voyage to**   *Add. MS. 19276, 55*
1617.   **the East Indies.**   *fols.*

Journal of the *Expedition*, in her voyage to India, with the *Dragon, Lyon* (having aboard her Sir Thomas Roe, Ambassador to the Great Mogul), and *Peppercorn.*

22 Jan.   List of the ship's company and passengers, with notes of what befell them.

f. 4.   24 Jan.   Sailed from Gravesend.

f. 7a.   5 June.   Anchored at the Cape.

f. 10.   22 July.   Anchored at 'Molahlye', Comoro Islands.

f. 13a.   19 Aug.   Reached Socotra. Notes on its productions, etc.

f. 17a.   17 Sept.   Anchored in Swally Road. Description of Surat. Reception of the Ambassador.

f. 19.   7 Oct.   Threat of an attack by a Portuguese armada.

f. 20.   30 Oct.   Sir Thomas Roe goes to Ajmer.

f. 22.   19 Jan., 1615-16.   Sailed from Swally. Notes on trade in Surat and other parts of India and Persia.

f. 28.   3 Feb.   Anchored at Calicut. Notes on Calicut, Cranganore, Cochin, etc.

f. 34.   1 May.   Arrived at Bantam. Notes on the place and trade.

f. 35a.   10 June.   Anchored at Priaman and, later, at Tecoe. Notes on Tecoe Factory, and on Achin and its government.

f. 39.   Sailing directions.

f. 41.   8 Oct.   At Bantam.   Notes on 'abuses' put upon the English by the 'Hollanders'.

f. 44a.   Notes on Portuguese trade in India.

f. 49.   2 Jan., 1616-17.   Anchored at the Cape on the homeward voyage and in February reached St. Helena.

f. 55.   19 May.   In the Downs.

An important document, supplementing information on a most interesting aspect of commercial rivalry.

1615, 22 Jan., 1614-15.	**Letter from George Cockayne and Francis Kelly, at Macassar, to [? the Company].**	*Cotton MS. Ch. III, 13, fols. 8-8a.*

This letter deals principally with trade in rice and cloth.

(?) 1615.	**A letter on the state of the affairs of the Europeans in the Mughal country.**	*Cotton MS. Titus B. VIII, fols. 235-36a*

Four closely-written pages with the end missing and no indication of the writer or writers.

1615.	**A few notes of a voyage in the *Samaritan*, East India Company's ship, commanded by Captain David Middleton, to the East Indies.**	*Egerton MS. 2121, fols. 11-12.*

These fragmentary notes are probably taken from O.C. 245, India Office Records, which gives an account of the voyage. The notes are preceded by a note on the use of nautical instruments, etc., and other memoranda, signed by Rowland Thomas.

1615, 10 April.	**Letter from 'Fra. Corsi' to Gioseph Baudo, a Jesuit at Milan, on the persecution of the Mission in India.**	*Cotton MS. Titus B. VIII, fols. 249-50.*

The letter is dated from Agra, is catalogued as from Fra. Corsi, but is signed Joseph di Castro. It reports the closing of churches on account of disturbances, and the necessity for the Fathers to remain in hiding.

1615- **1616/17.**	**Letter Book of the English Factory at Surat in the years 1615, 1616.**	*Add. MS. 9366, 177 fols.*

This valuable MS. consists of 241 separate documents. Its title is somewhat misleading for it consists of letters signed by Thomas Kerridge in his official capacity as the Company's servant at Ahmadabad, July, 1615—Feb., 1615/16, as well as after he became head of affairs in Surat, in Feb., 1615-16. In the latter case the letters are penned in concurrence with his colleagues, and these extend from Feb., 1615-16 to Jan., 1616-17.

The letters are addressed to Surat, Agra, Ahmadabad and Broach. There are, besides, a considerable number written to Sir Thomas Roe, Ambassador at the Court of the Mogul, and two or three to the Company in England.

Some half dozen of the letters to Sir Thomas Roe and the Company have been printed by Mr. Wm. Foster in his *Letters Received*, Vols. IV and V, and Mr. Foster has also utilised Kerridge's correspondence with the Ambassador when editing the Diary of the Embassy for the Hakluyt Society.

A second copy of the letters from Feb., 1615-16 onwards is preserved at the India Office, *Factory Records, Surat*, Vol. LXXXIV, Pt. 1, and this vol. contains four letters of a later date than those in the B.M. Vol.

The whole series is intensely interesting and throws much light on the political and commercial relations of the East India Company, in Surat and the neighbourhood, in the early part of the 17th century.

To indicate adequately the matter to be found in the closely-written pages of this mass of correspondence would require a volume. For the present purpose it has been considered sufficient to catalogue the documents chronologically with location, date and name of addressee, and to note in the briefest fashion the chief points of interest in each document. The MS. is essential to the study of the early history of English intercourse with India, and it ought to be carefully analysed by a skilful scholar.

f. 3. [1615.] [The Emperor Jahangir] to King James I. Instructions have been given to his officials to encourage and protect English merchants. He asks for novelties from England.

f. 4. 26 July, 1615. Thomas Kerridge, at Surat, to W. Edwardes at Ahmadabad. He arrived at Surat 14 July. He gives an account of trade carried on under Mr. Aldworth.

The following letters were written mainly by Thomas Kerridge.

f. 4a-5. 5 Sept., 1615. From Surat to W. Edwardes, at Ahmadabad. Cause of high price of indigo. Death of Wm. Burrows. Quicksilver not yet sold.

f. 5-5a. 7 Sept., 1615. From Ahmadabad to W. Biddulph, at Surat. Directions for his proceedings on the arrival of the fleet from England. The Portuguese desire peace but it is refused by the Mughal Emperor.

f. 5a. 19 Sept., 1615. From Surat to W. Edwardes, at Ahmadabad. Report on the sale of quicksilver. A *farman* necessary to prevent seizure of goods.

f. 6. 24 Sept., 1615. From Surat to W. Edwardes at Ahmadabad. Rumour of a prohibition against buying and selling indigo.

f. 6-7. 26 Sept., 1615. From Ahmadabad to Capt. Wm. Keeling [at Swally]. Reasons why the lading for the fleet is not ready. Details of obstructions to trade.

f. 7a-8. 27 Sept., 1615. From Ahmadabad to Wm. Edwardes [at Surat]. Review of letters received and sent. 'The briefe of the Cargason sent to Mr. Edwardes.' This includes iron, lead, sword-blades, knives, hats, presents, etc. of the total value of [? Rs.] 23,661-18-11.

f. 8a-9. 28 Sept., 1615. From Ahmadabad to Capt. Wm. Keeling. Untrustworthiness of the Ahmadabad brokers, one of whom has absconded. Report of cloth provided.

f. 9. 5 Oct., 1615. From ditto to ditto. The King's *farman* to the Governor of Surat, Cambay and Ahmadabad received.

f. 9a-10. 6 Oct., 1615. From Ahmadabad to W. Edwardes [at Surat]. Report of investments at Agra. The cloths badly sorted.

f. 10-11. 8 Oct., 1615. From Ahmadabad to J. Brown [at Surat]. Death of Mr. Aldworth and present state of affairs at Ahmadabad.

f. 12-13. 8 Oct., 1615. To Sir Thomas Roe. Treats of relations with the Governor of Ahmadabad before the arrival of the Ambassador.

f. 13-14a. 10 Oct., 1615. From Ahmadabad to Capt. Wm. Keeling. Notes on the cargo to be procured for the homeward-bound ships, and on the disposal of goods brought from England.

f. 15.   10 Oct., 1615.   Note of the ports in Persia 'observed from Sir Robert Sherley'.

f. 15a-16a.   18 Oct., 1615.   [At Ahmadabad] to Capt. W. Keeling.   An amplification of the information already given on 10 Oct.

f. 17.   18 Oct., 1615.   Ditto to ditto.   Declines to meddle with private quarrels.

f. 17-17a.   21 Oct., 1615.   Ditto to Wm. Biddulph [at Agra].   Regarding the opening of Mr. Aldworth's papers.

f. 11a-12.   19 Oct., 1615.   From Ahmadabad to ditto.   General instructions.

f. 17a.   21 Oct., 1615.   From Ahmadabad to J. Browne [at Surat]. Regarding the purchase of indigo.

f. 18-18a.   21 Oct., 1615.   From Ahmadabad to Capt. W. Keeling. Concerning the cargo for the homeward-bound ships.

f. 19-19a.   21 Oct., 1615.   From Ahmadabad to Sir Thos. Roe.   The Ambassador is urged to procure 'novelties' to present to the Mughal Emperor.

f. 19a-20.   23 Oct., 1615.   From Ahmadabad to W. Edwardes [at Surat]. Reasons for continued high prices at Ahmadabad.

f. 20-20a.   25 Oct., 1615.   From Ahmadabad to Capt. W. Keeling. Regarding investments in cloth and indigo.

f. 20a-21.   26 Oct., 1615.   From Ahmadabad to W. Edwardes [at Surat]. He rejoices at the report of a rupture in the negotiations between the Portuguese and the Mughal officers.

f. 21a.   27 Oct., 1615.   From Ahmadabad to Sir Thos. Roe.   Acknowledging the receipt of a *farman* from the Mughal Emperor.

f. 21a.   27 Oct., 1615.   From Ahmadabad to W. Edwardes.   Reporting the proceedings of Sir Thos. Roe, etc.

f. 22-22a.   27 Oct., 1615.   From Ahmadabad to Capt. W. Keeling. Notes on trade in general.   Quicksilver not sold.

f. 22a-23.   4 Nov., 1615.   From Ahmadabad to Thos. Mitford [at Ajmer]. Comments on Mitford's unruly conduct and on the proceedings of the Ambassador.

f. 23.   6 Nov., 1615.   From Ahmadabad to W. Edwardes [at Surat] Deadlock in the 'indigo business'.

f. 26a-27.   6 Nov., 1615.   From Ahmadabad to W. Biddulph [at Agra]. Unimportant.

f. 23a.   7 Nov., 1615.   From Ahmadabad to T. Barber.   Notes difficulties with the Native Government.

f. 23a-24.   7 Nov., 1615.   From Ahmadabad to Capt. W. Keeling. Notes on the price of indigo.

f. 24.   9 Nov., 1615.   From Ahmadabad to Thos. Coryat.   Regarding books required by Coryat, etc.

f. 24a.   9 Nov., 1615.   From Ahmadabad to Wm. Edwardes [at Surat]. Reports what provision of goods has been made at Ahmadabad.

f. 25.   10 Nov., 1615.   From Ahmadabad to R. Baker, etc. [? at Surat], Reports what goods have been procured and notes by what methods they have been obtained.

f. 25a.   12 Nov., 1615.   From Ahmadabad to Wm. Biddulph.   Gives details of cloth to be procured.

f. 27.   12 Nov., 1615.   From Ahmadabad to R. Baker, etc.   Report on piece-goods provided at Ahmadabad.

f. 25a-26a.   16 Nov., 1615.   From Ahmadabad to Capt. W. Keeling. Reports what advances have been made in procuring cargoes for the fleet.   A present to be sent to Abdu'llah Khan.

f. 27a. 18 Nov., 1615. Ditto to ditto. Efforts have not been wanting to procure goods.

f. 27a-28. 19 Nov., 1615. Ditto to W. Edwardes [at Surat]. Investments hindered by the coming of the Jesuits.

f. 28. 23 Nov., 1615. Ditto to W. Biddulph. Cause of rise of prices in cloth.

f. 28a. 23 Nov., 1615. Ditto to R. Baker, etc. Concerning the investments.

f. 28a-29. 25 Nov., 1615. Ditto to ditto. Reports on the state of Portuguese trade at Goa.

f. 29-30. 25 Nov., 1615. Ditto to Capt. W. Keeling. Reports on the progress of the investment.

f. 30-31. 26 Nov., 1615. Ditto to ditto. Gives an account of piece-goods purchased.

f. 31-31a. 27 Nov., 1615. Ditto to ditto. Further reports of sales and purchases.

f. 31a-32. 28 Nov., 1615. Ditto to R. Baker, etc. [at Surat]. Note of goods despatched from Ahmadabad.

f. 32. 28 Nov., 1615. Ditto to W. Biddulph [? at Broach]. He is desired to provide transport for indigo.

f. 32a. 28 Nov., 1615. Ditto to W. Edwardes. Unimportant.

f. 32a-33. 29 Nov., 1615. Ditto to Capt. W. Keeling. Note of the amount of indigo, etc., procured.

f. 33. 5 Dec., 1615. Ditto to ditto. A rumour, of Portuguese competition at Cambay for piece-goods, denied.

f. 33a. 5 Dec., 1615. Ditto to W. Biddulph [at Broach]. Regarding customs payable on piece-goods.

f. 33a-34a. 6 Dec., 1615. Ditto to W. Edwardes [at Surat]. Gives an account of goods despatched from Ahmadabad, and of relationship with the Governor of that place.

f. 34a-35. 6 Dec., 1615. Ditto to Capt. W. Keeling. No efforts are spared to procure cargoes for the fleet.

f. 35. 6 Dec., 1615. Ditto to the Factory at Surat. Note on the variations in the content and price of a churl of indigo, etc.

f. 33a. 7 Dec., 1615. Ditto to W. Biddulph. Urging the speedy despatch of goods from [? Broach to Surat].

f. 33a-34. 7 Dec., 1615. Ditto to Capt. W. Keeling. Regarding goods obtainable and transport for the same.

f. 34. 11 Dec., 1615. Ditto to T. Mitford. Notes the delay in procuring indigo.

f. 36a. 11 Dec., 1615. Ditto to Capt. W. Keeling. Regarding transport for goods.

f. 36a. 14 Dec., 1615. Ditto to W. Edwardes [at Surat]. Reports the hindrances to the transport of goods by the Governor of Cambay.

f. 37. 17 Dec., 1615. Ditto to the factors at Surat. Note of what indigo has been despatched. Gives reasons why quicksilver will not sell.

f. 37a. 17 Dec., 1615. Ditto to Capt. W. Keeling. Reporting the difficulties met with in despatching goods.

f. 38-38a. 21 Dec., 1615. Ditto to J. Browne. Reporting a theft of indigo.

f. 39-39a. 21 Dec., 1615. Ditto to Capt. W. Keeling. Reports a favourable answer from the Governor of Cambay in reply to a complaint about double custom extorted.

f. 39a-40a.   22 Dec., 1615.   Ditto to W. Edwardes [at Surat].   Gives an account of charges for transit of goods.

f. 40a.   22 Dec., 1615.   Ditto to F. Fettiplace at [? Agra].   Notes the arrival of their 'discordant Caphila'.

f. 41.   25 Dec., 1615.   To J. Browne [at Surat].   An expected buyer of quicksilver proves useless.

f. 41-41a.   25 Dec., 1615.   To Capt. W. Keeling.   Gives details of his negotiations with the Governor of Cambay.

f. 41a.   25 Dec., 1615.   To W. Biddulph.   Gives details of unjust demands on the part of the Deputy of the Governor of Cambay.

f. 42.   28 Dec., 1615.   To R. Baker, etc., at Surat.   Carts for the transport of goods are delayed by the order of the Governor of Cambay.

f. 42.   30 Dec., 1615.   To J. Browne [at Surat].   He gives an account of how he 'cleared' the carts, and of the amount of piece-goods and indigo procured.

f. 42a.   30 Dec., 1615.   To the English at Broach.   An agreement regarding the payment of customs arrived at with the Governor of Cambay.

f. 42a-43.   30 Dec., 1615.   To Capt. W. Keeling.   Reports further difficulties with the Governor of Cambay.

f. 43-44a.   31 Dec., 1615.   To Sir Thomas Roe.   Gives very full details of abuses suffered by the English at Ahmadabad.

f. 44a-45.   4 and 6 Jan., 1615-16.   To J. Browne [at Surat].   Account of goods despatched to Surat.   He has been compelled to submit to the exactions demanded as 'Customes of Barroch'.   Also to the factors at Surat as follows.

f. 45-45a.   9 Jan., 1615-16.   Account of indigo for Surat and the price thereof.

f. 45a.   9 Jan., 1615-16.   To the factors at Broach.   Gives an account of the arrangement arrived at regarding customs.

f. 45a-46a.   9 and 13 Jan., 1615-16.   To Capt. W. Keeling.   Regarding goods procured and despatched and goods to be left at Ahmadabad at Keeling's departure.

f. 47.   13 Jan., 1615-16.   To the factors at Broach.   Sends certificates of sums paid for customs at Ahmadabad.

f. 48a.   21 Jan., 1615-16.   List of goods sent from Ahmadabad for the lading of the homeward-bound ships.

f. 47.   22 Jan. 1615-16.   To the factors at Surat with a list as above.

f. 48a.   22 Jan., 1615-16.   To the factors at Broach.   Regarding goods despatched and detained.

f. 49.   Goods not 'Costomed heer [Ahmadabad] to be Cleered ther (if demaunded)'.

f. 49-49a.   23 Jan., 1615-16.   A 'remembrance' sent to Mr. Martin Holt by Thos. Kerridge, with a list of goods sent from Ahmadabad. The list contains a detailed account of goods despatched, with the marks on the bales.

f. 47-48.   24 Jan., 1615-16.   Account of goods despatched from Ahmadabad, and of goods detained unjustly and excessive customs demanded for them.   Kerridge announces his impending departure for Surat.   [Two letters.]

f. 50.   25 Jan., 1615-16.   To Sir Thos. Roe.   Congratulates him on his success in his negotiations.   Reports the release of M. Withington arrested by the Governor of Ahmadabad.

f. 50-51. 2 Feb., 1615-16. To Capt. W. Keeling. Notes the wrongs suffered by the English at the hands of the Governor of Cambay. Gives prices of goods at Ahmadabad.

f. 51. 3 Feb., 1615-16. To the factors at Surat. Relates measures taken for 'clearing' carts laden with the Company's goods.

f. 55a. 14 and 18 Feb., 1615-16. A recommendation of and certificate to Thomas Kerridge as principal factor in the Mughal Emperor's dominions.

f. 51a. 16 Feb., 1615-16. To Capt. W. Keeling. Unimportant.

f. 51a-54a. 18 Feb., 1615-16. General letter from the factors at Surat to the Company, per the *Lyon*. There are no signatures. This document contains a chronicle of events, both political and commercial, since March 1614-15. List of goods laden on the *Lyon*.

From this point to the end of the volume (Add. MS. 9366), there is another copy of Kerridge's letters. It is preserved in the India Office and entitled *Factory Records, Surat*, Vol. LXXXIV, Part I. The letters are numbered 1-156 inclusive.

f. 56. 21 Feb., 1615-16. Thomas Kerridge, at Surat to [? N.] Bangham, etc. He is desired to ascertain the prices of quicksilver and elephants' teeth, and the quantities available.

f. 56-56a. 23. Feb., 1615-16. Ditto to Sir Thomas Roe. Describes the ill-treatment received by the English from the late Governor of Surat.

The succeeding letters are all from Thomas Kerridge, and his colleagues at Surat, unless otherwise stated.

f. 56a. 23 Feb., 1615-16. To W. Biddulph. Note of the sailing of the Company's ships for England, and of the departure of Mr. Edwardes.

f. 56a-57. 24 Feb., 1615-16. To Sir Thomas Roe. Contains nothing of special interest.

f. 57-57a. 26 Feb., 5 and 8 March, 1615-16. To Mr. Farwell, etc. [at Ahmadabad]. They are to make use of the *farmans* received from the Ambassador in their relations with the Governor of Cambay.

f. 58. 7 March, 1615-16. A letter of recommendation to 'Malam Cymey', master and pilot of the *Samady Ruzzauy*.

f. 57a. 9 March, 1615-16. To [? the English Consul at Aleppo]. Requesting him to forward a packet to the Company.

f. 58-61a. 10 [or 11] March, 1615-16. General letter to the Company. Printed, from the copy in *Factory Records, Surat*, Vol. LXXXIV, in Foster's *Letters Received*, Vol. V, pp. 291-303.

f. 61a-62. 17 March, 1615-16. To Mr. Bangham. Regarding goods provided at [? Burhanpur] and prices of the same.

f. 62-62a. 20 March, 1615-16. To Lucas Antheunis [at Masulipatam]. Notifies the settlement of the factories of Surat, Ahmadabad, Agra and Burhanpur, and the progress of trade, etc.

f. 63-63a. 23 March, 1615-16. To Sir Thomas Roe. The Ambassador is begged to obtain satisfaction for abuses suffered by the English from local Governors.

f. 62a-63. 24 March, 1615-16. To W. Biddulph. The accounts kept at Ajmer are irregular. Gives news received from Masulipatam.

f. 63a-64a. 4 [or 5] and 15 April, 1616. To J. Browne, etc. [at Ahmadabad]. Instructions regarding goods to be provided and comments on hindrances met with in procuring them.

f. 64-65. 17 April, 1616. Directions to Mr. Samuel Saltonstall, charging him with the convoy to Burhanpur.

f. 65-65a.   18 April, 1616.   To Mr. Bangham.   Note of goods to be provided and an account of injuries suffered by the English at Surat from the new Governor.

f. 66-66a.   29 April, 1616.   To J. Browne [at Ahmadabad].   Regarding satisfaction to be obtained for injuries from the Native Government, the provision of indigo, etc.

f. 66a-67.   30 April, 1616.   To Mr. Bangham.   He is urged to dispose of the Company's quicksilver and sword-blades.

f. 67-68.   2 May, 1616.   To J. Browne, etc.   [at Ahmadabad].   Commiserates him for being forcibly dispossessed from the house occupied by the Company's servants, and urges him to continue the investment.

f. 68-68a.   3 May, 1616.   To Sir Thos. Roe.   Reports the obstructions met with from the custom-house officer at Surat.

f. 68a-70.   3 May, 1616.   To W. Biddulph.   He is to be Chief at Agra and conduct the investment there.

f. 70-71.   11 May, 1616.   To Mr. Bangham.   China commodities from Masulipatam are unprofitable to the Company owing to excessive charges for transport, etc.

f. 71-72.   14 May, 1616.   To J. Browne, etc.   Remarks on the tactics of the Portuguese, who endeavour to enhance the price of Sarkhej indigo.   The purchase of 'looteas' indigo approved.   [Two letters.]

f. 72-73.   17 May, 1616.   To Lucas Antheunis, at Masulipatam.   Comments on the threatened attack by the Portuguese on the English and Dutch settlements on the Coromandel Coast.

f. 73-73a.   24 May, 1616.   To Mr. Bangham.   Expresses surprise that the 'coming of the Army' has made it more difficult to dispose of goods.

f. 73a-76a.   26 May, 1616.   To Sir Thomas Roe.   The greater part of this letter has been printed in *Letters Received*, Vol. V, pp. 320-21, from the copy in *Factory Records, Surat*, Vol. LXXXIV, Pt. I, No. 29.

f. 76a-77a.   26 May, 1616.   To Wm. Biddulph.   Reasons for considering Ajmer a good centre of trade.

f. 77a-78.   7 June, 1616.   To J. Browne [at Ahmadabad].   It is hoped that the newly-acquired favour with Sardar Khan will accelerate the sale of cloth in that place.

f. 78a-79.   8 June, 1616.   To ditto.   A note on the coins usually current at Burhanpur.

f. 79.   12 June, 1616.   To Mr. Bangham.   Regarding arrangements made with brokers who procure goods.

f. 80-80a.   14 June, 1616.   To J. Browne [at Ahmadabad].   Notes on abuses suffered by the Company for many years owing to a misunderstanding.

f. 80a.   20 [or 21] June, 1616.   To [? J. Browne, etc.].   A copy of the King's *farman* for restitution of indirect customs has been sent to Broach.

f. 81.   Note of payments for customs and duties in 1615.

f. 88.   19 July, 1616.   Consultation in Surat.   A debate on the question of the advisability of the withdrawal of the ambassador from Court in case he should fail to secure restitution of wrongs for the English.

f. 81a-87.   23 July, 1616.   To Sir Thomas Roe.   Recording events subsequent to the 5th July and commenting on the proceedings of the ambassador.   A long, interesting document with allusions to contemporary historical events in N. India.

f. 87-87a. 24 July, 1616. To J. Browne [at Ahmadabad]. News from Court. Arrival of a Dutch ship at Swally.

f. 88a-90. 24 July, 1616. To Wm. Biddulph. Orders for the government of the factory at Agra, and for Biddulph to repair to Ajmer. Many other points are also touched on.

f. 90a-91. 31 July, 1616. To Mr. Bangham. Regarding sale of goods, news of the arrival of the Dutch ship, etc.

f. 91-95. 7 and 8 Aug., 1616. To J. Browne, etc. A long letter dealing with customs, sale of goods, Portuguese and Dutch trade, etc.

f. 95-95a. 11 Aug., 1616. To Sir Thos. Roe. Remarks on the Dutch and Portuguese and their attempts to trade as in the previous letter.

f. 95a-96. 11 Aug., 1616. To Wm. Biddulph. Only the best indigo to be procured. Details of ' the business ' at Broach.

f. 96-98. 15, 20 and 23 Aug., 1616. Copies of letters from T. Barker, etc., at Surat, to T. Kerridge, etc., at Broach. Reporting what has occurred at Surat since Kerridge left that place for Broach.

f. 90-90a. 24 Aug., 1616. Ditto to T. Mitford. Regarding piece-goods.

f. 98a-100. 28 Aug., 1616. Ditto to T. Kerridge, etc., at Broach. Concerning the amount of goods to be provided at Surat.

f. 100-100a. 31 Aug., 1616. Ditto to T. Mitford. News of the departure of the Dutch ship with a small cargo.

f. 100a-1. 31 Aug. and 1 Sept., 1616. Ditto to Mr. Bangham. Reports T. Kerridge's departure for Broach and relates occurrences at Surat.

f. 101-1a. 1 Sept., 1616. Ditto to T. Mitford. Regarding Ibrahim Khan's letter and its effect on the customs officers.

f. 101a. 6 Sept., 1616. [? Ditto] to Mr. Bangham. Contains nothing of special interest.

f. 102-3. 17 Aug., 1616. Thomas Kerridge, at Broach, to J. Browne, etc. He answers various letters from Ahmadabad in detail and recounts his own measures to secure restitution of excessive charges at Broach.

f. 103a-5a. 18 and 23 Aug., 1616. T. Kerridge, etc., at Broach, to R. Barker, etc., at Surat. They give orders concerning the sale of quicksilver, vermilion, etc. Kerridge recounts his proceedings at Broach, his interviews with the Governor. He notes the rivalry of the Dutch, etc. [Three letters.]

f. 106. 23 Aug., 1616. Ditto to T. Mitford. Announces his intention to return to Surat shortly.

f. 106-7. 24 Aug., 1616. Ditto to J. Browne, etc., at Ahmadabad. He finds ' intollerable abuses and knaverye ' at Broach.

f. 107-7a. 26 Aug., 1616. Ditto to R. Barker, etc., at Surat. The authorities, at Broach conspire to weary the English by delays.

f. 107a-8. 26 Aug., 1616. Ditto to T. Mitford. Contains nothing of special interest.

f. 108-9. 29 Aug., 1616. Ditto to R. Barker, etc., at Surat. Remarks on the various kinds of *bafta* suitable for the European markets, etc.

f. 109-10. 1 Sept., 1616. Ditto to J. Browne at Ahmadabad. Mr. Farwell's perverseness and neglect of his duties is censured. Kerridge announces his impending return to Surat.

f. 110-11. 7 Sept., 1616. Thos. Kerridge, at Surat, to J. Browne, at Ahmadabad. Regarding debts to be collected, etc.

The remainder of the letters are all dated from Surat and are signed by Thomas Kerridge, unless otherwise stated.

2

f. 114-15.   22 and 26 Sept., 1616.   To Wm. Biddulph.   Comments on affairs at Agra and instructions for the conduct of the factory there.

f. 111-14.   23 and 26 Sept., 1616.   To Sir Thos. Roe.   Note of receipt of Mahabat Khan's *parwana* to his deputy at Broach, with a long account of affairs in general and remarks on the Ambassador's proceedings.   Reports the arrival of a fleet of the Company's ships.   [Two letters.]

f. 115.   27 Sept., 1616.   To Captain Pepwell.   Asking for particulars of the frigate captured by the Captain.

f. 115a-17.   28 Sept., 1616.   To J. Browne at Ahmadabad.   Regarding the provision of goods, the arrival of the fleet, etc.

f. 117.   — Sept., 1616.   To Mr. Bangham.   Reports the arrival of the fleet, the destination of the ships, and gives details of their cargo.

f. 117a-18a.   5 Oct., 1616.   To J. Browne at Ahmadabad.   Gives information as above and an account of what money has been received from England.

f. 119-19a.   11 Oct., 1616.   To [? Capt. Pepwell].   Asking him to defer sending the convoy [? from Swally to Surat].

f. 119a.   14 Oct., 1616.   To [? Capt. Pepwell].   Informs him of the obstructive action of the 'customer' at Surat, which is only a 'trick' to extort a large present.

f. 120.   14 Oct., 1616.   To T. Mitford.   Recommends Haidar Beg's men to his care.   Relates a report that a town belonging to Mir Ja'far in the *pargana* of 'Uepatt' had been set on by thieves.   [Two letters.]

f. 121.   14 Oct., 1616.   Note of goods provided and sent to Ahmadabad.

f. 120-21.   15 and 16 Oct., 1616.   To J. Browne, etc., at Ahmadabad.   Account of goods received by the fleet and sent to Ahmadabad.   Cause of a fall in prices.   Notes Browne's intended journey to Cambay.

f. 121-21a.   17 and 18 Oct., 1616.   To F. Fettiplace [at Agra].   He is urged to send frequent advices to Surat of his proceedings.

f. 121a.   18 Oct., 1616.   To J. Browne, etc.   Note of charges to be paid for hire of carts.

f. 122.   20 Oct., 1616.   To Francis Futter (or Fuller).   He is ordered to hand over Elephants' teeth to bearers authorised to receive them.   A broker is sent as an interpreter.

f. 134.   17 Oct., 1616.   To Mr. Bangham.   Contains nothing of special interest.

f. 122-22a.   22 Oct., 1616.   To Sir Thomas Roe.   A long, interesting letter, commenting fully on the proceedings of the Ambassador.

f. 123-23a.   22 and ? 23 Oct., 1616.   To W. Biddulph.   Notes that English cloth is unsaleable at Agra.   If the King removes to Mandoa, R. Hughes is to be sent there with a consignment of cloth.   Instructions regarding 'Midnall's' money.   [Two letters.]

f. 123a.   23 Oct., 1616.   To F. Fettiplace.   Regarding indigo to be procured at Agra.

f. 123a-24.   23 Oct., 1616.   To J. Browne, at Ahmadabad.   Respecting the purchase and sale of goods.   The result of Browne's journey to 'Doulca' and 'Courry' will be awaited.

f. 124.   25 Oct., 1616.   To [Capt. H. Pepwell].   He is begged to restrain his people from injuring the Company's trade in quicksilver and to prevent the continuance of their disorderly behaviour.

f. 124a.   25 Oct., 1616.   To T. Mitford.   Instructions for an investment in piece-goods.

f. 125-26. 28 Oct., 1616. To Lucas Antheunis, at [Masulipatam]. He comments on the letters received from Masulipatam, and relates what has taken place in the northern settlements.

f. 126-27. 28 Oct., 1616. To Sir Thos. Roe. Remarks on the tyrannical conduct of ' Zulphercar ' Khan, the promise of the King to sign articles confirming former grants, etc., etc. A long letter full of interesting details.

f. 127-27a. A particular note of commodities required for the Southwards, vendible in Surat.

f. 127a-28. 30 Oct., 1616. To J. Browne. Instructions regarding the investment of goods for England.

f. 128-28a. 30 Oct., 1616. To Mr. Bangham. He is to ascertain how much Biana indigo can be procured at Agra.

f. 128a-29. 30 Oct., 1616. To Wm. Biddulph. Regarding the purchase of indigo and the sale of English cloth.

f. 129. 30 Oct., 1616. To Sir Thos. Roe. Notes the despatch of a ship to Persia.

f. 129. 31 Oct., 1616. To [? T.] Meth[w]old. He is to go to Ahmadabad, where more assistance is needed.

f. 129a-30a. Commission and instructions to Edward Connock, T. Barker, etc., in the ' voyadge and imployments ' for Persia.

f. 130a-33a. 2 and 7 Nov., 1616. General letter from T. Kerridge and the factors at Surat to the Company. Printed in *Letters Received*, Vol. IV, pp. 334-42, from the copy in the India Office, *Factory Records, Surat*, Vol. LXXXIV, No. 97.

f. 134a. 15 Nov., 1616. To [Capt. H. Pepwell]. Reports that the frigate seized by him was laden by the Portuguese and can be held in reprisal for injuries done to the British nation.

f. 134a. 16 Nov., 1616. To T. Rastell. Giving an account of the frigate from Diu seized by the English fleet, and of an interview with the *Shahbandar* of Surat regarding the occurrence.

f. 135. 17 and 18 Nov., 1616. To [Capt. H. Pepwell]. Repeating the information given to T. Rastell. [Two letters.]

f. 135a. 18 Nov., 1616. To ditto. Relating a brawl that has occurred between his followers and the inhabitants of Surat.

f. 136-39a. 18, 19 and 20 Nov., 1616. To Sir Thos. Roe. The letter of the 18th and 19th, with the exception of the first eight paragraphs, is printed in *Letters Received*, Vol. IV, pp. 343-54, from the copy at the India Office, *Factory Records, Surat*, Vol. LXXXIV, No. 103. The letter of the 20th describes the altercations between Kerridge and the *Shahbandar*, of Surat, regarding the Portuguese frigate which Kerridge refuses to surrender.

f. 140a. 24 Nov., 1616. To T. Mitford. He is desired to send an account of goods ready for despatch to Europe.

f. 141. 25 Nov., 1616. To [Capt. H. Pepwell]. Relates the deadlock in the dispute between the *Shahbandar* and customs officer, of Surat, regarding the captured frigate. Either the Company's honour or their trade must be sacrificed.

f. 140. 26 Nov., 1616. To Wm. Biddulph. Urging a speedy despatch of investments from Agra.

f. 141-41a. 26 Nov., 1616. To T. Mitford. He is ordered to come to some arrangement with the *sarrāfs* for a supply of money.

f. 141a-43. 26 Nov., 1616. To J. Browne [at Ahmadabad]. Various remarks concerning the conduct of trade. The *parwāna* of the Governor of Cambay has been sent to Broach.

f. 143a. 26 Nov., 1616. Sorts of goods required for Sumatra and Bantam to be provided in Cambay and Ahmadabad.

f. 144-46. 29 Nov., 1616. To Sir Thos. Roe. Relates the difficulties caused by the seizure of the Portuguese frigate. The letter contains many other points of interest.

f. 146a-47. 30 Nov., 1616. To W. Biddulph. Treats of sale and purchase of goods.

f. 147-47a. 1 Dec., 1616. To [Capt. H. Pepwell]. Regarding the affair of the captured Portuguese frigate and the threats of the Surat authorities in consequence.

f. 147a-48a, 149a. 1 and 2 Dec., 1616. To Mr. Bangham. It is hoped that the coming of the Prince to Burhanpur will assist the sale of the Company's goods. Advice of the expedition to Persia, etc.

f. 148a-49 ; 149a-50. 1 and 2 Dec., 1616. To Messrs. Woolman, etc. [? at Bantam]. Acknowledging their letter of 15 July and giving news of occurrences at Surat, etc. Advice concerning goods. [Two letters.]

f. 150-51. 3 Dec., 1616. J. Browne [at Ahmadabad]. Regarding investments for the Company.

f. 151-51a. 4 Dec., 1616. To T. Mitford. Describes the difficulty of remitting the money required at Agra.

f. 151a-52. 5 Dec., 1616. To [Capt. H. Pepwell]. Indigo, etc., shall be sent up to the ships as soon as possible if not hindered. Remarks on obstructions by officials at Surat.

f. 152-52a. 5 Dec., 1616. To T. Mitford. Regarding despatch of goods and customs to be paid thereon.

f. 152a-54a. 6, 7 and 12 Dec., 1616. To [Capt. H. Pepwell]. They have been compelled to consent to the release of the captured frigate. Sir Thos. Roe disapproves of the expedition to Persia. Goods to be sent ashore from the ships. [Four letters.]

f. 155-61. 12 and 14 Dec., 1616. To Sir Thos. Roe. Reasons for the expedition to Persia, with a long explanation and many other details.

f. 161a-62. 13 Dec., 1616. To Wm. Biddulph. His opinion, that the cost of a permanent factory at Agra will not be justified, is endorsed, etc.

f. 162a-63. 13 Dec., 1616. By F. Fettiplace. Regarding the provision of goods.

f. 163-63a. 14 and 16 Dec., 1616. To [Capt. H. Pepwell]. Requesting delivery of lead. An account of indigo sent aboard, etc. [Two letters.]

f. 163a. 18 Dec., 1616. To T. Mitford. Regarding piece-goods.

f. 164-65a. 20 and 21 Dec., 1616. To J. Browne [at Ahmadabad] Regarding the sale of quicksilver and lead, the provision of goods, relations with the Governor of Ahmadabad, etc.

f. 165. 21 Dec., 1616. To [Capt. H. Pepwell]. Respecting the sending of Mr. Harbert, to join Sir T. Roe at Court.

f. 165a-66. 24 Dec., 1616. To T. Mitford. Regarding investments for Europe and goods suitable for the southern factories.

f. 166-66a. 25 Dec., 1616. To J. Browne [at Ahmadabad]. Account of money sent for investments.

Vol. LXXXIV of *Factory Records, Surat*, contains Invoices of Goods, Nos. 133, 138, 139, 140, which do not appear in the B.M., MSS.

f. 166a-67. 1 Jan., 1616-17. To T. Mitford. Relating to goods.

f. 167-68. 3 Jan., 1616-17. To T. Bangham. Regarding provision and sale of goods.

f. 168-69.   3 Jan., 1616-17.   To Mr. Terry.   Instructions for his procedure in his journey in charge of presents for the Emperor Jahangir.

f. 169, 169a-170.   3 and 12 Jan., 1616-17.   To Mr. Young.   Instructions to take precautions against attack in his journey from Burhanpur.

f. 169a.   11 Jan., 1616-17.   To [Capt. H. Pepwell].   Money furnished him to distribute among his people to satisfy claims.

f. 170.   12 Jan., 1616-17.   To T. Bangham.   Contains nothing of special interest.

f. 170a.   12 Jan., 1616-17.   To F. Futter.   He is ordered to apprise Mr. Young of his arrival at 'Dayta '.   Instructions for his conduct there.

f. 171-73a.   15 Jan., 1616-17.   To Sir Thos. Roe.   Note of presents despatched and of goods in readiness, with many other matters of interest.

f. 175a-76.   15 and 16 Jan., 1616-17.   To T. Mitford.   Respecting trade, etc.   [Two letters.]

f. 173a-74a [14] or 16 Jan., 1616-17.   To W. Biddulph.   The retention or dissolution of the factory at Agra, etc., discussed.

f. 174a-75a.   16 Jan., 1616-17.   To J. Browne, etc., [at Ahmadabad]. News of the arrival of the Agra *kāfila* at ' Dayta ', etc.

f. 176-76a.   21 Jan., 1616-17.   To ditto.   Regarding the sale and purchase of goods.

f. 176a-77.   [21] Jan., 1616-17.   To T. Mitford.   Congratulates him on obtaining the release of some dyers that had been imprisoned.

f. 177-77a.   24 Jan., 1616-17.   To F. Fettiplace.   He is instructed to barter cloth for indigo, etc., etc.

1615-19.   **Journal of Sir Thomas Roe during**   *Add. MS. 6115, 288*
             his Embassy to India.   *fols.*

The whole of the Journal and the greater part of the letters in this MS. have been printed in two volumes, issued by the Hakluyt Society in 1899 (Second Series, Vols. I and II) and edited by Mr. Wm. Foster, C.I.E.   The work is entitled *The Embassy of Sir Thomas Roe to the Court of the Great Mogul*, 1615-19, edited with contemporary records. The letters omitted contain matters of minor interest, and those abridged by the Editor are either unimportant or contain matter which is also found in other letters.

Besides the Hakluyt Society's volumes, a certain number of the letters in Add. MS. 6115, have been printed elsewhere, or are to be found among the I.O. Records.   The following are instances :

f. 58.   15 [should be 16] Oct., 1615.   Sir Thos. Roe to the Governor of Surat.   Printed in Foster's *Letters Received*, Vol. III, pp. 303-4, from the original letter, O.C., 303.

f. 54b.   20 Oct., 1615.   Sir Thos. Roe to the Viceroy of Goa.   Printed in *Letters Received*, Vol. III, pp. 197-99.

f. 70.   25 Jan., 1615-16.   Sir Thos. Roe to the E.I. Co.   Printed in Foster's *Letters Received*, Vol. IV, pp. 9-21, from the original letter, O.C., 335.

f. 96.   1 May, 1616.   Sir Thos. Roe to Prince Khurram.   Printed in Foster's *Letters Received*, Vol. IV, pp. 101-2 from O.C., 360.

f. 113.   23 July, 1616.   Sir Thos. Roe, at Ajmer, to L. Antheunis, at Masulipatam.   Printed from the original, O.C., 382, in *Letters Received*, Vol. IV, p. 143.

f. 126.   15 Oct., 1616.   Sir Thos. Roe, at Ajmer, to the factors at Surat. Printed in *Letters Received*, Vol. IV, p. 202.   Original O.C., 410. There are slight variations in the two versions.

f. 149.   27 Nov., 1616.   Sir Thos. Roe to Sir Thos. Smyth, Governor of the E.I. Co.   Printed in *Letters Received*, Vol. IV, p. 245, from the original, O.C., 410.

f. 153.   1 Dec., 1616.   Sir Thos. Roe to the Company.   Printed in *Letters Received*, Vol. IV, p. 249, from the original, O.C., 411.

f. 173.   4 Jan., 1616-17.   Sir Thos. Roe to H. Pepwell.   Printed in *Letters Received*, Vol. V, p. 317.   There is another copy in *Marine Records*, Misc., I.O. Records, Vol. II, p. 29.

f. 160.   5 Jan., 1616-17.   Sir Thos. Roe to T. Rastell, etc., at Surat.   The greater portion printed in *Letters Received*, Vol. V, p. 325.

f. 164.   16 Jan., 1616-17.   Sir Thos. Roe to Sir T. Smyth, Governor of the E.I. Co.   Printed in *Letters Received*, Vol. V, p. 328.

f. 166.   17 Jan., 1616-17.   Sir Thos. Roe to W. Robbins, at Isfahan.   Printed from the original, O.C., 434, in *Letters Received*, Vol. V, p. 50.

f. 170.   28 Jan., 1616-17.   Sir Thos. Roe to Sir Thos. Smyth.   Printed in *Letters Received*, Vol. V, p. 333.

f. 175.   10 and 12 March, 1616-17.   Sir Thos. Roe to the factors at Surat.   Printed in *Letters Received*, Vol. V, p. 335.

f. 186.   25 April, 1617.   Ditto to ditto.   Printed in *Letters Received*, Vol. V, p. 200.   Copy also in O.C., 467.

f. 180.   7 April, 1617.   Sir Thos. Roe, at Mandoa to the factors at Surat.   Printed in *Letters Received*, Vol. V, pp. 338-44.

f. 207.   21 Aug., 1617.   Ditto to W. Robbins, at Isfahan.   Printed in *Letters Received*, Vol. VI, pp. 75-76.   Another copy, O.C., 530.

f. 207.   21 Aug., 1617.   [Ditto] to [Sir Paul Pindar at Constantinople].   Printed in *Letters Received*, Vol. VI, pp. 298-301.

f. 270.   6 Oct., 1617.   Sir Thos. Roe, at Mandoa to the factors at Agra.   Printed in *Letters Received*, Vol. VI, pp. 105-7.   Another copy, without PS., O.C., 543.

f. 264.   29 Sept., 1617.   Sir Thos. Roe, at Mandoa to the factors at Surat.   Printed in *Letters Received*, Vol. VI, pp. 301-7.

1615,   **Unsigned letter.**   *Cotton, Ch. III, 13,*
29 April   *fols. 10-10a.*

This contains a brief account of the voyage of the 'Tomazin', one of General David Middleton's fleet.

1615-16.   **(1) A true relation of my voyage**   *Egerton MS. 2121,*
11 April-   **for Succadana, Patani and Japan**   *fols.15-44a, 45-66a.*
7 Sept.,   **in the *Hosiander*.**
1615.

11 Sept.,   **(2) A brief relation of a voyage for**
1615—   **'Ossica, Meaco and Surungona'.**
13 March,
1615-16.

Both sections very much damaged and parts of pages quite destroyed.

1615-22.   **Diary of Richard Cocks, head of**   *Add. MS. 31300-1.*
                        the English factory at Firando
                        [Hirado], Japan.

This Diary, which includes the dates 1 June, 1615, to 24 March, 1621-22 has been edited by Sir Edward Maunde Thompson and printed by the Hakluyt Society in two Vols. (Series I, Vols. LXVI, LXVII), London, 1882.

1616-17, 9 Feb., 1615-16. 24 Jan., 1616-17.	**Journal of a voyage for Surat and other places in the East Indies, with a fleet of six East India Company's ships, under Captain Benjamin Josep.**	*Egerton MS. 2121,* *fols. 84-100.*

The MS. is badly stained and partly destroyed,

? 1616.	**An undated, mutilated fragment. This is probably a portion of the Company's instructions to William Keeling.**	*Cotton MS. Otho E.* *VIII, fols. 254-* *63.*

The person to whom the instructions are addressed is ordered to choose four principal places where responsible persons should reside, such as Surat, the Coromandel Coast, Bantam and Patani; and directions are given as to which part of the country each should control. If a factory is established at Mocha, a chief is to be appointed there also.

The fragment concludes with an interesting account of trade on the Coromandel Coast, in Bengal and Peru, apparently derived from the reports of Peter Floris.

In the *Calendar of State Papers, East Indies,* 1513-1616, p. 300, this document is conjecturally assigned to 1614, with a suggestion that its contents were addressed to Jourdain. See Foster, *Letters Received,* IV, xv.

The MS., as stated above, is much mutilated, and the top of every page is burnt off.

1616, 5 May.	**A resolution recorded on board the** *Clove* **respecting the East India Company's trade at Tidore.**	*Cotton MS. Ch. III,* *13, fol. 11.*

1616, 6 Nov.	**Copy of a commission by Henry Pepwell, commander of the Company's fleet, to Alexander Childe, captain of the** *James,* **for a voyage to Jask in Persia.**	*Egerton MS. 2121,* *fol. 103a.*

Badly damaged. For a good copy see O.C., 408, I.O Records, printed in Foster's *Letters Received,* Vol. IV, p. 225.

1616, 10 Dec.	**Copy of a protest by the factors landed in Jask, Persia, against Alexander Childe, master of the** *James.*	*Egerton M.S. 2121,* *fol. 104.*

Mutilated. See O.C., 413, I.O. Records for a good copy and Foster's *Letters Received,* Vol. IV, p. 255, for a printed version.

1616, 17 Dec.	**Consultation of factors in Persia.**	*Egerton M.S. 2121,* *fols. 104a-5a.*

Mutilated. For a good copy see O.C., 416, I.O. Records. Cf. Foster's *Letters Received,* Vol. IV, p. 263, for a printed version.

[1618,]   Translation of a letter from the   *Add. MS. 4155, fol.*
[Feb.]   **Great Mogul to King James I.**   *100.*

In Sir Thos. Roe's hand. Abstracted in Foster's *English Factories*, 1618-21, pp. 22-23. Printed in *The Embassy of Sir Thomas Roe*, ed. Foster, Hak. Soc., Vol. II, p. 557. There is another version of this letter, with slight variations, Add. MS. 29975, fol. 37.

1618,   Notes on the Dutch business bet-   *Add. MS. 12498, fol.*
20 Dec.,   ween the King's Commissioners   *335a-36.*
1618,   **and those for the States General.**
and 5 Jan.,
1618-19.

1618-19,   The complaints of the English   *Add.   MS.   12498,*
11 Jan.   merchants of the Company of the   *fols. 327-33.*
East Indies against the Hol-
landers delivered to Sir Julius
Cæsar.

The merchants contest the claims of the Dutch to a monopoly of trade in Ternate, Banda and the Molucca Islands generally. They complain that the Dutch gave the ruler of Pulicat to understand that they were pirates. They give details of the unwarrantable actions of the Dutch with regard to Pularoon and of other unfriendly actions towards their ships in the East Indies.

1618-19,   Tabular statement of the complaint   *Add. MS. 12498, fol.*
16 Jan.   of the English against the Dutch.   *338-39.*

The complaint contains a list of injuries done to the King's Majesty in his dominions by word and deed, and to his subjects, their persons and estates.

1618-19,   The Complaints of the Hollanders,   *Add. MS. 12498, fols.*
18 Jan.   etc., against the subjects of the   *317-25.*
Great King of Great Britain, *viz.*,
against the Company of the East
India Merchants.

The English are accused of assisting the enemies of the Dutch in Amboyna, Banda, Ternate, etc., of violent conduct towards the Dutch in Bantam, of obstructing them in Siam and Macassar and Succadana. Details of all the injuries complained of are set out at length and reparation demanded.

1618-19,   The business between the State of   *Add. 12498, fol. 315.*
18 Jan.   the Lowe Countries and the East
India Merchants of England.

15 Feb. Note of heads of points to be inserted in the Treaty. Private articles between the two Companies to be appended by the King and the States General touching the Moluccas.

1618-22.   Papers relating to the differences   *Lansdowne MS. 151.*
between the English and Dutch
East India Companies.

This is a most important MS., throwing vivid light on the Anglo-Dutch rivalry in the East. Compare also Calendar of State Papers, *East Indies*, by W. N. Sainsbury.

The folio number given first is the number as paged by the Museum authorities and the number following within brackets is the original number on the MS. and the one referred to in the Catalogue of Lansdowne MSS.

f. 307 (258). [1619.] Measures necessary for the establishment of trade at Bantam.

f. 308-9 (259-60). [1619.] The State of the question between the English and Dutch trading to the East Indies. The views of both parties stated at a conference of the Commissioners.

f. 293-300 (242-47). 2 [? June] 1619. Articles of the Treaty between the English and Dutch concerning their trade to the East Indies. Thirty articles. In English. Signed in London by Dudley Diggs, etc., and J. Van [? Goch], etc.

f. 301-6 (251-54). 7 July, 1619. Order for the execution of certain articles of the Treaty between the English and the Dutch, with an explanation of the same.

f. 286, 289 (235, 238). 21 April—30 May, 1620. Extracts taken out of several joint consultations of the English and the Dutch in the Indies after the arrival of the ship, the *Bull*, and before the arrival of the *Vrede*, proving both Publication and Execution of the Treatie.

f. 285, 290 (234, 239). 23 Sept., 1621. Complaint of the treatment of English merchants by the Dutch in the East Indies, especially at Sumatra, followed by remarks in Latin.

f. 272 (219). [1622.] Concerning the restitution of ships after publication of the Treaty in the East Indies on the part of the English Company farther alleged out of the Texts and express words of Law. The 'words of Law' are quoted in Latin.

f. 311 (262). [? 1621-22.] The State of the Losses and Hindrances of the English East India Company by the Dutch.

f. 260 (208). 1622. The demands of restitution by the English from the Netherlands East India Company, the total being £179,683-18-0. The demands of restitution by the Netherlands from the English East India Company, the total being £1,838-6-7.

f. 287-88 (236). 2 Jan., 1621-2. A meeting called to advise what breaches 'our merchants can assigne of the last articles and their performance, that wee may deal with the States accordingly'.

f. 277-82 (225-27). 6 Jan., 1621-22. The complaints of the East India Company of London against the East India Company of the Netherlands, with a list of goods brought into Holland, 20 March, 1621-22.

Endorsed : ' The Remonstrance of the wronges done by the Dutch to the English in the East Indies contrary to the articles of the last Treaty between the two nations'.

f. 312-17 (263-67). 19 Jan., 1621-2. A representation of the reasons produced by those of the Company of the Lower Countryes to demonstrate that the English Company have no right to pretend that restitution of goods taken from them in the East Indies ought to be made in Europe.

f. 255 (202). 10 May, 1622. A declaration of the Dutch—their denial of the restoring of our ships after the arrival of the *Bull* and the *Vrede*.

f. 256-57 (203-4). 15 May, 1622. Answer of the English to the protest and papers of the Dutch concerning their pretended offer to restore our ships in the Indies.

f. 273-76 (220-23). 24 Aug., 1622. A summary of the proceedings of the Commissioners touching the E.I. trade, recapitulating events from 6 Jan., 1621-22.

f. 265-71 (211-14).   4 and 19 Sept., 16 Oct., 9, 11 and 28 Nov., 12 Dec., 1622.   Meetings of the East India Commission.

Offers made by the Dutch respecting the English demands regarding Bantam, Lantour, etc.   Recapitulation of what took place on the subject in Jan., April and May, 1620.   Discussions on the various points in dispute.

f. 251-52 (198-99).—[? Oct.] 1622.   The opinion of my [cut off] concerning the business of [cut off] ult., October, 1622.

The Ambassadors of the States General demand that in all undertakings in the East Indies the English shall bear half the charge, as well as receive half the profit, and cite the siege of Bantam as a particular instance.   Their Lordships determine that the English shall bear only that proportion of the charge fixed by the Council of Defence according to the Treaty.

f. 253-54 (200-1).   28 Oct., 1622.   A particular declaration of the state of the business of Bantam between the Dutch and the English.

' Proofes that the English Company have noe wayes beene defective in procureinge the Trade of Bantam both by faire means and also by the beseidginge of Bantam so farre as they were enjoyned by the Councell of Defence in India.'

f. 261-62 (208-9).   16 Dec., 1622.   The points necessary to be considered of in the Reglement of Trade for the Future.

These concern the 20 ships of defence, forts, Pularoon, Lantore, place of residence for the English Council of Defence, punishment of the people belonging to each Company. The building of forts to be respited for two years more on both sides, and any built by either since the last Treaty to be demolished.

f. 263-64 (210).   16 Dec., 1622.   The state of the questions depending, as yet undetermined between the English and Dutch E.I. Companies concerning restitution.

f. 283 (232).   27 Dec., 1622.   ' Reasons drawen from severall and experimentall grounds whereby the English E.I. Co. doe prove their offers made to the Netherlands Companie of twentie pounds per last fraight and ten per centum for assurance, to be reasonable '.

f. 319-20 (270-71).   10 May, 1622.   Particulars of the names, burthen and value of the ships taken by the Netherlands E.I. Co. in India from the English E.I. Co., which have been demanded and not restored, with reasons why restitution should be made, and proofs of divers demands for the same.

f. 323-30 (275-80).   21. Jan., 1621-2.   Answer to the Dutch reasons against restitution of goods taken from the English E.I. Co. and carried into Holland.

Proofs that these goods were brought into the Netherlands (fol. 326), and reasons why restitution is demanded in Holland (fols. 327-30).

f. 331-32 (281-82).   2 Jan., 1619-20.   Articles of the Treaty (Nos. 1-23) between the English and the Dutch touching the Trade of the East Indies.

f. 334-61 (284-307).   April-May, 1622.   Papers concerning the controversy between the English and the Dutch respecting the restitution of the ship, *Black Lyon*, burnt by the English, and her goods.   These papers are six in number :

April, 1622.   (1) A brief state of the controversy between the English and the Dutch concerning the restitution of the *Black Lyon* (fols. 335-36).

[April] 1622.   (2) Discourse by Henry Marten concerning the *Black Lyon* and her goods, disclaiming any responsibility on the part of the English.   [fols. 340-43.]

12 April, 1622. (3) An appendix or answer to the Dutch propositions for restoring the *Black Lyon* (fols. 338-39).

2 May, 1622. (4) The sum of the difference [dispute] concerning the *Black Lyon* digested into three questions (fols. 338-39).

4 May, 1622. (5) The reply of the Dutch touching the *Black Lyon*, with proofs why the ship should be restored without any question (fols. 348-54).

6 May, 1622. (6) The answer of the English to the replies of the Dutch concerning the *Black Lyon*.

The papers in the above MS. do not appear in strict chronological order, but they all deal with the same subject, and I have thought best to catalogue them in the order in which they appear according to folios.

1618/19-	**Register of Letters of the Factors**	*Egerton MS. 2122,*
1619/20.	**of the East India Company**	*212 fols.*
	at Surat, *viz.,* Thomas Kerridge,	
	Thomas Rastell, Giles James and	
	others, February, 1618-19, to February	
	1619-20. Much mutilated and damaged.	

Nearly the whole of this MS. has been used by Mr. William Foster in his *English Factories*, 1618-21. A chronological list is given below with the name of the writer and addressee, and a reference to the pages in Mr. Foster's volume, where abstracts or copies will be found. This work will be styled, for the sake of brevity, *E.F.*

f. 1-25. 9 and 15 Feb., 1618-19. T. Kerridge and T. Rastell, at Surat, to the Company (*E.F.* pp. 50-60). [Badly damaged and many portions gone. There is an abstract of this letter in *Factory Records, Misc.* (I.O. Records), Vol. I, pp. 6 ff.]

f. 26-27. 15 Feb., 1618-19. T. Kerridge and T. Rastell aboard the *Dragon*, in Swally Road, to the President (*E.F.*, p. 65). [Much damaged and portions entirely gone.]

f. 27-28. 15 Feb., 1618-19. T. Kerridge and T. Rastell and G. James, aboard the *Dragon*, in Swally Road, to Wm. Nicholls, at Achin (*E.F.*, p. 64-65). [This is a badly damaged copy of O.C., 754 (I.O. Records).]

f. 28-29. 15 Feb., 1618-19. Directions from the Surat factors to Messrs. Salbank, Heynes and Wallis, bound for the Red Sea (*E.F.*, p. 66). [Badly damaged.]

f. 29. 15 Feb., 1618-19. Directions to Mr. Fursland and other merchants of the fleet (*E.F.*, p. 66). [Badly damaged.]

f. 29-32. 26 and 28 Feb., 1618-19. T. Kerridge, T. Rastell and G. James, at Surat, to the factors at Ahmadabad (*E.F.*, pp. 75-76). [Damaged.]

f. 51-52. [— Feb.] 1618-19. Goods to be provided for Persia (*E.F.*, p. 76).

f. 52. 6 March, 1618-19. T. Kerridge to [Wm.] Marten, at Broach (*E.F.*, p. 76).

f. 52-55. 8 March, 1618-19. T. Kerridge, T. Rastell and G. James, at Surat, to the factors at Masulipatam (*E.F.*, pp. 76-78).

f. 55-57. [— March, 1618-19.] Goods sent for England in the *Royal Anne*: (1) on account of the Old Joint Stock ; (2) on account of the New Joint Stock. Goods shipped to the southward in Captain Bonner's fleet. Goods sent to the Red Sea in the *Lyon* (*E.F.* pp. 61-64).

f. 57-62.   12 and 13 March, 1618-19.   T. Kerridge, T. Rastell and G. James to the Co., dated at Surat (*E.F.*, pp. 78-83).   The original of this letter O.C., 777 (I.O. Records), is partly written in a cipher.

f. 62-64.   15 March, 1618-19.   T. Kerridge, at Surat, to the factors at Mocha (*E.F.*, p. 83).

f. 64-66.   16 March, 1618-19.   T. Kerridge, T. Rastell and G. James to the factors at Agra, dated from Surat (*E.F.*, pp. 84-85).

f. 66.   17 March, 1618-19.   Ditto, do., do., at Surat, to Wm. Marten, at Broach (*E.F.*, p. 85).

f. 66-67.   17 March, 1618-19.   Ditto to the factors at Ahmadabad, (*E.F.*, pp. 85-86).

f. 67.   22 March, 1618-19.   Pass given by the Surat factors to a Surat junk (*E.F.*, p. 86).

f. 67-68.   26 March, 1619.   Directions from the Surat Council to Robert Hutchinson proceeding to Baroda (*E.F.*, p. 87).

f. 68.   26 March, 1619.   T. Kerridge, T. Rastell and G. James, at Surat, to Wm. Marten, at Broach (*E.F.*, p. 87).

f. 68.   1 April, 1619.   Ditto to ditto (*E.F.*, pp. 87-88).

f. 68-69.   2 April, 1619.   Ditto to John Bangham (*E.F.*, p. 88).

f. 69.   4 April, 1619.   Ditto to the factors at Masulipatam (*E.F.*, p. 88).

f. 69-71.   6 and 7 April, 1619.   Ditto to Wm. Biddulph [at Burhanpur] (*E.F.*, pp. 88-90).

f. 71.   6 April, 1619.   Ditto to the 'officers of Suratte' (*E.F.*, p. 90).

f. 72.   7 April, 1619.   Ditto to John Bangham, at Burhanpur (*E.F.*, p. 90).

f. 72.   8 April, 1619.   Petition of the English residents, at Surat to 'the Lord Cancana, Shield of the Soulders' (*E.F.*, pp. 90-91).

f. 73.   8 April, 1619.   T. Kerridge, T. Rastell and G. James, at Surat, to the factors at Agra (*E.F.*, p. 91).

f. 73-74.   10 April, 1619.   Ditto to the factors at Ahmadabad (*E.F.*, pp. 91-93).

f. 75-76.   [April] 1619.   Goods to be provided for Bantam (*E.F.*, p. 93).

f. 76.   11 April, 1619.   T. Kerridge, at Surat, to Wm. Martin, at Broach (*E.F.*, p. 93).

f. 76-77.   12 April, 1619.   T. Kerridge, T. Rastell and G. James, at Surat, to Wm. Biddulph [at Burhanpur] (*E.F.*, p. 94).

f. 77.   15 April, 1619.   Ditto to Robert Hutchinson, at Baroda (*E.F.*, p. 94).

f. 78-79.   [April] 1619.   Goods to be provided for Sumatra (*E.F.*, p. 94).

f. 79-80.   20 April, 1619.   T. Kerridge, etc., at Surat, to Wm. Martin [at Broach] (*E.F.*, p. 95).

f. 80-81.   21 April, 1619.   Ditto to R. Hutchinson [at Baroda] (*E.F.*, p. 95).

f. 81.   25 April, 1619.   Ditto to ditto (*E.F.*, p. 95).

f. 81.   29 April, 1619.   Ditto to ditto (*E.F.*, p. 96).

f. 82.   29 April, 1619.   Ditto to Wm. Martin [at Broach] (*E.F.*, p. 96).

f. 82.   3 May, 1619.   T. Kerridge, at Surat, to J. Bangham [at Burhanpur] (*E.F.*, p. 96).

f. 83.   4 May, 1619..   T. Kerridge, T. Rastell and G. James, at Surat, to ditto (*E.F.*, p. 97).

f. 83-85.   4 May, 1619.   T. Kerridge, at Surat, to Francisco Soares [at Bijapur].   In Portuguese.   (Abstracted in English in *E.F.*, p. 97).

f. 85.   6 May, 1619.   T. Kerridge and T. Rastell, at Surat, to the factors at Agra (*E.F.*, p. 97).

f. 86. 11 May, 1619. T. Kerridge, at Surat, to R. Hutchinson [at Baroda] (*E.F.*, pp. 97-98).

f. 86. 12 and 13 May, 1619. T. Kerridge, T. Rastell and G. James, at Surat, to Wm. Martin [at Broach] (*E.F.*, p. 98).

f. 87. 14 May, 1619. Ditto to R. Hutchinson [at Baroda] (*E.F.*, p. 98).

f. 87. 14 May, 1619. Ditto to the factors at Broach (*E.F.*, p. 98).

f. 88. 21 May, 1619. Ditto to ditto (*E.F.*, p. 99).

f. 88. 22 May, 1619. Ditto to ditto (*E.F.*, p. 99).

f. 88-90. 23 May, 1619. Instructions from T. Kerridge and T. Rastell to G. James proceeding to Burhanpur, enclosing a list of goods to be provided in Burhanpur and Dharangaon for Persia (*E.F.*, pp. 99-100).

f. 90-91. 26 May, 1619. T. Kerridge and T. Rastell, at Surat, to the factors at Broach (*E.F.*, p. 100).

f. 91-93. 29 May, 1619. Ditto to ditto (*E.F.*, 100-2).

f. 93-95. 6 June, 1619. Ditto to Francis Fettiplace, etc., at Agra (*E.F.*, pp. 102-3).

f. 95-97. 6 June, 1619. Ditto to Wm. Biddulph, at Agra (*E.F.*, p. 103).

f. 97. 7 June, 1619. T. Kerridge, at Surat, to W. Biddulph and F. Fettiplace, at [Agra]. They are directed to ' participate ' letters sent from Surat. The messengers to await a reply.

f. 97-98. 8 June, 1619. T. Kerridge and T. Rastell, at Surat, to the factors at Broach (*E.F.*, p. 104).

f. 98-99. 13 June, 1619. Ditto to ditto (*E.F.*, p. 104).

f. 99. 18 June, 1619. Ditto to [Giles] James, at Burhanpur (*E.F.*, p. 104).

f. 100. 20 June, 1619. T. Kerridge, at Surat, to the factors at Ahmadabad (*E.F.*, p. 105).

f. 100. 29 June, 1619. T. Rastell and R. Hutchinson, at Surat, to T. Kerridge, at Broach (*E.F.*, p. 105).

f. 104. 1 July, 1619. T. Kerridge, at Broach, to the factors at Surat (*E.F.*, p. 105).

f. 104. 5 July, 1619. Ditto to ditto (*E.F.*, p. 106).

f. 101. 5 July, 1619. T. Rastell, at Surat, to T. Kerridge, at Broach (*E.F.*, p. 106).

f. 101-2. 10 July, 1619. T. Rastell and R. Hutchinson, at Surat, to T. Kerridge, at Broach (*E.F.*, p. 106).

f. 105-6. 12 July, 1619. T. Kerridge, etc., at Broach, to the factors at Surat (*E.F.* p. 107).

f. 106. 14 July, 1619. Ditto to G. James, at Burhanpur (*E.F.*, p. 107).

f. 107-8. 14 July, 1619. T. Kerridge, at Broach, to W. Biddulph, at Agra (*E.F.*, p. 107).

f. 108. 15 July, 1619. T. Kerridge, W. Martin, etc., at Broach, to the factors at Surat (*E.F.*, pp. 108-9).

There are two folios numbered 108.

f. 108-9. [? 15] July, 1619. T. Kerridge, at Broach, to the factors at Ahmadabad (*E.F.*, p. 109).

f. 102-3. 16 July, 1619. T. Rastell, at Surat, to T. Kerridge, etc., at [Broach] (*E.F.*, p. 109).

f. 108. [23] July, 1619. T. Kerridge and T. Rastell, at Surat, to [the factors at Broach] (*E.F.*, p. 111).

f. 108. 5 August, 1619. Ditto to ditto (*E.F.*, p. 111).

f. 111-12. 9 and 10 August, 1619. Ditto to Wm. Biddulph, at Agra (*E.F.*, p. 111).

f. 112-13. 10 August, 1619. Ditto to G. James, at Burhanpur (*E.F.*, p. 112).

f. 114. 14 August, 1619. Ditto to the factors at Broach (*E.F.*, p. 113).

f. 114-17. 16 August, 1619. Ditto to the factors at Ahmadabad (*E.F.*, p. 113).

f. 118-19. 17 August, 1619. Ditto to the factors at Broach (*E.F.*, p. 113).

f. 117. 18 August, 1619. T. Kerridge, at Surat, to W. Martin, at Broach (*E.F.*, p. 113).

f. 118. [? Aug.] 1619. T. Kerridge to Is-haq Beg, Governor of Surat (*E.F.*, p. 114).

f. 119. 20 August, 1619. T. Kerridge and T. Rastell, at Surat, to the factors at Broach (*E.F.*, p. 114).

f. 117-18. [21] August, 1619. Ditto to the factors at Ahmadabad (*E.F.*, p. 114).

f. 119-20. 23 August, 1619. Ditto to the factors at Broach (*E.F.*, p. 114).

f. 120-21. 25 August, 1619. T. Kerridge, at Surat, to G. James [at Burhanpur] (*E.F.*, p. 114).

f. 121-24. 26 August, 1619. T. Kerridge and T. Rastell, at Surat, to the factors at Masulipatam (*E.F.*, pp. 114-15).

f. 124-27. 2 [6] August, 1619. Ditto to Wm. Methwold, at Masulipatam (*E.F.*, p. 115).

f. 124. 27 August, 1619. T. Kerridge, at Surat, to G. Ball, at Masulipatam (*E.F.*, p. 116).

f. 127. [? 30] August, 1619. T. Kerridge and T. Rastell, at Surat, to the commander of the English fleet at Masulipatam (*E.F.*, p. 117). [Damaged.]

f. 127. 30 August, 1619. T. Kerridge, at Surat, to A. Spalding, etc., at Masulipatam (*E.F.*, p. 117). [Damaged.]

f. 127-28. 31 August, 1619. T. Kerridge and T. Rastell, at Surat, to the factors at Ahmadabad (*E.F.*, p. 117).

f. 128. 31 August, 1619. Ditto to the factors at Broach (*E.F.*, p. 117).

f. 129-30. 1 Sept., 1619. Ditto to G. James, at Burhanpur (*E.F.*, p. 117).

f. 130-32. 1 Sept., 1619. Ditto to [Wm. Biddulph] at Agra (*E.F.*, p. 118).

f. 132. — Sept., 1619. T. Kerridge, at Surat, to the factors at Broach (*E.F.*, p. 119).

f. 132-33. — Sept., 1619. Ditto and T. Rastell to the factors at Ahmadabad (*E.F.*, p. 119).

f. 133-34. [7] Sept., 1619. Ditto to the factors at Broach (*E.F.*, p. 119).

f. 133-34. 8 Sept., 1619. Ditto to the factors at Broach (*E.F.*, p. 119).

f. 134. 10 Sept., 1619. [T. Kerridge and T. Rastell] at Surat, to [G. James] at Burhanpur (*E.F.*, p. 119).

f. 135. 11 Sept., 1619. T. Kerridge to the Acting Governor of Surat (*E.F.*, p. 120).

f. 135-36. 11 Sept., 1619. T. Kerridge and T. Rastell, at Surat, to the Bantam Council at Masulipatam (*E.F.*, p. 120).

f. 136. 11 Sept., 1619. T. Kerridge, at Surat, to the factors at Masulipatam (*E.F.*, p. 120). [Damaged.]

f. 137. 14 Sept., 1619. Ditto to Is-haq Beg, Governor of Surat (*E.F.*, p. 120).

f. 137-38. 15 Sept., 1619. T. Kerridge and T. Rastell, at Surat, to the factors at Broach (*E.F.*, p. 121).

f. 138. 16 Sept., 1619. Ditto   do.   (*E.F.*, p. 121).

f. 138. 17 Sept., 1619. Ditto   do.   (*E.F.*, p. 121).

f. 138-40. 17 Sept., 1619. [T. Kerridge] at Surat, to the factors at Ahmadabad (*E.F.*, p. 121). [Damaged.]

f. 138. 17 Sept., 1619. T. Kerridge and T. Rastell, at Surat, to Wm. Biddulph (*E.F.*, pp. 121-22). [Damaged.]

f. 141. 19 Sept., 1619. T. Kerridge, at Surat, to J. Bangham, at Burhanpur (*E.F.*, p. 122). [Damaged.]

f. 141-42. 25 Sept., 1619. T. Kerridge, T. Rastell and G. James, at Surat, to J. Bangham, at Burhanpur (*E.F.*, p. 122). [Damaged.]

f. 142. 25 Sept., 1619. T. Kerridge, at Surat, to Robert Tottle (*E.F.*, p. 122). [Damaged.]

f. 140-41. 25 Sept., 1619. T. Kerridge, T. Rastell and G. James, at Surat, to the factors at Ahmadabad (*E.F.*, p. 123).

f. 142-43. 30 Sept., 1619. T. Kerridge, at Surat, to W. Biddulph [at Agra] (*E.F.*, p. 123). [Damaged.]

f. 143. [2] Oct., 1619. Ditto to the factors at Broach (*E.F.*, pp. 123-24).

f. 143. 2 Oct., 1619. Ditto to the commander of the English ships at Surat Bar (*E.F.*, p. 124).

f. 144. 6 Oct., 1619. Ditto to the factors at Broach (*E.F.*, p. 125). [Damaged.]

f. 144. 6 Oct., 1619. Ditto to the commander of the fleet (*E.F.*, p. 144). [Damaged.]

f. 144-45. [6 Oct.] 1619. Ditto to [the factors on board the ships]. (*E.F.*, p. 125). [Damaged.]

f. 146-47. [7 Oct.] 1619. [Ditto] to the factors at Ahmadabad (*E.F.*, pp. 125-26). [Damaged.]

f. 147-48. 7 Oct., 1619. Ditto to Wm. Biddulph (*E.F.*, p. 126). [Damaged.]

f. 145-46. 7 Oct.. 1619. Petition to Prince Khurram (Shah Jahan) (*E.F.*, pp. 126-27). [Damaged.]

f. 148. 8 Oct., 1619. T. Kerridge, T. Rastell and G. James, at Surat, to the factors at Masulipatam (*E.F.*, p. 127).

f. 154. [? 8 Oct.] 1619. Ditto to W. Martin, at Broach (*E.F.*, p. 127).

f. 150. [? 8 Oct.] 1619. Ditto to the commander of the fleet at Swally (*E.F.*, p. 128).

f. 150-51. 9 Oct., 1619. Ditto to [the Bantam Council] (*E.F.*, p. 128). [Partly illegible.]

f. 154. 9 October, 1619. T. Kerridge, etc., to Wm. Martin and R. Lancaster [at Broach] (*E.F.*, p. 128). [Damaged.]

f. 151-52. 9 October, 1619. T. Kerridge, at Surat, to [? Capt. Martin Pring] (*E.F.*, p. 128).

f. 152-53. 10 Oct., 1619. T. Kerridge, etc., at Surat to [Capt. J. Bickley] (*E.F.*, p. 152).

f. 153. 10 Oct., 1619. Ditto to the merchants arrived in the fleet (*E.F.*, p. 128). [Damaged.]

f. 154. [? 10 Oct.] 1619. T. Kerridge, at Surat, to [? Capt. Bickley] at Swally (*E.F.*, p. 129). [Damaged.]

f. 154. 12 Oct., 1619. Ditto to [Wm. Martin, at Broach] (*E.F.*, p. 129).

f. 155. [? 13] Oct., 1619. Ditto to Messrs. [? Ewing] and Dyer or here [on board the fleet at Swally] (*E.F.*, p. 129). [Much damaged.]

f. 155-56. [? 18] Oct., 1619. Ditto to J. Browne, etc., at Ahmadabad (*E.F.*, pp. 129-30). [Much damaged.]

f. 156-57. 18 Oct., 1619. Ditto to [Wm. Martin] at Broach (*E.F.*, p. 130). [Much damaged.]

f. 157. [? 19] Oct., 1619. Ditto to J. Browne, etc., at Ahmadabad (*E.F.*, p. 130). [Damaged.]

f. 157.   19 Oct., 1619.   Ditto to W. Biddulph [at Agra] (*E.F.*, pp. 130-31).   [Much damaged.]

f. 159.   20 October, 1619.   Petition from the Surat factors to Afzal Khan (*E.F.*, p. 131).

f. 160.   [20 Oct.] 1619.   Petition from the Surat factors to the Prince (*E.F.*, p. 131).   [Much damaged.]

f. 160.   22 Oct., 1619.   T. Kerridge, at Surat, to [Robert] Young (at Swally] (*E.F.*, p. 132).   [Damaged.]

f. 160.   22 Oct., 1619.   Ditto to the commanders and masters of the fleet (*E.F.*, p. 132).   [Damaged.]

f. 161.   22 Oct., 1619.   Ditto to Wm. Martin, at Broach (*E.F.*, p. 132). [Damaged.]

f. 161.   [? 28 Oct.] 1619.   Ditto to Capt. Bickley, at Swally (*E.F.*, p. 132). [Damaged.]

f. 161-62.   28 Oct., 1619.   Ditto to the Captain of the Guards [? at the Watering Place] (*E.F.*, p. 132).   [Damaged.]

f. 162.   [? 28] Oct., 1619.   Ditto to J. Browne, etc., at Ahmadabad (*E.F.*, p. 133).   [Damaged.]

f. 162a.   — Oct., 1619.   Ditto to Mr. Baker, etc., concerning goods for Persia.   [Much mutilated.]

f. 162a-68.   29 Oct., 1619.   [Ditto] to ditto.   Sir Thos. Roe left for England, 17 Feb.   Remarks concerning commerce.   The names of numerous commodities mentioned.   [Much damaged.]

f. 168.   [? Oct.] 1619.   T. Kerridge and T. Rastell to [? Mr. Baker (or Barker), etc.].   Sending specie, etc.   [Much mutilated.]

f. 168a.   [1 Nov.] 1619.   T. Kerridge and T. Rastell, at Surat, to Wm. Martin, at Broach (*E.F.*, p. 133).   [Damaged.]

f. 167-73.   [? Nov.] 1619.   T. Kerridge, T. Rastell and G. James to the Company.   [Almost entirely illegible and partly torn away.]

f. 173-75.   [? 3 Nov.] 1619.   Commission to Capt. Bickley for a voyage to Persia (*E.F.*, pp. 133-34).   [Partly illegible.]

f. 175.   7 and 15 Nov., 1619.   T. Kerridge, etc., at Surat, to the factors at Broach (*E.F.*, p. 144)   [Damaged.]

f. 176.   [? 15 Nov.] 1619.   Ditto to Mirza Jam Quli Beg, Captain of Surat Castle (*E.F.*, p. 145).

f. 177-78.   [? 15 Nov.] 1619.   Ditto to ditto.   (*E.F.*, p. 145).   [Damaged.]

f. 179-81.   16 and 18 Nov., 1619.   Ditto to Wm. Biddulph, etc., at Agra (*E.F.*, pp. 145-46).   [Much damaged.]

f. 177-78.   [? Nov.] 1619.   Petition of T. Kerridge, etc., to the Prince [Shāh Jahān] (*E.F.*, pp. 146-47).   [Much damaged.]

f. 178.   [Nov.] 1619.   Ditto to Afzal Khan, the Prince's Diwan (*E.F.*, pp. 147-48).   [Much damaged.]

f. 181-82.   20 Nov., 1619.   T. Kerridge, at Surat, to Wm. Martin, at Broach (*E.F.*, p. 14).

f. 182-85.   22 Nov., 1619.   T. Kerridge, etc., to J. Browne, etc., at Ahmadabad (*E.F.*, pp. 148-49).   [Much damaged.]

f. 185.   22 Nov., 1619.   T. Kerridge, at Surat, to Wm. Biddulph, etc., at Agra (*E.F.*, p. 149).   [Damaged.]

f. 185.   [? 22] Nov., 1619.   T. Kerridge and G. James, at Surat, to Wm. Martin, etc., at Broach (*E.F.*, p. 149).

f. 185.   23 Nov., 1619.   Ditto to ditto (*E.F.*, p. 149).   [Damaged.]

f. 186.   25 Nov., 1619.   Ditto to ditto (*E.F.*, p. 149).   [Much damaged.]

f. 186-88.   30 Nov., 1619.   Petition of the English, at Surat, to [Jamshed] Beg, appointed Governor of Surat (*E.F.*, pp. 150-51).   [Damaged.]

f. 188.   2 December, 1619.   Ditto to J. Young, at [?], (*E.F.*, p. 151). [Illegible.]

f. 188.   6 Dec., 1619.   Ditto to Wm. Martin, etc., at Broach (*E.F.*, p. 152).

f. 189-91.   [? 8] Dec., 1619.   Ditto to Wm. Biddulph, at Agra (*E.F.*, pp. 154-55).   [Much damaged.]

f. 191-92.   9 Dec., 1619.   Ditto to J. Browne, at Ahmadabad (*E.F.*, p. 153).   [Much damaged.]

f. 192.   9 Dec., 1619.   Ditto to Wm. Martin, at Broach (*E.F.*, p. 155). [Much damaged.]

f. 192-94.   10 Dec., 1619.   Ditto to Wm. Methwold, etc., at Masulipatam (*E.F.*, pp. 158-59).   [Much damaged.]

f. 194.   10 Dec., 1619.   Ditto to ditto (*E.F.*, p. 159).   [Much damaged.]

f. 194-95.   10 Dec., 1619.   Ditto (in Portuguese) to George Griger, at Masulipatam (*E.F.*, p. 159).   [Much damaged.]

f. 195.   [? 10] Dec., 1619.   Ditto to all English chiefs (*E.F.*, p. 159). [Much damaged.]

f. 195.   12 Dec., 1619.   Ditto to Wm. Biddulph, at the Court (*E.F.*, p. 160).   [Much damaged, part quite illegible.]

f. 197.   13 Dec., 1619.   [T. Kerridge] at Broach, to T. Rastell and G. James, at Surat (*E.F.*, p. 160).   [Much damaged.]

f. 196.   15 Dec., 1619.   T. Rastell and G. James, at Surat, to T. Kerridge, at Broach (*E.F.*, p. 160).   [Much damaged.]

f. 197.   [? 17] Dec., 1619.   T. Kerridge, at Broach, to T. Rastell and G. James, at Surat (*E.F.*, p. 166).   [Damaged.]

f. 197.   [18] Dec., 1619.   T. Kerridge, at Broach, to J. Browne, etc., at Ahmadabad (*E.F.*, pp. 166-67).   [Damaged.]

f. 198.   24 Dec., 1619.   T. Kerridge, T. Rastell and G. James, at Surat, to Wm. Methwold, etc., at Masulipatam (*E.F.*, p. 167).   [Much damaged.]

f. 199.   25 Dec., 1619.   Ditto to Wm. Martin, etc., at Broach (*E.F.*, p. 167).   [Much damaged.]

f. 188.   [? 27] Dec., 1619.   Ditto to ditto (*E.F.*, p. 151).   [Damaged.]

f. 199.   1 Jan., 1619-20.   [T. Kerridge] at Surat, to Wm. Martin, etc., at Broach (*E.F.*, p. 178).   [Much damaged and partly illegible.]

f. 200.   [? Jan.] 1619-20.   Estimate of funds available at the various factories for investment (*E.F.*, p. 178).   [Much damaged.]

f. 201.   10 Jan., 1619-20.   Goods to be provided at Lahore, Agra and [? Samana] (*E.F.*, p. 178).   [Much damaged.]

f. 202.   [? Jan.] 1619-20.   Goods to be provided at Ahmadabad, Cambay, Dholka, etc. (*E.F.*, p. 178).   [Much damaged, partly illegible.]

f. 203.   [? Jan.] 1619-20.   Goods to be provided at [? Broach] (*E.F.*, p. 179).   [Much damaged.]

f. 204.   13 Jan., 1619-20.   [T. Kerridge, etc.] at Surat, to J. Browne etc., at Ahmadabad (*E.F.*, p. 179).   [Much damaged.]

f. 205.   [13] Jan., 1619-20.   [Ditto] at Surat, to the commander of the fleet at Swally (*E.F.*, p. 179).   [Damaged.]

f. 205.   13 Jan., 1619-20.   [Ditto] to [Wm. Martin, etc.] at Broach (*E.F.*, pp. 179-80).   [Damaged.]

f. 206.   [? 13 Jan.,] 1619-20.   [Ditto] at Surat, to [Capt. Bickley, at Swally].   [Illegible.]

f. 206.   14 Jan., 1619-20.   Ditto to ditto (*E.F.*, p. 180).   [Damaged.]

f. 206.   [?] Jan., 1619.   Ditto to ditto (*E.F.*, p. 180).   [Damaged.]

f. 206.   18 Jan., 1619-20.   Ditto to Capt. Bickley, at Surat (*E.F.*, p. 180). [Much damaged.]

f. 207.   [?] 19 Jan., 1619-20. Ditto to [?] 'Seryne' (*E.F.*, p. 180). [Much damaged.]

f. 207.   21 Jan., 1619-20.   T. Kerridge, at Surat, to [John] Weddell, at Swally (*E.F.*, p. 180). [Much damaged.]

f. 208.   22 Jan., 1619-20.   T. Kerridge, etc., at Surat, to Capt. Bickley, at Swally (*E.F.*, p. 181).   [Much damaged.]

f. 209.   22 Jan., 1619-20.   Ditto to Wm. Biddulph, at [the Court] (*E.F.* p. 181).   [Much damaged, partly illegible.]

f. 210-11.   [? 22] Jan., 1619-20.   Ditto to the factors at Agra (*E.F.*, pp. 181-82).   [Much damaged, partly illegible.]

f. 209.   [? 22] Jan., 1619-20.   T. Kerridge, at Surat, to [Walter] Harvey [at Surat] (*E.F.*, p. 182).   [Much damaged.]

f. 209.   23 Jan., 1619-20.   Ditto to [?] (*E.F.*, p. 182).   [Much damaged.]

f. 212.   [?] Jan., 1619-20.   Ditto to J. Browne, etc., at Ahmadabad (*E.F.*, pp. 182-83).   [Much damaged, the greater part illegible.]

1619.   **Articles du Premier Traité fait**   *Stowe MS. 133, fols.*
                   entre La Compagnie des Mer-   *75-78.*
                   chants Anglois et celle des Hol-
                   landois   traffiquants   es   Indes
                   Orientales.

7 July.   Thirty-one articles, clearly written in seventeenth century French, and dated and signed.

[1619].   **Duplicate of the above (Stowe MS.**   *Add. MS. 12498, fols.*
                     133), with date and signatures   *348-53.*
                     missing.

1620.   **Reasons to prove that it is not the**   *Harl. MS. 1579, fols.*
                   East India Trade which doth   *79-80.*
                   consume the Gold, Silver, Coyne
                   or other treasure of this kingdom, but
                   rather that it is an excellent means
                   greatly to increase the same.

The writer shows that no gold has been exported since the foundation of the Company, and only a proportion of the silver permitted, but that exports of cloth have increased and that trade has been opened in hitherto unknown centres. The increase of trade between 1617 and 1620 is specially emphasised. The writer anticipates many of Mun's arguments, and is specially skilful in analysing the effects of the consumption of precious metals. Compare my *East India Trade in the XVII Century.*

1620-25.   **Petition of William Bragge, cloth-**   *Reg. MS. 17, B. x.*
                      worker of Eastcheap, for satis-   *119 fols.*
                      faction of claims against the East India
                      and Summer Island Companies. Partly
                      in the name of his late brother Matthew,
                      who sailed to India with Sir Henry
                      Middleton.

There are letters from 18 August, 1620, to 20 April, 1621, addressed to Sir Thomas Smyth, Governor of both Companies, prefixed by an appeal to James I. The whole is interlarded with a mass of Scriptural quotations applied to the case.

1621-22.   **Disputes between the English and**   *Add. MS. 30069, 127*
  Dutch East India Companies,   *fols.*
  1621-22. A Register of Proceed-
  ings which passed in the Treatie
  with the Dutch in Anno 1621.
  M. Aldran Hallidon, Governor.

The narrator sets forth that, having failed to obtain restitution from the Dutch for damages inflicted by them, contrary to Treaty, the East India Company appealed to the King, who demanded that the Dutch should select Deputies from the States General and the Netherlands E.I. Co. to meet his Commissioners and the Governor and Deputy Governor of the E.I. Co., together with certain members of the Court of Committees. In consequence, the Dutch Deputies arrived in England, in December, 1620, and, after an audience with the King, Committees were appointed to go into the question of reparations with the Dutch.

The Governor of the E.I. Co. produced an abstract of the losses and damages suffered in consequence of the failure of the Dutch to surrender ships that had been seized.

f. 3a-15. 2 Jan., 1620-21. Statement of violation of certain articles of the last Treaty by the Dutch. Answer of the Dutch to the complaints. Points debated : charges of the Fort at Pulicat, restitution of ships, freedom of trade at Bantam, etc.

f. 16-34. 20-25 Jan., 1620-21. Reciprocal restitution of ships and goods debated with arguments on both sides.

f. 34a-36. 'Coppye of the new complaints sent to the Kinge contayninge a relation of the takeinge of the islands of Lantore and Pooleroun'.

f. 36a-38a. Reasons showing the English offers of freight and assurance to the Dutch to be reasonable.

f. 39-69. 7 Feb., 1621-22. Restitution of goods brought into Holland demanded by the English E.I. Co. The amount of freight to be paid by the Dutch, the price of pepper, etc., debated, with special reference to the case of the *Black Lyon*.

f. 69a-81. Exception taken by the English to charges made against them by the Dutch before the Treaty, with reasons for their non-liability to restore the goods of the *Black Lyon*.

f. 82-90. 10 May, 1622. Answer of the English E.I. Co. to a paper of Protest delivered by the Dutch on that date.
  15-31 May, 1622. Further debates on the restitution of ships.

f. 90a-99. 4-29 June, 1622. Meetings between the English and Dutch merchants for valuation of ordnance, ships and ships' provisions, debates concerning restitution, etc.

f. 99-104. 1 July, 1622. Agreement signed by both parties on the First Article of the Treaty, Reciprocal Restitution.
  3 July, 1622. Signed agreement delivered to the Lords Commissioners in French and English. Points of disagreement debated, especially that regarding the restitution of the *Expedition*.

f. 104a-8. Second complaint of the English E.I. Co. against the Dutch for injuries done after the publication of the Treaty at Jacatra and recently come to their knowledge.
  1 August, 1622. Petition to the King about Lantore and Pularoon delivered and referred to the Lords Commissioners. Opinion thereon.

f. 109-10. 27 Aug., 1622. The order for the Dutch to pay for goods seized, not ratified by the Lords Commissioners. Valuation of goods and other points debated.

f. 111-16.   The Dutch complaint against the English touching the islands of Banda. They contend that the English have no right to Pularoon.
4 Sept., 1622.   The English reply to the above.

f. 116a-19.   9 Sept., 1622.   Discussion regarding Pularoon. The English and Dutch views set forth.

f. 119a-23.   12-14 Sept.   Rejoinder of the English to the Dutch complaints about Pulicat.

f. 123a-24a.   Demands of restitution by the English from the Dutch.

f. 125-26.   Further complaints against the Dutch.

This MS. is mainly concerned with the English side of the case and has very little to say for the Dutch point of view.

1621.   **Tract entitled, 'A Discourse of Trade from England unto the East Indies: answering to diverse objections which are usually made against the same'. By T.M., 4to, 58 pp. printed.**   *Harl. MS. 7310, fols. 78-109.*

This is a copy of Thomas Mun's well-known treatise.

1621-22.   **Letter Book of Correspondence of Factors of the East India Company 1621-22.**   *Egerton MS. 2123, 144 fols.*

Like Egerton MS. 2122, nearly the whole of this volume has been incorporated by Mr. William Foster in his *English Factories*, 1618-21, and 1622-24. The MS. has therefore been treated in the same way as Eg. 2122 and the references to Mr. Foster's abstracts are noted in the same way, viz., *E.F.*, with appropriate page. [Much mutilated and decayed.]

f. 47a-48.   2 Aug., 1621.   Robt. Young, at 'Semiane' to the President and Council at Surat (*E.F.*, pp. 257-58).   [Much mutilated.]

f. 54-55a.   22 Aug., 1621.   Wm. Biddulph and J. Young, at Agra, to the President and Council at Surat (*E.F.*, pp. 260-61).   [Damaged.]

f. 59a-63a.   27 Aug., 1621.   Wm. Methwold, etc., at Masulipatam, to the Council at Surat (*E.F.*, pp. 264-66).

f. 70-71a.   [? 8] Sept., 1621.   Wm. Biddulph and J. Young [at Agra] to the Council at Surat (*E.F.*, pp. 266-68).   [Much damaged.]

f. 83-83a.   12 Sept., 1621.   Capt. J. Weddell, at Swally, to [the President at Surat] (*E.F.*, pp. 300-1).   [Damaged.]

f. 49-52.   16 Sept., 1621.   E. Heynes and R. Hutchinson, at Burhanpur, to the Council at Surat (*E.F.*, p. 269).   [Much mutilated.]

f. 52a-53.   [? 18] Sept., 1621.   Ditto to ditto (*E.F.*, p. 270).   [Damaged.]

f. 48a.   18 Sept., 1621.   Capt. J. Weddell, etc., aboard the *Jonas*, off Daman, to the Council at Surat (*E.F.*, p. 271).   [Much mutilated.]

f. 53a.   23 Sept., 1621.   W. Martin, G. Pike, etc., at Broach, to the Council at Surat (*E.F.*, p. 273).

f. 57a-59a.   26 Sept., 1621.   [E. Heynes] and R. [Hutchinson] at Burhanpur, to the Council at Surat (*E.F.*, pp. 273-75).   [Damaged.]

f. 56-57.   27 Sept., 1621.   [Capt. J. Weddell] aboard the *Jonas*, at Swally, to the Council at Surat (*E.F.*, p. 279).   [Damaged.]

f. 65a-69a.   27 Sept., 1621.   J. Bickford, etc., at Sarkhej, to the Council at Surat (*E.F.* pp. 278-79).   [Much damaged.]

f. 57. 27 Sept., 1621. W. Martin, etc., at Broach, to ditto (*E.F.*, p. 278).

f. 56. 28 Sept., 1621. N. Bannham, aboard the *Whale* [at Swally] to ditto (*E.F.*, p. 279). [Damaged.]

f. 73. 29 Sept., 1621. R. Barker and J. Offley, at Baroda, to ditto (*E.F.*, p. 279). [Damaged.]

f. 64a-65. 30 Sept., 1621. Capt. J. Weddell, aboard the *Jonas*, to ditto (*E.F.*, p. 279). [Damaged.]

f. 65a. [? 30] Sept., 1621. R. Tottle [at Swally] to ditto (*E.F.* p. 280). [Much damaged.]

f. 72. 1 Oct., 1621. W. Martin, etc., at Broach, to ditto (*E.F.*, p. 280). [Damaged.]

f. 73a-74a. 2 Oct., 1621. E. Heynes and R. Hutchinson, at Burhanpur, to ditto (*E.F.*, pp. 280-81). [Damaged.]

f. 72. 3 Oct., 1621. Ditto to ditto (*E.F.*, p. 280). [Much damaged.]

f. 73. 3 Oct., 1621. G. James, at Surat, to President Rastell, at Swally (*E.F.*, p. 282).

f. 75. 3 Oct., 1621. J. Bickford, etc., at Ahmadabad, to the Council at Surat (*E.F.*, pp. 281-82). [Damaged.]

f. 75a-76. 4 Oct., 1621. Ditto to ditto (*E.F.*, p. 282). [Damaged.]

f. 84-84a. 5 Oct., 1621. E. Heynes and R. Hutchinson, at Burhanpur, to ditto (*E.F.*, pp. 282-83). [Damaged.]

f. 77-77a. 6 Oct., 1621. J. Bickford, etc., at Ahmadabad, to ditto (*E.F.*, p. 291). [Damaged.]

f. 86a. 7 Oct., 1621. R. Hutchinson, at Burhanpur, to ditto (*E.F.*, p. 293).

f. 85-86a. 7 Oct., 1621. E. Heynes and R. Hutchinson, at Burhanpur, to ditto (*E.F.* pp. 292-93). [Damaged.]

f. 79a-80. 7 Oct., 1621. R. Barker and J. Offley, at Baroda, to the President and Council at Surat (*E.F.*, p. 291). [Damaged.]

f. 76a. 7 Oct., 1621. T. Quince, at Broach, to ditto (*E.F.*, p. 291). [Damaged.]

f. 80-80a. 8 Oct., 1621. R. Lancaster, at Cambay, to ditto (*E.F.*, pp. 293-294). [Damaged.]

f. 75-75a. 8 Oct., 1621. Capt. J. Weddell, at Swally, to [ditto] (*E.F.*, p. 294). [Much damaged.]

f. 78a-79a. 9 Oct., 1621. W. Martin, etc., at Broach, to ditto (*E.F.*, p. 94). [Damaged.]

f. 76a. 9 Oct., 1621. Capt. J. Weddell, on the *Jonas*, at Swally, to the [President] at Surat (*E.F.*, pp. 294-95). [Damaged.]

f. 77a-78. 10 Oct., 1621. Ditto to ditto (*E.F.*, p. 295). [Damaged.]

f. 87. 10 Oct., 1621. Ditto to ditto (*E.F.*, pp. 295-96). [Damaged.]

f. 90a-91. 10 Oct., 1621. R. Jeffries, etc., at 'Deugar' near Chaul, to the President and Council at Surat (*E.F.*, pp. 296-97). [Damaged.]

f. 78-78a. 10 Oct., 1621. Capt. J. Weddell on the *Jonas*, at Swally, to [ditto] (*E.F.*, p. 295). [Damaged.]

f. 78. 10 Oct., 1621. Ditto to ditto (*E.F.*, p. 295). [Damaged.]

f. 88. 12 Oct., 1621. J. Bickford, etc., at Ahmadabad, to ditto (*E.F.*, p. 301). [Damaged.]

f. 82-83. 12 Oct., 1621. W. Martin, etc., at Broach, to ditto (*E.F.*, p. 300). [Damaged.]

f. 88a-89. 13 Oct., 1621. E. Heynes, at Burhanpur, to ditto (*E.F.*, p. 303). [Damaged.]

f. 89-89a. 13 Oct., 1621. Ditto and R. Hutchinson to ditto (*E.F.*, pp. 302-3). [Damaged.]

f. 80a-82.   13 Oct., 1621.   Capt. J. Weddell [at Swally] to [ditto] (*E.F.*, pp. 301-2).   [Damaged.]

f. 84.   14 Oct., 1621.   W. Hoare, at Swally, to ditto (*E.F.* p 306).

f. 88a.   15 Oct., 1621.   R. Lancaster, at Cambay, to ditto (*E.F.*, p. 306). [Damaged.]

f. 86a.   15 Oct., 1621.   Capt. J. Weddell, aboard the *Jonas*, to ditto (*E.F.* p. 306).

f. 93.   17 Oct., 1621.   J. Bickford, etc., at Ahmadabad, to ditto (*E.F.*, pp. 306-7).   [Damaged.]

f. 93a.   19 Oct., 1621.   R. Barker and J. Offley, at Baroda, to ditto (*E.F.*, p. 308).   [Damaged.]

f. 90.   19 Oct., 1621.   J. Hopkinson, at Surat, to [President Rastell, at Swally].   (*E.F.*, p. 307).   [Damaged.]

f. 90-90a.   19 Oct., 1621.   Ditto to ditto (*E.F.*, p. 307).   [Damaged.]

f. 91-92a.   19 Oct., 1621.   W. Martin, etc., at Broach, to the President and Council at Surat (*E.F.* pp. 307-8).   [Damaged.]

f. 94.   21 Oct., 1621.   Ditto to ditto (*E.F.*, p. 308).   [Damaged.]

f. 98a-99a.   22 Oct., 1621.   J. Salbank [at Ahmadabad] to ditto (*E.F.*, p. 309).   [Much damaged.]

f. 95-96.   22 Oct., 1621.   J. Bickford, etc., at Ahmadabad, to ditto (*E.F.*, pp. 308-9).   [Damaged.]

f. 94-94a.   23 Oct., 1621.   Capt. J. Weddell, aboard the *Jonas*, to ditto (*E.F.*, p. 310).   [Damaged.]

f. 97a-98.   23 Oct., 1621.   R. Lancaster, at Cambay, to ditto (*E.F.*, pp. 309-10).   [Much damaged.]

f. 95.   23 Oct., 1621.   Capt. R. Blyth, etc., on the *Jonas*, at Swally, to ditto (*E.F.*, p. 310).   [Damaged.]

f. 96a.   24 Oct., 1621.   Ditto to ditto (*E.F.*, p. 311).   [Much damaged.]

f. 96a-97.   24 Oct., 1621.   W. Hoare, aboard the *Dolphin*, to ditto (*E.F.*, p. 311).   [Much damaged.]

f. 101a-2.   24 Oct., 1621.   J. Bickford, etc., at Sarkhej, to ditto (*E.F.*, pp. 310-11).   [Much damaged.]

f. 100.   25 Oct., 1621.   W. Hoare, etc., to ditto (*E.F.*, p. 311).   [Much damaged.]

f. 100a.   [26] Oct., 1621.   T. Kerridge, aboard the *Hart*, to ditto (*E.F.*, pp. 311-12).   [Damaged.]

f. 103-3a.   27 Oct., 1621.   J. Salbank, at Cambay, to ditto (*E.F.*, p. 312). [Much damaged, part torn away.]

f. 101.   28 Oct, 1621.   W. Martin, etc., at Broach, to the President and Council at Surat (*E.F.*, p. 312).   [Much damaged.]

f. 102-2a.   29 Oct., 1621.   T. Kerridge, aboard the *Hart*, to ditto (*E.F.*, p. 312).   [Much damaged.]

f. 109a.   30 Oct., 1621.   J. Salbank [at Cambay] to ditto (*E.F.*, p. 313). [Damaged.]

f. 104-4a.   31 Oct., 1621.   T. Kerridge, aboard the *Hart*, to ditto (*E.F.*, p. 313).   [Much damaged, part torn away.]

f. 105.   [? 31] Oct., 1621.   Capt. Blyth, aboard the *London*, to [the President and Council at Surat].   [Practically every part of the letter torn away but signature and date.]

f. 105.   [? 31] Oct., 1621.   [Capt. J. Weddell, at Swally] to ditto (*E.F.*, p. 313).   [Much damaged.]

f. 106-7a.   31 Oct., 1621.   W. Martin, etc., at Broach, to ditto (*E.F.*, p. 313).   [Much damaged and torn.]

f. 108a-9.   [31 Oct.] 1621.   [The factors at Ahmadabad] to ditto (*E.F.*, p. 314).   [Partly torn.]

f. 108-8a. [? 1 Nov.] 1621. R. Blyth, etc., at Swally, to ditto (*E.F.*, p. 314). [Much damaged.]

f. 109-9a. [? 2 Nov.] 1621. [? Wm. Blunderstone] to ditto (*E.F.*, pp. 314-15). [Much damaged.]

f. 110a. 2 Nov., 1621. W. Martin, etc., at Broach, to ditto (*E.F.*, p. 315). [Torn and much damaged.]

f. 110. 3 Nov., 1621. T. Kerridge, aboard the *Hart*, to ditto (*E.F.*, p. 315). [Damaged.]

f. 87-87a. 13 Nov., 1621. J. Salbank and R. Lancaster, at Cambay, to ditto (*E.F.*, p. 329). [Damaged.]

f. 113. 10 Mar., 1621-22. W. [Methwold], etc., at Masulipatam, to ditto (Abstracted in *English Factories*, 1622-24, p. 59). [A fragment.]

f. 113a-14. [?] April, 1622. R. Young [at Agra] to ditto (*E.F.*, pp. 74-75). [Damaged.]

f. 115a-16. 26 April, 1622. Ditto to ditto (*E.F.*, pp. 75-76). [Damaged.]

f. 116-16a. [? 27] April, 1622. R. Hughes [at Agra] to ditto (*E.F.*, pp. 78-79). [Damaged.]

f. 113a. 6 May, 1622. [N. Bangham] at Burhanpur, to ditto (*E.F.*, p. 79). [Damaged.]

f. 111-12. 9 May, 1622. [Ditto] to ditto (*E.F.*, p. 79). [Fragment only.]

f. 113. 14 May, 1622. W. Martin etc., at Broach, to ditto (*E.F.*, p. 85).

f. 115-15a. 15 May, 1622. [Ditto] to ditto (*E.F.*, p. 86). [Damaged.]

f. 114. 16 May, 1622. N. Halstead, etc., at Ahmadabad, to ditto (*E.F.*, p. 86).

f. 116a. 17 May, 1622. N. Bangham, etc., at Burhanpur, to ditto (*E.F.*, pp. 86-87). [Damaged.]

f. 114a-115. [? 21] May 1622. W. Martin, etc., at Broach, to ditto (*E.F.*, p. 87.)

f. 117-17a. 23 May, 1622. N. Bangham and R. Hutchinson, at Burhanpur, to ditto (*E.F.*, pp. 87-88). [Damaged.]

f. 117. 29 May, 1622. W. Martin, etc., [at Broach] to ditto. (*E.F.*, p. 88). [Damaged.]

f. 117a-18a. 5 June, 1622. N. Halstead, etc., at Ahmadabad, to ditto (*E.F.*, pp. 88-89). [Damaged.]

f. 121-22a. 5 June, 1622. R. [Hughes] at Agra, to ditto (*E.F.*, pp. 89-91). [Damaged.]

f. 118a. 6 June, 1622. N. Halstead, etc., at Ahmadabad, to ditto. [Damaged.]

f. 112. 10 June, 1622. W. Martin, etc., at Broach, to ditto (*E.F.*, p. 91). [Fragment only.]

f. 118a-19a. [12] June, 1622. Ditto to ditto (*E.F.*, p. 92). [Much damaged.]

f. 123a-24. 12 June, 1622. J. Parker, at Narwar, to ditto (*E.F.*, pp. 91-92).

f. 112-12a. 14 June, 1622. W. Martin, etc., at Broach, to ditto (*E.F.*, p. 92). [Much damaged.]

f. 120a. 18 June, 1622. N. Halstead, etc., at Ahmadabad, to ditto (*E.F.*, pp. 92-93). [Damaged.]

f. 120. 19 June, 1622. W. Martin, etc., at Broach, to ditto (*E.F.*, p. 93). [Damaged.]

f. 124-27. 20 June, 1622. R. Hughes, at Agra, to ditto (*E.F.*, pp. 93-94). [Damaged.]

f. 121. 23 June, 1622. N. Bangham, at Burhanpur, to ditto (*E.F.*, p. 95). [Damaged.]

f. 127-27a.   24 June, 1622.   J. Parker, at 'Ventora' to the President and Council at Surat (*E.F.*, pp. 95-96).   [Damaged.]

f. 122a-23a.   25 June, 1622.   N. Halsted, etc., at Ahmadabad, to ditto (*E.F.*, pp. 96-97).   [Damaged.]

f. 120-21.   29 June, 1622.   W. Martin, etc., at Broach, to ditto (*E.F.*, p. 97).   [Damaged.]

f. 127a-28.   30 June, 1622.   W. Methwold, etc., at Masulipatam, to ditto (*E.F.*, pp. 97-98).   [Damaged.]

f. 124.   6 July, 1622.   W. Martin, etc., at Broach, to ditto (*E.F.*, p. 98). [Slightly damaged.]

f. 128a.   7 July, 1622.   G. Pike, at Broach, to ditto (*E.F.*, p. 99). [Damaged.]

f. 128a-29.   7 July, 1622.   N. Bangham, etc., at Burhanpur, to ditto (*E.F.*, p. 99).   [Damaged.]

f. 129a-30.   11 July, 1622.   N. Halstead, etc., at Ahmadabad, to ditto (*E.F.*, p. 100).   [Damaged.]

f. 130-30a.   15 July, 1622.   Ditto to ditto (*E.F.*, p. 100).

f. 130a-31.   16 July, 1622.   W. Martin, etc., at Broach, to ditto (*E.F.*, p. 100).

f. 129-29a.   19 July, 1622.   Ditto to ditto (*E.F.*, p. 101).

f. 131-31a.   24 July, 1622.   N. Halstead, etc., at Ahmadabad, to ditto (*E.F.*, p. 101).

f. 131a-32a.   27 July, 1622.   W. Martin, etc., at Broach, to ditto (*E.F.*, p. 108).

f. 132a-33.   1 Aug., 1622.   R. Hughes, at Agra, to ditto (*E.F.*, p. 108).

f. 133a.   1 Aug., 1622.   W. Martin, etc., at Broach, to ditto (*E.F.*, p. 108).

f. 134.   6 Aug., 1622.   N. Halstead, at Ahmadabad, to ditto (*E.F.*, p. 109).

f. 134-35.   10 Aug., 1622.   Ditto to ditto (*E.F.*, p. 109).

f. 135-36.   15 Aug., 1622.   W. Martin, etc., at [Broach] to ditto (*E.F.*, p. 110).   [Damaged.]

f. 136a-37.   17 Aug., 1622.   J. Parker, at Burhanpur, to ditto (*E.F.*, pp. 110-11).

f. 137-37a.   17 Aug., 1622.   N. Bangham, etc., at Burhanpur, to ditto (*E.F.*, pp. 111-12).

f. 138.   21 Aug., 1622.   W. Martin, etc., at Broach, to ditto (*E.F.*, p. 115).

f. 138a-39.   23 Aug., 1622.   N. Bangham, etc., at Burhanpur, to ditto (*E.F.*, p. 115).

f. 139-39a.   24 Aug., 1622.   W. Martin, etc., at Broach, to ditto (*E.F.*, p. 116).

f. 139a-40.   27 Aug., 1622.   Ditto to ditto (*E.F.*, p. 116).

f. 145-54.   27 Aug., 1622.   Copy of General Letter from the factors at Batavia to the Company, sent per the *Lesser James*. See O.C. 1076, 1077 (I.O. Records) for the original.

f. 155-68a.   [? Sept.] 1622.   Corrected draft of letter from the Co. to the [factors at Batavia].   [Imperfect. Beginning and end missing.]

f. 140-40a.   1 Sept., 1622.   W. Martin, etc., at Broach, to ditto (*E.F.*, p. 118).

f. 140a-41.   R. Davis, aboard the *Richard*, to ditto (*E.F.*, p. 123).

f. 141.   12 Sept., 1622.   N. Halstead, etc., at Ahmadabad, to ditto (*E.F.*, p. 123).

f. 141a.   12 Sept., 1622.   R. Davis, at Surat Bar, to ditto (*E.F.*, p. 123).

f. 141a-42.   14 Sept., 1622.   W. Martin, etc., at Broach, to ditto (*E.F.*, p. 124).

f. 142. 14 Sept., 1622. R. Davis, at Surat Bar, to ditto (*E.F.*, p. 124).

f. 142a. 20 Sept., 1622. R. Lancaster, etc., at Ahmadabad, to ditto (*E.F.*, p. 125).

f. 143. 20 Sept., 1622. Ditto to ditto (*E.F.*, pp. 124-25).

f. 143a. 20 Sept., 1622. T. Hawke[ridge] at Swally, to ditto (*E.F.*, pp. 125-26).

f. 143a-44. 23 Sept., 1622. R. Lancaster, etc., at Ahmadabad, to ditto (*E.F.*, p. 126).

[1623.] **The Cruelty of the Dutch at Amboyna to the English.** (With a full-page pen and ink illustration.)   *Sloane MS. 3645.*

A printed version of the above, with a reproduction of the illustration, is entitled, ' A true relation of the unjust, cruel and barbarous proceedings against the English at Amboyna in the East Indies, by the Netherlandish Council there,' etc., etc. The 3d. impression. Published by authority. London, 1632. Small 4to. Printed by G. Purslowe for Nathaniel Newberry.

1623, 12 Dec.   **Copy of the English Protest exhibited to the Dutch Governor-Genl.** Peter de Carpentier and Council in Jacatra (Batavia), signed by Geo. Gunning, Richd. Welldon, Geo. Bruen.   *Add. MS. 12496, fols. 1-45.*

The writers protest against the violation by the Dutch of the articles agreed on between James I and the States General in 1619, and cite the following instances : The exaction of customs in Batavia. Forced payments on arrack and fish in Banda. Prohibition of the sale of slaves unless ' excise ' was paid for them. Intolerable exactions in the Moluccas, Amboyna and Banda. Assertion of legal authority over British subjects. Interference with trade at Bantam. The underhand action of the Dutch with regard to an attack on Macao. The separation of two Dutch ships from the fleet in 1622 to serve their own purposes in the Red Sea, whereby the combined fleet was scattered and could not inflict a decisive blow on the Portuguese. The refusal of the Dutch to restore the island of Pularoon according to agreement, etc., etc.

O. C. 1128 (I.O. Records) is a fragment of the original protest with the signatures of Gunning, etc., and an attestation that the document was exhibited to the English and Dutch Commissioners on the 24 July, 1654.

1623, 20 Dec.   **Protest by Thomas Brokeden, Henry Hawley and John Gomring [Gunning] dated in Batavia,** against Hermann van Speult, Govr. of Amboyna, for his treatment of British subjects on that island.   *Add. MS. 12496, fols. 45-46.*

See O. C. 1137 (I. O. Records) for the original of this MS.

1624.   **A Guarantee of indemnification from the Ambassadors of the States General to the Dutch E.I. Co. Signed in London by the**   *Add. MS. 22865, fols. 83.*

Dutch Ambassadors and Representatives of the Netherlands E.I. Co.

(In Dutch.)

1627-37.   The Mundy MSS.   *Harl. MS. 2286, Add. MSS. 19278-81.*

Copies of portions only of this remarkable work exist at the British Museum. The original and complete MS. (Rawl. A. 315) is to be found at the Bodleian Library, Oxford, and will be fully described in the Bibliography of 17th Century MSS., dealing with British India, contained in that library.

1627-34.   *Harl. MS. 2286.*

This is a contemporary copy, made for Sir Paul Pindar, of Relations I—XIX (1608-34), the first three Relations dealing with Mundy's early life and European travels before he entered the service of the E.I.Co., (1608-27), and the remainder, Relations IV—XIX, describing Mundy's first voyage to India and his service as factor at Surat, Agra, Patna, with his return to England in 1634.

This MS. contains no tracings of the illustrations that are found in the original.

1628-30.   *Add. 19278, 18 fols.*

This is a late copy of Relation V, ' Some Passages at Suratt '. It contains no illustrations.

1630-
1630-1.   *Add. 19279, 40 fols.*

This is a late copy of Relation VI, ' A Journey from Suratt to Agra '. It contains no illustrations.

1631.   *Add. MS. 19280, 25 fols.*

A late copy of Relations VII and XV, the former entitled ' A Journey from Agra to Cole ', and the latter, ' Of Agra : Whatt Notable there, etc '. It contains no illustrations.

1636-37.   Voyages to the East Indies, China, etc.   *Add. MS. 19281, 212 fols.*

A late copy of Relations XXI-XXVI, inclusive. It describes the voyage of a fleet sent out by Sir William Courteen for trade in India and China. Mundy was employed as a merchant, and he recounts the experiences of the fleet. Relation XXVI, does not complete the story, as it ends while the ships were still in China.

This copy contains the ' China Characters ' but no tracings of the author's illustrations.

For details of the portions of the MS. already printed and edited, see the note on the original in the Bodleian collection.

1627-28.   Complaints against the Dutch for wrongs done to the English since the Treaty of 1619, with special reference to the massacre   *Stowe MS. 133, fols. 191-237, 251, 255.*

at A m b o y n a. Counterclaims from the Dutch and replies thereto.

Fols. 191-98, 251, 255 deal with Amboyna. Fol. 235 contains 'Pointes sur lesquels Sa Majesté se declare touchant le fait des Indes Orientales'. The remaining folios are mainly concerned with reprisals in European waters. The whole MS. is in French.

1630.   **Letter from Charles I to the Shah**   *Add. MS. 11310.*
Sufi, the Emperor of Persia.

The letter was sent by William, Earl of Denbigh, to congratulate the monarch on his accession and to cement the friendly relations that had obtained in the days of the preceding monarch, Shah Abbas.

1631-32.   **Four Journals of the** *Mary.*   *Add. MS. 18649, 52 fols.*

f. 1-18a. 2 Feb., 1630/1-9 Oct., 1631. ' A Journall kept in the *Marye*, being the daily course and distance that she went, from . . . the Downes untill wee came . . . on the coast of India.'
f. 19-37. A duplicate of the above.
f. 38-43a. 28 April—30 May, 1632. Journal from Surat to Masulipatam. Brief remarks on the Danes' Castle at Trincomalee. At Armagon, Mr. Norris and Mr. Cartwright came on board.
f. 44-50a. 29 June—2 Sept., 1632. Journal from Masulipatam to Gombroon. Anchored in Jask Road on the 15 Sept. Heard news of war between the Portuguese and the Persians.
f. 51-52a. 23 Oct.—28 Nov., 1632. Journal from Persia to Surat.

These Journals contain very little information beyond courses, distances, observations, remarks on currents, land sighted, etc.

O.C. 1407 (India Office Records) contains an account of the early part of the voyage up to 9 Dec., 1631, and O.C. 1455 gives an account of the voyage from Surat to Armagon and Masulipatam, and thence to Persia up to the 12 Oct., 1632.

1632-34.   **Journal of five ships, the** *Charles,*   *Sloane MS. 3492, 35*
Jonas, Dolphin, Hart **and** *Swallow*   *fols.*
from England to Surat [by Thomas Clements].

14 March, 1631/2—3 May, 1634.

7 April, 1632. Sailed from the Lizard.

13 June, 1633. Reached Bantam. Then follows a diary of movements in India until 3 May, 1634.

[1632.]   **A Brief Relation of the Great Citty**   *Sloane MS. 948, No.*
of Jaggarnat in Bengalla, taken   *6.*
ont of a booke Intituled Newes from
the East Indies written by William
Brutten [Bruton], printed 1638, London.

This MS. is only an extract (pp. 28-35) of the work of William Bruton, quartermaster of the *Hopewell.* A copy of *Newes from the East Indies* is among the rare books in the British Museum, Press Mark, C. 32, d. 5. It has also been reprinted in Vol. VIII of Osborne's *Travels,* and in Vol. V of Macklehose's Edition of *Hakluyt's Voyages.*

C. R. Wilson has, moreover, quoted freely from the work in his *Early Annals of Bengal*, Vol. I.

1635. **Journal kept by Thomas Clements, midshipman of the *Hart*, bound for England.** *Sloane MS. 3492, fols. 36-38a.*

2 Feb.—16 March, 1634-5.

2 Feb. 1634-5. Sailed with the *Swan* for Cape ' Bone Sprance '. The Journal breaks off abruptly on the 16 March.

For the Log of the *Jonah* (or *Jonas*), see I.O. Marine Records, Vol. LVII, also O.C. 1444, 1492, 1509, for letters written aboard that ship ; and for letters written on the *Charles*, see O.C. 1442, 1469.

1637. **Account of a naval engagement between the Portuguese and the Dutch, off Goa, Jan., 1637.** *Add. 28461, fols. 19-25.*

In Portuguese. See also Add. MS. 20944, fols. 138-45a, which is a printed account, also in Portuguese.

1637-39. **Receuil Historique.** *Stowe MS. 988, No. 6.*

Abstract of the travels of Adam Olearius, in Persia, 1637, and of the travels of T. A. Mandelslo in India, China, etc., 1638-39. From a French translation, published 1656-59.

17th century. **Collections out of various authors.** *Sloane MS. 2350, 54 fols.*

Printed extracts from Mandelslo, Purchas, Thevenot, etc., etc.,

1650-51. **Journal kept by Charles Wilde, Purser of the *Bonitta*, bound from England to the island of Assida on the west side of St. Lawrence, and thence to Fort St. George.** *Sloane MS. 3231, fols. 1-41a.*

4 Feb., 1649-50. Sailed from Blackwall dock.

11-16 June, 1650. In St. Augustine's Bay.

24 June—4 July, 1650. Very full entries, describing the ship's route, an account of the Island of Assida, etc.

9 July, 1650. Sailed for Johanna, Comoro Island.

20-21 July, 1650. Account of Johanna, with a sketch of the island.

22 Aug., 1650. Description of Trincomalee.

26 Aug., 1650. Anchored at Fort St. George.

28 Dec., 1650. Sailed for Gombroon (Bandar Abbas).

11 March—16 April, 1651. At Gombroon.

24 May, 1651. Anchored at Madras.

17 Dec., 1651. Reached Bantam.

4 Jan., 1651-2. The writer was transferred to the *Ann*, bound for England.

The Journal is embellished with coloured sketches and draughts of bays, contours of hills, islands, etc. It has been abstracted in Foster's *English Factories*, 1646-50, pp. 272, 273, and 1647-51, pp. 5-7.

1652.   **Journal of the ship *Ann*, from Ban-**   *Sloane MS. 3231,*
            tam to England, by Charles   *fols. 42-55.*
            Wild, passenger.

4 Jan., 1651-52.   Transhipped from the *Bonitta* to the *Ann*.

29 Jan., 1651-52.   Sailed from Bantam.

28 July, 1652.   Anchored at Plymouth.

See O.C., 2273 (I.O. Records) for a letter from on board the *Ann* to the Company.

c. 1655.   **Wilde of East Indian Trade (Title**   *Sloane MS. 3271, 5*
            on cover of vol. No title inside).   *fols.*

Richard Wylde's remonstrance to the Lord Protector on the East India Trade.

This is an exceedingly rare tract, and is important for the study of the Company's trade. Compare my *East India Trade in the XVIIth Century.*

1654-70   **Travels of Richard Bell (and John**   *Sloane MS. 811, 64*
            Campbell) in the East Indies,   *fols.*
            Persia and Palestine.

f. 2-18b.   1.   An account or journal of the travels of Richard Bell in the Moguls' country in India, and his residence in the Court of Shah Jahan, the Emperor, and father of Aurangzeb, to both of which he was gunfounder, several years, from 1654 to 1668 ; as also an account of John Campbell and others residing in that country.

f. 18b-45b.   2.   Another journal of the said Richard Bell's travels to Prester John's country, Persia, etc., in 1667.

f. 45b-63.   Account of the voyage and travels of Richard Bell from Lisbon to Jerusalem and other places, in Anno 1669.

The whole of this MS. has been printed verbatim in the *Indian Antiquary*, Vol. XXXV, pp. 131-42, 168-78, 203-10 ; Vol. XXXVI. pp. 98-105, 125-34, 173-79 ; Vol. XXXVII, pp. 156-70.   It is edited, with a preface, by Sir Richard Temple and contains valuable notes contributed by the late Mr. William Irvine.   The part played by John Campbell in the events recorded, the proportion of 'travellers' tales' and important historical facts contained in the narrative, and the estimate of the value of the MS. as a whole, are set forth by the editor.

1657-   **List of the Governors, Deputy**   *Add. MS. 38871, 88*
1708/9.   **Governors and Committees of**   *fols.*
            the Old E.I.Co. from 1657 when
            incorporated to 1708 when "that
            Co. determin'd."

f. 1-14.

f. 15-16.   List of the names of the Old and New E.I.Co's., chosen to be of the Court of Managers for the United Trade, July, 1702-18, March, 1708-9.

f. 16-88.   List of the names of the Court of Directors from 1708-9 to 1858.

1658-65.   **Negotiations of Sir George Down-**   *Add. MSS. 22919-*
            ing.   *20.*

The following documents throw further light on Cromwell's attitude towards the Company, while Downing's activity and zeal are no less manifest. Thurloes' letters to Downing are particularly important.

N.B.—The numbers of folios given are those of the revised paging in pencil.

f. 27-29. 3 May, 1658. Answer (in French) by the States General to the protest delivered by Sir George Downing, on the 21st March, on behalf of merchants trading to the East Indies, who complain of ill-treatment on the part of the Dutch.

The States General defend the conduct of their servants in the East. They set forth that the Javanese in Bantam had broken the peace concluded with them, and had burnt the houses and sugar factories of the Dutch, compelling the latter to have recourse to arms and to blockade the town and river of Bantam. That they courteously warned the English of this design and did not refuse to allow them to provision their ships for Europe as stated in the protest. Further, they deny that Pularoon has been destroyed, that they have offered 30,000 dollars for the monopoly of the pepper trade, or that the alleged injuries done to English vessels has any foundation. Nevertheless, they have sent orders to their Governor-General, directing that if any of their commanders shall be found guilty of the charges brought against them, or of any violation of the Treaty of 1654, they shall be rigorously punished. They maintain that the complaints of the English merchants are groundless, and suggest, in case of their continued dissatisfaction, that their cause shall be tried in a court of law.

f. 66. 3 Dec., 1658. J. Thurloe (Treasury) to Sir George Downing. Sends papers and instructions with reference to the three E.I. ships taken by the Dutch. No details given.

f. 68. 24 Dec., 1658. Ditto to ditto. Respecting the three ships as above.

f. 72. 7 Jan., 1658-59. Ditto to ditto.

His Highness and the Council want to know what is to be expected of the Dutch in the 'East India business' as 'the Eyes of all the Nations are upon it'.

f. 75. 4 Feb. 1658-59. Ditto to ditto.

He has received news of the agreement about the Bantam ships. The owners demur to the ten weeks allowed for payment. An early settlement is desired.

f. 86. 4 March, 1658-59. Ditto to ditto.

Agreement about the three E.I. ships ratified by the Protector. Further petitions from the E.I.Co. for restitution, apart from the three ships. The Ambassador is to do the best he can for them.

f. 207. [1662.] Demands of John South, of London, merchant, for loss and damage sustained by and from the Netherlands E.I. Co. in the East Indies.

The demands are for £4,000 worth of goods on board the *Nostra Signora di Rimedia*, which ship was taken at Macassar, Celebes I, and carried off by the Dutch to Batavia.

f. 209-12. 30 April, 1662. Complaint of the owners of the *Advice*, which was let on freight to the E.I. Co., in 1658, for a voyage to Bantam and back.

They complain that the ship arrived at Bantam but that the Dutch would not permit her to unlade or lade goods there or even provision the ship. That, in consequence, the cargo was unladed by stealth, at Lampoon, 26 leagues from Bantam. That owing to the obstruction of the Dutch, the ship's return was delayed and she was forced to make the voyage in the winter to the detriment of her gear, the loss of her passengers' goods and the payment of extra demurrage by her owners.

f. 236. 11 July, 1662. Letter from Sir Richard Ford, in London, to Sir George Downing.

Expresses appreciation of Downing's activity on behalf of the E.I. Co. The Company's servants at Bantam have been ordered to attempt to regain possession of Pularoon.

f. 239. [1662.] [Torn fragment.] A paragraph (in Latin), touching the delivery of Pularoon, according to the articles of treaty of 1654.

f. 248-50. 5-15 Sept., 1662. Letter (in French) from the Dutch Ambassadors at Chelsea 'au Greffier Ruysel' stating that they are empowered to agree to all the articles in question, between the Dutch and English, except as regards the claims of the English for the *Bonne Esperance* and *Henry Bonaventure*.

f. 263. 9 Nov., 1662. Deposition of J. Hurstaerdt, commander of the Dutch East India fleet, that he prevented the English E.I. Co.'s ship from going to Porcat, because the king of that place was an enemy of the Dutch, but that the vessel in question, the *Hopewell*, had been provided with wood and water. [In French.]

f. 265. 6 Dec., 1662. Protest by James Snow, and the officers of the *Hopewell*, against Jacob Hurstaerdt, head of the Dutch factory at Cochin, for his refusal to allow their ship to proceed to Porcat. [In French.]

f. 266. 31 Dec., 1662. Protest by George Oxenden and Council, at Surat, against Jacob Hurstaerdt and the Netherlands E.I. Co., for their action with regard to the *Hopewell*.

1663.   *Add. MS. 22920.*

f. 13-14. 17-27 Sept., 1663. Sir George Downing, at the Hague, to the States General. [In French.]

He protests against the States General, for the action of their agent, on the coast of Africa, in refusing to allow the *Charles* and *James* to take in slaves or to trade at Cormantin, on the coast of Guinea, on the pretext that the English E.I. Co. was at war with the inhabitants on the coast of Africa. There is further correspondence in the volume about the above affair, but it refers entirely to the African Company.

f. 15. 17 Nov., 1663. Copy of a protest by the E.I. Co.'s factors at Porcat (Porakad) against the Governor of Cochin for his action regarding the *Hopewell*.

They complain of obstruction in trade to their ship and also to the *Leopard*, and of the conduct of the Dutch in overawing the native ruler and forbidding him to have commercial relations with the English.

f. 35. 7-17 April, 1664. Lord Denzil Holles, at Paris, to Sir Geo. Downing.

He complains of the attitude of the Dutch towards the English, their refusal to restore Pularoon, their attempts to obstruct British trade on the coast of Guinea, etc.

f. 42. 5 June, 1664. Answer of the States General (in French) to the protest of the English regarding the *Hopewell*.

They declare that they have enquired into the matter but go into no particulars and only express a hope that for the future the relations between the two countries may be amicable.

[1659.]   **Receuil Historique.**   *Stowe MS. 988, fols.*
                                                       11b-24b.

No. 4.   Abstract of the travels of R. Knox in Ceylon [1659] from a
French translation published in 1693.

1659.   **Journal of the** *Coast* **frigate from**   *Sloane MS. 3672,*
                 Cape Agulhas to India.   *fols. 67-69a.*
16 July—17 August, 1659.

The ship touched at St. Lawrence (Madagascar) and again at Johanna, Comoro
Island where the Log breaks off.   It contains nothing of special interest.

1661.   **A proposal for removing spices**   *Egerton MS. 2395,*
                 and other plants from the East   *fols. 337-39a.*
                 to the West Indies.
Endorsed : Sir Richard Ford's Paper.

1661-68.   **Journals of the voyages of the**   *Sloane MS. 2943, 60*
                 ship *Greyhound* **from the East**   *fols.*
                 Indies to England,

Catalogued : ' An Indian portefeuille of black paper, bound after the fashion of the
Indians, with part of a ship's journal and some accounts '.   The MS. is almost illegible.

1661,   **Copy of the Letters Patents grant-**   *Sloane   MS.   2178,*
3 April.   **ed by His Majesty Charles II to**   *fols. 35-44.*
                 the Governor and Company of
                 Merchants of London trading to
                 the East Indies.

1661-63.   **A Briefe Relation of a Voyage**   *Lansdowne MS. 213,*
                 from St. Helena on the Coast of   *fols. 435-41.*
                 Africa to Bantam in India, begun
                 the 6th day of May, 1661, and
                 from thence to England.   With
                 the most remarkable observations and
                 passages which happened during the
                 said Voyage.   Written by Captain John
                 Dutton, Governor of the Islands of
                 St. Helena and Pularoon.

f. 435.   6 May, 1661,   Embarked in the *African* with his family and
      attendants and Capt. Brouse, commander of the ship.
f. 435a.   26 July, 1661.   Arrived off Java.
29 July, 1661.   Anchored at Bantam.   ' Mr. Page came aboard us '.
f. 435a-36.   30 July, 1661.   Dutton landed with much ceremony and re-
      mained at Bantam until Jan., 1661-2 ' during which time severall
      Occurrences happened relating to the English Trade and Commerce
      with the Kings and Chiefs of the Countries adjacent, not much
      pertinent to the present Relation '.   No details of these occurrences are
      given.
f. 436.   1 Jan., 1661-62.   Sailed in company with the *London*.
11 Jan., 1661-62.   Anchored at Jappara.

16 Jan., 1661-62. A Dutch ship, the *Elephant*, Commander Peter Daniell, suspected to be a spy, arrived.

f. 436. 4 Feb., 1661-62. Anchored at Macassar. Dutton was entertained in the Company's house by Messrs. Turner and Mohun.

17 Feb., 1661-62. Agent Hunter came on board.

19 Feb., 1661-62. Sailed from Macassar.

23 Feb., 1661-62. Entered the Strait of 'Bottoun'.

27 Feb., 1661-62. A skirmish with the natives.

f. 436a. 11 March, 1661-62. Anchored at Pularoon.

12 March, 1661-62. Van Dam, Governor of Vero, was notified of Dutton's arrival and returned an 'impertinent answer'.

17 March, 1661-62. A further application was made to the Governor of Vero for the surrender of Pularoon, but he refused and 'slighted our Gracious Sovereign's Commission'.

20 March, 1661-62. A Protest sent to the Governor.

21 March, 1661-62. Left Pularoon. Anchored before Vero.

31 March—14 April, 1662. Constant altercations with the Dutch, who set guards on the English ships.

14 April, 1662. Sailed from Vero.

f. 437. 26 April, 1662. Anchored at the town of Bottoun. Friendly relations with the King and his son.

27 April, 1662. Sailed from Bottoun (Boutton).

3 May, 1662. Anchored at Macassar. During his stay there Dutton was jeered at by the Dutch for his inability to take Pularoon.

5 June, 1662. Sailed from Macassar.

15 June, 1662. Anchored at Jappara.

19 June, 1662. Sailed for Bantam.

23 July, 1662. Agent Hunter visited the Sultan of Bantam.

f. 437a. 1 Oct., 1662. Embarked on the *London*, Captain Bowen commander.

f. 439. 22 Jan., 1662-63. Anchored at St. Helena.

f. 439a. 1 Feb., 1662-63. Sailed from St. Helena.

f. 141a. 24 April, 1663. Anchored at Falmouth.

1661-80. **Reports on the E.I. Co's. affairs in Bengal.** *Add. MS. 34123, fols. 42-50.*

The MS. deals with the trade of that Province, its currency and weights and measures. It contains a list of the chiefs of the Company's factories, a copy of the agreement made between the agent and Council of Fort St. George and 'Chim Cham and Chintamundsaw' a firm of merchants, 3 Sept., 1679, also a copy of the regulations drawn up by Streynsham Master for conducting the Company's affairs in the Bay of Bengal, 12 Dec., 1679.

1661-62. **Warrant for the East India Company to correct disorderly persons.** *Sloane MS. 856, fols. 10.*

Letters and Warrants of Charles II.

1662. **An answer to some of the Enquiries formerly sent into the East Indies.** Brought in by Mr. Colwell, October 21, 1663, but written at Bantam, November 14, 1662. *Sloane MS. 698, No. 28, fols. 36a-38.*

This document treats of the following commodities, their use and properties : Betel, Arbor Tristis, Macassar poison, camphor, birds'-nests, rhinoceros horn, ' pedra de porco ', ambergris. A pencil note in the margin refers to ' Birch, 1. 318 '.

1662-63.   **Journal of a voyage in the** *Dolphin*   *Egerton MS. 1852,*
16 July,   **from Batavia to Japan,** and thence   *fols. 3-119.*
1662—16   by Malacca to Ceylon, up the west
May, 1663.   coast of India and returning to Ceylon.

[In Dutch.]

[1663.]   **Orders for masters of ships bound**   *Sloane MS. 4436,*
         for the East Indies and other far   *fols. 128-29.*
         voyages.

These directions relate to observations of the compass, tides, eclipses of the moon, soundings, charting, etc., with special orders to observe the eclipse of the moon on 8 August, 1663.

[? 1664.]   **Supplement au Discours de M. le**   *Add. MS. 22920, fols.*
         Chevalier Downing sur des Avis   *82-83.*
         qui sont venus icy depuis a
         l' Ambassadeur Extraordinaire
         d' Angleterre.

This unsigned document (in French) recapitulates the attitude of the Dutch towards the English in the East from the time of the massacre at Amboyna and the capture of Pularoon onwards. It is endorsed : ' Paper given by M. Holles to French King with my memoriall'.

1664.   **Answer returned by Sir Philberto**   *Sloane MS. 698, No.*
         Vernatti, residing at Batavia in   *54, fols. 94a-96a.*
         Java Major, to certain enquiries sent
         thither by order of the [Royal] Society
         recommended by Sir Robert Moray.
         Read before the Society the 27th of
         July, 1664.

(Note in pencil in the margin): ' Printed in Sprat's *History of the Royal Society*, p. 158'.

1664,   **Lord Holles, in Paris, to Sir Geo.**   *Add. MS. 22920, fol.*
12 Aug.   **Downing.**   *44.*

The writer states that he is afraid ' these passages ' in the East Indies will make ' the Accommodation ' between England and the States General more difficult.

1664,   **Resolution of the Estates General**   *Sloane MS. 3112, fols.*
25 Sept.   **concerning the ships** *Hopewell,*   *1-4.*
         Leopard, Charles, James **and** *Mary.*

Answers (in French) to be given to Sir George Downing, Envoy Extraordinary of Charles II, in reply to his complaints on behalf of the E.I. Co., regarding the conduct of the Dutch in refusing to allow the *Hopewell* and *Leopard* to put in at Porca (Porakad), and also in obstructing the *Charles, James* and *Mary* on the coast of Guinea.

The States General do not allow that their servants have acted illegally, but, in order to preserve the peace concluded on 14 Sept., 1662, they are willing to grant concessions and to arrange for reasonable compensation.

1664-65.   **Abstract of the log of the** *African*   *Harl. MS. 4252, 2*
            to Surat, Capt. T. Harman, begun   *fols. upside down.*
            23rd March.

[1665.]   **A Brief of the desires of the E.I.**   *Add. MS. 17018,*
            Co. to the Rt. Hon'ble the Lords   *fols. 199-200a.*
            Commrs. appointed by H.M. to
            treat with the Dutch Ambassa-
            dors.

The document recapitulates what has taken place between the English and the Dutch in 1619, 1622 and 1654 with regard to the Island of Pularoon, and the Commissioners are urged to take action to enforce the restitution of the Island since the fears of the petitioners have been aroused by the preparation of a large Dutch fleet with an unknown design.

1665.   **Regulations for the Charter of the**   *Add. MS. 31146, fols.*
            E.I. Co.   *3-3a.*

These consist of 32 articles and treat of the stock of the present and old Co., subscriptions, rights of members, etc., etc.

1665,   **Letter of the States General to the**   *Add. MS. 22920, fols.*
9 April.   **King of France.**   *114-16.*

They resent the arrest of their ships in French ports and deprecate the attitude of the English East India Co. in inciting the French against them.

1665,   **Sir John Webster to Sir George**   *Add. 22920, fol. 121.*
23 April.   **Downing.**

He writes from Amsterdam and states that reports are current there of atrocities committed by the English on the Dutch in Guinea. He comments on the price of the E.I. Co's stock.

1665,   **Letter from the Committees of the**   *Add. MS. 22546, fol.*
21 Aug.   **E.I. Co. to the Commissioners of**   *243.*
            the Navy.

They report the arrival of five of their ships from the Coromandel Coast.

1665.   **The seizure of the** *Slothany* **and**   *Harl. MS. 1509, fols.*
            Phœnix, **two Dutch East India**   *191-229,*
            ships, by ships of the Royal
            Navy. Papers and correspondence
            thereon.

f. 191a. 21 Sept., 1665. Special order of the Lords Commissioners to the Commissioners of the Port of London acquainting them with the taking of two Dutch East India ships.

f. 192a-96. 21 and 23 Oct., 1665. Instructions regarding the safeguarding of the prizes and their cargoes.

f. 197a. 26 Oct., 1665. Negotiations with the E.I. Co. respecting the sale of the two prizes.

f. 198.   26 Oct., 1665.   The E.I.Co's. articles about two prizes taken by
them (eleven articles) with the answer of the Lords Commissioners
of Prizes thereto.

The E.I. Co. claim the custody of the goods of the said ships and agree to lend the
King money raised on the value thereof. The Commissioners object against allowing
the Co. sole control of the goods and discretion as to the amount to be levied for His
Majesty's use.

f. 200.   30 Oct., 1665.   Order of the Lords Commissioners to the
Commissioners of the Port of London, empowering them to give
up the goods from the East India prizes to the E.I. Co., with the
exception of copper and saltpetre.

f. 199a.   31 Oct., 1665.   Articles agreed on between the Duke of
Albemarle and the Commissioners for prizes on the one part, and
the E.I. Co., on the other part, respecting the two East India prizes,
the *Slothany* and the *Phœnix*.

f. 200a-1a.   1 Nov., 1665.   Second articles presented by the E.I. Co.,
with observations by the Lords Commissioners for prizes thereon.

f. 203a.   1-5 Nov., 1665.   Further correspondence on the above subject.

f. 206.   14 Nov., 1665.   A bargain concluded with the E.I. Co.

f. 229a.   20 March, 1665-66.   Opinion of the Lords Commissioners touching the sale of the goods found in the East India ships.

The folios noted in this MS. are those given in pencil by the Museum authorities.

1666,
23 June.

**Warrant for seizing . . . thirty
hundredweight of Pepper em-
bezzled out of the East India
Prize Ship, the Golden Phœnix, and
carried unto Mr. Wright and Mr.
Gregorie, merchants in London.**

*Harl. MS. 1510,
p. 551*

1666,
29 June.

**Order for payment of £200 apiece
unto the Lord Brounker and Sir
John Mennes, and of £100 apiece
to Charles Bennet and Richard
Kingdom, Esqrs., as His Majesty's
reward for their going on board
the two East India Prize Ships
Slothany and Golden Phœnix, and
securing and landing the goods
from the same.**

*Harl. MS. 1510,
p. 554*

1667-68.   **The Case of Thomas Skinner.**   *Stowe MS. 303, fols.
1-65.*

A Particular Journal of the Proceedings in the House of Peers between Thomas
Skinner, a private merchant trading to the East Indies, and the East India Company,
heard and argued at the Bar of the said House in the years 1667 and 1668.

Fols. 2, 3, 6, 7, 8 refer to trade in India in 1657-59 and to Thomas Skinner's
proceedings at Jambi.

19 Jan.   **The Case of Thomas Skinner.**   *Harl. MS. 4319, 59*
1666/7—   *fols.*

1668,
9 May.

The case of Thomas Skinner against the E.I. Co. in the House of Lords, with copies
of numerous documents.

1667-69.   **Skinner v. the E.I. Co.** Proceedings   *Add. MS. 25116, 75*
in Parliament in the case of Thomas   *fols. 4to*
Skinner against the E.I. Co. Proceed-
ings of the House of Lords.

f. 3-5. 30 Oct., 1667. Petition of T. Skinner to Parliament read.

f. 6. The E.I. Co., ordered to put in their answer.

f. 6-7. 7 Nov., 1667. Rejoinder of the E.I. Co., to the accusation of
T. Skinner.

f. 7. Council on both sides to be heard.

f. 7-8. 2 Dec., 1667. T. Skinner's petition referred to the Judges for
report.

f. 8-9. 4 Dec., 1667. Opinion of the Judges.

f. 9. 13 Dec., 1667. Council to be heard on the whole matter.

f. 9-10. 16 Dec., 1667. Case to be heard on the 17th.

f. 10. 17 Dec., 1667. The Company ask for time to prepare their
answer.

f. 10-11. 11 Feb., 1667-68. Case to be heard.

f. 11-18. Answer of the E.I. Co. to T. Skinner's complaint.

f. 18. 18 Feb., 1667-68. Case adjourned.

f. 19-21. 20 April, 1668. £5,000 awarded to T. Skinner.

f. 21-22. Paper signed by Robert Blackborne, the Company's secretary,
and delivered to the House of Commons, said to be libellous.

f. 22-34. 29 April and 1 May, 1668. Robert Blackborne, Wm. Moses
and Sir Samuel Barnardiston examined with regard to the said
paper.

f. 34-38. 2 May, 1668. Sir Samuel Barnardiston and other members of
the Court of Committees examined regarding a petition drawn up
against the decision in the case of Skinner v. the Company, but
which was subsequently destroyed.

f. 38-41. 4 May, 1668. The rights and privileges of the House of Lords
to be vindicated before the adjournment of the House.

f. 41-44. 5 May, 1668. Petition of the E.I. Co. to the House of
Commons regarding the case of T. Skinner.

f. 44-56. The same debated.

f. 57-87. 6 May, 1668. Debate on the privileges of the House resumed.
Petition of Thomas Skinner showing that the E.I. Co. refuse to carry
out the decree of the Lords and pay him the compensation awarded,
read.

f. 88-89. T. Skinner's petition considered.

f. 89-100. Petition of E.I. Co. to the House of Commons debated.

f. 100-1. It was decided that the entertainment by the House of
Commons of the scandalous petition of the E.I. Co. was a breach of
privilege.

The greater part of these proceedings resolves itself into a question of privilege
between the Lords and Commons.

f. 107-14. 9 May, 1668. Sir Samuel Barnardiston, Sir A. Riccard, Sir R. Wynn and Sir C. Boone brought to the bar of the House as delinquents. Sir S. Barnardiston fined for alleged libel against the Lords and the others reprimanded.

f. 115-16. 17 April, 1668. Proceedings of the House of Commons. Petition of the E.I. Co. to the House of Commons, setting forth their grievances.

f. 116-24. 24 April, 1668—9 May, 1668. The same debated and the examination of the case of Skinner *versus* the Company before the House of Lords, and their finding with regard to the same said to be a breach of privileges of the House of Commons, and the second petition by the Company to the Commons no breach of privilege, as regards the Lords.

The case of Thomas Skinner, merchant, was as follows : He took a ship, the *Thomas*, on a trading voyage to India in 1657-58, the trade being then open. The ship reached Jambi, where Skinner hired a house, stored his goods in a warehouse and purchased the Island of Barella from the King of Jambi. He there built a dwelling-house and entered into contracts for planting pepper, etc. In May, 1659, the agents of the E.I. Co. seized his ship, goods, houses and 1,521 dollars. He estimated the loss at £17,172, besides ' vast charges'. He also complained of violence done to his person. From the year 1661, onwards, he petitioned the King of England for justice, and failing to get redress, brought his case before the House of Lords. The Lords awarded him damages and then the matter resolved itself into a question of privilege between the two Houses.

1668.   **Resolutions of the House of Com-**   *Egerton MS. 2543,*
          mons and House of Lords in the   *fols. 207-8a.*
          case of Thomas Skynner.

An extract from Add. 25116, described above.

No date   **The Case of Thomas Skynner, mer-**   *Harl. MS. 7310, fols.*
c. 1669.   **chant, against the East India**   *190-90a.*
             Company. Praying leave to bring
             in a Bill to be passed into an Act of
             Parliament. Printed.

For printed version of the whole case, see ' The grand question concerning the judicature of the House of Peers stated . . . And the case of T. Skinner . . . complaining of the East India Company . . . related. 1669. 8vo. British Museum Press, Mark 288-a. 12.

1667-69.   **Log of the *London*, Captain John**   *Sloane MS. 3668, 40*
             Privett, from England to Bantam   *fols.*
             and back.

28 Jan., 1666-67. The log begins in the Thames.

27 Aug., 1668. The ship anchored off Bantam.

19 Sept., 1668. The King of Bantam was saluted with 15 guns.

17 Oct., 1668. The ship sailed for England.

 4 Jan., 1668-69. Anchored at St. Helena.

14 Jan., 1668-69. Sailed for England.

22 Jan., 1668-69. Anchored at Ascension Island.

26 Jan., 1668-69. Sailed thence.

10 April, 1669. Anchored at Erith.

This journal is an ordinary seaman's log and contains no matter of special interest.

1667-72. THE MARSHALL MSS.

There are eight MSS. in the British Museum attributed to John Marshall. They are : Harleian MSS. 4252, 4253, 4254, 4255, 4256 ; Add. MSS. 7037 (now O.R. 17 A.K)., 7039, 7040.

Harl. MS. 4252 is a copy made by Marshall of the captain's journal of the voyage of the *Unicorn* to Madras, and thence to Bengal, in 1667-69. In this ship Marshall sailed as a factor in the service of the E.I. Co.

Harl. MS. 4253 contains Marshall's account of the Hindu religion, gathered from his intercourse with a Brahman at the Company's factory at Kāsimbāzār, where Marshall was stationed from 1672 until his death in 1677. It also contains part of his translation of the *Bhagavat Purana*.

Harl. MS. 4254 deals with occurrences and notes made at Patna from 1668-72. Some of the entries are in the form of a diary but the greater part are scraps of information jotted down at random with no attempt at arrangement.

Harl. MS. 4255 is similar in character to 4254, but of a later date, covering the period, 1671/2-1672.

Harl. MS. 4256 contains a copy of 16 fols. of No. 4253 and a continuation of Marshall's translation of the *Bhagavat Purana*.

Add MS. 7037 (O.R. 17 A.K.) is a later copy of Harl. MSS. 4253 and 4256.

Add. MS. 7039 contains extracts from Harl. MSS. 4254 and 4255.

Add. MS. 7040 contains extracts from Harl. MS. 4254.

C. R. Wilson has two references to the Marshall MSS. in his *Early Annals of Bengal*, Vol. I, pp. 375, 381, foot-notes, but he speaks of the author erroneously as a ' superstitious sailor '.

Sir Richard Temple has freely used Marshall's *Notes and Observations* in his edition of the *Diaries of Streynsham Master* (Indian Records Series), and in his *Countries round the Bay of Bengal* (Hak. Soc. ed). He has also given a brief biography of Marshall in his *Correspondence of Richard Edwards*, (*Notes and Queries*, 12 S III, 263, 1917), and *Bengal Past and Present*, Vol. XVII, pp. 162-64.

Marshall's account of the famine at Patna, in 1670-71, has been quoted both by Sir Richard Temple in *Countries round the Bay of Bengal* and by Sir Theodore Morison in his *Economic Transition of India*, 1911.

In the detailed description of Harl. MSS. 4254 and 4255 given below, the various subjects dealt with in a discursive fashion have been grouped under their several headings for facility of reference.

The Marshall manuscripts have been strangely ignored by scholars. Marshall was probably the first European who studied the language, philosophy and religion of the Hindus, and his Diary is essential to the understanding of many of the local customs, and important events of the period. See my article, in the *Journal of Indian History*, No. 1, Vol. I.

1667-69. The Marshall MSS., Journall to *Harl. MS. 4252, 28* East India in Ship *Unicorn* *fols.* 1667-68 [1669].

f. 1a.   Sketch of the Island of Teneriffe.

f. 2.   29 Dec., 1667. Sailed from Blackwall for the coast of Coromandel. At Erith and Gravesend found the rest of the fleet, eight ships in all.

f. 2a.   Feb., 1667-68.   Joined by the *Diligence*.
10 March 1667-68.   Sailed from the Downs.
f. 3.   16 March 1667-68.   The ships part company.
f. 3a.   Note on the orders for the re-taking of Fort St. George, held in rebellion by Sir Edward Winter.
f. 4a.   Description of Madeira and its Governor.   Notes on Englishmen residing there.
f. 5a.   2 April, 1668.   The soldiers on board, for the reduction of Fort St. George, refused to pick oakum and were compelled to do so.
f. 6a.   8 April, 1668.   At St. Jago, Cape Verd Island.   Description of the island.
10 April, 1668.   Price of provisions at St. Jago.
f. 11a.   6 June, 1668.   Capt. Harman protests against the other ships for not keeping in company with him.
f. 13.   29 June, 1668.   Comments on birds seen.
f. 14.   Drawings of Cape Falso and of the land near the Cape of Good Hope.
f. 16a.   Drawing of the coast of Mauritius.
f. 16a-17.   30 July 1668.   Description of Mauritius.
f. 21.   28 Aug., 1668.   Protest against the desertion of the *Unicorn* by Capts. Price and Wilde.
Sketch of the South-East Coast of India.
12 Sept., 1668.   Anchored in Madras Road.
5 July, 1669.   Sailed from Masulipatam to Bengal.
9 July, 1669.   Anchored in Balasor Road.
13 July, 1669.   Reached Balasor town.

Following the Log, bound upside down, is a portion of the Log of the *African*, in her voyage to Surat, in 1664-65, under the command of Capt. T. Harman.   See *ante*, under the date, for a note on this fragment.

1675.   ' A familiar and free Dialogue bet-   *Harl. MS. 4253, 40*
wixt   Joh   John   Marshall   and   *fols.*
Muddoosoodun Rauree Bramin
at Cassambuzar in Bengal [1] in East
India, begun the 18th March, 1674-5 '.

f. 1-8.   The creation of the world.   The difference between ' Addirb' the Omnipresent and ' Dirb' the corruptible.   The creation of woman, then man.

These matters are treated in a series of questions between John Marshall and the Brahman.

f. 9.   25 June, 1675.   Account of Muddoosoodum Raure[e], Bramine : ' Account of the Hindoo book called Srebaugabatporam '.

Then follows Marshall's version of the Brahman's interpretation of the sacred book. He begins with the evolving of the creation in the mind of God and the making of ' Rosagum, Hittagum and Tomagum ', who merged into one woman called ' Addea ', for whom God created ' Manapurse '.

1675.   **The Marshall MSS., contd.**   *Harl. MS. 4253,*
contd.

Marshall's marginal notes summarise the information obtained from the Brahman's account of the *Bhagavat Purana*.   The chief of these are :

f. 10-15.   Heaven and earth divided.
  ' Berna, Besna, Manadeeb.'
  ' Berna ' to make ' Deutas '.
  ' Keyshub ' created and ' Additee Ditte ' and ' Kudroo ' for his wives.
  ' Inder ' born to ' Additte '.
  ' Burna ' made astrologer.
  ' Inder ' a raja.
  Creation of ' Bismavera '.
  ' Howa ' born of ' Addittee ' and cut into seven pieces or Wind, 49
      more children born to ' Addittee '.
  ' Bisooa Burma' the world's artificer, born.
  ' Urrun ' redness born.
  ' Burrun ' owner of water born.
  ' Cubbere ' keeper of riches born.
  ' Astologopaulo ' (governor of the eight parts of the heavens) born.
  Fire, water and souls created.
  ' Bostookie ' a snake with 1,000 heads, created.
  ' Shurma ' the origin of dogs, created.
  The earth created.
  ' Addea's ' children who are ' Dutas ' contend with the ' Dittees '.
      Heaven given to the former and earth to the latter.
f. 15-18.   Number of the ' Usras ' weakened by a trick.
  Origin of poison.
  ' Nilcunt ', why so called.
  How the moon was made.
  Origin of goodness, badness, long life, increase, precious stones.
  Brahmans created—their duties.
  How the ' Dutas ' circumvented the ' Usras ' and how one of the latter
      became immortal.
f. 18-23.   ' Indra' king of the ' Dutas '—wives created for them.
  Origin of man and of woman.
  The 27 wives of Chand, the moon.
  Transformation of ' Sobbona ' pursued by ' Oftob ' and children born
      to them.
  How ' Sumitcher ' earned his nickname and became lame.
  The inhabitants of the fourth, fifth and sixth heavens.
  Distinctions made in men, beasts and things heretofore of identical
      pattern.
f. 24-32.   Creation of castes.
  Divisions of Brahmans—servants for their use.
  Origins of the seasons of the year.
  Rajahs.
  ' Sangur's ' fight with the sun.
  How the sea and fresh water were made.
  Divisions of time.
  Feud between ' Manhadeeb ' and Dick—' Manhadeeb's ' wife ' Suttie'
      casts herself into the fire.
  ' Manhadeeb ' becomes a *faqir*.
  ' Birna' expels Indra from the heavens and alters the course of the sun.
f. 33-40.   ' Suttee ' reincarnated and called ' Parbati.'
  How Parbati regained her husband and was married again to
      ' Manhadeeb '.
  Parbati's son, ' Cortick ' kills ' Birtur' and restores Indra to his kingdom.
  ' Bissoroo ' born and killed by Indra.

Indra's ' evil ' passed on to earth, water, women, trees.

The value of the above MS. lies in the fact that it represents Hinduism as understood by a Christian in the seventeenth century. In spite of the many unsuccesful attempts to reproduce names, as given by his informant, the MS. is remarkable as the work of an Englishman who had been in India for only five years and during that period had been mainly occupied with mercantile duties.

1667/8-   **The Marshall MSS., contd.**   *Harl. MS. 4254.*
1671/2   **Memorandums concerning India from September 11th, 1668, to January 1st, 1671-2. Per J. M.**

ASTRONOMICAL AND MATHEMATICAL NOTES

f. 5.   Easy problems stated and solved.
f. 5a.   Eclipse of the sun at Masulipatam, 20 April, 1669.
   Notes on the Hindu almanac.
f. 6a, 10a.   Height and declension of the sun, 30 Aug., 1669 and 1 June, 1670.
f. 15, 23.   Eclipses of the moon, 15 March and September, 1671.
f. 16, 26a-27.   Hindu names for constellations and stars and notes thereon.
f. 23.   11 Sept., 1671.   Variation of the sun at Patna.
f. 26a.   Variation of the sun at the Cape and Mauritius.

BOATS

f. 3a. *Bajras* described.
f. 4 (reverse).   ' Purgos ' described.

COINS

f. 2a.   Coins at Balasor—cowries.
f. 6a.   Different kinds of rupees.
f. 10a.   A table of coins at Patna.
f. 13a.   Table of coins.
f. 14a.   Dollars, sicca rupees, etc.
f. 14a.   Cowries, abassin, ' cuppan '.
f. 21a.   Coins of Nepal.
f. 2 (reverse).   Coins of Fort St. George.
f. 3 (reverse).   Coins in use at Masulipatam.

DIARY

f. 28-29.   1667-68 Marshall's entertainment by the E.I. Co., his sponsors and securities.
f. 29-31.   10 March, 1667-68—20 Sept., 1668.   His account of his voyage to India in the *Unicorn*, with notes on Madeira, St. Jago, Mauritius and tornadoes, etc.
f. 5a.   20 April, 1669.   An eclipse of the sun at Masulipatam.
f. 4 (reverse).   5 July, 1669.   Arrived at Balasor.
f. 5-6 (reverse).   14 Feb.—5 March, 1669-70.   Description of a journey from Balasor to Hugli, with notes on objects of interest, etc.
f. 7-8 (reverse).   28 March—9 April, 1670.   Journey from Hugli to Rajmahal, with descriptive notes.
f. 9-13 (reverse).   11—22 April, 1670.   Journey from Rajmahal to Hajipur, with descriptive notes.
f. 14 (reverse).   27 May, 1670.   Observation of the sun at Singhiya.
f. 6.   1 June, 1670.   The rains began at Patna.

f. 14 (reverse). 29-30 July, 1670. At 'Bimkalattee' seven *kos* from Singhiya ; note on an engraved pillar

f. 16 (reverse). 10 Aug., 1670—5 Jan. 1670-71. A journey from Jahanabad to Hugli, Balasor, Pipli, and back to Hugli.

f. 12. 7 Sept., 1670. The English saltpetre boats stopped by the Governor.

f. 17-18 (reverse). 17-27 Sept., 1670. Account of a journey by river from Patna to Hugli.

f. 13a. 9 Feb., 1671. Mr. Vincent's son born.

f. 15. 15 March, 1671. Eclipse of the moon at Hugli. Dutch Governor, Van Leen, present when Marshall took his observation.

f. 16. 29 March, 1671. A day of penance for the Hindus.

f. 19-27 (reverse). 3-23 May, 1671. Account of a journey from Hugli to Patna, with descriptive notes, remarks on the difficulty of obtaining *dastaks* and on the dues extorted.

f. 27 (reverse). 24 May, 1671. Arrived at Patna.
25 May, 1671, Rode to Singhiya.

f. 17. 31 May, 1671. Bought a ' Brahmin ' slave boy at Patna.

f. 17, 18a, 19a, 20, 21a. 6 June, 1671. The rains came in at Patna. Notes on their long duration.

f. 19a, 23. 1 Aug., and 10 Sept., 1671. Saw the hills of Nepal.

f. 22, 22a. 18-25 Aug., 1671. River Gandak overflowed the banks of the factory at Singhiya.

f. 23. 2-3 Sept., 1671. Periodical storm at Patna.

f. 23. 10 Sept., 1671. Eclipse of the moon at Jahanabad.

11 Sept., 1671. Variation of the sun at Patna.

24 Sept., 1671. New moon—the ' Hotty ' over.

f. 23, 23a. 7 and 15 Oct., 1671. Brief violent storms.

f. 24a. 6 Nov., 1671. Hindu ' washing festival ' at Hajipur.

f. 26, 31a. 17 Nov., 1671. Cold weather came in at Patna.

For a diary of the famine at Patna, 1670-71, see under Famine.

FAMINE AT PATNA IN 1670-71

Full details of the famine are given in scattered notes on fols. 17, 17a, 19, 20, 20a, 22a, 23, 26, 31a, 33a.

FAQIRS

f. 8a, 24a, 18a. Their marvellous powers.

f. 9. A female Hindu *faqir*.

f. 18a. Their method of assuaging hunger.

f. 24a, 25, 25a. Their manners, customs, and habitat.

FOLKLORE

f. 6. Influence of the moon.
Direction of glances.

f. 10a. Belief regarding a star in Charles's Wain.

f. 11a-12. Signs of health, sickness and death.
Charms to hinder men from being angry.
Charms to make a vision appear.
Charms to cause money to stay by a man.
Charms to render hidden money inviolable.

f. 14a. A worm charm.

f. 18a. Propitious days for journeys.

f. 21. Humours in man's body in which certain months may predominate.

f. 31a, 32.   Hindu charms.
f. 15 (reverse).   Why alligators have no tongues.

FOLK-MEDICINE

f. 10a.   Test for the 'bay' and remedy for it.
f. 13, 17a, 26.   Remedies for sore eyes, colic, etc.
f. 13a, 27a.   Remedies for stone.
f. 13a.   Remedies against witchcraft, toothache, etc.
f. 14a.   A medicinal wood—a remedy for cholera and hæmorrhage.
f. 15a 'Dhauts' or digestions.
f. 17.   Remedy for 'Tenesmus'.
f. 17a, 27a.   Remedies for gout.
f. 18.   Antidote for the bite of a 'Coa'.
f. 18, 27a.   Remedy for 'French pox'.
f. 18a.   Cure for madness.
   Cure for weak joints.
f. 22.   'Aukkapaut' leaf, an aperient.
   Hindu theory of the circulation of the blood.
f. 23a.   'Singreny' a disease of the digestive organs.
f. 24a.   Remedies against fire, sun, etc.
f. 25a.   Remedy to prevent dysentery.
f. 27-27a.   Remedies for dropsy, etc.

GEOGRAPHICAL NOTES

f. 2a.   Old name for Balasor.
f. 2a, 9.   Notes on the Ganges.
f. 14.   Account of distances from Delhi to Patna.
f. 17, 25.   Distances between Patna, Benares and Nepal.
f. 19a.   Various names for the mountains beyond the Mogul's dominions.
f. 25a.   Note on Jagannath pagoda as a landmark.
f. 31.   Latitude of Patna.
f. 32.   Size of the earth according to the Brahmans.
f. 2-3 (reverse).   Description of St. Thomé and St. Thomas's Mount.
f. 3.   „   Masulipatam.
f. 3-4.   „   Madapollam and Verasheroon and of the
   English factories there.
f. 4.   Description of Pettipolee.
                „   Balasor Road, River and Factory.
                „   'Ramana'.
f. 6 (reverse).   Description of Hugli.
f. 8-9 (reverse).   „   Rajmahal.
f. 13-14 (reverse).   „   Hajipur and account of distances travelled.
f. 14 (reverse).   „   Note on an engraved stone pillar at 'Bimkalattee' or 'Bimsclub'.
f. 15 (reverse).   Muhammadan tomb, near 'Bursla'.
f. 27 (reverse).   Account of distances travelled from Hugli to Patna.
   See also under Diary for accounts of journeys.

HINDUS

f. 4a.   Hindu notions of England.
f. 5a.   Teaching paid in kind by Hindus.
f. 20a.   Hindu justice.
f. 23a.   Hindu ingratitude.
f. 24-24a.   Hindu notions concerning palmistry.
f. 25.   A Rajput's wife.

f. 26.   Hindu seas, seven in number.
f. 27a. How Hindu physicians prescribe for sick women.
f. 28.   Hindu query as to relationship.
f. 32.   Hindu reckoning of time.
    See also under Religion.

HISTORICAL NOTES

f. 4a.   Account of Tamerlane (Timur).
f. 13a. Note on the pride of Khwaja 'Osomangee' who fought with the King of India but was overcome.
f. 25.   Names of the Rajas of Katmandu, etc.
f. 26.   Aurangzeb's treasury; amount contained therein.
f. 31-31a. Akbar's encounter with a *yogi*.

JAPAN

f. 21a. Gold dust, a product.
         Restrictions on the Dutch factory.
         Japanese hatred of Christians.
         Remarks on a Scotchman who had been in Japan.
         Justice and honesty of the Japanese.

KASHMIR

f. 12-12a. Description of physical features, productions, houses, inhabitants, music, boats, religion, etc.
f. 21a. Fir trees of Kashmir.

LANGUAGE

f. 16a. Note on the Chinese and Japanese languages.
f. 20.   'Naggery' language, why so called.
f. 21.   Origin of the word 'Hindu'.
f. 25a. Derivation of Jagannath.
f. 32-32a, 33a. 'Sanskrit or Nagari' letters and figures.

LEGENDS AND STORIES

f. 5.   Story of the Judgment of Solomon as told at Pegu.
f. 8a.   Stories of the inhabitants of Kashmir.
f. 11.   'Mamidarif's' story of fourteen in a mosque in a thunderstorm.
f. 14a. Notes on mermaids at Mozambique.
f. 20a. Story of the three Brahmans and the burned and resurrected maiden.
         Story of the Flood at Patna, 4733 years before 1671.
f. 24.   Story of the *faqir* and his would-be helpers.
f. 26a. A story of Muhammad.
f. 31a. Story of Akbar's encounter with a *yogi* and the consequent change in his nature.
f. 14-15 (reverse). Legend of 'Bim'.

MANNERS AND CUSTOMS

f. 6a-7. Marriage and burial customs of Muhammadans and Hindus. *Sati*.
f. 16-16a. Hook-swinging at Hugli.
f. 18-18a. Naming of children.
f. 18a. Child-bearing in India.
f. 24a. Washing festival at Hajipur.

Meteorological Notes

f. 2.   Hot winds at Fort St. George and Masu'ipatam.
Rains at Masulipatam.

f. 6.   Rains began at Patna, 1 June, 1670.

f. 17, 18a, 19a.   Rains began at Patna, 6 June, 1671.
Between 700 and 800 people killed in Patna, c. 1661, by the falling of walls during the rains.

f. 19.   Note on monsoons.

f. 19a.   Duration of rainy season in 1671.

f. 20a.   5, 7, 22 and 23 Aug., 1671, the only fine days (except two) since 6 June.

f. 26, 31a.   17 Nov., 1671.   Cold weather at Patna.

Miscellaneous

f. 9.   A plague of flies at Jahanabad.

f. 12a.   Notes on a greyhound, born in the *Rainbow*, in 1669.

f. 13a.   Method of melting amber.

f. 13a.   Eunuchs never bald.

f. 17.   Sealing-wax can be bent.

f. 19.   Position of bodies seen floating on the Ganges.

f. 26a.   How the ship's cooper was burnt when opening a cask of water.

f. 33.   Travelling charges between Patna and Agra.

Muhammadans

f. 7a-8, 9.   Their laws and customs.

f. 8.   Usury forbidden by ' Moors '.

f. 26a.   Three kinds of Musalman Shekhs.
Two kinds of Musalmans.

f. 24, 31.   Their ' leachery '.

See also under Religion.

Natural History

f. 5a.   Engendering and capture of Elephants.

f. 8a.   Prodigious size of snakes at Nepal.

f. 13a.   ' Gosomph ' a creature like a lizard.
Arbor sentila, a tree of death.

f. 16a.   A sword-fish.

f. 17.   ' Futchoa ' a fish.

f. 18a.   Small oxen and large goats at Patna.

f. 19-19a.   Description of a musk-cat and habitat of the animal.

f. 22.   ' Bya ' a bird, its hanging nest.

f. 25.   Tigers and their habitat.

f. 26.   ' Harrealls ' green and yellow pigeons, described.

Nepal

f. 8a, 18a.   Huge snakes.

f. 8.   Conveyance of passengers from Patna.

f. 10.   Musk.

f. 21a.   Fir trees.

f. 22, 25.   Customs, clothes, houses, government, etc.
Names of hills in the neighbourhood.

f. 23.   Plan of elevation of hills.

Pagodas

f. 9a.   At Masulipatam.

f. 12.   Origin of the Jagannath pagoda.

Patna (with Hajipur, Nanagur and Singhiya)

f. 9a. 'Sasugos' a garden, at Patna.

f. 9a. Description of the Company's factory houses at Hajipur and Nanapur.

f. 20a. Price of provisions, at Patna, in 1671.

f. 21a, 25. Fir trees driven down from Kashmir to Patna by the 'freshes'.

f. 23. Periodical 'hotty' or great storm, at Patna.

f. 33. Coaches, oxen and horses ply between Agra and Patna.

Pegu

f. 5a. Method of pleading at Pegu.

f. 5a. Story of the Judgment of Solomon brought from Pegu.

Productions and Merchandise

f. 4a. Growth of rice at Dacca.

f. 10, 19a, 25. Musk, how sold, at Patna, and whence obtained.

f. 12a. Rapid growth of barley in Patna.

f. 15. Valuable properties of 'Coco Maldiva'.

f. 15a. Ambergris from Johanna.

f. 16a. 'Dootura' seeds.

f. 18. Price of elephants' teeth at Patna.

f. 18a. Saffron from Nepal and Kashmir.

f. 19a. Fine earthenware from Minapur, near Hajipur.

f. 21a. Price of gold dust.

f. 22a. Rock salt mines between Lahore and Kandahar.

Recipes

f. 12a. To make glue. To clear water.

f. 17. To prevent a dog from growing.

f. 18a. To preserve tombstones.

f. 20. To cool water with saltpetre.

f. 28, 33. To make an 'oyle bandgir' an aperient.

Religion, Religious Beliefs and Philosophy

f. 2a, 9. Sanctity of the Ganges.

f. 3-4, 19, 21, 23a. Story of the creation and fall of man.

f. 5a. Age of the world.

f. 5a-6. Temptation and fall of Adam.

f. 7a. *Faqirs.* See also separate title.

f. 10a. 'Mamidarif' on human credulity—similarity of men to sheep, different religions—prayers of Muhammadans and attainment of heaven by Hindus.

f. 11-11a. Remarks on the Muhammadan religion.

f. 12. Birth, re-incarnation and death of Krishna.

f. 16-16a. Hook-swinging at Hugli.

f. 18, 23a. Hindu belief in three humours in the body and five senses.

f. 22. Hindu 'mudds' or follies.

Transmigration of souls.

f. 22a. Sacrifice of a kid by the 'saltpetre boatmen'; the ceremony described.

f. 23-23a, 31a. Hindu belief in four 'Auguns' or stomachs in man.

f. 23a, 24a, 28. Hindu notion of God.

f. 23a. Growth of the world.

f. 24, 24a. 'Sloka' for the six actions betokening 'lightness' in men.
f. 24a. Hindu 'washing festival' at Hajipur.
f. 25a-26. 'Ruttons' or chief things created by God.
f. 27. Ghosts not the souls of men.
f. 28. The nine bodies of Krishna; his reappearance in a different form.
f. 31, 32. Hindu idea of the constituents of man.
f. 32a. No free will doctrine among Hindus.
    Remarks on the soul of man.
f. 33a. Three things professed alike by Brahmans and Moguls.

WEIGHTS AND MEASURES

f. 2. Maund and candy.
f. 2a. Hugli maund; Patna maund; weights and measures at Patna.
f. 6. Barleycorns, covids 'dun' 'course'.
f. 7a. Measure of time by 'Gurries'.
f. 10a. Measures at Patna.
f. 11, 13. Different kinds of *gaz*.
f. 14a. Table of weights at the various factories.
f. 17. Length of a 'Saut'.
f. 21a-22. Stilliard for weighing gold and silver.
f. 10. Weight of a great seer.
f. 15a, 32. Hindu measurements and reckoning of time.
f. 18. A 'Ruttee'.
f. 22a. Length of a *kos*.

Note.—Where an entry under the same heading occurs on more than one folio, it is frequently a duplicate, the author having probably forgotten that he had already recorded it. Many of the remarks consist of three or four lines only, and the longest of them seldom exceeds a full page. The writing throughout is crabbed and in many places difficult to decipher.

The above remarks apply to the remainder of Marshall's *Notes and Observations* (Harl. MS. 4255), for a description of which see below.

1672. **Notes and Observations of East India** *Harl. MS. 4255*
taken per John Marshall from Jan. *30 fols.*
1st Anno Domini, 1671-2.

ASTROLOGICAL AND ASTRONOMICAL NOTES

f. 2. Number and nature of Nakshatras and their connection with the naming of children.
f. 2. Effect of the place of the moon at the time of birth or marriage.
f. 2a. Diagram of the Nakshatras.
f. 3. Position and discord of planets, with table.
f. 3a. Table for making a horoscope from the place of the moon at the time of birth.
    Resolution of Horary questions.
f. 4. What planets befriend each other.
f. 4a-5. Table of 'Rosses' and 'Nachutters' with explanation.
f. 5. Endowments of the planets.
    Conjunction necessary for a 'native' to become a King.
    Explanation of 'Coljoog'.
    Source of Indian astrology.
f. 5a. Diagrams and horoscopes for a nativity.
f. 6a. A table to determine a man's thoughts.
f. 7. A table to show the effect of the planets.
f. 8a. Horoscope to show in what hour in each day the planets rule.

f. 9a. Length and reign of each planet.
How to pacify the planets.
f. 10-10a. Table of the reigns of the planets and their good and evil influence.
f. 11. A wife's 'Ross' the seventh 'house' from her husband's.
f. 11a-12. Table of good and bad planets, with notes of exceptions.
f. 12. Weapons of the planets.
f. 12-12a. Table of friendly and enemy 'houses'.
f. 12a. Good and bad 'gurries' for each 'Ross'.
f. 12a. Planets under every 'Nachuttur'.
f. 13. Good and bad 'Nachutturs'.
Casting a nativity.
How to know whether a man or his wife will die first.
f. 13, 18a, 20. Good and bad planets.
f. 13a, 20. Tables of planets and their effects.
f. 14. Places of planets and exceptions.
Twelve 'houses' their place and influence.
f. 14a, 15a. Planets that shorten life.
Table of good and bad Nakshatras for natives.
f. 15. What planets go in each 'house' and what planets shorten life.
f. 15, 18a, 19. How to determine a man's age.
f. 15a. To determine the time of day.
f. 16. Table of position of the planets on 1 January, 1671-72.
f. 16, 16a. Signs of good fortune.
f. 16. Table of daily motion of the planets.
f. 16a, 20. Length of the reign of the planets.
f. 16a. The sun's motion.
f. 17. How to know what islands governed the year when a man was born.
f. 17a, 18, 18a. 'Ross' and 'Burge' which govern a man's nativity.
f. 18. Table to cast a horoscope.
f. 18a. What planets see each other.
Marriage omens from the planets.
To find out what planet reigns at each 'gurry'.
Those born under certain planets will die in foreign countries.
f. 19-19a. Influence of various planets.
f. 20. 'Houses' and their effects.
f. 25. 'Cornebepauk' a book of destiny to try fortunes; Horary question.
f. 25-25a. To determine a man's age by Nakshatras and by 'Burge'.
f. 25a. To find what creature a man's soul inhabited in a previous existence.
f. 25a. Names of the 27 'Joogs' and 27 'Nachutturs'.
f. 26. To find the 'Nachuttur' the moon is in.
Result of the meeting of 'Joog' and 'Nachuttur'.
f. 26-26a. To ascertain what 'Joog' reigns.
f. 26a. Names of the days and nights called 'Tuttorra'.
To ascertain fortunate days.
Table of what every 'Ross' gets and spends in the year 1672.
The master of the planets.
f. 26a-28. Hindu almanac for 1672 translated.
f. 27a. Division of plenty and scarcity.
f. 27a-28. To find in what 'gurry' the moon entered into 'Nacshuttur'.
f. 28. How long sickness lasts in each 'Nachshuttur'.

(The account was received by Marshall from 'Ramnaut, an able astrologer Brahman'.)

Names of the periods between new and full moon.

f. 30.   Propitious days for travelling.

BHUTAN

f. 8.   The residence of a revered Brahman.

Manners and customs in Bhutan.

f. 20a.   'Batista de Joan's' information about Bhutan.

'Mucteer de Isaac's' remarks on the religion, manners, customs, method of trade, etc., of Bhutan.

f. 21.   How travellers from Bhutan to Russia sustain themselves without food.

f. 22.   Natural productions of the country.

f. 22a.   Goods saleable at Lhasa.

The Lama and his government.

DIARY

f. 5.   — Jan., 1671-72.   Very severe weather in Singhiya.

f. 7a.   12 Jan., 1671-72.   A great storm at Singhiya.

— Aug., 1671.   A flood at Ellabasse [Allahabad] in which over 17,000 persons perished.

f. 11.   15 and 16 Jan., 1671-72.   Cold and windy weather.

f. 17.   1 Feb., 1671-72.   The weather begins to be warm.

f. 18a.   4 Feb., 1671-72.   A storm of wind at Singhiya and a little rain.

f. 23a.   3 March, 1671-72.   Eclipse of the moon at Singhiya.

f. 24a.   6 March, 1671-72.   A meteor seen at Patna, its import.

f. 25a.   15-18 March, 1671-72.   Stormy weather.

FAQIRS AND YOGIS

f. 14a.   Their method of answering questions.

f. 16a.   Venerated by the Hindus.

f. 21.   Note on a *faqir* at Patna.

FOLKLORE

f. 6.   A Persian belief in six unlucky days each month.

f. 6.   Signs of death.

Signs of victory against enemies.

Signs of good digestion.

f. 7a.   Why elements are made of different natures.

f. 8a-9, 18.   A test to know who will be victor in a fight.

f. 9.   An unlucky birthday.

f. 10a.   Hindu charms and conjuring tricks.

f. 15a.   Reason for the saltness of the sea.

f. 18a.   Marriage omens from the planets.

To know how many arrows are in a sheaf.

f. 21a.   The blind cannot dream.

f. 23a.   'Shearcerree' from a lion's head, a charm against evil.

f. 24.   A charm to retain a friend.

f. 25.   Tests for a witch.

f. 25a.   Three men that are unfortunate.

f. 28a.   Charm of 62 against evil or enemies.

                 ,,   20   ,,   snake-poison.

                 ,,   72   ,,   evil.

                 ,,   50   ,,   for a crying child.

f. 29.   ,,   100 against enemies, evil and to beget love.

f. 29-29a. Charm of 34 against devils and enemies.

f. 29a-30. ,, 34 ,, devils and enemies and all evil things: the 'highest of all Hindoos Magick'.

Marshall received the above from 'Ramnaut, Brahman at Modufferpore, near Mossee'.

f. 30. Charm of 15 to open any lock. Propitious days for travelling.

FOLK-MEDICINE

f. 2. 'Ghowpant' a cure for wounds.
f. 9. Remedy for indigestion.
f. 10a, 11. Antidotes for scorpion and snake bites.
f. 11. Cure for the French pox.
f. 16a. Cause of indigestion.
f. 21. A cure for stone.
f. 21a, 22a. Remedy for dysentery.
f. 22a. ,, ,, small-pox.
f. 22a, 23a, 26. ,,˙ ,, ague.
f. 22a. ,, ,, gout.
f. 23a. ,, ,, bladder trouble.
  ,, ,, worms.
  Tonic properties of iron.
  Tonics and stomachics.
  Remedy for 'morgee' or falling sickness.
f. 24. 'Killed' minerals used by a Brahman doctor at Patna.
f. 30. An Arab saying about salves and wounds.

GEOGRAPHICAL NOTES

f. 21a. Distance from Isfahan to Smyrna.
f. 21a, 22. Distance from Patna to Lhasa and from Lhasa to 'Sullur' with names of the peoples of those countries.
f. 22a. Note on Kashmir and its inhabitants.
  See also under Bhutan and Nepal.

HISTORICAL NOTES

f. 7a. August, 1671. A flood at Allahabad. The Nawab refused entrance to the Fort to all refugees who could not pay five rupees, and was, in consequence, turned out by the king.
f. 21. Sunyasis, at Benares, cut to pieces by order of Shah Jahan.

LANGUAGE

f. 16. Notes on words of the same sound in many languages but of different signification.
f. 21a. Names of figures in 'Lossa' (Lhasa) language.
f. 25a-26. Origin of the name, Turkoman or Turks.

LEGENDS AND STORIES

f. 7a. Story of why Adam refused and afterwards accepted gold from the devil.
f. 21. Story of a drunkard and the Mogul king's elephant.
f. 24. Stories of the raja, the woman and the *faqir*, and of the blacksmith's wife and the *faqir*. [These stories are noted but not related.]
f. 30. Story of Alexander the Great.

MANNERS AND CUSTOMS

f. 2. Naming of children.
f. 7a. 'Cheraukcush' a Persian marriage custom.

f. 8.   Manners and customs at 'Button'.
Parsi funeral cermonies.
Killing of frogs by Parsis.

MISCELLANEOUS

f. 14a.   Musk merchants are shortlived.
f. 15a.   Note of letters written to 'Mr. Lovell' and 'Dr. More'.
Thought-reading in rupees and annas: a card trick.
f. 16, 16a.   Names and lengths of Muhammadan months.
f. 16.   Hindu months and their names.
f. 17, 18.   Methods of telling the time.
f. 17a.   Hindu notion of sky colour and green.
f. 20a, 21a.   Notes on information from 'Batista de Joan'.
Note on 'Mucteer de Isaac' and his extensive travels.
Commencement of a letter by a Brahman.
f. 24a-25.   Length of days.
f. 25.   Muhammadan law of succession to property.
f. 28a.   No method known for 'killing' quicksilver.

NATURAL HISTORY

f. 6.   Snipe, wagtails and robins seen in Singhiya in winter.
f. 22.   Musk-deer in Bhutan.

NEPAL

f. 22.   Physical features and government of the country.

PARSIS

f. 8.   Their funeral customs.
f. 9.   Their fires.

PRODUCTIONS AND MERCHANDISE

f. 17.   Japanese lacquered ware and Patna lacquered ware.
f. 19.   Cultivation of opium—whence obtained.
f. 22.   Musk from Bhutan.
Gold dust from Bhutan—used as currency.

RECIPES

f. 16a.   To 'blue' iron and prevent it from rusting.
f. 23.   For Leachery.
To prevent milk from curdling.
To cleanse poisoned wells.
To reduce the size of women's breasts.
f. 24a.   To make Hindu varnish.
To make bows.
f. 26.   To make 'Seat burgee', a remedy for ague.
f. 28-28a.   To 'kill' gold, silver, copper.
To test if a mineral is well 'killed'.
f. 30.   To gild with quicksilver.
To make wine or vinegar.

RELIGION AND PHILOSOPHY

f. 6.   A Brahman notion regarding breathing the name of God.
f. 9.   Uneasiness caused by the predominance of either 'By', 'Pit' or 'Cuff'.
f. 15.   Teaching and preaching of the Brahmans.
The cause of diversity in human nature.

f. 17.   Various kinds of 'By', 'Pit', and 'Cuff'—the body governed by five 'Rojas'.

f. 17a.   Six tastes and their names.

f. 18.   Notes on the state of life after death.

f. 19, 20.   A Brahman's remarks on the uselessness of prayer.

f. 19.   'Beade', the Hindu Book of the Law.

f. 19a.   Origin of the rite of circumcision and of the 'Mautherbuckts'. 'Sherrum', Shame, a net of trouble.

f. 20.   Eighty-four lacks of lives.

f. 20a.   Melancholy is non-existent. Five 'Boots' or Devils.

f. 20a, 21.   God's essence.

f. 21.   Sunyasis, philosophers. Five 'Darts of women'. Three kinds of existence. Creation of Heaven and Hell.

f. 21a.   Consistency of soul matter. How conscience is bred.

f. 24.   Man's soul will remain male. Four spirits or? 'Bursuns'. The infinity of God. Whither man's evil goes. The deceitfulness of riches.

f. 24a.   A theory of pain.

1675-77.   *Harl. MS. 4256, 230 fols.*

f. 1-16.   Duplicate of Harl. MS. 4253.

f. 17-48.   Continuation of the Translation.

f. 49-51.   MS. Index of names.

f. 52.   'Bramins Poran Liber B.'

f. 53.   The Sri Bhagavat Puran translated into English by John Marshall from a version of the Sanskrit original.   (This is the title as catalogued by the B.M. authorities.)

f. 54-98.   The Translation continued.

f. 99.   'Bramins Poran Liber C.'

f. 100.   'A Continuation of Muddoosoodun Rauree Bramin's Account of the Hindoos Book called Sreebaugabut poran.'

f. 100-46.   The Translation continued.

f. 147.   'Bramans Poran Liber D.'

f. 148.   Title as on fol. 100.

f. 148-90.   The translation continued.   It ends: 'Hither writ 160 pages and left 63 to writ of that book called Serebaugobut Poran.   Here ended the 18th June 1675.'

f. 191.   'Bramins Poran Liber E.'

f. 192.   Title as on fol. 100, with the date, 29th May, 1677.

f. 192-230.   Continuation of the Translation.

1674-75.   **The Sri Bhagavat Puran translated into English by John Marshall from a Persian version of the Sanskrit original.**   *Add. MS. 7037 (now O.R. 17 A.K.), 254 fols. or 510 pages.*

This MS. is a modern copy of portions of Harl. MSS. 4253 and 4256.

pp. 1-16.   A copy of Harl. MS. 4253, fols. 1-8, with slight variations in the spelling of the title and no marginal notes.

pp. 17-83.   A copy of Harl. MS. 4253, fols. 9-40, with slight variations in the spelling of the title on fol. 9 and with no marginal notes.

pp. 83-217.   A copy of the first section of Harl. MS. 4256.

pp. 218-367.   A copy of the second section of Harl. MS. 4255 entitled: 'A Continuation of Muddoosoodun Rauree Bramin's Account of the Hindoos Book called Sreebaugabut poran—translated per John Marshall and brought from Liber A the 14th July 1674.'

p. 367.   This ends with the words: 'Ended and carried to Lib. C 22th March 1674-75.'

pp. 360-510.   Title as before 'brought from Liber B the 22th March 1674-75.' Ends: 'Ended here 30th April, 1675 and carried? rest to Liber D.'

1675-77.   **A late copy of portion of Harl. MS. 4256.**   *Add. MS. 7038 (now O.R. 17 A.K.), 317 fols.*

pp. 511-814.   'A Continuation of Muddoosoodun Rauree Bramin's Account of the Hindoos Book called Sreebaugabut poran—translated per John Marshall and brought from Liber C the 30th of April, 1675.'

pp. 815-1099 and 2000-44.   'A Continuation, etc., brought from Liber D the 29th May, 1677.' The MS. ends with the words: 'Explicit Sunker Liber or the Bramin's Poran or Booke.'

1667-72.   **Cursory remarks from the Papers of J. Marshall on the Customs and popular Astronomy of the Hindoos, etc.**   *Add. MS. 7039, 39 fols.*

This MS. contains extracts from Marshall's MSS., Harl. MSS. 4254 and 4255.

f. 1-37.   Extracts of astrological and astronomical notes, notes on languages, opium, *faqirs*, Brahmans, geographical notes, etc., taken from Harl. MS. 4255.

f. 38-39.   An extract from Harl. MS. 4254, fol. 28-29, concerning Marshall's election as a factor in the service of the E.I.Co.

1667-72.   **Extracts from a MS. 'intituled' 'Memorandums concerning India from Sepr. 11, 1670 to January 1st, 1671-2 Per John Marshall.'**   *Add. MS. 7040, 25 fols.*

This is a small notebook containing extracts from Harl. MS. 4254, chiefly Marshall's remarks on the Hindu religion. On fol. 25 there is a note on the author, his education and the value of his MSS.

c. 1668.   **Papers by Lord Guildford on the Charter of the East India Company, *temp*. Charles II.**   *Add. Ms. 32518, fols. 191, 192-203, 255-56, 257.*

c. 1668.   **Considerations concerning the Charter of the East India Company.**   *Add. MS. 32518, fol. 191.*

?c. 1668.   **An Essay upon the East India**   *Add. MS. 32518, fols.*
Company.   *192-203.*

The writer sets forth the inconveniences and injustices of the present East India trade as carried on under the charter of the Co. He accuses Sir Josiah Child of opposing any change, and he proposes various reforms which are, in his opinion, necessary.

?c. 1668.   **Objection to dissolving the East**   *Add. M.S. 32518,*
India Company and Considera-   *fols. 255-56.*
tions thereupon and the advant-
ages by the dissolving or regula-
ting them.

The writer urges that free trade is desirable but admits that trade with the East cannot be carried on without a license.

?c. 1668.   **Further remarks on the East India**   *Add. MS. 32518, fol.*
Company's trade extracted out   *257.*
of a quarto, paper-bound book
marked H.C.

The passages quoted show how the Company's permission to their servants to engage in private trade is of advantage only to the principal merchants, in other words, to those who are senior in standing.

1668,   **Memorial of Lord Robert South-**   *Add. MS. 34331, fols.*
Decr.   **well, Envoy Extraordinary from**   *96-97a.*
Charles II to the Prince of Port-
ugal concerning Bombay and the
English East India Company.

The writer states that the Government of the Island of Bombay has been handed over to the E.I.Co. He requests that the Viceroy of Goa and the respective Portuguese Governors under his jurisdiction may be 'encouraged' to 'continue his friendship and civility' to the English, and in all points comply with the 11th and 12th articles of the Treaty of Marriage, a copy of which is annexed.

1668/69-   **Log of the** *Sampson,* **Capt. Samuel**   *Sloane MS. 3814.*
1670.   **Chamblett, to Surat and home, 13**
March 1668/69 to 9 May 1670, kept
by John Kempthorne Junr., son
of Rear-Admiral Sir John Kemp-
thorne.

This is an ordinary seaman's log, kept with exactness but not with the detail of Kempthorne's later Journals. It contains nothing of historical interest.

For another Journal of the same ship in a later voyage, kept by Capt. Chamblett see Sloane MS. 3668, fol. 42.

c. 1670.   **Traitte de la navigation aux Indes**   *Sloane MS. 3210,*
Orientalles Divisé en deux parties,   *41 fols.*
La première, Des Moissons, ou Vents
reguliers, La Segonde, Des Tems
propres pour Naviger d'un lieu à
l'autre. Fait par l'ordre et a l'usage
de S. A. R. Monsieur le Duc d'York.

The first part of this document, 32 quarto folios, deals with monsoons (meaning winds and seasons), currents, rainfall, tides, etc. The second part, fols. 33-41, deals briefly with the favourable seasons for making a voyage to India, the penalty incurred by losing a monsoon, and the places where pilots are necessary.

1670.   **Voyage to Achin.**   *Sloane   MS.   3668,*
                                                       fols. 112-18.

Neither the name of the ship nor the name of the commander is given.

4 May, 1670.   The log begins in sight of Achin.

9 July, 1670.   The log ends.

This Journal contains an account of the islands in the Straits of Malacca and off the Malay Peninsula, with illustrations. It appears to form part of the log which follows, fols. 119-122. If so, it is a portion of the log of the *Bonaventura* kept by Edward Colthurst, the ship being owned by Robert Fleetwood.

1670-71.   **Log of the** *Bonaventura,* **owned by**   *Sloane   MS.   3668,*
               Robert Fleetwood, from Siam to   *fols. 119-22.*
               Masulipatam; the journal kept by
               Edward Colthurst 30 Oct., 1670-17 Jan.,
               1670-1.

This Journal contains nothing of special interest.

1671.   **Abstract of Capt. [Benjamin]**   *Sloane   MS.   3668,*
               Browne's Journal in the *Ann*   *fol. 161.*
               from England to Bantam, 28 June-
               12 Sept., 1671.

1671-78.   **Proceedings of the Commissioners**   *Harl. MS. 1511.*
               for Prizes.

f. 80.   6 Aug., 1672.   The Dutch E.I. ship *Kluit,* taken by the *Richmond,* now in the Humber. Directions to place officers in the prize vessel to ensure the safety of her contents.

f. 123a.   15 Aug., 1672.   Instructions for the Sub-Commissioners of Prizes to take charge of the *Papenburg,* a Dutch East India prize, with a view to secure her contents.

f. 123b.   16 Aug., 1672.   Letter to the E.I. Co., with regard to the sale of the cargo of the *Papenburg.*

f. 124a.   29 Aug., 1672.   Goods from the prize ships to be delivered to the Husband of the Co.

f. 125b.   10 Sept., 1673.   All Dutch prisoners taken in East India ships, 'now come from Kinsale', to be delivered up to the E.I. Co., so that an exchange can be arranged with those taken by the Dutch in the *Hannibal* and *Experiment.*

f. 125b.   10 Sept., 1673.   The Commissioners of the Customs and the E.I. Co. to adjust articles about the management of the goods taken in the *Papenburg* and the other three East India prizes.

f. 126.   10 Sept., 1673.   The copper and saltpetre in the *Papenburg* to be delivered to the officers of the Ordnance. The goods in the *Alphen, Armes of Camphir* alias *Terveer,* and *Europa* to be delivered to the E.I. Co.

f. 127a.   15 Sept., 1673.   Captain Richard Munden to be desired to render a strict account of the goods in the *Alphen, Europa* and *Arms of Terveer* seized by him off St. Helena.

f. 127b.   20 Sept., 1673.   Note about the cables and anchors of the four East India prizes.

19 Sept., 1673.   Powder and ordnance to be removed from the four vessels.

f. 128b.   26 Sept., 1673.   The *Papenburg* to be valued and delivered over to the Commissioners of the Navy for their use.

f. 129, 141.   25 Sept., and 1 Oct., 1673.   Arrangements between the Crown and the E.I. Co. as to the disposal and relief of the Dutch prisoners taken on the four prize ships.

f. 129b.   25 Sept., 1673.   Instructions regarding the plunder taken from the Dutch prize ships by English sailors and the unlading of the cargoes or discharge and gratification of the crews and supernumeraries.

f. 130a.   10 Oct., 1673.   Custodians of the prize ships rewarded.

f. 131a, 142b.   16 Oct.–14 Nov., 1673.   Goods of the prize ships disposed of to Edward Nelthorp and Co.

f. 136b.   28 Oct., 1673.   A tenth part of the proceeds of the four Dutch East India ships taken as prizes to be set apart for the flag officers.

f. 137b, 139a.   29 Oct., 1673.   Articles of Agreement between the Crown and the E.I. Co. for selling the four Dutch prize ships (13 clauses).

f. 155a.   27 Feb., 1673-74.   Article 6 of the above enforced.

f. 140a.   6 Nov., 1673.   The *Alphen, Arms of Terveer* alias *Camphir*, and *Europa* to be delivered to the officers of the Navy for His Majesty's use.

f. 140b.   6 Nov., 1673.   Money realised by the sale of goods belonging to the four East India prizes to be paid to the Receiver-General.

f. 146b.   22 Dec., 1673.   Sir Richard Munden recommended to His Majesty in consequence of the retaking of St. Helena and the capture of Dutch ships by him.

f. 149a.   22 Dec., 1673.   Notes about goods taken out of the ships by him. 24 Dec, 1673.   £2,500 reward paid to him.

f. 157b.   26 March, 1674-75.   Instructions with regard to the disposal of Dutch ship *Arms of Rotterdam* taken by Captain Wetwang, commander of the *Newcastle* frigate, on the 25th Feb.

1672-82.   **Customs paid by the East India Company. Total for the 11 years, £431,668. 5. 6½.**   *Add. MS. 17019, fol. 44.*

1672-77.   **Tonquin Journal 25 June, 1672– 26 June, 1677.**   *Sloane MS. 998, 116 fols.*

The MS. begins :

' A Journal Register of all the Transactions in the first Settlement of a Factory there and the Negotiation of Mercantile Affaires for the Honble. English E.I. Co. Agitated per Mr. Wm. Gyfford Cheife, etc.   Factors there beginning the 25th of June, 1672.'

This MS. narrates the settlement of a factory at Tonquin and chronicles the events in connection with it. It also contains copies of outward letters to Bantam, and the Co's remarks on methods of trade, dealings with the ruler of Tonquin and his ministers, lists of goods purchased, etc.

1673-1791. East India Company's Records, *Add. MS. 38872,*
July 30, **Vol. II. Committee of Shipping** *fols. 1-92.*
1673—25 **Ship Book.**
May 1791.

Account of E.I.Co.'s ships sent to India, with dates of sailing and number of tons, guns and men, commanders, value of cargo, etc.

1675. *CVIII. 78.*

Seal of the Governors and Company of Merchants of London trading to the East Indies.

No date **Seals of the E.I. Co.** *CXXXVI. 74-77.*
[?17th cent.]

1675. **Account of Asia 1675.** *Sloane MS. 1836,*
fols. 26-103.

Apparently taken from some printed work. Fols. 60-81 deal with India and Further India. The MS. contains nothing useful for the History of British India as the writer touches only on Portuguese settlements and on those but cursorily.

1675, A description of the Diamond *Egerton MS. 2543,*
27 Nov. **Mines in India.** *fols. 224-29.*

The following are noted : 'Quoleur, Codawillkull, Mallabar, Buttepalem, Ramiah Gurem, Muttampellee, Currure, Jonagerie, Muddemurg, Visiapore, Donee, Gazzerpellee', etc., etc. The MS. is dated at 'Munnemerg'.

1677, **Order in Council concerning the** *Add. MS. 34332,*
26 Oct. **Portuguese in Bombay.** *fol. 110.*

Representing that the English in Bombay are suffering from the imposition of unjust duties, that an application to the Viceroy of Goa has procured no redress, that these duties being levied contrary to Treaty His Majesty forbids his subjects to pay them. The Court of Portugal to be informed thereof.

1677/78- **Log of the** *New London,* **Captain** *Sloane MS. 863, fols.*
1678. **John Daniel.** *3-50.*

29 Jan., 1677/78—31 July, 1678, from Madras to St. Helena and thence to England.

This is an ordinary seaman's log, kept by Jacob Bevan. It contains a sketch of Ascension, but nothing of special interest.

See O.C. 4693 (I.O. Records) for a protest by Capt. John Daniel, dated Swally Marine, 26 Jan., 1679-80, against the President and Council of Surat for deficient lading.

1678. **Proposals for freedom of trade in** *Add. MS. 14002, fols.*
India and navigation in Eastern *205-13.*
waters for English, French, Dutch
and Portuguese.

In Portuguese.

1678/79- **Extracts from the Vansittart** *Add. MS. 34123, fols.*
1695. **Papers.** *30-40.*

1679-80. Trade reports from Fort St. George and the Coast of Coromandel, with ' Directions, etc., received from Mr. Pitts'.

1680. Coins current in 'Indostan, Persia, Golconda, Visapore, etc'. with their weights, fineness and value.

1684. Trade reports.

1694. Ditto.

1695. Cargo of the *Morning Star* from Amoy.

c. 1679.   **Directions for sailing from Balasor Road to Hugli.**   *Sloane MS. 3668, fol. 40a.*

c. 1679.   **Directions for sailing up and down the River Hugli.**   *Sloane MS. 3668, fol. 41.*

c. 1679.   **Unsigned Memorandum concerning the coast in the neighbourhood of the Jagannath Pagoda, with illustrations.**   *Sloane MS. 3668, fol. 161a.*

1679.   **Memories of our voyage to the East Indies in Ship *Commerce* A.D. 1679.**   *Sloane MS. 1704, fol. 23.*

Undated notes of occurrences as far as the Comoro Is., merely entries of arrival, departure, sight of land and deaths on board.

1679-80.   **Log of the *Caesar*, Captain Jonathan Andrews, to Bantam and back, kept by Wm. Pearse, copied by John Kempthorne.**   *Sloane MS. 3668, fols. 123-54, 160a.*

13 May, 1679. The Log begins in the Thames.

13 June, 1679. Sailed from Falmouth.

29 Sept., 1679. Anchored at the Cape. Two sketches (fols. 15a and 16) of the 'Table Land' and the 'Shadow of Table Bay'.

6 Oct., 1679. Sailed from the Cape.

13-14 Dec., 1679. Brief description of Sumatra and the Island of 'Engano'.

24 Dec., 1679. Anchored in Bantam Road.

10 Jan., 1679/80. Four Dutch Ships at Bantam.

24 Feb., 1679/80. Draught of the Straits of Sunda.

25 Feb., 1679/80. Sailed from Bantam.

25 May, 1680. St. Helena.

19 June, 1680. Ascension.

6 Sept., 1680. Downs.

An Abstract of the voyage from the Lizard to Bantam is given on fol. 160a.

1679.   **Extract from the Political Papers of Lord Strafford.**   *Add. MS. 31146, fol. 11.*

31 Oct., 1679. At a Court of Committees for the Hon. E.I.Co. Orders and Rules to be observed by all Persons in the Company's Service.

Five paragraphs. Printed.

This document is concerned with the following points: the faithful use of the Company's money, prompt payments, overpayment of salary, discharge of bankrupts or insolvents from the Company's service.

1679- **1681/82.**	**Journal of the ship** *Berkeley Castle,* **Capt. Wm. Talbot, kept by Benjamin Harry, Chief Mate. Voyage to Madras and Bengal.**	*Sloane MS. 3668, fols.* *89-111.*

19 Nov., 1679.　Log begins at Erith.

2 Sept., 1680.　Anchored in Balasor Road, having put in at Madras and Masulipatam.

25 Jan., 1680-81.　Sailed from Balasor.

21 Feb., 1680-81.　Anchored at Madras.

9 March, 1680-81.　Sailed from Madras.

5 July, 1681.　Anchored at Mauritius.

12 July, 1681.　Sailed thence.

7 Nov., 1681.　Anchored at St. Helena.

17 Nov., 1681.　Sailed thence.

13 Jan., 1681-82.　Arrived in the Downs.

The log is embellished with drawings of rocks, islands, elevations, etc.

1679-80.	**Letter from the Council at Fort St. George to Agent Master in Bengal, dated 9 Jan., 1679-80, giving an account of events at Madras since the departure of the Agent.**	*Add. MS. 34123, fols.* *49a-50.*

1679/80- **1681.**	**Log of the** *Sampson,* **Captain Samuel Chamblett, to Madras and Bengal.**	*Sloane MS.　3668,* *fols. 42-88.*

1 Jan., 1679-80.　Log begins at Gravesend.

13 July, 1680.　Anchored at Fort St. George.

23 July, 1680.　Anchored in Masulipatam Road.

2 Sept., 1680.　Anchored in Balasor Road.

28 Dec., 1680.　Sailed thence.

9 Jan., 1680-81.　Anchored at Masulipatam.

13 Jan., 1680-81.　Sailed thence.

20 Jan., 1680-81.　Anchored in Madras Road.

2 Feb., 1680-81.　Sailed for England.

12 May, 1681.　Reached St. Helena.

17 May, 1681.　Sailed thence.

25 May, 1681.　At Ascension Island.

27 May, 1681.　Sailed thence.

16 Aug., 1681.　In the Downs.

22 Aug., 1681.　The Log ends.

This ship met with ' interlopers ' in Balasor Road and on the homeward voyage.

c. 1680.	**An account of the navigation from Johanna to Ceylon through the Eight Degree Channel, together with an abstract of the** *Sampson's*	*Sloane　MS.　3668,* *fols. 159a-60.*

voyage from the Cape to Ceylon
in June and July, 1680.

1680. ' A Treatise concerning the East
India Trade: being a most
profitable Trade to the Kingdom.' Written at the instance of
Thomas Papillin.

*Harl. MS. 7310, fols.
51-56.*

A printed tract of 27 pp., published 1680, reprinted 1696. There are copies also
among the B.M. printed books. Press Marks, 1029. h.30 and 1029. e.8 (15).

1681-82,
1 July,
1681–30
June, 1682.

Abstract of the ships and value of
cargoes sent out by the E.I. Co.
to Surat, Fort St. George, Bay of
Bengal and Bantam.

*Add. MS. 15898, fol.
134.*

1681. A Journal of a voyage to the King-
dom of Tonquin bordering upon
China in the East Indies by Capt.
Robert Knox.

*Lansdowne MS. 1197,
fols. 12-13.*

21 Sept., 1681. Sailed from the Downs in the *Tonquin Merchant.*

This MS. is only a fragment with a detailed description of St. Jago, in the midst of
which it breaks off.

1682.
14 March,
1681/82–12
April, 1682.

An unsigned relation of what
passed at Bantam in March, 1682.

*Lansdowne MS. 1152,
fols. 84-85.*

The chief points in this narrative are :

The intervention of the Dutch during differences between the old King of Bantam
and his son.

The seizure of Bantam by the Dutch, 28 March, 1682, after a previous unsuccessful
attempt, owing to the treachery of the young prince.

An order to the English (31 March) to leave Bantam. Their goods stopped by the
Dutch.

The English factory ransacked by the Dutch (11 April) and the English compelled
to leave on the 12th April.

The English flag dishonoured by the Dutch.

1683. Letter from Lord Sunderland to
Mr. Chudleigh about the Bantam
business, to be delivered by Sir
John Chardin.

*Lansdowne MS. 1152,
fol. 86.*

22 April, 1683. Mr. Chudleigh is informed of the anger of King Charles
II at the action of the Dutch in Bantam and is desired to assist Sir
John Chardin, the Deputy of the E.I. Co., who is to demand repara-
tion from the States General.

1683. Letter of protest from Charles II,
dated 26 April, 1683, per the Earl

*Lansdowne MS. 1152,
fol. 86a.*

of Sunderland, to the States
General, to be delivered by Sir John
Chardin, the Deputy of the E.I. Co.,
complaining of the action of the Dutch
in Bantam.

1683.
May, 1683.

Copy of the Memorial given by Sir John Chardin in Holland about the Bantam business.

*Lansdowne MS. 1152,
fols. 88-91.*

The memorial relates (in French) the events contained in the unsigned narrative
(*ante*, fols. 84-85 of this MS.) and adds that the *China Merchant* reached Bantam on the
9th May, that the young King of Bantam would have received her Captain, but that the
Dutch refused to allow him to land.

1683.
17 June,
1683.

Extract from the Register of the Resolutions of the States General.

*Lansdowne MS. 1152,
fol 96.*

A copy of the reply of the Seventeen to the representations of Mr. Chudleigh, Envoy
Extraordinary of Charles II., and Sir John Chardin (delivered 25 May and 2 June respectively) to be handed to these two emissaries.

1683.
7-17 June,
1683.

The Reply of the States General concerning the Bantam business (in French).

*Lansdowne MS. 1152,
fols. 93-104.*

They recapitulate relations between the King of Bantam and themselves during the
last 25 years and declare that the seizure of Bantam was the consequence of the bad faith
of its ruler, that the English report of events is incorrect in almost every detail, that the
Dutch befriended them wherever possible, and that what damage they sustained was the
result of internecine troubles. Of the refusal to allow the *China Merchant* to land they
have no details.

1683.
July, 1683.

Project of an agreement between the English and Dutch East India Companies about the Bantam business (in French).

*Lansdowne MS. 1152,
fols. 105-7.*

The chief point of this proposal was that neither the English nor the Dutch should
enter into trading agreements at Bantam to the exclusion of the other.

1682-83.

Log of the *Persia Merchant*, Capt. John Bowers, from England to Surat and thence back to England in company with the *President*, Capt. Jonathan Hyde, 15 April, 1682–13 Dec., 1683.

*Sloane MS. 1070, 127
fols.*

An ordinary seaman's journal, containing, in addition, accounts of goods sold and
bartered to the crew during the voyage.

1682-84.

Log of the *Charles*, Capt. John Preston, to Bombay and Surat, with a description of the Maldives, 25 Oct., 1682–5 Aug., 1684.

*Sloane MS. 3672, 66
fols.*

f. 1.   25 Oct., 1682.   Sailed from the Downs.
f. 3a.   19 Nov., 1682.   Anchored at St. Jago.
f. 4.   23 Nov., 1682.   Sailed for the Cape.
f. 9a.   25 Jan., 1682-83.   Anchored in Saldania Bay.   Sketch of Bay and directions for getting into it.
f. 10a.   31 Jan., 1682-83.   Sailed for the Maldives.
f. 19.   23 April, 1683.   In sight of the Maldives.   Sketch of the islands as they appeared when nearing them.
f. 20.   25 April, 1683.   Sent a boat ashore for cowries.   Remarks on the islands.
f. 21a-22a.   Sketches of the shape of the islands and remarks on their nature.
f. 23.   2-5 May, 1683.   Ineffectual attempts to obtain an audience of the ruler of the Maldive Islands.
f. 24a.   Sketch of 'Maldivia Road'.
       25 May, 1683.   Sailed from the Maldives.
f. 26.   Sketch of 'Point Galla' and description.
f. 26a.   1 June, 1683.   Anchored in 'Point Galla' Road.
f. 29.   Sketch of the coast of Tutacorin.
f. 29a.   5 July, 1683.   Anchored at Tutacorin and, 10 July, sailed thence. Sketch of the 'Land at Anchor in Tutacorin' by Nathaniel Warren.
f. 38.   26 Aug., 1683.   Anchored at Cochin and, 3 Sept., sailed thence.
f. 40a.   6 Sept., 1683.   Anchored off Calicut.
f. 41.   10 Sept., 1683.   Sailed from Calicut and anchored in Tellicherry Road.
f. 42.   17 Sept., 1683.   Sailed for Bombay.
f. 44.   26 Sept., 1683.   Anchored in Goa Road.   Description of the place.
f. 45.   30 Sept., 1683.   Sailed out of Goa Road.
f. 47a.   19 Oct., 1683.   Anchored at Bombay.
f. 48a.   22 Oct., 1683.   Sailed for Surat.
f. 50a.   1 Nov., 1683.   Anchored at Swally.
f. 51.   25 Jan., 1683-84.   Sailed for Bombay.
f. 51a.   1 Feb., 1683-84.   Unable to land at Bombay on account of a revolution there.
       2 Feb., 1683-84.   Sailed for England.
f. 59.   27 April, 1684.   At St. Helena.
       6 May, 1684.   Sailed thence.
f. 59a.   13 May, 1684.   In Ascension Road.
f. 66a.   4 Aug., 1684.   Anchored in the Downs.

This Log is unusually discursive and informing, and the geographical notes are interesting, those on the Maldives and the coast of Malabar being especially valuable.

See also the Diary and letter of the Supercargoes of the *Charles*, I.O. Records, O.C. 4938 and 4984.

1682-1701.   Papers relating to the East India Company.   *Add. MS. 22185, 60 fols.*

This is a miscellaneous collection containing:—
f. 1.   Ships appointed for the year 1682 with commanders and tonnage.
f. 2.   Ships that may be got ready for East India.
f. 4.   An account taken out of the Company's Books in Jan., 1682-83.
f. 7.   Stock belonging to the Honble. E.I.Co., both in England and in India, calculated the 30 June, 1685.

f. 8.   Copy of His Excellency General Child's letter to 'Oransha', the Great Mogul, dated in Bombay 1688, requesting redress of grievances.

f. 10.   The Mogul's *farman* (undated).

f. 11.   Five questions and answers about the E.I.Co. in Bengal (undated).

f. 12.   A List of the names of all the Adventurers in the Stock of the E.I.Co. 1689 (printed).

f. 14.   A List of names of the Courts of Assistants.

f. 15.   Committee to be appointed to examine who procured the Commission to execute martial law at St. Helena, 6 Nov., 1689.

f. 17.   9 Nov., 1689.   General account of the E.I.Co.

f. 19.   Petition of the E.I.Co. to Parliament praying for monopoly of trade to the East Indies and protection against Interlopers (undated).

f. 21.   Fair copy of the same, endorsed 19 Nov., 1689.

f. 23.   Several proofs of illegal trading by the E.I.Co. brought forward by Messrs. Johnston, Bonnell, White and Pitt and Capt. Nicholson.

f. 25-26.   Copies of clauses in letters from John Vaux to his father and brother dated Surat, 22 January, 1690-91.   The writer states that on the death of the General and Lieut.-General the conduct of the war fell to him, that he opened negotiations with the Mughal and concluded a peace on the 28 Feb., 1689-90, but that he is held as a hostage.   He desires relief from England.

f. 27.   A Brief Account of the Great Oppressions which the Managers of the E.I.Co. have acted on the Lives, Liberties and Estates of their Fellow Subjects . . . Humbly offer'd as Reasons for Establishing a New Joint-Stock (printed together with a copy of the Mughal's *farman*, for which see fol. 10).

f. 29.   Heads of complaints exhibited against the E.I.Co. by the House of Commons dated 13 November, 1691.

f. 33.   Proofs of the above complaints.

f. 37.   Unsigned speech to the House of Commons concerning the danger the East Indies trade is in by the ill management of the Governor and Committee.

f. 38.   Some Heads humbly proposed for the regulation of an E.I.Co. (undated).

f. 40.   Ditto.

f. 41.   29 Propositions about the Dead and Quick Stock of the E.I.Co. (undated).

f. 43.   Methods and Regulations proposed for the Settlement of an E.I. Co. (undated).

f. 45.   An Address to be made to His Majesty to dissolve the Old Company.

f. 46.   Oath of the Subscribers for themselves.

f. 47.   Oath of Governor and Deputy.

f. 48.   Oath of Subscribers for others.

f. 49.   Oath of Admission.

f. 50.   Oath of the Committees.

f. 51.   Three Proposals pursuant to the regulating a Company to trade to the East Indies.

f. 52.   Articles proposed for the E.I.Co. to agree to.

f. 53.   List of the Committees that held up the Stock taken from the printed list of Adventurers 1691.

f. 54.   1 Dec., 1692.   Court at Whitehall.   Liberty granted to the E.I.Co. to send out 6 ships, half the number requested, and half the number of men desired.

f. 56. 28 Dec., 1694. Heads of the New Charter for the E.I.Co.

f. 58. Account of revenues of Fort St. George, Fort St. David and Bombay, and customs of Persia, ending April, 1697.

f. 59. Extracts from letters in April and June, 1698, between Bombay, Surat and Persia, regarding the piratical actions of Captain Kidd and his consorts.

f. 60. List of the Company's ships sent to India 1698-1701 with details of men, tonnage, cargo, etc.

The writing of this MS. on several folios is difficult to decipher.

c. 1683.	**Observations of Mr. John Davis on voyaging from Achin to Teco and Priaman.**	*Sloane MS. 3668, fols. 156a-59.*

1683.	**Memorandum of Capt. Lake, Commander of the *Prudent Mary*, of his voyage from Ceylon to Point Palmeiros and thence to Balasor Road, 5-21 April, 1683.**	*Sloane MS. 3668, fols. 155-56.*

1683.   *Harl. MS. 1243, fol.*
July 1683.   *178.*

Warrant to pay the E.I.Co. for saltpetre purchased by the Master of the Ordnance, by means of customs due from the Company, on goods imported by the Company (one paragraph).

1683.   *Harl. MS. 1243, fol.*
July, 1683.   *178.*

Royal Permission to the Lords Commissioners of the Admiralty to grant commissions to the E.I. Co. against the young King of Bantam and his subjects or any infidel Prince, within the limits of the E.I. Charters, that shall make war on them (one paragraph).

1683-85.	**Sir Thomas Grantham's voyage to the East Indies in the *Charles the Second*, 21 August, 1683–25 July, 1685.**	*Harl. MS. 4753, 42 fols.*

The ship put in at St. Jago (Cape Verd Islands), St. Helena, Straits of Sunda, Batavia, Surat, and Bombay (twice), and sailed thence to England via St. Helena and Ascension. There are long entries of Sir Thomas Grantham's proceedings on shore, especially at Hippens Island, of which he took possession.

f. 2. 12 May, 1684. Sir Thomas Grantham anchored in the Straits of Sunda and took possession of Hippens Island for King Charles II. and renamed it Carolus Secundus, but was met by an English vessel with orders to abandon the Island since peace had been concluded between England and Holland.

He therefore provisioned at Batavia and proceeded to the Gulf of Persia, where he had a commission to seize interlopers.

Remarks on the weakness of the Dutch fleet.

f. 9. 11 June, 1684. Letter from Grantham on the *Charles the Second* at Princess Island to the Dutch Commodore Heer Haron at Bantam.

6

30 Aug., 1684.   Anchored at Gombroon.
18 Sept.   Anchored at Muskat.
26 Oct.   Anchored at Swally.
f. 13-19.   29 Oct.   Copy of Commission and Instructions from the President and Council at Surat to Sir Thomas Grantham to reduce the rebels in Bombay.
f. 20.   3 Nov.   Anchored in Bombay Road.
f. 20-33.   Details of measures taken for the reduction of Keigwin's rebellion and the recovery of Bombay for the Co.
18 Dec., 1684.   Commissions delivered to officers of the garrison.
26 Dec.   Sailed from Bombay for Surat, returned to Bombay.
5 Jan., 1684-85.   Sailed for England.
f. 38-39.   Copy of the pardon granted to Capt. Richard Keigwin and the officers, soldiers, etc., of Bombay.
f. 40-42.   Propositions relating to the officers, soldiers and inhabitants of Bombay, signed by Sir Thomas Grantham.
7 May.   Reached St. Helena and settled differences there.
25 July, 1685.   Anchored in the Downs.

See also I.O. Records, O.C. 5186, for Sir Thomas Grantham's letter from Muscat to the Company of 23 Aug., 1684, and O.C. 5234, 5235, for his correspondence regarding the *Bristol*, interloper, and O.C. 5236, 5250, 5256-62, 5282, 5301, for his Commission to reduce the rebels at Bombay and subsequent action thereupon.

1683/84-   **List of the Company's ships.**   *Sloane MS. 3671,*
1686.   *fols. 2a-3.*

8 Jan., 1683/84–17 Nov., 1686.   Tabular list of the Company's ships (70 in all), with date of sailing, number of men, tonnage, guns, soldiers on board, names of Commanders, value of cargoes outward, places to which the ships were assigned and value of cargoes home.

[? 1684.]   **'The Deplorable Case of the**   *Harl. MS. 7310, fols.*
Poor Distressed Planters of the   *309-9a.*
Island of St. Helena under the
Cruel Oppression of the East
India Company.'

A printed pamphlet.   See also a copy in the British Museum Library.   Press Mark, 8223, d. 43 (4).

1684-92.   **THE CASE OF THOMAS SANDYS**
The E.I.Co. *versus* Thomas Sandys.   *Harl. MSS. 1222,*
4139.
Lansdowne MSS.
650, 1219.
Add. MS. 10615.

The action was brought by the Company because Thomas Sandys, not being a member of the Company, had traded to the East Indies without a license.

[1684.]   **Extract of the declaration of the**   *Harl. MS. 1222, No.*
E.I.Co. against Thomas Sandys.   *13, fol. 123.*

1684-85. **Case of the East India Company against Interlopers.** The Governor and Company of Merchants of London trading to the East Indies against Thomas Sandys. *Harl. MS. 4139, No. 4, fols. 107-245.*

f. 107-10a. Mr. Holt's opinion—'Whether or no an Accusation lies by the Company upon the Charter, for that the Defendant not being a member of the Company has traded into the East Indies without licence of the Company.' Mr. Holt's argument was in favour of the Co. (See also Harl. MS. 1222, No. 20, fol. 206a.)

f. 111-24a. Sir George Treby's argument in the Case. This was in favour of the defendant.

f. 125-62. Mr. Solicitor General's argument in favour of the Company. (See also Harl. MS. 1222, No. 12.)

f. 162-63a. Remarks of the Lord Chief Justice, who adjourned the Case from Trinity to Michaelmas Term. (See also Harl. MS. 1222, No. 15, fol. 166 and Lansdowne MS. 1219.)

f. 164-92a. The Case resumed and restated. The opinion of the Attorney-General, Sir Robert Sawyer, that 'the Action is well brought for damages.'

f. 193-207a. Mr. Williams' argument in favour of the defendant.

f. 208-9a. 31 Jan., 1684-85. The case was resumed in Hilary Term and the question was restated by Mr. Justice Walcott. (See also Harl. MS. 1222, No. 17.)

f. 209a-11a. Mr. Justice Holloway's opinion. (See also Harl. MS. 1222, No. 18.) He maintained that the case resolved itself into the question whether the King's subjects could trade to 'Infidel Countries' without a royal license. He argued in the negative and maintained the Company's right to bring an action against Sandys.

f. 211a-18. Mr. Justice Wilkins' opinion in favour of the King and the Company. (See also Harl. MS. 1222, No. 19.)

f. 218-45. The Lord Chief Justice's summing-up. He decided that the action was 'well brought'.

This case created a great stir and was well argued on both sides, the points in question being, as the Lord Chief Justice affirmed, very important—on the one hand the King's prerogative, the privileges of the East India Company and their joint trade ; on the other hand the benefit of private individuals and unrestricted trade.

1684-85. **Proceeding of the East India Company** *versus* **Thomas Sandys.** *Lansdowne MS. 650, 270 fols.*

f. 1-35a. Statement of the case in Latin with a recital of the Charter of Charles II to the Company of 13 April, 1672 (in English).

f. 83-130. Mr. Pollexfen's argument in favour of the defendant. (See also Harl. MS. 1222, No 14.)

The remainder of the MS. is a duplicate of Harl. MS. 4139 described above.

1684-85. **A Manuscript containing 'all the Proceedings in His Majesties Court of Kings Bench upon an action brought there by the East** *Add. MS. 10616, fols. 1-324.*

India Company against Thomas
Sand[y]s '.

This MS. is almost identical with Lansdowne MS. 650 described above.

[1684.]   **Separate opinions in the Case of**   *Harl. MS. 769, fols.*
Thomas Sandys. Mr. Attorney   *1-12a.*
General's argument for the East India
Company against Interlopers.

1684.   **The Solicitor-General's argument.**   *Harl. MS. 1222, No.*
12.

19 April, 1684.   He maintained that the Company's right to trade was
well founded upon the King's Letters Patent and therefore begged
for a judgment for the plaintiffs.

1684.   **Mr. Pollexfen's argument on**   *Harl. MS. 1222, No.*
behalf of Thomas Sandys.   *14, fol. 125.*

19 April, 1684.   He endeavoured to prove that the Charter of the E.I.Co.
was against the Statute of Monopolies and that the defendant could
lawfully carry on a free trade in the Indies.

1684.   **Speech of the Lord Chief Justice**   *Harl.   MS.   1222,*
and opinion of the other Judges   *No. 15, fol. 166.*
in the case of Thomas Sandys
versus **the E.I.Co.**

The further hearing of the Case was deferred till the Michaelmas Term as the cause
was declared to be of ' as great consequence ' as any that had ever been tried in
Westminster Hall.

1684   **Lord Chief Justice Jefferies in the**   *Lansdowne MS.*
great case of monopolies relative   *1219.*
to the East India Company, 1684.

Five sheets, incomplete.   *Vide* State Trials, VII, 555, for a more perfect copy
(Note in Catalogue).

See also ' The Argument of the Lord Chief Justice concerning the . . . case of
Monopolies between the East India Company . . . and T. Sandys, etc.' 1689.
Folio. B. M. Press Mark, 5805. cc. 2.

1684-85.   **The Opinion of the Judges of the**   *Harl. MS. 1222*
King's Bench in the Case be-   *No. 16.*
tween Thomas Sandys and the
East India Company, 31 Jan.,
1684-85.

1684-85.   **The Opinion of Mr. Justice Wal-**   *Harl. MS. 1222, No.*
cott in the case of Thomas   *17, fol. 195.*
Sandys.

31 Jan., 1684-85.   The Grant made by the Crown to the Company and the prohibition
of Interlopers holds good ; consequently the action was justified.

1684-85.   **The Opinion of Mr. Justice Charles**   *Harl. MS. 1222, No.*
            Holloway in the case of Thomas   *18, fol. 196b.*
            Sandys.

31 Jan., 1684-85. His opinion was in agreement with that of Mr. Justice Walcott and he therefore held that the action was justified.

1684-85.   **The Opinion of Mr. Justice**   *Harl. MS. 1222, No.*
            Wilkins.   *19, fol. 119.*

31 Jan., 1684-85. He agreed with Mr. Justice Walcott that the action was justified.

1684-85.   **The Opinion of the Lord Chief**   *Harl. MS. 1222, No.*
            Justice Sir Thomas Holt on the   *20, fol. 206b.*
            case of Thomas Sandys.

31 Jan., 1684-85. He agreed with Mr. Justice Walcott that the action was justified.

1692.   **Judge Rookebye's Argument in the**   *Harl. MS. 1222, No.*
         case of the E.I. Co. *versus* **Thomas**   *6, fols. 69-78.*
         Sandys.

' Thomas Sandys and others laded a ship in England with intent to trade in places within the limits of the East India Company's Charter.' The Company's agents petitioned the King for the ship to be arrested and prevented from setting out until security was given in the Admiralty that she should not be sent to the East Indies or trade within the limits of the Company's Charter. An order was obtained from the King to this effect. In consequence the plaintiff brought an action against the defendants. The Judge's opinion was that the ' action was maintainable ' and that judgment should be given for the plaintiffs because ' the ship was arrested in the body of the country '.

1684-86.   **Journal on board the ship** *Barnard-*   *Sloane MS. 854, fols.*
         iston, **bound for Surat and Gom-**   *1-63.*
         broon, Thomas Parramore Com-
         mander.

The Journal begins 25 April, 1684, and ends at Gombroon (Bandar Abbas), 10 May, 1685. It is an ordinary seaman's journal with several gaps in the dates, and contains nothing of special interest.

1684-85.   **Journal kept on the** *Frances* **to St.**   *Sloane MS. 855, fols.*
         Jago, Isaac Carver Commander,   *1-31.*
         the *Phoenix* **towards India, Cap-**
         tain John Tyrrell Commander,
         the *Bristol* **towards Surat, Capt.**
         Richard Hoder Commander, and
         the *Phoenix* **again.**

The Log begins 22 September, 1684, and ends 10 June, 1685. It is illustrated with a few coloured draughts. See Sloane MS. 854, which follows, for a fuller account of this voyage.

1684-86.   **Journal kept by Jacob Bevan, Mid-**   *Sloane MS. 854, fols,*
         shipman, on board the *Frances*   *64-133.*

to St. Jago and the Cape of Good Hope, 1 December, 1684–1 January, 1684-85, Isaac Carver and Mr. Benge Commanders ; afterwards on board the *Phoenix* frigate towards Surat, 18 January, 1684/85–17 May, 1685 ; then on board the *Bristol* towards Bombay and Surat 5 June–18 September, 1685 ; lastly on the *Williamson* to England 22 January, 1685/86–3 May, 1686, Captain Richard Warner Commander.

Two days off St. Jago the *Frances* was seized by H. M. Frigate *Phoenix* and her Commander was detained on board the man-of-war, and the Log is continued in the *Phoenix* to Surat. At Johanna, Comoro Is., the *Dragon*, Capt. Fenn, and the *Bristol*, an interloper, were encountered. The latter, Capt. William Andrews Commander, was seized on the 4th May, 1685. The Log is continued in the *Bristol*, prize ship. She sprang a leak, encountered bad weather, and sank on the 4th June, 1685. The Log is then continued in the *Phoenix* to Bombay, whence the writer sailed for Surat, was present in an action with a country ship, returned to Bombay, and eventually went back to England in the *Williamson*, Capt. Richard Warner. The homeward voyage is chronicled as far as St. Helena.

The Log which is of unusual interest, is embellished throughout with coloured draughts of islands, harbours, headlands, etc. There is also a sketch of the *Bristol* as she sank.

1684-87.   **Log of the *Kempthorne* to Madras and home, kept by Captain John Kempthorne, son of Rear Admiral Sir John Kempthorne (died 1679).**   *Sloane MS. 3670, fols. 130.*

f. 1.   A 'Table of Multiplier of Dollars ' made by ' Mr. Henry Mose, Factor and Merchant at Fort St. George ', with explanation.
f. 3.   Dimensions of the *Kempthorne*.
f. 5.   List of the men deceased and time they served on the ship.
f. 7.   11 Oct., 1684.   Sailed from Gravesend.
f. 18a.   22 Dec., 1684.   At St. Jago.
f. 59.   19 Dec., 1685.   Anchored in Madapollam Road, having touched at Porto Novo and Achin.
f. 60.   30 Jan., 1685-86.   Sailed for Persia from Masulipatam.
f. 70a.   19 March, 1685-86.   At Cochin.
f. 72.   4 April, 1686.   At Calicut.
f. 79.   12 May, 1686.   Anchored off Muscat.
f. 80a.   26 May, 1686.   Off Ormuz.

There is a gap in the Journal here and it is resumed later at Fort St. George.

f. 82.   9 Oct., 1686.   Sailed from Fort St. George.
f. 110.   3 Feb., 1686-87.   At St. Helena.
f. 129a.   24 May, 1687.   Off Portland.

This is a detailed Log full of valuable geographical notes. It is especially interesting on account of the Captain's persistence in making the voyage to Persia when his passengers opposed it as being too late in the season for safety.

For the charts and drawings belonging to this Journal, see Sloane MS. 3665, described among the Maps and Plans, *infra*.

1684-86. **Log of the** *Williamson***, Capt. Rich-** *Sloane MS. 1045, 76*
ard Warner, to Surat and Bom- *fols.*
bay.

f. 1.   14 April, 1684.   Set sail from Start Point.
f. 7.   Sketch of Bona Vista, Cape Verd Is.
f. 7.   14 May, 1684.   Anchored at St. Jago.
f. 7a.   17 May, 1684.   Set sail from St. Jago.
f. 21a.   4 Sept., 1684.   Anchored in Bombay Road.
f. 22.   Coloured drawing of Bombay Road and Castle.
f. 22a.   6 Sept., 1684.   Sailed for Surat.
f. 23a.   Elevation of Valentine's Peak.
f. 24.   Anchored in Swally Hole.
f. 25.   30 Sept., 1684.   Sailed for Calicut.
f. 25a.   5 Oct., 1684.   Met with the *Bristol*, interloper.
f. 26a.   11 Oct., 1684.   Anchored off Goa.
f. 27.   13 Oct., 1684.   Anchored in Karwar Road and sailed again.
f. 28.   Thirty sketches of Mangalore and Mount Dilly.
f. 28a.   21 Oct., 1684.   Anchored in Calicut Road.
f. 29.   Description of Calicut.
f. 29a.   25 Oct., 1684.   Sailed from Calicut.
f. 30.   26 Oct., 1684.   Anchored in Tellicherry Road.
        30 Oct., 1684.   Sailed for Surat.
f. 31.   5 Dec., 1684.   Anchored in Goa Road.
f. 31a.   8 Dec., 1684.   Sailed thence.
f. 33.   17 Dec., 1684.   Anchored in Swally Hole.
f. 35.   Draught of Surat and Swally.
f. 37a.   21 Feb., 1684-85.   Took in 132 passengers.
        24 Feb., 1684-85.   Sailed for Gombroon.
f. 40a.   Sketch of Cape Jask.
f. 41a.   23 March, 1684-85.   Anchored in Gombroon Road.
f. 43.   22 April, 1685.   Took aboard 105 passengers.
        23 April, 1685.   Sailed from Gombroon.
f. 46.   10 May, 1685.   Anchored at Surat river's mouth.
f. 47.   24 May, 1685.   Sailed for Karwar.
f. 48.   31 May, 1685.   Anchored in Karwar Road.
f. 50.   23 Aug., 1685.   Sailed for Bhatkal.
f. 51.   30 Aug., 1685.   Anchored at Bhatkal.
f. 51a.   8 Sept., 1685.   Sailed for Onore (Honawar).
f. 52a.   12 Sept., 1685.   Anchored at Onore.
f. 53.   16 Sept., 1685.   Sailed from Onore.
f. 53a.   20 Sept., 1685.   Anchored in ' Murgee ' Road.
f. 54.   29 Sept., 1685.   Sailed thence.
f. 54a.   1 Oct., 1685.   Anchored at Karwar.
        2 Oct., 1685.   Sailed for Goa.
f. 55.   4 Oct., 1685.   Anchored at Goa.
        5 Oct., 1685.   Sailed thence.
f. 57a.   25 Oct., 1685.   Anchored in Swally Hole.
f. 61.   1 Jan., 1685-86.   Sailed for England.
f. 70a.   25 April, 1686.   At St. Helena.
f. 71a.   Sketch of the South side of Ascension Island.
f. 75a.   28 June, 1686.   The Log breaks off.

1685,   **Extracts out of several Books of**   *Sloane MS. 2295, 50*
etc.   **Voyages, published 1685, 1687,**   *fols.*
     1688, etc., etc.

The MS. consists of a numbers of long extracts closely written in very small writing.

1685-86.   **Journal of a voyage of the E.I.**   *Add. MS. 19282, fols.*
     Co's. ships, *Samson* **and** *Society,*   *1-12.*
     from Surat to Persia, and of the
     return to Surat, with account of ex-
     penses, etc., by Samuel Annesley, one
     of the Supercargoes, 21 April, 1685–21
     Jan., 1685-86.

At Gombroon (Bandar Abbas) the factors met with Agent Hedges, with whom they had a slight altercation. Difficulties arose with the Portuguese concerning a slave boy purchased by Capt. Leidger of the *Samson*. At Cong there was a slight altercation with the Dutch. At Basra Annesley had an interview with the ' Bashaw'.

The remainder of the Journal is occupied with an account of the discharge and disposal of the cargoes of the ships and the relading of them for Surat. The second and third sections of the MS. contain statements of accounts of the voyage.

c. 1687.   **Instructions for sailing from Point**   *Sloane MS. 3670, fols.*
     de Galle on the S.W. of Ceylon   *131-55.*
     towards Jaffnapatam, along the
     Coast of Coromandel, to Pipli in
     Bengal.

These Instructions are by Capt. John Kempthorne. They are detailed, and valuable as giving an accurate contemporary description of the Coast and preserving old names of landmarks.

1687.   **Letter from Richard Salwey,**   *Sloane MS. 3672, fols.*
     Supercargo of the *Bauden,* **dated**   *70-73.*
     22 Oct., 1687, at Johanna, Comoro
     Islands.

The writer gives an account of the engagement of the *Bauden* with a French pirate ship near St. Jago, Cape Verd Is., on 28 Oct., 1686, and of the subsequent misfortunes that befell the ship. A list of the ' Dead and Deserted ' follows.

1687.   **Miscellaneous (Lowe) Papers rela-**   *Add. MS. 20240.*
     ting to St. Helena, 1687-1820.

f. 1.   3 Aug., 1687. Extracts from the Honble. Co's. letters regarding the execution of martial law.
       1673-1714. Extracts from Laws, Ordinances and Constitutions for the good Government of the Island.

The MS. contains but little 17th century information of value.

1688.   **Letter from Capt. Henry Benson**   *Sloane MS. 3672, fols.*
     of the *Jonas,* **left at Johanna, dated**   *73a-74.*
     18 June, 1688, giving an account
     of his outward voyage and of his
     losses by sickness.

1688. Letter from Jos. Wake (or Wale) *Sloane MS. 3672, fol.* in Johanna Road, dated 22 July, *74.* 1688, giving an account of occurrences on his arrival at Delagoa from Bombay and of the storm encountered after leaving that place.

1688-89. Journal of the *Kempthorne*, com- *Sloane MS. 3671, fols.* manded by Capt. John Kemp- *5-70.* thorne from England to Bombay, 2 Sept., 1688-21 May, 1689.

f. 5. 4 Sept., 1688. Sailed from the Thames.
f. 36a. 20-22 Jan., 1688-89. Sketch of elevations of islands seen.
f. 42a. 11 Feb., 1688-89. Off Tristan da Cunha Island.
f. 48a. 6 March, 1688-89. Off the Cape of Good Hope. Sketch of Table Mt.
f. 57. 8 April, 1689. Sketch of 'the appearance of the Island of St. Christopher'.
f. 59. 13 April, 1689. At Johanna, Comoro Islands.
f. 60. Sketch of Johanna and bay.
f. 60a. 22 April, 1689. Sailed from Johanna.
f. 68. 21 May, 1689. Anchored in Bombay Road, where eight of the Co's ships were riding.

With the exception of the Castle and about two acres of ground, Bombay was found to be in the hands of the Sidi.

1688. Letter, dated 12 Oct., 1688, left at *Sloane MS. 3672, fol.* Johanna by William Freke of the *74a.* *Ann*, bound from Fort St. George to Mozambique.

See I.O. Records, O.C. 5690, for an account of the loss of the ship.

1688-89. Journal of a voyage from Bengal *Egerton MS. 283,* to Madras with letters, etc., re- *fols. 2-26.* ceived concerning Capt. Wm. Heath's Transactions in the Right Hon. Co.'s affairs, 8 Nov., 1685—5 March, 1689.

f. 21. 11 Oct., 1686. William Heath to Job Charnock and Governor and Council, in the Bay of Bengal. Written aboard the *Resolution* at Chuttanuttee. He authorises a letter to the Nabob, offering the services of 10 ships of war for twelve months, provided the Nabob confirms their old privileges and permits their building a fort. If this permit be not speedily given, they are to state they will depart, as their orders are 'to stay no longer here in fenceless Factories'.
f. 21-21a. 28 Oct., 1688. C. Eyre and R. Braddyll at Dacca to Job Charnock, etc. They anticipate a favourable answer from the Nabob to their petition, and request that a delay of 25 days be allowed them.
f. 23. Nov., 1688. Ditto to ditto. The Nabob's *parwana* not yet obtained although they have promised him to transport 1,000 horse

and 2,000 foot on his behalf. They ask for further delay, which would be greatly to the Co.'s benefit.

f. 21a. 3 Nov., 1688. Ditto to ditto. They are in a fair way of securing their requests. The Nabob has given his promise and a *parwana* is expected in a few days.

f. 22a. 10 Nov., 1688. William Heath to [?] He sends a letter to 'Mellick' to be translated and forwarded.

f. 22a-23. 17 Nov., 1688. H. Stanley and John Haynes at Balasor to Job Charnock, etc. They complain that they have been neglected. They state that the Co.'s servants could easily have been got on board the ships, but no orders were received. Now threats have been used, and at the first attempt to escape all will be killed or carried up-country. They are imprisoned in their own houses, under a strong guard.

f. 22. 18 Nov., 1688. Ditto to ditto. Repetition of the previous letter. The Governor is willing to treat for peace and the 'Naib' is on the way with terms, or the English may be left to trade in peace as formerly.

f. 23a-24a. 20 Nov., 1688. C. Eyre and Roger Braddyll at Dacca to Job Charnock, etc. The Nabob's answer sent by peons, who returned without delivering it, is now sent by 'Dauk'. The charge against them of neglect is indignantly denied. They declare that they have used every effort to fulfil their mission. They are now in close confinement. They urge the need of awaiting the issue of this treaty.

f. 3. 24 Nov., 1688. Two French ships captured.

f. 8. 27 Nov., 1688. Treated with the Governor, who threatened death to all English on shore on the first attempt to land a force.

29 Nov., 1688. Account of fighting on shore.

3 Dec., 1688. Negotiations with the Governor.

4 Dec., 1688. Balasor occupied by the Governor's forces. The Co.'s servants carried off.

f. 25. 4 Dec., 1688. **Translation of an Obligation given to the Nawab Bahadur Khan by Messrs. Eyre and Braddyll. Received from Dacca, 4 December, 1688.**

The main conditions of the 'obligation' were that, should their trading privileges be confirmed and land granted them for the erection of a fort, they would furnish transport for 1,000 horse and 2,000 foot for the Nawab, convey them to Arakan, and assist the Nawab in the seizure of fortresses there.

4 Dec. 1688. *Parwana* **from the Nawab Bahadur Khan to Capt. William Heath, received from Dacca, 4 Dec., 1688.**

The Nawab acknowledges the receipt of a promise of free transportation of his men and horses to Arakan. In return he will send 'Bohurnmull' to treat with the English.

f. 25a. 4 Dec., 1688. Mir Mahmud 'Ummee', *Faujdar* Balasor, to the Agent of J. Charnock. The men sent to the fortifications are landed. Three *parwanas* have arrived from the Nawab. The Agent is desired to send a person to confer with him.

f. 26. 4 Dec., 1688. 'Bohurnmull' to the Agent. The Nawab is pleased with the promise of transport for his forces and has granted his *parwana*, which is sent herewith.

f. 8-8a. 11 Dec., 1688. Consultation—Present: Messrs. Charnock, Ellis and Peachie. As there are no hopes of using the Co.'s treasure at Balasor, they decide to send it to the Coast, but Capt. Heath would not permit this to be done.

21 Dec., 1688. The Company's fortifications demolished—all forces re-embarked.

23 Dec., 1688. Sailed from Balasor.

18 Jan., 1688-89. Off Chittagong. Messengers sent to the town and a conference held.

f. 12a-13. 21 Jan., 1688-89. Consultation of all the Commanders of the Co.'s ships and the Agent and Council. Discussion as to the advisability of attacking Chittagong. It was decided that the town could be taken, but probably could not be held. See also I.O. Records, O.C. 5657.

f. 15a-16a. 26 Jan., 1688-89. Consultation—Present: Messrs. Charnock, Ellis and Peachie. Note of injuries received in Bengal by the E.I.Co. and of the power in the hands of Capt. Heath. The Council would have stayed longer at Chuttanuttee to treat with the Nawab's agent but Capt. Heath's impatience caused the loss of goods and men. He intends to leave Chittagong without waiting for answers to letters or receiving provisions and water.

f. 17-17a. 26 Jan., 1688-89. Letter from J. Charnock, F. Ellis and J. Peachie, on board the *Defence*, to Capt. Wm. Heath. The messengers sent on shore have been well treated and have been asked to await the Nawab's answer to the letter sent by them. A new Governor is expected immediately. They suggest waiting for six days to provision and water the ship. An agreement might then be concluded. So good an opportunity of settling the Co.'s affairs may never recur. A survey of 'Sundiva' is most desirable.

26 Jan., 1688-89. Sailed from Chittagong.

4 Mar., 1688-89. Reached Madras.

The above is a valuable document, and throws further light on Job Charnock.

The account of Captain Heath's proceedings and his attempts to supersede and discredit Job Charnock is related at length in the *Diary of William Hedges*, Vol. II, by Yule. It is also dealt with by C. R. Wilson in his *Early Annals of Bengal*, Vol. I.

1688-89. '**The Diary of George Weldon and Abraham Navarro's Journey up to the Court of the Great Mogull** in prosecution of the Treaty of Peace before by them and Mr. Higgins begun with Meer Nazams and Cozzy Ibrahim at Daman and Bassein in the presence of John de Sequeira de Faria, Capt. Genll. of the Portuguese nation, etc.' *Sloane MS. 1910, No. 3, fols. 45-58.*

A most valuable document, giving a vivid account of the country.

This document consists of two Diaries with the above title.

f. 45-46a. The first, 27 Nov.–21 Dec., 1688 is occupied with an account of events in the journey from Bombay to the King's camp at 'Peergoon' in the Deccan. It contains notes of the route, condition of the towns traversed and remarks on contemporary events. From 'Peergoon' the ambassadors travelled with the army to 'Jerrebe', where they had a conference with the Nawab, Asad Khan, who promised to act as intermediary with the King and to deliver the Company's petition to him. Here the Diary breaks off.

f. 47-57a. 29 May–23 Sept., 1689. The second Diary is entitled:

'A Diary of all accurrances of our expedition to Daman in order to the makeing a peace betweene the English nation and the Mogull, begun the 29th May, 1689.'

f. 47-47a. On these fols. there is a detailed account of the journey to Daman, where the party arrived on the 7th June and had a conference with the Captain-General of the Portuguese.

f. 48-49. A long delay ensued, the events of each day up to the 7th July being chronicled. 'Antonia de Gaurde Coutte' was then sent to Surat to endeavour to expedite matters.

f. 50-50a. A conference was held on the 23rd July, 1688, between Qazi Ibrahim and Mir Nazim (who pretended to have powers to treat) and the Company's emissaries, but it was inconclusive.

A further conference was held on the 24th July, when certain points of agreement were decided on.

The English demands were stated and debated on the 25th July and again on the following day.

After much controversy the ambassadors decided, on the 14th August, to return to Bombay for further instructions.

f. 55. 21 August, 1688. The ambassadors arrived at Bombay.

30 Aug., 1688. They set out for Bassein, and arrived on the following day.

1 Sept., 1688. Negotiations were continued, and eventually concluded, with Mir Nazim.

23 Sept., 1688. The envoys received sealed copies of the agreement and took their leave.

1688.   **Letter from Capt. Joseph Haddock**   *Egerton MS. 2521,*
         dated 17 Dec., 1688, on board the   *fols. 57-58a.*
         ***Princess of Denmark* at Balasor, to**
         his brother, Sir Richard Haddock.

He gives an account of the proceedings at Hugli and Balasor, of the imprisonment of the Co.'s servants, and of the outrages committed by the Mogul officers, etc., etc.

1689-93.   **'A Journall of our Intended**   *Add. MS. 18989, fols.*
         Voyage by God's Assistance in   *1-117.*
         the Good Shipp *Benjamen*, Leo-
         nard Browns, Commander, from
         England towards East India, in
         the servise of the Honerable India
         Company', 11 April, 1689–2 Nov.,
         1693.

f. 2. 15 April, 1690. Sailed from England.

f. 40. 28 May, 1690. At 'Henry Kenery'.

6 June, 1690. At Bombay. Between June and September several deaths are noted.

f. 43a. 7 April, 1691. The *Kempthorne*, Capt. Kempthorne, and the *Rebecca* at Surat.

f. 44. 24 May, 1691. Weighed for Achin.

f. 45a. 11 June, 1691. Off Achin.

f. 57,58. 14 Nov., 1691. Account of the Malay method of killing wild hogs; description of darts. Threatening attitude of the Malays on shore. These people said to be there for purposes of robbery.

18 Jan., 1691-92. Sailed for Surat.

23 Sept., 1692. Sailed from Carwar.

16 Oct., 1692. At Swally.

24 Oct., 1692. Received news of the capture of the *Samuel* by the French.

14 Feb., 1692-93. Weighed for Bombay and thence towards England.

14 March, 1693. At the Cape.

31 Oct., 1693. Plymouth.

f. 118. Account of Letters sent in the Co.'s 'pacquett' to the East India House.

f. 120-33. Instructions by Admiral Edward Russell for the better ordering the sailing of the fleet—with Index.

For the numerous drawings in this Journal, see under Maps and Plans.

1689.	**Letter from Capt. John Kempthorne aboard the** *Kempthorne* **in Johanna Road outward bound, with an account of his voyage, dated 21 April, 1689.**	*Sloane MS. 3672, fols. 74a-75. f. 74a.*
	Letter from Capt. Charles Masters of the *Diana* **outward bound left at Johanna, with a brief account of his voyage, dated 23 April, 1689.**	*f. 75.*
1691-92.		*Sloane MS. 1689, 30 fols.*

Dr. Brown's account of his voyage from ?Madras to the Cape, Comoro Islands, Surat and the Malabar Coast, 23 June 1691–8 May, 1692.

The Journal is mainly occupied with medical details and the treatment of the crew, but there are interesting remarks on birds and fish and on the Cape. The first page (damaged) does not appear to belong to the rest. It is dated 10 April, 1691.

1692-93.	**The Journal of the** *Samuel* **(27 Jan., 1691/92–23 July, 1693), Freke Commander, in a voyage from London to Madras; taken on its passage by a French East Indiaman and ransomed. Drawn up by Charles Low, purser.**	*Lansdowne MS. 224, 58 fols. (bound up with No. 243).*

3 Feb., 1691-92. List of names of officers and crew and 23 soldiers. Left England.

27 Feb., 1691-92. Reached Madras (?).

27 Feb., 1691-92. Reception at Madras (?)—customs there. European inhabitants, trade, etc.

8 March, 1691-92. A man detained on shore on pretence of his being born there; could not recover him and he was left behind. Note of the cost of provisions and difficulty of procuring them. Note on penances and sufferings in the name of religion.

26 March, 1692. Sailed for the Cape.

2 July, 1692. Arrived at the Cape.

10 July, 1692. Sailed for Madras.

14 July, 1692.   Fought a French ship but was forced to surrender. The vessel was plundered and the men stripped even to their shirts. The Captain was compelled to buy the ship.   These events are fully described.

Here follows an 'Account of happenings while prisoner in a French ship.'

4 Nov., 1692.   At Surat.   Negotiations for the ransom of the ship taken by the French.

11 Nov., 1692.   A description of *faqirs*.

20 Nov., 1692.   A description of a fowl called a 'Cullum'.

1 Jan., 1692-93.   Baptism of '3 Black girls and a blackman'.

6 Jan., 1692-93.   Marriage of Mr. Colt.   A journal of daily events follows.

f. 24a.   1 March, 1692-93.   News received of a victory over the French fleet.

f. 25.   6 March, 1692-93.   Account of a festival in honour of the victory.

f. 27.   8 April, 1693.   Edward Bellamy, writer, being drunk and abusive, was publicly 'drubbed by His Honour'.

f. 29.   19 May, 1693.   At Bombay.

f. 29.   29 May, 1692.   Forced by weather into 'Sangazera River'.   An altercation between Captains Beere and Brangwin.

f. 33.   3 June, 1693.   Mr. Bentik [*sic*] copied his Journal from Croxon's, 'having kept none'.

Here follows an account of proceedings while at 'Sangazera River'.

f. 51.   9 August, 1693.   Set sail.

f. 52.   17 August, 1693.   At Karwar.

f. 57a.   31 June, 1693.   At Bristol.

The Journal described above contains much more information than an ordinary seaman's log and is well worth a close examination.

1692.   **Mr. West's note relating to the**   *Lansdowne MS. 846,*
        state of the E.I.Co., in 1692.   *No. 82, fols. 80-81.*

14 Nov., 1692.   The Company reject all the material particulars as to the King's power in the new regulations.   The King recommends to Parliament to establish the trade on such foundations as are likely to preserve and advance it.

17 Nov., 1692.   Judge's opinion thereon.

10 Dec., 1692.   Absurd resolutions.

18 March, 1692-93.   Submission of the Company.

1692.   **Resolutions regarding stockhold-**   *Sloane   MS.   2902,*
        ers and their votes, private con-   *fols. 143-44.*
        tracts, payments of dividends,
        etc., dated 7 Dec., 1692.

1692-95.   **Memoranda respecting the Trade**   *Add. MS. 5540, fols.*
        of the E.I.Co., 1692-95.   *111-11a.*

This includes a list of ships sent to the Indies May 1692 – ? 1695, with names of commanders, destination, tonnage, value of cargo, etc.

1693.   **'A   Discourse   concerning   the**   *Harl. MS. 7310, fols.*
        East India Trade.'   *271-78a.*

A printed pamphlet.   There is a duplicate on fols. 271-71a of the same MS.

1693. **Copy of Charter granted to the East India Co. dated Nov., 1693.** *Harl. MS. 7310, No. 5, fols. 262-69.*

1693-94. **Heads for a Bill to establish the East India Trade in a regulated Company.** *Harl. MS. 7019, No. 5, fols. 23-24.*

1693-94. **The East India Trade, 3 Jan., 1693-94.**

A printed pamphlet. See also in the catalogue of printed books in the B.M., Press Mark 816. m. 11 (81 and 82).

c. 1695. **Copy of the Bill brought by the East India Company into the House of Commons for the settling of their Charter.** *Add. MS. 5540, fols. 107-9a.*

1695. **Treatise on the trade of India by Samuel Baron, dated Fort St. George, June 1695.** *Add. MS. 34123, fols. 40-42.*

The Treatise deals with trade in Bombay, Surat, Persia, the Malabar Coast, Pegu, Achin, etc.

1695-1696/97. **Extracts from Court Minutes 18 June, 1695-22 March, 1696/97 relating to a petition to the King about regulating the votes of adventurers.** *Sloane MS. 2902, fol. 142.*

1695. **'Act for a Company Trading to Africa and the Indies', 26 June, 1695.** *Harl. MS. 7310, fols. 182-85a.*

A printed pamphlet. There is another copy in Harl. MS. 6847, fol. 140.

1695. **'To preserve the East India Trade.' Dated 10 Oct., 1695.** *Harl. MS. 7310, fols. 153-54a.*

A printed pamphlet by T. Neale, printed in the Old Bailey, 1695. There is a duplicate copy on fols. 177-78a with an additional sheet at fol. 179, and another copy on fols. 191-92a of the same MS.

1695. **A Subscription of £60,000 for a trading voyage to East India, to** which is appended the signatures of the subscribers and the amount subscribed by each, 15 Oct., 1695. *Add. MS. 17477, fols. 53-56a.*

1695-96. **Brief abstracts of Petitions and Parliamentary Proceedings, 14 Dec., 1695—31 March, 1696.** *Stowe MS. 246, fols. 1-2.*

These concern the Scotch East India Company, the settlement of trade to the East Indies, the import of Indian silks, etc.

1695-96.   'Copy of a Bill for restraining the   *Add. MS. 5540, fols.*
wearing of all wrought Silks,   *113-14.*
Bengalls, and dyed, printed and stained
Calicos imported into the Kingdome of
England, of the product and manufacture of Persia and the East Indies,
brought into the House of Commons
by Sir Henry Hubbart 7th and 8th
Gulielmi Tertii but sunk in the House
of Lords.'

1695-96.   Queries offered to the House of   *Sloane MS. 5540, fols.*
Commons against the E.I.Co. by   *115-16.*
John Cary, merchant, which were
spoken to in the House Anno 7th and
8th Gulielmi III, when the Confirmation of that Company's Charter was
under debate.

The querist opposes the importation of East Indian goods to the detriment of home
manufactures.   He objects to the monopolies created by a Joint Stock Company and
begs the House to restrict the powers of the E.I.Co.

1696.   'A paper concerning the Charter   *Harl. MS. 7310, fols.*
granted by the King to the   *175-76a.*
E.I.Co., dated 14 Jan., 1695-96.
From Mr. Matthew Andrews.'

1695-96.   Statement of the debt and credit   *Add. MS. 5540, fol.*
of the East India Company,   *111a.*
February 1695-96.

1695-96.   A memorial concerning the East   *Harl. MS. 1223, No.*
India trade, for preserving the same   *6, fol. 157a.*
in a Company to be erected by authority
of Parliament, addressed to Sir Wm.
Trumbal, Secretary of State, by
Doctor Charles Davenant.   Dated 6
Feb., 1695-96.

1696.   A History of remarkable things in   *Harl. MS. 5245, 24*
a voyage to the East Indies.   *fols.*

This document is concerned principally with dreams, portents, jugglery, etc., and
contains very little matter dealing with the East Indies.

1696.   A small quarto tract of 20 pages   *Harl. MS. 7310, fols.*
entitled, 'A letter to a Friend   *35-44a.*
concerning the East India Trade.'
Printed.   Stationers Hall.

See, for another copy, among the printed books in the Library of the B.M., Press
Mark, 1029. i. 31.

1696. '**Proposals for setling the East India Trade.**' *Harl. MS. 7310, fols. 67-80a.*

A tract of 22 quarto pages, printed in 1696. There is a duplicate on fols. 279-89a, and another copy in the B.M. Library, Press Mark 1029. k. 37.

c. 1696. **Paper relating to Bribes given by the E.I. Co.** *Harl. MS. 7310, fol. 199.*

c. 1696. '**Second Breviate against the E.I. Co.**' *Harl. MS. 7310, fols. 195-98.*

This MS. contains objections urged against the formation of the Co., with answers thereto.

c. 1696. **A Letter written to a Member of Parliament concerning the East India Trade.** *Harl. MS. 7310, fols. 290-93a.*

A printed tract.

c. 1696. '**Proposals humbly offered to the consideration of the Honble. House of Commons** for settling the East India Trade in a new National Joynt Stock by Act of Parliament.' *Harl. MS. 7310, fol. 270.*

A printed tract. There is a duplicate on fol. 310.

c. 1696. '**Heads of a Scheme whereby to establish the Present East India Company for the Preservation of Trade**', etc. *Harl. MS. 7310, fols. 174-74a.*

A printed tract.

c. 1696. '**Eleven Queries . . . relating to the Bill for Prohibiting the wearing of East India silks and printed and dyed calicoes.**' *Harl. MS. 7310, fols. 169-69a.*

A printed tract.

c. 1696. '**Copy of Bill to declare Free Trade for the East Indies.**' *Harl. MS. 7310, fols. 193-93a.*

It begins, 'Whereas all the subjects of England have and always had ', etc., and ends, 'Contrary in any wise notwithstanding '. Printed.

c. 1696. '**Bill in Parliament for Establishing an East India Co.**' *Harl. MS. 7310, fols. 4-26a.*

A MS. copy, with numerous blanks. It begins, 'Whereas the trade to the East Indies is necessary and beneficial ' and ends, 'next sessions of Parliament '.

1696. **Some accounts of the East India Company.** *Harl. MS. 7310, fols. 157a-59.*

These contain debtor and creditor accounts dated 21 Feb., 1695-96.

1696-99.   **List of the cargoes of ships arriv-**   *Sloane MS. 2902, fols.*
ing from the East Indies, July   *147-49.*
1696-August 1699.

Printed.

1696.   **Account of diamonds per the**   *Sloane MS. 2902, fol.*
Sarah **to be sold by the candle at**   *150.*
the E.I.Co's House, 10 Novem-
ber, 1696.

c. 1697.   **'Querical Demonstrations writ by**   *Harl. MS. 7310, fols.*
Prince Butler, author of the   *170-70a.*
Eleven Queries.'

A printed pamphlet. See *ante,* in the same MS., fols. 169-69a., c. 1696, for the
' Eleven Queries '.

c. 1697.   **'Proposals for a more Beneficial**   *Harl. MS. 7310, fols.*
and Equal Establishment of a   *173-73a.*
Regulated Company to carry on
the Trade to the East Indies.'

A printed pamphlet.

1697-98.   **Letter, dated Amsterdam, 16 March,**   *Add.   MS.   28940,*
1697-98 (in French), beginning   *fols. 227-37.*
' Monsieur ' and unsigned, giving the
writer's sentiments on the establishment of the Scotch East India Company and on the damage to trade
likely to ensue therefrom.

1697-98.   **Copies of Representations made**   *Harl. MS. 1324, fols.*
by the Turkey Company to the   *22, 51, 53.*
King and the Lords Justices, regarding woollen manufactures, on the
following dates, 31 August, 1696, 19
January, 1697-98, 9 August, 1698.

The Turkey Company complained of the interference by the East India Company in
their sale of woollen manufactures in Persia. They begged that the new E.I.Co. might
not be under an obligation to export ' draperies '.

1697.   **Copy of a Representation made by**   *Harl. MS. 1324, fols.*
the Commissioners for Trade   *37-50.*
and Plantations regarding the
general state of the trade of this
Kingdom, dated 23 Nov., 1697.

f. 40.   In 1696 the French King imposed heavy duties on all East Indian
goods and limited their import to certain ports.
f. 40a.   List of imports from the East Indies, 1670-88.
f. 44a.   By an Edict of 19 Oct., 1696, France has confirmed the above
impositions.
f. 45a.   Remedies proposed to alleviate the inconvenience of exporting
bullion to the East Indies.
f. 50.   Danger to trade from the Scotch East India Company.

1697-98.   **Copy of a Report made by the Commissioners of Trade and Plantations upon the Turkey Company's Memorial** about the interference of the East India Company in the 'vent' of the woollen manufacture in Persia, dated 19 January, 1697-98.   *Harl. MS. 1324, fols. 51-52a.*

The E.I.Co. is obliged by Charter to carry to the Indies £100,000 worth of manufactured goods. These are largely sent to Persia from India and thus trade is taken away from the Turkey Co. The Commissioners recommend that the E.I.Co. be instructed to find a market in China, Japan or elsewhere, and that they be prohibited from selling English woollen goods in Persia.

1698.   **Copy of Representation from the Commissioners for Trade and Plantations to the Lords Justices on the Turkey Company's petition** that the new E.I.Co. may not be under any positive obligation of exporting draperies, dated 9 August, 1698.   *Harl. MS. 1324, fols. 53-54a.*

The representation recommends an alteration in the clause of the old Charter which provided that the E.I.Co. should export a fixed amount of woollen goods. They suggest that the New Company's obligation to transport woollen goods to India be limited to 10 per cent of the annual value of their trade and that none of the goods be sold in Persia.

c. 1698.   **'The Case of the East India Co.'**   *Harl. MS. 7310.*

A printed tract tracing proceedings from Oct., 1691, to 11 Nov. [1697].

1698-1702.   **Embassy of Sir William Norris to the Emperor Aurangzeb, Dec. 1698-1702.**   *Add. MS. 28943, 31302.*

The account of the Embassy contained among the MSS. at the British Museum is confined to (1) the official papers (credentials, instructions, etc., inaugurating the Mission) with letters from the Company to the Ambassador after his departure ; (2) Minutes of Council held at Masulipatam from the arrival of Sir William Norris until his departure for the Mogul's Court ; (3) copies of correspondence between the Ambassador and the President and Council at Masulipatam. To complete the history of the Embassy recourse must be had to the India Office Records, *Factory Records, Misc.,* Vols. 19, 20 (Norris's Letter Books), and to the O.C. collection from No. 6728 onwards. There is an account of the Embassy in Bruce's *Annals,* Vol. III, and short notices in Wilson's *Early Annals of Bengal,* Vol. II., pp. 152-53, and Love's *Vestiges of Old Madras,* Vol. II., pp. 5-6.

N.B. Add. MS. 28943 contains, with one exception, duplicates of a portion of Add. MS. 31302.

Add. MS. 31302.

f. 4-5a.   29 Dec., 1698.   Covenants between the English East India Company and Sir William Norris.

f. 2.   31 Dec., 1698.   King William III's instructions to his Ambassador.

f. 5a-8.   [Dec., 1698.]   Directions and instruction given by the English E.I. Co. to Sir William Norris.

f. 8.   [Dec., 1698.]   List of the names, stations and salaries of the persons to attend the Ambassador.

f. 8a.   [Dec., 1698.]   Inventory of silver plate for the use of the Ambassador.

f. 1a.   1 Jan., 1698-99.   Commission to Sir William Norris from William III to be his Ambassador to the Great Mogul and other Princes in India.

The Ambassador is authorised to conclude agreements respecting trade, etc.

There is a duplicate of the Commission in Add. MS. 28943, fols. 4-4a.

*Add. MS. 28943, f.
3.*

f. 3.   1 Jan., 1698-99.   Copy of the King's Warrant to the Chancellor of England to Affix the Great Seal of England to a commission of Sir William Norris, Bt.

This document does not appear in Add. MS. 31302.

Add. MS. 31302.

f. 3.   1 Jan. 1698-99.   Letter from King William III to the Great Mogul. Credential letter authorizing the Ambassador to conclude a Treaty of friendship and commerce.

There is a duplicate in Add. MS. 28943, fols. 6-7a.

f. 3a-4.   1 Jan., 1698-99.   Letter from King William III to the Great Mogul.   Credential Letter of Edward Norris, Secretary to the Embassy, who is authorised to act as Ambassador in case of the death of Sir William Norris.

There is a duplicate in Add. MS. 28943, fols. 7a-8a.

f. 8a-9a.   3 Jan., 1698-99.   Edward Norris chosen Secretary to the Ambassador.

Directions from the Company to him in case of the Ambassador's death.

f. 10-11.   3 Jan., 1698-99.   Instructions to Thomas Harlewyn and Mr. Blackett, stewards of the Embassy.

f. 11.   3 Jan., 1698-99.   Instructions to Thomas Thurgood, an assistant to the Embassy.

f. 11a-12.   3 Jan., 1698-99.   Adiell Mill to keep account of expenses and presents.

f. 12-13.   5 Jan., 1698-99.   Directions for using the telescopes.

9 and 10 Jan., 1698-99.   Two letters from the Company to the Ambassador at Portsmouth.

10 Jan., 1698-99.   Letters from the Company to Messrs. E. Norris, Harlewyn, Thurgood.

f. 13a-14.   17 Jan., 1698-99.   Letter to the Ambassador at Portsmouth.   25 Feb., 1698-99 and 4 Apl., 1699.   Letters to the Ambassador after his departure.

f. 15.   4 Apl., 1699.   Letters to E. Norris, Thomas Harlewyn and Thomas Thurgood, from the Company.

f. 16-26.   28 Apl., 1699—6 Aug., 1702.   Sixteen letters from the Company to Sir William Norris.

f. 29-44.   23 Mar., 1699/1700–22 July, 1700.   Minutes of Council held at Masulipatam by Sir William Norris, Ambassador.

f. 45-56. 1 Oct., 1699–31 May, 1700. Copy of the President and Council's Accounts for Equipage, Necessarys, etc., for the Embassy, with an account of what was returned.

f. 58-99. 3 Jan., 1700/1–20 Mar., 1701/2. Copies of correspondence between the Ambassador and the President and Council at Masulipatam.

1608-99. **Copy of King William III's Commission to Edward Littleton, to be Consul at the Bay of Bengal dated 1 Jan., 1698-99.** *Add. MS. 28943, fols. 8a-9a.*

1698/99-1699. **An Account of what has passed in the Treaty between the New and Old East India Companies.** *Harl. MS. 7019, No. 7, fols. 27-33.*

23, 27 and 28 March, 1699. Powers exchanged. Valuation of dead stock agreed on. Resolutions regarding the forts and factories in possession of the two Companies. 13 and 20 July, 1699. Statement of the privileges, grants and revenues of the two Companies. Resolutions regarding the Union of the Joint Stock of the two Companies.

c. 1699. **'Proposals to both Houses of Parliament for the establishment of an East India Company.'** *Harl. MS. 7310, fol. 165.*

A printed pamphlet.

1699. **Letter from the Portuguese Envoy to King William III, dated 3 May 1699.** *Add. MS. 28943, fols. 137-38.*

He complains of the Treaty between the English and the Governor of Surat, which, he avers, may impair the peace between the Portuguese and the English.

This MS. is a draft with numerous corrections.

1699-1709. **Official Letter Books of the Honble. Thomas Pitt, Governor of Fort St. George, Madras, 21 Oct., 1699–21 Oct., 1709.** *Add. MSS. 22842-22850.*

This series of nine volumes consists of copies of letters written by Thomas Pitt, some 1,500 letters in all. There is an index of names at the end of each volume. With the exception of the letters (147) contained in Add. MS. 22846, entitled 'Country letters', the correspondence is carried on with persons in England, principally past and present servants of the Company. Historically, the collection is extremely valuable and, except by Sir Henry Yule, in his life of Pitt in *Hedges' Diary*, it has been little used by students. Pitt's correspondence includes such names as Sir William Langhorne, Elihu Yale, President Beard, William Hewer, George White and other outstanding characters connected with the E.I.Co.

1699-1709. **Bills of Exchange drawn by Thomas Pitt.** *Add. MS. 28853.*

1698- 1704/5.	Invoices of Goods shipped by Thomas Pitt.	*Add. MS. 22854.*

1698-1700.	Invoices of Goods shipped by Thomas Pitt and others.	*Add. MS. 22855.*

1704-8.	Invoices of Goods shipped by Thomas Pitt and others.	*Add. MS. 22856.*

c. 1700.   'A Regulated Company more   *Harl. MS. 7310, fols.*
National than a Joint Stock in   *166-66a.*
the E.I. Trade.'

A printed pamphlet. See among the printed books in the B.M., Press Mark, 816. m.
11 (71), for another copy.

c. 1700.   'The Arguments for a Regulated   *Harl. MS. 7310,*
Company, or open Trade to the   *fols. 155a-56a.*
East Indies Answered. With
Reasons why a Joint Stock will
best carry on, and preserve that
Trade.'

A printed pamphlet. There is a duplicate on fols. 171a-72.

c. 1700.   'Reasons against Establishing an   *Harl. MS. 7310,*
E.I. Co. with a Joynt Stock ex-   *fols. 168-68a.*
clusive to all others.'

A printed pamphlet. For another copy see B.M. General Catalogue, 816 m. 11
(57).

c. 1700.   'Reasons . . . for establishing the   *Harl. MS. 7310 fols.*
present East India Company by   *167-67a.*
Act of Parliament.'

A printed pamphlet. See also B. M. General Catalogue 816 m. 11 (56).

c. 1700.   'Reasons proposed for the en-   *Harl. MS. 17310,*
couragement of all People to   *fols. 297-300.*
under-write to the New Subscrip-
tions appointed to be made to the late
East India Company's Stock.'

A printed pamphlet.

1701-2.   **A Brief View of the Weight and**   *Lansdowne MS.*
Consequence of the General   *1234, fols. 1-38.*
Trade and of some Considerable Plans
in the Indies addressed to King William
III. Unsigned. Dated 1 Jan., 1701-2.

This is a general essay on trade and its possibilities, with a scheme for 'permission
trade', the whole very vague and with little direct reference to the East Indies.

MAPS AND PLANS

The following maps and plans are undated, but appear to belong to the first half of the 17th century or thereabouts.

Map of India. *Add. MS. 5027 A, fol. 101a.*

A small map showing Ceylon and islands, with coast names only.

Map of the Indian Seas, with part of India, and the East Coast of Africa. *Add. MS. 5414 No. 11.*

A large number of coast place-names are given.

A coloured Map, on vellum, of the East Coast of Asia, with the adjacent islands, from Sumatra to Japan. *Add. MS. 5415, I. i.*

Plans of Bona Esperanza. *Add. MS. 5027A, fols. 20-24, 109.*

These give very little detail.

Plan of the City of Daman on the Malabar Coast. *Add. 5027A, fol. 50b.*

The names in the plan and the written description accompanying it are in Portuguese.

Plan of the Island and City of Goa on the Malabar Coast, with part of the Island of Salcette. *Add. MS. 5027A, fols. 52b-54b.*

Names, etc., in Portuguese.

Plan of the City and Fortification of Chaul, a Portuguese possession on the Malabar Coast near Bombay. *Add. MS. 5027A, fols. 55b-56.*

Plan of the City and Fortress of Thana. *Add. MS. 5027A, fol. 57b.*

Plan of the Town of Bassein. *Add. MS. 5027A, fols. 60b-61.*

Plan of the City of Cochin, situated on a peninsula of the Malabar Coast. *Add. MS. 5027A, fol. 58b.*

Map of Bengal. *Add. MS. 5027A, fol. 63.*

The map shows coast and islands, but gives very few place-names.

A Dutch Map of Japan. *Add. MS. 5414 No. 9.*

A large, clear map showing inland and coast towns, mountains, etc.

A Coast Map of Asia, the Malay Ar-   *Add. MS. 36667A.*
chipelago, etc., from Arabia to Japan.
Names in Dutch.

A large number of coast place-names are inserted.   The map is divided into squares
and has an index of names.   Size 6 ft. 2 in. x 4 ft. 6 in.

Portuguese Chart, comprising the   *Add. MS. 36667B.*
Islands South of Arabia (*see the*
previous MS.) from Sumatra to the
Moluccas.

Very few place-names, except those on the North coast of Java, are given.   A vellum
roll.   Size 2ft. 6 in. x 3 ft. ½ in.

A Portuguese Chart, comprising the   *Add. MS. 36667C.*
North Coasts of Sumatra and
Borneo, Philippines, Formosa and the
corresponding Coast of Asia.

Very few place-names are given.   A vellum roll.   Size 2ft. 4½ in. x 2ft. 11 in.

Dutch Chart of the North Coast of   *Add. MS. 36667D.*
Java, including Bantam to the West,
and Batavia to the East.

It contains very little detail.   A vellum roll.   Size 1 ft. 5 in. x 3 ft. 5¾ in.

1646.   **Livro do Estado da India Oriental.**   *Sloane MS. 197.*

This valuable and beautifully executed MS. is in three parts, the third of which is
entitled: 'Livro de Antonio Bocarro, Guardamor de Archivo Real da India', etc.

It contains coloured plans of the Portuguese possessions on the W. coast of India, including Diu, Daman, Mahim, Bassein, Thana, Chaul, Mangalore, Cananore, Cranganore,
Cochin, etc.

n many cases a description accompanies the plan.   A series of tracings of the plans
has been made for the Map Department in the India Office, and a printed list of the
names is to be found in the *Catalogue of MS. and Printed Reports, Field Books, Maps,*
etc., p. 95.

1650.   **Plan of Batavia on the North-West**   *Add. MS. 5027A,*
of Java.   *fol. 73.*

c. 1661.   **Maps executed by Dutchmen.**   *Add. MS. 34184, 101*
fols.

A quarto volume bound in vellum entitled, 'Dutch Portolano c. 1660', containing
49 coloured maps and views, 17 of which are of India, Further India, and the islands of
the Malay Archipelago, etc.   Size 7 in. x 9 in.   Some of the maps bear a very striking
resemblance to those in Add. MS. 5027A, Vellum, fols. 101, etc. *q.v.*   These maps are
valuable for old place-names.

f. 32a-33.   Coast of 'Guadel' and 'Gouzarate' from 'Cabo Salque' to
'Dioue' with numerous place-names.
f. 34a-35.   Mogoll—a map of Hindustan and Ceylon, showing 'Cuncan',
'Canara', 'Coromandel', 'Orixa', with numerous coast towns.

f. 36a-37. Bengala, showing the Bay of Bengal, Arakan, Pegu and the
Tenassarim Coast with the Andaman and Nicobar Islands.

f. 38a-39. Map of Siam—very few places marked—coast line and
islands indicated.

f. 40a-41. Cambodia and ' t'Siompa' (Champa).

f. 41a-42. T'siompa—with many coastal place names.

f. 44a-45. Couchinchuna—coast with a few names.

f. 46a-47. Tonquin.

f. 54a-55. Malacca and Sumatra—with many names.

f. 56a-57 & 58a-59.   Java.

f. 60a-61. Malay Archipelago with Philippine Islands.

f. 62a-63. Celebes.

f. 64a-65. Banda.

f. 66a-67. Coloured view of 'Neyro', one of the Banda Islands with its
fort.

f. 68a-69. 'Poulou Row and Poulo Ay.'

f. 72a-73, 74a-75 & 82a-83. Amboina.

1663.   **Dutch Chart of portions of the**   *Add. MS. 36667A.*
East Indies, N. Coast of Borneo,
Philippines and Coast of Cochin China
by John Blaeu.

A vellum roll.   Size 2 ft. 9¼ in. x 3 ft. 1 in.   The map gives very little detail except
for Cochin China.

1667.   **Chart, on vellum, of the Island of**   *Add. MS. 9047G.*
Sumatra and the adjacent coasts,
drawn in 1667, by John Blaeu. Size
30 in. x 38 in.

c. 1680.   **'The South Coast of the Island**   *Add. MS. 5222, No.*
Selebes and the West Coast of the   *11.*
Island Zeyllyer.'

An unsigned coloured and gilt chart of the south coast of ' the western leg ' of the
Island of Celebes, with the west coast of the Island ' Zeyller ' (Salayer), on a scale of
11 in. to a degree.   The writing is that of Thomas Bowrey.   Size 6 ft. 7 in. x 1 ft. 5 in.

c. 1680.   **Philippine Islands, Celebes and**   *Add. MS. 5222, No. 7.*
Formosa.

An unsigned chart, with very little detail, in Thomas Bowrey's writing.

1681.   **'The Island of Zeyloan with the**   *Add. MS. 5222, No.*
opposite coast of the Carnatic.'   *17.*

A chart of the island of Ceylon with ' The Bay of Totecoryn'.   Drawn by Thomas
Bowrey.   Size 3 ft. x 2 ft. 4 in.

1682.   **Tenasserim.**   *Add. MS. 5222, No.*
13.

A chart of the coast of Tenasserim from 9° 30' to 14° 30' North Latitude, showing
the Andaman and Nicobar Islands.   Drawn by Thomas Bowrey in Madapollam, 1 Dec
1682.   Size 2 ft. 10 in. x 2 ft. 4 in.

1685.   **'Golfe of Persia.'**   *Add. Ms. 5222, No. 15.*

A chart of the Persian Gulf, drawn by Thomas Bowrey, on a scale of 6 in. to a degree. Size 2 ft. 4 in. x 1 ft. 8 in.

c. 1686.   **Mindanao.**   *Add. MS. 5222, No. 9.*

An unsigned chart, in Thomas Bowrey's writing, with very little detail.

1686.   **A Chart of 'Amoy Bay on the**   *Add. MS. 5222, No.*
          coast of China.'   *14.*

A chart drawn by Thomas Bowrey and copied from a chart made by J. N. (John Nicholson) aboard the *Advice*, 20 Dec., 1676. The chart extends from 23° 50' to 24° 30' North Latitude. It shows 'the isle of Amoy' and part of 'the isle of Quenoy'. Size 2 ft. 7 in. x 1 ft. 8 in.

1687   **A large Chart of the Island of For-**   *Add. MS. 5222, No.*
          mosa, with the Pescadores and part of   *16.*
          the opposite Coast of China.

Drawn by Thomas Bowrey. Size 2 ft. 6 in. x 2 ft. 6 in.

1687.   **A Chart of the River of Hugly**   *Add. MS. 5222, No. 8.*
          drawn by Thomas Bowrey in
          Fort St. George, 1687.

Size 2ft. 6 in. x 1 ft. 8 in. This is the most detailed of all Bowrey's charts. It has been reproduced and described with his MS. (1669-79) *Countries Round the Bay of Bengal*, published by the Hakluyt Society and edited by Sir Richard Carnac Temple.

c. 1687.   **'Straits of Sincapura.'**   *Add. MS. 5222, No.*
                                              10.

An unsigned coloured chart on a scale of 8 in. to a degree, showing the Straits of Singapore and part of the coast of 'Malaya', with remarks on the products obtainable. The writing is that of Thomas Bowrey. Size 1 ft. 10 in. x 1 ft. 4 in.

c. 1688.   **Coloured drawing of the Bay and**   *Sloane   MS.   3671,*
          Island of St. Jago, Cape Verd   *fol. 4.*
          Islands.

1688-90.   **Kempthorne's Sea Views, etc.**   *Sloane   MS.   3665,*
                                                  76 fols.

This book of maps belongs to Sloane MSS. 3670 and 3671 (already described), which contain the Journals of Captain John Kempthorne in the *Kempthorne* 1684-89.

The maps, plans and drawings are, for the most part, coloured. The earlier folios contain illustrations of European and African ports. The following deal with India and the Indian Seas :

f. 34a Elevation of the Comoro Islands ; f. 35 Plan of Johanna ; f. 39a-40 Achin and Pulo Wai ; f. 41 Billiapatam ; f. 42 Batacala (Bhatkal) ; f. 43 Onore ; f. 44 'Merice'; f. 45 Carwar ; f. 46 Goa; f. 47 Mauritius ; f. 48 Philippine Islands ; f. 60, 69 Malay Archipelago and Straits of Singapore ; f. 70 Balasor River and Town ; f. 75 Straits of Sunda.

1689-93.   Log of the *Benjamin.*   *Add. MS. 18989, 117 fols.*

The Journal has already been described. It contains the following illustrations :

f. 5 Sketch of Plymouth Sound ; f. 7a Madeira ; f. 9 ' The Road ' of Madeira ; f. 13a St. Jago Road ; f. 16a ' Anibo ' Island, 3 small sketches ; f. 20, etc. Coast of Angola, etc. ; f. 27a St. Helena ; f. 30a Cape of Good Hope, The Table ; f. 34a St; Lawrence (Madagascar) ; f. 35a ' Mohelia', Comoro Islands ; f. 39a, etc. Small sketches ; f. 41 Land round Bombay harbour ; f. 41a The Island of Bombay and Salsette ; f. 43a Swally Hole from the anchorage of the ship ; f. 46a Achin Road ; f. 50a Coast of Malacca ; f. 54a Malacca Road ; f. 57 Carimon Island ; f. 66 Kedah Bay ; f. 72 ' Tinga Patanam, the Dutch Factory House ' ; f. 77 Carwar Road ; f. 78a Goa Road ; f. 97a Table Bay ; f. 116a St. Mary's Sound, Scilly Islands.

1696.   Chart of the West Coast of Hindo-   *Egerton MS. 741.*
stan. By John Thornton, 1696.

A coloured map, showing coast indentations, towns, capes, etc. It contains numerous remarks on the country, land elevations, etc., and directions for navigation.

Size 1 ft. 6 in. x 12 ft.

1700.   North Coast of Java.   *Add. MS. 5222, No. 6.*

A chart of part of the north coast of Java, showing Batavia and Bantam.

Drawn by Thomas Bowrey in 1700. Size 2ft. 6 in. x 1 ft. 4 in.

MAPS AND PLANS PROBABLY OF LATE SEVENTEENTH AND EARLY EIGHTEENTH CENTURY

The following maps and plans, all undated, appear to belong to the end of the seventeenth century or to the first half of the eighteenth century.

Whampoa, Canton, China : with   *Add. MS. 31343B.*
soundings.

Very little detail beyond soundings—a few names only. Size 23 in. x 50 in.

Maps of Centre of Indostan, from   *Add. MS. 31343C.*
Delhi to Allahabad.

Showing rivers, mountains and towns. Size 17 in. x 29 in.

' General Map of the Calcutta   *Add. MS. 31343K.*
Lands.' Surveyed by Capt. Claud
Martin.

Numerous names. The Company's lands are shown ; good, cultivated and marshy ground, etc., noted, also names of parganas, roads, villages, etc., etc. ; 30 in. x 60 in.

The Provinces of Midnapur and   *Add. 31343R.*
Bishenpur, Bengal—with their
environs.

Rivers, mountains, districts, and a few towns are marked. Size 20 in. x 30 in.

Map of the Western Jungles belonging to the Province of Midnapur.

Add. MS. 31343S.

Rivers, mountains and a few towns are marked. Size 20 in. x 24 in.

Plan of the Road from 'Carumnassah' to Allahabad.

Add. MS. 31343AA.

Numerous place-names along the road and river are given. Size 20 in. x 28 in.

'Plan of the Road to Bargur by the way of Chacundeh and from Burgur by Sourajepour to Bara, from the Gaut of Mahaveh.'

Add. MS. 31343CC.

The towns on the route are marked. Size 16 in. x 42 in.

Map of Road from Balasor to Sumbulpur.

Add. MS. 31343DD.

The map shows mountains, river, road and towns. Size 20 in. x 30 in.

Map of China—with adjacent Islands.

Cotton MS. Aug. I vol. 2, No. 45.

There is a note appended giving the number of cities and villages and other items of interest.

Besides the above MSS. which (with the exception of Add. MS. 18989) contain only maps and plans, sketches (pen, pencil and coloured) of islands, harbours, etc., elevations of hills, etc., are to be found in the following ships' journals already described :

1650-51.	Log of the *Bonita*.	*Sloane MS. 3231.*
1667-69.	Log of the *Unicorn*.	*Harl. MS. 4252.*
1678.	Voyage to Achin.	*Sloane MS. 3668.*
1677/78-1678.	Log of the *New London*.	*Sloane MS. 863.*
1679-80.	Log of the *Caesar*.	*Sloane MS. 3668.*
1679-1681/82.	Log of the *Berkeley*.	*Sloane MS. 3668.*
1682-84.	Log of the *Charles*.	*Sloane MS. 3672.*
1684-85.	Log of the *Frances*.	*Sloane MS. 855.*
1684-85.	Log of the *Frances, Phoenix*, etc.	*Sloane MS. 854.*
1684-86.	Log of the *Williamson*.	*Sloane MS. 1045.*
1688-89.	Log of the *Kempthorne*.	*Sloane MS. 3672.*

DOCUMENTS ON SEVENTEENTH-CENTURY BRITISH INDIA, IN THE PUBLIC RECORD OFFICE, CHANCERY LANE

DOCUMENTS ON SEVENTEENTH-CENTURY BRITISH INDIA, IN THE PUBLIC RECORD OFFICE, CHANCERY LANE

BROADLY speaking, whilst the Records of the inner administration of the East India Company are to be found at the India Office, the records of its relations with the State, its influence on the foreign policy of the Home Government and the consequent intricate treaty negotiations with different powers (the Dutch in particular) must be sought at the Public Record Office. There, too, the traces of the rival companies and traders may be met with. It may be noted that the Public Record Office, until William Noel Sainsbury utilized its materials for his *Calendar of State Papers, East Indies*, was strangely neglected by students of Indian history. Since then its resources have been tapped by Sir George Birdwood, Sir William Foster, and many others.

The new classification of Records at the Public Record Office is as far as possible a geographical one; but a large proportion of the earlier documents do not admit of such a division.

Save for the important *Colonial Series—East Indies* (now C.O. 77) we must not hope to find the documents or references relating to the East Indies as a separate section. The enquirer may even be met by a well-meant remark that there is little relating to India at the Public Record Office.

Moreover, the long and bitter rivalry between the English and Dutch East India Companies, their temporary co-operation, and the immense importance attached by both to the spice trade in the Moluccas; also the fact that for a time the headquarters of the English Company as well as of the Dutch were in Java (at Bantam and Batavia)—all these factors make it undesirable, if not wellnigh impossible, to separate the early documents relating to the Moluccas and Java in particular, from those more strictly concerning the English Factories on the continent of India.

Throughout the negotiations and treaty preliminaries between England and Holland after the restoration of Charles II, Pulo-run is one of the cardinal points insisted upon on behalf of the East India Company.

In 1662, Lord Treasurer Southampton reported to the King (on Sir Nicholas Crispe's petition concerning the importance of and duties on spices) that the Dutch had the sole trade for many years. 'The English cannot import them from Holland because they import them not from the place of their growth; the East India Company themselves having no capacity to do it until they be restored to Poleroon, or gain some of the Spice Islands.'

To deal profitably with the history of British India, the connection with Europe cannot be ignored. From the beginning of the sixteenth century, the economic and commercial history of the chief European nations and their naval and colonial history are practically inseparable.

The relations of the East India Company with the Portuguese, the French, the Dutch, the Danes, and other European rivals in the Eastern trade are reflected not only in the records of the Company itself, but in those of the States, and in the foreign relations of the latter, and the inter-relation of all these countries. Whilst, in the sixteenth and early seventeenth centuries, Portugal is the great colonising power, in the middle of the century the history of the Dutch colonies, and especially of the Dutch East India Company, is of extreme importance. In 1664, in his Memorial to the States-General, Sir George Downing, the English envoy, could state that the whole of the complaints against Holland were, in a manner, complaints against the East and West India Companies of that country.

Hence the documents concerning the various developments and relations must be sought in the great store-house of State Records, not only under the sections dealing exclusively with the colonial correspondence of the East Indies (now C.O. 77), but in the general series of *Domestic State Papers* and in the *State Papers—Foreign*, relating to each country concerned.

The State Administration in England was not divided into definite Departments until the end of the period with which we are dealing. Until 1782, Home affairs were administered by two Secretaries of State, Northern and Southern, but, whilst in the eighteenth century it was the Southern Secretary who had charge of the Colonies, in the seventeenth century the distinction was by no means so clear. The separation even between Domestic and Foreign departments was not absolute. The classification of State Papers as Domestic or Foreign was made in the reign of James I. There is no definite class of *State Papers: Colonial*, although from 1699 the Colonial Records take the place of such.

The data for the early history of the East Indies must therefore be searched for at the Public Record Office in the comprehensive General series in which they are included, not only as separate volumes in a class, single documents in bound volumes, or loose papers in partly classified bundles, but as individual entries in books or component parts of General Correspondence.

As in the *State Papers: Foreign*, the despatches of the English ambassadors and agents abroad are of great importance, so in the *State Papers: Domestic*, the correspondence of Secretaries of State must be consulted. To Sir Joseph Williamson, Keeper of State Papers, and later Secretary of State, we owe the collection and preservation of the great wealth of documents for the reign of Charles II. To him are due also several systematic collections arranged under subjects containing selected copies of documents in chronological order for the elucidation of particular questions. These may be consulted with great advantage, even though the originals of some of the papers may be found scattered elsewhere (e.g. *State Papers: Foreign: Archives*, No. 219).

A list of Secretaries of State will be found printed in P.R.O. *Lists and Indexes*, No. XLIII, pp. v-viii, and one in Haydon's *Book of Dignities*. This and similar lists of ambassadors and officials at home and abroad are especially useful in tracing the continuity of a subject. Their correspondence is often indexed under names alone.

The official *Guide to the Various Classes of Documents preserved in the Public Record Office*, by Mr. Scargill-Bird contains no detailed description of the documents specially relating to the East Indies.

The Search Rooms of the Public Record Office contain in addition to the printed 'Calendars' of abstracts of various series a large number of lists and inventories, both printed and manuscript. In 1892 appeared the first of an official series of *Lists and Indexes*, which, in conjunction with the Calendars, will, 'in course of time, form a catalogue of the National Archives' (cf. 51st Report of the Deputy-Keeper of the Records, p. 10). A '*List of Lists*' compiled in 1906 was placed in the Literary Search Room, but, since the date of the Royal Commission on Public Records in 1911, the lists there available have been considerably supplemented and completely rearranged.

The successive rearrangements and re-classifications of the archives, due in many cases to the incorporation of new material or to the correction of misdescriptions, and the consequent alteration of references, have, however, made necessary the use of 'Keys'. A note communicated to the Royal Commission in 1912 by the Deputy-Keeper of Public Records as to the references which have been altered in Official Calendars, Lists, or Indexes, includes, amongst others, the following 'Calendars in which some part of the references no longer holds good'.

Calendar of State Papers, Domestic.
Calendar of State Papers, Colonial.
Calendar of Treasury Books and Papers.

8

It also states that, 'apart from the local records or State Papers which have been calendared, many volumes, rolls or bundles have been used and cited in various works, and the references to these documents are now, in many cases, obsolete.'

As regards the Colonial Office Records, the old printed lists have been re-arranged and catalogued in *Lists and Indexes*, No. XXXVI.

The present notes are necessarily based chiefly upon the Official Lists, Calendars and Reports, and printed authorities, but have been supplemented by direct examination of selected original documents.

COLONIAL OFFICE RECORDS

The principal series of documents at the Public Record Office relating to British India will be found in the *Colonial Office Records—East Indies*, now C.O. 77.

No. 36 of the *Public Record Office Lists and Indexes*, published in 1911, supersedes the List of Colonial Office Records printed in 1896.

The documents now therein listed, though generally known as Colonial Office Records, also comprise such of those derived from the Board of Trade, relating to the early committees and councils in charge of trade and plantation affairs, as have not been dispersed or lost.

When it was decided to issue the Colonial Calendars, the books and papers, letters, loose memoranda, etc., were sorted and rebound in chronological order, many volumes of manuscripts already bound being broken up for the purpose. (This last method was subsequently adandoned.)

The papers described as *Colonial Correspondence*—now *Original Correspondence—Secretary of State*, were those which accumulated in the offices of the Secretaries of State who administered the Colonies. These papers ultimately reached the Colonial Office, and thence the Record Office. In addition there was a collection of office books from various sources, classed as *Entry-Books*, amongst them those containing papers earlier than the year 1688, which had escaped being broken up. The whole of the records were rearranged, and as far as possible classified geographically, for the compilation of the new list, No. 36, except in the case of papers already calendared by Mr. Noel Sainsbury. The earlier references therefore became obsolete. To obtain the new reference when only the former is known, the List itself should be consulted; but a Key based thereon, giving new and old references for the main East Indies Class (C.O. 77), is appended. *A Key to the Colonial Entry-Books* is now printed, with

an account of their history, in C. S. S. Higham's ' *The Colonial
Entry-Books—a Brief Guide to the Colonial Records in the Public
Record Office before 1696*'.

A brief abstract of every document of the East Indies
original correspondence, down to the year 1634, is contained in
the *Calendar of State Papers—Colonial Series—Indies, China and
Japan* [and Persia], edited by W. Noel Sainsbury.   This series is
continued in date from 1635, in the unofficial *Calendar of the
Court Minutes, etc., of the East India Company*, edited by Miss
E. B. Sainsbury, with Introductions and Notes by Sir William
Foster, C.I.E., which has now reached the year 1667.   The latter
include documents in the Public Record Office, besides those in
the India Office, British Museum, etc., and in the sixth volume
a large proportion of the papers is contributed by the Public
Record Office.   *Letters Received by the East India Company from
its Servants in the East*, begun in 1896 by Mr. Danvers, as a
verbatim edition of the early correspondence from 1602-15, was
continued by Sir W. Foster to the year 1617.   Another official
series of the India Office, edited by Sir W. Foster, was begun in
1902, *The English Factories in India*.   It also includes Record
Office documents as well as ' all those either emanating from or
directly relating to the English factories in India, which could
be found either in the Archives of the India Office, or in the
MSS. Department of the British Museum'.   This series begins
with the year 1618 and the volume last published relates to the
year 1664.

The papers calendared by Mr. Sainsbury comprise not only
those in the Public Record Office, but also many in the British
Museum and the India Office, relating to the early voyages for
the discovery of a north-east or a north-west passage to India,
the establishment of the East India Company, the settling of the
different factories in the peninsula of India and the most important
islands of the Indian Ocean, Sumatra, Java, Borneo and Celebes,
the development of English trade and influence in Malacca, Cambodia, and Siam, and the opening up of trade with Persia, China,
and Japan.   The difficulties with the Spaniards and Portuguese
appear in the first volume, and the violent opposition of the Dutch
occupies a prominent position.   The abstracts embrace those
derived from documents in the Colonial Series, the Domestic
Series of Records, and extracts from the Holland Correspondence
and that of Spain, Portugal, and France.   Where a document
relating to the East Indies is calendared in both Mr. Sainsbury's
Colonial Series and the Calendar of Domestic Papers, the abstract
is generally more full in his Colonial Series.   Where periods over-
lap, the Series edited by Sir W. Foster, which include numerous

documents previously unknown to students, are generally to be preferred, but not always for individual purposes. Comparatively few of the Foreign documents at the Public Record Office are embodied, and the more limited scope of the English Factory Series necessarily excludes the continuous and detailed record of the contentions with the Dutch.

Documents relating to the East Indies will also be found in the other Series of Official Calendars interspersed among those dealing with other subjects.

COLONIAL CORRESPONDENCE—EAST INDIES
NOW C.O. 77

C.O. $\frac{77}{5}$ (Formerly *East Indies* 4a, 1634, old reference Vol. IV, No. 112) is a parchment exemplification of the East India Company's Charter of 20 James I, reciting earlier Letters Patent of 13 James I, concerning the appointment of Chief Commanders and the punishing of capital offences. Provision for the Revocation of the Power. Cf. *Calendar of State Papers, Colonial—East Indies*, 1630-34, No. 526.

C.O. $\frac{77}{8}$ (1655-63) Original Correspondence—Secretary of State. Contains *inter alia* (1661-62):

E.I. Co.'s demand for delivery of Polo Run by the Dutch. Refusal of the Dutch Agents.

E.I. Co.'s Petition to the King *re* damage received from the Dutch. Arbitration requested before ratification of the Treaty.

States-General's Proceedings *re* Ships *Bona Esperanza* and *Henry Bonaventure*. Bombay: Complaints of A. de Mello de Castro against Earl of Marlborough and Captain Minors. Captain Ambrose Browne's Journal (extracts). Cf. C.O. $\frac{77}{7}$.

C.O. $\frac{77}{9}$ (1663-65) Original Correspondence—Secretary of State. Contains *inter alia*:

Bombay: Non-surrender to English (1663, October 31). Complaint made in Portugal as to non-surrender. Letter to Sir Abraham Shipman, enclosing one to Viceroy of Goa.

Petition and Memorial of the Inhabitants to King Charles II; an account of hardships suffered [? 1663]. Cf. C.O. $\frac{77}{19}$.

C.O. $\frac{77}{10}$ (1666-67) Original Correspondence—Secretary of State. Comprises original documents (in many instances in duplicate) and copies of letters relating chiefly to:

Bombay: The King's possessions there, Fishery Rights and Customs, and disputes with the Portuguese.

Sir Gervase Lucas's Reports: His Commission, Instructions and death. Amongst Sir Gervase Lucas's letters may be noted that of 2nd March 1666-67 (C.O. $\frac{77}{10}$ f. 90) to the King, giving an account ' of y^e affairs in these parts'. After referring to the change of Councils in the E.I. Co., he gives his opinion that ' so long as your Majesty continues that Company your affairs in these parts will never answer your great designe and noble interests of advancing Trade. . . . As well English as others in these parts are taught to believe they are a body apart from your Majestie's Authority or Government '.

Henry Gary's Reports to the King and various authorities (important). His differences with Humphrey Cooke.

Danger of Dutch attempts.

E.I. Co.'s Proposal to take over Bombay from the Crown.

Annual Revenues under King of Portugal, and of King Charles on Island of Bombain, 1667 . . . etc.

Soldiers: Names of 21, and monies due to E.I. Co. for Pay, Diet, etc.

E.I. Co.: Dissensions between E.I. Co.'s servants in India, especially at Fort St. George. Sir Edward Winter and George Foxcroft. Complaints of affronts offered by Mr. Humphrey Cooke, Governor of Bombay, to the English factory at Surat. Complaints concerning the ship *Love* sent out by Mr. Andrews.

Fort St. George, Madras: Full series of documents relating to dissension between Sir Edward Winter and George Foxcroft. (Cf. Love, *Vestiges of Old Madras*, etc.)

Dutch in India and East: Claim to have defeated English and slain Duke of York, Prince Rupert, etc.

Captain Henry Young's Petition for particular service done to Lord Bellamont in Persia and the East Indies.

C.O. $\frac{77}{49}$ (Formerly *C.O. East Indies*, 15), described as ' 1661–1695—Charters, grants, petitions, Orders in Council, Board of Trade correspondence, etc '.

This is one of the original leather-bound series of General Office Books of the ' Lords of Trade ', i.e. of the Committee of Trade and Plantations of the Privy Council appointed in 1675. On a stamped panel on the front cover it is described as ' Entries relating to the East India Company '; it is thus referred to in the List of Books belonging to the Committee, drawn up in 1696 by William Popple, clerk of the new Board of Trade, on taking them over from John Povey.

It is described on an inner title-page as ' Journal and Entries Relating to the East India Company ', and contains a map, on Mercator's projection, of the Eastern hemisphere (Africa, the East Indies, New Holland, etc). The loss of the Original ' Map of Bombaim ' given by the Portuguese Ambassador on the first ' Overture of Bombaim ' is referred to—pp. 128, 134.

An Index of the chief matters contained ends the book. The documents are mostly connected with Bombay, its surrender to Great Britain and difficulties with the Portuguese.

The ' Journal ' was apparently begun in 1675-76 in connection with these difficulties, but the first 120 pages, approximately, contain copies of earlier documents bearing on the subject:

pp. 1–46. Charter of the East India Company [3 April, 1661].

47–75. Charter for the Island of Bombay, 27 March, 1668.

76–93. Grant of St. Helena to the E.I. Co., 16 Dec., 1673.

93–106. ' Coppie of H.M.'s Charter to the E.I. Co.' [2nd Charter] 5th October, 1676.

108–13. Petition of the E.I. Co. about Bombain. Title: ' On the 2nd of March, 1675. The Petition of the E.I. Co. setting forth severall hardships received from the Portuguese at Bombain is Read, As also a State of their case as followeth . . .'

114–21. ' Bombain described, how transferred to his Majestie, How afterwards to the Company, what Injuries suffered from the Portugeas, what Address made to the Vice Roy of Goa, what Answer returned by him, what opinion given by the President and Council thereon, And lastly the Sovereignty of the whole Haven and Islands asserted.'

pp. 122–24. '11th Article of yᵉ Treaty of Marriage with Portugall' in November, 1663, in Latin and English. [Also the 15th Article.]

129-33. 'On the 16th of Jan., 1676 [i.e. 1677] their Lordships take the business of Bombain into their further consideration, and cause the Draught of Sir Abraham Shipman's Commission and Instructions to be read as followeth . . .'

139-53. Surrender of Bombay. Paper containing the whole Process of the Surrender as it was made on the 27th February, 1664-65. Translation of documents out of the Portuguese certified by Lucas Emans, Notary Public.

158–63. Report about the Jurisdiction and Dependencies of Bombain by Sir Robert Southwell to their Lordships [including the description and expense of Maim Bandora].

167–87. Representation of the Governor, etc., of the E.I. Co. to the Right Hon. the Lords of the Committee for Trade and Plantations [with Inventory of Contents], dated 12 Feb., 1676 [1677]. Account of their possession of Bombay, etc. Capitulation forced on Cook by Antonio de Mello : Ports Rights. Forts—Charge and Expense of Forts, etc., etc., 12 special points submitted, etc. The notes by J. Williamson about Bombain *S.P. Dom. Chas. II.* 366, p. 305, abstracted in *Calendar of S.P. Dom. Charles II.* 1676-77, p. 552, under the same date, are evidently based on this document.

188-89. Petition of the Governor, etc., of the E.I. Co. to the Lords of the Committee for Trade and Plantations. Further abuses of the Portuguese. Refusal of Portuguese to grant passes to 'Jauncks' for Gombroon.

190-95. Privy Council, 23 Feb., 1676-77. Report of the Lords of the Committee . . . on the complaints from the E.I. Co. touching injuries received by them at Bombain from the Portuguese, dated 12th February, 1676-77. [Apparently not calendared in *Cal. S.P. Domestic, Charles II,* nor in the *Acts of the Privy Council.*]

195-99. King's letter to Don Lodovico de Mendoça Ffurtado, Vice-Roy and Captain-General of India, in pursuance of Orders of Feb. 23rd, 1676-77 (Latin). 10th March 1676-77.

200-29. Alvaro Pires de Tavora's complaint against the E.I. Co. for

238-46. injuries at Bombay. His case, and a series of documents, Orders, etc., relating thereto. Orders in Council referring him for Redress to the Courts of Judicature at Bombain. [Not all calendared; but cf. Sir J. W. Williamson's *Notes of Arguments before the Privy Council in the Case of Alvaro Perez* [*sic*]. *State Papers Domestic, Charles II.* 366, in *State Papers Domestic, Calendar Charles II,* 1677-78, p. 190.] His submission to the E.I. Co. and restoration to his Estate.

230-34. Customs and Tolls of Bombay. Order in Council, 26 Oct., 1677. Containing—Report from the Lords of the Committee to the King in Council.

234-37. King's Letter to the Prince Regent of Portugal about the Customs (Latin).

246. Secretary Conventry's Letter to [Gerald Aungier] the E.I. Co.'s President of Surat on behalf of A. P. de Tavora. 13 March, 1677-78.

N.B.—There is a long interval of time between this and the following entries in a new hand, which seem to have been made after the date to which they refer, possibly *circa* 1690.

247. Report of the Attorney-General, R. Sawyer, to the King concerning Interlopers and the E.I. Co.'s Petition. 16 Nov., 1682.

pp. 248-49. Order and Report from the Lords of Committee for Trade and Plantations, of 13 Nov., 1680, *re* Pepper. [Duplicate Document . . . In Margin *vide* Petit and Lib. Trade, Vol. I, p. 221.]

249-56. 'Minutes of the Council. 18 Sept., 1690.' Permits for the ships of the E.I. Co. to sail, 1690-94.

251-52, Saltpetre, Price and Purchase from E.I. Co.
253.

256-57, Elihu Yale's (late President of Fort St. George) Petition to come
258-59. to England referred to the Committee for Trade and Plantations. Minutes of the Committee upon hearing Mr. Yale and the E.I. Co., 2nd March, 1694-95.

KEY TO COLONIAL CORRESPONDENCE: EAST INDIES
(From the Official Lists and Keys)

[Old Reference East Indies]		[New Reference C.O. 77]	
1	1570-1621	1	Miscellaneous Correspondence [now described as Original Correspondence — Secretary of State].
2	1622-23	2	,, ,, ,, ,,
3	1624-25	3	,, ,, ,, ,,
4	1626-34	4	,, ,, ,, ,,
4a	1634	5	Exemplification of the Govr. and Company of Merchants of London—East India Co.'s Charter 20 Jas. I.
4b	1635-42	6	Miscellaneous Correspondence (see description above).
4c	1643-45	7	,, ,, ,, ,,
5	1655-62	8	,, ,, ,, ,,
6	1663-65	9	,, ,, ,, ,,
7	1666-67	10	,, ,, ,, ,,
8	1668-70	11	,, ,, ,, ,,
9	1671-73	12	,, ,, ,, ,,
10	1674-77	13	,, ,, ,, ,,
11	1678-86	14	,, ,, ,, ,,
12	[Wanting]		
13	[Undated]	15	Elizabeth—Charles II.
14	1660-64	C.O. $\frac{389}{1}$	Entry-Book [really 1663-64].
15	1661-95	C.O. $\frac{77}{49}$	Charters, grants, petitions, Orders in Council, Board of Trade correspondence, etc.
16	1689-1744 now divided into two 1689-1725	16, 17	Miscellaneous Correspondence.

COLONIAL ENTRY-BOOKS

C.O. $\frac{77}{49}$ has been referred to as an Entry-Book, and as dealing exclusively with affairs relating to the East Indies. It has under the new topographical arrangement been assigned to class C.O. 77 ; but other so-called Colonial Entry-Books will be found to contain, amongst other matters, documents relating to the Indies.

A large number of the Entry-Books formed part of the collection belonging to the Lords of Trade. This was passed on by them to the Board of Trade which succeeded them in 1895. Arbitrarily divided in former arrangements of records at the Public Record Office between the Colonial and the Board of Trade sections, the collection no longer exists as a series.

Most of the books of the different Councils and Committees for Foreign Plantations and Trade before 1670 have been lost, some having at one time been in private hands ; the few remaining are derived from many different sources.

A Standing Committee of the Privy Council to deal with Plantation affairs was appointed in 1660, and in the same year, and co-existent, a Council of Plantations, and a Council of Trade (cf. C.O. $\frac{389}{1}$).

In 1670 the Council for Foreign Plantations was established. The King's Intructions to the Commissioners (July, 1670) will be found in C.O. $\frac{389}{4}$. In 1672, the King extended the powers and membership of the Council, instructing the Attorney-General to prepare a Bill under the Great Seal, appointing a ' Standing Council . . . for all the affairs concerning the Navigation, Commerce or Trade as well Domestique as Forreigne ' . . . and for all Foreign Colonies and Plantations, excepting Tangier (see C.O. $\frac{389}{4}$). In 1675 complete control over Plantation affairs was restored to a Standing Committee of the Privy Council commissioned as Lords of the Committee for Trade and Plantations, but generally known as ' Lords of Trade '. Sir Robert Southwell was the first Secretary. The Journal and Entries of their dealings with the East India Company are contained in C.O. $\frac{77}{13}$ (q.v. ante).

In 1696 the Board of Trade was established, and a large number of the records of the Lords of Trade were handed over to it by John Povey on their behalf. The list of these drawn up by William Popple, and a brief history of the Entry-Books, will be found in Mr. Higham's Colonial Entry-Books, the history of the various controlling bodies, in C. M. Andrews' British Committees, Commissions and Councils of Trade and Plantations, 1622-75 (Johns Hopkins Press, Baltimore, 1905).

Among the Colonial Entry-Books, still extant, to be found amongst the Colonial Records, the following may be instanced in addition to C.O. $\frac{77}{13}$:

C.O. $\frac{324}{3}$. A small leather-bound notebook, formerly listed as a Colonial Entry-Book, Plantations, General, 98. It bears the stamp of the Colonial Office, and was at one time No. 77, Plantations. This was Sir Joseph Williamson's private notebook, when Secretary of State. Colonial Calendar, 1675-76, pp.

154-63, contains a full résumé. We here extract from the original the entries relating to India, in abstract only.
The book is begun from both ends, pages 1-12 being blank except for a few miscellaneous notes. A new paging in pencil then begins.

p. 3. contains an incomplete List of Contents.
    65, Bombaim. 2 [? March], 1675-76.
      E. Indies Pet[ition].
      Yᵉ Port and Island of Bombaim Sovereignty and Property in this by yᵉ King's Grants they complain . . .
p. 66. Notes relating to ' Bombaim ' and Portuguese (2 pages).
    67. Caranjah and Tanna. '*N.B.*Yᵉ opposite shores to Tanna and Caranjah are in [the hands?] of yᵉ R[aos] princes, not yᵉ Portuguese.' Suggestion that the King should propose to the Portuguese to yield the other islands, etc., 'which would oblidge yᵉ Portuguese to quit those dominions '.

At the opposite end of the Book is written: Plantacoñs—For. Dominions. 30 pp. of notes + 1 page of notes on p. 45.
C.O. $\frac{389}{1}$ (formerly C.O. East Indies, Vol. 14, 1660-64, at one time ' P. 11, T. 174 '). This is the only surviving entry-book of the Council for Trade of 1660. The title-page inside the leather cover indicates its provenance: ' At his Majesties Councel for Trade: att Mercers Hall, London: 1660.'
A copy of the Patent for a Councell of Trade 7 Nov. 12 Chas. II [i.e. 1660] is at the beginning of the Book before the paging begins. (See *Cal. S.P. Dom. Chas. II*, Nov. 7, 1660.)

f. 8. East India Company's Petition to the King (1660) relating to Polo-Roone, the founding of a factory there by King James's consent, ' untill by the violent intrusion of the Netherlands East India Company the Petitioners were totally deprived thereof '. . . . Resolve ' by the Permission of God and your Majestie to possess and plant the said Island of Polo-Roone with all possible speed '. . . Petition to his Majesty 'to graunt his Majesty's Royall Commission under your Greate Seale impowering them to possess and plant the said island for use of the said Company, and to substitute and commission thereunto such persons as from time to time shall be found needful by your Petitioners both as to military and civill power for the performance of so hopefull a designe '. . . (Copy 1½ pp. in all), followed by Council of Trade Minute 27 Nov., 1660. Resolution of Council of Trade on Petition recommending that the matter contained in it be granted.
f. 10. ' Exportation of Gold and Silver in forreigne Coine and Bullion. The Opinion and humble advice of His Majesty's Council for Trade ' (1¼ pp.). Cf. *Cal S.P. Dom.*, 12 Dec., 1660.
f. 11-13. ' Reasons and Arguments for the free exportation of Gold and Silver in forreigne Coine and Bullion.' Four reasons given, the fourth makes particular reference to the East Indies (6 pp.).
f. 23. E.I. Co.'s Petition to the Council for Trade (Copy):
    ' Freedom of Trade to be granted to the E.I. Co. at the Spanish plantations on the Manillas, Phillipines and Molucco Islands in East

India.' Petition of Council to recommend to His Majesty that 'in the Articles now to be made with the Spanish Embassador it may be provided that this Company may have like freedom of Trade to all yᵉ said Spanish plantations and factories in East India, as to any port or place of the said King his Dominions in Europe (1 p.).

f. 24-26. E.I. Co.'s Petition. History of Spice Trade. Narrative of the 'Rise and Proffitts, impediments and losses of the East India trade and great damages and wrongs from the Dutch, and Petition that before the present Treaty of Alliance with the Embassador of the United Provinces be concluded your Petitioners may have their demands of damage done them by the Netherlands East India Company adjusted and fully satisfied' (7 requests). 1660-61 (5½ pp.). The original of this is in East Indies Vol. V, 3 Jan., 1660-61.

f. 27-29. Report of the Council for Trade to the King on the above Petition, with Reasons and answers for advice given for protection of the E.I. Co.'s trade (5½ pp.).

f. 75-76. 'Instructions for yᵉ Councill of Trade.' (12 numbered Paragraphs, 3½ pp.) A duplicate is calendared [? *Cal. S.P. Dom.*] 1660, Nov. 7.

C.O. ³⁸⁹⁄₄ (formerly C.E.B. 93). It is labelled on cover: Colonial Entry-Book—Plantations General 1663-1664'; but it comprises three Letter-Books now bound in one, removed from *Trade Papers*, Nos. 126, 127, 128. The former *T.P.* 126 is the Out-letter book of Secretary Arlington, 1662-65; and *T.P.* 127, that for the year 1670-74. The former *B.T. Trade Papers*, 128, is the Out-letter book of Secretary Sir Joseph Williamson for 1674-78.

Each of these Letter Books had its independent paging marked in ink, but they are now re-numbered in pencil, No. 126 being continuously paged, No. 127, after an interval of blank pages, beginning a new numbering of leaves (pages 42 and 43 being wrongly bound between 57 and 58), and the new paging of No. 128 being continuous with that of No. 127. There is no table of contents.

Former *T.P.* No. 126. 'Bombaim affairs therein':

pp. 40-41. To Sir Abraham Shipman at Angediva. 26 Nov., 1663: 'Season of year not permitting to His Majesty to send succour he proposeth to do so in due time . . . His Majesty's support in making his complaints in yᵉ Court of Portugal . . .' with enclosure of 'a new power from His Majesty for yᵉ taking possession of yᵉ same place and Island . . .' (2 pp.).

43. To Sir George Oxenden, President of the E.I. Co. at Surat: Secretary's letter recommending good offices to Sir Abraham Shipman enclosing letter to Sir Abraham Shipman (1 p.).

44. King's letter to Sir George Oxenden to same effect. 26 Nov., 1663 (1 p.).

45. To Mr. Gary, Merchant of Goa. 26 Nov., 1663: Secretary's letter transmitting His Majesty's recommendation of all good services to Sir Abraham Shipman (1 p.).

49-50. To Sir Abraham Shipman. 14 March, 1663-64: Recapitulating letter of 26 Nov. . . . with addition suggesting that with the succour received he may 'make a shift to subsist well enough till upon a new representation of your condition His Majesty can take new resolutions . . .' (nearly 2 pp.).

pp. 51.   Postscript to the above, enclosing Bill of Exchange for 14,550 pieces of $\frac{8}{8}$ . . .

52-54.   Alderman Blackwell's Bill for 14,550 pieces of $\frac{8}{8}$ and letters of advice to Sir G. Oxenden relating thereto.   March 12 and 14, 1663-64.

55.   To Sir G. Willoughby :
Permission to return.   1663-64.

Former *T.P.* No. 127 :

pp. 1-2.   King's Letter to the 'Pengram Sultan of Jambee' concerning the trade of 'Our East India Company unto whom we have solely committed . . . the management of the trade of Our Kingdom to all the parts of the East Indies, and Correspondence with all the princes there . . .'
Refers to 1,000 parcels of pepper taken from the E.I. Co. and asks for orders, and care that no other injury shall in future be done to them.   31 [22nd] Jan., 1670.

3-5.   King's Instructions to Commissioners for Foreign Plantations [July, 1670] . . . 'Coppies of all previous Commissions and Instructions to Government, etc., to be procured, transcribed and entered in a book provided for the purpose, etc.'
Nine numbered 'Heads', possibly more given or intended, as there is no date or signature to the document (5 pp.), followed by several blank pages.

70-74.   King's Letter.   Warrant to Attorney-General to prepare Bill 'to pass the Royall Signature and Great Seale in these words . . . [appointing Standing Council] for all affaires concerning the Navigation, Commerce or Trade as well Domestique as Forraigne of these our Kingdomes and our said Forraigne Colonies and Plantations respectively . . . or which may at any time hereafter come into our hands . . . (Tangier onely excepted) and whether held immediately or by any other by vertue of Charters, etc. . . .' with full powers to the said Council.   Anthony, Earl of Shaftesbury to be President, Thomas Lord Culpeper Vice-President; John Evelyn a member (9½ pp.).   103 to 108 blank.

Former *T.P.* No. 128, 1674-78 : begins with new continuous paging on p. 109.

pp. 127, 129, 136, 137-38, 141.   Secretary Sir J. Williamson's repeated requests to ambassadors in Germany and envoys in the Mediterranean to send news and specified information relating to their respective countries and neighbouring lands.

156 and 157.   King's letter to the King of Bantam.   31 Dec., 1677.
Refers to the letter sent to the E.I. Co. giving an account of the murder of their Agent White, Mr. Willoughby and Mr. North.   'Hopes that impartiall justice will be done upon the Authors thereof', and requests protection for the present Agent, Robert Parker.   Thanks for a present of pepper.   A return of 150 'Barills of Powder' being sent (2 pp.).

158-61.   Blank.

161-73.   Transferred from *America and West Indies :* once *Plantations Gen.* No. 488, relate only to America, West Indies and Tangiers.

C.O. $\frac{389}{8}$ (former C.E.B. 95). This, formerly *Board of Trade, Trade Papers* 129, was the Out-letter Book of Secretaries Arlington and Coventry, 1674-80. It contains nothing relating to the East Indies.

STATE PAPERS: DOMESTIC

The *Calendar of State Papers—East Indies*, etc., containing documents culled from various classes and sources, ends with the year 1634.

The *State Papers—Domestic* contain the records of the Home Administration, and scattered amongst them are many relating to the East India Company. The Public Record office *Lists and Indexes*, No. XLIII (1914), forms the 'List of volumes of State Papers relating to Great Britain and Ireland, including the Records of the Home Office, 1782-1837, preserved in the Public Record Office', and supersedes List No. III, published in 1894. The new list now includes the series of Letters and Papers, Foreign and Domestic, of the reign of Henry VIII, also the Records of the Home Office and the Signet Office, to the year 1837, inclusive. In the new arrangement of papers, the designation of many described previously as Home Office Papers has been corrected, although this has entailed the 'scrapping' of printed references in the *Calendars of S.P. Dom.* for the reign of William and Mary.

In addition to the Records of each reign, loose papers, letters and drafts, grouped under the name of the sovereign, there are large classes arranged under subjects or according to the nature of the Records, such as Docquets, Naval, etc., and Various. The large and important series of *Entry-Books* comprises several groups. The large 'Unclassified' group begins in Vol. I (1661-62) with the letters, both Domestic and Foreign, of Secretary Sir E. Nicholas, whose letters are also contained in No. 10.

The same 'Unclassified' group contains King's Letters, and also Petitions. No. 39 (1672-73) contains Secretary's Letters, and documents relating to the War with Holland. A large number relate to warrants and passes.

The *Criminal Entry-Books* (Correspondence and Warrants) contain no records within the period with which we deal. The same may be noted of the Treasury Accounts.

The *Domestic Entry-Books* (Secretaries' Letter Books) now form from 1685 to 1782 a consecutive series embodying the two concurrent series of Letter Books which belonged to the two Secretaries of State who, up to the latter date, administered Home Affairs. From 1661 to 1685 their Letter Books will be found in the Unclassified Series, Nos. 1, 10, 17, 39, 43, 56, 62, 64, 68.

King's Letters were classed as a special series only after 1688. Early Royal letters must be sought in the General Series. Soon after the Restoration we find *Entry-Books of King's Letters* (one 'Secret') though not in unbroken sequence. *State Papers, Domestic—Entry-Books*, Nos. 3, 10, 24, 31, 42 (Unclassified) contain Royal letters for the period 1661-79, and Nos. 162 and 163 the Letter Book for the years 1676-89.

Drafts or Copies of King's letters will also be found in *State Papers, Foreign*, e.g. in *S.P. For. Holland*, 170 that of King Charles II to the States-General *re* the Ships *Bonaventure* and *Bon Esperance*; others in the C.O. Records.

Royal letters from foreign princes are included until 1689 in the General Correspondence of *State Papers, Foreign*.

Petitions 'previously bound in alphabetical orders in 3 separate series, amounting together to 35 volumes', were from the year 1671 incorporated in the Domestic Series. Entry-Books of Petitions are listed under *State Papers Dom. Chas. I*, Nos. 323, 403 (1636-40); *State Papers Dom. Entry-Books*, Nos. 13, 18, 33, 37, 46, 55, 61, 71 (1666-88); and Nos. 235-38 (1688-1702). A book of *Petitions and Miscellanea* (Committee of Trade), *S.P. Dom. Jas. II*, No. 5.

Navy Board papers after 1673 have been placed amongst the Admiralty Records.

The printed *Calendars of State Papers, Domestic Series*, are nearly complete from the reign of Edward VI (1547) to 1703. The year 1688, that of the Revolution, was originally intended to be the limit to the work. The still uncalendared intervals comprise the years from 1683 to 1689 and 1697 (William III) to 1702. The word 'Domestic' was chosen to designate the papers in the State Paper Office forming the correspondence of Home Affairs; the word 'Calendar' was intended to express their chronological arrangement. The methods followed, however, are not uniform throughout. The principle adopted in the earlier volumes was 'that of indicating rather than describing the contents of the papers', so that abstracts are short and often incomplete. In the preparation of the volume for 1591-94 of Queen Elizabeth's reign, it had already been found advisable to give more full descriptions.

For the reign of Charles I, the mass of papers was very considerable, including, as it did, many of a private character. In the first volume for this reign, the references to the East Indies (already frequent from the last years of Elizabeth) become fairly numerous.

The Papers of the Interregnum required special treatment. The first volume of Calendars of the regular series for this period deals principally with the records of the Council of State. Although the portions of the Order Books relating to colonial affairs have been omitted, we find references to a special 'Committee on the East India business', and in it and the subsequent volumes the East India Company, its trade, its ships, the purchase from it of saltpetre for the manufacture of gunpowder, a proposed loan, etc., are mentioned.

The Papers relating to the reign of Charles II (now calendared on the more extended plan) were immensely increased in bulk by the incorporation, with the Domestic Series, of whole series of documents either recently transferred to the State Paper Office, or rearranged. These classes included undated Papers, Petitions, Legal, Parliamentary and other Miscellanea, Board of Trade papers, Papers relating to the Navy, Papers transferred from the Foreign Series, etc. A very large number of entries from bound volumes, selected as 'Domestic', were embodied and placed in their chronological positions (amongst them many from the Papers of the Levant Company).

With the volume for the year 1671, it was decided to calendar the whole contents of the *Entry-Books*, thus including also those entries which relate to Foreign and Colonial affairs. Mention is made not only of the East India Company, but of the Dutch and French East India Companies and their ships.

From June 1673, Navy Board papers, previously classed as Domestic papers, were restored to the Admiralty records.

The Calendars and Lists and Indexes should themselves be consulted, not only for further details, but for the exact references to particular volumes. The following notes serve as suggestions only :

State Papers : Domestic—Interregnum

The history of the Colonies during this period still requires investigation. No copy of Cromwell's charter to the East India Company is known to exist. It was probably deliberately destroyed, thus sharing the fate of the original Parliamentary records of the Interregnum. Of the Acts and Ordinances from 1649-60, the Record Office possesses only printed or manuscript copies. The MSS. *Index of State Papers, Miscellaneous*, in the Search Room, contains much additional matter. *S.P. Dom., Supplementary*, 101, 103 refer to prizes in the Admiralty Court, etc.

State Papers : Domestic—Charles II

1665-66. The *Papers* and *Entry-Books* contain many documents relating to the sale of the Dutch East India prize ships and advances of money by the East India Company to the King on the prize goods.

1665. *S.P. Dom. Chas. II*, $\frac{449}{77}$. Contains the Draft Contract between the E.I. Co. and the Navy Commissioners (1682) for the use of two ships to bring home from Angediva the survivors of the King's forces.

1670. *S.P. Dom. Chas. II*, $\frac{273}{158}$. Mentions a report of the French King's resolve to trade to the East Indies.

1674. *S.P. Dom. Precedents* 1. f. 7. Provides for the Annulment of Letters Patent of 1643 granted to the inhabitants of Cornwall which might hazard the loss of English East Indian trade ; the latter 'being carried on by forts and factories' required special provision. (Cf. *Calendar S.P. Dom. Chas. II*, 1673-75, p. 291.)

1675. *S.P. Dom. Entry-Book* 43, p. 16. Two articles given in by the Dutch ambassador as the utmost he can yield in the matter of trade in the East Indies.

1677-78. *S.P. Dom. Chas. II*, $\frac{396}{171}$. Notes by Sir J. Williamson about the origin and history of the East India Company.

1682. The *Domestic Papers* of this year (the *Calendar* of which is in process of printing) contain *inter alia* much interesting information as to the E.I. Co.'s affairs, derived not only from the *Entry-Books*, but from two series of *News Letters* to Newcastle correspondents, from the Papers of Admiralty : e.g. Greenwich Hospital, 2 :—Great fear for safety of East India ships which recently sailed. Value of drugs, pepper and silk at E.I. Co.'s sale. Arrival and reception of the King of Bantam's embassy. French King's declaration concerning East India trade. King Charles's promise of support to the E.I. Co. Difference between the 'Turkey Company', and the E.I. Co. and H.M.'s attitude towards a new charter.

A large number of Sir Joseph Williamson's Notebooks and his Journals from 1667 to March 1669 are amongst the Domestic Papers of this reign. *S.P. Dom. Chas. II*, 396, No. 171, contains notes by Sir J. Williamson about the origin and history of the E.I. Co.

State Papers Dom. Chas. II, Nos. 420-450, are still uncalendared. A large number of these are undated.

Among the parchments and pamphlets of Case F (1660-77) is a list of goods from India containing many strange designations.

State Papers : Domestic—Jas. II

Nos. 1, 3, 4 (1685-88). Contain Letters and Papers.
No. 5. Petitions and Miscellanea (Committee of Trade).

State Papers : Domestic—William and Mary

There are two separate Collections for this period—the one known as *King William's Chest*, from their origin in his private cabinet, the second as *S.P. Dom. William and Mary*. The papers of the former collection begin in 1670 and continue to 1698 and later ; the letters and Papers of the second cover the period 1689-1702.

It is essential to consult the new List and Index and the Key to the references of this period, many of the latter having been altered since the Calendars of the William and Mary series were begun.

The *Calendar of State Papers—William and Mary*, and that of William III have now reached the year 1697, the volume for which is in progress. The letters preserved in *King William's Chest* are extremely important as regards foreign affairs in general, and those also of the Earl of Portland (written in French, whilst on a mission to Holland); but, their contents being outside the scope of the Domestic Calendars, they are barely touched upon therein.

S.P. Dom. King William's Chest 14, No. 42, contains an important Report by Sir John Somers, Lord Keeper to the King, on the Charter and Reconstruction of the E.I. Co., 12 Sept., 1693. (*Cal. S.P. Dom. William and Mary* 1693, 323-24.)

S.P. Dom. William and Mary 1, No. 56. Proceedings in the House of Commons, and reference to a Committee of the House, of a Petition of Charles Price and others respecting the seizure of their ship *Andaluzia*, first in India, and again in England, by the East India Company ; also of one from John and Thomas Temple for the sinking of their ship, the *Bristol*. The said Committee to consider the whole affairs of the E.I. Co.

S.P. Dom. William and Mary 2, No. 89. A printed abstract of the case of Samuel White against the oppressions of the E.I. Co.

S.P. Dom. William and Mary 7 and 8 for the year 1697, and *S.P. Dom. Entry-Book* 275, contain many references to the dangers of trade with the East owing to the war with France ; the convoying of ships ; the public transports of joy on the conclusion of the Treaty of Ryswick and the hope of ' very brisk trade ' on the cessation of hostilities at sea. Arrival of a fleet with a cargo of East India goods worth 6,000,000 pieces of eight ; and arrival of 15 Dutch East Indiamen.

S.P. Dom. Entry-Book 275, p. 315. Petition of E.I. Co. against pirates in India and their encouragement by the Governor of New York. Proceedings of the Lords Justices thereon, 5 Oct., 1697.

STATE PAPERS: FOREIGN

The State Papers relating to Foreign Affairs at the Public Record Office up to the year 1577 are all arranged in a single chronological series. From the year 1578 (date of the foundation of the State Paper Office by Queen Elizabeth) they are classified separately under countries, the general correspondence from English ambassadors and agents abroad being placed, where possible, with the papers of their place of origin.

These records are un-calendared from 1585 to 1702.

Public Record Office List and Indexes, Vol. XIX (1904) forms the List of State Papers, Foreign, preserved in the Public Record Office.

The chief classes included are:

Foreign Entry-Books, containing copies or extracts of Out-letters.

Foreign Ministers in England. This series begins only in 1689; the letters are Memorials from foreign envoys previous to that date being included in the General Correspondence.

News Letters, i.e. 'unsigned despatches, copies of foreign gazettes and news-sheets' sent by Agents abroad, classed under place of origin.

> The news contained in them is by no means restricted to the country whence they were sent. Those from Paris and The Hague are of particular interest for our purpose. Sir J. Williamson was not only an industrious collector of foreign news, but in 1674-75, he issued repeated instructions to the Mediterranean agents to forward news, etc., of their respective countries and neighbouring ones, specifying the information required.

Royal Letters. Up to the year 1688 drafts of King's letters to foreign rulers, as well as the letters of foreign princes, will be found in the General Correspondence of *State Papers : Foreign*, under their respective countries. From 1689 the separate collections classed as *Royal Letters* include little beyond an exchange of courtesies.

Treaty Papers and *Treaties* form two important classes, supplemented by the *Archives* of British Legations abroad. Treaty correspondence with Secretaries of State is comprised in the General series, not in these classes.

The *State Papers : Foreign* relating to Portugal, Spain, France and Holland all need to be consulted for various periods. Nor should it be forgotten that Denmark had her share in early colonization, and that Bergen in Norway was one of the havens of refuge of the E.I. Co.'s ships.

State Papers: Foreign—France

The history of early French expeditions to the Indies is authoritatively traced in Charles de la Roncière's *Histoire de la*

9

Marine française. Volume IV discusses the colonial programme of Henri IV and the attempts to carry it out, down to the year 1622. References are given to the Calendars of State Papers, Colonial and Domestic, for the periods treated, but the original documents of the Public Record Office do not appear to have been examined. No work of equal authority for the early French attempts in Eastern colonization exists in English.

Colbert's colonial policy, the foundation of the French East India Company in 1664, and the first settlement in Pondicherry, are dealt with in Vol. V. The authorities quoted therein are almost exclusively French and foreign ; but the records of the Public Record office also contain evidence of Louis XIV's determination to have a share in the East Indian Trade.

The Public Record Office possesses a series of copies (sent to England by Chauran) of the letters which Abraham van Wicquefort wrote from Holland to Paris, 1661-62. Lous XIV acted as Mediator between England and Holland in the treaty negotiations of 1665-66, and considerable light is thrown on English-Dutch relations by the letters of Van Beuningen, the Dutch envoy in Paris.

The records from 1688 to 1697 show traces of the difficulties encountered by Indian trade through war with France.

State Papers : Foreign—Holland

These are of supreme interest for this period, and the material is very extensive. The despatches of the English envoys at The Hague are of great importance, in particular those of Sir George Downing, appointed Resident at The Hague by Cromwell, re-appointed at the Restoration, and after the Dutch war sent again as ambassador from 1671 to 1672.

His correspondence is, unfortunately, scattered, his letters to Clarendon and Secretary Nicholas being chiefly in the Bodleian and British Museum Libraries. A few of his letters to Nicholas for the year 1662 are to be found at the Public Record Office ; those to Arlington from 1663-66 are nearly complete in the *S.P. Foreign: Holland Correspondence.* Verbatim extracts are printed in Dr. Nicolaas Japikse's *De Verwikkelingen tusschen de Rupublick en Engeland van* 1660-65 (Leiden, Thesis, 1900), which deals with differences between the Dutch and English from 1660-65, leading up to the second Dutch war.

For the years 1661-65 the Public Record office also contains a long series of letter-reports from Holland to the English Government from their Dutch correspondent, Van Ruiven, under the *nom de plume* of Bacquoy.

State Papers: Foreign—Holland, Vols. 60-220, contain the Letters and Papers for the years 1600-99.   Undated documents for the years 1660-85 are under No. 219. Nos. 221-23 (1689-97) contain the correspondence of Matthew Prior, Dr. W. Aglionby, Lord Dursley, Earl of Athlone, Lord Villiers, Abraham Kirk and Sir Joseph Williamson.

The following documents serve to illustrate the contents of this class:

S.P. For. Holland, Vol. 170 (1664):

p. 3. Charles Gringand to J. Williamson. 1 April, 1664 (old style). Though Sir George Downing requested the States-General to give satisfaction as to the list of Damages and other English pretensions, they left town without doing anything.

6-7. Sir George Downing. 1 April, 1664. His talk with De Witt *re* list of damages, the 15th Article of late Treaty: business of the *Hope-well*, *Leopard*, *Charles and James* . . . (4 pp.)

14. Spanish Ambassador (Gamaria), 8 April, 1664. Promise of Spanish King's joint aid with the States against Mediterranean pirates.

16, 18, 20, 22. Four copies of French Report of Occurrences. 14 and 15 April, 1664, between Sir George Downing and Duke of Holstein. A question of precedence.

31, 52. Sir G. Downing to Sir H. Bennet. His own account of the above.

35-37. Sir G. Downing to Sir H. Bennet. 8 April, 1664. *Inter alia*, Dutch nettled at the House of Commons discussion concerning question of obstructing Dutch trade . . . . p. 37, East Indies affairs discussed with De Witt. (5½ pp.)

54-57. Sir G. Downing to the same. 15 April, 1664. p. 55, Business of the Treaty for the East India and African trade. Towns of Amsterdam, Rotterdam and Horne deputed by the States of Holland to deal therewith.

58. Charles Gringand to J. Williamson. 15 April, 1664. 'Here is still great talk of a warre . . .'

60. R. Duke (The Hague) to J. Williamson. 15 April, 1664 . . . 'East India Actions are fallen 28 p. cent att Amsterdam . . .' (1 p.)

76-78. Sir G. Downing to Sir H. Bennet. 22 April, 1664. Again the question of precedence with the Duke of Holstein's Coach, the Courtesies due to Ambassadors, Residents, etc.

81. R. [? C.] Duke to J. Williamson. 22 April, 1660. 'The King of France has brought 4 ships at Amsterdam . . . It is said also that he is sending a fleet of saile to Madagascar to settle a colony there, it being a fitt place for him to pirate in, it being a place going to and from the East Indies.' (1 p.)

92-93. Sir G. Downing. 29 April, 1664. *Inter alia*, p. 93, 'a private conference with 2 or 3 of the principall of them whereby to trye how neere we can come to understand each other both as to the satisfaction for what is past and a reglement for the future in the East Indies and upon the Coast of Africa'.

96. Sir G. Downing to Sir H. Bennet. 29 April, 1664. 'East India Actions are fallen this week to 409 so that you see what opinion yᵉ people here have of a warre with England.' (2 pp.)

99. R. Duke to J. Williamson. 29 April, 1664. East India affairs at The Hague, Amsterdam, etc.

111-16. Sir George Downing to Sir H. Bennet (with enclosures). 6 May 1664. States of Holland satisfied with H.M.'s answer to Parliament.

Discussion of damages, etc. with De Witt.   List of damages to be ready in a few days.   Disagreement as to *Bona Esperanza* and *Henry Bonaventure.*

p. 117. R. Duke to J. Williamson.   6 May, 1664.   Dutch satisfaction. List of damages.   (1 p.)

119. Memorial of Sir G. Downing to States-General of United Provinces, 7 May, 1664, demanding speedy justice and reparation for injuries . . . Particularly deals with East India Company, and precautions for the protection of English trade in future.   (2 pp.)

122-27. 'Mons. Bacquoy', 10 May, 1664.   General Dutch news. Indignation of States-General at English demands. (11 pp.) Endorsed 'Matters prefatory to ye warre with England'.

130-32. Mons. Bacquoy. 12 May, 1664 and 13 May, containing Extracts of Resolutions of the States-General.

144. C. Gringand to J. Williamson.   13 May, 1664.   General news.

145. R. Duke to J. Williamson. 13 May, 1664. 'East India business. The States-General appointed 24 Commissioners to consider y^e business of *Bona Esperanza*, etc., in particular.'

148. Translated 'Extract out of y^e Register of the Resolutions of the H.M. the States-General.'   13 May, 1664.   Deliberation 'to desire y^e Lords of Holland to give order in their Province that the English may have expedition of Justice'.   ($\frac{1}{2}$ p.)

149. Sir George Downing to Sir H. Bennet. 13 May, 1664. Dissatisfaction in the provinces of Low Countries other than Holland. '"Why then" say they, "should we engage ourselves to spend our monies to maintain y^e insolences and violences of the East India Company" . . .'

152-55. Mr. Bacquoy.   17 May, 1664.   Reports news concerning English and Dutch.

156-60. Mr. Bacquoy. 29 May, 1664. Reports upon Sir George Downing's conferences with the Deputies of the States-General on the 25th of same month, *re* ships *Bona Esperanza* and *Henry Bonaventure*. (p. 159 ff.)

163-65. Sir G. Downing to Sir H. Bennet. 20 May, 1664. Reports meeting with Deputies of States-General *re* ships *Bona Esperanza* and *Henry Bonaventure*, and the meaning of the words *litem inceptam prosequi* in the 15th Article of the late Treaty; also a subsequent conference. Full discussion. An important document. ($4\frac{1}{2}$ pp.)

167. Notes [? of Sir J. Williamson].

168-72. Sir G. Downing to Sir H. Bennet. 20 May, 1664. Further report. Poleroon also mentioned.

170. (Inserted in the above) Chas. Gringand, 20 May, 1664. Reports Sir G. Downing's meeting and the Resolutions of the States-General; also concerning the words, *litem inceptam prosequi.*

173. Translated 'Extract of Resolutions of H.M. Lords States-General of the United Provinces' 27 May, 1664. Lists of damages caused to Dutch and English to be exchanged. No other pretensions to be produced by either side after the exchange of lists.

179-86. Mr. Bacquoy. Report 25 May, 1664, *re* Dutch E.I. Co., with copies of their letters to the States-General and one of Secretary Cuneus. (Important.)

187-88. States-General to King Charles II, 4 June, 1664, about the ships *Bona Esperanza* and *Henry Bonaventure*. (4 pp.)

p. 196. Mr. Bacquoy. 31 May, 1664. Concerning the ships *Bonaventure*
   and *Esperanza*. (6 pp.)
   205 to end. King's letter to States-General, *re* ships *Henry Bonaventure*
   and *Bona Esperanza*, May, 1664. Draft.

S.P. Foreign—Holland, Vol. 178 (1665-66). Of the numerous
papers in Dutch, the important ones in relation to East Indian
affairs are the despatches from Paris of Van Beuningen, relating
to treaty negotiations and the English and Dutch rival claims for
reparations, Poleroon, etc., and the conditions proposed by France
as Mediator.

S.P. Foreign—Holland, Vol. 179 (1666-67). Out of 84 papers
in Dutch, only 7 or 8 relate to East Indian affairs; but, as before,
Van Beuningen's are important.

The General correspondence of each country forms a distinct class under its own name, but these classes do not embrace
the whole of the records relating to the country.

The Foreign Entry-Books constitute a very important series
of 271 volumes comprising *Secretary's Letter-Books, King's Letters,
Précis-Books*, etc.

Vols. 17-19 include France (1669-89) Secretary's Letter-Books ;
Vols. 60-70, Holland (1672-1703), Vol. 65 (1674) containing the Journal of
   the Marine Treaty with Holland.
Vols. 164-200 of the Miscellaneous section include from 1603-1700 King's
   and Secretaries' Letter-Books dealing with more than one country,
   and including France, Holland, Denmark, Spain and Portugal. Vols.
   176-80 are the Journal of the Committee of Foreign Affairs, 1667-78.
Vol. 239 contains Instructions to Ambassadors, 1676-79.

S.P. Foreign—Foreign Ministers in England as a separate
class beginning in 1689, contain little relating to our period.
Volumes 1, Denmark (1684-1780); 37, Portugal (1684-1710); and
60, Sweden (1683-1709) have papers before that date. All earlier
correspondence is embodied in the General Series.

Foreign Ministers, 21, Holland (1689-1712) contains nothing
relating to the East Indies within the period. The papers before
1700 are connected with Admiralty appeals and seizures of ships
not engaged in Eastern trade.

S.P. Foreign—News-Letters. As we are reminded by a note
in the List, ' News-Letters are classified as far as possible according to their place of origin, but often contain despatches from
other quarters.'

Vols. 1-7 comprise Flanders, 1572-1711 ;
Vols. 9-23, France, 1580-1702 ;
Vols. 70-86, Italy, three series, from Genoa, Rome and Venice, covering
   the whole 17th century. Nos. 87-89 comprise Italian gazettes, 1664
   to 1684.
Vols. 90-92, Spain and Portugal, 1580-1731 ;
Vols. 95-98, miscellaneous advices.

Vols. 45-63 contain a long series for Holland from 1584 to 1706, and No. 122 Copies and Despatches sent by Dutch agents abroad to The Hague, 1662-68.

Royal Letters as a distinct class have already been referred to. In some instances entries before the dividing year 1689 will be found here.

State Papers: Foreign—Treaty Papers

Vols. 36-50 concern Holland, 1593-1623—1684-1716;
Vols. 8-15 relate to 17th century France;
Vols. 57-58 to Portugal, from about 1640 to 1777;
Vols. 64-66 to Spain, from 1597 to 1719;
Amongst the *Treaty Papers—Miscellaneous*, we may mention those relating to Breda, Vol. 73 (1667); Cologne, 75 and 76 (1673). See also for the Cologne Treaty *Archives* 219-38, and *State Papers Foreign—Germany (States)* No. 60, which includes negotiations at Cologne, 1673-74. The Grand Alliance (Holland, Empire and England) 1689-1702, in Vol. 104 for Ryswick (1697), see *Archives*, 257.

S.P. Foreign—Treaties. Reference should be made to *List and Indexes* XIX for the details of Treaties with Denmark, France, Portugal and other countries.

Of the long series of treaties with Holland the following are amongst the most important: No. 300 (1654), Treaty of Peace and Alliance between the Commonwealth of England and the States-General; 306 (1668), Treaty of Navigation and Commerce between Great Britain and the States-General; 313 (1674), Marine treaty between Great Britain and the States-General; 315 (1675), Articles between Great Britain and the States-General for preventing disputes between the British and Dutch East India Companies, and Ratification; 316 (1675), Declaration as to 9th Article of late Treaty; 317 (1677), Treaty between Great Britain and the States-General; 325 (1689) Naval Agreement, and 328 (1689) treaty between the same Powers for a renewal of former Treaties, and 329 (1689), respecting naval captures.

Of treaties with Portugal, that under No. 386 (1656) is the ratification of the Treaty with the Commonwealth of 1654.

No. 545 (*Marriages*) 1661, contains the ratification by Portugal of the Treaty of Marriage between Charles II and the Infanta, with the secret article for the surrender of Bombay.

Of treaties with Spain, Nos. 465 (1630), 466 (1667) may be instanced.

Copies and extracts of treaties (1639-1709) will be found under *F.O.* 95: *Miscellaneous—Treaty Papers* (cf. *Foreign Office Records*, List 41).

State Papers: Foreign—Archives (of British Legations).

Vols. 7-18 (1631-41) contain Gerbier's *Entry-Books*.
Vol. 26 France (1698) contains the Earl of Portland's *Journal*.

The series from Holland is again of great interest:

Vols. 92 and 93 (Holland) 1607-10 contain Sir Ralph Winwood's *Entry-Books*.

Vols. 94, 95, 96 (1616-18), Sir Dudley Carleton's *Entry-Book* and *Note-book*.

Vol. 97 (1624-25), the Earl of Oxford's.

Vol. 98 (1653), Negotiations with the Dutch Deputies.

Vol. 99 (1654), Proceedings at the treaty negotiations between the English and Dutch Commissioners.

Vol. 100 (1667-71), Papers relating to the Triple Alliance, and 101 (1672), the Entry-Book of Lord Arlington and the Duke of Buckingham.

Vols. 107-218 contain the important series of documents of the Levant Company from 1580, including the Charters from Jas. I and Chas. II.

Vols. 209-57 include the Treaty Papers of Sir J. Williamson's Collection (219-32 relating to the Cologne Treaty), and that of Sir Leoline Jenkins (233-38, Cologne ; 239-56, Nimeguen) ; 257 (1697) Sir J. Williamson's Journal relating to the Treaty of Ryswick.

For the Letters and Papers of Mr. Davaux, 1672-99, see F.O. 95, Nos. 543-77.

State Papers: Foreign—Archives. Vol. 219. One of Sir Joseph Williamson's special *Entry-Books* relates specially to East Indian Affairs. Inside the cover in his own handwriting is the following note : ' England and Holland. The Two E. Indy Companys. Copys of Papers put into my hands and otherwise layed by me together in order to ye Treaty at Cologne. 1673. J.W.' This volume apparently contains, arranged in chronological order, all the Petitions, Correspondence, etc. relating to the disputes between the two Companies, English and Dutch, from 3 April, 1668, to Oct. or Nov., 1669. The ' Discussions of the Various Articles ' are annotated. Table of contents at end of volume.

pp. 1-3. E.I. Co.'s Petition to the King touching ' things impracticable and doubtful in ye Treaty Marine', 3 April, 1668. ' Order of H.M. in Counsel on said Petition ' (same date).

3-7. ' Memorial presented to y^e Lords of y^e Councell, for Trade, and reported to His Majesty in Councill, April 10th, 1668.' Impracticability of 8th Article especially in India ' where there is no Admiralty in being, nor any Marine Officers . . .' ($4\frac{1}{2}$ pp.)

90-91. 'Memorial delivered to Lord Arlington, and Mr. Secretary Trevor, 2d July 1669, with the Articles drawn up together as y^e Companie's final proposals . . .'

91-97. The final Articles delivered with the foregoing Memorial. ($5\frac{1}{2}$ pp.) The volume includes letters from Van Beuningen and Sir W. Temple : two Memorials concerning Macassar, 10th and 13th May, 1669 ; and Dutch Articles transmitted by Sir W. Temple.

The *Transcripts* of State Papers and Manuscripts relating to English affairs existing in the Foreign Archives in Venice, etc., at the Record Office, and the *Calendars* of similar papers should also be consulted. The Calendar for the collections in

Venice and the libraries of north Italy has reached the year 1636. The last volume contains several references to the affairs of the English and Dutch Companies.

The List of Foreign Office Records to 1837 (P.R.O., *Lists and Indexes*, XLI, 1914), is a continuation of the List of *State Papers : Foreign*, No. XIX, 1904. The Class *Foreign Office, Miscellaneous*, i.e. F.O. 95, includes some collections dating from the seventeenth century, to which reference has already been made under *Treaty Papers*.

STATE PAPERS : MISCELLANEOUS

(*Domestic and Foreign*)

This large supplementary collection (a manuscript list of which is on the shelves of the Literary Search Room) includes many documents of great interest, in bundles still uncalendared, as well as bound volumes. They include a large number of notebooks and papers from Sir. J. Williamson's Collection, and Admiralty and Admiralty Court Papers for the Interregnum and the reign of Chas. II.

S.P. Miscellaneous, Nos. 97, 98 and 243 form an important collection of intercepted Dutch papers sent from Batavia in 1672. The contents of the three large bundles (now scattered between the three) fall into two related series. By far the largest consists of full legal documents and correspondence, and the appeal to the 'Bewinthebbers' of the Dutch E.I. Co. by Daniel Wichselhuijssen, Ordinary Councillor of Justice, in his prolonged litigation with Pieter Anthonis Overtwater, President of the Dutch E.I. Co. in Batavia, and Christian Poleman, whom he accused of private trade.

The legal documents (some of which are in duplicate) are dated from 1667 to 1672, and comprise amongst the evidence, letters or interrogatories of Daniel Six, Monsieur Bogaart, etc.

In parcel 'No. 13' of Bundle 243 is a very long report signed Daniel Wichselhuijssen, to the Dutch E.I. Co. in Holland concerning 'Matters to the Company's advantage in the East Indies': 192 points annotated in the margin and several special enclosures, labelled from Liber A. to Liber H. Liber E. relates to private trade. 'Pallia-cut, Bengal, Surat' are included. Liber H. includes 'Proof that India cannot be kept except by a chartered company', and refers to the English and French.

Bundle 243 also includes the original despatches addressed by the President and Council at Batavia, 31 July, 1672, to the 'Bewinthebbers' of Amsterdam, Zeelandt and Delft respectively, two in the original wrappers, as sent by the English ship the *Advance* via Bantam and England. (The copies addressed to the Chambers of Enckhuijsen, Rotterdam and Hoorn are in Bundle 98.) Every copy bears the original signatures of the Governor-General, Joan Maetsuyker and seven members of the Council. The copy addressed to Amsterdam contains the List of Documents to Zeelandt. Of the seven entries, Nos. 2, 3, 4 and 7 are missing. No. 1 is the original letter above referred to, dated 31 July, 1672. No. 5, of which the only copy is now paged 1-12, contains certified copies of protests between the [Dutch] and the officers of the French fleet near ' Trincquemale '. No. 6, of which one copy also is present, contains copies of resolutions concerning the French in and near Ceylon. The English Company is referred to.

No. 1, the ' Original Despatch ', is a general report and includes paragraphs relating to ' Macassar ', Banda, Amboina, Ternate, Timor, ' Bima ', Palembang, Banca, ' Jambij ', Siam, ' Tonquin ', Japan, Malacca, West Coast of Sumatra, Bengal (p. 77), Coromandel (pp. 78-79), Ceylon (79-85), ' Tutucuryn ' (85), Malabar (85-86), ' Wingurla ' (86, refers to Portuguese in Goa), Surat (88-89, with reference also to the French), Persia (90-91), the Cape of Good Hope (91), and Batavia (92-94).

The same bundle, 243, also includes a letter from P. A. Overtwater, President in Batavia, 31 July, 1672, with the original seal.

RECORDS OF PARLIAMENT AND COUNCIL

Privy Council

The Proceedings of the Privy Council and the Orders in Council are recorded, though not always completely, in the Registers which contain the Proceedings before the Sovereign in Council, from the year 1598, and also those before Committees of the Council. The volumes from 1604 to May 1613 were destroyed by fire in 1618.

P.C. 2. Nos. 27-32 include James I, Vols. 1-6 ; Nos. 33 to 53, Charles I, Vols. 1-18, August 1645 ; Nos. 54 to 70, Charles II, Vols. 1-17 ; Nos. 71 and 72, James II, Vols. 1 and 2 ; and Nos. 73 to 78, William III, Vols. 1-6.

The Privy Council Registers had been printed complete to the year 1604 in the *Acts of the Privy Council of England*, 1542-1604, edited by Sir J. R. Dasent. A new series has been begun, of which two volumes have been published, relating to the years 1613-16 and 1616.

The separate *Colonial Series* of Calendars (the first volume of which appeared in 1909), comprises selected extracts and refers chiefly to the American Colonies.

Vol. I (1613-80) of the *Acts of the Privy Council—Colonial Series*, contains very little relating to the East Indies.

Vol. II (1680-1720) contains reference to the suppression of piracy in the East Indies in 1696-98.

Vol. VI (1676-1783) (Unbound Papers) contains a petition of the E.I. Co. (1696) and a Memorial, respecting the prevention of illegal trade by ships from the East Indies.

ACTS AND ORDINANCES OF THE INTERREGNUM

Of the Acts and Ordinances of the Interregnum from 1649 to 1660, the Record Office possesses only manuscript or printed copies, and the originals are not amongst the Records of Parliament, but appear to have been deliberately destroyed. A collected edition of the *Acts and Ordinances of the Interregnum*, 1642-60, was edited by C. H. Firth and R. S. Rait for the Statute Law Committee in 1911.

Of the two references to India the most important is to be found in the provisions of the Act of October, 1651 (which has been called the First Navigation Act), and the special proviso exempting ' East-India Commodities loaden in the Shipping of this Nation '.

In the Act of 9 Sept., 1652, calling home seamen serving abroad, seamen serving in the East Indies were allowed time for their return.

LEGAL RECORDS

Besides the Chancery Records, practically all the judicial records are technically in the custody of the Master of the Rolls. A summary of those of the various courts is contained in *Appendix II* (5) to the *1st Report of the Royal Commission Public Records*.

Although the local jurisdiction of the courts established in the Settlements was emphasized at an early date, many questions relating to the East India Company or to its servants will be found in the records of the higher Courts.

A large proportion of the Chancery Proceedings have already been indexed: comparatively few of the Exchequer Records have been calendared.

CHANCERY PROCEEDINGS

Chancery—(Equity Records) comprise Bills petitioning for redress where none could be obtained under Common Law, and Answers to these Bills.

The Bills and Answers in Chancery for the so-called ' Bridges Division ' for the period 1613-1714, comprising over 61,000 files, have now all been numbered and indexed under the plaintiffs' surnames. Public Record office *List and Indexes*, Nos. 39, 42, 44 and 45, form an Index to these Chancery Proceedings. In Vol. II, D. H. (No. 42) will be found a number of

entries referring to proceedings relating to money, in which the
Governor, etc., of the East India Company appear as plaintiffs,
and the following as defendants:

		Bundle No.
Ballard, John, and another (answer)	1695	157/26
Blake, William, and another	1670	57/16
,, ,, ,, ,, ...	1671	585/40
Carter, Jerome (answer)	1649	399/104
Chambers, Sir Thomas, and others	1668	52/20
,, ,, ,, (answer)	1669	54/35
Chappell, Roger	1666	420/92
,, ,, (answer)	1667	585/38
Clobery, Sir John, Kt., and Dame Anne his wife	1670	59/15
Cooke, Sir Thomas, Kt., and others	1695	168/57
,, ,, ,, ,, ...	1696	290/48
,, ,, ,, ,, ...	1697	157/57
,, ,, ,, ,, (answer)	1698	141/25
Dandy, Henry, and others	1694	157/4
Dunkin, Michael	1677	475/18
Firebrace, Sir Basil, and another	1697	129/8
,, ,, ,, (answer)	1697	293/16
Herne, Sir Joseph, Kt. (answer)	1698	364/44
Ken, John	1668	53/24
,, ,, (answer)	1668	585/40
Knipe, Edward, and another	1649	399/105
Lewis, Simon, and another	1678	475/19
Littleton, Edward, and others	1683	475/21
Mainstone, William	1675	475/17
,, ,, (answer)	1676	585/43
Perry, John	1695	157/7
Sambrooke, Samuel, and Mary, widow ..	1682	475/20
Stanton, Thomas, and others	1667	585/42
Wood, Edward, and others	1661	420/91

Amongst those who were bold enough to appear as plaintiffs
against the Governor, etc., of the East India Company may be
mentioned—John Gourney in 1675 (489/65), Urban Hall and
others in 1696 (367/39), Mary Hallett, widow, in 1669 (610/55);
and between 1703 and 1710, Edward Denham, John Frampton,
and David Edwards.

ADMIRALTY COURT RECORDS

No printed list of Admiralty Court Records is amongst
those of the Public Record Office. There are, however, a few
17th century Indexes and Calendars.

Select Pleas in the Admiralty Courts to the year 1602 have
been edited by Mr. R. G. Marsden in the Selden Society's
Publications. Extracts from the books and records of the
High Court of Admiralty and the Court of the Judges Delegates,
1584-1839, etc., are contained in his work, *Report of Cases*

determined by the High Court of Admiralty, issued in 1885. In 1899 *A Digest of Cases relating to Shipping, Admiralty and Insurance Law, from the reign of Elizabeth, to the end of* 1897, was also published by him.

Admiralty Secretary's Out-letters relating to Admiralty and Vice-Admiralty Courts and Business, from 1689 to 1702, will be found amongst the Admiralty Records, under Admiralty Secretary's Out-letters, Nos. 1045-48.

Accounts of receivers of prizes (1664-77) will be found under Audit Office Accounts. *A.O.* 3-3 (1) and (2).

The List of *Admiralty Records* in the Public Record Office, Vol. I., are printed in *Lists and Indexes,* No. 18 (1904).

Admiralty—Greenwich Hospital, 2, contains an interesting series of *News-Letters* to two Newcastle correspondents, with frequent references to East Indian matters.

NAVY BOARD RECORDS

Papers of the Navy Commissioners or Navy Board were included in the *Domestic State Papers* throughout the Commonwealth and Protectorate, and for the reign of Charles II until June 15th, 1673, date of the Duke of York's resignation of the office of Lord High Admiral, and were calendared as such. *Navy Board Papers* after that date have now been placed amongst the records of the Admiralty in the Public Record office.

For In-letters before 1822 see *Indexes* from the Admiralty, 1660-1822, Nos. 1-131. For In-letters 1688-1815 see *Admiralty Secretary's Out-letters.*

EXCHEQUER K.R.—PORT BOOKS

These documents, as disclosed in evidence before the Royal Commission on Public Records, are invaluable for the study of colonial settlement and expansion, the identification of names of ships, and the growth of export and import trade, and are of assistance in the genealogy of shipmasters. Their historical value is increased by the non-survival, as a class, of the original Customs Accounts, 'Exchequer Accounts (K.R.) Customs' from the time of Elizabeth.

The Port Books were issued yearly to all customers under an order of Queen Elizabeth giving very elaborate instructions for a new procedure. The parchment books were issued 'in tin boxes under the Exchequer Seal and were known as " the Queen's Books " because of the great importance in which they were held. In these books were to be entered, on the information of the merchants importing goods into London, the name of the ship and of its master, whence freighted, the bulk and number of

parcels of merchandise, their nature, and other particulars.'
(*First Rept. Roy. Com. Public Records*, Vol. I, Pt. II, App.
IV, 14.)

Exchequer, K. R.—*Port Books, I*, relate to the Port of London
and comprise 160 Bundles (Bundles 11 to 160 covering the period
1600-96), each Bundle, with very few exceptions, embracing
several numbers or volumes. It is therefore essential to consult
the MSS. List in the Search Room to find the volume desired.
References to the E.I. Co.'s. ships and goods to and from the
East Indies are numerous. *Port Book, London*, 52/1, 1667-68,
may be given as an instance.

BOARD OF CUSTOMS AND EXCISE

A typed MSS. List of the Records is on the shelves of the
Search Room at the P.R.O. The Inspector-General's Accounts
of Imports from 1696 to Christmas 1702 are to be found under the
reference, *Customs 2*, 1-10; the Ledgers of Imports and Exports
for Michaelmas 1697 to 1701, under *Customs 3*, 1-5.

Accounts of Farmers and Commissioners of Customs for
1638-41 will be found under *Audit Office Various Accounts*
(*Customs*), *A.O.* 3, No. 297, those for 1672 under No. 303 (9). No.
304 (7) contains Fines for uncustomed goods for the years 1667-
68.

The Treasury Records, *Customs, England and General*, comprise, under the reference T. 38, 349, charges of account in divers
ports *temp.* Elizabeth; 340—Abstract of yearly receipts 1679-
1761; 347—Yearly accounts of various duties, 1691-1700. See
List and Indexes XLVI.

TREASURY

The records of the Treasury are listed in Public Record
Office *Lists and Indexes*, No. XLVI. 'Lists of the Records
of the Treasury, the Paymaster-General's Office, the Exchequer
and Audit Department and the Board of Trade, to 1837, preserved in the Public Record Office (1921).'

The introduction contains a description of the various
series, and a table showing where correspondence with various
offices may be found when the titles of the series do not
sufficiently indicate this. India before 1832 is in the General
Series under the reference T. 27, which contains 16 volumes for
the years 1668-1702.

The earlier history of the Treasury is contained in the
Introduction to the *Calendar of Treasury Papers*, 1729-30.

T. 1 (1557-1837) *Treasury Board Papers*, are the In-letters
of the Treasurer with occasional minutes and reports; T. 27
Treasury: Out-letters, General.

The Treasury Books and Papers have been calendared in two different series: The *Calendar of Treasury Papers*, Vol. I. (1557-1667) to Vol. VI (1720-28), edited by Joseph Redington and comprising In-letters; and the *Calendar of Treasury Books and Papers* edited by Dr. W.A. Shaw, Vol. I, 1729-30, etc. The latter is outside the Period with which we deal; but his *Calendar of Treasury Books*, begun in 1904 and still in progress, commencing with Vol. I, Charles II, 1660, has now reached Vol. IX, for the year 1692. This series contains for the Period 1660-72 only documents in the Public Record Office, from 1672 to 1678, also papers outside it. The Records included in Vol. VIII are described as 'Letters Patent, Privy Seals, Royal Sign Manuals and Warrants, Treasury Warrants, Commissions, Orders, Letters, Memorials, Reports and other Entries: all not of the nature of Treasury Minutes'.

A gap in the Treasury Minutes at the Public Record Office extended from 1672 to 1696, and for the period 1672-78 the missing volumes were either in the possession of the Duke of Leeds (descendant of Lord Treasurer Danby) or at the British Museum. Leave to incorporate these documents was therefore obtained.

Reference to the excellent indexes of the series will disclose a very great number of entries relating to the East India Company and connected subjects.

Amongst Treasury Records we may mention the following:

T. $\frac{27}{16}$ (1698-1702) contains several entries relating to the E.I. The Semi-Official papers of Lord North forming the series of T. 49 *Miscellanea—East India Papers*, begin only with the year 1702. T. $\frac{48}{21}$ (7) Loose documents in a large bundle of the Lowndes Miscellaneous papers comprise several documents of interest.

'Draft Letters Patent constituting the [East India] Company by writ of Privy Seal.' (Endorsed East India Company 1698.) Pigott, 5th September, 10 Will, annotated in pencil: 'There are 2 drafts, the 2nd imperfect. The first I think with marginal notes by Lowndes. The 2nd is apparently the corrected draft with marginal guides.' (Printed, 24 pp.)

The constitution of the Dutch East India Company [undated? 1698]. A very clear account in English. (1 p. and a few lines.)

Letter from Court of Directors of the E.I. Co. to William Lowndes *re* appointment of Mr. Walker as Lieutenant in their service on William Lowndes' recommendation.

H.M.'s order to Lords Commissioners of the Treasury to sell H.M.'s Stock in the Old East India Company, $\frac{15}{26}$ August, 1701.

Warrant for Privy Seal for sale of shares in East India Company. (Undated draft.)

Attorney-General (Ed. Ward) on the rights of the Crown *re* the E.I. Co.'s Petition, 5 William and Mary. Refers to Charter of Chas. II., 3rd April, 13 Chas. II. Relates to Interlopers and the share of the

Crown in Seizures; with a Schedule of 'some shipps and vessells with their tack, apparell, freight, and goods seized upon by the E.I. Co. since the year of Our Lord 1680', by Capt. Andrews, Capt. Tyrell, and others. Mention is also made of 'All the Stores of the Interlopers at Suratt' under the Charge of Mr. Banister and others. (Copy, 43 pp.)

Heads for Articles of Agreement between the two East India Companies (i.e. Old and New) . . . 1701. (MSS. Draft, $3\frac{1}{2}$ pp.)

Fair copy of the same under 46 heads, 'proposed to be inserted in a Tripartite Indenture to be firmed under the Great Seale of England and the Common Seales of the two Companies.' ($4\frac{1}{2}$ pp.)

Tripartite Indentures of Union between the two East India Companies (Old and New), 1701. Reference is made to doubts raised as to the validity of former charters, financial agreements with the State, etc, (Draft, 68 pp.)

Quinquepartite Indenture of Conveyance of the Dead Stock of the two East India Companies (i.e. the Old and New), 22nd July, 1702. Bombay held as of the Manor of East Greenwich in Free and Common Socage on yearly payment of £10. Recites rights and possessions of the Old East India Company. (Printed, 17 pp.)

ACCOUNTS

Declared Accounts—Audit Office

(Cf. P.R.O. *Lists and Indexes*, II)

Bundle 1540. Lotteries, Annuities, etc. Roll, 31 July, 1698-1700; refers to Monies raised by lottery for the payment of annuities, and for settling the East Indian trade.

Bundle 1948. Pepper, Roll 1, 1 Oct., 1640–31 March, 1641, contains accounts of pepper purchased from the East India Company.

Trade, etc.

Bundle 2303 contains amongst other the following accounts:

Date	Name of Accountant, etc.	Roll
1673	J. Lock, Secry. and Treasurer to the Council for Trade and Plantations	2
1674 June— March, 1675	T. Bedford, Secry. to the Commissioners to treat with the Commissioners of the Netherlands	3
1696 March— March, 1701	W. Popple, Commission for Trade and Plantations	1

Public Record Office documents and Calendars are included in the long list of records examined and discussed in Professor William Robert Scott's authoritative work, *The Constitution and Finance of English, Scottish and Irish Joint-Stock Companies to 1720*, 3 vols., Cambridge University Press, 1910-12.

Details of the classes of Record Office documents consulted are given in the full list of *Authorities*—MSS., Collections of Papers, Official Publications, Books, Articles and Pamphlets, prefixed to Volume I. The financial history of the East India Company and of its joint-stock rivals is fully treated.

APPENDIX

Published Calendars of Records and uncalendared intervals:

	First Year	Last Year
Calendar of State Papers, East Indies	..	1634 (end)
Letters Received by E.I. Co. from Servants in East	..	1617 (end)
English Factories in India	1618	1664
Calendar of Court Minutes, etc. ..	1635	1663
Calendar of State Papers, Domestic (Edw. VI–Chas. I)	1547	1649
Calendar of State Papers, Dom., Commonwealth	1649	1660
Calendar of State Papers, Dom., Charles II. ..	1660	1682 in progress
Calendar of State Papers (uncalendared to William and Mary, 1689)	..	..
Calendar of State Papers (uncalendared to William and Mary)	1689	1697 in progress.
Calendar of State Papers, Foreign	1558	1585
Calendar of State Papers (uncalendared to Anne, 1702)	..	..
Calendar of Treasury Books (W. A. Shaw, edit.) ..	1660	1692 in progress.
Calendar of Treasury Books and Papers	1587	1728
Acts of the Privy Council	1542	1616
Colonial Series	1613	1720
Unbound Papers	1676	1783

MSS. RELATING TO THE EAST INDIES IN THE BODLEIAN LIBRARY

MSS. RELATING TO THE EAST INDIES IN THE BODLEIAN LIBRARY

1599-1600. **Travels of Sir Anthony Sherley in Persia** [Published 1613]. *MS. Ashmole 1809.*

1600. **The chiefe places where ... Spices do grow in the East Indies, gathered ... by R. Hakluyt.** *Western MS. 3338 (now MS. Arch. Selden B. 8), No. 6, fols. 84-93.*

f. 86. Some notes on the value of diamonds and pearls.
f. 89. Notes by Hakluyt of the best merchandise to bring from the East Indies to Spain.
f. 93. Notes of the best merchandise to take from Spain to the East Indies, etc.

1601. **Letter from Sir Thomas Cornwaleys to Sir John Hobart of St. Mary's Spital,** dated Brome, 17 Aug., 1601. *MS. Tanner 285, fol. 10.*

He mentions that an Ambassador has been sent to the Pope from Persia to pray His Holiness to send emissaries to preach and convert.

1605. **Charter granted to the East India Company by James I.** *MS. Rawl. D. 701.*

1609. **Abstract of the Patent granted to the East India Company,** 31 May, 1609. *MS. Tanner LXXV, fol. 322.*

1610-67. **The Travels of Peter Mundy, Cornishman.** *MS. Rawl. A. 315.*

The greater part of this valuable MS. is concerned with India and the East.

From 1628 to 1634 Mundy was in the service of the East India Company. His experiences during that period have been edited by Sir Richard Temple and printed by the Hakluyt Society (Second Series, No. XXXV, *The Travels of Peter Mundy*, Vol. II) in 1914.

From 1635 to 1638 Mundy was in the service of the Courteen Association and accompanied a fleet which sailed to the Malabar Coast, Sumatra, China, Mauritius, Madagascar, St. Helena and Ascension. These adventures have also been edited by Sir Richard Temple and printed by the Hakluyt Society (Second Series, Nos. XLV, XLVI, *The Travels of Peter Mundy*, Vol. III, Parts I and II) in 1919.

In 1655 Mundy made a third voyage to India (Malabar Coast) in the *Aleppo Merchant*, a Separate Stock ship. This portion of the MS. is in course of preparation for the Press and will be issued uniformly with the preceding volumes as Vol. V (Vol. IV being concerned with Europe only) as soon as completed.

The remarkable powers of observation evinced by Mundy, and his wonderful accuracy in chronicling what he saw and heard, serve to render his MS. of the highest historical value.

c. 1624. **Reply to a remonstrance of the** *MS. Rawl. C. 280.*
Dutch East India Company in
which they justify their proceedings
against the English at Amboyna.

1626. **Letter from T. Lydgate to the** *Western MS. 27569*
E.I. Co., dated 22 November, 1626. *(now MS. Bodl.*
313), fol. 32.

He petitions to be employed as a scholar. The letter contains remarks on the erection of a factory and the planting of a Colony on the East Coast of Africa, notes on the Equator, etc.

1629-96. **Moral Blazonry, a Poem by** *Western MSS. 16493*
Robert Fleming on the Company *(now MS. Rawl.*
of Scotland trading to Africa *Poet. 202), fol. 16.*
and the Indies.

1631-32. **Licence to the E.I. Co. to transport** *MS. Rawl. D. 918,*
foreign and English gold to the *fol. 138.*
East, dated February, 1631-32.

1636-37. **Papers connected with Sir William** *MS. Rawl. A. 299,*
Courteen's Expedition to India *fols. 188-225.*
and China, 1635-38.

f. 188. 14 February, 1636-37. A coppie of a letter from Beer Buddra Naige [Vira Bhadra Nayak] Kinge of Mallinar [Malnad], dated the 14th of February, 1636, translated out of the Canara language into Portuguez, and Englished.

This letter is reproduced in the *Travels of Peter Mundy*, ed. Temple, Vol. III, Pt. I, p. 74.

f. 188a. 1 March, 1636-37. A second lettre from the Kinge [of Bhatkal].

This letter is also reproduced in the volume noted above, p. 92.

f. 189. 12 March, 1636-37. A third letter from the Kinge.

Reproduced on p. 93 of the volume noted above.

f. 190-198 (198-200 blank). 14 April, 1636–1 April, 1637. Journall conteyning the memorable passages in the voyage of the shipps *Dragon*, *Sunn*, *Katharine*, *Planter*, *Ann* and *Discoverie* for East India. Begunne from the Downes, le 14 April, 1636.

This document is a duplicate of *State Papers, Dom. Chas. I*, CCCLI, No. 30, at the Public Record Office. Nearly the whole of the account has been incorporated in the volume of *The Travels of Peter Mundy* noted above.

f. 200b—205 (206 blank). 1636 [?1637]. Accounts of merchandise sold during the voyage. Endorsed : A Calculation of what goods are sould, and what Remayne for the proceede of the Voyage. These accounts give the values of the goods sold in 'Sherefins, Tangs, Vints, Basaks', and in £. s. d.

f. 207. 4 May, 4 and 17 June, 1636. Consultations held aboard the ship *Dragon* on the outward voyage. (Duplicates on fol. 214.)

f. 208. 17 July, 1636. A Coppie of the Directions for Rendezvous, etc. given Mr. Miller, Master of the *Ann*, with the provisions ordered to be delivered her le 17th July, 1636. [The *Ann* was unable to keep up with the fleet and was left behind to find her way alone to Goa.] (Duplicate on fol. 215.)

f. 208-10. 26 September, 1636. Consultation held aboard the ship *Dragon*. Publication of orders by the Commanders of the fleet. Three consultations were held on board the ship on this date.

f. 210-11. 1 and 14 Nov., 1636. Further Consultations held aboard the *Dragon*.

f. 211, 213. 3 March, 1636-37. Ditto. 9 March, 1636-37. Ditto.

f. 212. 16 March, 1636-37. 'Commission and Directions for our Lovinge Freinds, Mr. Anthony Vernworthy appointed Cheefe Marchant of the Factory of Baticala, for the better mannaging of all such affaires and occasions of moment as may happen in the tyme of his Residence there.' Signed by John Weddell and Nathaniel Mounteney.

Printed in *The Travels of Peter Mundy*, ed. Temple, Vol. III, Pt. I., pp. 103-5.

f. 216. 4 April, 1637. Commission and Instructions for Captain Edward Hall, Commander of the *Planter*.

f. 218-21. 19 December, 1637. 'Coppy of the general Lettre sent to the Company per the Shipp *Katharine* from Macao, le 19th of Dec., anno 1637.'

Printed in *The Travels of Peter Mundy, op. cit.* as Appendix D, pp. 475-88.

f. 222. Invoice of goods shipped aboard the ship *Planter*.

f. 223-24. An undated copy of an answer to a letter from the President and Council of Surat, written at Goa.

The portions in the collection of papers noted above that have not been used by Sir Richard Temple are those that do not bear directly on Peter Mundy's Journal.

1640. **Log of the *Frances* to Madagascar.** *MS. Rawl. A. 334.*
An ordinary seaman's journal.

1640-43. **A booke containing the knowledge** *Western MS. 27766*
of divers precious Stones and *(now MS. Bodl.*
Druggs. *51), 46 fols.*

f. 18. A description of 23 precious stones and the 'true worth of cleare and neat diomonds . . . taken the 7th of July 1643'.

f. 22. A description with prices of 28 drugs sold in England, and remarks on comparative weights in London and foreign places. By N.B. [? Nicholas Buckridge.]

c. 1640- **Collections by Archbishop Usher,** *Western MS. 27611*
50. **chiefly relating to chronology,** *(now MS. Add.*
sacred and classical. *C. 297).*

f. 61. Note, signed by William Methwold regarding the current measures of time in the East Indies.

c. 1645. **'The Case of several of His Majes-** *MS. Rawl. D. 916,*
tys Subjects of Great Britain who *fol. 158.*

have a just, legal and equitable demand
on the East India Company of Holland
for the principal sum of £151612 sterling besides the Interest thereof for
many years past.'

The claim is for ships belonging to Sir William Courteen and Sir Paul Pindar,
seized in 1643-44.

1646. **Memorandum of the sailing of the** *MS. Ashmole 846,*
Loyalty from Carwar, 18 April, *fol. 153.*
1646, with the names of six men
who died on the voyage.

1646. **An account of the voyage and** *MS. Ashmole 846,*
state of the ship *Loyonesse* **by** *fols. 155-56.*
'Jos. Brookhourn', captain, dated
Saldania Bay, 1 Oct., 1646.

(Copy) See O.C. 1999-2001 (India Office Records) for account of this ship in St.
Augustine's Bay, Madagascar, in Aug. 1646.

1646-47. **Epistuncula Jos. Thomps[on] ad** *MS. Ashmole 178,*
Lillium de annulo perdito cum *fol. 206.*
figura ab es inde posita, 6 January,
1646-47.

1647-64. **'Some writings belonging to Mr.** *Western MS. 36883*
Nicholas Buckeridge relating *(now MS. Eng.*
cheifly to Persian affairs during his *hist. c. 63), 90 fols.*
stay at Gombroon [Bandar Abbas] and
his residence at Ispahaun : collectted
by his son B[aynbrigge] Buckeridge.'

This MS., which is damaged by damp, contains valuable remarks relating to trade
in the 17th century, directions for Voyages in the Indian Seas, Journals of travel, etc.
The most important items are :
N. Buckeridge's petition to the ' Ettaman Doulett '.
A set of *farmans* from the King of Persia, ' Shaw Sephi '.
A list of *farmans* with translations of certain of them into Latin, English, etc.

f. 15, 34, 80.   Lists of prices of commodities in Persia and in England in
1658-59.
f. 27.   An account of the river ' Quadran'.
f. 29, 30, 66.   Directions for buying taffeta, diamonds and pearls.
f. 35.   Accounts kept by John Lewis at Isfahan, 1647-48, with a list of
presents, prices of horses, etc.
f. 43, 44, 56.   Journal of voyages to Macassar in 1655-57 and instructions for such voyages.
f. 46.   Dry measures of Cochin.
f. 50, 51, 73.   Voyage to Mozambique, 1651.
f. 54.   Instructions for Nicholas Buckridge at Mocha.
f. 59.   Consultation held at Bender [Bandar Abbas] 1659.
f. 73.   Instructions for Mr. Buckridge for the Coast of Sofala.
f. 73.   Contains a good impression of the seal of the E.I. Co.
f. 75.   A list of presents, prices of goods, at Isfahan, etc.

f. 81.   A list of the Company's yearly charges in India, Persia, etc.
This MS. also contains some Dutch and Portuguese documents at fols. 58 and 61.

1650-51.   **Joseph Thompson to Elias Ash-**   *MS. Ashmole 826,*
mole describing his voyage to   *fols. 245-46.*
the East Indies. Dated Bantam, 31
January 1650-51.

At the Cape some time was spent in repairing their ship, the *Golden Fleece.*
Bantam was reached 25 Nov., 1650.   A short account of Bantam is given.   The writer
thanks ' my Lady ' for her ' Morefield favours '.

1653,   **Copy of an Agreement between**   *MS. Rawl. C. 366,*
22 Dec.   **the E.I. Co., and Sir John Jacobs**   *fol. 98.*
and others, the late farmers of the
Customs.

The farmers admit that £90,859 is due to the Company on bonds, the 29th
Aug. 1640.   They agree to pay £18,450 and to give security for the remainder.   The
Company accept the terms, of which full details are given.

[1654.]   **Translations of Remonstrances of**   *MS. Rawl. A. 15,*
the Netherlands E.I. Co., against   *fol. 542.*
the E.I. Co., of England.

They complain that the English began to reckon their pretended damages from
1620 although they fail to observe the Treaty of 1619.   They hope that the Protector
will enforce the observance of the said Treaty.   The States-General desire that their
request may be communicated to their Commissioners in London.

[The document is very faint and damaged.]

1655,   **Copy of an order by Oliver**   *MS. Rawl. A. 261,*
9 May.   **Cromwell respecting the sale of**   *f. 44.*
the island of Pulo Run, by the
English E.I. Co.

The Protector orders that ' an instrument for the delivering up of Polaron Island,
with an acquittance ' for the £85,000 to be paid shall be drawn up and given to the
Ambassador of the United Provinces.

1655.   **Report delivered to Oliver Crom-**   *MS. Rawl. A. 28,*
well, June, 1655, from a Com-   *fol. 710.*
mittee of reference, respecting the
sale of Pulo Run, with the opinion of
Dr. Walker.

This document is printed in Birch's *Thurloe Papers,* III, 515.

1655.   **Statement regarding the East India**   *MS. Rawl. C. 366,*
Co.'s debt.   *fols. 111, 117.*

f. 111.   The debt arose from a glut of pepper, few purchasers and the
King's pressing need for money, which necessitated forced sales.
f. 117.   30 Oct., 1655.   It was agreed, on the motion of Nathaniel Wyche,
that £6,000 should be paid to the creditors of Sir Job Harby.

1658.   **Translation of a letter from the**   *MS. Rawl. A. 58, fol.*
Netherlands E.I. Co. to their   *272.*

Govr.-Genl. and Council of India,
dated 12 April, 1658.

They have received complaints that acts of hostility against the English E.I. Co., in violation of the Treaty of Peace of 1654, have been committed, and they enjoin a strict and punctual observance of the said Treaty.

1658-60. **Copy-Book of Letters received at** *MS. Rawl. C. 395,*
Fort St. George. *110 fols.*

This book contains letters from Surat and Rajapur, from the factories subordinate to Fort St. George (Masulipatam, Peddapalle, Viravasaram, Madapollam), and from the Bay of Bengal.

All the letters have been abstracted by Mr. William Foster, and the abstracts (in MS.) are bound in the volumes of the India Office Records catalogued as Factory Records, Miscellaneous, Vols. 29-31.

Further, Mr. Foster has utilized all the matter of interest in his *English Factories in India*, Vol. X.

1661. **The Charter of Charles II to the** *MS. Rawl. B. 516,*
E.I. Co., dated 13th yr. of his reign *fols. 1-15.*
(1661) with Table of Contents, fol. 16.

1660. **Fragment of the Log of the** *MS. Rawl. C. 963.*
***American* in November, 1660.**

See the Log of the *Nathaniel*, 1678-79.

1661-91. **List of amounts of Dividends paid** *MS. Rawl. A. 245,*
by the E.I. Co. from 1661 to 1691. *fol. 2.*

No names of shareholders are given.

1661-97. **Account of appointments of Agents** *MS. Rawl. 747 D.,*
at Fort St. George. *fols. 171-71a.*

A few lines are devoted to remarks on each Agent and the document is endorsed 'Secretary's Report to the Committee of 11'. It is signed by Robert Blackborne, Secretary, and dated East India House, 23 April, 1698.

1662-97. **Dividends paid by the E.I. Co.** *MS. Rawl. D. 747,*
fols. 140-41.

1663. **Reply of the States-General of the** *MS. Ashmole 857, pp.*
United Provinces to King Charles *234-35.*
II's letter of the 18th December, 1662,
relative to the surrender of Pulo Run.
Dated Hague, 18th January, 1663, N.S.
(French.)

They assure His Majesty of their desire for friendship with England. They enclose their orders to their General in India as a proof of their good faith in carrying out their agreement.

1664. **Mercantile accounts kept by Will-** *MS. Ashmole 1809.*
iam Smyth in the year 1664.

[1667.] **Note of Proceedings in the Case of** *MS. Rawl. D. 658,*
Thomas Skinner v. the E.I. Co. *fol. 21a.*
in the House of Lords.

For a full account of the Case, see Brit. Mus. MSS., Harleian MS. 4319.

1668. **Account of the French East India** *MS. Rawl. A. 478,*
Company (in French). *fol. 59.*

A brief note only.

1668. **Grant to the East India Company** *MS. Rawl. B. 516,*
of the Island of Bombay, 27 March, *fols. 17-27.*
1668.

Begins : 'Charles the Second by the Grace of God ', etc., and ends, ' in the twentyeth
yeare of our Reigne '.

See also MS. Rawl. B. 516, fols. 17-27, for another copy : and C.O. 77/49 (P.R.O),
pp. 47-75.

[1669.] **Complaints to the Company from** *MS. Tanner XLIV,*
Fort St. George. *fols. 94, 95, 100.*

Letters from the Factors at Fort St. George to Daniel Sheldon in Bengal together
with a Remonstrance to the Company, complaining of the sending out of two laymen to
officiate as clergymen.

1669. **Court at Whitehall, 13 Oct., 1669.** *MS. Tanner XLIV,*
fol. 162.

Concerning a complaint by factors and others at Fort St. George and Masulipatam
against Hoare and Thompson, ' two schismatical and seditious ministers'. Order
promulgated for their recall.

1670. **Bill of Lading of the** *Berkeley* *MS. Rawl. A. 303,*
Castle **from Swally Marine for** *Art. 47, fol. 236.*
England, 13 Dec., 1670.

1670. **Bill of Lading of the** *Constantinople* *MS. Rawl. A. 303,*
Merchant **from Bantam for Eng-** *Art. 47, fol. 229.*
land, 29 Dec., 1670.

1670-71. **Bill of Lading of the** *Ann* **from** *MS. Rawl. A. 303,*
Bantam to England, 30 Jan., 1670-71 *Art. 47, fol. 277.*

1673. **Money lent to Charles II by the** *MS. Rawl. D. 864,*
unanimous consent of the E.I. Co. *fol. 59.*

1673. **Accounts of an engagement be-** *MS. Rawl. A. 185,*
tween the English and Dutch *fols. 386-91.*
fleets in the neighbourhood of
Masulipatam, 22 August, 1673.

f. 386-87. Account by Captain Goldsborough of the *Antelope*, taken
by the Dutch. He imputes the disaster to the rashness of Capt.
Basse. The *Antelope* sank the day after her capture. Casualties, 16
killed and wounded.

f. 388-89. Account by Capt. Jonathan Hide, Vice-Admiral, dated 'Ship *Dannida*, Metchlepatam Bay, 21 Sept., 1673'. He was 'laid for dead', and recovered to find the Dutch in possession of his ship. Capt. Basse could 'easily have shunned engaging'.

f. 390-91. Account by Capt. William Basse, Admiral of the fleet. He is of opinion that if the whole fleet had 'stood to the enemy, we might have worsted them', but four of the captains 'bore away', and his defenceless condition compelled him to do likewise.

See O. C. Nos. 3835, 3836 (India Office Records) for two other accounts of this action, and O. C. 3824 for Capt. Basse's ?original account of the same.

1673.	**Charter of Charles II. dated 16 Dec., 25th of his reign, granting St. Helena to the Co.**	*MS. Rawl. B. 516, fols. 28-35.*

1674-75.	**Minutes of the proceedings of the Royal Commissioners** appointed to treat with the Dutch Deputies regarding trade and navigation and the Treaty regulating the East India trade of both nations, 27 July, 1674 – 8 March, 1675.	*MS. Rawl. A. 302, fols. 7-75.*

The meetings were held at Fishmongers' Hall, and a list of those present at each meeting is given.

The proceedings are concerned with the 12 propositions presented by the E.I. Co. 'importing their desires' with respect to the Treaty:

(1) Concerning the besieging and blockading of towns, cities, etc.

(2) Reciprocal non-interference with trade.

(3) Contracts with natives.

(4) Procedure if either country be at war with any native power.

(5) Passports.

(6) Losses and damages to be adjusted by an umpire. See also C. O. $\frac{77}{49}$ (P. R. O.), pp. 76-93.

(7) The island of Dam to belong to the English E.I. Co.

(8) Native residents to remain undisturbed.

(9) Privileges in the ports of either nation.

(10) Subjects of both nations to be undisturbed in their trade with Indians.

(11) Bribery of native officials to be prohibited.

(12) Procedure in case of war between England and Holland.

These points are fully discussed with many references to the Treaty Marine.

11 March, 1674-75. The Articles were finally presented to the King after the Dutch Commissioners had left the country, before which the English and Dutch Commissioners dined together on the date noted above.

1676.	**Charter of Charles II, dated 5 Oct., 28th of his reign, granting additional privileges to the Company.**	*MS. Rawl. B. 516, fols. 56-57.*

1675-76.	**Journal of a voyage to and from Surat, kept on board the merchant ship *Ann*,** Samuel Chamblett commander, by John King.	*MS. Rawl. A. 299, fols. 28-74.*

The log, which is an ordinary seaman's journal, begins 11 March, 1675, and ends June, 1676. The ship sailed from Gravesend and returned to Woolwich. See O.C. 4164 (India Office Records) for instructions, 17 Jan. 1675-76, for the homeward voyage.

1676-77. **Fragment of the Journal of the** *MS. Rawl. C. 963.* **Nathaniel in January 1676-77.**

See the Journal of this ship in 1678-79.

1678-79. **Journal of a voyage in the mer-** *MS. Rawl. C. 963,* **chant ship** *Nathaniel,* William *fol. 67.* Stannard commander, from Gravesend to Madras and back to England, 1 January, 1677-78—20 September, 1679.

This is an ordinary seaman's journal. At the end of the MS. is the fragment noted above. At the beginning of the MS. is one leaf of the Log of the *American,* bound from [?Swally] to ' Sinda', and thence to Gombroon. The captain's name is not given.

1679-80. **Coins of India.** *MS. Rawl. C. 841,* *fol. 1.*

'A collection of coins now current in the Kingdoms of Indostan, Persia, etc., with their severall weights, fineness and values at this present 1679-80.' [One page only.]

c. 1681. **Case between the E.I. Co., and the** *MS. Rawl. A. 183,* **Turkey Companies concerning** *fol. 232.* the right of the latter to trade with Mocha.

The chief points urged are the following :

Queen Elizabeth's grant to the Company of Merchants of England trading into the Levant, that they and no others should trade within the Grand Seignior's Dominions, was confirmed by King James I.

Mocha is in the said Dominions.

Sulaiman the Magnificent conquered Aden (where Mocha is situated) and held it until the year 1632.

Charles II, by Letters Patent of 3 April in the 13th year of his reign, granted all the trade beyond Cape Bona Esperanza, including Mocha, to the E.I. Co.

The E.I. Co. for the last sixteen years have ' declined ' the said port and have forbidden any trade thither by their factors in India.

His Majesty's Commission of 30 Nov., 1664, ordered a trade to Mocha.

In 1664, therefore, a ship was sent thither, but miscarried on the homeward voyage, since which time the Company have not traded there.

In view of the above statements these questions are propounded :

(1) Admitting that the Turkey Company's grant was the earlier, can the E.I. Co. prohibit the Turkey Co. from trading to Mocha.

(2) Whether the E.I. Co. can seize the ship now expected from Mocha by virtue of their grant.

1681. **Propagation of the Gospel in the** *MS. Tanner* **East.** *XXXVI, fols. 57,* *67, 86.*

21 June, 1681. Letter from Dr. Fell to Archbishop Sancroft regarding the intention of the Company to raise money for the propagation of the Gospel in the East.

1 July, 1681. Report of the Committee appointed to consider Dr. Fell's propositions.

6 Aug., [1681]. Letter from Dr. Fell to Archbishop Sancroft. The appointment of clergy to serve in the East is vested by the Co. in the Archbishop of Canterbury and the Bishops of London and Oxford.

1683-85. **Case against Thomas Sandys for trading to the East Indies** contrary to the Company's Charter (A. 193), with Pleadings and Judgment in the case (C. 130). [And see below.] *MSS. Rawl. A. 193 and C. 130.*

1683. **Pleadings in the case of Thomas Sandys** *versus* **the E.I. Co.** *MS. Rawl. D. 747, fols. 20-135.*

Duplicate of MS. Rawl. C. 130 noted above. See also Harl. MSS. 769, 1222, 4139 and Lansd. MS. 1219 (Brit Mus.) and All Souls Coll. MS. 210.

1683. **Commission and Instructions from the E.I. Co. to Sir Thomas Grantham** for declaring war against Persia, dated 27 July, 1683. *MS. Rawl. A. 257, fols. 69-70.*

The Commission gives the following reasons for the attitude of the Company :

By the Charter of Charles II of 3 April, 1661, the Company are empowered to make war on non-Christian countries.

By ' ancient stipulation ' with the King of Persia, the Company have the right for ever to half the customs of the port of Gombroon and other privileges in return for the help given by the English in taking the island of Ormus from the Portuguese.

Only 1,000 tomands, instead of 40,000, have been paid cf late, so that a debt of 150,000 tomands has accrued.

Sir Thomas Grantham is therefore authorized to make war upon the King of Persia.

When he has taken what he thinks due to the Company, he may make peace with the King, provided that he exacts the payment of the 150,000 tomands and receives a promise of payment of the half-yearly customs. In return, the English will protect the King against the Portuguese.

Sir Thomas Grantham's sailing orders :

He is to sail to St. Helena, Pepper Bay and Bantam, where he will meet with ships under Sir John Wetwang and Captain John Nicholson. He is then to proceed on his Persian voyage and finally to make his way to Bombay and Surat.

1683. **Further instructions to Sir Thomas Grantham regarding his procedure at Bantam,** dated 1 August, 1683. *M.S. Rawl. A. 257, fol. 79.*

He is to be careful to keep on friendly terms with the Dutch at Bantam and to victual his ship and procure arms and ammunition without their knowledge.

See also O.C. 5186 (India Office Records) 23 August, 1684, for Sir Thomas Grantham's letter to the Company, with a brief account of his proceedings ; also O.C. 5186, 5234,

5235, 5236, 5250, 5256-5262, 5282, 5301 ; MS. Rawl. A. 257 (Bodl. Lib.) ; MS. All Souls Coll. 210.

1683.   **Sir Josiah Child to Secretary Black-**   *M.S. Rawl. A. 303,*
            borne, dated 8 Aug., 1683.   *fol. 260.*

He orders that the bills of Wm. Coke and Basil Herne be referred to Messrs. Serle and Jarrett for examination.

1683.   **Instructions from the E.I. Co. to**   *MS. Rawl. A. 257,*
            their Agent and Council at   *fols. 81-93.*
            Bantam and Batavia, dated 24 Aug., 1683.

The main points in these voluminous instructions, 94 in number, are :

The object in sending Mr. English and the *Beaufort* and *Amoy Merchant* before the rest of the fleet to Bantam.

Method of treating with the King of Bantam for delivering up ' Pollypanjany and Hippins ' Islands and the fort, city and country of Bantam.

The appointment of a Governor, etc., after such cessions.

What the ships are then to do.

The sealed orders.

Building of houses.

No interference to be permitted with native religions.

Ammunition.

Orders to be carried out if it shall prove true that the ' Old King hath retaken Bantam'.

Wherever they may settle and fortify, the same rules are to hold good as to government, &c.

Hippins Island to be called Carolus Secundus.

Regulations regarding building, the importing of slaves, guns, collection of revenue, marriage of soldiers with the native inhabitants, English planters, Dutch settlers, etc., etc.

1683.   **Commission from Charles II to**   *MS. Rawl. A. 257,*
            Captain John Nicholson for a   *fol. 95.*
            mission to Bantam, dated 5 Oct., 1683.

See above, Sir Thos. Grantham's Commission.

1683-1711.   **Lists of the ships of the E.I. Co.**   *MS. Rawl. D. 747,*
                                                        fols. 136, 189, 382,
                                                        384, 386.

These lists give the name of the vessels and their commanders, tonnage, number of men and guns, cargoes outward, designation ; also, in some cases, dates of sailing and return.

1683-84.   **Abstract of a letter to King Charles**   *MS. Rawl. A. 257,*
               II from the inhabitants and   *fol. 97.*
               soldiers of Bombay, with com-
               plaints against the E.I. Co., dated 28
               Jan., 1683-84.

1684.   **Address to King Charles II con-**   *MS. Rawl. A. 257,*
                   cerning   an   insurrection   at   *fol. 72.*
                   Bombay, dated 15 August, 1684,
                   signed by four members of Council
                   acting as a Committee of Secrecy.

This, with the preceding, and three following, entries, deals with Keigwin's rebellion
at Bombay.   Further voluminous information on the subject is to be found in the O.C.
collection (India Office Records) for the year 1684.

1684.   **Order from King Charles II to**   *MS. Rawl. A. 257,*
                   Captain Richard Keigwin and   *fol. 75.*
                   others to restore Bombay to the Com-
                   pany, dated 23 Aug., 1684.

1684.   **Commission from King Charles II**   *MS. Rawl. A. 257,*
                   to the President and Council of   *fol. 77.*
                   Surat for reducing Bombay in case of
                   further resistance, dated 25 Aug., 1684.

1684.   **Instructions to the officers at Surat**   *MS. Rawl. A. 257,*
                   for the reduction of Bombay,   *fol. 91.*
                   dated Aug., 1684.

1685.   **Order from King James II to the**   *MS. Rawl. A. 257,*
                   insurgents at St. Helena to deliver   *fols. 178, 180.*
                   up the Island to the Company, dated
                   14 April, 1685.
                   Commission to the Governor-
                   General, etc., at St. Helena to
                   proceed against the insurgents
                   according to martial law, dated 14
                   April, 1685.

1685.   **Sir Josiah Child to William Addis,**   *MS. Rawl. A. 303,*
                   dated 6 May, 1685.   *Art. 51, fol. 238.*

He notes the death of Isaac Tillard, our ' former [shipping] correspondent ', and
requests Addis to act in his place at Plymouth should any ships arrive or depart.

1686-87.   **War with the Mogul.**   *MS. Rawl. A. 257,*
                                                           fols. 253-70.

   f. 253.   Case of the Company for declaring war against the Great Mogul,
by Sir Benjamin Bathurst.   The Company had a *farman* for trade
and paid only two per cent custom until the Dutch and Interlopers
persuaded the Mogul to impose 3½ per cent; both at Surat and
in Bengal.
   The Company originally had privileges and power to recover their
debts ; now they have to apply to Darbars or Courts of Justice, and
are compelled to pay one half in order to recover the other half of
the whole due to them.
   The Company can get no satisfaction for the £160,000 owed them
by the Mogul.

The Dutch say that they will force the Mogul to exclude the servants of the Company and all Europeans from the Bay of Bengal, by making war upon his subjects there.

By their Charter the Company have a right to make war upon heathen nations, but a further Commission direct from the King is desirable.

f. 255. Draft of a Commission to the King's ships to make war on the Great Mogul in behalf of the E.I. Co.

f. 256. List of ships designed to be sent out with the above Commission.

f. 259. Instructions from the Company to their Agent and Council in Bengal respecting war with the Mogul, approved by King James II, January, 1686-87.

f. 270. Instructions to the Councils of Surat and Bombay respecting the same, approved by the King.

1687. **List of ships abroad, 1 May, 1687.** *MS. Rawl. A. 189, fol. 119.*

1687-89. **Log of the** *Royal James and Mary* *MS. Rawl. A. 323,* **from Gravesend to Bombay,** Commander James Cooke, 4 Aug., 1687— *127 fols.* 14 Feb., 1688-89.

4 Aug., 1687. Departed Gravesend.

30 Sept., 1687. Reached St. Jago. Owing to a drought, very little beef to be obtained.

30 Oct., 1687. Cape of Good Hope. Sheep, barley, etc., taken on board.

8 Jan., 1687-88. Some bales of the Company's cloth put out from the hold to air. A storm such as the writer was 'never in before', and hoped 'never to be in again'.

1 April, 1688. Saw 'Zeloan'. Rough drawings of the coast of the island.

5 April, 1688. Some drawings of the coast near Cape Comorin.

19 April, 1688. Off Tegapatam, on the Malabar Coast. Sent a man ashore at Retora to visit the Company's factory there. He returned with Mr. Daniel Acworth, chief of the factory, and Mr. Caleb Travers, who came on board. A description of 'Brinjon' and of the coast about Retora follows. The officials from Retora reported that, although they had been entreated to establish a factory there by the Queen of Attinga, their flag had been cut down, probably at the instigation of the Dutch. The Queen of Attinga next sent her delegates aboard the *James and Mary*, and much consultation ensued, after which the Queen renewed her promise of protection to the English.

23 May, 1688. Arrived at Bombay.

1 June, 1688. Attended the trial by Court-martial of Lieut. James Dare, who was ordered to be 'discarded the Company's service', and to be sent home.

17 July, 1688. Captain Jacob Barber, who had been sent to rescue three soldiers who had fled from a ship to Thana, returned to Bombay after having been subjected to many insults.

10-16 Aug., 1688. The Company's cordage, nails, ironware, etc., were unloaded.

17 Aug., 1688. John Gladman and John Jesop were sent on board to inspect the quicksilver which had been running out of its package.

8 Oct., 1688.   Sir John Child, General of India, came on board to go to Surat.

31 Aug., 1688.   The Company's woollen goods inspected.

20 Oct., 1688.   Thomas Michell declared to be President of India.   The *Mirbar* or customs officer came on board to attend the General regarding the answer he was to carry to the Govr. of Surat respecting the conclusion of a peace.   The General deferred his answer until he should arrive at Surat.

22 Oct., 1688.   Preparations made in case of an attack by the 'Moors'.

24 Oct., 1688.   The General left the ship to go on the *Worcester*.

29 Oct., 1688.   The General refused to go to Surat to receive the King's *farman*, in spite of a promise of a safe conduct.

30 Oct., 1688.   The General went ashore, well armed.

31 Oct., 1688.   Further Consultations about the King's *farman*, 'not to the General's liking'.

2 Nov., 1688.   Orders for ships to be kept ready for defence in case of an attack.

3 Nov., 1688.   Propositions made to the General about the King's *farman*.

13 Nov., 1688.   An agreement reached.   The King's *farman* to be expected in 40 days.

11 Dec., 1688.   Arrival of the *Shrewsbury*.

24 Dec., 1688.   Some men from the *James and Mary* and *Shrewsbury* attacked by Frenchmen.

26 Dec., 1688.   News received that Agent Harris and Mr. John Gladman, Agent-designate for Persia, with others, were confined as prisoners by the Governor of Surat, and that there was a design to seize the General.

30 Dec., 1688.   By the General's orders, all the ships sailed from Swally Bar and anchored in the mouth of Surat river.

4 Jan., 1688-89.   The *James and Mary* sailed for Bombay 'with intent to apply to the Mogul about their grievances'.   Notes of encounters with various ships.

20 Jan., 1688-89.   Anchored at Bombay.   Various consultations.   Certain vessels examined for corn, etc., and seized.

12 Feb., 1688-89.   News of the severe treatment of the imprisoned Agent and his companions.

14 Feb., 1688-89.   The Journal breaks off abruptly.

1687-1710.   Lists of the Company's Servants (both of the Old and New Companies) with their salaries.   *MS. Rawl. D. 747, fols. 139, 164-68, 296, 379-80.*

These include :

f. 164-65.   1686   Bombay.
              1687   Surat—Calicut.
              1690   Gombroon and Persia.
              1692   Carwar.
              1693   Indrapura—York Fort.
              1694   Fort St. George—Fort St. David—Vizagapatam.
              1695   Chuttanutte—Ballasore.

f. 166-68.   1698   Fort St. Gerge—Fort St. David—York Fort—Sillebar.

f. 139, 296, 379, 380.   [1700], 1702, 1710.   Officers employed by both Companies.

1687-88.   **Abstract of advice from Fort St.**   *MS. Rawl. A. 302,*
         George, via France, dated 21 Jan.,   *fol. 91.*
         1687-88, including a letter from the Bay
         to the Fort, dated 26 Aug., 1687.

An advantageous peace concluded for the Company on better terms than ever before on account of the taking of several of the Nawab's ships by the English. The English lost but few men, though several died from sickness which had overspread the whole Coast of Coromandel and was due to the rotting bodies of those who had died of famine and plague. The Mogul has taken possession of Golconda and its King. Fort St. George in a good posture of defence. Nawab Shaista Khan, the Mogul's uncle, is recalled, and also the Surat Governor, for ' abusing ' the English. They have sent £80,000 on the *Resolution* and 50,000 dollars on the *Williamson* to Bengal, and 40,000 Pagodas to the West Coast. They have great hopes of future prosperity.

1688.   **Original copy of a representation**   *MS. Rawl. A. 171,*
         from Dr. St. John to the King   *fols. 52-59.*
         [James II] on the affairs of Hindustan
         and of the E.I. Co. Dated aboard the
         Success, 18 July, 1688. Enclosed in a
         letter from Dr. St. John to John
         Pepys, dated Windsor Castle, 29 Aug.,
         1688.

The MS. is very closely written. It contains a long account of Aurangzeb's wars with Sumbhaji, the siege and capture of Bijapur, the siege and capture of Golconda in 1687, the Embassy to Shah Sulaiman, etc.

The writer dilates on Aurangzeb's aversion to all Christians.

He gives an account of affairs in the Bay of Bengal and describes the bad state of the factory at Surat, and reports a better state of affairs there under a new Governor.

He remarks on relations between the Portuguese and the Mogul, the action of the French in Siam and the state of Dutch trade in India.

He complains of the despotic attitude of Sir John Child at Bombay and of the Company's ill-treatment of himself. (This MS. would probably repay for the work of transcribing *in extenso.*)

1689-1700.   **Bills of Exchange drawn on the**   *MS. Rawl. D. 747,*
            Company for providing Bullion.   *fols. 261-64.*

1690.   **Copy of a Letter of Complaint**   *MS. Rawl. D. 747,*
         against President Elihu Yale to   *fols. 234-50.*
         the Company, sent by the *Defence,*
         dated 20 Oct., 1690, and signed by
         Thomas Wavell, John Cheney, William
         Fraser and Thomas Gray.

This copy is dated 25 May, 1691, and the signatories remark : ' We could largely add to the same purpose, but that we know it would be unpleasant to your Honrs.'

(Abstract of the above on fols. 215-20, and duplicate of the Abstract on fols. 222-31.)

c. 1690.   **The East India Trade and Manu-**   *MS. Rawl. A. 400,*
         factures beneficiall to England.   *fols. 1-29.*
         Proved by severall Arguments Collected

11

on Occasion of a late Petition from
the Weavers to prohibit the same.

The writer maintains that the Petition of the Weavers needs 'some answering'.
He quotes an author (unnamed) who (urged by Mr. Pollexfen) writes to prove :

1. That the E.I. Trade in general is beneficial to England.

2. That the Importation of the Manufactures of India adds to the main stock and
wealth of England, and is not in general prejudicial to woollen manufactures.

3. That a prohibition of Indian manufactures will be destructive to that trade in
general, and 'hazard its being utterly lost to this Kingdome'.

The writer gives details of money saved by the reduction of the price of goods from
France, Holland, etc., owing to the trade of the East India Company in India and also to
their trade in China and Japan. The trade gives employment to many workers, and
'breeds good seamen'. The gain on goods bought in India is about a third of what they
would cost here. The prohibition of E.I. silks would hinder the woollen manufacture
and would cause the price of silks from France, etc., to rise again. The Dutch would then
be able to put their own rates upon their calicoes.

The effect of prohibition on the E.I. trade would be disastrous, for the profit of the
trade not only affects the Adventurers, but also the country. The Dutch would be the
gainers in India.

The conclusion arrived at is that the trade is really an advantage to the weavers.

1691-92. **Minute-book of the proceedings**   *MS. Rawl. C. 449,*
of the Committee for procuring   *fols. 1-35.*
the establishment of a new East
India Company, held at the Sun
Tavern, at the Bell in Nicholas Lane,
and at the Red Lion in Cornhill, from
12 October, 1691 to March, 1692, and
from 6 October to 26 December, 1692.

12 Oct., 1691.   Resolved to apply for a new Charter on a new Joint
Stock, not to graft : Sub-Committee to propose a Petition.

13 Oct., 1691.   Committee appointed to get the King's leave to address
Parliament.

14 Oct., 1691.   Heads of grievances against the Old Company read.

15 Oct., 1691.   Heads of grievances again discussed, and form of
preamble.

16 Oct., 1691.   Discourse of grievances and preamble.

17 Oct., 1691.   Grievances read and corrected. Copies of the Charters
of the Company ordered to be delivered. Bill in Parliament to be
prepared.

19 Oct., 1691.   Ordered that a copy of the Octroy of the Dutch E.I. Co.
be obtained and that Mr. Finch be attended with the grievances next
day.

20 Oct., 1691.   Draft of a Petition to Parliament read. Ordered that it
be signed forthwith. Charters of the E.I. Co. from Charles I and
James II read.

21 Oct., 1691.   Preamble confirmed. Form of words in which each
person shall subscribe to the preamble settled. Mr. Ince to find a
room for taking the subscriptions. The engrossed Petition produced
and signed by those present.

22 Oct., 1691.   The Petition to be carried up to the Lords. Grievances
read and ordered to be printed.

23 Oct., 1691. Orders as to attending the King about the Bill to Parliament.

24 Oct., 1691. Printed grievances read. Sir Christopher Musgrave to be asked to present the Petition, and, failing him, Sir John Guyse. The *farman* to be printed at the end of the grievances.

26 Oct., 1691. The King gives leave to deliver the Petition to Parliament.

27 Oct., 1691. The Duke of Bolton intending to subscribe £10,000, books are to be sent to him to that end.

28 Oct., 1691. Proofs of Capt. Pitt's charge against the Company debated.

29 Oct., 1691. Scheme of the Company's finances proposed. A Committee appointed for the same.

30 and 31 Oct., 1691. No full Committee.

2, 3 and 4 Nov., 1691. Ditto.

5 Nov., 1691. The condition of Surat to be enquired into. Copy of the E.I. Co.'s Order of Council, for permission to send out six ships lately built, to be obtained. Arguments used on behalf of the Co. to be examined.

6 Nov., 1691. Oppressions of the Company to be considered, so that proofs against them may be prepared. A paper read, of the objections made by the [Old] Company against the intended settlement. The Charter of 35 Charles II to be examined.

7 Nov., 1691. Heads of the Company's objections against the intended settlement read. Grievances, with proofs annexed, also read.

9 Nov., 1691. Committee of Accounts to prepare their accounts.

10 Nov., 1691. Report of a difficulty in obtaining a copy of the Charter of 35 Charles II. Ordered that the same must be obtained and a copy made.

11 Nov., 1691. Certain members were desired to attend Mr. Finch that evening.

12 Nov., 1691. The question put, whether the Committee would stand by such Members of Parliament as should engage in proposals to the House about the Committee's readiness to send out ships and stock for carrying on trade : carried.

13 Nov., 1691. Heads of the Petition against the E.I. Co. to be drawn out, pursuant to the order of Parliament : done accordingly.

14 Nov., 1691. Heads and proofs of the Petitioners' complaints read and approved.

17 Nov., 1691. Nothing done.

22 Feb., 1691-92. Resolved that some of the Committee wait on Sir Charles Musgrave, etc., about an address to the King, to determine the Old Company at the end of 13 years.

23 Feb., 1691-92. Order that the Company's Charter be delivered to the Members of Parliament who are to promote the address to the King.

—March 1692. Report of those summoned to attend the Cabinet Council.

6 Oct., 1692. This Committee to proceed in the same affair they began last Session of Parliament, namely, the procuring an E.I. Co. on a new Joint Stock, clear of all encumbrances. Agreed to raise £10 a man more for a fund for the expenses of the same.

21 Oct., 1692. Resolved that Lord Nottingham attend His Majesty for a speedy settlement of a new E.I. Co.

2 Nov., 1692. It was reported that a ' Person of honour ', having the King's permission to send 300 seamen in three or more ships to the

East Indies, gives the benefit of the same to this Committee upon their importing [blank] tons of saltpetre for the King. It is agreed that the offer be accepted, if it can be done without prejudicing the proceedings in Parliament for a New Co. Preamble drawn up to that effect.

3 Nov., 1692. The 'Person of honour' attended on. Petition to Parliament read.

7 Nov., 1692. The 'Person of honour' again attended on concerning the saltpetre. Capt. Pitt is desired to obtain the *Essex* and the *Royal Mary* for the New Co. if the owners will sell.

8 Nov., 1692. Concerning the above vessels. The owners are willing to sell. Seven managers appointed to arrange the business of the saltpetre.

9 Nov., 1692. Discussion as to the Petition to Parliament and the seven managers.

11 Nov., 1692. Nothing done.

14 Nov., 1692. Resolved that, in pursuance of the Petition to Parliament, the prosecution thereof shall be for obtaining a Bill for a New Company.

15 Nov., 1692. Draft of the Bill read and corrected.

18 Nov. 1692. Agreed that three persons chosen by the Board of the New Co. shall meet three persons appointed by the Old Company to debate matters.

22 Nov., 1692. Names of four masters of ships agreed on to transport 300 men to India.

24 Nov., 1692. Sir C. Levinz, Sir T. Powys and Sir B. Shower to be retained on behalf of the New Company here assembled.

25 Nov., 1692. Discourse about surveying the ships.

26 Nov., 1692. Report on the delivery of papers to the 'Hon. Person'.

30 Nov., 1692. No full Committee.

2 Dec., 1692. Ditto.

5 Dec., 1692. Order for 12 copies of the Order of Council and 10 of the Regulations to be provided.

8 and 12 Dec., 1692. No full Committee.

13 Dec., 1692. Mr. Coulson to prosecute the business of the ships with the 'Hon. Person'.

16 Dec., 1692. Discourse about docking the ships, etc.

20 and 21 Dec., 1692. No full Committee.

22 Dec., 1692. Appointment of new Chairman. Discourse about the 'Hon. Person's' ships.

23 Dec., 1692. Discourse about the said ships.

26 Dec., 1692. The names, of those fit to be appointed for the Committee in the Bill to be brought before Parliament, to be taken from the Subscription Book.

Resolved that the Bill in Parliament be vigorously proceeded with. With regard to the setting out of two ships for the Indies, each Member of Committee can be concerned therein or not, as he pleases.

1692-94.	**Sixty-one letters and notes to Rob-bert Blackborne, Secretary to the Old Company,** from Sir Josiah Child, 1692-94, with some scattered notes of earlier date.	*MS. Rawl. A. 303, Art. 47, fols. 202-311.*

These last appear in their chronological order.

f. 295. 4 April, 1692. Recommends the bearer, Mr. Read, as a Sergeant for Fort St. George and to go on board Capt. Newnam's ship at once. Dated from Wanstead.

f. 247. 10 May, 1692. Encloses draughts of what he thinks the Company should send immediately overland to Surat. He thinks they should give the security demanded by the Barons of the Exchequer. Captain Heath must fit the *Defence* for sea, to sail with the *Resolution*.

f. 250. 5 June, 1692. Concerning abatement of freight on pepper from Surat. Dated from Streatham.

f. 207. 6 June, 1692. Concerning 'our Adversaries' and prize money. He had opened the whole matter to His Majesty formerly. Dated from Wanstead.

f. 297. 2 July, 1692. If the Company can have 5 per cent for their saltpetre, it may be enough from their Majesties, although private persons give 5½ per cent.

f. 287. 15 July, 1692. Sir Josiah Child is going to Cannons. He hopes that he and Mr. Woolly will continue the correspondence. Dated from Wanstead.

f. 301. 22 July, 1692. He hopes that the Company will send out this winter at least four three-decked and eight two-decked ships. Dated from Cannons.

f. 203. 10 Aug., 1692. The Directors should insist on having twelve ships for the winter's exports, but at any rate five are absolutely essential. The *Resolution* should sail in October for Bombay, three more to the Fort and the Bay, and one to St. Helena and Bencoolen.
'The Lords may do with us what they will, as they have for 50 years past to my knowledge, to the great detriment of the Country and Company.'

f. 300. 1 Sept., 1692. Recommends Josiah Cliff to go to India as a factor by the next ships.

f. 210. 15 Oct., 1692. Concerning stores for their next shipping. 'I see noe consistance in the Bill for a new Company, and beleive it will come to nothing.' Dated from Streatham.

f. 223. 18 Nov., 1692. He does not doubt the Company's business will 'go to their content'. They should have 'Casa Punos a witness in their cause'.

f. 311. 26 Nov., 1692. He recommends Job Bright to go in the next ships for India. Dated from Wanstead.

f. 235. 3 Dec., 1692. The *Resolution* and *Defence* to go to Surat. Lead, cloth and kintlage to be provided for them, but no tin.

f. 304. 21 Dec., 1692. List of names of persons to 'give Mr. Norrey'. Dated from Streatham.

f. 288. 22 Dec., 1692. Requests that Mr. John 'Fidsherbert' may be entered for a factor for Fort St. George by the next ship. Dated from Streatham.

f. 224. 22 Dec., 1692. Concerning: a certain Indulgence; list of Stores; soldiers wanted at Bombay; the Company's settlement by Act of Parliament. Dated from Streatham.

f. 218. [? 1692.] Enclosing a draft of two letters for the Committee to correct, concerning matters of trade at Ispahan and Capt. Heath's accounts.

f. 219. [? 1692.] The three ships at Gravesend should be despatched immediately.

f. 262.   [? 1692 or 1693.]   List of ships about which Mr. Snelgrove has informed Sir Josiah Child, among them the *London* Frigate, etc.

f. 307.   5 Jan., 1692-93.   A recommendation to William Morris for factor to Bengal or Madras, and to his brother Bezaliel Morris to accompany him as a writer.   Dated from Streatham.

f. 303.   11 Jan., 1692-93.   Satisfactory news from India.   Arrival of the *Dorothy* from Madras.   Dated from Streatham.

f. 292.   3 March, 1692-93.   He hopes the Co. will be successful in their petition to Parliament.   He advises that 'Coja Panuse' should be paid without delay.   He desires that Mr. Bright, Sir Job Charlton's kinsman, now going to India as a factor, may change one of his securities for another, etc.

f. 286.   22 March, 1692-93.   He recommends that Mr. Cormell be permitted to go aboard his ship.   Dated from Wanstead.

f. 291.   22 March, 1692-93.   He desires that Capt. Heath's account may be settled, as otherwise he cannot go to sea.   He must consult the Govr. and the Dep. Govr. before finishing the Genl. Letter.

f. 293.   1 April, 1693.   An order for Mr. Poole, who was to go to Surat but was left behind, to sail in the *Defence*.   Dated from Wanstead.

f. 214.   11 April, 1693.   Notifying the transmission of letters to London.

f. 248.   13 April, 1693.   Concerning the bond of Mr. Poole's friend.

f. 267.   24 April, 1693.   He advises the departure of the Co.'s four 'Coast and Bay' ships.   There should be no danger from one Interloper since twenty have been baffled formerly.   He proposes that Capt. Oyles be ordered to fit his ship for India, with any other two or four to be found: protection could easily be obtained for six ships.   Dated from Wanstead.

f. 231.   25 April, 1693.   Mr. Charnock is to be advised that the Interloper has only permission to go to Madeira.   Dated from Wanstead.

f. 208.   19 Aug., 1693.   He returns all letters and papers except the abstract of the Fort Letter, which he keeps because he sees that Mr. Yale 'hath put in a charge against' Mr. Fraser, whom he is confident is an honest man.   Dated from Cannons.

f. 205.   8 Sept., 1693.   Concerning the sailings of the *Dorothy* and the charge for her freight.   Dated from Cannons.

f. 275.   22 Sept., 1693.   Regarding the sealing of a bond.   The Co.'s business is 'often in his thoughts' during his 'country leisure'.   Dated from Cannons.

f. 294.   9 Oct., 1693.   An introduction for the bearer to the Committee of buying of goods.   Dated from Cannons.

f. 279.   12 Oct., 1693.   He has agreed for an eighth part of Capt. Rang's ship, which is to go to Fort St. George and Bengal.

f. 211.   19 Oct., 1693.   Concerning the freighting of ships.   Sir John Morden is to be informed that the *Kempthorne* will be either laden or sold immediately.   A reference to Mr. Lightborn's 'second proposal'.

f. 309.   21 Oct., 1693.   The Co. and owners of the ship are willing that Capt. Oyles should depart from Gravesend the 20th Nov., and out of the Downs on the 20th Dec.   He need not carry kintledge.   Dated from Cannons.

f. 302.   5 Nov., 1693.   Concerning the selling of lead by the Duke of Bolton.

f. 265.   7 Nov., 1693.   He has 'discontinued Courts' for so many years that he is not willing to recommence attendance at them.   He

will, however, give advice. He thinks it best to obtain the opinion
of each individual adventurer as to whether such investor wishes the
return of the money invested or to be credited for the same in the
Co.'s books. Dated from Wanstead.

f. 264. 30 Nov., 1693. Remarks concerning the cargo of the *Dorothy*.

f. 249. 1 Dec., 1693. He has lent the King £6,000 on the Million
Act. He is about to purchase land which will absorb all the money
he receives from the Company, so that he cannot lend more than
£5,000. Dated from Wanstead.

f. 308. 5 Dec., 1693. He recommends that, at Capt. Heath's request,
the *Amity* have the same terms regarding her stay at St. Helena as
were accorded to the *Benjamin*. Dated from Wanstead.

f. 202. 13 Dec., 1693. He hopes that the Govr., does not intend to
buy two interloping ships, which would be a dead loss in time. The
freights this year are heavy. The Co. owe a voyage to the
Wanstead Frigate. Dated from Wanstead.

f. 222. 18 Dec., 1693. Concerning the sending of a new Chief to
Bencoolen. Remarks on the assassination of the Govr. of St.
Helena. Keeling suggested to fill his place. Dated from Streatham.

f. 259. 22 Dec., 1693. Sir John Goldsborough's project concerning a
Protestant Portuguese Church at Fort St. George is being carried
out and the English Liturgy is now being translated at Oxford.
Remarks on the proposition by ' Coja Panuse ' to calender various
goods.

f. 241. 26 Dec., 1693. The bearer, William Hicks, recommended as a
writer for India. Dated from Wanstead.

f. 230. ? 11 Jan., 1693-94. The petition of Elizabeth Child for the
Company's charity (though no relation of Sir Josiah) is recommended
to the Governor.

f. 281. 11 Jan., 1693-94. He returns the sealed packet with additions to
the Letter to Bengal and Madras. He enquires if Galloway is a safe
port. The *Dorothy* must not stop at Tonquin. Remarks about the
Protestant Portuguese church at Fort St. George. He has added to
the Fort Letter a clause about the numerous new adventures. The
same should be repeated to Surat and Bengal. It is reported that
Mr. Heath is about to creep out in an Interloper. If this is true, he
is not fit to be a factor. Dated from Wanstead.

f. 305. 15 Jan., 1693-94. Advice as to the sailing of the *Thomas*, the
sending out of bullion and the coining of it. The *Thomas* should
take out at least £50,000 for Surat. Directions about the cargo of
the *Thomas*. A paragraph to be added to the letter to Persia about
sending money to Surat and one to the Fort about coining silver into
rupees.

f. 289. 24 Jan., 1693-94. He sends a paragraph to be added to the
Bengal letter. He remarks on goods bought of the Armenians at
great profit to the Company. Dated from Wanstead.

f. 204. 29 Jan., 1693-94. Advice as to the sailing of Capt. Janaper,
the sailing of the *Martha, London* frigate and *Thomas*. The long
services of Mr. Ackworth, Chief of ' Retora ', should be brought to
the notice of the Company.

f. 276. 5 Feb., 1693-94. The Company's sealed orders should be
furnished to Mr. Langley as he is going where there is no settled
Council. He has been requested to procure certain stuffs.

f. 212. 9 Feb., 1693-94. Capt. Raynes must be at the head of the outgoing fleet. Next in command to him, Captains Hatton and Oyles. Remarks on the cargoes of the *Martha* and *Success* and on the treasure on board the *Nassau* and *Mary*. He suggests that a letter be written to Sir John Goldsborough and Council to send down the £30,000 required to Bengal by the *London* Frigate. As regards the indulgence requested by Capt. Hatton, the Co. will defer considering it until they know the result of the decision of Parliament with regard to their Charter.

f. 215.   20 Feb., 1693-94.   Concerning a present for the Governor of Surat, and a gratuity to Mr. Addis from the Co. for his services.

f. 226.   21 Feb., 1693-94.   He returns drafts of petitions to Parliament with remarks.   Note of the lading of saltpetre on the *Berkeley Castle* and the *Samson.*

f. 209.   3 March, 1693-94.   He requests a charterparty for the *Tonquin* of which he and Capt. Heath are owners, the Commander being Mr. Page Cable [? Keble].   Dated from Wanstead.

f. 232.   6 April, 1694.   If the *King William* sails for Surat on the 1st September, she may put in at St. Helena and carry rafts, deal boards, etc. also young people desirous of settling on the Island.   Dated from Wanstead.

f. 285.   12 April, 1694.   A recommendation of Mr. Waring to serve as a writer in India and to sail by the next Surat ships.

f. 266.   25 April, 1694.   Concerning Dr. Woodrif's bill and the binding of books.   Dated from Wanstead.

f. 310.   24 May, 1694.   Concerning the adjustment of all ships' accounts, the bill for the *Benjamin* and *Tonquin* : the shipping of soldiers on the Company's ships.   The *Tonquin* or any other ship cannot be expected to carry two tons for one.   Dated from Streatham.

f. 219.   30 May, 1694.   The Captain of the *Mocha Merchant* to be Admiral of the outgoing fleet, the Capts. of the *Tonquin* and the *Benjamin* to be next in rank.   Dated from Streatham.

c. 1692.   **Account of memorials for convoys**   *MS. Rawl. A. 449,*
          delivered to the Admiralty by the   *fol. 26.*
          Company and what ships have been
          appointed for that purpose.

1692.   **Resolutions of a Committee of the**   *MS. Rawl. A. 303,*
          Old Company for regulating the   *fols. 109-10.*
          East India trade. Dated 10 Dec.,
          1692.

1. The East India trade to be carried on by a Joint Stock.

2. The sum necessary for the purpose not to be less than £1,500,000 nor more than £2,000,000.

3. The duration to be for 21 years.

4. Joint Stock to be made up by new subscriptions.

5. No subscription to be less than £100 or above £10,000.

6. Subscribers of £500 to have one vote.

7. No subscriber to have more than one vote.

8. The Governor to subscribe not less than £5,000.

9. The Deputy Governor to subscribe not less than £1,000.

10. The export of the Co. to amount to at least £100,000 of goods.

11. No private contracts for goods to be permitted except for saltpetre for the use of the Crown.

12. The Company to sell to the King yearly 500 tons of saltpetre at £35 per ton.

13. No foreigner to have any interest in the Company or to be employed abroad.

14. No contract for transfer of stock to be valid unless executed within a week.

15. No lot exceeding £500 to be put up at a time, except jewels.

16. Dividends to be paid in money. No dividend to be declared without leaving the original stock entire.

The above was read a second time and agreed upon. It was moved that a Bill be brought in upon the said resolutions : ordered.

1692-94. **Six letters and notes to Mr. Woolley from Sir Josiah Child.** *MS. Rawl. A. 303, fols. 200, 233, 243-46, 290.*

f. 246. 31 Aug., 1692. A copy of Capt. Dorrill's charter desired.

f. 313. 1 Sept., 1692. He has received letters and newspapers ' which please continue to send, as I must take some measures in the Co.'s affairs from the more public occurrences upon which ours depend. Forget not to get a bill for B wharf signed next Court.' We have been ' almost 1½ years out of that money '. Dated from Wanstead.

f. 243. 5 Sept., 1692. 'The Govr. and Deputy Govr. agree that you should give an order to Capt. Oyles to survey the new ship at Mr. Dorsett's dock, which please dispatch.'

f. 244. 21 Sept., 1692. ' Pray hasten your Brother's Charterparty with the Company's Secretary, and if you can get the ship into the Downs next month she may go to China.' Dated from Wanstead.

f. 245. 3 Oct., 1692. It ' mightily imports ' the Company to hasten their ships ' with all speed '. Their ports to be fixed later, but the *Resolution* and *Defence* will be enough for ' Surat side '. Dated from Streatham.

f. 290. 1 Nov., 1692. He has looked over the Packet. He expected before this to hear that the pirates in India, who comprise all nations, Danes, Dutch, English and French, would cause trouble. He hopes that the disturbance was over before the *Kempthorne* came away. As to Sandys' many actions, the best way to bring him to reason would be a short Bill in Chancery. Dated from Wanstead.

f. 200. 27 April, 1693. He returns a letter with his signature. ' If I leave out what the Govr. would have altered, need write no private letter.' ' Nothing but an additional stock will do the Company's business and the dispatch of our ships before the season is lost.'

f. 233. 22 March, 1693-94. He has perused the charterparty for the *Tonquin* sent to him by Capt. Heath, ' wherein I have made some alterations.' The dates appointed for the departure of the ship from Gravesend and the Downs cannot possibly be complied with, but the *Tonquin* will be as forward as any. Dated from Wanstead.

1692-93. **Wm. Thorowgood to Secretary Blackborne.** Dated Wanstead, 21 March, 1692-93. *MS. Rawl. A. 303, Art. 58, fol. 280.*

Sir Josiah Child desires that the bearer, Mr. Bright, may go to Surat in the *Defence.*

1693.   **Case respecting a new Charter.**   *MS. Rawl. D. 747,*
                                                             fol. 137.

1693.   **Thomas Lewes to George Boun,**   *MS. Rawl. A. 303,*
                 dated 29 March, 1693.   *Art. 60, fol. 312.*

He desires that the Court may be ' moved ' to supply £500 for the pay of the soldiers on the Company's ships.

1693.   **Orders of the Court of the E.I. Co.**   *MS. Rawl. D. 747,*
                                                            fol. 143.

13 April, 1693. The Govr. presents his charges in the affair of a new Charter. The same to be settled.

24 Nov., 1693. The Govr. presents his charges in the affairs of management. The same to be paid.

c. 1693.   **Miscellaneous entries regarding**   *MS. Rawl. D. 747,*
                 the East India Co.   *fols. 396-400.*

Mr. Culliford's draught for the Court of Directors. Report about lead sheathing. Silver on board the men-of-war arrived in England. Abstract from the Letter Book of monies remitted to Holland and Cadiz. Regulations of the E.I. Co. with regard to their powers as an Incorporated Co.

1693-95.   **Sir Thomas Cooke's Accounts**   *MS. Rawl. D. 747,*
                 with the Co., 1693-95.   *fols. 153-57.*

1693-98.   **Memorandums relating to the**   *MS. Rawl. D. 747,*
                 Case of the Old East India   *fol. 175.*
                 Company.

Notes regarding the Company's Charters, issues of subscriptions, taxes imposed on them, with remarks on the effect likely to be produced by a dissolution of the Company.

1693-94.   **Sir Benjamin Bathurst to Secretary**   *MS. Rawl. A. 303,*
                 Blackburne, 10 Jan., 1693-94.   *Art. 48, fol. 216.*

The Admiralty have ordered the *Hampshire* to convoy the *Tonquin* under Captain Knox.

The five men imprested on the *Mary* are likely to be returned.

1693-94.   **Copy of bond £300 for the safe**   *MS. Rawl. D. 747.*
                 return of the *Dorothy*, dated 18
                 January, 1693-94.

Similar bond, undated concerning the *A*[?*nn*] of Lo[ndon]. Portion of a similar bond, undated.

1693-94.   **Orders of the Court of the E.I. Co.**   *MS. Rawl. D. 747,*
                                                             fol. 143.

22 Jan., 1693-94. Particulars of the disbursement of £30,000 laid before the Court—the said monies to be paid.

1693/94-   **Notes of ships from January, 1693-**   *MS. Rawl. D. 747,*
1699.   **94 to September, 1699.**   *fol. 181.*
      A few lines only.

1694. Report of a Committee appointed   *MS. Rawl. D. 747,*
to inspect the Books of the (Old)   *fol. 145.*
East India Company.

1694-95. Report of a Committee appointed   *MS. Rawl. D. 747,*
1 March, 1694-95 to inspect the   *fols. 145-52.*
Books of the Company as above.

1694-99. Payments for customs.   *MS. Rawl. D. 747,*
fol. 162.

1694-99. Description of the diamond mines   *MS. Rawl. A. 334,*
on the Coast of Coromandel.   *fol. 44.*

The MS. contains details of weights and prices and methods of trade in diamonds.

1695. A Coppy of a Protest delivered   *MS. Rawl. D. 916,*
President Annesley, etc., Councill   *fol. 161.*
att Surat 18 April, 1695. By R. B.

The protest concerns the sale to some Armenians of a bale of damaged cloth out of
the ship *Thomas* for near £1,000 less than its value.

1695. Parliamentary enquiry respecting a   *MS. Rawl. A. 82,*
charge of bribery on the part of   *fol. 78.*
the Company, April, 1695.

This MS. is concerned with the examination of Sir Thomas Cooke as to monies paid
to prevent the establishment of a new Company.

Begins : ' 23 April, 1695. All the Committee appointed by both houses of Parliament
pursuant to the Act of Parliament for Examination of Sir Thomas Cooke. The
Committee being met in the Exchequer Chamber, the Earle of Pembroke Lord Privy
Seale being first in quality acted as Chairman.'

p. 78 ends : ' Earl of Torrington. I doe not see you are like to reap any benefit by
asking of Questions. If he hath any thing further to offer I would be glad he would
speake it or withdraw.

' And accordingly he declareing he had nothing further to offer he withdrew.'

Charge : ' As to two sums of £67,000 and £10,000.' Sir Thomas Cooke to be
imprisoned until they are discovered ; £4,000 paid to one'man, £10,000 to Mr. Tissen and
another sum to him ' for service of the Company for preventing of a new Company
and for services about the Old Charter.' Also sums to Sir Basil Firebrace and others.
Sir Thomas Cooke is asked how these sums were disposed of. He replies that they were
used for the service of the Company and to prevent Interlopers and to obtain a Charter.
This is not considered a sufficient explanation. Mr. Richard Acton, who advanced
£10,000, cannot give any account of the transaction owing to his head being affected by
a fall from his horse.

The questioning of Sir Thomas Cooke is continued and the case is apparently not
completed in this MS. See also Harl. MS. 7310, fol. 199 (Brit. Mus.).

1695. Copy of a letter from J. D. Dolben, a   *MS. Rawl. A. 302,*
merchant at Canton to [?] dated 11   *fol. 126.*
November, 1695.

He congratulates the addressee on selling his cloth. He reports that merchants at
Amoy have ' sent their Factors hither ' to buy up considerable quantities of silk, but the

Hoppo has put a general embargo on them, hoping thus ' to prejudice the so much envied trade ' of that Port.   He gives the prices of taffetas, satins, velvets, etc.

1695.   **Proposals for the Conversion of**   *MS. Tanner XXIV,*
              the Indians to Christianity.   *fols. 17, 32.*

1695-98. **State of the Proceedings of the**   *MS. Rawl. D. 747,*
              E.I. Co., against S i r T h o m a s   *fol. 158.*
              Cooke, Sir Basil Firebrace, Sir
              Richard Acton, Sir John Chardin,
              etc.

1696.   **Order of the Court of 22 May, 1696.**   *MS. Rawl. D. 862,*
                                                          fols. 14, 15.

Concerning the validity of Sir John Goldsborough's directions as to the destination of the *Sampson.*   Opinion of the Court to be taken.

1696.   **Order of the Court of 13 Oct., 1696.**

Sir Thomas Rawlinson appointed to supervise monies which shall be issued henceforth out of the Treasury.

1696.   **Sir Josiah Child to Sec. Blackborne,**   *MS. Rawl. A. 303,*
              dated 14 Oct., 1696.   *fol. 206.*

Concerning freight charges ; the case of Samuel Richardson and his ill treatment by the factors in India ; a grant of money must be made to the town of Halsted ' to keep the poor alive '.

1696.   **Messrs. Musgrave, Boulton and**   *MS. Rawl. D. 747,*
              Goodriche to the East India Com-   *fols. 159-60.*
              pany, dated Office of Ordnance, 17
              October, 1696.

Concerning the King's saltpetre.

1696.   **Orders of the Court of the E.I. Co.**   *MS. Rawl. D. 747,*
              dated 21 Oct., 1696.   *fol. 161.*

300 tons of the Company's saltpetre to be reserved for the King—the remainder to be sold.

1696-1702. **Expense of Establishments at Fort**   *MS. Rawl. D. 747,*
                St. George, May, 1696—July, 1702.   *fol. 209.*

1697.   **An account of what was agreed**   *MS. Rawl. D. 862,*
              upon by the Owners of the Ship   *fol. 17.*
              Thomas in order to fit her to India
              this 10th Aug., 1697.

An order of the Court.   List of Committee chosen to oversee.

1697, etc. **Lists of officers with Salaries in the**   *MS. Rawl. D. 747,*
                Factories and Forts.   *fols. 164-68.*

1697-98. **List of Supercargoes sent to China**   *MS. Rawl. D. 747,*
              with the names of their ships   *fol. 179.*
              18 June, 1697—8 November, 1698.

1697-98. Minute Book of the Bullion Com- *MS. Rawl. C. 439,*
mittee of the East India Com- *fol. 37.*
pany.

1697-98. Orders of Courts of the Old Com- *MS. Rawl. A. 302,*
pany, 1697-98. *fols. 77-81, 94, 98,*
124, 132-38, 218-
22, 228, 238-46,
253a.

These deal with a variety of subjects, such as the regulation of the expenditure of
Seamen's wages, debts of mariners, victualling of the Company's ships, increase of stock,
payment of dividends, assets and liabilities of the Company, lists of investors with
amounts subscribed, representation to Parliament of the 15th June, 1698 (for which see
under that date), minutes of standing orders, proposal to advance £200,000 for the service of the Government, etc. etc.

1699-1700. Diary of Sir William Norris, Bart. *MS. Rawl. C. 912,*
fol. 913.

Begins : 'September 12th, 1699. Att 4 of the clocke in the afternoone wee
arriv'd in Porto Novo Roade on the Coast of Coromondell which was the place I was
first to touch att by the Directions of the Company.'

Ends : 'Ruilo Chawn [who] promisd to send his secretary to treate of ceremonys
this day faild and has all alonge shuffled and delayd.'

'This day I ordered Mr. Halowin my treasurer to bringe me in an exact account of
all the Charge of Carts and Hackerys from Surat to the Emperors Laschar which is as
follows.' [Account follows.]

Closing words : 'From Bouramporee to Parmellaw, Corse 65-8 days march.'

(See also O.C. 67 *et seq.* (India Office Records) for a number of letters respecting
the Embassy of Sir William Norris. The Embassy has been fully dealt with by Mr.
Harihar Das.)

1697-1702. Expense of Establishment at *MS. Rawl. D. 747,*
Bombay, August, 1697—July, 1702. *fols. 210-11.*

1697-1702. Money paid for Taxes. *MS. Rawl. D. 747.*

1698. Report to the House of Commons *MS. Rawl. A. 302,*
from their Committee appointed *fols. 230-31.*
to examine into the affairs of the
Old Company, June, 1698.

The Committee find, after examining the books of the E.I. Co., that the original Stock
was £369,891-5-0.

Reports of various General Courts in 1680 and 1681 respecting dividends. Dividends from 1685 to 1691 furnished to the Committee, but no stated accounts or valu-
ations upon which any of the said dividends were made can be found. The
Company's Accountant has been examined. He knows of no such book of accounts,
but states that upon the arrival of their ships, the Co. made general computations for
dividends.

The Committee further enquired into the state of the Company's affairs about the
time of the new subscriptions, 1693, i.e. what was owing to the Co. and what sums
were advanced by the adventurers.

The Committee lays before the House the lists of subscribers, with the respective sums subscribed, distinguishing old adventurers from new. The total subscription money amounted to £1,220,314-13-5, which was afterwards reduced, according to the Charter, to £744,502-6-2.

Between 11 Jan., 1693 and 21 May, 1698 several adventurers sold out their whole stock to the amount of about £118,278-8-7.

The Committee report that what is owed on bond from 30 Nov., 1694 to 30 Nov., 1697 and their debt upon bond to 31 March, 1698 (to which time their books are balanced) is £631,554-19-10. The sum owing for customs is estimated at £44,177-9-4, and that due on sundry ships' accounts £10,191-7-3.

The Committee furnish an estimate of the Company's cash and credit in goods, etc.

On enquiring as to how the £744,000 was disposed of, the Committee were told that it was impossible to furnish a particular account, as it was all mixed up with 'the other monies'.

[References are given at various points of the Report to papers designated A to K.]

1698. **Representation from the Com-**   *MS. Rawl. A. 302,*
mittee of the Company to the   *fols. 131-32.*
House of Commons, 15 June, 1698.

The Committee, in answer to a report made to the House of Commons by a Committee appointed to inspect the books of the E.I. Co., state :

That in 1691 an account of the Co. laid before the House amounted to more than £744,000.

That many of the adventurers offered themselves as securities for this amount.

That the Company continued to send out large and rich ships to India in order to make it appear at the time of calling in of the 50 per cent. on the 3rd May, 1693, that they had estate to that value.

To carry on the trade, it was agreed, on the 3rd May, 1693, that 50 per cent. should be advanced by the adventurers and repaid them again, with the agreement of new subscribers, as appears by Orders of the General Court.

[Here follow the Orders of the General Court of 3rd May, 1693.]

1698. **Representation of the Committee**   *MS. Rawl. A. 303,*
of the E.I. Co., holden 15 June,   *fols. 236-39.*
1698, to the House of Parliament,
in answer to a Report made to this
House by their Committee appointed
to examine the East India Company's
affairs.

The whole of the document is concerned with the accounts of the Company. Orders of the General Court of 3 May, 1693 are quoted and also those of 10 Nov., 1693. A full copy is given of the General Court of 16 Nov., 1693, containing the long preamble offered to their Majesties' Charter of Regulations, which is concerned with provisions for obtaining the new subscription.

Then follow reports of the General Court of Adventurers of 8 and 20 Dec., 1693 and 1 Jan., 1693-94.

1698. **Memorial from the Subscribers to**   *MS. Rawl. A. 303,*
the New Company to the House   *fol. 165.*
of Commons, 20 June, 1698.

Concerning the two million pounds to be raised by the Bill for settling the East India trade. The subscribers having already underwritten £1,350,000 ask for a preference for their several sums so subscribed, and that they may be obliged by the Bill to make good the same. [Duplicate on fol. 221.]

1698. **Two copies of the Letters Patent granted to the English (or New) East India Company,** dated 5 Sept., 1698.   *Western MS. 29777, (now MS. Eng. Hist. b. 1), fols. 12, 106.*

1698. **Draft of the Memorial of the E.I. Co. to the Lord of the Treasury** about the saltpetre reserved for His Majesty, Sept., 1698.   *MS. Rawl. D. 747, fol. 170.*

1698. **List of repairs required to the** *East India Merchant,* 6 Oct., 1698.   *MS. Rawl. D. 747, fols. 173-74.*

1698. **List of the Company's Servants at their several Factories in the East Indies.**   *MS. Rawl. D. 747, fol. 169.*

1698. **List of provisions necessary for the East India Company's ships.**   *MS. Rawl. D. 747, fol. 182.*

[? 1698.] **Allowances of victuals made to the King's ships** compared with what the Commanders of the E.I. Co. allow to their ships.   *MS. Rawl. D. 747, fol. 183.*

[1698.] **Representation from the Company to the House of Lords,** in answer to some propositions respecting the unprofitableness and disadvantage of the East India trade.   *MS. Rawl. A. 302, fols. 161-63.*

The Company represent :

That the spice trade having been cut off by the Dutch, they have only lately ' advanced in Callicoes, silks, drugs, etc.' Other points in the Representation relate to the export of bullion ; the sending out by the Company of throwsters, dyers, etc. ; the dealing in commodities tending to interfere with the trade of Great Britain ; the trade of India and its liability to interfere with other foreign trades ; the amount of bullion sent to India ; the annual charge of the Company which is stated to be about £100,000 ; prohibition of goods manufactured in India ; the settlement of the East India trade by Act of Parliament in a Company by a joint stock.

[1698.] **Twenty-eight Bye-laws proposed by the 'Committee appointed by the General Court** of the English Company tradeing to the East Indies, to prepare By-lawes' [dated 1698 or early in 1699].   *MS. Rawl. A. 303 fols. 73-76.*

The Bye-laws relate to the keeping of the Seal and the cash ; the cost of transfers ; the Court of Directors to meet once a week ; annuity money ; persons not licensed by the Co. not to use the Company's ships ; the licensing of traders ; the withdrawing of a Director if concerned in any debate ; the Directors and the Company's servants to take no fees ; election of Directors ; inspectors appointed to inspect the actions of the Directors ; the buying of ships ; Directors not to own ships after Michaelmas 1699 ; penalties for not remitting money when called for ; allowances for prompt payment ; yearly balance ; the making of payments ; printed lists to be delivered before the annual election of Directors ; no note of Directors to be taken ; no members to trade outside the Joint Stock ; a Committee to inspect Bye-laws ; orders for India to be signed by 13 Directors ; orders for the election of Directors ; penalty for breach of these laws.

[? 1698.]   Arguments against the importation   *MS. Rawl. A. 303,*
            from India of silks and manu-   *Art. 23, fols. 117-*
            factured goods, as destructive to   *19.*
            home trade [dated c. 1698-1700].

The document contains long arguments against the importation from India of silks, etc., and also against the settling of the trade in the East India Co. for 21 years.

[? 1698.]   Arguments in favour of the East   *MS. Rawl. A. 303,*
            India trade and the importation   *Art. 21, fol. 115.*
            of silks, calicoes, etc. [dated about
            1698-1700].

The arguments controverted are that :

1. The goods are not necessities.

2. Their use prejudices the English manufactures.

3. Their use hinders the employment of British workers.

4. Their manufacture takes money out of the kingdom.

The writers sum up by hoping that the question will be settled by Act of Parliament.

[? 1698.]   Lists of the names, stations and   *MS. Rawl. A. 303,*
            salaries of the Presidents, Chiefs,   *Art. 31, fols. 145-*
            Merchants, Factors, Writers and others   *46.*
            in India in the Service of the Hon'ble
            the English Company trading to the
            East Indies [dated about 1698].

[? 1698.]   State of the Case of the East India   *MS. Rawl. D. 747,*
            Company.   *fol. 137.*

[A portion only.]

1698-1700.   Monies imprested since 1 May, 1698,   *MS. Rawl. D. 747,*
            continued up to 1700.   *fol. 208.*

The ' severall persons ' mentioned in this document are chiefly attorneys.

1698-1700.   List of ships abroad.   *MS. Rawl. A. 245,*
                                     fol. 87.

1698-1705.   An abstract showing the General   *MS. Rawl. D. 747,*
            State of the Old East India Com-   *fols. 343-44.*
            pany's affairs on the 1st May, in each
            year from 1698-1705.

1698-1707.	Abstract as above from 1698-1707.	*MS. Rawl. D. 747, fol. 344.*
1698-1709.	Account of transfer money received.	*MS. Rawl. D. 747, fol. 363.*
1698-99.	Petition of the Company to Parliament, March, 1698-99.	*MS. Rawl. D. 747, fol. 177.*
1698-99.	Petition of John Oakley to be employed by the E.I. Co.	*MS. Rawl. D. 747, fol. 405.*
[1698-99?]	Petition of Thomas Jackson to be employed by the E.I. Company (undated).	*MS. Rawl. D. 747, fol. 404.*
1699.	A Narration of Mr. Samuel Glover and Mr. Andrew Goodman concerning their voyage from Madras to Succadana.	*Western MS. 16428 (now MS. Bradley 24) pp. 57-70; 73.*

4 Jan., 1698-99. Sailed from Madras.

Put into Batavia for provisions.

13 May, 1699. Anchored in the Bay of Succadana. Traded with the son of the Sultan. News of prows coming from Bantam on a warlike expedition.

Engagement between the 'Bantamers', assisted by the Dutch, and the people of Succadana.

Messrs. Glover and Goodman were compelled to leave their ship and were pursued by the enemy, of whom they killed thirteen. The ruler of Succadana lent them a 'gunting' in which to go to Malacca, but they were intercepted by the 'Bantamers' who seized their goods and handed them over to the Dutch. On arrival at Bantam they were imprisoned and afterwards shipped to Malacca whence they eventually reached Madras in the *Humphrey and Charles*.

p. 73. Tables of merchandise, accounts of Mocha, Succadana (1703), Delagoa Bay, etc.

1698/9-1699.	Minutes of Proceedings of the Committee of the Old Company appointed to negotiate with a Committee of the New Company, 22 March, 1698-99 to 22 December, 1699.	*MS. Rawl. A. 302, fols. 167-84.*

22 March, 1698-99. Meeting of the Grand Committee of 52 appointed by the General Court of the Company of Merchants of London Trading into the East Indies (Old Company).

Instructions for the Committee of Seven appointed to meet the Committee of Seven of the New Company, were given. Extracts were read of the Resolutions passed at a General Court of Adventurers, 13 Jan., 1698-99, expressing their willingness for a coalition, and that the Grand Committee of 52 be advised.

7 Feb., 1698-99. General Court of Adventurers.

Nomination of the Committee of Seven (named). Resolutions as to their instructions, and as to appointing more than seven if the New Company do likewise.

12

17 March, 1698-99.   General Court of Adventurers.
    One member of the Committee of Seven found to be unqualified;
another appointed.   The Grand Committee empowered to give written
instructions to the Seven.
17 March, 1698-99.   Grand Committee of Fifty-two.
    Resolutions as to arrangements for meeting the Committee of Seven
of the New Company.
22 March, 1698-99.   Grand Committee of Fifty-two.
    Resolution that five of the Seven shall be a quorum.   Memorandum
that the two Committees of Seven met on the following day and
made an agreement as to the Minutes, etc.
27 March, 1699.   Grand Committee of Fifty-two.
    Resolutions as to secrecy.   Report of the meeting of the Committees
of the two Companies.
21 Feb, 1698-99.   General Court of the New Company.
    Nomination of the Seven of Committee (named).   Instructions to
be received from the Grand Committee of Forty-eight of the New Co.
7 March, 1698-99.   General Court of the New Company.
    Grand Committee of Forty-eight empowered to act.
22 March, 1698-99.   Grand Committee of Forty-eight, New Company.
    Five of the Seven to be a quorum.
23 March, 1698-99.   Committee of the two Sevens.
    Agreed that all transactions shall be in writing.
    Heads to be discussed:
    (1) Terms to be made for the £315,000 subscribed by Mr. Dubois.
    (2) Valuation to be put on Dead Stock of the Old Company.
    The following propositions to be made to the Committee of Seven
of the New Company:
    (1) A sum to be agreed on for carrying on the trade as a General
United Joint Stock.
    (2) The proportion of the Old Company in the United Joint stock
to be as £315,000 shall bear to the sum agreed on as an annual
necessary export to India.
28 March, 1699.   Grand Committee of the Old Company.
    Resolution that the value of the Dead Stock be reckoned at £350,000.
Papers produced enumerating the Dead Stock.
    Their Committee of Seven request the Committee of Seven of the
New Co., to put forward in writing their proposition concerning the
two heads above mentioned; otherwise the two propositions are to be
withdrawn.
    It is reported that the Committee of Seven of the New Co., agree on
the points concerning the valuation of Dead Stock as per the meeting
on the 23rd March.
30 March, 1699.   Grand Committee of the Old Company.   Concerning
papers regarding the propositions as above, to be delivered to the
Committee of the Old Company.
    Here follows an account of the Dead Stock, with a list of all
Factories, Forts, etc., Privileges, Revenues, etc., but no details of
the actual value of the same.
3 April, 1699.   Meeting of both the Committees of Seven.   Resolutions
concerning valuation of stock, etc., exchanged.
4 April, 1699.   Meeting of the Grand Committee of the Old Company.
    Report of the meeting of the New Company's Committee of Forty-
eight on the 24th March and their resolve that the £315,000

subscribed by Mr. Dubois be admitted as if it had been originally subscribed. They are willing to come to an agreement regarding Dead Stock if they can be furnished with further particulars to enable them to judge of its value.

10 April, 1699. Meeting of both the Committees of Seven.

The New Company deliver a paper passed by the Grand Committee on the 6th April.

19 April, 1699. Meeting of the Grand Committee of the Old Company.

In answer to the proposition delivered at a Grand Committee of Forty-eight on the 6th April and to other Propositions and Papers, the Committee state that:

(1) It is impossible to name what sum of money the trade may require, as it is capable of enlargement.

(2) That two millions having been settled by Act of Parliament, any subscriber hereafter admitted ought not to expect more than his proportion, but if such subscriber should desire a greater portion than the £315,000 subscribed by Mr. Dubois, the Old Company will endeavour to procure it for him.

(3) Concerning Dead Stock, the Committee desire to know (i) the value of each Fort, etc., (ii) what the privileges and immunities were; (iii) whence the revenues arise.

26 April, 1699. Grand Committee of the Old Company.

Answers agreed on to the Paper from the New Company, dated 6 April, which answers were delivered to the New Company.

28 April, 1699. Meetings of both Committees of Seven.

The Old Company delivered a Paper, dated 26 April, to the New Company, being an answer to a Paper, dated 6 April.

18 May, 1699. Meeting of both Committees of Seven.

The New Company delivered a Paper dated 11 May, in answer to a Paper from the Old Company of 26 April.

30 June, 1699. Meeting of the Grand Committee of the Old Company.

The answer of the Grand Committee of Forty-eight dated 11 May, read. This was in answer to the Paper received from the Old Company, dated 26 April.

6 July, 1699. Grand Committee of the Old Company.

A collection of all transactions ordered to be made and to be presented to the General Court.

13 July, 1699. Meeting of the Committee of Forty-eight, New Co.

A message to be sent to the Old Company reminding them of the Paper from the New Company dated 11 May.

20 July, 1699. Meeting of the Grand Committee of the Old Company.

A resolution passed that an answer be sent to the New Co., stating that their proposals and replies do not show a disposition to unite the interests of the two Companies. The Grand Committee nevertheless desires a further conference in order to frame favourable terms.

28 July, 1699. Meeting of both Committees of Seven.

A paper dated 25 July delivered by the New Company to the Company.

3 Aug., 1699. Grand Committee of the Old Company.

Answer read from the Grand Committee of the New Co. of 25th July. They are surprised that the Old Company thinks that they do not show a disposition to unite. They cannot but think they have shown themselves ready to treat on terms both just and reasonable.

A Memorandum inserted here that occurrences between 3rd Aug.

and 14th Dec., will be found in the 'general Minute Book belonging to this fair one '.

20 Dec., 1699.   Grand Committee of the Old Company.

Resolution that both the Committees of Seven shall meet on ' Friday next '.

22 Dec., 1699.   Meeting of both the Committees of Seven.

'After some discourse wherein nothing was put down in writing, they all adjourned to the Rummer.   Both sides forbore any further discourse.'

1699.	**Heads of Charterparties agreed on for the Coast and Bay and ships** taken up for the year 1699.	*MS. Rawl. D. 747, fols. 202-3.*

1699.	**List of six ships with 'Bags— gross—tare a l l o w e d—N e a t e'** **March—Sept., 1699.**	*MS. Rawl. D. 747, fol. 206.*

A few lines only.

1699.	**An account of woollen manu- facture expected by the E.I. Co. since 11 Nov., 1693** and whence consigned, dated 20 Dec., 1699.	*MS. Rawl. D. 747, fols. 191-92, 193.*

[A similar account of same date on fol. 193.]

1699.	**Account of gratuities and fees to the King's Patent Officers** for the year 1699.	*MS. Rawl. D. 747, fols. 254-55.*

Endorsed 1699-1700.

[?1699.]	**Arguments for and against the E.I. trade in silks, etc., with reference to home manufacture.**	*MS. Rawl. A. 303, fols. 117-19.*

The chief arguments discussed and confuted are :

That such importation of Indian goods will (1) take the place of English manufactures ; (2) divert money abroad ; (3) hinder the consumption of home manufactures ; (4) lead to monopolies.

Regulations are proposed to avoid the evils above mentioned.

See also fol. 115 of the same MS. noted above.

[?1699.]	**Regulations of the Charter with proposed alterations.**	*MS. Rawl. A. 452, fol. 1.*

These Regulations were comprised under 26 heads as follows :

1. Subscriptions for £744,000.
2. To be paid within 3 months.
3. Each subscriber to take oath that the money subscribed is for the persons named.
4. If over £744,000 be subscribed, each subscriber to reduce proportionably.
5. No member to subscribe more than £1,000, including his present stock.
6. One-third of the amount to be paid down.

7. A subscriber of £500 may have one vote ; of £4,000, two ; of £6,000, three ; of £8,000, four ; of £10,000, five. None to have more than five votes.

8. Members to be incorporated by name of the 'Governor and Company of Merchants of London trading to the East Indies.'

9. Subscribers of £500 to choose the Governor, Deputy Governor and Committee. Governor and Deputy Governor to subscribe not less than £4,000. The Committee not less than £1,000.

10. The Governor, Deputy Governor and Committee to be chosen annually.

11. The Governor, Deputy Governor and Committee to take the oath of fidelity.

12. Every subscriber shall take his freedom, and pay a fine of £5, and take the oath.

13. All persons free of the former Company and subscribers to the present Stock to be admitted gratis.

14. The Company to make bye-laws.

15. A General Court to be called by the Governor or Deputy, the same to have casting votes.

16. No licences to be granted to trade to the East Indies on private account.

17. No private contracts for sale of goods to be allowed.

18. No lot of goods to exceed £500.

19. Their Majesties to have 500 tons of saltpetre annually at — per ton.

20. Yearly export of goods, etc., not less than £100,000.

21. All dividends to be paid in money.

22. The accountant to keep the book for the entry of stock.

23. All transfers of Stock to be entered in a book to lie open all day.

24. The Charter to last for 21 years and no longer.

25. A book of new subscriptions to be laid open before the end of the said 21 years.

26. The Company shall recommend Parliament to pass an Act for them to enjoy the monopoly of trade to the East Indies between Cape De Bona Esperanza and the Straits of Magellan.

1699.   **Copy of a letter from Surat on the**   *MS. Rawl. A. 302,*
              affairs of the Company. 18 April,   *fols. 247-47a.*
              1699.

This concerns the acknowledging of the New Company ; Mr. Colt's dealings with the Governor of Surat, and the imprisonment of him and the Council ; the Governor's demands for restitution of what was taken in the late wars ; his threats to seize the Company's effects ; the robbing of a ship worth 1,400,000 rupees laid to the charge of the Company ; the impending ruin of the Company's trade unless the arrival of the expected Ambassador produces a favourable change in the state of affairs.

1699.   **Coynes, Weights, and Measures of**   *MS. Rawl. A. 302,*
              India.   *fols. 249-50.*

Metchilipatam, 14 July, 1699.

Value of pice in relation to cash and the rupee, of the rupee and the fanam to the pagoda, etc., and of the pagoda to English standard gold.

Weights : Cash in relation to seer ; seer to the maund cutcha ; pice to cash and oz. troy weight.

Gold and silver weight, Sicca rupees in relation to seer, and troy weight.

Ballasore, 13 Aug., 1699.

Weight of Sicca rupees in relation to troy weight; of pice in relation to seer bazaar and avoirdupois; and of the bazaar maund in relation to avoirdupois.

Hughley, 10 Oct., 1699.

Sicca rupees of Rajamaul and of Madras in ounces; Teculls, Cattees, and Peculls in ounces.

Long Measure: various kinds of ' Guz '.

Weights: maund, seer, rupee.

Muxoadavad, 17 Dec., 1699.

Value of cutcha pice, pucca pice, seer bazaar, maund, ' anoe '; of Covads, Bega of ground, ' Russa ', course in miles, etc.

f. 250.   Other notes on various comparisons of the coins, weights, etc. mentioned above.

1699.	**Draft of the Commission to Sir Charles Eyre as President in the Bay of Bengal** sent per the *Fame*, dated 20 Dec., 1699.	*MS. Rawl. D. 747, fols. 204-5.*
1699-1700.	**Seven receipts for pay received of John Dubois,** July, 1699—Oct., 1700, signed by Charles Davenant.	*MS. Rawl. D. 747, fols. 195-201.*
1699-1703.	**Heads of Collections from Accompts given in to the House of Commons** from the Custome House, 1699-1703.	*MS. Rawl. A. 302, fols. 329-30.*
c. 1699.	**Miscellaneous notes concerning goods exported, value of coins,** with a list of commercial papers ' sayd to be Mr. Langley's.'	*MS. Rawl. A. 303, Art. 29, fols. 134-43.*

f. 134.   Rough notes of exports of the Old and New Companies, Michaelmas 1698—Feb., 1699.

f. 135.   Rough notes of the value of bales of broadcloth, pepper, etc.

Notes as to the money due on freight, extent of the Dutch ell, value of the rupee, seer of 20 pice weight, customs rate, etc.

f. 137.   Notes of the value of current monies at Amsterdam.

f. 138.   Notes on the value of the ducat.

f. 141.   'Abstract of Papers, etc.   Sayd to be Mr. Langley's papers, marked No. 9 received from the *Fleet* frigate, perused per Mr. Sandford, Mr. Williams and W. T., 28 Dec., 1697.'

'A waste Ledger.'

'A Ledger begun to be framed containing an account of the Contents of each Bale of Cloth and how disposed off, but the creditt parte not posted.'

'Account of Goods packt up and shipt on board the *Dorothy*,' etc.

f. 143.   ' Invoice of Goods shipt on board the *Dorothy* and consigned to Mr. Samuell Langley on account of Thomas Magle, 8 Feb., 1693-94.'

1699-1700. **Letters that passed between the** *MS. Rawl. A. 302,*
New and Old East India Com- *fols. 185-217.*
pany's servants in the East Indies
after the arrival of the former from
July 1699 to January following.[1]

Sir Nich. Waite, Consul to the Mogul (translation). Translation of a
Persian certificate written by the 'Voqnavees Moola [? for] Abdul
Gaffore,' merchant of Surat.

28 July, 1699. John Pitt from the *Degrave*, to President Thomas Pitt.
28 July, 1699. President Pitt, Fort St. George, to John Pitt.
28 July, 1699. John Pitt, on the *Degrave*, to President Pitt.
7 Aug., 1699. John Pitt, Consul, Metchlepatam, to Thos. Lovell and
others of the Old Company at Metchlepatam.
20 Aug., 1699. John Pitt, Metchlepatam, to President and Council at
Fort St. George.
14 Sept., 1699. Thos. Pitt and others, Fort St. George, Madras, to John
Pitt.
28 July, 1699. Sir Edwd. Littleton, Ballasore, to John Beard and others.
29 July, 1699. Sir Edwd. Littleton, Ballasore, to John Beard.
7 Aug., 1699. John Beard and others, Chuttanuttee, to Sir Edwd.
Littleton.
7 Aug., 1699. John Beard, Chuttanuttee, to Sir Edwd. Littleton.
28 Aug., 1699. Sir Edwd. Littleton, Ballasore, to John Beard.
28 Aug., 1699. Sir Edwd. Littleton, Ballasore, to John Beard and others.
4 Oct., 1699. John Beard, Chuttanuttee, to Sir Edward Littleton.
4 Oct., 1699. Sir Edwd. Littleton, Hugly, to John Beard, agent at
Calcutta.
25 Oct., 1699. Sir Edwd. Littleton, Hugly, to John Beard, and others.
6 Oct., 1699. John Beard and others, Chuttanuttee, to Sir Edwd.
Littleton.
2 Feb., 1700. Sir Wm. Norris, Ambassador, Metchlepatam, to Saml.
Woolston, Factor of Old Company,
1 Feb., 1700. Sir Edwd. Littleton, Hugly, to John Beard and others.
6 Feb., 1700. John Beard and others, Chuttanuttee, to Sir Edwd.
Littleton.
11 Jan., 1700. Sir Nich. Waite, *Montague*, to Sir John Gayer.
16 Jan., 1700. Sir John Gayer, Bombay Castle, to Sir Nich. Waite.
11 Jan., 1700. Sir Nich. Waite, *Montague*, to Sir John Gayer.
15 Jan., 1700. Sir John Gayer and others, Bombay Castle, to Sir Nich. Waite.
22 Jan., 1700. Sir Nich. Waite, *Montague*, to Sir John Gayer and others.
23 Jan., 1700. Saml. Richardson, Secretary, to Benj. Mewse and Chidly
Brooke, enclosing : 22 Jan., 1700. The President and Council (Old
Co.), Surat, to Sir Nich. Waite.
23 Jan., 1700. Benj. Mewse and Chidly Brooke, to President and Council
at Surat.
23 Jan., 1700. Sir Nicholas Waite, *Montague*, to Stephen Colt, etc.
22 Jan., 1700. Benj. Mewse and Chidly Brooke, Surat, to President and
Council at Surat.
25 Jan., 1700. President and Council at Surat, to Sir Nich. Waite.

1699-1710. **Accounts of bullion exported.** *MS. Rawl. D. 747,*
fols. 298-310, 335-
36, 366-67, 407.

---

[1] It is impossible to abstract these without practically reproducing the MS.

1699-1700-   Orders of the Court of the East   MS. Rawl. A. 747,
1702-3.   India Company.   fols. 312-30.

Proceedings of the General Courts of the Old Company relating to a proposed union with the New Company on the following dates : 6, 13, 27 January ; 7, 10 February ; 10, 17 March, 1699-1700, 6 July, 1699, 12 March, 1699-1700 ; 6, 23, 31 Dec., 1700 ; 27 Jan., 1700-1 ; 17, 23, 24, 26, 30 April, 1701 ; 2 Jan., 1701-2 ; 25, 27 April, 1702. The proceedings contain among other matters relating to the Union, an address to the King, resolutions sent to the New Company, definition of the powers of a Committee of Seven, transfer of stock, Instrument of Union. See also MS. Rawl. A. 302, fols. 167-84, 22 March, 1698-99—22 Dec., 1699.

[? 1700.]   Coins, weights and measures of   MS. Rawl. A. 302,
**   India.   fol. 249.**

[? 1700.]   A remembrance of the Coynes and   Western MS. 3965
**   Weights with measures currant   (now MS. Casau-**
**   in the Dominions of the Grand Mogul. bon 20), 10 fols.**

At the end are notes and directions for Merchants' Accounts.

1700.   Odd accounts for dyeing cloth, etc.,   MS. Rawl. D. 747,
**   May—July 1700.   fol. 207.**

1700.   Account of presents received from   MS. Rawl. D. 747,
**   the 'Etheopian Embasseder and   fols. 252-53.**
**   charge we were att', received 28**
**   June, 1700, per Northumberland.**

1700.   Letter of Elihu Yale to the Com-   MS. Harl. D. 747,
**   pany, dated 26 July, 1700.   fols. 213-14.**

Concerning the charges brought against him in his capacity as President of Fort St. George.

1700,   Orders of the Court.   MS. Rawl. D. 863,
14 Aug.   fol. 62.

Regarding repairs to ship *Sidney.*

1700.   Abstract of Bills of Exchange   MS. Rawl. D. 747,
**   drawn by Messrs. Ash, Welch   fols. 265-66.**
**   and Cook of Cadiz on the Old East**
**   India Company between August and**
**   December, 1700, on account of Bullion.**

1700.   Account of the parcels of gold sent   MS. Rawl. D. 747,
**   out in Chest B. to Fort St.   fols. 259-60.**
**   George, Nov., 1700.**

1700,   Orders of the Court of the East   MS. Rawl. D. 747,
31 Dec.   India Company.   fol. 267.

Notice of a recommendation by the King for the two Companies to confer with a view to Union.

1700.   Account of Stock bought of vari-   MS. Rawl. D. 747,
**   ous persons.   fols. 268-76.**

1700.   **Proposal for the number of ships,**   *MS. Rawl. D. 747,*
tonnage and value to be ' sett   *fol. 256.*
out this present year 1700 '.

c. 1700.   ***Farman* granted by the Governor**   *MS. Rawl. A. 326,*
of Surat to Thos. Lucas, granting   *fol. 106.*
freedom of trade.

c. 1700.   **Directions about purchasing jars,**   *MS. Rawl. A. 303,*
cups, etc., in China, with rough   *Art. 30, fol. 144.*
sketches of patterns.

    Descriptions are furnished regarding colour, shape, material, etc. The MS. has no date.

c. 1700.   **Directions for sailing from the**   *MS. Rawl. A. 334,*
Coast of Coromandel to Batavia   *fol. 22.*
and to and from other ports in the
East Indies, etc.

    (In the same hand as fol. 44., diamond mines 1694-99.)

c. 1700.   **Memoirs of East India.**   *MS. Rawl. A. 334,*
fols. 72-79 (9 pp.).

    f. 72-78.   These ' memoirs ' include descriptions of the chief ports and commercial cities of the East, e.g. Muskat, Gombroon, Surat, Bombay, the ports on the Malabar Coast, with remarks on Ceylon, Achin, Malacca, Johore, Siam and China.

    f. 79.   Instructions to supercargoes for carrying on trade with Mocha.

c. 1700.   **Sailing directions to various places**   *MS. Rawl. A. 334,*
from the east coast of Africa,   *fol. 65.*
Madagascar, Surat, etc.

c. 1700.   **Account of drugs imported from**   *MS. Rawl. A. 334,*
East India and Africa.   *fol. 69.*

c. 1700.   **Fragment of a ship's trading jour-**   *MS. Rawl. C. 841,*
nal at Banjar and ' Tartaso'.   *fols. 25-26.*

    A brief view of the Weight and   *MS. Rawl. C. 840,*
Consequence of the General   *fols. 1-57.*
trade, and of some considerable places
in the Indies.

    The remarks are divided under five general Heads, viz., the interests of Spain, Portugal, France, Holland, and England, possessions in the Indies, etc.

    The remarks on Spain relate mostly to the West Indies and America. Those on Portugal relate to Brazil, etc. Those on France to America, Hispaniola, etc. Those on Holland (a short account) to Guiana, East Indies (no places named), etc. The remarks on England relate to Africa, America, Bermuda, Jamaica, East Indies in general (no places named).

    The whole is a warning of the dangerous consequences that may arise from the joint interests in the Indies, etc., of France and Spain, owing to the late union of their Crowns in the House of Bourbon.

1700-1.   **Bills of Exchange August, 1700—**   *MS. Rawl. D. 747,*
            February 1700-1 (No names).   *fols. 202-12.*

1700-1.   **Messrs. Senoretts Account for**   *MS. Rawl. D. 747,*
            Bullion supplied to the E.I. Co.   *fol. 277.*
            Jan., 1700-1.

1700-1.   **A letter from a stranger proposing**   *MS. Rawl. D. 747,*
            several things relating to the Old   *fols. 278-79.*
            East India Company's advanage,
            dated 23 January, 1700-1, addressed
            to 'Wm. Ewer [Hewer] Esq., at the
            Old East India House, Leadenhall
            Street.' Signed E.F.

The letter contains propositions concerning the raising of stock, dividends, etc.

1701.   **Account of bullion received from**   *MS. Rawl. D. 747,*
            abroad for the year 1701.   *fols. 257-58.*

c. 1701.   **Description of Achin in Sumatra.**   *MS. Rawl. A. 334,*
                                                  fol. 76.

[1701.]   **The case of Adam Codey, on the**   *MS. Rawl. A. 303,*
            behalf of his son William Codey,   *fol. 83.*
            a Supercargo in China, respecting
            china ware, etc., brought home by
            him.

Statement as to certain goods from China brought home in the *Fleet* frigate by William Codey.

Adam Codey acts for his son who is ill at Aix-la-Chapelle, and who is unwilling that certain China ware and fans should be included in the Company's stock. Various witnesses are summoned who attest that the goods were marked with young Codey's mark and that they were his own private property.

The document is undated, but as the voyage of the *Fleet* frigate to Amoy and back was begun 20 Oct., 1698 and ended 3 Feb., 1700-1 the 'Statement' should probably be dated as above, viz., 1701.

1701-2.   **Draft agreements and other papers**   *Western MS. 29777*
            relating to the Union of the two   *(now MS. Eng.*
            English E.I. Co.'s.   *Hist. b. 1), fol. 67.*

1701-2,   **Orders of the Court of Directors.**   *MS. Rawl. D. 863,*
20 Feb.   *fol. 66.*

Respecting a cargo of indigo which is said to be worthless.

1701-2.   **Voyage of the** *Macclesfield* **to and**   *MS. Rawl. C. 841,*
            from Borneo.   *fols. 4-25.*

Log begins 14 Aug., 1701 and contains descriptions of the Cape Verd Is., Bombay, Surat, Muskat, Madeira, St. Helena, etc., with remarks on manners and customs of the various peoples. It contains 42 very closely written pages.

[See O.C. 7832 (India Office Records) for a letter from the Supercargoes of this ship to the Co. dated 21 Jan., 1701-2.]

1702. E.I. Co.'s allowances of provisions. *MS. Rawl. D. 747, fols. 185-88.*

The list on fol. 185 is dated 14 Oct., 1702. The succeeding lists have no date.

1703. Accounts of goods remaining unsold in Leadenhall Warehouse and Botolph Wharf, July, 1703. *MS. Rawl. D. 747, fols. 331-34.*

c. 1703. Lines on the Union of the two Companies. *MS. Rawl. D. 832, fol. 185.*

c. 1706. Petition from two Armenian merchants, 'Babba' and 'Maller' to the Company for payment of bills of exchange. *MS. Rawl. D. 863, fol. 139.*

1706. Court of Committees, 26 July, 1706. *MS. Rawl. D. 747, fol. 239.*

Heads of the proposals of the Old E.I. Co. regarding the Union of the two Companies.

1707. Account of Cargoes received at Amsterdam from the East Indies. *MS. Rawl. A. 302, fol. 374.*

1707. Court of Committees, 29 April, 1707. *MS. Rawl. D. 747, fol. 347.*

Mr. Dubois appointed to inspect the accountant's .office and the Company's accounts.

1707. Order of Court. *MS. Rawl. D. 747, fol. 347.*

1708. Old Company's State of Cash, 1 May, 1708. Order for money to be paid out, 27 October, 1708. *MS. Rawl. D. 747, fols. 354-55.*

1709-10. General Courts held 10, 17 Nov., 1709, 29 March, 26 May, 1710. *MS. Rawl. D. 747, fol. 376.*

Proceedings respecting the shares of the United Company.

(Early 18th century.) View of the English cemetery at Surat. *MS. Rawl. B. 376, fol. 352.*

(Early 18th century.) Description of Surat. *MS. Rawl. A. 334, fol. 73.*

MAPS

17th-18th century. Twelve folded maps of parts of the Indian Ocean and Malaysia. *Western MS. 30632 (now MS. Maps, Indian Ocean, a. 1).*

f. 1. (*a*) The coasts of India, Burma, the Malay Peninsula and Sumatra, by John Blaeu, Dutch, 17th cent.

f. 2. (*b*) The Coast of Malabar (English), 18th cent.

f. 3. (*c*) Siam, Cochin China, Borneo and the Malay Peninsula, by John Blaeu, 1679.

f. 4. (*d*) Siam, Cochin China, Borneo and the Malay Peninsula, by Augustine Fitzhugh, for Capt. Stephen Barber, 1697.

f. 5. (*e*) Cochin China, Formosa, Borneo (English), c. 1700.

f. 9. (*i*) S. Borneo and Java by John Thornton, 1701.

f. 10. (*j*) S. Borneo and Java (Dutch), first half of 18th cent.

f. 11. (*k*) S. Ccast of Java (Dutch), c. 1700.

f. 12. (*l*) Sumba, Floris and Timor (Dutch), c. 1700.

f. 13. (*m*) New Guinea to Celebes and Timor (Dutch), c. 1700.

? Late 17th century.   **Chart of the soundings round Pulo Condore I.**   *Western MS. 16428 (now MS. Bradley 24), 1. p. ix.*

c. 1700.   **Draught of the Island of Negrais on the coast of Burma.**   *MS. Rawl. A. 302, fol. 67.*

MSS. RELATING TO THE EAST INDIES AT ALL SOULS COLLEGE, OXFORD

MSS. RELATING TO THE EAST INDIES AT ALL SOULS COLLEGE, OXFORD

1619.   **The Treaty of the Dutch and English East India Companies,** signed 8 July, 1619, sealed with the seal of the City of Amsterdam, 16 August, 1619, S.N.

Signed at end—' De Haen.' 31 Articles.

MS. All Souls College, 256, fols. 53-58.

1624.   **The States General to his Majestie about the businesse of the East Indies.** Dated the Hague, 12 December, 1624.

MS. All Souls College, 220, fol. 60.

Concerning affairs at Amboyna. They wish to preserve the former friendship and amity between the two countries. They have given orders that all those summoned to the ' procès Jugement et execution d'Amboyna ' shall have good and sufficient ground that all the affairs of justice may be carried out in good faith. They hope that his Majesty's subjects will act in a similar manner.

1661.   **Extract of the East India Company's Charter granted the 13th April, 1661.**

MS. All Souls College, 234, fols. 305-11.

No date.   **' Notes of the East Indie ships now bound forth and of the Shipps** imployed to Newfoundland.'

MS. All Souls College, 222, fol. 60.

One page only. The list of ships includes the *James, Jonas, Star, Eagle,* and two pinnaces. The amount of powder carried is stated.

1667-85.   **Collections of projects for, and drafts of, treaties between England, Holland,** and other foreign powers, containing much relating to the affairs of the E.I. Co., communications of foreign ambassadors, etc.

MS. All Souls College, 243.

f. 1-17.   Rough draft of a treaty between the English and Dutch, consisting of 43 (*alias* 38) articles. At the beginning is written: ' 3rd Project. Being amended upon the Lordes first meeting. Mar. 31.' [No year given. Some of the articles relate to the E.I. Co.]

f. 18.   ' Art. of the East India trade.' Query if Sir George Downing's [endorsement].

That the English and Dutch may freely trade with any people or nation, within the limits of the Charters of the English and Dutch East India Companies.

That it will be of great honour and reputation to his Majesty to regain Pulo Run, Dam, Cormantine and Surinam.

f. 22.   Extracts from the Treaty between the English and Dutch East India Companies, concluded in June, 1619.

f. 24.   'Art. [XV] of the Flag Lat. drawen by my Lord Ambassador Sept. [16] 73 ' (Latin).

f. 26-29.   Articles from the Project of the Treaty of Peace at Aix, 1673, as given in by the East India Company 3 April, 1673.' Nos. XXXV—XLIII.

f. 36-39.   [Endorsed] 'My Latin Draught of the Article of Commerce Jan., 1673-74.' ' East India Trade and Commerce.'

f. 40.   Four articles, without date, in Latin, concerning freedom of trade, etc.   Begins: 'Conventum et Concordatum est quod ubique locorum tam intra ditiones et fines hinc Societatis Anglicanae etc.'

f. 53.   Another rough draft of the same.

f. 69.   'A short memorial delivered to the Plenipotentiaries.' A brief abstract of 'the Articles of most moment to the Company,' viz., 1-6, 7, 8-10.   No. 7 is concerned with 'mutuall reparation of Losses ', etc. No date.

f. 70-73.   Conditions under which the King of England and the King of France consent to make peace with the Dutch. 17 July, 1672 (French).

f. 74.   'The original demaund of the King of France' (English). Eleven items.

f. 75-76.   ' VIIth Article of his Majesties Propositions at Boxtel Camp, July, 1672.' 'Third Article of the Marine Treaty of Breda, 21-31 July, 1667.'

f. 77-79.   'Demands of the East India Company brought from London.' Proposed Articles (10) of agreement between the English and Dutch for satisfaction of damages sustained by either Company since the Peace of Breda, 1667.

f. 81-82.   Another copy of the same.

f. 80.   'The Reasons following are inserted at the end of each of the foregoing Articles.'   The 'Reasons' are comments on the demands noted above.

f. 98-99.   'The Protest of the Admirall Rycklof Van Goens and the Dutch Counsell of Ceylon, etc., sent to the French Roy of India Monseyr De La Haye.'   Signed by Van Goens and the Council.   Dated 'On Board the *Tulpenburg* in the Outward Bay of Trinquenemale, May 15th, 1672.'

f. 99-100.   'Answere to the foregoeing Protest received, May 16th, 1672.' Signed: 'De La Haye.'

f. 101-3.   'Reply to the next preceding Letter.'   Signed : 'Ryckloff Van Goens.   In the Fort of Trinquenemale, May 20th, 1672.'

f. 104-5.   'Answere to the former letter dated May 20, 1672 in the Fort of [blank].'   Signed : 'De La Haye.' Trinquenemale, 27 May, 1672.

f. 106.   'Extract Out of the General Resolution of India, taken 12 July, 1672.'
Concerning affairs relating to Ceylon, the Naval force of the French appearing there, and Ryckloff van Goens. Dated Batavia 'in the Castel ', 31 July, 1672.

f. 107-10.   'Contract of Peace . . . in the name of the Dutch East India Company . . . and the great Samorin, King of Calecut together with a cessation of Armes beetweene the said King and the King of Cochine.'   6 and 11 Feb., 1672 (Copy).   Signed by the Samorin and 'Henry van Reede at Drakesteyne.'

f. 111-12.   Rough draft of a treaty concerning the English in the East Indies and Guinea (Latin).
Endorsed: 'Trade Indies.   Sept. 9th, 1673.   Sir Leslie Jenkins draught at first but not liked.'

f. 127.   Article thirteen of an agreement made by the East India Company, relating to the purchase of certain goods, the whole to amount to £33,700: they will advance £5,000 on account on Thursday 30 October, the sum to be paid to Richard Mounteney at their house in Leadenhall Street, London, and will advance another £5,000 on 6 Nov. following.   No date.

f. 128-31.   Copy of 'Treaty agreed between the English and Dutch about the East India and Bantam trade.   2nd June, 1619.'

f. 132-40.   'By the Company of merchants of London trading to the East Indyes.   Instructions for Sir John Chardin, Knt., relating to the late transaction of the Dutch East India Company at Bantam and the injuries and Losse susteyned by this Company by reason thereof.'   London, 4 May, 1683.[1]

f. 149-56.   Ratification of the treaties with Holland, by James II, 17 Aug., 1685.

Among them is: '5 Articulus and Controversias inter communitates Anglicanam et Belgicam, quæ in Indiis Orientalibus commercia faciunt antevertendas vel amicabiliter componendas, conclusas Londini $\frac{8}{18}$vo die Martii Anno Domini 1674-5.'

1668-69.   Collections of papers respecting the Treaty Marine.   *MS. All Souls College, fol. 205.*

f. 1.   April, 1668.   Petition of the East India Company to the King, touching the Treaty Marine.
3 April, 1668.   Order of His Majesty in Council on the above.
9 April, 1668.   Memorial presented to the Privy Council.

f. 2.   8 July, 1668.   Order of His Majesty in Council on the Company's proposals.   Reports of the Lords Committee upon same.

f. 3.   15 July, 1668.   Order of His Majesty in Council, giving Particulars proposed by the East India Company.

f. 7.   23 Oct., 1668.   'A Paper in Answer to some Objections made by the Dutch.'

f. 8.   5 Dec., 1668.   'The Abstract of a Letter from Sir William Temple communicated to the Governour from Sir John Trevor,' with the Company's answer to the same.

f. 9.   4 Jan., 1669, S.N.   'A Letter from Sir William Temple to the Lord Arlington, Hague.'

f. 10.   'The Company's Answer to the foregoing Letter.'

f. 11.   1 Dec., 1668.   'Answer to the Articles proposed to the Lords States General by the Ambassador Temple.'

f. 12.   No date.   'Sir William Temples lettre.'
'Compas. memoriall with a Draught of all the Articles desired to be insisted on by the Lord Ambassadour.'

f. 14.   31 Jan., 1669.   'Monsr. Van Beuninghams letter to Mr. Secretary Trevor.'   Amsterdam.

f. 16.   No date.   'Answer to Monsr. Van Beuninghams lettre.'

---

[1] See also for the Commission C.O. $\frac{77}{14}$, fol. 146 (P.R.O.); and for Sir John Chardin's 'Memorial' to the Dutch, etc., Lansd. MS. 1152, fols. 88-91, 96 (B.M.).

f. 19.   12 March, 1668-69.   'Answer to the Heads of a Letter, received
from Sr. William Temple.'

f. 21.   10 May, 1669.   'A Memoriall concerning Macasser delivered to
Mr. Secretary Trevor.'

13 May, 1669.   'Second Memoriall concerning Macasser delivered
to the Secretary of State.'

f. 23. $\frac{7}{17}$ June, 1669.   'The Company's observations on Sir Wm. Temples
letter delivered to the Secretaries of State.'

f. 24.   2 July, 1669.   'Memorial delivered to the Lord Arlington and
Mr. Secretary Trevor at Goring house, with the Articles drawn up
together as the Company's finall proposall.'

'The finall Articles delivered with the foregoing memoriall.'

f. 27.   9 July, 1669.   'Memorial presented to the Lord Arlington.'

f. 28.   'The Dutch Articles.   The Articles transmitted by Sir Wm.
Temple mentioned in the foregoing.'

f. 29.   27 July, 1669.   'The following article was drawn by direction of
the Lord Keeper and his Majesty's Principal Secretary of State at a
meeting at Essex house and delivered with the ensuing lettre, viz.'

f. 30.   1 Oct., 1669.   'Mr. Van Beuningham's letter to Mr. Secretary
Trevor.'   Hague.

f. 33.   16 Oct., 1669.   'Answer to Mr. Van Beuningham's lettre delivered
to Mr. Secretary Trevour.'

f. 35.   'Mr. Secretary's answer to the foregoing letter of Mr. Van
Beuningham.'

1673-   **Copies of Admiralty Papers.**   *MS. All Souls*
? 1675.   **Papers relating to the affairs of**   *College, 208.*
            the East India Company with
            draughts respecting the flag, etc.

f. 81.   27 May, 1673.   Letter from John Banks Governor and Nath.
Herne Deputy, acquainting 'Their Excellencies' of the taking of St.
Helena by the Dutch East India Company.   London.   'Cargo and
Vallue of 4 East India Ships taken by the English.'   [Few lines
only.]

f. 82.   9 June, 1673.   'His Majesties Order to us to insist for the Restitution of St. Helena.'   Whitehall.   Signed at end 'By his Majesties
Command Arlington.'

'Puncta Commercii generalia': concerning trading in time of war,
restoration of the island of Dam, etc. (Latin).

f. 83.   'Puncta Commercii' marked in margin 'No. 1°', similar to the
preceding (Latin).

'Puncta Commercii in Indiis,' 'No. 2°', similar to the preceding.

f. 84.   15 Jan., N.S. 1673-74.   '1st Draft Commerce delivered to the
Mediators at Cologne.'   Begins: 'Ne autem in negotiationibus
mercatoriis extra Europam.'   Similar to the preceding (Latin).

f. 89-90.   'Articles for the two East India Companies': 12 in French.
Articles of an agreement between the English and Dutch.   Begins:
'Il a este convenu que par tout dans les Limites des chartres ou
lettres d'Ottroy des deux Compagnies des Indes Orientales d'Angleterre et d'Hollande comme aussy sur la Coste de Guniée.'   The
last article concerns the restitution of the island of Dam.

f. 91-94.   'Reasonings upon the Termes of Places *blocked up* and
Invested in the East Indyes.   Vide de eadem re treaty Book p. . . .'

Begins: 'Nor can we allow that that which hath been agreed to and settled in the treaty marine of the 1st of December, 1674, ought so to debarre and Conclude Us in this point that we cannot still demand the words *Besieged, Environn'd,* or *invested* in french *Blocquées* or *Investies,* in the 4th Article of that treaty, to be explaind in Order to prevent differences which is the great End of all Treaties.'

Then follows a long treatise concerning blocking and besieging places, with references to the Dutch.

1674-76. '**A Journal or Narrative of the Proceedings between the Commissioners** appointed by His Majestie and the Commissioners Deputed by the States Generall Pursuant to the Treaty of Peace made at Westminster 9/19 of Feb., 1673/74, concerning a Treaty Marine to be observed throughout all the World. And also an Article perticularly relating to the English and Dutch East India Companyes. Concluded in the year 1674.'   *MS. All Souls College, 265.*

At the top of the page is written in pencil: 'Owen Wynne, Vol. 65 : Duplicate.'

f. 1. 6 July, 1674.   Minutes of meeting of the English Commissioners.

f. 2. 21 June, 1674.   Copy of the Commission of King Charles II. Dated Windsor (Latin).

f. 4. No date.   Notes regarding the meetings, the place where they are to be held, etc.

f. 4-11. 23, 27, 30 July, 1674.   Minutes of the meetings of the Commissioners. 'Propositions of the E.I. Co.' on the 27th July.

f. 12. 4 Aug., 1674.   Minutes of meeting of the Commissioners.

f. 12a. 5 Aug., 1674.   Meeting of the English and Dutch Comissioners at Villiers House, Westminster.

f. 14. 6 Aug., 1674.   Names of the Commissioners furnished to both the English and Dutch.

f. 14-19. 7, 11, 12, 14 Aug., 1674.   Minutes of the meetings of the English Commissioners.

f. 23. 16 May, 1674.   'The Tenor of the forementioned Resolution.' In Dutch, followed by a translation.

f. 25-28. 20, 27, 28 Aug., 1674.   Minutes of the meetings of the English Commissioners, with 'Ordines generales Foederatarum.'

f. 32. 1 Sept., 1674.   Minutes of the meeting of the English Commissioners.   Fourteen Articles drawn up (Latin).

f. 41. No date.   'Formula Literarum—Commeatus vulgo Passiportus' (Latin).

f. 44-49. 8, 9, 15, 19, 21 Sept., 1674.   Minutes of the meetings of the English Commissioners.

f. 51, 58. No date.   Eleven Articles in Latin.

f. 67. No date.   Propositions, Petitions, notes regarding ships, etc.

f. 71, 53, 55, 59. 22, 24, 25 Sept., 1674.   Minutes of the meetings of the English Commissioners.

f. 59-62. 24, 25 Sept., 1674.   The opinions of Sir Robert Wyseman and Dr. Lloyd regarding the Deposition of Robert Lock, Captain of the *Royal Oak,* E.I. Co.'s ship, dated 25 April, 1667, made before

Thos. Bedford, Notary Public, concerning the Island of Dam, with other matters connected with that Island.

f. 65, 68, 73. 28 Sept., 6 and 7 Oct., 1674. Minutes of meetings of the English Commissioners with (fol. 70) eight Articles in Latin, and (fol. 73) seventeen Articles in Latin.

f. 85-102. 8, 15, 18, 19, 22 Oct., and 9 Nov., 1674. Minutes of the meetings of the English Commissioners and discussions on the Articles mentioned above.

f. 103. No date. Answer of the Dutch Commissioners (in Latin) to a paper of the 22 Oct., 1674.

f. 113, 120. 23 and 24 Nov., 1674. Minutes of meetings of the English Commissioners, thirteen Articles (in Latin) and reasons given for the said Articles.

f. 123. Nov., 1674. List of 'Concessions' made by the 'States General to several Articles on 1 December, 1668.'

f. 125. 26 Nov., 1674. The Committee attended the King.

f. 126-41. 26, 27, 28, 30 November, and 2 Dec. 1674. Meetings of the English Commissioners, with the Dutch present on the 27th November.

f. 142. 1 Dec., 1674. 'Tractatus Marinus . . . Londini conclusus primo die Decembris, 1674.' Sixteen Articles (Latin).

f. 159-60. 3, 11 Dec., 1674. Meetings of the English Commissioners.

f. 163-71. 14, 15, 16, 17 Dec., 1674. Meetings of both the English and Dutch Commissioners.

f. 173-81. 18 Dec., 1674, 12, 15, 18 Jan., 1674-75. Meetings of the English Commissioners.

f. 187. 24 Jan., 1674-75. Meeting of the English Commissioners, who attended the King.

f. 187-89. 6, 13, 23 Feb., 1674-75. Meetings of the English Commissioners. Accounts presented.

f. 190. 18 Feb., 1674-75. Long article in Dutch, signed De Haze, Van Muning, Graafiand, Boogaert, etc. Translation of the same in English.

f. 224-29. 26 and 27 Feb., 1, 2, 3, 7 March, 1674-75. Meetings of the English Commissioners. On 3 March they attended the King.

f. 229. 8 March, 1674-75. Meeting of the English and Dutch Commissioners.

f. 230. 8 March, 1674-75. 'Articulus . . . Conclusus Londini octavo die Martii, 1674.' Signed by Culpeper, Downing, Ford, Thomson, Jollife, Corver, Santyn, Beyer, van Vossen, Duvelaer, Michielzen.

f. 236. No date. Accounts for hire of furniture at Fishmongers Hall, etc.

f. 237. 11 March, 1674-75. Mr. Bedford delivered to the English Commissioners a warrant signed by King Charles II, dated Whitehall, 11 March, for payment of expenses.

f. 238. 11 March, 1674-75. Commissioners' warrant for payment of expenses.

f. 241. 'The answer given by the Commissioners to Mr. Secretary Williamson the 24th of September, 1675.' Signed, Ford, Jollife, Downing, Thomson, Buckworth.

f. 241a. 8 Jan., 1675-76. 'A Letter sent by Mr. Secretary Williamson about the point of Revisions.' Dated Whitehall.

f. 242. No date. Extract of Sir William Temple's letter to 'Mr. Secretary' 'about Revisions'.

f. 242a. 16 Feb., 1675-76. 'The Answer of the Commissioners to

Mr. Secretary Williamson's letter of the 8th of January, 1675-76 and the extract of Sir William Temple's letter.'

f. 245.   29 April, 1676.   'The Copy of a second Privy Seale authorizeing the officer of his Majesties Exchequer to make and give allowance of the summe of 1,182*li.* 12*s.* 9*d.*, in Mr. Bedfords Account which summe be paid to the Commissioners to buy them Plate according to his Majesties former warrant.'   Dated Westminster 28th of Charles II.

f. 246a.   19 June, 1676.   'The Copy of a Letter sent by Mr. Secretary Williamson to Sir George Downing.'   Dated Whitehall.

f. 247 to end of MS.   4 June, 1676.   'A Copy of the translation of the Resolution of the States about Revisions.'

[? 1680.]   **'A Project to raise the King a benefit out of the East India trade, without impeaching the Merchants.**   *MS. All Souls College, 211, fol. 11.*

'An estimate shewing what benefit his Majesty may make by the trade to the East Indies, and neither touch the King's Honour, decrease his Customes, nor tax the Company with any charge or losse worth the speaking of, nor disturbe or alter the course they are now in which are the most materiall things that may be objected.'

The first project sets forth that every holder of £100 stock shall lend his Majesty £10 gratis for three years.

The second project suggests that, as often as the Company takes £100 to admit adventurers of £1,000, they should give this £100 to the King or refuse admittance to the adventurer.

Four other projects of a similar nature follow.

1680.   **Copy of 'His Majesties Commission to Prince Rupert, Lord Chancellor Finch,** etc., to treat with the Dutch Ambassador about the business of trade between the Dutch East India Company and our African Company' (Latin).   Dated Whitehall 26 April, 1680.   *MS. All Souls College, 211, fol. 41.*

After the project for a Treaty with the States General made two years since, and Theod. and Leyden and Leewen having been appointed legates by the Dutch to make the project into a Treaty of Navigation and Commerce, the King appoints Prince Rupert, Baron Finch, John Earl of Radnor, and others, to be his deputies to treat with the States General concerning the matter.

1680—   **Papers of the Proceedings of the**   *MS. All Souls Col-*
1685-86.   **English and Dutch Commission-**   *lege, 234.*
ers appointed in behalf of England and the States to decide upon the differences existing between the English and the Dutch East India Companies in reference to the kingdom of Bantam.

pp. 102-5. 13 Oct., 1680. 'Extrait de la lettre generalle du Gouverneur et des Conseillers des Indes de Batavia le 13 Octobre, 1680, ecritte a l'assemblee de Messieurs Les Dix sept, registrée dans le livre des Lettres de Batavia arrivée avec la flote del'an 1681.'

pp. 106-7. [? 1682.] 'Lettre de Paducca Siry Sultan Aboen Nasser Abdul Capar qui a commandement sur tout le Royaume de Bentam a Hiay Aria Monga Sadana que Dieu veille [sic] garder en ce monde et en l'autre.'

pp. 107-12. [? 1682.] 'Lettre de Paducca Siry Sultan Aboen Nasser Abdul Cahar a Hiay Aria Mangon Sadana, pour estre Delivrée au Gouverneur General et a l'Amiral.' Attested 28 April, 1685.

p. 126. [1682.] 'Traduction d'une lettre du Roy Sultan Abdul Elkahaar Aboe Ennazaar escrite au seigneur Major Martin.' Attested 28 April, 1685. Also one from the Regence de Batavia to the young King of Bantam.

p. 127. 1682. 'Traduction de la lettre du Jeune Roy de Bentam, escrite au noble Seigneur Maior [? Martin] et apportée le 9 Mars, 1682 a 4 heures du matin.' Attested 28 April, 1685.

pp. 161-63. 1682. 'Extrait tiré des remarques faites par moy sousigné, des choses les plus remarquables arrivées pendant mon voyage a Batavia en Hollande en l'an 1682.' Signed, Daniel Heins. Attested 28 April, 1685, by Velters.

pp. 164-65. [1682.] 'Extrait d'un bref rapport fait a Monsieur Corneille Speelman et aux autres Conseillers des Indes par François Tack touchant beaucoup de choses qui se sont passées pendant son séjour a Bantam.'

p. 165. [1682.] 'Autre Extrait du meme rapport contenant la lettre du Resident françois le Sieur Guilhem.'

p. 166. 1682. 'Extrait d'un livre nommé The Civil Wars of Bentam or an Impartiall relation, etc. Imprimé a Londres chez H. C. pour Tho. Malthus à l'enseigne du Soleil dans le Poultrey l'an 1682.'

pp. 166-67. 1 Jan. to 30 Sept., 1682. 'Extrait du Journal de Batavia commençant le premier Janvier, etc., finissant le derneir de Septembre, 1682 ' (fol. 818).

pp. 121-25. 1 Jan. to 30 Sept., 1682. Extract from the Journal as above (fol. 441).

pp. 128-30. 1 Jan.—30 Sept., 1682. Extract from the Journal as above (fol. 275).

p. 130. 6 March, 1682. 'Lettre de Leurs Seigneurs escrite au Vieux Sultan de Bantam.' Dated 'L'Isle de Grande Java.' Attested 28 April, 1685.

pp. 113-18. [11] March, 1682. 'Traduction de la lettre de Paducca Siry Sultan Abd El-Cahar Abboe Ennazaar Roy de Bentam au Con-seiller Corneille Speelman Gouverneur General des Indes du Pays bas, etc., escrite en date du 11e du mois Rabeallawel a compter de la fin du mois de l'an 1093 qui est selon notre style le [11] de Mars, 1682.'

p. 31. 1 April, 1682. 'Extrait du livre des Deliberations.' Signed Gosnall, Hodges, Burdett, Fisher. Dated at Bantam.

pp. 31-34. 1 April, 1682. Attestation of William Smith, commander of Le Retour and James Jefcot, commander of the Formosa, also of James Harrison 'tonnelier' of Le Retour. Dated Bantam. Further attestations of Gosnell, Knipe and Burdett on 11 April (French).

pp. 168-69. 3 April, 1682. Letter from Edward Barwell, Nicholas Wayte,

Charles Sweeting, etc. to the Dutch E.I. Co., dated Bantam. Attested 28 April, 1685.

pp. 119-20. ? April, 1682. 'Lettre du Roy Sultan Abdul Elkadaar Aboe Ennazaar au . . . le Major Martin, laquelle est un extrait de la traduction d'une autre lettre escrite auparavant par sa Majesté au dit Major.' Attested true copy, 28 April, 1685.

pp. 34-35. 4 April, 1682. Two 'Depositions authentiques du Capitaine Jean Fisher.'

pp. 30-31. 20 June, 1682. 'Extrait d'une lettre du Capitaine Jean Utbers à Monsieur Ed. Rudge Directeur de la Compagnie des Indes Orientales d'Angleterre datée à Polofe.'

pp. 147-48. 25 June, 1682. Deposition of 'Pangeram Aria Dipa Ningerat et Key Aria Singa Weeiaya tous deux Ambassadeurs du Roy de Bentam' before David Regulet notary public, at Batavia.

pp. 154-55. 29 June 1682. Deposition of 'Martinas Dias de Malacca et françois de Tutucoryn.'

pp. 155-59. July, 1682. Similar deposition of David Soleman, merchant.

p. 170. 5 Oct., 1682. 'Extrait de la lettre du Gouverneur General et du Conseil de Bantam a L'Assemblée des Dix Sept.' Attested 28 April, 1685.

pp. 149-54. 6 Nov., 1682. Deposition of 'Le Sieur Michel Vanden Buisch battelier et Nicolas Maurits chef Pilot tous deux au service de la Compagnie et employez sur le vaisseau nommé *Europe*.'

pp. 131-46. 1683. 'Extraits des considerations de Mr. St. Martin sur le Memoire que Mr Chevalier Chardin presente de la part de la Compagnie des Indes Orientales d'Angleterre aux Seigneurs Estats Generaux des Provinces Unies en L'an 1683 au sujet de Bentan.'

pp. 39-42. 16 April [1683]. 'Attestation de Mr. Nicolas Waite cydevant Marchand à Bantam aux Indes Orientales.'

pp. 36-39. 'Attestation de Mr. Charles Sweeting cydevant Marchand et du Conseil de la Compagnie des Indes Orientales à Bantam.'

pp. 100-1. 17 Aug., 1683. Extrait d'une lettre de Messieurs Les Estats Generaux des Provinces unies du 17 d'Aoust, 1683.'

pp. 16-20. 23 Dec., 1683. 'A breif memoriall of the late transactions at Bantam extracted from the Companys Generall letter by the *Amoy Merchant*, dated from Batavia the 23rd December, 1683 and from Mr. Charles Sweeting of the 17th ditto (English).

pp. 42-48. 25 June, 1684. 'Relation d'Amboise Moody qui a demeuré cinq ans à Bentam et y a esté detenu cinq mois prisonier par les Hollandois.'

p. 160. 21 Dec., 1684. Letter from Daniel Heins stating that he is sending an abridged account of affairs at Bentam. Attested at Amsterdam 28 April, 1685.

p. 3-6. 21 April, 1685. Commission of the Dutch Commissioners (Latin).

pp. 7-9. 9 Aug., 1685. Commission of the English Commissioners (Latin).

p. 1. 3 Sept., 1685. Meeting of the English Commissioners at the Lord Treasurer's lodgings in Whitehall. Sir Josiah Child and Sir Benjamin Bathurst called in on behalf of the E.I.Co.

p. 1. 10 Sept., 1685. Metting of the English and Dutch Commissioners at Whitehall. Commissions read. The Dutch desire the English to send them a memorial of their demands.

pp. 11-15. 15 Sept., 1685. Copy of complaint of the English E.I. Co.

to the Commissioners. Nine articles. Signed by Governor Ashe, and Child, Bathurst and Sambrooke (English).

p. 11. 17 Sept., 1685. The memorial of the E.I.Co. in English and French received.

pp. 11-15. 18 Sept., 1685. Various French papers delivered to the Dutch, including the memorial of the 15th September.

pp. 20-25. 18 Sept., 1685. Complaint of the E.I. Co., as on pp. 11-15 (in French) delivered to Mons. Heinsius.

pp. 49-99. 13 Oct., 1685. 'Replique de Messieurs les Commissaires de Hollande faite à Westminster.'

pp. 191-215. 13 Oct., 1685. 'Translate of the Dutch Instructours reply.' Signed G. Hooft, Jacob van Hoorn, Fr. Blocquery, A. Pacts (English).

pp. 216-37. 22 Oct., 1685. 'The answer of the English and East Indian company' (French). Translation of the preceding (English). Signed Ashe, Child, Sambrooke, Bathurst.

pp. 239-63. 19 Nov., 1685. 'The Dutch Rejoynder to the answer of the Inglish.' Signed Hooft, Van Hoorn, Blocquery, Pacts (French). Translation of the same (English).

pp. 264-65. 26 and 29 Nov., and 2 Dec., 1685. Reports of meetings of the English and Dutch Commissioners.

pp. 266-83. 2 Dec., 1685. 'English last paper' (French). Translation of the same (English).

pp. 274-86. 2 Dec., 1685. 'Dutch last paper which concluded the papers' (French). Translation of the same (English).

p. 287. 4 Dec., 1685. Report of the Meeting of the Commissioners (English).

pp. 288-91. 9 Dec., 1685. Letter from the Court of Committees of the East India Company to the Commissioners appointed to treat of the differences between the English and Dutch.

pp. 298-99. 22 Dec., 1685. 'Extrait du Registre des Resolutions des Hauts et Puissants Seigneurs des Etats Generaux des Provinces unies des Pais bas.'

p. 292. 28 Dec., 1685. Report of a meeting of the Commissioners. Various letters sent.

p. 294. 30 Dec., 1685. Report of a meeting of the Commissioners when the General Committee of the E.I. Co. attended.

p. 300. Dec., 1685. 'Act to prolong the term of treating with the Dutch (English).

pp. 295-96. 2 Jan., 1685-86. Letter from the Court of Committees of the E.I.Co. to the Commissioners appointed to treat of the differences between the English and Dutch.

p. 297. 7 Jan., 1685-86. Report of a meeting of the English and Dutch Commissioners.

p. 303. 8-18 March, 1685-86. Paper signed by both the English and Dutch Commissioners, attesting their inability to agree within the time prescribed. They therefore leave judgment to the King of Great Britain and the States General to be terminated according to the tenor of the convention of 8-18 March, 1674-75.

[? 1682.]   **Papers having reference to the East**   *MS. All Souls Col-*
                  India Co.   *lege, 239.*

f. 436-37. Unsigned letter to Sir Leslie Jenkins concerning matters discussed with him the day before, relating to alterations in ' the present

East India Company', which 'I observed stuck with his Majestie.'
The letter also refers to the New Charter, new subscriptions, controversy between the East India Company and the Turkey Company,
etc. The letter is dated 8 June, but the year is missing.

f. 451-52. A paper without title or signature suggesting that the East
India Company's patent being under debate, his Majesty himself
should put £200,000 into the stock. The sum need not come out of
his own purse but could be lent him upon the credit of the Co. The
writer brings forward arguments in favour of this scheme. The
letter contains a mention of the year 1680, but the document is
undated.

f. 453. 17 April, 1682. Paper referring to the petition of the E.I. Co.
heard by the Privy Council, to new money subscribed, and expressing a hope that the New Charter may be determined and that the
money subscribed may be taken into the trade under it. The writer
conceives that thereby no prejudice will arise to (1) His Majesty's
Government, (2) his revenue, (3) the East India trade.

f. 454. 'The two Questions proposed.'
1. 'What expedient they would offer to make the trade of the
East India Company lesse prejudiciall to the Nation than it is now
said to be.'
2. 'What they will offer for the particular Government of a new
Company, that the power may lie in the hands of such only as shall
be well affected to the present Government.'
Answers to the above. No date.

f. 455. An unsigned letter relating to the new subscriptions for the
East India Company, to the silk trade and to the prejudice of the
Turkey merchants against the same.

1682-86.   **Various Papers respecting the dis-**   *MS. All Souls Col-*
            pute between the English and   *lege, 273, fols. 1-37.*
            Dutch East India Companies concern-
            ing Bantam.

f. 29-32. 23 Sept., 1682. 'A Brief Memoriall of the late transactions at
Bantam extracted out of the Companies Generall Letter by the *Amoy
Merchant*, dated from Batavia, 23rd September 1682, and from Mr.
Charles Sweeting of the 17th do.'

f. 1-2. 14 March, 1682-83. Petition of the E.I. Co. to the King, followed
by a narrative of events in Bantam, the first date being 14 March
1682-83 and the last, 12 April [1683]. There is no date to the
Petition.

f. 4-5. 14 March, 1682-83. Paper giving an account of affairs in Bantam.
Begins : 'Que la guerre stant survenue entre le vieux Sultan de
Bentam et le jeune Sultan son fils.' First date, 14 March, 1682-83, last
date, 9 May [1683].

f. 3. 26 April, 1683. Letter from King Charles II to the States General
concerning affairs in Bantam. Dated Hampton Court (French).

f. 3a. [No date.] Unsigned letter from one of the King's emissaries to
the States General, detailing the state of affairs in Bantam and praying
them to withdraw their army from that place (French).

f. 5a. 25 May, 1683. 'Extraict du registre des resolutions des Hauts et
Puissants Seigneurs Estats Generaux des Provinces Unies des Pais
Bas.'

f. 6.   25 May, 1683.   Letter from the States General to King Charles II, signed Van Wyngaend and H. Fagel, in answer to one of the 26 April, 1683 (French).

f. 7.   16-26 May, 1683.   Unsigned letter from [?] the Danish Ambassador to the States General concerning the Danish E.I. Co. at Bantam. Dated from The Hague.

f. 7-11.   16-26 June, 1684.   The Ambassador of the States General, Arn. van Cittrs, to Charles II, concerning affairs at Bantam.   Dated from Windsor (French).

f. 12.   15 Aug., 1684.   Reply from Charles II to the above.   Dated from Windsor.

f. 13-13a.·   No date.   Passport to the Commissioners from the States General and the Dutch E.I. Co., permitting them to leave England (French).   Followed by the names of the Commissioners.

f. 14-16.   27 Feb., 1684-85.   Official passport from King James II to the Commissioners as above.   Dated Whitehall (Latin).

f. 17.   No date.   Letter from the States General to King [James II], praying that the Commissioners may have access to his presence (French).

f. 18.   21 April, 1685.   Ditto to ditto, with the same request.   Dated, The Hague (French).

f. 20-22.   21 April, 1685.   Orders for the Commissioners.   Dated, The Hague.   Begins : ' Ordines Generales Faederatarum Belgii Provinciarum Universis et singulis ', etc. (Latin).

f. 19-20.   21 April, 1685.   Extract of an unsigned letter from the States General, dated from The Hague, naming their Commissioners, stating the time to be accorded to them, etc. (English).

f. 19.   13 May, 1685.   Letter signed Middleton to Ashe, Govr. of the E.I. Co. stating that the King desires the Co. to appoint Commissioners to meet the Dutch Commissioners about the Bantam affairs (English).

f. 23.   No date.   Letter from ' Sultan Abdull Fathee Abdull Fattah King of Terteassa Atman Surah', praying him [? Charles II] to assist him against the Dutch who are fighting with Sultan ' Annome ' against him.

f. 23-24.   20-30 May, 1685.   Letter signed by the Dutch Commissioners Hooft, van Hoorn, Blockquery, Paets, to ' Amplissimi et Nobilissimi Domini ', dated at Westminster, concerning the conference to be held, praying that Latin may be the language employed (Latin).

f. 24.   25 May, 1685.   Letter signed Ashe, Child, Bathurst and Sambrooke (of the Court of Committees of the E.I. Co.) in answer to the preceding.   They consider that the French language will be a more convenient medium than Latin, in which to conduct the conference (Latin).

f. 25.   27 May, 1685.   Commr. Hooft, etc. to Govr. Ashe, dated Westminster, concerning the projected conference (French).

f. 26.   1 June, 1685.   Govr. Ashe, etc. to Commr. Hooft, etc.   Dated London.   Concerning the conference and affairs at Bantam (French).

f. 26a.   5 June, 1685.   Commr. Hooft, etc. to Govr. Ashe, etc. Dated Westminster.   In reply to the above (French).

f. 27.   10 June, 1685.   Govr. Ashe, etc. to Commr. Hooft etc. Dated London (French).

f. 28.   11 June, 1685.   Commr. Hooft etc. to Govr. Ashe, etc.   Dated Westminster (French).

f. 28a.   17 June, 1685.   Govr. Ashe, etc. to Commr. Hooft, etc.   Dated
London (French).

f. 32-34.   24 June, 1685.   Letter signed Childs, Bathurst and Sambrooke,
to the Commissioners for determination of differences concerning
Bantam between the English and Dutch East India Companies.

f. 34-35.   [June, 1685.]   'The English East India Company's demands
from and upon the Dutch East India Company for damages sustained
by them, by reason of the surprize of Bantam.'   The damages
are estimated at £355,775.   Signed by Child, Bathurst and Sambrooke.

f. 36.   8-18 March, 1685-86.   'Last Account about Bantam.'   Signed by
the English and Dutch Commissioners at Whitehall (French).

1683.   *MS. All Souls Col-*
lege, 210.

f. 145.   1 Aug., 1683.   Copy of Letters Patent granted by the King to
his Majesty's Commissioners for 'executing the office of Lord High
Admirall of England to Impower them to grant Commissions to such
commanders of ships as shall be recommended by the East India
Company, and approved of by the King to aid and assist them and
their forces against the young King of Bantam and his subjects or
against any other Infidell Prince or Princes whatsoever.'   Dated
1 Aug., 35 Charles II.

f. 142.   14 Aug., 1683.   Copy of a Warrant from the Lords Commissioners of the Admiralty for issuing a Commission to Sir Thomas
Grantham, Kt., Commander of the ship *Charles,* to aid and assist the
E.I. Co. and their forces, etc. against the young King of Bantam and
his subjects, or any other Infidel Prince, etc.   Dated from Derby.

f. 143.   15 Aug., 1683.   Commission granted to Sir Thomas Grantham
as above.

f. 143a.   15 Aug., 1683.   A like Commission granted to Captain John
Nicholson, Commander of the *Beaufort.*

f. 145.   14 Sept., 1683.   Copy of Letters Patent identical with that given
above, dated 1 August, 1683.

f. 146.   6 Oct., 1683.   Copy of a Warrant for issuing a Commission
to Captain John Nicholson, Commander of the *Beaufort,* for aiding
the East India Company against the young King of Bantam.

f. 147.   6 Oct., 1683.   Commission granted to Captain John Nicholson
as above.

f. 149.   6 Oct., 1683.   Like Commissions granted to Captain William
Dyke, Commander of the *Rochester*, and to Sir John Wetwang,
Commander of the *Royal James.*

For other MSS. connected with Sir Thomas Grantham's Mission to Bantam, see Harl.
MS. 4753 (British Museum); Original Correspondence, Nos. 5186, 5234, 5235, 5236, 5250,
5256-62, 5282, 5301 (India Office Records); MS. Rawl. A. 257 (Bodleian Library).

1683-85.   The Case of Thomas Sandys.   Re-   *MS. All Souls Col-*
port of the Pleadings and Arguments   *lege, 210, pp. 1-73,*
in the King's Bench, 35, 36 Car. II, in   *contd. as fols. 74-*
the case of the East India Company of   *125.*
merchants against Sandys.

p. 1.   Begins 8 November, 35 Chas. II.
For the E.I.Co. against Sands the Interloper.   Mr. Holt's pleading.

p. 23.   Trinity Term, 35 Chas. II. Rot. 126.
          Sir G. Treby for Sands.
p. 61.   Easter Term, 36 Chas. II, 19 April, 1684.
          Mr. Finch for the E.I. Co.
f. 76.   Mr. Pollexfen for Sands.
f. 103. Mr. Williams for Sands.
f. 152-73. East India Company *versus* Sandys.   The Lord Chief
          Justice's Judgment against Sandys.

1684.   **Case of the E.I. Co. *versus* Thomas**   *MS. All Souls Col-*
          Sandys, 31 January, 1684.   *lege, 220.*

f. 14-31.   Arguments of Mr. Justice Walcot, Mr. Justice Holloway and
          Mr. Justice Wilkins.

Note.—For other MSS. dealing with this case, see Harl. MSS. 769, 1222, 4139, Lansd.
MSS. 650, 1219, Add. MS. 10615 (British Museum); MSS. Rawl. A. 193, C. 130, D. 747.

[1683.]   **Copy of Charles II's Confirmation**   *MS. All Souls Col-*
          of the Charter of the East India   *lege, 229, fols. 254-*
          Company (undated).   *57.*

f. 257a. 22 July, 1683. Warrant under Royal Sign Manual to the E.I. Co.
          to seize any ships, etc., which shall be brought from, or conveyed to
          any place within the Company's limits contrary to their former
          charter, one moiety of the forfeiture to be the King's, the other the
          Company's. The warrant also grants them the government of Forts,
          etc. and confers on them power to make peace or war, etc.

PRIVY COUNCIL REGISTERS

PRIVY COUNCIL REGISTERS

1600.   **Letter, dated 16 Sept., 1600, from**   *P.C. 2/25, fol. 366.*
             the Privy Council to Sir John
             Harte, Kt., Alderman Banneringe, and
             the rest of the Adventurers in the
             intended voyage to the East Indies.

The Adventurers desire to 'set forth' 6 ships and 6 pinnaces for the above voyage. Her Majesty having considered the request, approves the voyage and gives permission for preparations to be made.

1600.   **Letter from the Privy Council to**   *P.C. 2/25, fols. 399-*
             the Adventurers in the intended   *400.*
             voyage to the East Indies.

Although Her Majesty's permission has been given for the furtherance of this voyage, proceedings have apparently been 'stayed' upon a rumour that the voyage will not be permitted. The Adventurers are informed that Her Majesty's permission having been given, it cannot be withdrawn without dishonour, and they are therefore encouraged to hasten all preparations.

1600-1.   **Letter from the Privy Council to**   *P.C. 2/26, fol. 41.*
             the Attorney General, dated 4 Jan-
             uary 1600-1.

Stating that the Commission under the Great Seal for making new coinage for merchants going to the East Indies is defective and praying for a speedy correction, or the whole voyage may be endangered.

1600-1.   **Order in Council dated 11 January,**   *P.C. 2/26, fol. 33.*
             1600-1.

Great difficulties having been caused to the newly chartered E.I. Co., owing to subscribers who formerly promised subscriptions retracting their promises, they are now ordered to furnish their promised contributions 'by Satterday nexte' or they shall be committed to prison until they comply.

[*Note.*—The Registers from 1604 to 1612, were destroyed by fire.]

1613.   **Letter from the Privy Council to**   *P.C. 2/27, fol. 94a.*
             Sir Daniel Dunn, Judge of the
             Admiralty, dated 14 Oct., 1613.

Reporting the mutinous conduct of the crews of East India ships and suggesting measures to be taken to prevent the hazard of the loss of ships and goods.

1613.   **Letter from the Privy Council to**   *P.C. 2/27, fols. 95-*
             Lord Chichester, Lord Deputy of   *95a.*
             Ireland, dated 7 Nov., 1613.

Reports the seizure as a pirate of the E.I. Co.'s ship *Peppercorn* at Waterford on her return voyage and the imprisonment of her captain, Nicholas Downton, and members of his crew. It is ordered that the vessel and prisoners be released and assistance rendered them.

A similar letter of the same date was sent to the Earl of Ormond.

1613.   **Letter from the Privy Council to**   *P.C. 2/27, fols. 104a-*
                   Sir Thomas Edmondes, Kt., H.M.   *5.*
                   Ambassador with the French King,
                   dated 29 Nov., 1613.

Regarding the unpaid balance of the loss on the *Union*, wrecked and plundered off Brittany in 1611, on her return from the East Indies.

1613-14.   **Letter from the Privy Council to**   *P.C. 2/27, fols. 119,*
                   Sir Richard Sands, Kt., dated 11   *124.*
                   Jan. 1613-14.

Orders regarding goods landed at Queenborough from the E.I. Co's ship *Pearl*, wrecked on the coast of Ireland.

A similar letter, dated 13 Jan., regarding goods from the same ship taken to Wales.

1613-14.   **Order in Council, 17 March, 1613-14.**   *P.C. 2/27, fol. 137a.*

A ship, illegally freighted for the East Indies by Englishmen and foreigners, about to sail from France, is forbidden to proceed. Eustace Man is to be sent back to England.

1614-15.   **Warrant of Privy Council,** dated 20   *P.C. 2/27, fols. 259a-*
                   Jan., 1614-15.   *60.*

Transportation of 17 persons (named) to be delivered to the Govr. of the E.I. Co. for conveyance to the East Indies or other parts beyond the seas. (See also 24 March 1616-17.)

1614-15.   **Order in Council,** dated 12 February,   *P.C. 2/27, fol. 270.*
                   1614-15.

Forbidding interloping trade in the countries included in the Charter of the E.I. Co.

1615.   **Letter from the P.C. to the Lord**   *P.C. 2/27, fol. 309.*
                   Admiral, dated 14 May, 1615.

Requesting the 'stay' of two ships lately built at Shoreham and intended for the East Indies.

1615.   **Letter from the P.C. to Sir Thomas**   *P.C 2/27, fols. 311-*
                   Edmondes, H.M. Ambassador in   *11a.*
                   France, dated 21 May, 1615.

Information has been received of a ship now at Brest, preparing for the East Indies, having obtained a Commission from the French King : detriment to the E.I. trade and probable piracy expected therefrom. The voyage to be prevented and the merchants sent to England.

1615.   **Letter from the P.C. to Sir Thomas**   *P.C. 2/28, fol. 23.*
                   Edmondes, dated 19 June, 1615.

He is requested to take steps at all times to prevent vessels from being fitted out for the East Indies in any part of France to the prejudice of the E.I. Co.

1615.   **Order in Council,** dated 3 December,   *P.C. 2/28, fol. 113.*
                   1615.

Permitting £500 to be sent to Ireland to bring home the *Hope*, lately from the East Indies.

1616-17.   Order in Council, dated 20 January,   *P.C. 2/28, fol. 143.*
            1616-17.

Enjoining the Lord Treasurer to permit the unloading of a quantity of quicksilver, elephants' teeth and vermilion, brought in two Dutch pinks by the merchants trading to the E. Indies.

1616-17.   Warrant of the Privy Council,   *P.C. 2/28, fols. 601-2.*
            dated 24 March, 1616-17, for the
            transportation of criminals.

Persons condemned to die for 'robbery or felony (willful murther, rape, witchcraft or Burglary onely excepted),' who may be considered 'fitt to be imployed in forreine discoveryes or other services beyond the Seaes ' may be certified in writing by Judges or Serjeants in Law, and may be reprieved and employed as proposed. But if they refuse to go, or if they return before the time limited, they shall be subject to the execution of the law as first adjudged. In pursuance of this power, John Browne is reprieved and appointed to be delivered to Sir Thomas Smith, Govr. of the E.I. Co. or his Assignees, to be conveyed into the East Indies or other parts beyond the seas.

There are several similar transportation orders in the succeeding volume, P.C. 2/29.

1617.   Proceedings of the Privy Council,   *P.C. 2/29, fol. 70.*
         29 June, 1617.

Permission is granted to the E.I. Co. to purchase silver bullion and Spanish money recovered from a wreck off Sussex in order to furnish money for their next voyage to the East Indies provided they do not exceed the yearly transportation of £30,000.

1617.   Proceedings of the Privy Council,   *P.C. 2/29, fol. 140.*
         12 Oct., 1617.

Enquiry to be made into the allegations that the E.I. Co. have obtained forcible possession of Leadenhall from the Merchant Staplers, that they have removed locks from their doors, and replaced them by others, etc., etc.

1618.   Proceedings of the Privy Council,   *P.C. 2/29, fol. 399.*
         24 May, 1618.

The East India Company, in conjunction with the Muscovy Co., is to advance a loan of 100,000 roubles to the Emperor of Russia.

1618.   Letter from the Privy Council to   *P.C. 2/29, fol. 507.*
         the Govrs. and Companies of the
         Merchant Adventurers and the East
         Indies, dated 6 September, 1618.

Information has been received that the Company's trade in the United Provinces is not profitable on account of the inconvenient situation of their staple. To enable His Majesty to form his own judgment, the Companies are required to report the value of their goods and debts now in the United Provinces, their nature and sort, etc.

1619.   Proceedings of the Privy Council,   *P.C. 2/30, fols. 241-*
         27 June, 1619.   *42.*

Regarding a controversy between the E.I. Co. and the Dutch as to building forts on the Isles of Molucca and Banda. The urgency on both sides nearly caused the breaking off of the Treaty. His Majesty suspends the question for three years for the benefit of his merchants and in order to compose the differences that have happened between them and the Dutch in the East Indies, where hostilities and much shedding of blood have occurred. His Majesty assures the Company of his favour and care towards them and of His Royal protection against all injury by others. If, at the end of the three years, the Dutch will not accommodate the merchants in the matter of forts, etc., His Majesty will break off the Treaty and provide what is most suitable.

1619-20. **Proceedings of the Privy Council,** *P.C. 2/30, fol. 414.*
4 Feb., 1619-20.

A return to be made of the articles of Trade to and from the East Indies and of the quantities exported and imported for the last four years.

1619-20. **Proceedings of the Privy Council,** *P.C. 2/30, fol. 434.*
28 Feb., 1619-20.

Proposition of a separation between the Muscovy and East India Companies. Remonstrance by the Muscovy merchants.

1620. **Letter from the Privy Council to** *P.C. 2/30, fol. 550.*
Sir Henry Martin, Kt., Judge of
the Admiralty, etc., dated 4 July, 1620.

The E.I. Co., in Dec. 1618, sent the *Bear* and *Star* to the East Indies, Thomas Berwick being in command of the former. On his arrival in India, Berwick allowed certain of the Company's ships to become a prey to the Dutch and also surrendered the *Bear* to them without resistance. Such conduct being deserving of punishment, Berwick has been placed in Newgate. The Company pray for 'legal course' against him.

Two more letters on the same subject were written on the 12th July, and 11th Dec., 1620. See fols. 563, 649.

1621. **Petition from the E.I. Co. to the** *P.C. 2/31, fols. 54-*
Privy Council, dated 16 June, 1621.   *55.*

They complain of the insufferable wrongs done to them by the Dutch in taking their ships and goods (of which they can get no restitution), using violence upon the persons of their factors in the East Indies, and otherwise breaking the Treaty. Sir Noel Caron, Ambassador Resident for the States General, is called before the Board and representations made to him of these matters. He is reminded of the promises formerly made that Commissioners should arrive last Whitsuntide for the settlement of differences and is informed that redress is expected. The Ambassador promises that the Commissioners shall arrive by Midsummer, with full authority to give satisfaction.

1621. **Letter from the Privy Council to** *P.C. 2/31, fol. 169.*
the E.I. Co., dated 19 Oct., 1621.

Engaging their favour and courtesy towards Danish merchants in the East Indies.

1621. **The charges of the E.I. Co. against** *P.C. 2/31, fols. 186,*
George Ball, while factor in the East   *197-98.*
Indies, heard by the Board, 9 Nov.,
1621.

It is ordered that the charges be put in writing and a due trial take place.

On 23 Nov., the E.I. Co. announce their intention to proceed against George Ball in the Star Chamber.

1621-22.   **Letter from the Privy Council to**   *P.C. 2/31, fols. 265-*
the King's Majesty, dated 9 Feb.,   *68.*
1621-22.

Regarding the E.I. Co. and the Ambassadors of the States General.

Note of a conference between the English Commissioners and those of the States
General to discuss the restoration and compensation for goods seized in the East Indies
and also property. The Dutch exorbitant in their demands. Long account of proceedings on the subject.

1622.   **Letters from the Privy Council to**   *P.C. 2/31, fols. 494-*
His Majesty, dated 19 and 24 Oct.,   *95, 501.*
1622.

Dealing with a proposed conference between the Ambassadors of the States General
and the King concerning the affairs of the E.I. Co. The importance of the subject
is emphasized as it involves a considerable revenue to the King. The Council's opinion
on the matter is expressed at length.

1622.   **Letters from the Privy Council to**   *P.C. 2/31, fols. 513-*
His Majesty, dated 19 Nov. and 3   *15, 526-27.*
Dec., 1622. Conference with the Am-
bassadors of the States General.

The following points were discussed : Disputes regarding Bantam ; pepper brought
into Holland ; restitution of goods at Lantore ; the exchange of reals of eight.

No satisfaction was obtained. The Ambassadors refused to permit the erection of
forts at Molucca, Amboyna and Banda, although the Treaty period had elapsed,
Long discussions had taken place, but no settlement was reached. The Ambassadors
had withdrawn to Newmarket, etc., etc.

1623-24.   **Declaration of King James of** 30   *P.C. 2/31, fols. 568-*
Jan., 1623-24.   *69.*

Regarding various points of the East India business. Freedom to both Companies
to erect forts in India under certain conditions, excepting only Molucca, Banda and
Amboyna ; forts built by the Netherlands Co. since the Treaty to be demolished ;
remarks on ships of defence, punishment of offences, payment and victualling of
garrisons, enforcement of courtesy and good treatment to English subjects by Govrs.
and others, etc., etc.

1623-24.   **Note of payment, on the 31st Jan.,**   *P.C. 2/31, fol. 572.*
1623-24 of £20,000 by the Ambas-
sadors of the States General to the E.I.
Co. in reals of eight (Spanish dollars).

1624.   **Proceedings of the Privy Council,**   *P.C. 2/32, fols. 407-8.*
5 Aug., 1624.

The E.I. Co. desire to be wholly separated from the Dutch and therefore wish the
Treaty to be declared void· They further desire to be allowed to erect forts in India and
to be guaranteed against loss from Dutch ill-usage. They request that a Dutch ship, now
in Plymouth from the East Indies (value £60,000) may be seized and also measures taken
to capture four other Dutch ships shortly expected, etc., etc.

The Council notes the Company's apparent hesitation as to accepting His Majesty's
offer to become an adventurer.

1624. **Report of the Deliberations of 27** *P.C. 2/32, fol. 456.*
September, 1624, on the Massacre
at Amboyna.

The inhuman cruelties and ignoring of treaties by the Dutch are emphasised, also
the fact that no reparation has followed remonstrance against their action. A resolution
to seize Dutch East India ships is approved.

1624. **Letter from the Privy Council to** *P.C. 2/32, fol. 456.*
the Duke of Buckingham, Lord
High Admiral.

A fleet is to be fitted out to seize Dutch East India ships, either outward or homeward bound, as a reprisal for the massacre at Amboyna.

1625-26. **Proceedings of the Privy Council,** *P.C. 2/32, fol. 614.*
28 January, 1625-26.

The E.I. Co. represent the refusal of the Dutch to give any satisfaction for the wrongs
done by them, especially at Amboyna. Their Lordships resolve to prosecute their
measures against the Netherlands Co.

1626. **Letters from the Privy Council to** *P.C. 2/33, fols. 85,*
the E.I. Company, dated 20 July, *87.*
and 4 August, 1626.

The Company is rebuked for remissness in managing their trade in the East Indies
and for resolving to abandon it.

Redress is ordered for wrongs and the members are ordered to continue in company
though they cannot meet at present, owing to the plague.

1626. **Proceedings of the Privy Council,** *P.C. 2/33, fol. 204.*
20 Dec., 1626.

A Letter to be sent to the Ambassador of the Low Countries, praying for freedom of
trade in Bantam for the E.I. Co.

1626-27. **Proceedings of the Privy Council,** *P.C. 2/33, fol. 230.*
12 Feb., 1626-27.

The E.I. Co. to be allowed to export gold to the amount of £30,000 in lieu of silver.

1626-27. **Letter from the Privy Council to** *P.C. 2/35, fols. 275-*
the President and factors of the *76.*
E.I. Co. residing in Persia and Surat,
dated 26 Feb., 1627-28.

H.M.'s Ambassadors, Sir Dodmore Cotton and Sir Robert Sherley, are to be transported
to Persia in one of the E.I. Co.'s ships outward bound, viz., the *Mary, Hart, Star,*
Hopewell and a pinnace called the *Scout.* They are to go merely as passengers, having
no control over the ships or goods ; and when landed they are to have authority only in
things pertaining to their Commissions.

1627. **Proceedings of the Privy Council,** *P.C. 2/35, fol. 349a.*
11 April, 1627.

Whereas on the 20th March last His Majesty granted permission to the E.I. Co to
transport to the Indies in English gold or silver coin the sum of £20,000 on condition that
within three months the said Company should bring into His Majesty's Mint the sum of

£25,000 foreign coin to be coined there, the Company only used His Majesty's favour to export £10,000. They therefore pray only to return £12,500, the just proportion. Agreed to.

1627.   Proceedings of the Privy Council, *P.C. 2/36, fol. 235a.*
19 December, 1627.

It is reported that large quantities of saltpetre are imported into England in the ships of the E.I. Co. and in those of the Dutch Company, now ' stayed ' at Portsmouth. It is ordered that all the saltpetre of both Companies be ' stayed ', being greatly needed, until the quality and value be tested, when further orders shall be given.

1627-28.   Letter from the Privy Council to *P.C. 2/36, fols. 251-*
the Surveyor of the Land Carri- *51a.*
ages, H.M. Customs in the Port of
London, dated 4 January, 1627-28.

Goods laden in the *Expedition* from the East Indies, the property of the East India Company, have been secretly landed in the Isle of Wight and elsewhere to the detriment of the Company and of H.M.'s customs. H.M.'s Warrant for the surrender of such goods has been defied. All such goods are to be seized, etc.

Further proceedings concerning the same affair in fols. 262, 281, 313.

1627-28.   Letter from the Privy Council to *P.C. 2/36, fol. 273.*
the Govr. and the E.I. Co., dated 25
Jan., 1627-28.

All vessels belonging to the said Company to be prepared for Government service in case of need.

1628.   Warrant, dated 30 May, 1628.   *P.C. 2/36, fol. 181.*

To free the E.I. Co. from their contract to bring in £40,000 in foreign gold, they having brought in a relative proportion.

1628.   Order in Council, dated 11 July, 1628.   *P.C. 2/38, fols. 297-*
98.

In accordance with former promises by His Majesty to the E.I. Co. of support and assistance in case of injustice on the part of the Netherlands E.I. Co., three of the said Company's ships were seized at Portsmouth as a reprisal for the Amboyna massacre. The Ambassador of the States General now definitely promises the arrival of an Embassy in Sept. next to settle all differences, and His Majesty therefore permits the release of the ships on this understanding, promising the East India Company future aid should the States not fulfil their promises.

1628.   Proceedings of the Privy Council, *P.C. 2/38, fol. 340.*
30 July, 1628.

The books printed by Nicolas Bourne, by order of the E.I. Co., touching the business of Amboyna, to be delivered to the East India Company, but not to be published.

1628.   Letter from the Privy Council to *P.C. 2/38, fols. 390-*
Lord Conway, dated 12 August, *91.*
1628.

Respecting the release of the Dutch ships detained at Portsmouth. Men-of-war sent to convoy them.

1628.   **Letter from the Privy Council to**   *P.C. 2/38, fol. 423.*
               Lord Conway, dated 27 August,
               1628.

Representation made by the E.I. Co. of the depressed state of their trade and their
doubts of being able to continue.

1628.   **Letter from the Privy Council to**   *P.C. 2/38, fols. 476-*
               Dudley Carleton Esq., His Majes-   *77.*
               ty's Agent with the States of the United
               Provinces, dated 23 Sept., 1628.

Representation to be made of the need for deputies to be sent to England, if further
evidence is needed of the Amboyna affair, to examine witnesses and receive documentary
evidence, including Captain Towerson's Bible and Thomson's Table book in which
appears certain writing. Speedy justice is demanded. Otherwise His Majesty must
enforce reparation.

1628.   **Order in Council,** 26 November, 1628.   *P.C. 2/38, fol. 602.*

Pamphlets, papers and pictures relative to Amboyna to be suppressed.

1628-29.   **Proceedings of the Privy Council,**   *P.C. 2/38, fol. 602.*
               26 January, 1628-29.

Hearing given to Thomas Smythwick of London, merchant, who complained of
the ill management of the trade to the East Indies by the Govr. and the E.I. Co. The
complainants were ordered to exhibit a Bill in Chancery for their private interests.
Another hearing appointed.

1628-29.   **Proceedings of the Privy Council,**   *P.C. 2/39, fol. 77.*
               6 February, 1628-29.

Full hearing given to Thomas Smethwicke, Anthony Withers, George Wynne and
others, pretending to be Adventurers in the E.I. Co. against the Govr. and Committees
of the said Company for mismanagement of the East India trade. It was decided that
the complaints were ' wholly calumnious '. The complainants were censured and the
Company ' fully exonerated and encouraged '.

1629.   **Proceedings of the Privy Council,**   *P.C. 2/39, fols. 473-*
               16 October, 1629.   *74.*

Licence granted to the E.I. Co. to transport 50 tons of saltpetre, brought from the
Indies, and 1,000 barrels of gunpowder made from the same.

1631.   **Seven letters from the Privy**   *P.C. 2/41, fols. 177-*
               Council, dated 28 September, 1631,   *78.*
               to various outports (Plymouth, Barn-
               staple, etc.) and to the Warden of the
               Cinque Ports.

Stating that great damage has been suffered by His Majesty and others through the
officers of the Company of merchants trading to the East Indies who have defrauded the
customs. The proclamation of 15 Feb., 3 Charles I, to be rigidly enforced.

1631-32.   **Proceedings of the Privy Council,**   *P.C. 2/41.*
               28 February, 1631-32.

The E.I. Co. having represented that they have brought large quantities of saltpetre from the Indies, which has been converted into gunpowder in larger quantities than they require, they request licence to transport 1000 barrels into Holland or other parts beyond the sea. This is permitted ' to foreign parts in amity with His Majesty'.

1631-32. **Proceedings of the Privy Council,** *P.C. 2/41, fols. 474-*
23 March, 1631-32. *75.*

The E.I. Co. prays permission to transport 100 tons of saltpetre to foreign parts. Granted.

1633-34. **Proceedings of the Privy Council,** *P.C. 2/43, fol. 502.*
21 February, 1633-34.

A similar petition for 500 tons. Granted.

1635. **Order in Council,** 18 November, 1635. *P.C. 2/45, fols. 228-*
29.

Whereas the E.I. Co. are by Letters Patent authorised to transport foreign silver to the East Indies to the amount of £100,000 which large quantity is sometimes difficult to obtain, and the trade in the Indies requiring gold, the Govr. and Committees have petitioned to be allowed to surrender their Letters Patent and receive in return new Letters Patent, by which they may have 'libertie to transporte the said one hundreth thousand pounds as well in foreigne silver as in foreigne golde, so as they exceede not in any one yeare in foreigne golde the sume of thirty thousand pounds.' Any deficiency in foreign gold to be made up in English gold. His Majesty having considered the matter, hereby grants their petition, and orders the Attorney General to prepare a draft for his signature.

1636. **Warrant of the Privy Council,** *P.C. 2/46, fol. 446.*
8 Nov., 1636.

Whereas the *Palsgrave*, E.I. Co's ship, lately returned from the East Indies, laden with cloves, pepper, calicoes, silk, indigo, sugar, etc., of great value, was cast away on the coast in the West Country ; these are to require all aid to be given to the agents of the E.I. Co., in securing the ship and everything belonging to her, and to secure the return of any goods, etc., removed from her.

1637. **Proceedings of the Privy Council,** *P.C. 2/48, fols. 398-*
November, 1637. *99, 509.*

Petition (undated) of John Massingberd to the P.C. read, complaining that a suit has been instituted against him in the Star Chamber for having transported gold abroad and declaring his innocence of the charge, having merely acted as agent for the E.I. Co., he himself being a merchant trading only to the East Indies.

The Attorney General is ordered to enquire into the charge and if it is proved to be unfounded, to deliver the petitioner from any trouble in the Star Chamber : in the meantime proceedings are to be 'stayed '.

1637-38. 12 Jan. Proceedings further 'stayed '.

1637. **Order in Council,** 6 December, 1637. *P.C. 2/48, fols. 435-*
36.

Granting full license to the E.I. Co., to export foreign silver and bullion of silver for their East India trade by their agents, Bateman, Massingberd and others.

1638.   **Proceedings of the Privy Council,**   *P.C. 2/49, fol. 213.*
25 May, 1638.[1]

His Majesty in Council heard the Govr., Deputy, and others of the E.I. Co. touching the present state and condition of their trade to the East Indies. H.M. appointed a Committee to enquire into the matters and to receive propositions for their encouragement, to regulate a method of trade, to settle differences with the Dutch, to consider how Mr. Courteen may be joined to the Co., etc.

1638.   **Proceedings of the Privy Council,**   *P.C. 2/49, fols. 411-*
2 September, 1638.[1]   *12.*

Four proposals made by the E.I. Co., including a request to be released from new imposts on East India commodities, and that they may have some part in the Molucca and Banda trade. Answers thereto by the King in Council.

1638.   **Proceedings of the Privy Council,**   *P.C. 2/49, fol. 487.*
7 October, 1638.

His Majesty informed the Govr. and Committees of the E.I. Co. that Mr. Courteen is building a ship of 500 tons to fetch home his stock from the Indies, and that he does not intend to continue to trade in those parts.

1639.   **Warrant of the Privy Council to**   *P.C. 2/50, fol. 565.*
Mr. John Young or any other ser-
vant of the E.I. Co., dated 31 July,
1639.

The East India Co., having complained of the great wrongs suffered by them by reason of the great private trade, both outward and inward, by persons not free of the Company, whereby His Majesty is also defrauded of his customs, etc., and the *Swan* having lately brought home great quantities of private trade to the detriment of the King and the Company, and other ships expected : this is to order measures to be taken for the seizure of such goods, and all assistance to be given to the said Company by His Majesty's officers.

1639.   **Proceedings of the Privy Council,**   *P.C. 2/51, fols. 11-12.*
2 November, 1639.

Order to ' stay ' Captain Bell in the *Southampton*, now leaving the river, bound to parts beyond ' the Cape Bona Speranza ' until enquiry has been made and further orders issued.

1639.   **Proceedings of the Privy Council,**   *P.C. 2/51, fol. 12.*
2 November, 1639.

After a long debate on the complaints of the E.I. Co., a Committee was appointed to consider the best means of procuring a new subscription and upholding the East India trade : to report in writing.

1639.   **Proceedings of the Privy Council,**   *P.C. 2/51, fols. 165-*
10 December, 1639.[2]   *68.*

Remonstrance having been made by the E.I. Co. regarding injuries received from the Dutch, losses caused by the depredations of Cobb and Ayres, and impositions upon East

---

[1] Abstracted in *Court Minutes of the E.I. Co.*, 1635-39, pp. 295, 298.
[2] Abstracted in *Court Minutes of the E.I. Co.*, 1635-39, pp. 351-52.

India commodities, with patents granted to other parties to trade beyond the Cape of Good Hope, the Company now pray for the renewal of their Charter with privileges : otherwise the trade must fall wholly to the Dutch. Answer by His Majesty under five headings. A new Charter promised. Subscription book and preamble to be prepared and presented for His Majesty's approval, etc., etc.

1639-40. **Proceedings of the Privy Council,** *P.C. 2/51, fols. 245,*
15, 19, and 29 Jan., 1639-40. *251, 266.*

Preamble to a book of subscription for a new E.I. Co. to be considered.

Preamble agreed on. Committee to meet.

The shutting up of the Third Joint Stock, and commencement of a further Adventure in a new Joint Stock. Preamble to new subscription quoted.

1660-61. **Proceedings of the Privy Council,** *P.C. 2/55, fol. 170.*
15 March, 1660-1.[1]

A Petition of the Governor and Company of Merchants of London trading to the East Indies having been read, together with a narrative of their losses by the Dutch, the whole was referred to a Committee, to be pressed upon the attention of the Dutch Ambassadors.

1661, 21 August. *fol. 350.*

The matter was again referred to the Dutch Ambassadors.

1661, 23 October. *fol. 414.*

Complaints of the same nature and list of further damages referred to the said Ambassadors.

1661. **License from the Privy Council,** *P.C. 2/55, fol. 429.*
4 November, 1661.

Authorising Alderman Backwell to furnish the E.I. Co. and others with £80,000 worth of foreign coin and bullion to transport abroad for the advance of their trade.

[Similar licenses were granted on the 3rd August, 1662 (P.C. 2/56, f. 83) and on the 15th April, 1663 (P.C. 2/56, f. 386) to Francis Meynell, Sir Thomas and Robert Vyner for £30,000 and £60,000, and there are numerous other instances which have not been noted.]

(For an Order of this date, see *Court Minutes,* 1660-63, p. 145.)

1661. **Order in Council** of 11 December, *P.C. 2/55, fols. 480-*
1661.[2] *81.*

The E.I. Co. having represented that, in spite of His Majesty's Charter and exclusive privileges granted to them, certain persons are sending private ships to India, both from England and from foreign parts, to the prejudice of H.M. and the Co., and desiring that public proclamation may be made of their exclusive rights, the petitioners were ordered to attend the Attorney General, who is to consider the matter and report.

1661. **Proceedings of the Privy Council,** *P.C. 2/55, fol. 506.*
27 December, 1661.[2]

---

[1] Abstracted in *Court Minutes of the E.I. Co.,* 1660-63, p. 102.
[2] For abstracts of the above documents, see *Court Minutes,* 1660-63, under their several dates. See also p. 251 of the same vol. for an abstract of and Order of 6 June, 1662, respecting two ships belonging to William Courteen.

A Committee appointed for the ' transaction of all Affayres relating to Bonne Bay in the East Indies '.

1661-62. **License from the Privy Council to**   *P.C. 2/55, fol. 512.*
the E.I. Co., dated 10 Jan., 1661-2.[1]

Permitting the export in this year for India of £30,000 in foreign coin and bullion of silver and gold, over and above the £50,000 limited by their Charter, to furnish lading home for four of His Majesty's Royal ships from India.

1661-62. **Order in Council** of 7 February,   *P.C. 2/55, fol. 539.*
1661-2.[1]

The Master of the Ordnance is to send on board the *Couvertine*, bound for ' Bonne Bay in the East Indies ', 4 whole Culverins, 4 demi-Culverins, and 500 shot for the use of His Majesty's forces there.

1661-62. **License from the Privy Council to**   *P.C. 2/55, fols. 552-*
Sir Thomas Vyner and Robert   *53.*
Vyner, dated 21 February 1661-2.[1]

To supply the E.I. Co. and others with £50,000 in gold and silver of foreign coins and bullion to advance their trade abroad (see also *supra* under date, 4 Nov., 1661).

1662.   **Proceedings of the Privy Council**   *P.C. 2/46, fol. 6.*
8 June, 1662.[1]

The E.I. Co. are ordered to wait on the Committee of the Privy Council with reference to the complaint against the Dutch respecting Pulo Run.

1662.   **Order in Council** of 31 October, 1662.[1]   *P.C. 2/56, fol. 184.*

The E.I. Co. understanding that a list is to be made out of damages sustained from the Dutch and also of their complaints, to be submitted to an umpire, the Company request the appointment of proper persons on both sides to receive the complaints.

His Majesty orders the E.I. Co., to report to Sir George Downing and promises the future appointment of an umpire.

1662.   **Proceedings of the Privy Council,**   *P.C. 2-56, fol. 232.*
28 November, 1662.[1]

Petition of the E.I. Co., read, complaining against the commanders, officers and seamen of their ships for carrying on a large private trade to and from the East Indies, and stating that a confederacy has been formed to obstruct their trade. Referred for consideration.

1662-63.   **Order in Council** of 13 March, 1662-63.   *P.C. 2/56, fol. 340.*

That £1,000 sterling in pieces of eight be sent to ' Bonne Bay ' for His Majesty's forces there, and that a letter be sent to the President of Surat commending the said garrison to his care, and notifying that Bills of Exchange on this account will be accepted to the amount of £4,766.

---

[1] For abstracts of all the above documents, see *Court Minutes*, 1660-63, under their several dates.

1663.   **Proceedings of the Privy Council,** *P.C. 2/56, fol. 372.*
          1 April, 1663.[1]

The E.I. Co., ordered to bring in to the Board a 'medium' of the customs of Ormuz since the year 1611.

1663.   **Proceedings of the Privy Council,** *P.C. 2/56, fol. 586.*
          21 October, 1663.[1]

Petition of the E.I. Co. read, stating that an Edict has been promulgated in Spain prohibiting the importation of any East India commodities into the Spanish Dominions, unless brought by the Netherlands E.I.Co. The E.I.Co. is ordered to wait upon the Secretary of State who will draw up instructions to the Ambassador to be sent to Spain, so that due care may be taken for the protection of the trade of the Company.

Complaints received from the E.I.Co. of injuries done to them by the Dutch. A Committee appointed to consider proposals for the prevention of 'mischiefs which threaten the ruine of their trade by the exorbitant power of the Dutch in the East Indies', and also for the preservation of their trade and the protection of His Majesty's subjects trading thither.

1664-65.   **Proceedings of the Privy Council,** *P.C. 21/58, fols. 16,*
          13, 25, and 27 January, 1664-65.   *28, 31.*

Ordered that the case of Thomas Skinner be heard at this Board on the 20th inst.

Report of the case made to His Majesty in Council. The Attorney General ordered to attend on the 27th to give his opinion.

Ordered that the Committee formerly appointed do state the case of Mr. Thomas Skinner and the E.I. Co., and bring it to this Board on February 1st.

1665.   **Proceedings of the Privy Council,** *P.C. 2/58, fol. 95.*
          12 April, 1665.

Mr. Thomas Skinner having complained of injuries received from the E.I. Co., the Committee has examined the Case and now present their report. Ordered that the report be sent to the Lords Chief Justices, etc., to see whether he is entitled to relief.

State of the case. In 1657, Skinner sent a ship to India, which arrived at Jambi in 1658. He purchased two warehouses, goods, and the island of 'Barcella', built a house, etc. In 1659, the servants of the E.I. Co. forcibly seized his shop, warehouses and goods, assaulted his person, broke open and robbed his house, etc.

1665.   **Proceedings of the Privy Council,** *P.C. 2/58, fol. 248.*
          27 August, 1665.

Petition of Thomas Skinner, praying for relief, read. Ordered : That this business be taken into consideration and 'some expedient found out for the petitioners reliefe against the oppressions of the said East India Company '.

1665-66.   **Proceedings of the Privy Council,** *P.C. 2/58, fol. 354.*
          21 February, 1665-66.

Proposals considered from the E.I. Co. about the sale of His Majesty's prize goods taken out of the ships, *Slothany* and *Phoenix*. Referred to the Lords Commissioners for prizes.

---

[1] For abstracts of the above documents, see *Court Minutes* 1660-63, under their several dates.

1665-66.   **Proceedings of the Privy Council,**   *P.C. 2/58, fols. 370-*
2 March, 1655-66.   *71.*

Report read from the Lords Commissioners for Prize Goods as to Proposals of the
E.I. Co. regarding the sale of His Majesty's Prize Goods from the ships, *Slothany* and
Phoenix.

Report : Proposals as to time of sale, price, etc., approved ; three persons appointed
to be present at the sale, etc.

Order in Council, in accordance with the above report. Also permitting any goods
so sold to be exported ' to any parts beyond the Seas ', at any time before Midsummer
next.

1665-66.   **Order in Council** of 16 March, 1665-66.   *P.C. 2/58, fol. 385.*

Touching the payment of customs for the spices taken in the East India Prize Ships,
the *Slothany* and *Phoenix*.

1665-66.   **Proceedings of the Privy Council,**   *P.C. 2/58, tols. 387-*
23 March, 1665-66.   *88.*

As the East India Company ' have slighted the orders of this Board and not complyed
with any References or Mediators ' regarding the complaints of Thomas Skinner, a
Committee is appointed to send for some of the Company and treat with them for Mr.
Skinner's ' relief for the Losses and Damages he hath suffered under them.'

1666.   **Order in Council** of 5 December,   *P.C. 2/59, fol. 228.*
1666.

Granting protection, notwithstanding the present embargo, to the E.I. Co's ships,
the *London, Bantam*, and *Charles*.

1666-67.   **Order in Council** of 8 March, 1666-67.   *P.C. 2/59, fol. 220.*

Appointing a Committee, to enquire into the complaints of the E.I. Co. regarding
irregular proceedings against themselves, their factors and servants (in the East Indies).

1666-67.   **Order in Council,** of 20 March, 1666-67.   *P.C. 2/59, fols. 344-*
47.

The petition of the E.I. Co. complaining of damage received in the East Indies :
(1) at Bombay by Mr. Humphrey Cooke ; (2) in the Red Sea by the ship *Love* ; (3) at
Fort St. George by Sir Edward Winter. This having been referred to a Committee,
they report :

(1) Upon the misdeeds of Humphrey Cooke, who is already recalled.

(2) Damage not proved, but the future safeguarding of the Company's Charter
suggested.

(3) Witnesses examined on the conduct of Sir Edward Winter. Summary of
deductions. The Co. request that Foxcraft may remain as Govr. at Fort St. George
until they send a successor.

The Committee recommend the granting of the Company's petition.

Ordered : The Governor of Bombay to aid and assist the Company. Security to be
taken from ships going to the Red Sea. Sir Edward Winter dismissed from the
Government of Fort St. George and recalled home : his person and estate to be carefully
guarded. Mr. Foxcraft to continue one year longer, etc., etc.

The above points are treated with considerable detail and the whole document is of
much interest.

1667. **Order in Council** of 6 December, 1667.   *P.C. 2/60, fol. 79.*

Touching the commission and instructions to the E.I. Co. for the reduction of Fort St. George in the Indies which is held against them by Sir Edward Winter.

1667. **Order in Council** of 13 December,   *P.C. 2/60, fol. 89.* 1667.

Touching His Majesty's surrender of Bombay to the E.I. Co.   Six Articles agreed to. Draft of the Charter to be prepared and submitted to His Majesty in Council.

[This document is a copy of *Home Series, Miscellaneous,* Vol. 42, pp. 151-52, India Office Records.]

1667. **Order in Council** of 13 December,   *P.C. 2/60, fol. 90.* 1667.

The E.I. Co. petitioning for leave to export sulphur, gunpowder, saltpetre and camphor, His Majesty in Council orders stated quantities to be permitted to pass the Customs.

1667-68. **Proceedings of the Privy Council,**   *P.C. 2/60, fol. 172.* 7 February, 1667-68.

The Draft of the Bombay Charter referred to the Lords of Trade and Plantations.

1667-68. **Order in Council** of 14 February,   *P.C. 2/60, fol. 182.* 1667-68.

Granting the E.I.Co. licence to export to Bombay a further 100 barrels of gunpowder.

1667-68. **Order in Council** of 4 March, 1667-68.   *P.C. 2/60, fol. 211.*

Mr. Attorney General to attend the Council to-morrow with the Draft of the Patent for granting Bombay to the E.I. Co.   The same to be considered.

Proceedings of the Privy Council, same date.

The above draft referred to the Lords of Trade and Plantations.

1667-68. **Order in Council** of 6 March, 1667-68.   *P.C. 2/60, fol. 216.*

The Lords of Trade and Plantations having reported that the Patent granting Bombay to the E.I. Co. is fit to pass the seals, it was ordered to be prepared and engrossed, a clause being added binding the E.I. Co. to pay £10 per annum to His Majesty as a rent for the said island.

1668.   **Order in Council** of 3 April, 1668.   *P.C. 2/60. fol. 256.*

Petition from the E.I. Co. read regarding the Treaty Marine with Holland for the settlement of the trade in India.   The present provisions are declared to be impracticable and insufficient.

Ordered that it be considered by a Committee.

1668. **Order in Council** of 8 April, 1668.   *P.C. 2/60, fol. 260.*

That the officers of the Customs do deliver up the bond for £200 to the King of Persia's factors and allow their goods to be shipped, duty free on the E.I. Co's. ships.

1668. **Order in Council** of 8 July, 1668.   *P.C. 2/60, fol. 377.*

That the Petition of the E.I. Co. on the provisions of the Treaty Marine be submitted to a Committee of Trade.

1668. ### Order in Council of 15 July, 1668. *P.C. 2/60, fols. 387-88.*

Sir William Temple to have instructions to insist upon an alteration of the Treaty Marine with Holland, upon the petition of the E.I. Co.

[This document includes two articles ' doubtful and impracticable ' and four articles of ' things not provided for ', with remarks on them by the Lords of the Committee of Trade.]

1669. ### Order in Council of 1 October, 1669. *P.C. 2/62, fol. 2.*

On the petition of Thomas Winter, on behalf of his brother, Sir Edward Winter, complaining that the E.I. Co. have not obeyed His Majesty's orders concerning the differences at Fort St. George. The petition to be sent to the Company who are to answer in writing to the Board on the 8th inst.

1669. ### Order in Council of 8 October, 1669. *P.C. 2/62, fol. 9.*

The petition of Thomas Winter [see above] and the answer of the E.I. Co., together with another petition of Thomas Winter for a copy of the answer being read, it was ordered that a copy be supplied as desired and the case considered by a Committee on the 11th inst.

1669. ### Proceedings of the Privy Council, 8 October, 1669. *P.C. 2/62, fol. 9.*

' His Grace the Archbishop of Canterbury having this day offered to the Board a Letter and Remonstrance sent unto him from some Factors and others belonging to the E.I. Co., complayning against Two Sismatical and Seditious Ministers sent unto them, who by their unsound Principles and Turbulent Spirits do much disquiet the Factory there ', it was Ordered that the Govr., etc., of the said Company attend His Majesty in Council on the 13th inst, touching the said complaint.

1669. ### Proceedings of the Privy Council, 13 October, 1669. *P.C. 2/62, fol. 15.*

The Archbishop of Canterbury's letter and remonstrance against Hooke and Thompson, two seditious ministers at Fort St. George, having been read, and the Govr., etc., of the said Company having been heard, it appeared that the said two men were of ' ill Principles and unfit for their charge. The Company was ordered to recall them speedily and to send in their place two suitable men such as the Lord Bishop of London shall approve of.'

1669. ### Order in Council of 17 November, 1669. *P.C. 2/62, fol. 44.*

On the petition of Thomas Winter, Esq., regarding the differences between his brothers Sir Edward Winter and George and Nathaniel Foxcraft at Fort St. George. Nothing has been done as yet and the Company endeavour to delay action until the departure of their ships which may postpone matters for two years, etc., etc. It was ordered that the Committee for Trade do meet tomorrow to examine the whole matter and report, so that the business may come to an issue before the departure of the ships.

1669. ### Order in Council of 17 November, 1669. *P.C. 2/62, fol. 45.*

Read a Petition of Lieut. Francis Chuseman on behalf of himself and eighteen other persons, preferring complaints of ill-treatment received at Fort St. George, at the hands of George Foxcraft and his son, Nathaniel.

Ordered that a Committee examine the whole matter and report speedily.

1669.   **Report of the Committee for Trade**   *P.C. 2/62, fol. 50.*
              and Plantations *re* the Case of Sir
              Edward Winter and George and Natha-
              niel Foxcraft.

It is recommended that (1) Commissioners (named), be sent out under oath to examine the whole matter ; (2) arrangements should be made for the disposal of any goods belonging to Sir Edward Winter which may be found in the Company's hands ; (3) that George Foxcraft be allowed to remain in India until the next homeward ships ; (4) that Nathaniel Foxcraft be recalled by the shipping of this season ; (5) that Sir Edward Winter be treated fairly and sincerely, etc. etc.

The above report approved by His Majesty in Council and an order issued in accordance therewith.

1672.   **Order in Council** of 1 October, 1672.   *P.C. 2/63, fol. 316.*

Granting licence to the E.I. Co. to export 250 tons of saltpetre.

1673.   **Order in Council** of 9 April, 1673.   *P.C. 2/63, fol. 410.*

Sir Edward Winter having represented his losses caused by the E.I. Co., which Company has now instituted a suit against him to the amount of £20,000, it is ordered that his business be taken into consideration on the 23rd inst.

1673.   **Proceedings of the Privy Council,**   *P.C. 2/64, fol. 24.*
              23 May, 1673.

Sir Edward Winter petitioning for a hearing of his differences with the E.I.Co. it was ordered that the matter should be taken into consideration on the 28th inst.

1673.   **Proceedings of the Privy Council,**   *P.C. 2/64, fol. 138.*
              3 December, 1673.

Iron ordnance permitted to be exported by the E.I.Co. for one year on the payment of a duty of 5/- per ton.

1676.   **Order in Council** of 3 November, 1676.   *P.C. 2/65, fol. 364.*

Upon the petition of Abdella Shaw, merchant, subject of the Sultan of Johanna, complaining of injuries received in 1670 by Captain South, and also by one Captain Varloe, supposed to be of the E.I.Co., it was Ordered that Captain South and the E.I.Co. be at the Council, prepared with their answers on the 10th inst.

On the 10th November the Proceedings were deferred until the 17th November.

1676   **Order in Council** of 22 November, 1676.   *P.C. 2/65, fol. 381.*

That Captain South do pay £40 to the E.I. Co. to be employed towards the ransom of six subjects of the Sultan of Johanna, which he carried off the said island and sold at the Barbadoes.

Abdella Shaw complained that the Sultan of Johanna, desirous of exhibiting his complaints against Captain South to His Majesty, contracted with Captain Philip Varloe for the passage of Abdella Shaw to England. Captain Varloe, however, carried the said

Abdella Shaw to Barbadoes and left him without money or provisions, and he was compelled to sell one of his servants in order to pay his passage to England.

Ordered : That it be referred to the E.I.Co. who are to endeavour to prevail on Capt. Varloe to recompense Abdella Shaw ; if he shall refuse, they are to report to this Board.

1676-77.   **Proceedings of the Privy Council,**   *P.C. 2/65, fol. 438.*
17 January, 1676-77.

Alvaro Pires de Tavora's reply to the answer of the E.I. Co. respecting his complaints of hard usage at Bombay referred to the Committee of Trade.

1676-77.   **Report of the Lords Committee of**   *P.C. 2/65, fols. 491-*
Trade and Plantations, 12 Febru-   *92.*
ary, 1676-77.

Complaint of the E.I. Co. of injuries received at Bombay from the Portuguese, of the arbitrary taxes imposed at Thana and Carinjah and of refusal of redress by the Viceroy of Goa.

Letter proposed to be written to the Viceroy remonstrating with him and advising of a letter to be sent to the King of Portugal. Such arbitrary taxes cannot be endured and the E.I. Co. are ordered to refuse payment, etc., etc. [This document is copied from C.O. $\frac{77}{18}$, f. 165.]

1676-77.   **Proceedings of the Privy Council**   *P.C. 2/65, fols. 491-*
and Order, 23 February, 1676-77.   *93.*

Report of the 12th February (as above) read and approved. A Letter to be prepared accordingly. The E.I. Co. to be required not to pay the duties demanded at Thana and Carinjah. The Company prayed that additional clauses might be inserted in the letter, begging for the withdrawal of the prohibition of passes to Gombroon. Approved by His Majesty.

1677.   **Report of the Lords of Trade and**   *P.C. 2/66, fol. 47.*
Plantations touching the complaints of
Don Alvaro Peres de Tavora against the
E.I. Co., 12 June, 1677.

The complaints of de Tavora having been considered, together with witnesses for both sides, the Committee decide that as justice has not yet been denied him in any formal trial in India, he should be left to apply for justice to the Courts in Bombay.

1677.   **Order in Council** of 15 June, 1677.   *P.C. 2/66, fol. 47.*

Upon the Report of the Lords of Trade and Plantation of 12 June, 1677 (see above) it is ordered that Alvaro Pires de Tavora apply for redress of injuries to the Courts at Bombay.

1677.   **Report of the Lords of Trade and**   *P.C. 2/66, fols.*
Plantations *re* the possession of   *152-54.*
Bombay by the E.I. Co., 25 October,
1677.

Resumé of former reports—remarks on injuries sustained from the Portuguese in Bombay and the consequent measures of His Majesty and the E.I. Co. No redress has been obtained from the Viceroy of Goa. Taxes are levied arbitrarily contrary to the Treaty. The King of Portugal is to be requested to stop these unjust proceedings as being in opposition to the Treaty of Marriage.

1677.   **Order in Council** of 26 October, 1677.   *P.C.   2/66,   fols.*
152-54.

Report of 25 October (as above) read, regarding the securing the quiet possession of Bombay to the E.I. Co. The Report approved. A Letter to be written to His Majesty's envoy in Portugal to secure the effect thereof.

[This document is a copy of C.O. $\frac{77}{13}$, fols. 270-71 and 274.]

1679.   **Order in Council** of 24 September, 1679.   *P.C. 2/68, fol. 211.*

A petition having been read from the E.I. Co. concerning Manoel Brandon de Lyma who murdered his servant, Peter Rangall, at Fort St. George, and was condemned to death, but appealed to His Majesty and was sent to England, and the petitioners desiring directions in the case : Also a Petition having been read from Manoel Brandon de Lyma praying to be set at liberty : It was ordered that the matter be examined into on His Majesty's return from Newmarket.

1679.   **Order in Council** of 17 October, 1679.   *P.C. 2/68, fol. 237.*

A Petition from Manoel Brandon de Lima having been read, praying His Majesty's pardon for killing his servant : It was ordered that the Petition be forwarded to the E.I. Co. for their report and also for them to give their reasons for ' Limiting appeales in some Criminall Causes '.

1679.   **Proceedings of the Privy Council,**   *P.C. 2/68, fol. 293.*
28 November, 1679.

Approving of the draft of a letter to the several Agents and Factors of the E.I. Co. at Fort St. George and other places in India, forbidding them to give any assistance to an interloping ship called the *Expectation*, Commander William Alley, in confederacy with John Smith, James Harrington and others.

A draft of the letter is annexed.

1679-80.   **Order in Council** of 27 February,   *P.C. 2/68, fol. 407.*
1679-80.

Permitting Thomas Rolt, President of the English Factory at Surat, to transport 30 small brass guns for presents to several Indian Princes.

1681.   **Order in Council** of 8 June, 1681.   *P.C. 2/69, fol. 300.*

Upon the Petition of the E.I. Co. regarding the ship *Arcana Merchant*, John Hall, late Master, arrested for trading within the Company's limits.

Ordered that the persons interested do attend His Majesty in Council on the 16th inst.

16 June, 1681 (fol. 302), further proceedings in the above business.

1681.   **Order in Council** of 6 November, 1681.   *P.C. 2/69, fol. 390.*

On the Petition of the E.I. Co. for the ' stay ' of the *Head* frigate and *Golden Hind* from trading to the East Indies—the Petition to be reported upon by the Attorney Solicitor General, when His Majesty will declare his pleasure.

1681.   **Order in Council** of 11 November,   *P.C. 2/69, fol. 398.*
1681.

Report to be made on a petition of the E.I. Co., praying for a Royal Proclamation against Interlopers.

1681.   **Proclamation by the King,** 16   *P.C. 2/69, fols. 402-3.*
          November, 1681.

' For the Restraining all His Majesty's subjects but the East India Company to trade to the East Indies.'

1681.   **Licence to the East India Co.,** 23   *P.C. 2/69, fol. 407.*
          November, 1681.

To transport 66 iron guns to Fort St. George, Madras.

1681-82.   **Licence to the East India Co.,** 10   *P.C. 2/69, fol. 459.*
          February, 1681-82.

To transport 20 demi-cannon and 20 iron mortar pieces for the Sultan of Bantam.

1682.   **Licence to the East India Co.,** 25   *P.C. 2/69, fol. 553.*
          October, 1682.

To transport 1,000 cwt. of brass guns and 500 cwt. of iron guns to the East Indies.

1682.   **Order in Council** of 1 December, 1682.   *P.C. 2/69, fol. 586.*

That the allegations of the E.I. Co. against the ship *Expectation*, alias *Commerce*, of London, said to be bound for the East Indies to trade without the limits of the Company's Charter, be examined, and if found to be true, that securities be taken to prevent the same.

1682.   **Order in Council** of 13 December,   *P.C. 2/69.*
          1682.

The ship *Expectation*, alias *Commerce*, having sailed without clearing, orders are to be given to the Admiralty to ' make stop ' of the ship in the river or the Downs.

1682.   **Order in Council** of 13 December,   *P.C. 2/69, fol. 594.*
          1682.

That process be issued against the ship *Expectation*, to stop her until security be given not to trade within the limits of the Charter of the E.I. Co.

1683.   **Proceedings of the Privy Council,**   *P.C. 2/69, fol. 666.*
          28 March, 1683.

Petition read from Thomas Sands, Master of the *Commerce*, praying to be permitted to proceed on his voyage, referred to the Attorney and Solicitor General.

1683.   **Order in Council** of 11 July, 1683.   *P.C. 2/70, fol. 17.*

That the Attorney and Solicitor General do report on the proposed commission from the E.I. Co. to the commanders of ships going to Bantam.

1683.   **Proceedings of the Privy Council,**   *P.C. 2/70, fols. 57,*
          7 and 9 November, 1683.   *63.*

Read the Petition of Nicholas Barret, owner of the *Adventure*, praying that the ship now stopped in the River at the suit of the E.I. Co. may be allowed to proceed or that the Company may buy the same. Petition referred to the Company.

On 9 Nov., the above referred to the Court of Admiralty.

1683. **Papers relating to the East India** *P.C. 2/70.*
Company's complaints against
Thomas Pitt, Robert Dorrell and
Nathaniel Vincent, July—December,
1683.

f. 17.   11 July.   Orders for their arrest.
f. 18.   11 July.   Writs issued against them.
f. 19.   16 July.   Discharged upon bond. Complaints of the E.I.Co.
heard regarding their importing goods from places within the Company's Charter.
f. 33.   25 Aug.   Having refused to give new securities, the accused are
ordered into custody. The E.I. Co. ordered to exhibit their charges
against the three aforesaid.
f. 49.   24 Oct.   The accused are ordered to enter into new securities.
f. 57.   7 Nov.   The Company to answer Dorrell's petition against the
writ of the exeat.
f. 63.   9 Nov.   Dorrell's petition referred to the Court of Admiralty.
f. 81.   5 Dec.   Vincent and Pitt appear before the Council.
f. 83.   7 Dec.   Vincent and Pitt and the Co. to attend on the 12th inst.
f. 92.   14 Dec.   Vincent and Pitt to give bail.

1683-84. **Proceedings of the Privy Council,** *P.C. 2/70, fol. 123.*
27 February, 1683-84.

Read the Petition of Edward Wynne, praying leave for his brother, Owen Wynne to
go to Metchlepatam [Masulipatam] to look after the estate of his late brother, Maurice
Wynne, who died at that place. The request granted and the E.I. Co. are recommended
to give him a passage on the next ship.

1684. **Orders in Council** of 31 October and *P.C. 2/70, fols. 242,*
19 November, 1684.   *256.*

The E.I. Co. to answer Mr Wynne's petition for a passage, His Majesty's orders not
having been complied with.

An answer to the above ordered to be given on the 26th inst.

1684. **Order in Council** of 2 April, 1684.   *P.C. 2/70.*

Petition of Thomas Petit, complaining of Mr. John Child for seizing goods at Surat
to the value of above of £4,000 belonging to himself and others, referred to the E.I. Co.

1684. **Order in Council** of 5 December, 1684.   *P.C. 2/70, fol. 269.*

To the Lords of the Treasury, to direct the Lords Commissioners of the Customs to
prevent the importation of Red Sanders Wood from Holland, according to the petition of
the E.I. Co., who import it direct from the East Indies.

1684. **Order in Council** of 12 December, 1684.   *P.C. 2/70, fol. 274.*

Ordering writs of *Ne exeat Regnum* to be issued against Charles Price, John
Carpenter and Robert Gwillim for trading into the East Indies without license.

1684-85. **Proceedings of the Privy Council,** *P.C. 2/71, fols. 25*
6 March, 1684-85   *45.*

Petition of the E.I. Co. for leave to export 1000 cwt. of brass guns and 500 cwt. of
iron guns to fortify Fort St. George and Bombay and other purposes—Referred to the
Lord Treasurer.

1685,   **Order in Council granting the**
27 March.   **above petition.**

1684-85.   **Proceedings of the Privy Council,**   *P.C. 2/71, fol. 36.*
20 March, 1684-85.

Read a petition of the E.I. Co., against interlopers, giving instances of injuries received by them or through their influence. A Proclamation to be prepared to prevent these abuses and calling home such interlopers.

1685.   **Draft of Proclamation,** 1 April, 1685.   *P.C. 2/71, fols. 57-58.*

Forbidding trade within the limits of the Charter of the E.I. Co. Approved and ordered to be engrossed.

1686.   **'A Proclamation for the recalling**   *P.C. 2/71, fols. 298-*
all His Majestys Subjects from the   *99.*
service of forreigne Princes in East
India ', dated 11 July, 1686.

Draft of the above read and ordered to be prepared for His Majesty's signature. Copy annexed.

1688.   **Orders in Council** of 26 August, and   *P.C. 2/72, fols. 729,*
5 October, 1688.   *745.*

The E.I. Co., is ordered to return answer to the petition of John St. John, Doctor of Laws, late Judge of His Majesty's Court of Admiralty in the East Indies.
It is ordered that a copy of the E.I. Co's. answer be delivered to Dr. St. John.

1689.   **Proceedings of the Privy Council,**   *P.C. 2/73, fol. 85.*
29 April, 1689.

Permission for the ship *Benjamin*, Leonard Brown Master, to sail with advices from the E.I. Co., to their factors in the East Indies.

1689-90.   **Proceedings of the Privy Council,**   *P.C. 2/73, fol. 390.*
20 February, 1689-90.

Petition read from the E.I. Co., for protection of the *Modena*, bound to the East Indies. Referred.

1690.   **Order in Council** of 29 April, 1690.   *P.C. 2/73, fol. 429.*

That the E.I. Co's. ship, *Orange*, be permitted to proceed to the East Indies, and that protection be granted to her crew.

1691.   **Licence to the East India Company,**   *P.C. 2/74, fol. 220.*
30 July, 1691.

To send seven ships to the East Indies, viz., the *Modena, Resolution, Charles the Second, Berkeley Castle, Chandois* and *Williamson*, and the *Josiah*, advice boat—the seamen to be protected.

1691.   **Proceedings of the Privy Council,**   *P.C. 2/74, fol. 248.*
24 September, 1691.

The E.I. Co. report that they have 600 tons of saltpetre by them, which they will reserve for His Majesty's service, and if more should arrive, they will make it up to 1,000 tons.

1691-92. **Order in Council** of 4 February, *P.C. 2/74, fol. 324.*
1691-92.

That the ships of the E.I. Co., now going to the East Indies shall have commissions against the French.

1691-92. **Order in Council,** of 1 and 10 March, *P.C. 2/74, fols. 300,*
1691-92. *344.*

To stop the four outward bound ships of the E.I. Co., the *Charles the Second, Berkeley Castle, Modena* and *Sampson* until further orders.

To permit the above vessels to proceed.

1691-92. **Order in Council** of 10 March, 1691-92. *P.C. 2/74, fol. 344.*

To allow the ships of the E.I. Co., a convoy to the soundings if consistent with His Majesty's service.

1692. **Proceedings of the Privy Council,** *P.C. 2/75, fols. 23,*
3 November, and 1 December, 1692. *35.*

Petition read from the E.I. Co., praying for permission to send out 12 ships this year, with protection for the crews—grounds of the petition.

Ordered : That 6 ships be permitted to go, viz., the *Resolution, Defence, Princess of Denmark, Royal James and Mary, Armenian Merchant* and *Hawk*, but not to sail until the 15th January.

1693. **Proceedings of the Privy Council,** *P.C. 2/75, fols. 205,*
31 August, and 7 September, 1693. *218.*

Having read a petition of clothiers and woollen manufacturers of Gloucester, two petitions of several merchants, and a petition of several linendrapers and others of London trading in East India goods, praying for liberty to export their goods to any part of the East Indies, the said petitions were referred to the East India Company.

1693. **Proceedings of the Privy Council,** *P.C. 2/75, fol. 132,*
April—September, 1693. *etc.*

f. 132.   13 April.   Question raised as to whether the Charter of the E.I. Co. has been rendered void.   Referred to the Attorney and Solicitor General.

f. 192.   3 Aug.   The Company to be heard regarding their new Charter.

f. 197.   17 Aug.   Several merchants, etc., to be heard regarding the new Charter of the E.I. Co.

f. 218.   7 Sept.   The matter deferred.

f. 223.   14 Sept.   Ditto.

1693. **Proceedings of the Privy Council,** *P.C. 2/75, fol. 228.*
21 September, 1693.

Petition from the inhabitants of Cornwall praying for a free trade to the East Indies. Referred.

1693. **Orders in Council** of 28 September, *P.C. 2/75, fol. 235.*
1693.

Granting license to the E.I. Co. to send 12 ships to the East Indies, with protection for seamen and landsmen.

A new Charter granted to the E.I. Co. and ordered to be prepared.

1693.   **Draft of Charter to the East India**   *P.C. 2/75, fols. 236-*
                   Company, 28 September, 1693.   *42.*

1693.   **Order in Council** of 28 September,   *P.C. 2/75, fols. 242-*
                   1693.   *43.*

Mr. Attorney General ordered to take bonds from the E.I.Co. to the value of
£150,000 : list of names and amounts.

A form of bond is annexed.

1693.   **Proceedings of the Privy Council,**   *P.C. 2/75, fols. 256,*
                   12, 16 and 21 October, 1693.   *257, 263.*

The regulations of the Charter of the East India Company to be considered.

A question as to the price His Majesty should pay the Company for saltpetre referred.

Further consideration of regulations concerning the Charter.

1693.   **Proceedings of the Privy Council,**   *P.C. 2/75, fols. 263,*
                   21 October, 2 and 9 November, 1693.   *270, 275.*

In response to a petition from the E.I. Co., the ship *Redbridge* is stopped from going
to the East Indies, under pretence of sailing to Alicante in Spain.

The matter referred to the Admiralty.

The ship permitted to proceed.

1693.   **Order in Council** of 2 November, 1693.   *P.C. 2/75, fols. 269-*
                                                             70.

For the preparation of a draft of Regulations of the Charter of the E.I. Co., according to the Heads annexed.

The twenty-six heads of regulation follow.

1693-94.   **Order in Council** of 8 February, 1693-94.   *P.C. 2/75, fol. 333.*

Granting convoy to eight ships belonging to the E.I. Co., bound to the East Indies.

1694.   **Order in Council** of 27 September,   *P.C. 2/75, fols. 479-*
                   1694.   *87.*

For the preparation of a ' Charter of Regulations ' to the E.I. Co., as approved this
day.

A copy follows, entitled ' Charter of Regulations for the East India Company '.

1694.   **Order in Council** of 18 November,   *P.C. 2/75, fol. 508.*
                   1694.

Granting license to the E.I. Co., to send three ships to the East Indies, viz., the
King William, *Russell* and *Sceptre*, with protection for their crews.

A like Order was also issued for the ship *America*, Capt. Richard Lacock.

1694-95.   **Proceedings of the Privy Council,**   *P.C. 2/76, fol. 63.*
                   14 February, 1694-95.

Read the Petition of Elihu Yale, late President of Fort St. George, complaining of
injuries received in India, and praying permission to return home with witnesses and his
estate. Referred to the E.I. Co., for their answer.

24 Feb. (f. 72). Further demand to the E.I. Co., for their answer to the
   above.

28 Feb. (f. 75). The case referred to the Lords of Trade and Plantations. 3 and 17 March (f. 81, 85). The case ordered to be heard, etc.

1694-95. **Order in Council** of 14 and 21 March, *P.C. 2/76, fols. 90, 96.* 1694-95.

Calling on the E.I. Co., to answer the petition of Henry Tombes and Dionisia his wife, on behalf of John Nicks (now a prisoner at Fort St. George) and Katherine his wife, complaining of injustice and praying relief.
Referred to the Lords of Trade and Plantations.

1695. **Order in Council** of 12 September, *P.C. 2/76, fol. 278.* 1695.

Granting license to the E.I. Co., to send ships to the East Indies with 800 seamen and 400 landsmen.

1695. **Proceedings of the Privy Council,** *P.C. 2/76, fol. 206.* 31 October, 1695.

The petitions of the wives etc., of the commanders of five ships of the E.I. Co., prisoners in France, sent to the Commissioners of sick and wounded for report.

1695. **Order in Council** of 21 November, 1695. *P.C. 2/76, fol. 214.*

Requiring the E.I. Co., to answer the petition of Sir Francis Child, Robert Dorrell and Joseph Cope, praying leave to send to the East Indies for diamonds on the Company's ships, paying the usual customs to the Company and to His Majesty.

1695-96. **Proclamation,** 13 February, 1695-96. *P.C. 2/76, fols. 235-36.*

To arrest Roderick Mackenzie, for setting up a trade to the East Indies.

1696. **Order in Council** of 26 March, 1696. *P.C. 2/76, fol. 350.*

Permitting the E.I. Co., to send the *Sedgewick*, advice boat, to the East Indies, with protection for her men.

1696. **Proceedings of the Privy Council,** *P.C. 2/76, fol. 474.* 16th July, 1696.

On the petition of E.I. Co., setting forth that Henry Every, Commander of the ' *Fhancy* ' is turned pirate in the seas of India and Persia, and, with others, has captured the *Charles* and pillaged the subjects of the Mogul, etc., the draft of a proclamation is ordered to be prepared for the suppression of piracy.

1696. **Proceedings of the Privy Council,** *P.C. 2/76, p. 511.* 3rd September, 1696.

An account by the E.I. Co. of goods of English growth, produce of manufacture exported by the Company during 1695, referred to the Lords of the Treasury.

1697. **Order in Council** of 25 March, 1697. *P.C. 2/76, fol. 597.*

That the Lords of the Admiralty shall not grant Letters of Marque to ships bound to the East Indies until further orders from His Majesty.

1697. **Order in Council** of 30 December, 1697. *P.C. 2/77, fol. 143.*

That the Admiralty do grant Mediterranean passes to the three East India Company's ships, *Benjamin, Tonqueen* and *King William*, homeward bound.

1697-98.   Order in Council of 27 January, 1697-98.   *P.C. 2/77, fol. 153.*

Upon complaint of the Turkey Company of interference by the E.I. Co., the latter is to be told that carrying such quantities of draperies to Northern Persia is contrary to their Charter. Such cloth should be sold in India, China, Japan, etc., so as not to interfere with the Turkey Company.

Memorandum. ' This order did not issue.'

1697-98.   Order in Council of 17 February, 1697-   *P.C. 2/77, fol. 158.*
              98.

Referring to the Council of Trade, the petition of the E.I. Co. for making alteration in the votes of the Adventurers, and for permitting them to trade in diamonds, pearls, jewels, etc., etc.

1698.   Order in Council of 31 March, 1698.   *P.C. 2/77, fol. 166.*

That Letters Patent do pass to the E.I. Co. regulating votes of the Adventurers, and empowering the Company to grant commissions for trading in diamonds, etc.

1698.   Proceedings of the Privy Council,   *P.C. 2/77, fol. 217.*
              18 August, 1698.

Read the draft of a Charter to the E.I. Co. prepared by Mr. Solicitor General. The same approved and a warrant ordered to be prepared for the Great Seal.

1698.   Proceedings of the Privy Council,   *P.C. 2/77, fol. 276.*
              8 December, 1698.

A Proclamation read and ordered to be issued for the suppression of piracy in the East Indies. Copy of Proclamation annexed.

1699.   Proceedings of the Privy Council,   *P.C. 2/77, fol. 388.*
              2 November, 1699.

Read a return from the E.I. Co. of goods sent to the East Indies in one year, ending 29 September, 1699.

Note.—The *Privy Council Registers* consist of the following : 1600-3, Printed Calendars ; 1613-14, Printed Calendars ; 1615-99, MS. Volumes with Indexes.   The registers for the years 1604-12 have been destroyed by fire.

The *Colonial Series* consists of Printed Calendars for the years 1613-99 ; but this series contains practically nothing relating to the East Indies.

SOME SERIES OF SEVENTEENTH CENTURY RECORDS AT THE INDIA OFFICE

SOME SERIES OF SEVENTEENTH CENTURY RECORDS AT THE INDIA OFFICE

THE India Office, as recently pointed out by Sir William Foster,[1] C.I.E., now official Historiographer, contains the second largest accumulation of historical documents in the United Kingdom—a fact little known—and the range of subjects and countries to which they relate is but little recognised. The fact that the *Calendars of State Papers, Colonial*—East Indies, of Mr. W. Noel Sainsbury, to the year 1634 (including every document of the *Original Correspondence Series* to that year) were issued by the Public Record Office, and that many of the original MSS. calendared are to be found there, coupled with the general rule of centralization of Public Records in that storehouse of the National Archives, may have helped to mislead many students. Although the history of the Dutch in the East is so closely related with that of the struggle with England for supremacy in the trade of the East Indies, so distinguished an authority as Professor Blok, in his *Preliminary Survey of Archives in England relating to the History of the Netherlands*, does not mention the India Office Collections. The omission may have been a deliberate one, the examination of the India Office Records being reserved as within the purview of the specialist on Colonial History, whom Professor Blok considered it desirable to send to England. Whatever the cause, these Archives have not been included in the subsequent investigation of Dr. Brugmans, who, at the time of his visit to England, hampered by the want of detailed catalogues at the Record Office,as well as in some great English Libraries, found it an impossible task to examine every document, and was thereby led to the course of first cataloguing documents relating to certain selected periods of Dutch history existing at the Public Record Office. Neither Dr. Colenbrander nor Dr. Japikse quotes from any sources at the India Office, although letters and papers from the Bodleian, and various College Libraries, and from the Lambeth Archiepiscopal Library are reproduced or analysed in their works.

For a complete summary of the various series of Records at the India Office and indications of the contents of the most important among them, as well as an outline of their history and vicissitudes, the student must be referred to Sir William Foster's indispensable handbook, the *Guide to the India Office Records*, 1600-1858, issued in 1919, by the India Office.

Of the ten printed Press Lists of the present Record Department, three contain the documents of the period with which this report is immediately concerned, namely the Seventeenth Century:

List of the Marine Records (1896), by F. C. Danvers.

List of the Factory Records (1897), by F. C. Danvers.

General Records, 1599-1879 (1902), by Sir Arthur Wollaston.

The above lists were only printed for official use, and hence are not generally available ; but copies are on the shelves of the Reading Room in the

---

[1] Sir George Birdwood Memorial Lecture delivered at The Royal Society of Arts on 8 December, 1923 and subsequently published in the *Journal* of the Society, 4 January, 1924.

India Office Library. The Catalogue of the Library should also be consulted.

The notes given below relate mainly to documents not hitherto analysed or calendared or to series not already in process of publication, and are derived from direct examination of the originals; but a brief reference to the chief Seventeenth Century collections, based on the official lists and publications, may also be of some practical interest and is therefore appended as a preface to the more detailed description to follow.

In addition to the original records kept in the Record Department, important collections, such as the Mackenzie, the Orme, and the Philip Francis MSS. are preserved in the India Office Library. A detailed catalogue of the two collections of the Mackenzie MSS. by Mr. C. Otto Blagden was published in 1916 as Vol. I of the *Catalogue of Manuscripts in European Languages belonging to the Library of the India Office;* a catalogue of the Orme MSS., by Mr. S. Charles Hill was issued as Vol. II in the same year. It may be noted here that a Catalogue of the HOME MISCELLANEOUS Series of the Records, on a similar plan, is now being compiled by Mr. Hill.

Although the ORME MSS. consist principally of Eighteenth Century documents, there are a certain number relating to the Seventeenth Century, e.g.,

No. 260. Memorandum of Surat, 1660-61.

No. 263. Original Journal of the *Loyall Merchant,* Nicholas Millett, Commander, 7 April, 1663 to 26 July, 1664, containing an account of Sivaji's attack on Surat.

A manuscript index to Dutch voyages is also amongst the papers. A full index to the catalogue forms a guide to the contents of the papers, as far as they have been analysed.

Included in the MACKENZIE COLLECTION are many translations into English, of Dutch printed works and of Javanese MSS. The section known as the 'Private Collection' comprises matter in English, Dutch, French and Portuguese, though the first two languages largely predominate. Although a considerable portion of the material consists of copies or translations, there is much besides, and much that either is unique or exists elsewhere only in MS., e.g. copies or duplicates of Dutch records, of which the originals or other copies are preserved at Batavia. Some of the unpublished documents are 'of very considerable historical value'; among the more notable of these are those relating to the Dutch Government of the Coromandel Coast, with its centre first at Pulicat and later at Negapatnam, and especially a series (not quite complete) of reports of outgoing Governors, beginning in 1632 and ending in 1771.[1]

MARINE RECORDS

The Journals of all the East Indian Voyages of the East India Company, from 1600 to 1616, were in the custody of Richard Hakluyt, first Historiographer to the Company, and after his death came into the hands of the Rev. Samuel Purchas. In 1625, the latter published in four volumes, *Hakluytus Posthumus, or Purchas his Pilgrimes,* containing the materials drawn from the Journals and some other sources, the framing 'those materials to their due place and order', as he conceived them, being his own

---

[1] See Preface to the Catalogue of the Collection and Nos. 40, 47, 48, 54.

'Artifice'. Of the originals, many have been lost; others only exist as fragments; of those that remain many are damaged. The loss, originally due to neglect, was increased in latter years by wholesale destruction ordered by the Company in 1818 and 1860. The earliest Journal extant among the Records of the India Office, is a fragment due to an officer on board the *Ascension* (probably Falconer) covering but a few days (31 July—4 August 1605) of the Second Expedition.

Abstracts of the Ships' Journals, 1610-23, are contained in MARINE RECORDS, Section III, *Miscellaneous*, No. 3, q.v.

The reference numbers and description of all those preserved in the Record Department of the India Office will be found in the LIST OF MARINE RECORDS by Mr. F. C. Danvers, the Introduction to which should be studied as well as the notes in the *Guide* (p. 106 *et seq*).

Particulars of the Journals of the early voyages based on the above List are given below, and a number of the unpublished Seventeenth Century Journals have been selected for examination. All notes of any historical interest have been reproduced in full, and all portions of the Journals, other than the mere routine entries of an ordinary ship's log, have been extracted—generally *in extenso*. The contents are varied—the fight of the 22nd August, 1673, off the Indian Coast between the East India Company's fleet under Captain Basse and twenty Dutch ships; a mutiny at St. Helena against the Governor; minor mutinies on board ship; facilities for victualling at various places and the price of provisions; details of the Company's trade; incidents of the life on board; lists of seamen, soldiers and passengers; sufferings due to disease and deaths of seamen and passengers; occasional references to marriages; mentions of strange birds, beasts and fishes, some of abnormal size—these matters and much else are to be found recorded within the pages of the Journals.

Journals of Early Voyages

First Expedition—To Sumatra and Java.
    Commander: James Lancaster.
    Ships:
        Red Dragon (formerly *Mare Scurge*): Captain James Lancaster.
        Hector: Captain John Middleton.
        Ascension: Master William Brand.
        Susan: Master John Heyward.

    No original records at the India Office. Account in *Purchas*, Vol. I, Book 3, Ch. iii, from Journal of someone on board the *Red Dragon*. Reprint in *Harris' Voyages*, and in Works issued by Hak. Soc., No. LVI.

Second Expedition—for Discovery of N. W. Passage to India.
    Captain George Weymouth.
    Ships:
        Discovery: Captain George Weymouth.
        Godspeed: Master John Drew.

    Capt. Weymouth's original Journal missing, but printed in *Purchas*, Vol. III, p. 809. Condensed account in Hak. Soc. Publ., No. V.

India, Second Voyage—to Bantam and the Moluccas.
    Captain Henry Middleton.
    Ships:

Red Dragon: Captain Henry Middleton.
Hector: Captain Christopher Colthurst.
Ascension: Captain Roger Stiles.
Susan: Captain William Keeling.

Journals missing. Fragment of a Journal of the *Ascension* in *Marine Records*, I.
Account of the expedition published in 1606, by William Basse ; republished by Hak.
Soc., Vol. XIX.   Brief accounts in *Purchas* and *Harris' Voyages*.

Third Voyage—to the Indies.
    Captain William Keeling.
    Ships :
        Dragon: Captain W. Keeling.
        Hector: Captain Wm. Hawkins.
        Consent: Captain David Middleton.

Journals of Keeling and Hawkins' ships (some imperfect) in *Marine Records*, Vols.
III, IV, V, VI, and VIII.
Journals of Keeling, Hawkins and Middleton epitomised in *Purchas*, Vol. I, p. 188,
in *Harris' Voyages* and in Hak. Soc. Publ., Vol. LVI.

Fourth Voyage—1608.
    Captain Alexander Sharpeigh.
    Ships :
        Ascension: Captain Alex. Sharpeigh.
        Union: Captain Richard Rowles.

Sharpeigh's Journal in *Marine Records*, No. VII : Abstracts in Hak. Soc. Publ.,
LVI.   Two accounts of voyage by Thomas Jones and William Nichols, both on the
Ascension, in *Purchas*, I, p. 228.

Fifth Voyage—for Java and Banda, 24 April, 1609.
    Captain David Middleton.
    Ship :
        Expedition: Captain D. Middleton (formerly *Bonaventure*).
    Journal missing.   Account of voyage in *Purchas*, I, p. 238.

Sixth Voyage—1 April, 1610.
    Captain Sir Henry Middleton.
    Ships :
        Trades Increase: Captain Sir H. Middleton (destroyed at Bantam).
        Peppercorn: Captain Nicholas Downton.
        Darling.

Journals of *Trades Increase* in *Marine Records* X, XII ; and of *Peppercorn*, ibid.
IX, X, XI.
Particulars of voyage in Hak. Soc. Publ., LVI, *Harris' Voyages* and *Purchas*.

Seventh Voyage—1611.
    Captain Anthony Hippon.
    Ship :
        Globe: Captain A. Hippon.

Journal kept by P. W. Floris (Cape Merchant in the ship), in *Marine Records*, XIII.
An account in *Purchas*.

Eighth Voyage—1611.
    Captain John Saris.
    Ships:
        Clove: Captain J. Saris.
        Hector.
        Thomas.

        Journal of the *Clove* (1611-13) by Capt. Saris in *Marine Records*, XIV. Brief reference in *Harris' Voyages.*

Ninth, Tenth, Eleventh Voyages—One Expedition.
    Captain Thomas Best.
    Ships:
        Dragon: Captain T. Best.
        Osiander: Captain Thomas Aldworth.
        James.
        Solomon.

        Capt. Best's Journal, 1 Feb., 1612—15 June, 1614 in *Marine Records*, XV: Journals on the *Osiander*, 3 Feb, 1612—29 Aug., 1613, kept by Ralph Crosse, ibid. XVI: Extracts from another, 31 Aug., 1612—12 April, 1613, ibid. XVIII.

        Accounts of these voyages in Hak. Soc. Publ., LVI, *Purchas* and *Harris' Voyages.*

Twelfth Voyage—1611.
    Ship:
        Expedition: Captain Christopher Newport.
        No journal at the India Office. An account in *Purchas*, by Walter Payton.

Joint Stock Voyages

First Voyage—1614.
    Captain Nicholas Downton.
    Ships:
        New Year's Gift: Captain N. Downton.
        Hector.
        Merchant's Hope.
        Solomon.

        Two Journals of *New Year's Gift*, 1614-15 in *Marine Records* XIX, XXI. Journal of the *Hector*, 1614-17, ibid. XX.

Second Voyage—1614.
    Captain David Middleton.
    Ships:
        Samaritan.
        Thomas.
        Thomasine.

Third Voyage—1615.
    Captain Keeling.
    Ships:
        Dragon.
        Expedition.
        Lion.
        Peppercorn.

        This fleet took out Sir Thomas Roe to India as Ambassador to the Great Mogul.

Fourth Voyage—1616.
    Captain Benjamin Joseph.
    Ships :
        Charles.
        Unicorn.
        James.
        Globe.
        Swan.
        Rose.

Journals of these four voyages are published in *Purchas.*

Second Joint Stock

First Fleet—1617.
    Captain Martin Pring.
    Ships :
        James.
        Anne.
        New Year's Gift.
        Bull.
        Bee.

The Journal of the *Bull,* 5 Nov., 1617—29 Dec., 1618, kept by Robert Adams in *Marine Records,* XXV.

Capt. Pring's Journal of the expedition is published in *Purchas,* Vol. V.

Abstracts of Ships' Journals, 1610-23. See *Marine Records,* Misc. No. 2.

Journals of Later Voyages

1672-74. **Log of the** *London.* *Marine Records, Vol. LXXI.*

Vellum bound original cover. Lettered: ' Shipp *London* : Jornall of the Voyage Began August the 24th 1672 and Ended July the 27th 1674.'

On paper label : 1672. 24 August *London*, and the old reference No. 65 (and in pencil, 66). On inside of cover No. 103F.

The Journal contains 112 unnumbered pages, written continuously on both sides.

Title: A JOURNALL KEEPT BY WILLIAM BASS IN THE GOOD S[HIP] *London:* BELONGING UNTO THE HONOURABLE EAST INDIA COMPANY IN A VOYAIGE TO INDIA GOD ALLMIGHTY DERECKT US AND STEARE OUR COURSE : IN THE YEARE 1672.

24 Aug., 1672. ' Capt. John Proud by Order from the Honble. E.I. Co., gave me Persestion [*sic*] and the Command of thear ship *London.*'

26 Nov., 1672. ' All our fleet at Gravesend : *vizt: London*, Admirall ; Capt. Jonathan Hide in the *President*, Vice-Admirall ; Capt. Anthony Earning in the *Sampson*, Raire Admirall ; Capt. Thomas Andrews in the *Ceasar* ; Capt. Zachary Browen in the *Ann* ; Capt. Peter Westlock in the *Massinburgh* ; Capt. George Earwing in the *Bombay* ; Capt. John Goulsbrough in the *Antelope* ; Capt. Robt. Cooly in the *East India Marchant* ; Capt. William Cruft in the *Unity* : In all ten saile which god presarve.'

17 Dec., 1672. ' We satt saile ' from the Hope to the Downs.

22 Dec., 1672. ' This forenoon the *Massinburgh* came down by us and Capt. Westlock came aboard our shipp. I gave him his orders for putting his shipp into a postur of defence against an enemy, as allso fighting instructions, and he promised to gitt his men quartered, and to have all his Gunns Clear. . . .'

23 Dec., 1672. ' . . . About noon we Anchered at the boy of the Red Sand.'

28 Dec., 1672. ' This morning we mustred our men and found that we had aboard 115 men and boyes which is 10 more then our Established Number, and 10 souldiers. . . .'

3 Jan., 1672-73. ' This day discharged five men and sent them ashower, having now [after previous discharges] one board 100 men and boyes, and 11 souldiers.'

11 Jan., 1672-73. ' . . . We had a Consultation on board our shipp, all the Commanders being one board but Capt. Westlock, and it was agreed to touch at Ste. Agoe [St. Jago, Santiago], and In caise of sepperration that we doe not meat all at said Island then to make the best of our or thear way for the Island Johana and there stay six dayes or tell the 20th of May, which of them shall first happen. . . .'

18 Jan., 1672-73. ' . . . Came up with Capt. Mundin in the *Assistance* friggit, with three marchant shipps, men of warr and two fiour shipps, bound for St. Hellena to convoy the East India shipps home from thence. . . .'

3 Feb., 1672-73. ' . . . John Skiner foremastman departed this life ; his

16

distemper was mollincolly, being persest with strange fancis, and at last it turned to a feaver, which was his death.'

9 Feb., 1672-73. '. . . Anchered in Lapray road at the Island Ste. Agoe' [St. Jago, Santiago, Cape Verd Is.].

'Sent my boat ashower to know what newes and the Governor tould them that yisterday in the morning came into this place 3 Dutch shipps, 2 great and one small, all 3 shipps of warr: about 4 afternoon Capt. Mundin with his fleet coming about the point, the Dutch cutt thear cables and sett saile and Capt. Mundin after them, fireing at them and they ware in fight tell 10 night: the guns was heard, and thear was another Dutch Shipp of warr at St. Agoe town: he seing the other ingaged, did not goe out to his consoarts aide, but as soon as it was darke, satt saile and stered away from them by a wind. One of thear boats and men ware left behind and came to Ste. Agoe town. They tould this Governour, I me[a]n the Captains of the Shipps which ware att Lapray, that they had bin out of Holland 2 months, and came out 25 saile in Company, and ware all at the Cannarys and sepperated by foule weather, and they came to Ste. Agoe to look for the English and found a tartur. Our shipps tooke up all thear anchers and cables, and it was tould 2 of our Comanders which we sent ashower to give the Governor a vissitt, that at Ste. Agoe town they saw 7 shipps that morning we came into the road, soe that it may be conclueded that Capt. Mundin hath taken one of them. This afternoon called a Consultation . . . It was thought conveneant to hastin all our boats aboard, and saile assoonas we could gitt redy, not knowing how soone any of the other 25 Dutch shipps may arive hear. . . .'

10 Feb., 1672-73. '. . . Wee all satt saile from the Island Ste. Agoe, being 8 shipps besides my selfe. . . .'

3 March, 1672-73. '. . . This morning called a Consultation about the boatswain and his maite for abuseing of Mr. Housier, fourth maite, about the triming the sailes. They were seaverly checked for it and promised not to doe the like again. Allsoe this forenoon our foremast men, some part of them, wear gott togeather one the forecastle about alowance of bread, having but 17 pounds this weeke for 5 men and 18 pounds formerly, they refused to doe the woark which the boatswain comanded them. I sent the boatswain to them to bid them goe about thear buisnes, but they refused. Then I went foroud upon the forecastle with my hanger in my hand and drove them all of[f] and eavery man to his woarke. . . .'

16 April, 1673. 'Saw 3 shipps; spake with two of them shipps; it was the *Johanna* and *Barnedistant* from the Coast', the third being the *Rebeckah*. There had come out in company with them the '*Loayall Subject, Bartly Castle* and *Ann*. Capt. Fisher in the *Bartly Castle* they saw but 2 dayes before they mett with us. They told Capt. Brown that they was dead fraighted: thear was not goods to load them.' In November there went from 'Jefenypatan one Island Zeelone 25 Dutch shipps, but wheather they went they know nott; they did exspeckt them one the Coast [of Coromandel], but did not come thear.'

16 May, 1673. 'Anchored in the Road of Johanna with all our fleet, being in all 9 shipps. . . . We had 22 men that had the scurvy, 4 of which could not goe [walk], but ware carried ashower in cradills, and most part of our fleete in the same condition, some of them worse. . . .'

17 May, 1673. '. . . The ships heeled, sheathing mended and cleaned, took two boats of 'ballis' and one of water aboard. 'This day received a letter from the King [of Johanna, Comoro Is.] which was left by Capt. Richard Goodlad, bareing dated [*sic*] the 13th of August 1672, being bound for Surrat.'

19 May, 1673. Visit to the King and exchange of presents, every Commander receiving a bullock.

20 May, 1673. Cleared the ships. Bullocks, goats and provisions brought on board. A letter left on the Island to be delivered by the King to the next English ships arriving. Information that French ships have been at this island, nine two years ago and three the last year. Note of prices of several provisions. Oranges, lemons, limes and sweet potatoes may be bought for 'triffling things'. . . . 'We have not found soe faithfull deallings with the people as formerly, for at last when we ware to goe away, they brought very small cattle, and did not supply us with all things necessary; they ware very caustious in tacking of peeces of 8/8; none but Civill money [Spanish dollars] would pass with them.'

22 May—10 June, 1673. From Johanna towards Madras. Hindered by staying for the fleet.

11 and 13 June, 1673. A consultation as to the course.

16 June, 1673. 'Zelone' seen. 'The Land remarkable is a hill like unto Wesmester Abbe. . . .'

17 June, 1673. 'From Zelone towards Madarasaptam . . . Spake with 3 Junckes; carried them along with us.' On enquiry of the Portuguese pilots for Dutch letters or goods, a letter directed to Heer 'Ricklif von gonce, Admirall of 18 saile of Dutch shipps rideing at Negoptam' was, after a general Consultation on board the *London*, directed to be opened, but nothing of importance was found in it. It was also agreed to secure the junks and to tow them as they 'sailed very heavy'.

19 June, 1673. . . . One of the junks broke away, and 'being leakey, could not indure, soe left her.'

21 June, 1673. Received a letter from the Agent and Council of Fort St. George. A Consultation was called. On opening the letter, it was found that the 'Dutch did ride all the shower along from St. Thomay to Fort St. George, 12 shipps of warr and 2 small vessills; the pourport of the letter was, that if we thought ourselves not strong enough to deale with the Dutch, then to goe of[f] into the Sea and make the best of our way for Metchleptam. It was debated by us all wheather to goe for Madarasaptam and fight our way through the Dutch: but it was concluded by all that in regard the Companyes treasure was one board our shipps, and all thear conserns for this yeare, to goe for Metchleptam and thear receive farther orders to land our treasure.' It was decided to carry the junks with the fleet lest they should give information to the Dutch.

A Dutch flag was seen flying on land, on a factory to the north of 'Poole Cheze.'

Information was received from Mr. Harrison that another Dutch fleet of 8 sail, in addition to the first 14, 'all great shipps of fliboats', which had taken in goods at several places on the coast, were lying before St. Thomé and Fort St. George, 22 ships in all; that a French man-of-war of about 50 or 60 guns had fought her way through five Dutch men-of-war and had got to windward of them . . . 'Att

3 afternoon we saw the French shipp under saile, standing of[f] for feare of us; the Vice Roay Delahay was one board of her, as informed.'

24 June, 1673. Owing to difficulties experienced in towing the captured junks, it was, on consultation, decided to cast them off, and 'the parsons concernd was as willing to be cast of[f] as we to lett them goe. . . .'

26 June, 1673. . . . Anchored in Masulipatam Road . . . Sent a letter to Matthew Mainwaring, Chief of the Factory.

27 June, 1673. ' This forenoon Mr. Matthew Manwering came one board our shipp. Fired at his comeing and goeing 12 peece of Or[d]nance. In said boat sent our Chist of Gould and empty Caskes, with some other goods consigned for Foart St. George. . . .'

28 June, 1673. The greater part of the fleet ' wayed ' and went to the Southward. . . .

29 and 30 June, 1673. Provisioning.

3 July, 1673. Capt. Erwin sent an officer on board with the news that ' John Pounsted [Pounsett] which came over with Capt. Earwin, a dier ', had brought 2 or 3 letters from England for a Dutch merchant and had delivered them to the Dutch at Masulipatam.

A Consultation was called aboard to consider the advisability of riding off Masulipatam or weighing for ' Dew.' [Divy] point. The latter course was decided upon, subject to the consent of Mr. Mainwaring and the Council, and a request was sent for the Council to come on board for consultation, since no orders had been received from Fort St. George.

4 July, 1673. Received a letter from Mr. Mainwaring advising of the arrival of 12 Dutch ships south of Divy point, and thereupon all set sail, but later two members of Council came on board and a general consultation was held respecting the landing of the Company's treasure. It was eventually decided to retain the treasure on board and to anchor off Divy Point.

12 July, 1673. The fleet off ' Dew point '. This day received an order from Mr. Mohun and Council at Masulipatam concerning Mr. John Pounsett, who was kept in confinement. It was ordered that he should be removed on board the *Bombay Merchant* ; a copy of his letter which he sent ashore to Mr. John Whitehead, chaplain, and a ' certificate of his examination ' [were also sent aboard].

13-18 July, 1673. At the desire of Mr. Mohun and Council, consultations were held on board ' about goeing for Madarasaptam ' and returning to Masulipatam. The Commanders promised to use their best endeavours to reach Madras, if commanded to do so, but could give no undertaking as to time.

19 July, 1673. All the fleet set sail, bound for Madras. Several of Capt. Cruft's men, who had attempted to desert, and were on Capt. Hide's ship, sought to escape again, but being brought back on board their own ship, ' they began to mutiny and sware att strange raites.' Their complaints were examined by Capt. Basse, four other commanders and Mr. Hinmars, Second at Madras. Five of the men were sent in irons ' into five seaverall shipps '.

30 July, 1673. By the afternoon all the fleet except the *Unity* had anchored in Madras Road, also Capt. Westlock from England, ' which was wellcome newes unto us all.'

A French ' shollup ' with the Capt. Commanding in Chief under Viceroy Delahay came to bring a complimentary letter.

The Company's chest of gold and their goods were landed.

31 July, 1673. Captain Cruft in the *Unity* anchored in the Road.

4 Aug., 1673. M. Barron, Director General for the French, and later, Sir William Langhorne, Agent at Fort St. George, came on board and had a long private discourse in the Round House. M. Barron had come 'to borrow money of Sir William, but could not obtaine his desire, for Sir William would not furnish him with any betwixt 6 and 7 night.'

5 and 6 Aug., 1673. A consultation was held on board the *Unity* and seven of Capt. Cruft's men, including his mate, were sent on shore to be kept in irons. Four of Capt. Andrews' men ran away from the *Caesar*, in the ship's boat to Pulicat.

8 Aug., 1673. '. . . Mounser Barron, the French Derecter Ginerall sent to speake with me; it was to borrow 30,000 rupes of all the Comanders: but we had it not to lend him one such tearmes as neaver to receive it again.'

9 Aug., 1673. Set sail from Madras to Masulipatam.

15 Aug., 1673. Anchored in Muslipatam Road. A Consultation held on board Capt. Westlack's boat, the *Massingberd*.

19 Aug., 1673. '. . . This morning Mr. Moohune received a letter from Sir William Langhorne beareing [date] the 12th instant; gave account of 20 saile of Dutch shipps then in sight of St. Thoma, but wheather bound know not. I presently [immediately] ordered our shipps to be made cleare and put all things in hould. . . . Mr. Chambrelain came one board our shipp to give eavery Commander his dispatch. . . . About 4 he gave me mine and went. . . .'

20 Aug., 1673. The fleet set sail from Masulipatam towards Madras.

22 Aug., 1673. '. . . About 6 this morning saw the Dutch fleete consisting of 20 saile, 14 men of warr, 3 fliboats, 2 doggers and one hoye, which lay to windwards of the fleete. About 8 morning tackt to git all our Fleete into a line for our better defence against the enemy. . . . About 10 the Dutch fired at us. Then we began to ingaige: about ½ an houer past 6 afternoon the Dutch left of chaiseing and fireing at us, and we at them, we having the worst of it, by the loss of our Vice Admirall [Capt. Hide] Rair Admirall [Capt. Earning] and *Antelope* [Capt. Goldsborough], the which was accastioned by some of our fleete lying to leeward and doeing noe sarvise nor damnefying the enemy ; neither did they keepe malme [*sic*] all the time of the ingaigment, but came away and left thear flaggs (it was Capt. Andrews, second to the Rare Admirall : Capt. Goulsbrough his other second fought very stoutly and kept by his flagg and was lost with him), as allsoe others of my oawne devistion, and Capt. Hides ware a little space in a line, but bore to Leewards and theare lay, but did the enemy no damadge : Capt. Cooly wanting shott long before the ingaigment was over. Capt Hide, the Vice Admirall, fought very stoutly, being disabiled, boare away about ½ an houer past five afternoon. He was boarded by one Dutch shipp one his starboard quartur and another laide him one board amidship one his Larboard side. Our shipp being very much disabled : all our sailes and wriging shott to peeces, and mainemast shott in 3 places . . . and our ship verry much toarn

Ingaged with 20 sail of Dutch ships, of them 15 that fought.

Capt. Andrews lay to leeward of his flag all through the Engagement.

with shott : 5 men killed owtright, beside the sad accedent of powder
blowing up at 2 seaverall times bournd 18 of our men verry danger-
ously, sett the stearid [sic] and great Cabbin afire and gallerys
and the cloaths on the Quartur deck, and my coat one my back :
but by the Providence of God, we soone put all the fiour out, but
still kep[t] fireing our guns ; one the gundeck more wounded
with shott and splinters, with broaken leggs and thyes, 9, besides
seaverall others with small wounds, which was the reason of my not
staying to releive the Vice Admirall, or should I have staied longer to
ingaige, I might have bin in very great danger of loseing my
shipp, seeing none of my devistion stay by me but Capt. Browne,
and he was verry much disabiled.   He kept in his line all the time of
the ingaigment and fought well, but all the rest a very little time.
Capt. Earwin which lead the van, within an houer and a halfe
or two houers after we first ingaiged, bore away, having received
some shot under watter in hould, as he tould me the next day, and
come not up to ingaige any more, neither did Capt. Cruft, whoe
bore away with him ; but what his defects were I know not : little
to be seene one his sailes or rigging : onely he saith that [he] had a
shott in his foreyard.   Capt. Westlock neaver came up in his line
all day.   He was Capt. Hides second, but kept to Leeward of him,
and did not stay to his assistance.
    Capt. Coolys protence was he had noe shott, as whoule and demy
culvering in his shipp.
    ' This night, with what men we had left, being very much tired in
the time of Ingaigment, gott another foretopsaile to the yard . . .
also splist some of our runing riging. . . .   All the time of. the
Ingaigment the Dut[c]h had the wind of us, which was theare great
advantage.   They shott in thear guns small iron shott of 1, 2 or 3
pound each, 5 or 6 of them in a gun, as allsoe burr shott, which did
very much damnefy our riging, sailes, mast and yards.   Our long
boat and pinnis [were] shott away in the time of ingaigment. . . .'
23 Aug., 1673.   ' . . .   About 9 morning we bore to leeward to the rest of
our fleete ; at 11 forenoon we saw Capt. Browne and Capt.
Earwin.'   All the Commanders remaining went, by invitation, on
board Capt. Browne's ship to dine. . . . ' It was agreade by all the
Comanders to fall into the Southwards of S. Thoma for feare the
Dutch should follow us. . . .'   ' We having had a very great loss
alredy thinke its wisdome to presarve the remainder part if possible,
went away with our head sailes.'
    ' Died this day of thear wounds, viz. Thomas Newman, midship-
man, John Maijor, gunners maite ; Richard Maskcol and Luke
Woodly, foremastmen ; John Tincum, a souldier : in all 5 men.'
25 Aug., 1673.   ' . . .   This day Richard Joayce, a foremastman, his
right legg cut of[f] ; allsoe John Farmer, a souldier, died this
day. . . .'
26 Aug., 1673.   ' . . .   This forenoon sent my boat one board of Capt.
Cooly, my Cyrurgon in her, to desire his Cyrurgons advice as to
some of our men which waie wounded and burnt with powder. . . .'
27 Aug., 1673.   ' . . .   Mr. Henry Brewster, my cheife maite, died this
day of his wounds. . . .'
    Repairs to ship.
30 Aug., 1673.   ' Richard Kalinick, Thomas Carter, Francis Incknis and
John Williams died this day, all 4 of their wounds. . . .'

1 Sept., 1673.   Anchored in Madras Road.[1]
2 Sept., 1673.   'This morning came Leftenant Onnell [Oneal] Ensign
    Baites and Mr. Wm. Dickson, Gunner, to take an accompt of our men
    by order from Sir Wm. Langhorne, the which was dun.   About 10
    forenoon I went ashower in company with Capt. Browne and Capt.
    Earwin ; but Capt. Andrewes went ashower the day before to sett out
    his oawne valliantnes and gallantry.'
        Goods landed.
3 Sept., 1673.   'This day sent all our wounded and Burnt men ashower
    to the Foart; allsoe landed all the goods we had to land.'
4 Sept., 1673.   '. . .   John Steward departed this life, being ashower at
    the Foart, allsoe this day came Thomas Labrun aboard our shipp as
    one of the shipps Company in the Rumbe of the Trumpeters maite,
    Anthony Barton. . . .'
5 Sept., 1673.   'This day George Jackson departed this life being asho-
    wer at Madarasaptam, being one of our burnt men.   He makes the
    18 [th] man sence the ingaigment.'
6 Sept., 1673.   'This day [came] James Whenn and Wm. Faulkoner to
    goe in our shipp in the Rumbe of Mr. Martin.   These were 2 of Capt.
    Crufts men which ran away with his boat and have bin in Irons at
    Foart St. George, and   upon   theare   Submition   are   taken   one
    board. . . .'
8-10 Sept., 1673.   Lading treasure, goods, etc.
11 Sept., 1673.   Set sail for St. Thomé, bound for the Coast of Malabar.
    Henry Lawes and John Thomas, soldiers, left ashore at the Fort. . . .
13 Sept., 1673.   '. . .   Lay by for our fleete.   Sould our dead mens
    cloaths at the mast, att outcry. . . .'
25 Oct., 1673.   '. . .   Theare came a Clargo priest from the shower
    . . . and he tould us that Carnapole was 4 leags more Northerly
    . . . that theare ware noe English at Carnapole nor Poorcat
    [Porakad] and that thare ware Dutch, 2 or 3 at eavery towne upon
    this Coast, and a souldier or 2 at Poorcat. . . .   Sent our boate asho-
    wer to Carnapole to enquire wheather theare ware any goods in this
    place for the English. . . .'   A native who swam aboard, said the
    English ships might have water, cocoanuts or fish, 'but for goods,
    none was to be sent of [f] . . that the towne of Carnapole was
    6 miles up in the Country and that this was onely the fishing
    towne. . . .   Infoarmed that the Dutch have souldiers theare and will
    not permit any goods to be shippt of[f]. . . .'   It was decided to make
    for 'Pannany and Caillecutt '.
30 Oct., 1673.   . . . A boat came from 'Pannany ' on board, sent by the
    French Resident at that place with the information that 'theare was
    goods for us, and an Englishman ' in that place . . . that there were
    2 Dutch factors and 4 soldiers 'blacks, but in urope habit '.
1 Nov., 1673.   In 'Tannore ' Road . . . a Portuguese born in England
    came aboard from Mr. Bowcher.   A good quantity of pepper
    obtainable there. . . .
4 Nov., 1673.   'This day we did take in 37 bailes of pepper and 5
    tunns of watter . . .'
5 Nov., 1673.   Water and provisions shipped on board.   'This place
    affoardeth little else but pepper, rice and cocernuts ; some hens we
    gott, but very few.'

---

[1] For other accounts of the engagement with the Dutch, see O.C. Nos. 3834, 3835, 3836.

6 Nov., 1673.   Towards Calicut.   'Mr. (Randoll) Taylors Tombe Remarkable for the knowing of Callecut.'

8 Nov., 1673.   In Calicut Road.   Mr. Pettit came aboard, 'being fearfull
of some disturbance' about the pepper which had been detained two
days, and an order was given that all boats should be sent ashore
well manned and armed complete . . . 'but it proved nothing but
delayes'.   The Governor sent a present of cocoanuts plantains and
bananas. . . .

15 Nov., 1673.   In Biliapatan Road.   'This day was sent of[f] to our
fleete 150 baggs of pepper, which was that which this place doth
affoard, and about 10 bailes of Cardemums. . . .'

16 Nov., 1673.   '. . . Bought in this place bullucks per one doller and ½
per peece ; we had in all 9.'   No news 'from Mr. Pettit of sailing
from this place, which makes me much admire, having nothing to doe
nor noe goods to taeke in'.

20 Nov., 1673.   Four boatloads of goods taken in at Bhatkal.

21 Nov., 1673.   Six boatloads of pepper taken in at Onore (Honawar), one
for each ship.

22 Nov., 1673.   The captain went 'ashore at Onore to speake with Mr.
Sherlock about hoggs and watter.'   'Hoggs at 2 rupes per peece.'
Description of Onore harbour.   'Sent one chist of silver and 10 bailes
of Cloth ashore in the Cuntry boat.'   Made for 'Murge' Bay.
Pepper taken aboard.

24 Nov., 1673.   Mr. Sherlock and 'seaverall great men belonging to the
King of Cannanore came on board some of our fleete . . . with the
Kings Jenerall of his Army and Cheife Captain and Cheife
Marchant. . . .'

25 Nov., 1673.   Two chests of treasure sent ashore.

26 Nov., 1673.   Set sail from before 'Murge'.   Spoke with Capt. Niccols
in the *Revenge* from Bombay.

27 Nov., 1673.   Mr. Charles Bowridge left Chief at Carwar.

30 Nov., 1673.   'From Cape Ramus towards Bombay. . . . Mett the
Portengall fleet, consisting of 2 indiferant bigg shipps; all the rest
small friggits; these have lain before Muskcat in Arabia but did
nothing of execution the time they lay theare.'

6 Dec., 1673.   In Bombay Road . . . 'two Mores Kings shipps rideing at
the South end of Caringah with a fleete in the bay within Caringah,
belonging to Seathey'.

12 Dec., 1673.   'Satt saile from Bombay with all our fleete, Capt. Neccols
in company and allsoe the Cetch and hoy,' after having landed goods
and taken in water and provisions in the interval.

17 Dec., 1673.   Anchored before Swally Bar, off Surat.   A French man-
of-war in the mouth of Surat river.

19 Dec., 1673—9 Jan., 1673-74.   Landed goods, wine and beer, and received
on board goods for England, including 227 chests of Red Earth, 28
pieces of broken guns, 56 bales of indigo, etc.   Took in water, arrack
and provisions for the homeward voyage.   On the 31st December,
Capt. Anderson from Bantam in the King of Bantam's ship, the
Blessing, anchored in the Road.

10 Jan., 1673-74.   'This day received 6 small bailes, which filled up our
hoold.   We calked our hatchis up and fired a gunn being and [*sic*
? we] could take in noe more goods.'

14 Jan., 1673-74.   The fleet set sail from Swally Bar and arrived at
Bombay on the 17th.

19 Jan., 1673-74. '. . . Capt. Ustick and Mr. James Addams ware
aboard our ship and mustered our men and went betwixt decks to
see if our gunns ware cleare.'
20 Jan., 1673-4. The fleet set sail from Bombay for England.
Mr. Anthony Rooby a passenger on the *London*.
22 April, 1674. Anchored in St. Helena Road. There had been
a rumour before leaving Surat and Bombay that the Dutch had
seized St. Helena, but the Island was found to be in possession of
the English, having been retaken by Capt. Munden and his fleet at
the beginning of January, 1672-73, after the Dutch had been in
possession for four months. Details of the capture are given. On
the arrival of the fleet, a mutiny of the soldiers and some of the
inhabitants against the Govr. installed by Capt. Munden, under-the
Duke of York's commission, was in progress.
22-25 April, 1674. Detailed account of the mutiny and other occurrences
at St. Helena.
A Portuguese ship coming into the Road, refused to strike her
flag, though fired at.
The Commanders visited the 'new deputed Governor of the
mutenus souldiers and others', and after a consultation on board the
London, re-established Capt. Keigwin in his government. Details
regarding the fortification of the Island, etc.
26 April, 1674. 'This day we all dined with the ould Governor,
Capt. Keigwin. It was ordered that leftenant Burd should deliver up
his mutenus Commistion and it was burned by the Marshall at the
head of the Company in the Yard of the Foart, and Sargant Tailer
who was the head of the muteny was ordered on board our shipp;
soe by these two being taken of[f] the Island, it would be in the more
saifty and peecable condistion . . . and we did adwise Capt. Keigwin
not to be to[o] harsh in his Command, but to moddarate his pastion
and govern with love and meeknes, if possible to be dunn; the which
he promised should be done, nothing wanting in him. . . .' Two
Dutch prisoners brought on board.
27 April, 1674. Set sail from St. Helena.
3 May, 1674. Saw the Island of Ascension. Lay by.
4 May, 1674. '. . . Here we found not any letters, either English or
French: it hath been a custum to leave letters in this place. . . .
Tortouses turned in this bay against our ship 22, and in all the other
bayes 90, in all 112 tortouses.'
5 May, 1674. 'This night we turnded in all the bayes 42 tortouses. Our
men catcht much fish.'
6 May, 1674. 'This forenoon our boat fetcht all the tourtouses which
was turnded last night aboard. . . .' All the Commanders summoned
on board. . . . 'We had an accompt of all the Tortouses which
ware aboard all the shipps, 132, soe we propoused that eavery
shipp should have vizt., *London*, 88 men, tortouses 19; *Ceesar*, 108
men, tortouses 24; *Ann*, 93 men, tortouses 19; *Bombay*, 89 men,
tortouses 18; *Masinburd* 90 men, tortouses 19; *East India
Marchant*, 66 men, tortouses 17; *Unity*, 64 men, tortouses 16; in
all brought away 132 tortouses and men, in all, 599.' About 3 in
the afternoon all the fleet set sail for England.
19 May, 1674. '. . . Examined our bread and found but 2,100 lb. but
very much dust, and seaverall hoales eatin by the rats in the bailes.'
6 July, 1674. '. . . This forenoon we cetched an allbecor, waight 140
pounds.'

23 July, 1674. '. . . Anchered in the Downes with all our fleete. Found seaverall King shipps riding theare. . . . Sent Mr. Hide and Mr. Earning for London with the Companeys packquet. Could not gitt any pilott in the Downes. Found not any of the Companyes waiters hear.'

27 July, 1674, 'Anchered at Eriff. . . .'

[Log ends—112 pages.]

1674-77. Log of the *Bull*, etc. *Marine Records, Vol. LXXII.*

Vellum-bound. Lettering on paper label effaced. Former No. 85 and later 84. On reverse corner, 1674.

This volume is begun at both ends. The earlier voyage of the *Bull* begins at the opposite end of the volume, the pages not being numbered.

A R[E]CETTE FOR MASTING, YARDING AND RIGING A SHIP.

LINE OF BATTLE and Signals in case of attack. Signed THO: WARREN.

Title: A JOURNALL OF OUR VOYAGE BY GODS ASSISTANCE FROM BANTAM TO MANELA IN THE SHIP *Bull* PER JOHN HALLEWELL.

3 July, 1674. '. . . The Worshipfull Agent Dacces [*sic*] came a board; got under sale. . . .'

4 July, 1674. '. . . This night a Dutch Ship came a bord to serch for French men, but findeing none without passes, retorned.'

3 Aug., 1674. 'Came a great Galeon from New Spaine which anchored in the Caveeta.' Notes of distance and sailing directions thence to 'Marvelas'. 'The North side of the Island being very rocky and dangerous, there hath been 3 Portegeeze ships cast away this year; it is much if any man escaped death, for such as get to land the inhabitants kill.'

2 Sept., 1674. 'Set sale 3 Portegeeze shipps from the Caveeta bound for Macau. . . . A very great Storme, the wind at WSW lasted 24 houres.'

9 Sept., 1674. 'Two of the three Portegeeze shipps returned back, the other lost 10 leags to the Northward of Manelas.'

10 Sept., 1674. 'Came a small French ship from Siam, an Englishman owner of most of the cargo, his name Mr. Wyat, belonging to Tonkeen. The Spaniards imprisoned him and made price of ship and goods.'

30 Nov., 1674. Arrived at 'the Manelas', distant from 'Caveeta' 24 miles. 'Monys of Manelas, the doller, ½ doller, ¼ doller; 2 Royalls is ¼ doller, 12 Condereens are a royall, 24 Bareelias are a royall; 2 Bareelias make a Condereen.'

End.

SHIPP *Bull* FROM MANELLA TOWARD BANTAM.

16 Jan., 1674-75. Departed from 'Marvelas'.

7 Feb., 1674-75. Anchored at Bantam. 'At 11 a'clocke came the Sultna aboard, takeing the Cash and retorned.'

End.

[Here follows the Journal of the ship *America*, 1696, in another hand.]

A Journall of our Voyage by Gods Permission from Bantam to
Mallaca and from thence to Madrass in the ship *Bull*
belonging to the King of Bantam the 11th October, 1676.

19 Jan., 1676-77. 'Last night anchored in the roade [of Madras] . . .
finding in the roade the *Eagle*, Capt. Bonnell, the *Johanna*, Capt.
Bendall.'

27 Jan., 1676-77. 'Came in the *Faulkon*, Capt. Stafford, the *Surrat
Merchant*, Capt. Johnson.'

1 Sept., 1677. Set sail from Madras for Masulipatam (having been to
Porto Novo in the interval), and arrived there on the 5th September.

A Journall of our Voyage by Gods Assistance frome Metchlaptam
towards Bantam in the Ship *Bull* belonging to the King of
Bantam and kept by John Hallwell [1677].

1 Oct.—1 Dec., 1677. Nothing of note.

End.

[Here follows (fol. 13) the Journal of the Ship *Recovery* ' from Ballasore towards
Persia . . . kept by John Hallewell '.]

1679-82. Log of the *Jona*.   *Marine Records, Vol.
LXXV.*

Vellum-bound vollume lettered : ' President's Journall Per Jona. Hide Comd, for
Fort St. George begun 14th Novr., 1679, ended 13 Jany., 1681/2.'

Outer cover black basil, lettered LXXV : 32 cm. x 20 cm. : fols. 63 (pages 127).

8 Nov., 1679. ' Halled out of the Dock at Blackwall.'

14 Nov., 1679. ' Sayled to Erith.'

13 Feb., 1679-80. ' A Journall Kept in Ship *President* bound by Gods
Assistance for the Coast of Cormendell and Bay of Bengall being the
3d Voyage since the Ship was taken by the Dutch on the Coast of
Cormendell, then Commanded by my Father Capt. Jonathan Hide in
the year 1673.'

' Att 12 a clock ' sailed with four East Indiamen, ' severall Ginne
men ', etc., and a man-of-war.

15 Feb., 1679-80. ' From England towards Cape Bon Esprance.'

26 May, 1680. ' From Cape Legullis [Agulhas] towards the Coast
Cormendell.'

1 July, 1680. Off Porto Novo and Sadraspatnam. ' Here came of [f] to
us a Cattemeran with 3 or 4 blacks from Myn Heer Hemson, who
was cheif for the Dutch att Sandrassapatam. They desir'd our ships
name and whence we came. . . . Here we understood of the *Expectation*, Capt. Ally, being at Porta Nova, also that no other Europe
[ship] had been on this coast before us.'

' As soon as we came to Anchor [in Madras Road] a musyla came
on board with a letter from the Worshipfull Strensham Master Esqr.,
Governer of Fort St. George, which was to congratulate our safe
arrivall, and also to send some of his letters ashoar, but not to lett
any person come on shoar this night, it not being safe because of the
sufs. . . . Mr. Joseph Henmersh [Hinmers], late second in the Forte,
dyed in May last, Mr. Wm. Bridger 2d, Mr. Tim. Wilks 3d, being all
at present that are of the Councell here, Mr. Richard Mohon being
putt out at our arrivall.'

' At day light saluted the Fort with 11 guns ; they answered [with]
9 ; thanks 7 ; they with 1 ; we with 1 more.'

'About 8 Mr. Manwarring went on shoar; at his going fird 9 guns, I also carried the Companys packetts, etc. on shoar.'

'In the Road are severall contry ships, one being the *Good Hope* which Mr. Henry Oxended came in from Surrat, is now sold to Mr. Robert Freeman and bound for Atchin and Cudda [Queda]. Two days before us arrived Mr. Mohuns ship from Bantam, Mr. Holloway master, bound for the Bay, who informs us: of the death of Ajent Parker and Mr. Pains going for England, also that the Dutch have or are sending [an] Embassedor from Battavia to demand satisfaction from the Javes [Javanese] for Sundry things.

1st.   To demand satisfaction for there cutting off the Dutch Factor att Andergeley, a place to the Southward of Jambe, where all were put to death and the factory plundred.

2dly.   The Ilands of Lampoon from whence cometh all the Pepper.

3dly.   All the slaves that hath run from Battavia since the last war between them.

4thly.   The Castle that lyeth about a mile or 2 from Bantam towards Battavia.

5thly.   Pullapanjan Iland.

6thly.   Blood for blood ; they demand the men employ'd and the Pangrans that were the cause of cutting severall Dutch [i.e. cutting off (killing) several Dutch] that were in sloops and also the same for Andergely ; that they themselves may have the executing of the aforementioned Javes.   These demands not being answered by the Javes maketh the war between the Dutch and King of Bantam.'

6 July, 1680.   'This day about noon, Capt. Holloway in the *Pearle*, Mr. Mohuns his ship, sayl'd, himself [Mohun] being out [of] the Companys servis went in her, being bound for Metchlepatam and Bengall. Mr. Manwaring also went on board and took passage in her.'

In Madras Road and between Fort St. George and Masulipatam.

27 July, 1680.   'Metchlepatam Road. . . .   In the road was 8 or 10 Contry ships, also the *St. George*, a new ship, Mr. Clark, Master, laitly built in Methipolum [Madapollam] river, burthn'd about 400 Tuns.'

'Mr. Christopher Hatton who was cheife [of] the Factory dyed July the 17th.'

'Afternoon I went ashoar where I found Mr. John Tivell chief in the factory of Metchlepatam . . . and Mr. Ramsden steward, John Hethfeild Chirurgeon, being all the English that was at this time in the Factory.'

30 July, 1680.   'This day arrived here the *Polleron*, a Dutch ship from Battavia.'

31 July, 1680.   Sailed from Masulipatam Road for Bengal.

5 Aug., 1680.   Sailing directions for the Bay of Bengal.

7 Aug., 1680.   Anchored in Balasor Road.

Notes of events while in the Bay of Bengal.   Various deaths.

13 Sept., 1680.   The longboat, which had broken loose on the 6th in a storm. was recovered with the loss of only one man.

1 Oct., 1680.   This day arrived the *William and John*, Capt. Edward Cripps, Commander, a Interloper : he came out [of] England in March and was at Johanna with the Surrat ships, then went to Muscatt and there met with Capt. Pitts in the *Recovery*, who arrived here this day also.'

22 Oct., 1680.   'This day the *Recovery*, Capt. Pitts, sayl'd for Hugly.'

25 Oct., 1680. 'This day the Interloper sayld for Piply river.'

29 Oct., 1680. 'This morning Mr. John Biam, cheif of the Factory of Ballesore and Mr. Bugdon and his wife came of and went on board Capt. Chamblet.'

15 Nov., 1680. 'Today heard of the death of Capt. Ed. Crisp, Comander of the Interloper, who deceased the 12th at Piply and the 14th was interd at Balesore.'
Notes of several deaths among the crew.

14 Jan., 1680-81. Sailed from Balasor Road.

27 Feb., 1680-81. Anchored in Masulipatam Road. 'At this Factory Mr. Mauris Wynn cheife, Mr. Samuel Wales second, Mr. George Ramsden steward. Mr. John Tivell who was cheife when we weere heere befor in July dyed in Sept. 14th following, in 1680.' Note regarding Samuel White, master of the King of Siam's ship.

4 March, 1680-81. 'Mistress Manwaring and Mrs. White with there servants came on board us for to goe home in our ship.'

5 March, 1680-81. Anchored in Madapollam Road. Mr. John Feild, Chief of the Factory, Mr. Henry Croon Colborne second, Mr. John Clarke Steward.

21 March, 1680-81. Anchored in Madras Road. 'The *Bearkly Castle* arrived the 21st February and sayled hence 9th March.'

9 April, 1681. Sailed from Madras.

10 June, 1681. At a Consultation of the officers of the ship, it was decided to steer direct for Mauritius, 'the season of the year being past for getting aboute the Cape.'

17 June, 1681. Anchored at Mauritius. Notes of soundings. Sailing directions, Quoine Island, etc. Description of Quoine Island and details of provisions obtainable at Mauritius and animal life there.

9 July, 1681. The *Eagle*, Capt. Nathaniel Horsman, anchored at Mauritius.

14 July, 1681. 'The Govr. of the Island (Monsr. Isaaq Johanes Lametius by name) arrived here and went on board the *Eagle*. He demands ½ doller per goate and declareth to us Capt. Peck. paid soe when he was heere in the *Unicorne*, which I judge to be false ; by reason his demand[s] are so high we left off takeing goats and maintaine our ships Company with fish.'

25 July, 1681. 'The Govr. and Commander came on board us. We agreed to pay 1d per 11. of what goats flesh shall be delivered us by the hunts men.'

8 Sept., 1681. The *Eagle* and the *President* went out of the harbour.

9 Sept., 1681. 'The *Society* gott safe off and came out. . . . The Commanders entered into bond one with another to keepe Company to St. Hellena togeather on penalty of 50 lib.'

7 Nov., 1681. Anchored in St. Helena Road. 'Here found at anchor the *Barnardiston* from Bantam, Capt. Thomas Paremore Commander, who came out cheife maite, but Capt. Slaide being deceased at Bantam, the other succeed[ed]. Here we understand Capt. Chamblet saved his passage ; and the *William and John* Interloper, who was in the Bay, Capt. Taylor Commander ; the *Nathaniel* from Bantam sayled hence with Capt. Chamblet the 17th Aprill ; the 3 this Month, Capt. Ally in the *Expectation*, now called the *Comerce* sayled hence, who lost his voyage and wintred at Johana, where he see the Surrat and Coast ships, and left advice of Mr. Giffords goeing of in the *Bengalla* for to be Agent at Madderass.'

25 Nov., 1681. Off Ascension Island. By letters found there learned
that the Surat ships left the Island on the 3d and 4th May, the
Sampson from Madras and *Nathaniel* from Bantam on the 27th.
Notes of several ships that had put in at the Island.

3 Dec., 1681. ' Soon after noon came up with a Portegese flite (aboute
2 or 250 tonns) . . . he informed us of our haveing peace with all
nations but the Turke.'

13 Jan., 1681-82. Anchored in the Downs.
End of Journal.

127 + 6 blank pages.

1680-   Journal of the *Barnardiston*.   *Marine Records,*
81-82.   *Vol. LXXVI.*
Nov., 1680—
Jan., 1681-82.

Six pages blank.

A LIST OF THE SHIPS COMPANY IN THE *Barnardiston*, CAPTAIN JOHN
SLADE COMMANDER, FOR BANTAM AND CHINA.

The ages of the men are given. There were, besides, two passengers, Demengo
Merties and Silvester Francis, ' Blacks '.

Title : 'A DIRNUALL [diurnal] ACCOMPT OF A VOYAGE FROM ENGLAND
TO BAINTAM ONE THE ISLAND JAVA IN THE SOUTH SEA IN THE
SHIP *Barnardiston*, CAPTAIN JOHN SLEAD COMANDER BY ME
THOMAS PARRAMOER [purser] ANNO 1680.'

30 Aug., 1680. ' Cleared att Gravesent.'

1 Nov., 1680. After the entry for this date is a sketch of two fishes, one
of them a flying fish.

21 Jan., 1680-81. Sketch of the S. side of the Island St. Pauls.

26 Feb., 1680-81. Sketch of the S. part of Sumatra, with directions for
making it.

1 March, 1680-81. Anchored in Bantam Road.

24 July, 1681. Sailed from Bantam for England.

12 Nov., 1681. In St. Helena Road. ' This afternoon caim to anchor
the *Persimarchan*, Capt. John Bowers, from Bantam, whoe caime out
about 20 dayes after us, and gave us accompt that the desine of the
King of Baintam is altered in sendeing for England his shipp *Bombay*, and that his Imbasandrs is to com in the *London*, Capt. John
Daniell.'

14 Nov., 1681. A consultation on board the *Eagle* ' for keeping of Company and for the Mainigemen of the Squadron in cause [*sic*] wee should
be atracked by an enimie, the Senioritie to Capt. William Thompson
in the *Socitie*.'

17 Nov., 1681.   Note of ships that had arrived during the stay of the
Barnardiston at St. Helena.

Instructions for fighting in case of an attack. Sketch of the five
ships in their order for fighting.

' In case wee fight with our Larboard Tackes aboard, then the *Societie*,
Capt. William Thompson, Sinior, is to lead the vann ; if with ower
Starboard Tackes aboard, the *Persiamarchant*, Capt. John Bowers,
to lead the vann. Secondly, if intend to tack upon the Enemy, I will
spread the Jack flagg att the fore Topmasthead, and if I would have

the Reare to tack I will spread the same flagg in the Mizantopmast
shrouds and you are to keep the same saile as before.
When I will speake with all the Commanders I will put a Pendant
on the Mizan Peicke.'
Below is a spirited sketch of the six ships in line.
13 Jan., 1681-82. Anchored in the Downs.

1680-83.   Journals of the *Recovery* and *Susan-*   *M a r i n e   Records,*
          nah.   *Vol. LXXII.*

Title: SHIP *Recovery* FROM BALLASORE TOWARDS PERSIA GOD DIRECT
OUR COURSE. KEPT PER JOHN HALLEWELL.

27 Jan., 1680-81. Set sail from Balasor.
25 April, 1681.   Anchored in 'Comerone' road (Gombroon, Bandar
Abbas). Note of ships found in the Road.

Note—The Journal from 6 February is not in John Hallewell's hand.

21 May, 1681. 'Our Captain went sick ashore.'
10 June, 1681. 'Att 9 a clock at night Captain Storie departed this life.'
He was Commander of the *Agent.*

July, 1681.

Title: A JOURNAL KEPT PER ME JOHN HALLEWELL FROM COMEROON
TOWARDS MUSCATT. AND FROM THENCE TO BENGALL, IN THE SHIP
Recovery.

11 Aug., 1681. 'Att 4 in the afternoone yesterday Capt. Robert Cettel-
letan departed his life and att 5 this morning we houve him overboard he having layne sicke ever since the 21th May, fired 21 gunns.'

Feb., 1681-82.

Title: SHIP *Recovery* BEING BOUND FOR MALLDAVA GOD PROSPER:
JOHN HALLEWELL.

17 Feb., 1681-82. Set sail.
1 April, 1682.   Anchored at 'Malldava'.
24 April, 1682. Much sickness among the captain and crew.
21 July, 1682.   Set sail from 'Malldava'.

FROM BALLYSORE ROAD TOWARDS THE BRACES.

7 Aug., 1682. 'Waighed being weackly mand . . . Mr. Browne tackeing
chardge of our ship for Hughly . . . Mr. Hering came one board for
Hughly, butt hee not having any orders, I thought itt best with
Counsell from my ofissers to secure our shipp as soone as could bee.'
8 Aug., 1682. 'Wee stud to the Eadges of the braces, butt our Pillott
would not goe over.'
11 Aug., 1682. Anchored near 'Cookalle'.
12 Aug., 1682. The vessel grounded and was with difficulty got clear.
13 Aug., 1682. Anchored near the Diamond Sands.
Feb., 1682-83. Sailing directions from Point Palmeiras to the Downs.

Title: A JOURNALL OF OUR VOYADGE BY GOD'S PROMISSION FROM
BALLYSORE TOWARDS CAPE BONNE SPRANCE AND FROM THENCE
TO ENGLAND IN THE *Susanna* GOD DIRICTE OUR CORSE BY MEE
JOHN HALLEWELL.

6 Feb.—21 May, 1683. Log of the voyage to the Cape.

22 and 23 May, 1683. At anchor at the Cape. 'The 3 Ducth Shipps which ware homeward bound sett saylle this morning, one a great Square starnne shipp with a flagg att toppmast head, the other 2 fligh boats; all 3 came from Zealon. Our boat went ashore this day to aquainte the Governor of our wants which wass watter and fresh provissions, who sivilly made answer wee may have whatt the place aforded.'

30 May—24 June, 1683. From the Cape to Ascension Island.

'A shorte abstracte of the Severall voyadges and Imployments made in India per mee John Hallewell.'

Fifteen years since he left England in the *George* under Capt. Wm. Basse with whom he made two voyages.

He served in the *Philip* and *Ann* in President Aungier's service. In his first voyage from Bombay to Siam and back to Malacca he was taken prisoner by the Dutch, carried to Batavia and confined for 15 mos., then escaped to Bantam.

He made 3 voyages in the ships *Bull* and *Bombay Merchant*, in the King of Bantam's service.

Other voyages: 2 in a sloop of Agent Parker's; in the sloop *Mary* in Mr. Edmund Bugden's service from Bantam to Bengal; in the ship *Pearl* in Mr. Mohun's service from Bengal to Bantam and back; in the ship *Recovery* in Mr. Vincent's service (2 voyages).

25 June, 1683. The *Susanna* weighed anchor from Ascension for England.

End.

1686. *Marine Records, Vol. LXXXI.*

On inner paper cover lettered : 'Lost Ships, No. 1, 1686.'

'RECEIPTS FOR MONTHES PAY PAID SEAMENS RELATIONS WHO SERVE ON BOARD SHIPP *Loyal Adventure*, CAPT. Wm. GOODLAD, COMMANDER, 1685. LOST.'

40 pp. of printed receipts of payments.

1688. *Marine Records, Vol. LXXXV.*

Bound black basil. On the inner paper cover lettered : 'Blown up at Fort St. George.'

Receipts for monthly wages for the mariners belonging to the ship, *Persia Merchant*, Capt. Benjamin Brangwin Commander, 1688.

1688. Log of the *John and Rachel*, Cap- *Marine Records, Vol.* tain Robert Fox. 23 June—1 October, *LXXXVII.* 1688.

NATHANIEL BALL HIS BOOKE, 1688. A JOURNALL OF OUR WESTWARD VOYAGE TO LOOK OUT FOR THE SHIPPS EXPECTED HOME BY THE HONOURABLE ENGLISH EAST INDIA COMPANY IN THE *John and Rachel*, ROBERT FOX COMMANDER.

[The Journal ends on fol. 9 and contains nothing of interest.]

f. 10.   Notes of payments [? of seamen in ? 1702].

1695-96.   Journal of the ship *America*.   *Marine Records,*
Vol. LXXII.

Fols. 51-110, writing on one side only.

RULES FOR WORKIN AZAMETTS OR AMPLITUDES.

March, 1695.   Ship *America* from Tilbury bound for India, to be convoyed by the *Yorke* to Portsmouth, and there expected to join the ' Cadiz convoy '.

Title: A JOURNAL OF A VOIGE INTENDED FOR SURRATT IN THE SHIPP *America* IN THE HONBLE. EST INDIA COMPANYES SERVIS BEGUN THE 5TH OF MAY, ANNO 1695 FROM PORTSMOUTH.   Q.D.G.

Copy of Commodore Warren's sailing instructions for keeping company. Signals by day, etc.   Rendezvous at St. Helena.

9 May, 1695.   ' In site of Falmouth . . . wee mett with the *Falcon,* Captain Midleton, who is a Crewsar heare abouts ; he informs us thear are many French Privetears abroad.'

11 May, 1695.   ' This day wee dyned aboard the Captin.   Yesterday wee wear on board my Lord Hambleton, and in the afternoone he gave chase with his Nue Frigot the *Litchfeild* and came up with his Majestyes Shipp the *Waymouth* who had taken a French Privetear of fowerteen Guns and Eighty menn about 35 Leagues from Silley on Mundey last.'

17 June, 1695.   Teneriffe.   ' This afternoone Mr. Edward Smith the Consull of these Islands [Canaries] went aboard the *King William,* Captain James Thwaits Commander, with severall oather Merchants of this place.   Mr. Smith the Consull was marryed to Mrs. Mary Calvert, a passinger in the said ship bound for the Est Indese with Capt. James Thwaits the said Comander.'

26 June, 1695.   ' Paul Tattnall one of our midshipmen fell overbord out of the pinnis.   He was taken up but never came to life again, notwithstandin he vomited much salt wayter.'

27 June, 1695.   ' Yesterday in the evening we hove Paulle Tattnall overboard.'

Nov.-Dec., 1695.   From the Cape, eastward bound.   Much sickness on board and many deaths from scurvy.

Friday, 27 Dec., 1695.   ' Near the Coast of India.   Viztt.   Our Wesling made from Zealoan whear wee see the water discullered is 231 Myles with about 15 Leagues alowed for the distans from the Land, being Wee did nott see itt, was Les or 16 Leagues ; that to this day Noone I make out my Weslin to be 231 myle errors excepted.   Yesterday a great Long [log] of Timber Swim by the Ship that was full of Barnickles, suposed to be bloum from the Mallabar Iselands or the Main.   Wee looke uppon [it] as a Sine not to be farr from Land, which pray God send us a happey sight of, for wee are now in a Verey Weak condition, not have Tenn well men in all our Companye ; 27 is this day remaining alive, butt many of them are verey weake, not exspected to live.'

3 Jan., 1695-96.   On the coast of India towards Calicut.   ' Last night wee see one of the Mallabarr Boats which lay att a distans to vew us, which is one of thear Pyrotts who take all nations that they can overcome.'

Sunday, 5 Jan., 1695-96. 'Wee see Sacrefise Rock. . . . Wee stered . . . for Callecutt; in the Evening befoar Sunsett wee came to an Anckor in the Road. . . . Wee found no ships heare but the *Emrod*, one of the Companys small frigotts that belongs to Bumbay. They informe us that theare are five or six sayle of French Ships arived att Goa, and that the Duch are gone up toward that place with nine sayle ships from 40 to 50 guns and Eleven hundered men aboard of them and are resolved to fight them whear ever they meet them. Wee have lost in our passing from the Cannary Iselands sixteen Menn . . . from Plymouth . . . have not seen any Land all the Way . . . the first land wee see was the Mallabar Coast . . . wee have great reason to thank God for our safe ariveall our men being in a verey weak condition and had the last butt of water that I know of in the shipp a broach. Wee have liquise advised [*sic*] that Capt. James Thwaits in the *King William* is arived att Collumbo on the Iseland Zealon, but what condition he is in in respect to health cannott yett Learn.'

16 Jan., 1695-96. From Calicut towards Bombay.

About 8 a.m. 'Mr. John Burniston formerly cheif of Callicutt (who now resined the Facterey to Mr. Thomas Pen[n]ing) came aboard our ship, with Mrs. thear Wyves and Childeren came aboard our ship in order to sayle towards Tilla Chirre [Tellicherry] the next Facterey that belongs to our Honourable Company on the Mallabarr Coast.'

17 Jan., 1695-96. Abreast of Tellicherry, 'Wee fyred a gunn for the Companyes ship the *Emrod* to come out of the Roade who is laided with Peper and goes in company with us to Bombay.'

Anchored in Cannanore Road. 'The Governer of the place came aboard and carryed Mr. Burniston and his wife and childeren along with him, whear they stayed untill Munday in the evenin.'

21 Jan., 1695-96. Weighed anchor. 'Mr. Tho. Pennyng, Mr. Caleb Travers and his Lady with the oather Gentlemen thatt belonged to Callicutt and Tilla Cherre imbarked aboard the Briganteen . . . to land att Tilla Chirree.'

27 Jan., 1695-96. Off the island Anjidiv.

'A Canew came of[f] with a Pewn from Carwarr with a letter to Mr. Burniston withall to advise when the French shipps sayled fiom Goa and when the Duch ships that are bound up to Surrat passed by that place.'

1 Feb., 1695-96. Anchored near 'Caripalan wheare Savege [Sivaji] hath a strong Castle att the Rivers Mouth.'

13 Feb., 1695-96. Anchored 'not farr from a place called Kellsey and in site of one of Savegees Castles upon an Iseland that lyes verey near the main.'

14 Feb., 1695-96. Anchored near one of 'Savegee's Forts. Wee sentt the Callecutt Munchew [*manchua*] ashoar this morning to fill some wayter. In the afternoone she was seized on by five or six Savegees Boats and carryed to the Castle whear they plundered the Maister of all his Money and Cloose.'

15 Feb., 1695-96. 'One of the Savegees boats came aboard with severall of his Officers' with presents of provisions for Mr. Burniston, and the 'Munchew' arrived later on with wood and water received from the fort.

16 Feb., 1695-96. A boat was despatched with letters to Sir John Gayer,

General of Bombay, enquiring whether the French were cruising near that island.

17 Feb., 1695-96. Off Danda Rajapur, 'wheare the Sidde have a great Forte and the Magulls Menn a warr ly now theare.' Enquiry at one of 'Savegees Foarts' elicited the information that no French had been seen in the neighbourhood.

18 Feb., 1695-96. The Governor's 'Munchew' came aboard with a letter for Mr. John Burniston, and in the evening the *America* anchored near the Dutch fleet off the Island Hendry Kendry.

19 Feb., 1695-96. Sailed towards Bombay, passed the Dutch fleet of seven sail who were looking out for the French. 'Wee salluted thear Admerall with seven guns which he answered with five.' News was received that three sail of 'great French shipps' had lain off Bombay for several days, 'but when they got site of them [the Dutch fleet] they stud of[f] into Sea and the Duch after them about 20 leagues. The shipp *Thomas*, Capt. Pye Commander, one of our Companys ships laided with Pepper from the Mallabar Cost, being in theare companye, they left of thear chace and stud into the shoar and fell in with Dunda Rogapoar and arived att Bombay about two dayes before us. . . . Wee have great reason to thank God for a safe deliverance from the French, which if itt had not been prevented by the Duch they could not a amissed of us.'

20 Feb., 1695-96. 'This morning the Worshipfull Mr. John Burniston went ashoar in the Companyes Ballown and accompanyed with all the ships boats in the Harber. We fyred nine guns att his going of[f] and all the ships in the harbor fyered liquise. He was receved on shoar by most of the Gentlemen on the Place, with the Companyes Soogers all in Armes, and the Generalls Coach and Pallankeynes to carry him and his Lady and Childeren to the Forte whear he was received by the Generall and his Ladey and severall guns wear fyred of[f] att the Forte after he came theare.'

21 Feb., 1695-96. 'This morning I went on shoar to the Generall Sir John Gayer whear I receved an Order from the Counsell to send on shoar all the Companyes Chests of Treasure . . . which wear 27 Chests in all, and four delivered by the Generall Order to Mr. John Burniston and Counsell at Callicutt, which makes 31 in all, which is our Complementt wee broght from Eingland.'

28 Feb., 1695-96. 'Wee have not heard any moare news of ether the Duch or the French ships wheare they are, since our first ariveall here. The Generall had advise yesterday from the Magulls Corte that thear are Orders gon doune to Surratt for the releasin the Einglish Merchants that have been kept in Irons this five or six months att Surratt by reason of some Einglish Pyrots that robed and plundered the Magull[s] ships that came from Moca and abused his Women, and it is said heare by the Banjans thatt theare are liquise Orders given thatt the Trade shall go forward in the same nature as formerly.'

30 March, 1696. News from Goa received. Hunton, the Dutch Commodore, 'is comeing up to Surratt to meet the French and hath with him five Menn a warr and two Fyer ships. They all came from Zealone.'

6 May, 1696. 'This morning most of the Gentlemen went to a place called Mayam on this island to a great feast made by a Poarteguse Faddlgee [Fidalgo] of that place.'

7 May, 1696. 'This day the *Moca* Frigott, Capt. Edscomb and the *Benjamin*, Captt. Browns ship boath arived from Surratt in two day passidg. Captt. Brown the Commander of the *Benjam[in]* is in prison with the Merchants at Surat concerning the Einglish Pyrots who robed the Mooars ship from Moca.'

12 July, 1696. Off Ceylon. 'Did not prevale with the Governer last night to come into the Harber notwithstandin that hee called his Counsell together; itt was resolved to send to the Governor of Colombo first to have his consentt. . . . The Fovr. of Point Degall his name is Charles Bullenard.'

15 July, 1696. 'I went aboard the *Josia* in the harber and got Mr. Stanley and Capt. Bear to go ashoar along with me to wait on the [Dutch] Governer to know whether thear wear an Order come from Colombo or no for our going into the harber and he toald us thear was no Order come yett but every hower expected one. Wee see severall Ellefants shiped of which are going to the Coast of Cormedell; thear is two Duch ships in the Harber that carry 40 Ellifants each of them.'

16 July, 1696. 'This morning a boat came of from the shoare with a Pylott to carry us into the Harber. . . . Here are 5 Duch ships and the *Josia* and *Tonquen*, two English ships, boath from China.'

29 July, 1696. 'This night five of our men run ashoar in this Bay with our Pinnis which was almost staved in the Suff of the Sea. I went ashoare to the Duch Comadoar to desire him that they mite not be entertained in the Duch servis which he hath promissed me they should not.'

31 July, 1696. 'We heard no oather news of our men then that they are gon up towards the Hills for feare of being seised near the wayter side and conveyed aboard ship afterwards.'

17 Aug., 1696. Hunton, the Dutch Commodore, arriving from Tūtacor-in was forced by the weather to go away to 'Billegon the nextt sea Porte . . . which is much like to this place and the Duch have a small forte of tenn Guns.'

26 Aug., 1696. 'The peiple from the shoar reports that this morning about Six a clock they felt severall shakes of an earthquake and about Eight a clock the water fell away out of the harber at least Six Feett with an exterordnarey Curantt out for a small tyme thatt itt sunck most of the Boyes of the Anckors in the Harber, butt flowed in again in ½ a quarter of an hower, and drew in 7 or 8 men thatt weare fishin att the wayter side which wear all Drounded, liquise one Duchman thatt was standin upon the Rocks neare the Forte.'

9 Sept., 1696. From Ceylon towards the Cape.

2 Dec., 1696. 'Wee see a hauksbill turtle, a pritte large one.'

4 Dec., 1696. 'Severall Manga fallowders [*Mangas de velludo*, Velvet Sleeves] or ganitts which never flye farr from the Shoar . . . many black birds with white bills' seen.

1695-96—   Log of the *Madras Merchant*.   *Marine Records, Vol.*
1698.   *CVI.*

Black basil outer cover. Original vellum binding. 38½ cm. x 25 cm.

Lettered: '*Madras Merchants Journall* Capt. Benja. Prickman Comdr. to Fort St. George and Bengall: begun 9th Febry., 1695/6. Ended 27th April 1698.' Formerly numbered 91, then 92.

Pasted inside the inner cover is a label: 'No. 131 F. Zacariah Tovey his Book anno 1698.'

Title: A JORNALL OF OUR INTENDED VOYAGE BY GODS ASISTANCE FROM LONDON TO FORT ST. GEORGE ON THE COAST OF CORMANDELL AND FROM THENCE FOR THE BAY OF BENGALL IN THE SHIP *Madras Merchant* CAPT. BEN: PRICKMAN COMANDER, COMMENCING THE 9TH OF FEBRUARY ANNO DOMINI 1695/6. BY ME ZACHARY TOVEY SECOND MATT.

14 May, 1696. In the Middle of the Hope . . . 'the *Sidney* and the *East India Marchant* in Company.'

11 July, 1696. 'Yesterday . . . come to sale and all the fleet that were bound to the Westward with us from the Downes and 5 sale of men of warre for our Convoy.'

10 Aug., 1696. 'Our longbote went ashore for water at St. Helins.'

11 Aug., 1696. 'Came to sale and all the Dutch and English fleet that weere bound to the Westward, which might be about 2 hundred and 50 sale.'

7 Jan., 1696-97. 'Came to anchor in the road by Table land SSW and Pengewen [Penguin] Island . . . where we found our 2 consorts who left us the day we came in with the land and one Capt. Brown in the *Skilbana*, a Interloper bound for Bengall and 3 saill of frigots and a fire ship that came out with outer bound ships in May and on[e] homeward bound ship Capt. Laycock and they designe to saill the next month for St. Hellina.'

29 Jan., 1696-97. Sailed from the Cape, parting Company with a man of war and five homeward bound ships.

29 March, 1697. The ships met with a violent storm that continued so long that the course was lost. 'Wee see none of our Company in the storm. . . . At noon spoke with . . . the *East Inday Merchant*, Capt. Clark . . . the damage he had by the storm, lost all his topmast and his main top and 6 foot watter in the hould and 3 foot on the gun deck as the ship lay along and as the ship rould over floated all the Chests, so they were forced to cut holes in the dacks to let the watter doune . . .'

30 March, 1697. Saw 'Mohilla' and 'Joanna'. Dried some of the goods and bread.

2 April, 1697. Anchored at Johanna. Found the *Sidney*, *Skilbana* and Capt. Kyd in the *Adventure* galley, 'a Privitier and a sloop his Consort, bound the Lord knows where.'

16 April, 1697. 'This morning came to sail and all our Company with us and a Munday night last 5 of Capt. Clarks men run away with his pinnis and never hard aney thing of her afterwards and Capt. Kyd the priviter sailed from hence the 4th of this instantt and the slupe his consort.'

27 April, 1697. Parted company with the *East India Merchant* which was bound for Surat.

28 May, 1697. The *Skilbana*, interloper, parted company with the *Madras Merchant*, she being bound for Bengal.

1 June, 1697. Anchored off S. Thomé. Found the *King William*, Capt. Thwaites Commander. [For her Log see Vol. CXXXIX.] She had suffered from a storm and had been compelled to heave some of her guns overboard to lighten the ship. 'By report of some of their oficers they had 11 foot watter in the hould, which I cannot give

credit unto, she being a deep ladened ship before they were of[f] Zalone [Ceylon].'

13 July, 1697. 'This day came a chist of treasure for Fort St. Davids and an Iron gun of 49. 0. 14 weight.'

16 July, 1697. Set sail for Fort St. David.

18 Aug., 1697. Anchored in the road at Fort St. David.

24 and 25 Aug., 1697. Took aboard 'palmetara' trees for the Company.

26 Aug., 1697. 'This day came aboard . . . some Men and wemen slaves to go for Fort St. Georgs.'

29 Aug., 1697. Anchored in Madras Road. Found the *King William* laden for England.

30 Aug., 1697. 'Sent ashore . . . the 10 slaves and some of the Palme tres.'

2 Sept., 1697. 'Took in 423 peces of Tuthanag [*tutenaga*, spelter] and 25 pigs of Lead . . . and other things for Viz[ag]apatam.'

13—18 Oct., 1697. Landed goods at Vizagapatam.

17 Oct.—5 Nov., 1697. Took in wood, water and provisions.

8 Nov., 1697. Set sail for Achin.

5 Dec., 1697. 'All hopes of feechen Achiene is laid aside.'

29 Dec., 1697. A fire broke out in the bread room but a man 'trampled out and stifled it by a great providence.'

6 Jan., 1697-98. In the road of 'Projmong' [Priaman].

8 Jan., 1697-98. An attempt made to scrape the ship's bottom, it being 'like a mussell banck'. The purser went ashore with the Company's packet and six casks were carried ashore 'to trim and fille with water this place being the worst place I ever was at, for here is nothing to be had, as foules, bufelos, for the factors cannot get any to eat themselves ashore, for they go sumetimes two days and cannot get aney to eat.'

10 Jan., 1697-98. Richard Darly came aboard and carried off five chests that were consigned to him.

11 Jan., 1697-98. Water, pepper, butter, wine, etc. shipped aboard. 'A boat has 10 dolars for bringing abord 6 casks of water.'

13 Jan., 1697-98. Sailed for Bencoolen, and the next day anchored in the Road.

15 Jan., 1697-98. 'Yesterday in the evening our Pynis came abord from the Fort and brought word there was peper enought to load our ship.'

18 Jan., 1697-98. A buffalo and a turtle and much 'green traid' shipped aboard.

20 Jan.—4 Feb., 1697-98. The ship laden with pepper and other goods.

5 Feb., 1697-98. The Captain received his dispatch from the Govr. of York Fort to sail for England.

6 Feb., 1697-98. As the ship was about to weigh anchor, an interloping vessel, the *America*, bound for Borneo, appeared in the offing, and having lost her bearings, sent a pinnace to make enquiries at Bencoolen. The information regarding foreign relations that had been gleaned was 'that ther will be peace with the Frensch before we get home'; that the *Dorothy* and *Bedford*, East Indiamen, were taken in their outward bound passage, and that the *Tavistock* was supposed to be at Madras, 'and so this ship puts us of[f] sailing till she comes into the Road, we not trusting of him, ther being so many pyrats abroad.'

25 Feb., 1697-98. 'This morning our pinis went of[f] aboard the ship

to learn of a certain what she was and did, and with the sea breeze the ship came into the road and anchored by us and Capt. Spencer, Comander, and Super Cargo and Docter who imeadatly visited our Captain aboard of us and knowen our Captain lay sick and lame with the barbers [beri-beri]; and after they had satisfied our Captain of all the afairs in England and our Captain the affaires in the East Indeys, and at 12 a Cloak in the night they returned aboard their own ship designeing to saill in the morning with us with the Land breases; and so pray God send them to their desired port in safety and us a safe return and good passage to England in the Lords blessed time.'

28 Feb., 1697-98. Set sail from Bencoolen Road. The name of the island in the Road is said to be 'Pulle Tuckus.'

5 April, 1698. 'This evening at 8 a Clock Captain Benjamin Prickman deseased this life to our great greef, having been so long together as 17 years and comeing from Vizagapatam to the West Coast of Sumatra of[f] the head of Atchine got cold and came to be the Barbers which were the death of him.'

7 April, 1698. 'Yesterday in the afternoon at 4 a Clock our deseased Comander was buried and fired 14 guns; ther was 10 cross barr shot and 6 round shot to sink the corps, and every mase [mess] had a boule of punch at the buriall.'

27 April, 1698. Flocks of birds seen.

27 April, 1698. 'At 7 this morning Cape Doles bore NWbN, distant of[f] by judgment 9 leagues.'

End.

1697-99. Log of the Ship *Fame*, Robert   *Marine Records, Vol.* Betton, Captain.   *CXI.*

Vellum bound inside outer black basil cover. On paper label former Nos. 95 and 96. Inside the cover, No. 119 F.

TITLE: JOURNALL OF A VOYAGE FROM ENGLAND TO MADRAS AND FORT ST. DAVID, AND THEN FROM MADRAS BACK TO ENGLAND. KEPT BY JOHN CONWAY, 1ST MATE. BEGUN 1 FEB., 1697/8.

'A list of mens names belonging to and wente out by Gods Permition in the ship *Fame* For India Whereof Captain Robert Betton is Commander And God of His Infinite mercy sende us a good and Prosperous voiage.'

The list contains the names of 85 men, including the ship's officers and surgeon. There was also one passenger, Mrs. Mary Man, and 30 soldiers including a sergeant and corporal.

9 Feb., 1697-98. 'This day his worship [Thomas] Pitts came down who is goeing Governour of Fort St. George.'

10 Feb., 1697-98. 'At 6 this morning . . . weighed haveing in our Company the *Martha* Capt. Thos. Rains as Comadore and the *Anna*, Capt. Bridges, all 3 being bound to one port.'

13 March, 1697-98. 'This day wee caught 2 Turtles, each weighed 190 li.'

14 March, 1697-98. 'This Morning Our Captain sent his Honr. Pitts a Calapee of a Turtle.'

28 March, 1698. 'Wee saw a shipp bareing from us NWbN distant about 3 Leagues. Wee hoisted our Collours but he would show us none; wee supposed him to be from Portugall by his Bulk.'

29 March—1 April, 1698.　The strange ship kept in sight but would not speak with the *Fame*.

2—3 April, 1698.　Another sail in sight, also Portuguese. On the 3rd, 'both the Portugeze came in our Company and saluted us.'

4 April, 1698.　'This day all the Commanders of our shipps went on board the Portugeze and he saluted them verry nobly when they came away and he was answered by them again when come on board.'

9 April, 1698.　'This morning wee came up with 9 sail of Portugeze shipps which whaire bound for Brazel and allso with Capt. Flowers in the *London* Frigate for Borneo.'

25 April, 1698.　'This morning the *Martha* and *Anna* was ahead of us a considerable way. The *Martha* shortned saile for us, but I do suppose the *Anna* intends to make the best of her way and so leave us.'

6 July, 1698.　'About 2 a Clock yesterday in the Afternoon wee made the Cost of Cormandell, fine champion ground and full of trees. About 5 in the evening wee made Nagaptam [Negapatam], a factory possessed by the Dutch . . . Their was 3 Dutch shipps in the Road, one of which had a flagg at his maintopmast head.'

8 July, 1698.　Anchored in Madras Road.

18 Aug., 1698.　At Fort St. David.　'Imployed in taking in of watter and goods belonging to Capt. Throughton and Madam Gam[e]s who are going Passengers in us to Madderass.'

3 Oct., 1698.　'We have on board bound for England these following Passingers, viz.' [Here follow the names of 13 passengers.]

4 Oct., 1698.　Sailed from Madras for England. In furling the foresail an accident happened which injured three of the company.

7 Oct., 1698.　Richard Inge, Corporal, who was hurt in the accident on the 4th, died, also the Doctor, at whose burial 10 guns were fired.

15 Dec., 1698.　'This day I shott an albetross that was 10½ foot between the tips of her wings.'

25 Dec., 1698.　'This being Christmass day our Captain had all his Officers and Seamen too Dinner with him.'

31 Dec., 1698.　'A Corprosanct [St. Elmo's fire] appeared at our maintopmast head which was very large.'

4 Jan., 1698-99.　'This day it pleased Allmighty God to take to himself our Captain Robert Betton who hath bin sick ever since he came from India. I buried him as well as cou'd be don with desency on board. When wee committed his Body to the deep I fired 36 gunns, shott and all, and as by our Instructions, took the Command of the shipp my self and I pray God of his infinite mercy send us a good voyage.'

20 Jan., 1698-99.　Anchored in Saldanha Bay for refreshment.

21 Jan., 1698-99.　The Purser was sent on shore to get permission from the Governor of the Cape to obtain the required provisions. He brought word that the Governor pleaded a scarcity of fresh eatables, 'which is their custom when min[d]ed to raise their Price.'

22 Jan., 1698-99.　Anchored and 'saluted the fort with 13 gunns, in hopes to oblidge the Mighty Hogan Mogans, but after their Brutish manner they returned us 11 in answer under no Colours nor any of their shipps showed us any. . . . In the afternoon I went on shore and with me Mr. Thredcroft, one of the Counsell at Madderass to pay my respects to the Governer, who we understood was gon in to the Country.' After a long delay and much questioning, the Govr.

gave permission to water the ship, but refused to spare provisions. 'And so I was dismist without sitting down or being asked to drink, and I do intend they shall be as litle the better for me as possible I can.'

29 Jan., 1698-99. A ship came into the Bay, 'and seeing her to have English Collours I went on board and it proved to be the *America* an Interloper.'

30 Jan., 1698-99. Sailed from the Cape towards England.

31 Jan., 1698-99. Got all the firearms into the round house, having learned from 'Capt. Cullock, that was passinger on board the forementioned Interloper that his boatswains mate had made himself Commander of his shipp and in her 20,000 pound stock and had left him behind and his cheefe mait and whom woud not side with him in his viliany.'

13 Feb., 1698-99. 'This morning saw a small bird like a Tropick bird which they call a St. Hellena Pidgon.'

15 Feb., 1698-99. Anchored in St. Hellena Road.

16-28 Feb., 1698-99. Cleaned, provisioned and watered the ship.

1 March, 1698-99. Sailed from St. Helena.

5 March, 1698-99. It was decided 'to avoid the Island of Ascenstion least wee shou'd meet Pirots.'

23 April, 1699. Near the 'high peak on the Island Pico'.

25 April, 1699. Off the Island 'Grasiosia'. The Purser was sent on shore to get provisions, but the inhabitants would supply none 'without a bill of health from the last place wee came from,' although provisions were cheap and plentiful. They 'offered 2 sheep for the neckcloth about the Pursers neck. . . . This morning Thomas Hughs and John Berry made a mutony in the ship for which I put them in Irons.'

10 May, 1699. 'Wee are at present in great fear of wanting Victualls for wee have no bread nor other provisions except about 8 or 10 days Rice and Beef.'

12 May, 1699. Came up with the *Goodwill*, bound from Bideford to Newfoundland, whose captain spared them bread, peas and oatmeal.

22 May, 1699. Obtained a further supply of provisions from a French vessel from Toulon.

23 May, 1699. Mrs. Throughton died on board, and was buried on the evening of the same day.

30 May, 1699. Anchored in the Downs.

27 June, 1699. 'This day the ship being unlivered we were cleared by the King and Companys survayors riding then at Deptford Chain.'

MISCELLANEOUS

The descriptions in the official *List of Marine Records* (1896) are amplified, and in some instances corrected, in the selection of the most important of the series, noted in Mr. Foster's *Guide*, p. 107 *et seq.*, under the heading 'Miscellaneous'. The details given in the former are not necessarily duplicated or superseded, and both lists should be consulted.

MISCELLANEOUS, NO. I.

Large folio volume (dark basil binding), containing several manuscripts.

1609-1709.   **'Brief Historical Sketch of the**   *MS. I.*
**Management of the Shipping
Concerns of the E.I.C.'** [from
1600 to 1796].

ff. 1-17.   1600-1709, folios 1-17 relate to these years. The freights of ships to Surat and back in 1658 were £18 for coarse goods, £22 for fine.

The first MS., endorsed No. 1 ; Reg. No. 2573.

This MS. is referred to repeatedly by Mr. Danver in his Introduction to the *Marine Records List*, as his authority for various details.

1796 [?].   **'Memorandum containing a gene-**   *MS. III.*
**ral outline of the material and
leading points of the Shipping
Questions,** which for many years were
agitated in Leadenhall Street (said to
be by Mr. Bosanquet).'

Reg No. 2575.   Endorsed : (Private).

Although this MS. must approximately be dated 1796, and though it is connected with the policy of the E.I. Co. at that time, it contains references to earlier times (no dates are given) explaining (p. 9) 'the principles upon which the Shipping Concerns of the Company were conducted '. It is of particular value as having been written by one of the Directors, a fact mentioned by its author.

The extract below relates to a period following the renewal of the Charter by Cromwell. At that date (1657) most of the Company's ships were either lost or worn out.

p. 9, l.8.   'A certain number of ships, generally parted out in small shares among a variety of different Persons, were attach'd to the Company's Service. When a ship was worn out by having gone a certain number of Voyages, which was at first Four, but afterwards extended to Six, the Keel of a new Ship was permitted to be laid down upon the bottom of the Ship so worn out, or lost ; which was to be built under the Company's immediate inspection, and to be commanded
p. 10.   by the Captain of the old Ship so lost, or worn out, When the ship had been so rebuilt she came into the List of Fleet upon Service and was to be taken up in the Turn into which she came, by the Order established in the Rules of its Establishment. . . .'
p. 11.   This system practically restricted the Company in freighting ships to those expressly built for its service, and led to repeated conferences and heated discussions between the Court of Directors and the Body of Managing Owners (several of whom were often mem-

bers of the Court) 'to settle what Rate of Freight should be fixed as the price of the Season.' The evils of the system led to the ultimate destruction of the influence of the managing owners.

The remainder of the documents in this volume relate chiefly to the end of the 18th century (*circa* 1795-96), and include a 'Report on and Discussion of the Timber Trade of Malabar'. The 'Sketch of the present State of Oak Timber in England and the Sources ot Supply, etc.' contains notes on the Tonnage of Trading and Naval Vessels in the 17th century.

MISCELLANEOUS, NO. II.

Bound in red leather—contains several documents, some of which retain earlier covers.

Earlier cover, labelled: 'Voucher No. . . . shewing that the Paper cited as a Treaty in Bruce's Annals, Vol. I, p. , was but the Project of a Treaty.'

1615-16. Title within: 1615-16 **Letters from Sir Thomas Rowe and from other persons to Captain Pepwell.**

Addition in red ink: 'See revised title: . . . opposite Table of Contents, No. 4 B [which reads as follows: 'No. 4 B, 17th Century Copies of Letters from Sir Thomas Rowe . . . to Captain Pepwell, 1617 [? 1615-16], containing also other Letters with Drafts of Treaties. Another Project of a New Treaty also Unsigned Memorial of Agreement with the Zamorin and James I, King of England, Mar. 10, 1615.']

The Table of Contents contains a full abstract of each document with its date and place of origin ; 45 pages of Letters, etc., are followed by a later Index.

Sir Thomas Roe's Journal has been printed several times. The Articles of Agreement, 16 Nov., 1614, between him and the Company are reproduced in Sir George Birdwood's *First Letter Book*, pp. 446-49.

This volume also contains :

1620. **Commission to Captain Weddell and others.**

1621. **Ship, *Royal Exchauge*, Humphrey Fitzherbert, Company's Admiral, with Journal of the Fleet of Defence** from 2 July to 28 August, 1621, in a letter to the Company: Aboard the *Royal Exchange* in the Road of Batavia.

MISCELLANEOUS, NO. III.

[Modern] Abstracts of Ships' Journals preserved in the India Office (1610-23) numbered from 9 to 30. (Except 11 and 12, the numbers do not coincide with those in the official list ; e.g. No. 25 = *Marine Records*, XXX.)

Numbers 1-8, 11, 12, have been printed in the Hak. Soc. volume containing the *Narratives of the Voyages of Sir James Lancaster*. An 'Index—Indian Voyages Nos. 1-30' precedes the Abstracts.

Each Journal is abstracted, and followed by a short description of the Manuscript. There are also tables of storms encountered in the principal voyages.

The abstracts are not exhaustive, and the appreciations as to the value of the documents analysed need not be taken as final, e.g. No. 28 = *Marine Records*, XXXIV.

No. 12 = Ralph Crosse's Journal of the *Hoseander*, 1612-13 (*Marine Records*, XVI and XVIII).

No. 13 = Dodsworth's Journal of the *New Year's Gift*, 1614-15 (*Marine Records*, XIX).

No. 25 = Richard Swan's Journal in the *Roebuck* and the *Hart*, 1620-22 (*Marine Records*, XXX). Printed by Purchas, ' with some errors and omissions in his 1st vol. (p. 725).' See also *English Factories*, 1618-21, pp. 220 ff.

No. 26 = Richard Swanley's Journal in the *Exchange*, whilst attached to the Fleet of Defence, 1620-24 (*Marine Records*, XXXI).

No. 28 = Richard Swanley's Journal [in the *Jonas*], 1621-23 (*Marine Records*, XXXIV). Abstract in *English Factories*, 1618-21, pp. 271 ff.

MISCELLANEOUS, NO. XXVII (PART I).

1685-86.   The Committee of Shipping.

Red leather binding, lettered as above. Within, original vellum binding, lettered : Comittee for Shipping, 1685, 1686. [On a former label, 249.]

A note is inserted, ' This book should go with any other Volumes of the Committee of Shipping (1599 to 1834) as part of the Records of the old Shipping Office (abolished in 1834 in favour of the Marine Department) which were handed over to the Marine Department. There are not many of these Vols. but they are very valuable in many ways to any one writing an account of the E.I. Co. (Shipping, etc., etc.) prior to 1700.

' [Signed] CRUASON,

' 1882.'

A large proportion of the work of the East India Company was referred or delegated to Committees, at first 24 in number. The Shipping Committee was one of the most important of these. It came to an end with the Company's trade, in 1833. Its records were handed over to the Marine Department, and in 1860 the Minutes and Reports of the Committee, prior to 1813, were recommended for destruction.

But one volume of the Minutes for the 17th century, that for May, 1685— Dec., 1686, has been preserved, and now forms part of the *Marine Records, Miscellaneous* (Vol. 27, Part 1).

The more important portions of this document are extracted verbatim below, in particular the resolution obliging commanders of ships to obey orders of the E.I. Co.'s General Agent and Councils in all the Factories (p. 7), and the introduction of a new clause in the Charterparty for the purpose.

The range of subjects touched upon in the volume is very great, including the provision of all necessaries, from bread, beer, beef, brandy and brimstone, a ' Chirurgery chest for Priamon ' to bullet-moulds, badges for drummers, ' Blew Breeches and Blew stockings ' and red coats for the soldiers, cordage, guns and silk colours. We learn that the pensioners of the E.I. Co. apparently received 2s. 6d. a week from the Poplar Almshouse Fund, that passengers from London to St. Helena paid £6 each, and to India £8 ; and that surgeons were paid ' head money ' at 5s. and 3s. per passenger. The contemporary index prefixed is an efficient guide.

The pages are un-numbered.

i-xii.   A Contemporary Alphabetical Index of 12 pages.

f. 1.[1] Ornamental Title: 'Committee of Shipping and Plantations, 1685.
His Grace the Duke of Beaufort
Most Honble. Marquess of Worcester
Rt. Honble. Earle of Berkeley

Sr. Benjamin Bathurst	Sr. Thomas Daval Kn[t].
Sr. Henry Johnson Knt.	Richard Hutchinson, Esq.
Mr. Joseph Herne	Mr. Thomas Canham
Mr. John Paige	Mr. Wm. Sedgwick
Mr. George Boune	Mr. Tho. Rawlenson

'Or any three of them to direct the Makeing of Charter-partys And
to Provide Shipping and Necessarys for Plantations, And to
Examin the Accots. of the Paymaster of the Mariners, and to firm
Warrants for his Disbursmts. to Meet Every Court day in the
Afternoon, And at such other times as they shall apoint, And the
Care thereof is Comitted to Mr. Wm. Sedgwick.'

f. 2. 11 May, 1685. 'At a Comittee for Shipping, etc., Present
Mr. Wm. Sedgwick, Most Honble. Marquess of Worcester, Mr. George
Boune, Mr. Thomas Canham.

It is ordered that Capt. Wm. Basse and Mr. Edward Ely doe
forthwith goe to Gravesend and survey Ship *New*
Ship *New London*   *London*, and Report the same to the Comittee at
Survey and Extra-   his Returne on Wednesday next.
ordinary provisions.   And alsoe what Provissions Extraordinary will be
necessary for Passingers to Imbarque on said ship.

Capt. Eaton, then acquainted the Comittee that eight monthes
provissions more then already Provided will be sufficient for both
Passingers and Seamen.

Orders for Warrants.
[Here follow details.]

Ordered that a Report be made to the Court, that Mr. Fra. Tyssen
for the Ballance of Capt. Feilds Accot. have £129-14-6
Capt. Feilds accot.   (Total amt. of warrants).
Ballanced   Bills ordered to be paid By Capt. Basse: (for Iron
Crows, Compasses, Oyle, thin lead, Meale and Brim-
stone) £14-11-0.'

f. 3. 13 May, 1685. 'Present Mr. Wm. Sedgwick, Richard Hutchinson
Esq., Mr. Thomas Rawlenson. On reading the Petition of Richarp
Grove, mariner, who broke his leg in his servis on board ship
Lawrell, according to the Order of Court of the 11th of March last
past Capt. Wm. Basse was directed by this Committee to pay to said
Groves 2s. 6d. per week out of the Charity belonging to Popler
Almes houses.'

16 May, 1685. 'At a Committee for shipping, etc. Present, Mr.
Wm. Sedgwick, Sir James Edwardes, Sir Thomas Daval, Sr
James Ward, Richard Hutchinson Esq., Mr. Joseph
Complaint answered   Herne, Mr. John Paige, Mr. George Bowne, Mr. Tho.
by Capt. Swanly   Rawlenson. On a Complaint made that Shipp *Success*
was fully laden and could take in noe more Goods of
the Companys then what she had already received,
Capt. Wm. Swanley declareth that he will take in for the Compa.
420 Bales of Cloth, besides that already received.

It being required of him what Money he had taken up on Bottom-

---

[1] Original paging as given in index.

area, he informed them that he had taken up 1500 or thereabouts, of which he would give Mr. Herne, a more
sattisfactory Accot., he haveing not then his Pocket
Book about him, but at present he mentions, vizt.

Capt. Swanley money upon Bottomarea & Investment.

That he tooke up of a Jew whose name he *li.*

knew not ..	..	..	.. 500
of Sr John Norborrow		..	.. 200
Mr. Obadiah Sedgwick ..		..	.. 200
which he Invested into Liquors to the			
Vallu. of ..	..	..	.. £700
In Azedue ..	..	..	.. 150
Haberdashers Wares ..		..	.. 50
In Several other particulars,			
Ironmongers wares, &ca.		..	.. 150

Ann Plasted petitioner, gift.

To report to the Court that Ann Plasted Widdow
have 40s. out of the box.

f. 7.   31 July, 1685. 'Present, Mr. Will. Sedgwick, Most Hon. Marquess
of Worcester, Sir Henry Johnson Knt. Upon reading the Order of
Court of the 22nd July, It is ordered that a Report drawn by this
Committee be presented to the next Court, about obliging the Commanders of ships to obey such Orders as shall be given them by the
Company's General Agents and Councells in all the Company's
factories.'

5 August, 1685. 'Present, Mr. William Sedgwick, Mr. John Paige,
Mr. George Boune, Mr. Thomas Canham, Mr. Thomas Rawlenson.
Ordered that Jane Lambert whose husband was Castaway in Ship
Surrat Merchant, have 40s. given her out of the Poors Box.

'That the Petitioners John Delemo, Emanuel Robero, and John de
Cruz of Surat who came home in ship *East India Merchant* hath bin
considered of, and it is ordered that the 3 first ships bound for
Surrat be desired to ship each of them one, for wages and to be left
in India.

'That Capt. Hayward and the 4 Petitioners be brought home in
the *Henry and William* wait of [*sic*] the Comittee on Monday
Morning 9 a clock.'

9 Aug., 1685. 'Present, Mr. William Sedgwick [and 3 others] .
Upon Reading the Petition of John Combose, etc.,—John Combose
of Hambrough declareth that he served 9 monthes on board ship
Henry and William for which Capt. Hayward paid him but £6
and part of that paid in Clothes.

'Capt. Hayward saith he never made any Agreement with them for
Wages.

'This Committee taking into Consideration the sad condition of the
Petitioners, Cap. Hayward was required to make an Amicable end
with the four Petitioners and to discharge one of them out of White-
chapel prison that lyeth at his shute [suit].

'And to make them what further Consideration he can: the
Petitioners having declared they served 9 months or thereabouts.'

f. 8.   'According to an Order of Court of the 22 Instant whereby it is
referred to us to Consider how the Comanders of the Companys
shipping may be obliged to obey all such orders as shall be given
them by the Company's General President Agent and Councils in
India relating both to trade and Warfare, and to report our Opinion
thereupon Wee have perused the Charterparty now in use, and doe

humbly conceive that a Clause be inserted into the Charterpartys for the future, to the Purport following as Council shall advise, vizt.

'And it is further covenanted and agreed that the Comander of this ship in her Voyage Outward and Homeward bound shall observe and obey all such Orders and Instructions as shall be made and given him in Writing by the said Governor and Company or by their General and Council of Surat, or their President and Council at Foort St. George, or their Agent and Council in the Bay of Bengall, or the Major Part of any such Councils, the Generall President or Agent for the time, being one. And in case the said Comander or Master shall neglect or refuse to obey such Orders and Directions, and a Protest thereof being made by the Company, or by their General and Council at Surrat, or their President and Council at Foort St. George, or their Agent and Council in the Bay of Bengal, or the Major Part of such Counc[il]s respectively, the General President or Agent being one: The Governor and Company shall alow and Pay unto the said Part-Owners and Master only the sum of Tenn pounds per Ton for and upon all such Goods and Merchandizes as shall be Laden and brought home on the said ship for the use of the Company; and noe more, any Agreement in this Present Charterparty conteyned or any Law, Custom Usage or Pretence of Law or Equity, to the Contrary Notwithstanding.

'Wee have likewise perused the Surrat General of the 13th January last, received by the *East India Merchant*, and do find that they greatly complain of the Neglect of Comanders in not dispatching their lading soe early as they might, and alsoe of their backwardness, and refusal in complying with the Orders given them touching Interlopers &ca., And therupon have proposed that power may be given them to displace such Comanders upon Just Cause.

f. 9.   'On Consideration whereof we are of Opinion that the General and Council at Surrat may have Authority given them in the Cases aforesaid, as is desired, and that a Clause be drawn up by Council accordingly to be inserted in Charterparty.

'But whether the freight of ten pounds per ton proposed in the foregoing clause, or the other for displacing such Comanders may be most effectuall for redress of the Grievances complained of is humbly submitted to the Judgment of the Court.

'SIGNED WM. SEDGWICK,

'5th Aug., 1685.   'GEORGE BOUNE,

'THO. RAWLENSON,

'HENRY JOHNSON.'

19 Aug., 1685.   'Present, Mr Wm. Sedgwick [and 3 others].

'It is Ordered that the Petitioners Jane Davis, Dorcas Johnson, and Ann Peddy who desires [*sic*] to have passage to their husbands the Company's servants at Fort St. George, Attend this Comittee on Wednesday next.[1]

'It is Ordered that Sr. Peter Rich have Notice to Attend the Comittee on Wednesday Next, and in Case of his Absence that his servant attend in his roome.

---

[1] On the 28th it was ordered that they 'have liberty to goe to their husbands paying their Passages and that Thomas Lewis acquaint them that Children dye fast in those Long voyages.'

'It is Ordered that the Persons who petition for a Month's pay detayned from them by the Owners of shipp *Lawrell*, have notice that nothing wil be done therein, until the said ships Account be made up.

'It is ordered that Mr Beyer cause the Three Accounts of Capt. James Marine[r's] servants to be made up.

'It is ordered that the Warehouse In Crosby Square proposed by Mr. Clement Kettle for the Company's servis, be layd with loose deales, which are to be returned to the Landlord when the Company shall part with the said Warehouse, for which the said Landlord is to have 50 *li.* per Anno, he being to have a quarters warning when acquitted.

'It is ordered that Leftenant [*sic*] Gamble attend this Comittee every Wednesday.

f. 10. 'It is Ordered that Thomas Lewis Entertayn what Souldiers he can against October next, and that they cheifly be Artificers and Masons, Bricklayers Carpenters &ca.—all single men.

'That Inquirey be made what Gunns to be sent to Foort St. George: the Letter from thence of the 19th January, 1683/4 not expressing the demensions nor Qualetyes.

'It is Ordered that Capt. Poole attend the Comittee on Friday next by nine of the Clock. And that he prepare to Depart from Gravesend the 10th October next on a voyage for Tonqueen, and that he sattisfie the Committee what he wil let the ship for.

'It is ordered that Capt. Wetwang be ready to depart from Gravesend by the 10th October next, and that he make provission for 100 soldiers.

'It is ordered that several Charterparties be perused of the Bantam Shipping before the Reducement of freights.'

f. 54. 30th June, 1686. Sir Josiah Child Bt., Governor, and 11 others being present, it was unanimously agreed that every ship entertained in the Company's service should be half freighted by the Company outwards, i.e. 'the intire halfe of the ship shal be for the Companys goods,' the Master or Part owner to pay £6 per ton, if any of the Company's goods be left out; Commanders, etc. to pay port charges in India; £6 per ton to be paid on every ton of goods laden (by any persons whatsoever) on board the Company's shipping by their licence.

f. 55. 'And that such part of the Tonage laden by the Company not exceeding ¼ shal be in Lead, Iron, and (or) Guns, three Tons thereof to be reconed and accounted for one Ton of Goods.'

f. 56. 7 July, 1686. 'It is ordered that Tho. Lewes take care to provide forthwith for the Company, One Engine to make salt water fresh, with all other Materials thereunto belonging, to be laden on board ship *Bawden.*' [This engine cost £50 paid to Wm. Talbot.]

f. 65. 30 July, 1686. Chests of medicines were sent out for Bombay, etc., and it was ordered 'That the Auditor prepare an Alphabet for Medicines, and that he make a Column for the Pounds or Ounces of the severall sorts of Medicines and the lowest rate, which he is to Collect out of the Cheapest Bills.'

f. 66. 3 Sept., 1686. List of 'Stores wanting at the Island Bombay to be provided by order of Sir Josia Child, Barronet, Governour, and laden on board ship *Cæsar* and *Bengal Merchant*' including uniform, clothes and arms for the soldiers.

FACTORY RECORDS

THE important seventeenth century documents forming the chief part of this series were 'roughly calendared' by Dr. (afterwards Sir) George Birdwood whose *Report on the Miscellaneous Old Records of the India Office* (first printed for official use in 1879) should be read by all. The work of classification was continued by Mr. F. C. Danvers, and the Press List of the section was printed in 1897.

The two chief series relating to the period under consideration, are the seventy-one volumes of the *Original Correspondence*, 1602-1712, containing letters received by the Company from all its settlements, and the *Letter Books* containing the despatches of the Company to their settlements and agents. There are, besides, the various sections of records of individual Agencies and Factories.

The *Original Correspondence* is in course of publication either in full or in abstract form. From 1602 to 1617 the letters are printed verbatim in *Letters Received by the East India Company from its Servants in the East*, six volumes, 1896-1902, the first volume having been published in 1896 on the initiative of Mr. Danvers. From 1618 to 1654 abstracts of the letters from India (and some other places), contained in the *O.C.* Series, the correspondence in the *Letter Books* and the sectional *Factory Records*, are arranged in strictly chronological order in *The English Factories in India*, a series edited by Sir. William Foster. Documents in the Public Record Office, the British Museum and in Indian Record Offices are included, the 'unifying element' being supplied by an introduction. Publication was interrupted during the late war, and on resumption, it was found necessary to modify the above method in the volume for the period 1655-60, published in 1921. A point had been reached where the existing materials increased so greatly in number (the documents analysed reaching 500 for the year 1659, and 300 for 1660, instead of the early average of 75 to a year), that it became imperative to change the procedure and 'to extract merely those passages which seemed to merit preservation, and to connect them by a narrative which would at the same time embody the information obtained from other documents . . . (which it was) not necessary to quote in full.' The arrangement, partly chronological, and partly geographical, makes it easier to follow the course of events. Extracts from the same document often appear on different pages.

Besides the sources already mentioned in connection with the preceding volumes, use was made in the new volume of copies of letters received at Madras, 1658-60, now among the *Rawlinson MSS.* in the Bodleian Library, and of transcripts furnished by the Bombay Government. (See Preface to *English Factories in India*, 1655-60.) The last volume published covers the year 1660.

A detailed list of the *O.C.* Series from 1602 to 1709 forms volumes 711 and 712 of the *Home Miscellaneous* series.

Abstracts and extracts from the *Letter Books*, 1658-79, are contained in volumes 33-35 of the same (*Home Miscellaneous*) series, whilst a full calendar of all documents available from many sources for the years 1655-59 is now to be found among *Factory Records, Miscellaneous*, volumes 28-31. Volumes 19 and 20 of the last named section, containing material for the story of the Embassy of Sir William Norris, 1699 to 1702, have been freely used by Mr. Harihar Das for his volume on the subject, now in preparation.

GENERAL RECORDS

THE records within the period 1600-1700 contained in the *List of General Records* (1902) are the following:

	Period	Page in List	Observations
Charters	1536-1800	p. 76	Vols. 1-4, containing the Charters within the period, have all been printed.
Court Minutes	1599-	pp. 1-3	Nos. 1 (22 Sept., 1599) to 38 (27 April, 1702).
Court Minutes—Rough Notes	1621-1715	p. 6	Nos. 1 (Oct., 1621) to 3 (20 Nov., 1705). The Court Minutes are in course of publication, 1663 being the last issued.
Dutch Records	1596-1824	pp. 82-84	See below.
French in India	1664-1820	p. 85	Miscellaneous Correspondence, 1 vol. only within the period, i.e., 1 (1664-1810).
Home Correspondence Letters sent by the Court ('Miscellanies')	1699	p. 10	All the rest are outside the period.
Home Miscellaneous	1631-	pp. 92, 119	A Catalogue by Mr. S. C. Hill is in course of compilation.
Parchment Records	1498-1862	pp. 78-82	Nos. 2 to 58 cover the 17th century.
Portuguese Records	1500-1806	pp. 85-87	See below.
Treaties	1602-1834	pp. 77-78	Vols. 1 (1602) to 5 (1690-1751).

COURT MINUTES

(Vol. 1, 22 Sept., 1599 to Vol. 38, 27 April, 1702.)

THE contents of these volumes to the year 1663 have already been published in summarised form, the two first also *in extenso*.

Vol. 1, 22 Sept., 1599—10 Aug., 1603, published by Mr. H. Stevens as *The Dawn of British Trade in the East Indies*, in 1886.

Vol. 1A, 1600-19, *Miscellaneous Court Book*, edited under the title of *The First Letter Book of the East India Company*, by Sir George Birdwood and Mr. (now Sir) William Foster (1893).

Vols. 1 (1599-1603), 1A, 2 (31 Dec., 1606—26 Jan., 1610), and 3 (Dec., 1613—Nov., 1615) to 14 (1634) were abstracted in the Public Record Office, *Calendars of State Papers, East Indies*, by Mr. W. Noel Sainsbury.

Vols. 15 (1635) to 21 (and parts of 23 and 24) to the year 1663 are contained in the series *The Court Minutes of the East India Company*, by Miss E. B. Sainsbury (in progress).

Vol. 2A (1 March, 1611—4 May, 1620) and part of Vol. 3, added more recently to this collection, were not included in the Calendars of State Papers.

The reference numbers of the volumes not yet calendared and falling within the seventeenth century are here subjoined:

Vol. 23. United Joint Stock, 3 July 1650—7 April, 1669.

Vol. 24. New General Stock, 19 Oct., 1657—14 April, 1665.

Vol. 24A. Index to Vol. 24.

Vol. 25A. Committee Minutes, Accounts, etc., 1666-80.

Vols. 25-38. Old Company, 14 April, 1665—27 April, 1702.

Vol. 37A. New Company, 7 Sept., 1698—20 June, 1699.

PARCHMENT RECORDS

[Including Paper (Manuscript) Copies.]

THE seventeenth century documents beyond the dates of already existing calendars are as follows:

19A. 1654, 30 Aug. Certified copy of the Award of the English and Dutch Commissioners appointed under the Treaty of Westminster.

24. 1665, 14 Nov. Mandate of James, Duke of York, Lord High Admiral, to the Commissioners for Reprisals to sell the contents of the prize *Golden Phœnix*.

25. 1668, 6 Feb. Acquittance under the Great Seal to the East India Company, remitting to them the sum realised by the sale of the contents of two Dutch prizes, the *Slothany* and the *Golden Phœnix*.

26. 1668, 27 March. Letters Patent granting the Island of Bombay to the E.I. Co.

27. 1672, 7 Oct. Letters Patent for the payments, by instalments, of £92,000 due to the E.I. Co.

28. 1672, 7 Oct. Acquittance under the Great Seal to the E.I. Co., remitting certain monies due from them.

29. 1673, 27 Oct. Letters Patent ratifying an Agreement between Prince Rupert and others and the E.I. Co., for the sale of goods taken from certain Dutch prizes.

30. 1673, 16 Dec. Letters Patent granting the Island of St. Helena to the E.I. Co.

31. 1674, 6 March. Release from Prince Rupert and others of any further sums due on account of the sale of the above goods.

32. 1674, 13 March. Acquittance under the Great Seal to the E.I. Co., releasing them from all further claims on the same subject.

33. 1676, 21 Oct. Warrant under the Great Seal to the Commissioners, etc. of the Treasury and Exchequer for the repayment of £40,000 to the E.I. Co.

34. 1676, 5 Oct. Letters Patent confirming former privileges and giving power to coin money at Bombay.

35. 1678, 24 Jan. Warrant to the Commissioners, etc., of the Treasury and Exchequer for the payment of £60,000 to the E.I. Co.

36. 1678, 22 Nov. Warrant to the Commissioners, etc., for payment of £50,000 to the E.I. Co.

36A. 1680, 11 June. Counterpart of deed by which the E.I. Co. agreed to save harmless Sir John Banks and Sir Josiah Child in respect of a lease of the East India House.

37. 1682, 18 Sept. Warrant to Commissioners, etc., for payment of £15,372 to the E.I. Co.

38. 1683, 5 July. Warrant to Commissioners, etc., for payment of £40,463 10s. to the E.I. Co.

39. 1684, 12 Nov. To the E.I. Co. The King to John Petit, George Bowcher, Simon Cracroft and Edward Littleton, requiring their return to England to answer charges against them.

40. 1686, 12 April. Letters Patent confirming former Charters and authorising the Company to establish Courts of Justice, to raise military and naval forces, and coin money in India (copy only).

41. 1687, 30 Dec. Charter establishing a municipality and Mayor's Court at Madras (copy only).

42. 1688, 31 Jan. Acquittance under the Privy Seal to the E.I. Co., and to the owners of the ship *Andaluzia*.

43. 1689, 5 Sept. Hall and Wife v. Leigh and E.I. Co. Decree in Chancery.

44. 1689. Warrant under the Great Seal to the Commissioners of the Treasury and Exchequer, for payment to the E.I. Co., for saltpetre.

45. 1691, 19 Dec. Atwood, Halford and others v. Warr and the E.I. Co. Decree in Chancery.

46. 1693, 7 Oct. Letters Patent confirming the E.I. Co., in their powers and privileges.

47. Copy of No. 46.

48. 1693, 11 Nov. Letters Patent prescribing Regulations for E.I. Co. business.

49. 1694, 28 Sept. Copy of Letters Patent establishing further regulations.

50. 1695, 17 Jan. Byelaws, approved by a General Court.

51. 1697-98. Act 44, 9 and 10 Will. III for raising £2,000,000, etc.

52. 1698, 14 July. Letters Patent appointing Commissioners to receive subscriptions for the 'General Society' with Draft Charters.

53 and 54. 1698, 14-16 July. Roll of Subscribers to the £2,000,000, and two books of original subscriptions.

55. 1698, 3 Sept. Charter of Incorporation of the 'General Society'.

56 and 57. 1698, 5 Sept. Charter of Incorporation of the English Co. trading to the East Indies.

58. 1698, 13 Oct. Grant of Arms to the English Company trading to the East Indies.

THE FRENCH IN INDIA

THIS section of the General Records (p. 85) contains but one volume within the seventeenth century, i.e., Volume 1 (1664-1810), comprising Miscellaneous Correspondence, etc. References to the French, however, are numerous in the Dutch Records, as well as in those of the English East India Company. In the *Revue de l'histoire des Colonies françaises*, Mr. S. C. Hill gives 'a list of documents in the India Office records having a special interest for French students'.

PORTUGUESE RECORDS

THE Portuguese Records at the India Office consist of a large collection of transcripts obtained from the Lisbon Archives. Translations are available for all the volumes containing seventeenth century documents, a combined list of transcripts and the relative volumes of translations being given below.

These documents were utilised by Mr. F. C. Danvers in his work *The Portuguese in India, being a History of the Rise and Decline of their Eastern Empire*, two volumes, 1894, which contains a bibliography of authorities, including materials for the History of Portuguese India (*Subsidios* . . .) published by the Lisbon Academy of Sciences, as well as the *Livros das Monções* (1605-18).

Copies of letters from Portuguese Governors, etc., principally from Goa and Malacca, some in Portuguese, others in Dutch, with English translations or abstracts, are to be found amongst the *Hague Transcripts* [Dutch Records, B.I. 57, 3]. The unhappy condition of the Portuguese settlements is described in an intercepted letter of 1638-39 [Dutch Records, B.I. 57, 5]. Other Portuguese letters will be found in the Dutch Records for the years 1642 and 1644.

For the connection of Portugal with Bombay see *The Anglo-Portuguese Negotiations relating to Bombay, 1660-1677*, by Dr. Shafaat Ahmad Khan, first printed in the *Journal of Indian History*, Series No. 3, Sept., 1922, and reprinted in the Allahabad University Studies in History. The translations and transcripts from the Portuguese Archives to be found at the India Office, consulted for the purpose of the above mentioned work, yielded little of importance in this respect. Abundant material is, however, provided in the Letter Books and Correspondence of the East India Company and its agents.

Transcripts from the Lisbon Archives

Documentos Remettidos da India (*Livros das Monções*)

Transcripts	Translations	
No. 1. 1616-28	No. 1. Pt. 1. 1605-7	No. 8. 1632-35
2. 1628-35	1. Pt. 2. 1607-10	9. 1634-36
3. 1635-38	2. Pt. 1. 1611-12	10. 1636-39
4. 1637-43	2. Pt. 2. 1613-1614	11. 1636-38
5. 1643-51	3. Pt. 1. 1568 and 1602-14	12. 1637-38
	3. Pt. 2. 1615, 1616	13. 1639-40
	4. Pt. 1. 1616, 1617	14. 1641-43
	4. Pt. 2. 1617-19	15. 1643-46
	5. 1616-23	16. 1646-48
	6. 1623-30	17. 1649-51
	7. 1630-32	[Nothing of later date.]

Corpo Chronologico

Transcripts	Translations
No. 1. 1500-33	No. 1. 1500-28
[? 2.] 1535-1630	2. 1529-49
	3. 1548-163ᶜ

Gavetas Antigas

Transcripts	Translations
No. 1. 1514-1711	No. 1. 1514-29
	2. 1531-1711

Documents from Evora and Pombal Collections [Colleccaõ Pombalina]: and Viceroy's Letters [Cartas dos Vice Reis da India]

Transcripts	*Translations*	
No. 1. 1517-1806	Pombal Coll: and Viceroy's Letters.	No. 1. 1507-1806
	Documents from Evora Library. No. 1. 1572-1739	

[Antigo] Conselho Ultramarino

Transcripts	*Translations*
No. 1. 1614-1768	No. 1. Pt. 1, 1614

Noticias da India

Transcripts	*Translations*
No. 1. 1475-1744	Noticias da India (Five Volumes)

DUTCH RECORDS

East India Company's Records.　　*Dutch Records, A.*

Date

Vol. 1.	1596-1795.	Connections of the Dutch in the Eastern Seas.
„ 2-4.	1596-1795.	Treaties, etc., I, II, III.
„ 5.	1662-1864.	Treaties, etc., IV.
„ 6.	1617-74.	Miscellaneous Letters and Documents, I. (The other volumes in this series are outside the seventeenth century.)

Transcripts from The Hague.　　*Dutch Records, B.*

I. LETTERS FROM INDIA

Vol. 1.	1600-8	Vol. 20.	1655, 1656	Vol. 39.	1685, 1686
„ 2.	1607-16	„ 21.	1656, 1657	„ 40.	1686
„ 3.	1615-20	„ 22.	1657, 1658	„ 41.	1687-89
„ 4.	1621-23	„ 23.	1659, 1660	„ 42.	1688, 1689
„ 5.	1622-24	„ 24.	1660, 1661	„ 43.	1689
„ 6.	1621-25	„ 25.	1661, 1662	„ 44.	1689, 1690
„ 7.	1625, 1626	„ 26.	1662, 1663	„ 45.	1688, 1689
„ 8.	1626-29	„ 27.	1662-65	„ 46.	1689-91
„ 9.	1629-34	„ 28.	1665-67	„ 47.	1691-93
„ 10.	1634-37	„ 29.	1667-70	„ 48.	1691, 1692
„ 11.	1638, 1639	„ 30.	1670-72	„ 49.	1690-93
„ 12.	1639-42	„ 31.	1672, 1673	„ 50.	1693, 1694
„ 13.	1643-44	„ 32.	1673, 1674	„ 51.	1694, 1695
„ 14.	1644-45	„ 33.	1674, 1675	„ 52.	1696, 1697
„ 15.	1645-47	„ 34.	1674-79	„ 53.	1696, 1697
„ 16.	1646-51	„ 35.	1679-81	„ 54.	1697-99
„ 17.	1650, 1651	„ 36.	1681-83	„ 55.	1698, 1699
„ 18.	1652-54	„ 37.	1683, 1684	„ 56.	1698, 1699
„ 19.	1654, 1655	„ 38.	1684-86	„ 57.	1623-40, with list of the documents in this series up to 1694.

There is a translation of Vols. 1-29.

II. Letters from the 'Seventeens' to India
Vols. 1-4. (1614-1670).

There is a translation of each volume.

III. Letters from the Governor-General to Various Factories

Vol. 1.	1617-22	Vol. 6.	1663-66
,, 2.	1622-32	,, 7.	1668-80
,, 3.	1633-43	,, 8.	1681-86
,, 4.	1644-55	,, 9.	1686-99
,, 5.	1656-62		

There is a translation of Vols. 1-3.

Letters from India. *Dutch Records, B. I.*

As already noted, Vol. 57 of this series contains a list of documents in the First Series of *Hague Transcripts.* The rough and incomplete list (Vol. 57, No. 1) of the contents of 246 of the 564 Volumes and Portfolios, examined at the Hague for Mr. Danvers, comprises for the period 1595-1694 about 50 Volumes of Transcripts, containing several hundred documents, the list itself consisting of 119 MS pages as follows :

Vol. I, No. 1 (1595) to No. 797 (March, 1672), 41 pp.

No. 998 (1672) to No. 1283 (1694), 78 pp.

The first portion of the List of Contents is mainly a rough working list. From No. 998 onwards it is more systematically drawn up and contains additional details.

The first document mentioned relates to the first voyage of Cornelius Honkeman, between the years 1595-97. The Journals of several Dutch voyages from 1598-1600 are also to be found here.

B.I. Vol. 57 contains in addition :

2. Copy (in French) of Accord concluded between the English and Dutch Commissioners, 25 Jan., 1622-23.
3. Copies of letters from Portuguese Governors, etc., principally from Goa and Malacca, 1639 and 1640. Some in Portuguese, some in Dutch.
4. Translations of the letters in 3.
5. Undated Dutch letter describing the unhappy state of the Portuguese settlements, derived from Portuguese letters intercepted by the Dutch in 1638 and 1639.

Amongst a few of the subjects of interest contained in the later volumes of transcripts may be mentioned the following :

1674. Permission to coin gold at Negapatam.
French ships captured by the Dutch round Ceylon.
Proclamation of Peace by the States General.
1675. Agreement between the French and Dutch respecting San Thome.
1678. English and Dutch Correspondence.
1683. Report on the English by a Dutch spy. English and Dutch correspondence.
1685. List of native weights and measures.
Letter to the Dutch E.I. Co.
Protest by the Dutch E.I. Co.
Affair with the English at Indrapura.

1686. (Feb.): Letter from Hugli. (March—May, Sept.): Journal of Commander Pit.

1687. War of the English with the Mogul.

Notice of the blockade of Surat.

Since a translation of Volumes 1-29 of the Letters from India (*B. I*) covering the years 1600-70 of the Transcripts from the Hague, and one of the Letters from the Seventeen to India (*B. II*) to the same date exist at the India Office, and since the *English Factories in India* series has already reached the year 1660, and the *Calendar of Court Minutes*, 1659-63, has already been published, the volume of Transcripts containing documents of the years 1670-72 (*Dutch Records B. I, Vol. XXX*) has been selected for analysis and translation hereunder. The most important features of this volume are the expedition of the French Viceroy, De La Haye, the declaration of war by both England and France against the Dutch, and the commencement of hostilities in Ceylon and India.

The close connection of events requires the inclusion of many papers not originating in the Indian mainland. During these years, also, some of those papers relating to occurrences in Ceylon are so intimately associated with the French attempt to share in the East India trade on a large scale, that they cannot well be omitted.

LETTERS FROM INDIA, 1670-72.   *Dutch   Records   B. First   Series,   Vol. XXX.*

No. 781.   [? 167-] Native Regulations in Tonquin on the arrival of ships, and for trade with the Dutch. (Dutch, 3 pp.)   Undated.

No. 768.   4 July, 1670 (received).   Letter of Ossin bassa, son of Aly bassa in Basoura [? Basra] to the Governor-General Joan Maetsuyker in Batavia, received by the ship *Goylant*. (Dutch translation, 5 pp.)

No. 770.   7 Oct., 1670.   Treaty between the Baros chiefs and the Dutch E.I. Co.   Eight special Articles. (Dutch, 14 pp.)

No. 771.   28 Oct., 1670.   Hendrik Eggers, at Dansborg, near Tranquebar, to the Dutch Governor-General at Batavia, requesting exemption for the Danes from tolls or hindrance on passing the Straits of Malacca. (Dutch, 2 pp.)

No. 769.   12 Nov., 1670 (received).   Paducca Siry, sultan in Bouton, to the Dutch Governor-General Joan Maetsuyker, demanding the expulsion of 'Ternatenses'. (Translated from Malay into Dutch, 3½ pp.)

No. 783.   18 Dec., 1670.   Andries Bogaert and Council, Swally Beach, to Joan Maetsuyker, Governor-General and the Council of India at Batavia. [Extract.]

. . . Matters with the Government of these lands at a standstill as their Resident in Agra can give them no certain news, the King alone reading and dealing with the letters he received from the Prince at Orangabath [Aurangabad], and no others from that place being sent to Agra.   For a good while the Prince had a great force with him, amongst them a great number of Rajputs under the great Raja ' Jessingsen ' [Jai Singh], with which he had been at the attack of Brampour [Burhanpur], but had returned to Orangabath.   The accounts concerning his return say that ' Jessings ' was also very ill and that the others Ajmers [?] were said to have refused to follow

p. 2.   the Prince against his father, since which news arrived that ' Jessingsen ' had left for his own district with his people.   The King (it was first reported in Agra) who in September was to have marched against his son to Burhanpur and Aurungabad, afterwards to ' Dilly ' [Delhi], it was rumoured would then go even to Golconda ; as it was said that the King there had died without leaving heirs.

Some preparations said to have been made in Agra to commandeer camels and transport, but nothing further done, 'it being probable that the King and the Prince Sultan Masem [Mu'azam] have very little confidence in each other, and that each one seeks to save his own nest, and not to be surprized by the other or by Sivaji (who has caused an incredible fear in these nations) . . .

p. 3, l. 10.   The affairs of the French here in a bad way, the inland rulers and merchants having a great aversion for them. They have borrowed about 550,000 rupees here at ¾ per cent. interest, but without giving them credit or security or allowing them to leave as security what they wish to sell and promising more brokerage and interest besides—all this having been done for a long time—and with all the trouble and charges they have, after a long period, sometimes got together a few goods to send to France when they can pay for them. In Agra they have given orders to buy up '20,000 $r\frac{a}{a}$.' of musk under the above conditions. Their piece goods which they have purchased there and are said to consist of about '20 $r\frac{a}{a}$ Derria Caddys sola and atthara' have been hastily got ready.

With their ship, *St. Francisco* (which we hear had arrived on the [?] at Wingurla) they will no doubt obtain a good return. She has been a long time on her way hither, apparently waiting for her boat, sent

p. 4.   with 16 men to Goa, which was held up for some reason or pretext unknown. But their ship, *St. Paul*, which left France at the same time and touched at Madagascar, arrived here safely on the 18th of October last, and a few days before a hoy from the same place. So far it has only been possible to ascertain that 300,000 lbs. of iron were brought in the two bottoms, and it has been said three casks of silver.

p. 5.   With the foresaid *St. Paul* arrived Captain 'Mons. de Priaeumera' sent expressly by the King to bring letters to Mr. Caron, which were said to be full of His French Majesty's pleasure at all that was done in these lands under Mr. Caron's directions, and the said King's strong zeal to maintain the work of the Company and to continue it; and with that object he had caused a meeting of the Directors of this Company to be held and had presided over it. The authority and power of the said Mr. Caron over all the French nation here in India is strengthened, not only by the said letters, but by two 'Casjacken' from the King, thereby to be empowered to order the mighty proclamations and other executive acts necessary, if they in themselves do not enforce due respect, one lies in peril of death ('licht man des doots werden'). They now call their Company the Royal French Company, and by Order of their 'Conjugt' [? Conin Klijk, i.e., by virtue of their Royal title] they should everywhere have precedence before ourselves and the English, but that they cannot yet persuade these 'potentates'. . . .

pp. 6, 7.   The French in Madagascar and Bantam.

pp. 8, 9.   Persia.

p. 9, l. 6.   The English had received on the 2nd, 3rd and 10th October ships from England to Bombay (the *Berkeley Castle*, *Hannibal*, *Experiment* and *Loyal Subject*) with a large quantity of goods (detailed) and 200,000 $r\frac{o}{o}$ gold bullion, besides a large number of iron guns, anchors, hangers and other ship equipment. . . .

Signed: Andries Bogaert, Joost Clandt, Adriaen Pyck, G. Van de Voorde.   (Dutch, 8¾ pp.)

No. 772. 2 Sept., 1671. Extract of General Letter of Dutch Governor-General at Batavia to the 'Seventeens' . . .

p. 1, l. 12. Macassar.

Coromandel. Ship with elephants belonging to the King of Keda, carried off to Coromandel.

p. 2, l. 16. Surat news, dated 18 December, 1670, received 14 February, that 'the robber Siuragi' [Sivaji] had attacked the town in October, with a strong force of horsemen and footsoldiers, and had pillaged it for 3 days. . . .

p. 3, l. 20. Arrival at Batavia of two ships, the *Pouleron* and the *Cogge*, from Surat, on the 1st July and 5th August respectively, with a Return of f.733,237 : 13 : 13. A third ship, the *Amerong*, was still expected from thence by way of Ceylon with a cargo for Batavia worth f. 57,679 : 12 : 2, making a total of f. 790,917 : 5 : 15 for the three; besides which Surat has provided cash capital to the value of 523,310 guldens for Cochin and Ceylon, also doing some business upon interest ('negotiatie van eenige interest penningen') . . .

Signed. Joan Maetsuycker and five others. (Dutch, 3¾ pp.)

No. 782. 16 Oct., 1671. George Foxcroft, Agent and President of the E.I. Co. for Coromandel and Bengal and his Council. Formal Certificate of Receipt and Quitclaim respecting the seizure of a country boat and its cargo in Keda Road, and its conveyance to Batavia (on the ground that the King of Keda was at war with the Dutch E.I. Co.), the said ' praauw ' and specified articles having been returned with an indemnity. (Dutch translation, 4 pp.)

No. 778. pp. 1-4. 24 Oct., 1671. Andries Bogaert and Council at Surat to the 'Bewinthebbers.' [Extract.]

Troubles with the authorities at Surat. Attack on Dutch sailors by the followers of Miersie Conany on their refusal to allow four Moors on the Dutch skutes on the departure of Georguis Hartsinde. Subsequent attack in force of Miersie Conany's armed followers upon the sailors, and the Dutch Company's bamboo dwellings and warehouse, breaking open and pillaging the latter. Dutch complaint to the Governor and the 'Wackenewis' (whose daily duty it was to send news to the King) demanding damages.

p. 4. Visit of the Governor and Miersie Conany to the Dutch house to make peace; the Dutch however carried out their previously announced decision of writing to the King and other great men direct. As no answer was received, and also owing to the slackness

p. 5. of the Governor, the Moors became very insolent, and not only attacked the Dutch, but also fell upon the English and French with troops of 30 to 40 armed men, wounding and beating them. The Governor not only refused to hear any complaints, but caused it to be proclaimed with beating of drums, that no man of the French, English or Dutch nation was to carry arms, on pain of confiscation : on refusal, penalty of death—the slayer not to be punishable. 2° That no Moor was to serve any of the above nations, under heavy penalties and threat of pillage. As serious remedies were necessary,

p. 6. a consultation was held with the French and English, all removing with their principal people to Swally beach. In spite of all that had passed, the Moors perceiving this, exerted themselves to the utmost, with many promises, to induce their return. The Dutch only consented to do so after 42 days, after the Shabandar, the Customer and the chief merchants had been sent to them to treat respecting their

complaints, and with a written undertaking, sealed by the Governor and by themselves as envoys, promising publicly to proclaim a revocation of the previous order, and in addition had consented to
p. 7. several special articles favouring the Dutch in their relations with them. A few days later an answer was received to the previous complaint to the King, dismissing Miersie Bonany [*sic*] from his service, and seizing his revenues ; also charging the Governor, not only to investigate the damage done to the Dutch E.I. Co. in particular, but in future to give them greater satisfaction. The Dutch thereupon put in their claims not only for the damage done, but for the costs incurred in housing the goods for the recent Agra kafila in Ahmadabad, caused by the seizure of 660 camels by 'Badurchan and Delichan', previously referred to ; they also put forth pretensions for the 'extraordinary great expenses and damages (although the last are little or none) which [they] had been obliged to incur or suffer at the time in the previous year when Sewagie [Sivaji] had burnt and pillaged the town.' All which has been transmitted to the higher authorities with the Governor's recommendations. Whilst awaiting a reply, the Governor has sought to give them all satisfaction, and the Moors have refrained not only from attacking but even from insulting the Dutch. . . .   (Dutch, 8 pp.)

No. 776.   9 Nov., 1671 (received).   Ola of King of Porca to the Dutch Commander referring to the arrival of an English ship before Porca,
p. 2. whose brokers alleged that they had been sent by order of the English King to see the King of Porca and hand him a letter requesting permission to reside in the 'logis', to raise their flag, and to trade.   Refusal of the local authorities on account of their friendship and engagements with the Dutch.   Return of the English captains to their ship, and departure, after a fruitless attempt to see
p. 3. the King at 'Ambellapolle', asserting their desire to settle in this port on friendly terms with the Dutch, 'and if not we will settle there even though we English, French and Portuguese should come to differences with the Dutch.'   Request of the King for advice as to the action to be taken.   (Dutch translation, 3 pp.)

No. 775.   10 Nov., 1671.   Hendrik van Reede, Cochin, to the Bewinthebbers of the 'Seventeens' in Amsterdam.
pp. 2-47.   War with the Zamorin ; detailed account of the Siege of 'Cranganoor' [Cranganore], etc., and relations with Cochin.
pp. 47-55, and 84-86.   French relations with the natives at 'Mirzee', 'Cananoor', 'Craganoor', 'Pananie and Calicut'.
p. 55.   The Danes in Cannanore and Ceylon.
pp. 57, 61.   Favourable influence of the taking of Cranganore upon the pepper trade, and its importance for the trade of the whole of Malabar.
pp. 68, 69.   Tobacco monopoly in Cochin.   The rate for the present year 40,000 fanams higher.
pp. 80-84.   Cochinese fanams : complaints of base coinage issued by the Dutch East India Company : refutation of the allegations, etc.
p. 87.   The English [in Cannanore], greatly troubled by the disturbed state of the country, had also strengthened their dwellings with Nairs for their defence, and had placed six large guns ('prince stucken') and two small ship guns ('bassen') there, but few native ships having been there, and without their doing any trade of any importance. . . .   What the two nations yet take must be watched ; but by the experience of the Dutch themselves it is to be expected that they

will have little advantage there 'as the Moors, who there form the majority of the inhabitants, are not only merchants themselves, but also have strong equipments at sea, and can trade in pepper with greater profit than a few Europeans in India; so that we, trading in one and the same places, are not able to stand against them, since the [respective] charges on both sides are unequal, and the Moors being in their own land, are also content with much lower gains and

p. 88. [? can save]. This is not possible to Europeans, as everything is carefully reckoned, and even though the advantages of in and out trade were all equal, the Moors still trade more profitably, as they always act in person, without interpreters or brokers, through familiarity with the languages and knowledge of the countries, thereby having, except in their religion, a great advantage over the others.'

It rather appears that both the English and French do not take these matters into consideration; wherefore they still strengthen [? fortify] themselves towards a long stay, and still increase their charges, even to holding so many Nairs in their service. This, undoubtedly, will also embitter the country people all the more against them, as it is true that they are pressed into service against their will by the prince. . . .

pp. 89-91. Proposals for the Dutch defence and garrisoning of Cannanore. (Dutch, 91 pp.)

No. 773. 16 Nov., 1671. Extract of General Letter from Batavia to the 'Seventeen'.

p. 1. Wingurla. News received by the ships *Rotterdam* and *Voersichtighoijt* from the resident Rombout Lefer that, on the last of May, three ships had arrived in Goa from Portugal, and another on the 10th of April 'of preceding year' by which had come out a new Vice Roy named Luis Mendonsa Furtado [i.e., Luiz de Mendonça Furtado de Albuquerque, Conde de Lavradio], with many splendid titles, amongst them that of 'Restorer of Ceylon', which seems strange, since no war is known of between our country and them; but tidings are brought that a treaty of alliance has been concluded between Portugal and the French Crown, jointly to fall upon the

p. 2. United Netherlands, and to make a beginning here with the Mallabar Coast and the Island of Ceylon, for which the forementioned title seems to be intended. . . . A great number of ships are to come from France, amongst them twelve or more freighted in Hamburg. It appears from all this that the Viceroy is doing everything possible soon to get a large number of ships and the smaller men of war to sea and to prepare for war; but was ill provided with money and men, though nowise with courage and power. 'Some think that [the preparations] will not yet be intended for us this year, but that the said force will be employed against the Arabians. Nevertheless, we cannot do otherwise than keep on our guard, and hold everything ready for our defence, both by water and by land, as far as in our power, so that we may not be surprised unaware; and it were greatly to be wished that we were better provided with ships.' . . . (Dutch, 2 pp. and 7 lines.)

No. 777. 21 Nov., 1671 (received). Ola of the King of Marta to the Dutch Commander. An English ship had arrived in his port, those on board requesting speech with the King, asserting that they were friends of the Dutch. The King thereupon hastened to 'Carnapoly', but those in Dutch employ having informed him that the English were not their friends, he instantly returned to ' Mavelicare '.

The King's determination to maintain his contract with the Dutch : Request that the Dutch should send someone to carry on the Carnapoly trade on the same footing as at 'Calicoilan'. (Dutch translation, 1 p.)

No. 779.   6 Dec., 1671.   Treaty with Priaman.   Articles agreed between Commander Jacob Pits in the name of the Dutch Governor-General and Council of India.   Confirmation of previous treaties of 1664 and 1670.   Ten special articles or points.   In Article 5 *inter alia*:

p. 14.   Duty to be paid on goods at the following rates:
> '1 baar [bahar] pepper broght from without to be taxed Rixdaalders 3/4.
> '1 tayl [tael] of gold brought in as above Rd. 1/4.
> '1 tayl worth of cotton goods taxed as above . . .
> '1 tayl worth of coconut oil or other oils . . .
> '1 bahar benzoin medium sort taxed one 'pec' [? pecul].
> '1 catty camphor coss baros.
> 'Salt trading vessels 16 Rds. for each fathqm ('vadem') in breadth, Rd. 16.
> ' Rice and paddy are at present exempt from taxation as the natives require more of the seed than is brought in.'

pp. 16-18.   Article 7.   The native cotton trade and spinning to be discouraged in favour of Dutch monopoly and the encouragement of pepper growing. (Dutch, 21½ pp.)

No. 787.   7 Dec., 1671.   Treaty between native ' aulers ' (Regents of ' Chindrana ', Queen of ' Chiamba ', King of ' Malauwa ', and the King of ' Bengo ') with the Dutch, in Rotterdam Castle, Macassar.   Renunciation by these rulers of the supremacy of the King of Goa, and acceptance of the Dutch Company as sole overlord. (Dutch, 3½ pp.)

No. 774.   19 Dec., 1671.   Extract General Letter from Batavia to the ' 17 '.

p. 1.   Jambi.   The English still had a sum of 30,000 ra. outstanding with divers debtors, and had sought His Highness's help to an agreement towards the recovery, subject to a gift of one fifth of the amount, but had received an unfavourable reply, i.e., that they must await the day of judgment ('laestenoordeels ').

' One of the chief merchants, who had hitherto been a regular customer of the English, named Keey nebe Siry douta, had now been got over by our people to their side, and he obliged himself to by contract to deliver all his pepper to us, to the amount of quite 3,000 peculs per season, to be paid in piece goods at 4¼ riks daalers to the pecul . . . of which the said friends are thus deprived.'

p. 1. l. 25—p. 2, l. 5.   Malacca.

p. 2—p. 9.   Ceylon.   General relation of occurrences relating to Ceylon, Madura and Malabar.

p. 17.   'Though the great undertaking of the forementioned Viceroy, with his arrogant title of Restaurador came to nothing there where it is most probable ['daer't meest naer gelijcht '], it is nevertheless still intended to cause a demonstration to be made with the combined ships' force, to uphold reputation along the coast of India and Malabar ; to reassure wavering minds, so that they and other ill-natured or dissembling friends might clearly perceive that the [Dutch] Company is never unprepared to maintain acquired honour, respect and the mastery of the seas, to the uttermost against all the attacks of enemies, even though evil advisers (amongst them those who wish

us out of Ceylon) should not be a little disturbed to see so important
a fleet in the Road of Colombo, to set out which, everything else is
put aside, which is possible on our side.

pp. 18-19. Report of the Assistant Jacob Heresen on his experiences in
Mocha and Muscat in 1670. Possible advisability of negotiating a
military alliance with the Arabians against the Portuguese. Favourable treatment received there by the Dutch, preference given them
over French and English. Report of the preparation of a large fleet
by the Arabians with the alleged intention of attacking Goa. . . .

p. 19. Malabar. After long trouble with the Zamorin on the Coast of
p. 20. Malabar, the Dutch had been obliged to resort to arms : The Zamorin had been obliged to surrender several important fortified places,
and at last to give up the field with dishonour, to the resultant credit
of the Dutch name. Hopes of an equitable peace. Necessity of
keeping guard on the intentions of the Portuguese and French both
on this coast and in Ceylon, and of bringing everything into a state of
p. 21. defence. Great hopes that the enemy, if they come, will not find
them unprepared, and that the proud 'Restaurador of Ceylon' will
be driven to lay down his arrogant title. . . . Surat. Director
Bogaert and Council in several letters have given their opinion respecting the increase of Surat trade, especially that a greater number
of merchants should be sent there from the Homeland, considering
that it is more profitable for the Honourable Company, than
to send to other parts, without profit, the surplus cash obtained
from the sale of goods. 'We do not undervalue this advice, as it
coincided with the Company's opportunity ; but since this letter
announces that their trade in many profitable trading places and
round about is also in good condition, for which large sums are
required, it therefore seems to us that a moderate trade in Surat,
without exceeding the yearly demands both of the Homeland and
of the Indian districts most deserves approval. As to the surplus
capital, in India it is usually a matter of perplexity to send it as
'secours' to the places in greatest need, all being important. Surat
has had in the past year more than 1,328,000 guldens return, of which
they have paid out 523,000 guldens in cash ; and surely, if this can
be continued without raising money upon interest, we should
always have great promise from this trade, without regard to the
English, who have greater Returns there than we obtain, and send to
p. 23. Europe. In this the Company's capital does not allow us to compete,
lest we should neglect more important business and be unable to
provide the cargoes for the Fatherland, equivalent to assortment
of goods required for the yearly demands from India. This we
trust concurs with your High Mightinesses' sentiments. . . .'

l. 9. The English in Persia during the past year.

p. 24. The French in Persia. (Dutch, 24 pp.)

No. 784. 31 Jan., 1672. Governor-General Joan Maetsuyker and Council
at Batavia to the '17'. [Extract from General letter.]

Amboina. The English Agent at Bantam intended sending to
the East Coast of Ceram to settle a 'logis' (Factory) there.
Instructions had been given to the Dutch in Banda, and verbal
representations made through the Dutch Resident in Bantam to the
[English] Agent, that the Dutch through their absolute right and
possession of those lands could not admit anyone there, and that
they requested him to desist, so as to avoid unpleasantness and

vain expense. Answer was given thereto that the expedition was not intended thither, but only to Timor and some adjacent islands, and that this being done upon direct instructions from their superiors could not be set aside.

p. 2.   As the English perhaps have the island 'Babber' in view, an express is to be sent to the [Dutch] nearest Banda to take possession of it first and without delay.   This may have been suggested to the English by a certain Tiercq Backer, formerly a skipper in the Dutch E.I. Company's service, sent back to the Netherlands in the Fleet of the year [blank] without employment, who came out again last year in the service of the English, but was dismissed by them without long trial (his conduct being no more satisfactory than formerly with the Dutch in Bantam), and allowed to go over to the French directeur, François Caron, he being a drunken fellow.

Macassar. Their High Mightinesses know that there were hopes of a share of the Manilla trade in the Moluccas, through the padres in the island 'Chian', so far without result, but still not hopeless, if the 'Castillians' there were not disturbed by the Chinese.   Report
pp. 3-4. received through Jan Schot's ship of a conspiracy of the 'Coxinders', the Chinese inhabitants, etc. in Taijouan, and its relation to the outlook for the Dutch in the Manillas.

p. 4, l. 22. Jambi. The piracies of the Johor people, off and on the Jambi river, continue; but possibly without the King's knowledge.
pp. 5-6. It is not yet known whether he has decided to accept the Dutch offer of mediation.   The Jambi folk would have good reason for also putting armed forces to sea.   There was a report of the 'Laxamana' being ready to attack Jambi with a great force of vessels and men, and intending not to respect any ships the Dutch might have there.   Should this happen it would clearly prove that they have no thought of accommodation. News had come from Johor that a great number of 'Boegys', who had come from Macassar to Jambi a short time previously, had offered the Johorites help in order to conquer Jambi. . . .

p. 5, l. 12. Ceylon. Appearance of a joint war of France and Portugal rather increased than decreased, judging by copies of letters of 24 October from Surat, and 2 November from Wingurla [Vengurla], relating that in Swally Road 'there lay near each other 12 French ships, to wit 8 King's ships among them, 8 'Spiegelschipen' [ships with a square stern], 2 flutes and a hoy, and 4 of the Company's, which had arrived in succession from Madagascar, namely: 1, the *Crowned Dolphin* [a blank] on the 3d of September; on the 6th of October 6 big armed ships, named *Le Triomphe, La Flamme,* the *July* [? *La*
p. 7. *Julie*], *Navarre, St. Jean de Bayonne* (King's ships), and one of the [French] Company's; 2 flutes, *La Sultane* and *La Hope* [? *L' Espérance*]; 1 Roy, *St. Isaac.* On the 18th of October, of the Company's: 1 ship *St. Juan* [? *St. Jean*], 1 hoy, the *Neerstigheijdt* [*La Diligente*].

According to the most credible of many reports collected by Director Andries Bogaert, the French Company still expected from France and Madagascar 6 ships, namely 2 great ships, 2 flutes, and 2 hoys, and further the 3 ships which were in Bantam with the French Director Caron (these being fairly large); which had not yet been seen on the coast of India or elsewhere in Malabar, bringing up the total to 21; which is sufficiently large, and more than enough. From Vengurla

had come news, dated November 2nd, of the arrival from Portugal
and Goa of a very big Portuguese ship named the *Bom Jesus*,
p. 8. carrying 30 iron and metal guns, and 700 to 750 men, amongst them
many banished noblemen : that they were working hard to prepare
the big ships ; 4 or 5 small ones and over 40 war frigates lay ready
off the bar, but that the great fleet could not be ready before the first
half of December. The French seemed exceedingly busy at Surat,
and to have the intention of making their ships very fine, for which
purpose they were all beached, and 5 or 6 had taken down their top
masts. Meanwhile their people are carefully cherished, great
quantities of gunpowder laden, and other necessary provisions collected for the ships ready for their depature. The crews said to consist
at first of 3,000 men, now much less, owing to the great number of
deaths on the way out, the Admiral alone having lost, it is said, more
than 200 hands, besides having many sick amongst the 250 remaining
souls, and no more than 80 to 90 sailors, the rest soldiers
and nobles. Another had still 120 and the rest at least 80 to 60
p. 9. men aboard. The greatest ships are said to carry 60 metal
pieces, the others, each 40, 36 and 30 cannon, and the two King's flutes
the *Sultane* and *Hope* [? *L' Espérance*], to have been chiefly laden
with masts, palisades, 'stormleeven' [scaling ladders], mattocks,
shovels, grappling irons, and so forth. They boast freely in Surat : a
Monsieur de la Hope, commanding the King's ships in the quality of
Viceroy, is said to have received orders from his King to cause all
ships he may meet to strike their flags everywhere in honour of His
Majesty, even though it be at the cost of ship, life, goods, and stock.
The French Director Caron has notified the English Director, through
His Excellency, that he claimed the honours when he ran into the
'Chom' from his [i.e., the English] ship which lay there with the flag
at the masthead, and has thereupon received the reply that, so as to be
saved by his ships from many losses [? failures], he should give
orders to such effect, that they be carried out with guns only and not
p. 10. with the flag. Shortly after the Englishman ran out with flag flying,
saluting with 13 guns, answered by 7 ditto, the French flagship lying
nevertheless ready for action, as though ready to grapple with
the other ; but it was said there, that the bishop had advised
and begged His Excellency to desist ; whether this be so or
not, the English Director has not allowed the flag to be
brought to again on the ship *London*, which still remained in
the 'Chom', although the captain had caused all the goods to
be brought on deck which were laden for home, so as to discharge them. Director Bogaert was perplexed what to do in such
case with Their Honours' ships, and sought advice thereon by letters
of Oct. 14 from Heer van Goens, who was greatly occupied with
the matter with his Council in Ceylon. Finally, after serious consideration, it was ordered in Council, that in case of a meeting with
stronger French ships at sea, or in some open roadstead, it was
advisable for the Dutch ships to salute under protest of compulsion.
But if the French force were not the stronger, so that the advantage
lay on the Dutch side, then the captains were not to hesitate, but to
use the means provided by God and nature, not only defensively, but
offensively, and to exert their utmost powers to destroy the
aggressors. The Council at Ceylon earnestly begged to be informed
at the earliest opportunity of our sentiments and opinion [at Batavia]

19

for their further guidance on this point of honour, which is of the utmost importance for the respect and reputation of the Company amongst the 'Moors'. Whereupon, after due deliberation, we determined to concur in His Honour's decision, and to give orders, whilst matters were still in a state of uncertainty, for the captains to be careful to avoid all occasion of such encounters, as far as in them lay. And we have deemed it necessary to inform Your Honours of this matter with all its circumstances in detail.

p. 12.   There was great anxiety on account of the costly cargoes of the ships *Pulo Run* and *Ysselstein*, and it was to be wished that they had left Cochin (where they were on the 8th October), for Ceylon, instead of undertaking the voyage to Surat. But the skipper, van Osdorp, has reported to Colombo, that Their Honours' [ship] *Hase* intended to run into Bombay to ascertain there the trend of matters in Surat, and had he not again passed Vengurla safely, he surely would have returned from thence. Their Honours perceive, from the forementioned skipper's report in the Ceylon letter, that the English also were not without anxiety, Heer van Goens having sent an offer to Agent Foxcroft, through Heer Paviloen, that in case His Honour intended to send his ships to Surat, or Persia, or Galle, that they could sail in Company with [the Dutch] and thus the Triple Alliance

p. 13.   in Europe might be usefully observed; that is, that we, being wise through necessity, should be able to support each other in this matter. In such a case such action cannot be displeasing to Your Honours, since it appears to us from all circumstances, that it is no longer possible to doubt that the assembling of the French and Portuguese forces in India is definitely concerted in Europe, and they may perhaps all be about to unite now on the Coast of India. The exact time may come to our knowledge by and by, as well as the object of their enterprise, if any, whether against us, the Arabians, or any other.

According to the latest news from that place [? Ceylon] nothing is yet known for certain concerning their designs, the reports being very contradictory, the most probable being that their plans will depend upon the state of the Company's affairs either there or elsewhere. It therefore tends all the more to our security, that the

p. 14.   merchant Vertangen at Cannanore, and Commander Van Rhede from Cochin had informed Heer van Goens through Captains van Osdorp and Pittoor, that at Cannanore they had no difficulties at all and were not afraid of a powerful enemy; also that at Cochin and Cranganore they hoped to be quite ready before the New Year; and further, that Ceylon was in very good posture, though on the whole but very scantily provided with soldiers, but they hoped to discuss this later. In Ceylon, according to the latest letters, good progress was being made with the fortification of Negombo and Colombo . . . The naval force which still keeps together there has already been notified to Your Honours, and the speculations to which it gave rise.

p. 15.   In our separate letter of July 16th we asserted that Ceylon alone would require quite as many recruits as Your Honours were in the habit of sending for nearly the whole of India, the jealousy of the European princes against the Company being so great, and the eyes of the French being upon Ceylon . . .

l. 12.   Concerning the murder of Dutch people in the land of 'Cotiar' in the preceding year, and the betrayal of Dutch settlements in 'Arrandore', the King is held to be innocent . . .

pp. 16-27. Cayla [Kayal]. Difficulties with the natives and with 'Don Gaspar,' former Receiver of Jaffnapatnam, etc. Terms of agreement between the natives and the Dutch.

p. 27. Malabar. No fresh news received direct, but copies of letters from Commander Hendrik van Rhede to Hr. Rycklof van Goens in

p. 28. Ceylon, dated 29th December, sent by the flute *Osdorp,* telling of the satisfactory state of affairs there, but that the apprehension of war with France and Portugal was no less than before. The work on fortifications was being pushed forward as much as possible.

2 November last [1671] an English ship, the *Antelot* [*Antelope*] had anchored before Porcat, with the intention of settling a factory, but the Raja having refused to see them, they made another vain attempt at 'Carnapoly', and it was feared they might return in September. To prevent this, Commander van Rhede proposed a closer contract with the Raja, excluding foreign merchants. The said ship had gone thence to Cochin for provisions, which were granted her, and thence to Calicut. Time would show the reception received there . . .

l. 22. Persia. French undertakings in Persia not as brilliant as news from France would imply.

p. 30, l. 3. China. Their Honours' trade in China still very small, as only a few attempts at admission can be made . . .

Batavia Castle, 31 January 1672.

Signed: Joan Maetsuyker and 5 others.

(Dutch, 29½ pp.)

No. 788. 16 June, 1672. Ryckloff van Goens and others on the ship *Tulpenburgh*, in the N. bay of 'Trincquenemale' [Trincomalee] to the Governor-General and Council at Batavia. [Extract of letter.]

First attack of the Dutch upon the French and first bloodshed. The Dutch have 221 French prisoners and 15 French deserters. Measures necessary in consequence. Complaints of the French against their Admiral De La Haye. The French are treated by the Dutch similarly with their own men, the officers messing in the cabin, and the principal officers of the captured *Phénix* and *Europe* remaining with their crews on board their ships, without any Dutch guard. . . . (Dutch, 4 pp.)

No. 790. 19 July, 1672. Dutch translation of the Articles of Capitulation [proposed] by Monsieur de la Banoy, Commandant the Reverend Father Maurice, Franciscan friar, Intendant, and all the officers of the 'Isle de Son', which they were constrained to make to His Honour Ryckloff van Goens, Admiral General of the Dutch in the East Indies.

The fourteen articles include:

1. Restitution of all ships, sailors and soldiers arrested in the Indies, within 8 days, with munitions of war and provisions.

2. Restitution of the *St. Jean* within 24 hours, as an integral part of the agreement.

3. All officers, soldiers and other prisoners to be put on board the *St. Jean*, and to be sent back to France within the space of eight months from this day.

4. All runaway sailors and soldiers to be put on board the *St. Jean*.

5. The French departure from the 'Isle de Son' to take place with all the honours of war, flags flying, etc.

6. A month to be allowed for the retreat, during which period no Dutch or natives are to come upon the island.

7. No one to insult or trouble the French during the retreat upon any pretext; but in case the French meet with any difficulties, complaint may be made to the commander, and justice will be done by him in due course.

8. The French flag to be removed only after their departure from the inner bay of Trinquemale [Trincomalee].

9. The Dutch to allow the French to pass safely to Goa, and Surat, so as to arrive there by the 20th of September.

10. The Dutch to allow the French to be supplied with all necessary provisions for the said voyage upon payment, or if preferred, [they can be procured] from the Coromandel Coast, i.e., from San Thomé or Madras.

11. The natives sent by the King of Ceylon are to be landed in 'Cotjaar' within 24 hours, with the same securities demanded for the French themselves.

12. That the French shall have permission to take with them all appurtenances and tools remaining in the little ship the *Indienne.* . . .

13. That a valid pass be given the French for their security from hence to France, so that, if they meet with Dutch ships and are recalled, the Dutch may be held responsible for any damage or accident which might occur.

14. All the officers, soldiers and sailors now on the said island, to be put on board the same ship.

All which articles the undersigned demand may, as a matter of justice, be granted by Mynheer Ryckloff, Admiral General of the Dutch, since it can only lead to concord and good understanding between France and Holland.

On the Island 'de Zon', 19 July, 1672.

(Signed) De Bonnarde, Ravault, Villador, la Requette, le père Maurice, le père la Barde, Valeile, le Bories.

[Translation from the French into Dutch, signed, Davidt Butlere.]

p. 5. Articles appointed and settled by us undersigned, Ryckloff van Goens, Councillor of India, Superintendent, Admiral and Commander in Chief at sea and on land in matters of war, empowered by His Hon. the Governor-General Joan Maetsuyker and the Council of India for the Defence of the Island Ceylon, the Coast of Madura, Coromandel, Malabar, etc. . . . and others on the points presented by Mons. de la Baury, Commander, and the Rev. Père Maurice, etc., residing on the Company's island 'Dwers in de Wegh', lying in the mouth of their usual Winter bay, the fort and subordinate territory of Trinquemale [Trincomalee].

Agreement to restore the said island and bay to the E.I. Co. of the United Netherlands, forcibly seized and usurped by the French General De La Haye.

Articles 1, 2, 4 referred to the Sovereign Lords at home or the Govr.-General in Batavia.

3 and 9. Promise to send all such persons under arrest from Batavia to Holland to be sent on at the pleasure of the Sovereign Lord.

5. Honours of war to be granted the garrison. All else at the discretion of the Govr.-General in Batavia.

6. The island to be delivered by the evening of the following day, subject to an inventory of goods.

7. Granted.

8. Sent back.

10. All prisoners to receive, according to their respective qualities, both here and elsewhere, the same treatment as the officers and soldiers of the Dutch, as far as possible, and in accordance with Article 3.

11. The natives to remain at the disposal of the Dutch and at their discretion.

12. To be dealt with under Inventory by the Overlords in Holland or the Governor-General and Council.

13. Safe conduct against Dutch subjects assured.

14. To be accommodated on Dutch ships as opportunity and means permit.

'Done, resolved and agreed on the Company's Island, the 19th of July, 1672.'

Signed: Ryckloff van Goens, Laurens Pyl, Pieter de Graewe, Heere Symonse van Waerden, Jan Roelantse.

[In margin] for Confirmation; Martin Huysman, Prt Martensz Wiltvangh, Jan Fredricx, Jan Hendrick Boon. (Dutch, 8 pp.)

No. 789.   26 July, 1672.   Ryckloff van Goens and others, on board the
pp. 1-6.   *Tulpenburgh* off the inner bay of Trinquemala, to the Govr.-General and Council in Batavia.

Announces the departure of eight French ships from the said bay on 9th July. Seizure by the Dutch of the *St. Jean Baptiste* and of the island garrisoned by the French, called by the Dutch 'Dwers in den Wegh'. Since the danger of war with France seemed greater, it was thought inadvisable to release the prisoners, but to send them over to the 'Sovereign Lords' in Europe, so as to gain time, and remove them from the neighbourhood. Uncertainty of the Dutch Commander, owing to reports of the arrival of ten to twelve French King's ships and the threatened return of the eight French ships with provisions. No answer received from Jaffnapatnam. The King's lascars dying in great numbers at 'Cotjaar'. The French prisoners caused anxiety; also their ships, which it was difficult to keep seaworthy, the *Phénix* and the *St. Jean Baptiste* being excellent men of war. The greatest anxiety of all was due to the island 'Dwers in den Wegh', which had been fortified by the French. It was difficult to do more than place a garrison there.

The most urgent matter seemed to be to send over the *Europe* with 100 French to Malacca to Their Honours, according to agreement, so as to be free of these guests, in case of the arrival of more enemies, and as soon as news is received of the arrival of the French General De La Haye with his fleet on the Coromandel Coast (since it appears very probable that he has sailed thither), we should perhaps be able to follow him with eight or nine ships to watch his intentions, and to convoy the flutes *Oostdorp, Ysselstein, t'Wapen van der Veer,* and *Papenburg,* leaving the *Durchendam, St. Jean Baptiste, Phenix, t'Wapen van Batavia, Rammekens,* and the *Bears van Amsterdam* very sparsely manned to hold the inner bay, in the hope of succour from Your Honours (which we pray God may not be denied us!). The flute *Alphen* is to keep a watch for the coming of the French ships . . . and other measures taken. If the daily expected assistance arrives, six ships at sea, and 500 or 600 soldiers on land should suffice to guard these bays and territories until our
p. 8.   return from Coromandel. . . . However, Your Honours will be

pleased to treat the above as mere conjectures, since the French may, in the meantime, have gone through the Straits of Malacca to Batavia or elsewhere, or direct to Bengal or part of the way to Madagascar. It might happen that their ships . . . may fall upon us here, or it might come to pass that Your Honours' reinforcements may be so long withheld as to be no longer of any use here, but to be more necessary at Colombo or Galle, contingencies which would upset all our previous ' meditations '.

p. 8, 1. 24—p. 10.   It is impossible to find out how far ' Radja Singa ' has engaged himself with the French, or what treaties have been made with that nation. Great consequent difficulties will ensue if the main force of the weak militia be kept on the ships, whilst if they are to be employed on land, the ships remain almost defenceless, in which condition of weakness we have been for many years, and from which we pray God to be now saved and delivered. . . . Meanwhile our faithful Lascars are dispirited and worn out as a fourth of the 400 have perished in this one fight, our own people having lost no less, many of the rest still being very weak, and the captured French officers are particularly weak and failing, so that we badly need a change of air. We should have been in still worse plight had we not secured the French provision ships. The French here declare they have buried nearly 500 men in four months.

[Here follow further details of the French men and crews, their present force, etc.]

p. 12.   All the stores on the island ' Dwers in de Wech ', except those on the ships *St. Jean Baptiste, Phénix, Europe* and *Indiana* have been listed by a special commission, the principal being 112 iron guns, a great quantity of gunpowder, shot, handgrenades, some gun-carriages, large quantities of iron and lead, besides about 150 lasts of rice, 24 lasts of peas, a supply of wine and brandy. . . .

The highest command on the island was given over by the commander to a shorn priest or mendicant monk (Père Maurice) a stout, shameless, impudent fellow, who has given us much trouble, and still does so daily, railing and cursing so violently both us and our nation, that it would be almost unbearable, were it not that reason bids us suffer

p. 13.   and forbear, threatening to drive us in two years not only from this land but from the whole of India. The French have (as reported to us) written to France for 6,000 soldiers to command the island. The attentions we have rendered them and our particular care to avoid bloodshed as far as possible, are (construed and) blamed as fear of their king or faint-heartedness ; so that we have considered it necessary to silence this evil speaking person, since he is also a famous engineer whom it is not advisable to allow too much opportunity of examining our situation. He has therefore been shipped on board this flute. The other officers are amenable, and the commander, Monsieur de Banoy, of our religion. Several declarations have been made by the French proving that General De La Haye had instructions to occupy as many places as he thought fit on this island or elsewhere, in every case just beyond gun range of our forts.

p. 14.   The natives have also suffered much from the French, the people of ' Tammelganone and Cotjaar ' having all along remained faithful to us ; so that ' Cotjaar ' (which Lieutenant van der Houver had abandoned from mere fear of the French) was still garrisoned on our arrival and all difficulties on that account overcome. Our retreat having attracted the French there, Hensinga Wanna, the Dutch Company's great enemy returned, through whose advice two Frenchmen were sent with letters to the Raja. These were long held up by the latter, and not accepted by him until the news of the abandonment of 'Cotjaar,' and the assertion by the French that their King was the mightiest in the world, and that we were under his absolute power and pleasure, caused him to follow the advice of his evil counsellors. Of all which matters and many others His Honour Huysman and the Fiscal Montanier are to give sufficient proofs, which should reach Your Honours in due time, with the Inventories, our Resolution of the 21st inst. being annexed . . . (Salutations).

Signed: Rycklof van Goens, Laurens Pyt and 6 others. On the ship *Tulpenburgh*, anchored off the Inner Bay of Trincquenemale.

(Dutch, 14½ pp.)

No. 786, 31 July, 1672. Joan Maetsuyker and Council in Batavia to the 'Seventeens'. Extract from General Letter.

Ceylon. After the *Wytongh* had been sent off to Ceylon with the advices for Superintendent Rycklof van Goens on 16th April, the yacht *Fortuyn* arrived on the 29th from the said island, and on the 9th July the *Meercat* bringing several letters from his Excellency and the Govr. of Colombo, and one from Johan Bax dated 12th March, announcing that a fleet of 15 or 16 French ships had passed the same day from Surat along the Malabar Coast.

p. 2.   The last news was that they had gone to Trinquemale and occupied the inner bay with 9 large ships, 3 having been sent to Coromandel for provisions. The Admiral of the fleet was Viceroy De La Haye, associated with Directeur François Caron, undoubtedly the prime mover in the scheme. He announced that he was provided with special letters from the King of Kandy for the purpose. There can be no probability of truth in this, the contrary appearing from a letter received at the same time by Heer van Goens from the Court of Kandy.

Unfortunately, the main body of the Dutch fleet there, under Commander Adrian Roothaus, had left a few days before to convoy the cargo ships for Surat and Persia; otherwise they could have kept the French ships out of the bay.

p. 3.   It had been decided by His Honour, the Superintendent and Council assembled in Gall Town (by Resolution of April 28th), to maintain the (Dutch E. I.) Company's rights; for which purpose His Honour in person sailed to the said bay of 'Trinquenemale' with a fleet of 12 ships [names given], and it is hoped that they will be joined by certain other ships from home, and others from Surat and Persia.

p. 4.   And in order to assist this design as far as lay in our power, we have sent the three ships intended for Coromandel to Ceylon, adding the ships *Dordrecht* and *Oudtshoorn*, and have sent them 300 stalwart soldiers, divided into four companies, each under a lieutenant, ensign and 3 serjeants, the Superintendent in his last (forementioned) letter having asked for a qualified person to assist in the difficult work, Commander Adriaan Roothaus having died shortly after his return to Gall Town with the ships from the Malabar Coast, by which the Company has lost a pious and faithful servant. We have therefore once more taken into your service His Honour Cornelis Qualbergen, and have sent him with the above 5 ships. He had previously been at the Cape of Good Hope in quality of Commander.

p. 5.   Until the departure of the *Meercat* from 'Trincquenemale', no
actual hostilities had taken place on our side against the French,
except that we had intimated to them to leave the said inner bay, and
on their refusal had sought to cut off all provisions as far as possible.
For which purpose, one of the three ships sent for victuals was held
up on its return from Tranquebar, and deprived of sails and rudder,
so as to be able in any case to keep it in our power.   In this action
we cannot see that our people are in the least to blame, as no nation
can be obliged to admit so formidable a fleet of war ships in their
harbours, nor to tolerate it.   Besides, they had in the meantime
landed and driven off some of our guards, and had begun to fortify
here and there, and to throw up batteries on soil which was undoubtedly the Company's own, not only by conquest of the kingdom of
Jaffnapatam (from which it had always depended), but also by the
subsequent mandate of the King of Kandy, in as far as the latter may
have been necessary.

To give an account of the protests and debates between ourselves
and the said Viceroy would take too long; but copies of all the
documents are annexed, as well as all the resolutions taken by our
people in the matter, and some letters on both sides relating thereto,
in case they may serve Your Honours.

p. 7.   We shall be anxious to hear whether His Excellency persisted in
his attempt to drive the French from the wall, and to destroy their
fleet, and with what result; and an extract of our resolution concerning this is also annexed, in copy.

We cannot believe that the further help expected from France can
be as great as is asserted; and we [trust] that the difficulties with
them will be insignificant on our part, since it is to be expected that
the said nine ships will soon almost all lie powerless, as they already
have many sick, and many deaths daily, especially on all those vessels
whose transport can be held up by us.   Hence, much will depend upon
the good or bad disposition of the subordinates.   The admiral ship,
the *Triomphe*, can scarcely be kept afloat longer on account of leaks,
and the two ships they were still expecting with victuals from the
Coast have probably also fallen into our hands.

p. 8.   The above news was received by the flute *Clavers Kêrche* on the
24th inst.   Another letter from the said Heer Ryckloff van Goens
from 'Trincquenemale', dated 16 June, reports that the business with
the French remains mostly at a standstill, except that we had surprised a battery of fortification on a height on the E. point of the inner
bay, three of their men having been slain in the fight, and several of
ours wounded; that the first blood had been shed between them and
us, but to our advantage; and that they cannot impute it to anything
except their own actions, so unjustly undertaken against us.   Another
of the ships sent to Coromandel for provisions had been held up by
our people on its return, in the same manner as the first.   As to the
third, which was a hooker, a great number of men had deserted from
it, by which it may have been rendered powerless, and the supply of

p. 9.   victuals remains withheld.   These deserters had come over to us, as
they asserted, to escape from starvation and ill-treatment by the
Admiral.   They said that it was intended to remove to Coromandel
with five or six of the best ships, leaving others behind in the bay, with
300 soldiers to hold the posts on land, and maintain their acquisitions.
This would give us further trouble, owing to the injury they could

do the Company on the said coast, and to the costly cargo ships; also because in the meantime they might be allowed into the said bay, still further to fortify themselves there, as the natives all seem to have become favourable to them. These our fears we have also communicated to the Superintendent, and have also transmitted to His Honour the direction to use caution and judgment in the Hon. p. 10. Company's service, such as circumstances may demand.

What new protests have reciprocally been made between His Honour and the French Your High Mightinesses will see from the annexed copies. . . .

Batavia Castle, 31 July, 1672.

Signed: Joan Maetsuyker, Nicolas Verburgh, Laurens Pit, Pieter Antonissen Overtwater, Cornelis Speelman, Pieter van Hoorn, Jacob Cops, Willem Volger.

(Dutch, 9½ pp.)

No. 787A, 8 Oct., 1672. (Anthonie) Paviloen and Council at Palliacat to Joan Maetsuyker, Governor-General, and Council at Batavia.

p. 1. Details of letters received dated 14th, 16th April, 15th and 27th July, those of 14th June (in copy only, on the 17th of September, the originals sent by the English private yacht the *Fortune* not having yet arrived) from Ceylon, which all the ships had reached safely. The Lord be praised! [for this] as well as for the safety of all the Coast ships with their cargoes, and especially for the speedy voyage of the return fleet under the flag of Heer Ysbrandt Goshe to the dear Fatherland the preceding year, and the arrival of ships from p. 2. thence and elsewhere in Batavia.

According to advices received from Your Honours, we shall anxiously expect in January, besides a ship from Batavia via Malacca, and the usual Malacca yacht, the flutes *Kuylenburg* and *Uytdam*, with a large capital for our coast, for our Coromandel chest was at its very bottom when the gold now sent by Your Honours arrived. The general requirements [of goods] for the coming year 1673 for the Home country and India are very great, as Your Honours rightly say; and you request our opinion as to whether (owing to the troublous times) they should be carried out or no. We can give no definite answer, but after serious consideration, we think it would p. 3. be possible to execute the greater part, and especially the cotton thread and rough 'rond scherp', if we are not short of money; also perhaps the common 'guinea cloth', and the fine chintzes, but much might happen to prevent the fulfilment of this order. Other piece goods for Europe will probably fall short, since the English now employ greater capital therein than heretofore.

Six ships came this year from England to Madras, war not having yet broken out between France and our States at the time of their departure. They have brought out a stock of gold, silver and merchandise, amounting in value, it is said, to about 350,000 pagodas. p. 4. The five ships which first arrived have all been sent over to Masulipatam and Bengal and are to return thence together and to sail in company at the beginning of next year from Madraspatam for England. From news brought by the last ship, the *Barnardiston*, there appears to be some discontent between the King of England and our State, and that in order to allay it, an ambassador from Holland had come to London shortly before the sailing of the ship. Amongst the questions in debate, the chief was apparently that gun-shots had been exchanged between five of our men of war and theirs in the channel. . . .

p. 5.   A copy of letter No. 2, concerning the general insecurity of affairs as regards France, Portugal and England, sent by the Home authorities overland to India, and forwarded overland to Heer Rycklof van Goens, Superintendent in Ceylon, and also communicated to Director

p. 6.   Constantin Ranst in Bengal, is sent for information. The anxiety of watching for speedy news both by sea and by land is emphasised since the King of France has 'forced the war upon us'. Castle Geldria is a new and a weak fort with but a small garrison, and with an open town of strongly built houses on this side. The French need not trouble to respect the King of Golconda, should assistance reach them from France, either here or in the 'comptoirs in Sadrangapatnam, Masulipatnam and Bimelipatnam', for having already seized San Thomé, they can hope for no trade in his lands.

As regards the business of the King of Viziapore [Bijapur] they also have no reason to spare the factory of Tegenepatnam, and still less to leave the town of Nagapatnam untouched out of regard for the Tanjore Nayak or anyone else. This town would be an easy conquest, being of so great an extent, and with weak irregular fortifications, requiring a garrison two or three times as strong as it now possesses to hold it in its present condition for any length of time against a European enemy of tolerable strength.

p. 8.   In a letter of September 11th to us, His Honour writes: 'If Nagapatnam cannot be provided with militia otherwise that at present, and there should be war with France (since it is now rumoured that England and Portugal are to join in) I am decidedly of opinion, that the town should be made over to the Nayak of Tansjower [Tanjore] or another, and the sooner the better, upon condition of independence from Visiapore or Golconda; as otherwise the town will surely be lost, and Ceylon soon after would have to bear the brunt.' In the same letter His Honour writes: 'In Nagapatnam I have ordered Point Amsterdam to be enlarged by the tracing of a new Point [? lookout]. If Your Honour should wish to reduce the town to a moderate square or pentagon this will then prove very serviceable, whilst if the town remains so large, this is most important, since it is too badly exposed on that side to be defended on three sides by a small force unable, without fear of surprise, to command the attackers. But the opinion of the Singhalese engineers, Pieter Dunbeer and David Butler, sent last year

p. 9.   by His Honour, was not to make a most necessary improvement of the Nagapatnam fortification at that corner, but a general one.

Nevertheless work was to be begun on the said new Point near Amsterdam, at a cost of about 2,500 pagodas, this having already been explicitly ordered by Heer van Goens as Superintendent and Chief Commander, and that we should serve the Company's interests far better by reducing the fort of Nagapatnam than by repairing it, and by placing a suitable garrison as a frontier [defence] for the costly [settlement at] Ceylon on this side rather than to hand over the town to any native potentate.

There have been heavy expenses there this year caused by the construction of a turf 'fausse braie' with a breastwork on the inner side of the ditch, and the deepening and widening of the ditch, and the

p. 10.   continuation of the stone revêtement of the same begun on the town side. To do so on the other side would cost too much, and it is also impossible to cover it with turf, as sufficient is not to be procured hereabouts. We have no one on this coast skilled in the art of fortification. Therefore, if Your Honours should desire any particular alterations at Nagapatnam a suitable person should be sent there. . . .

p. 10, l. 13. Recapitulation of news of the French at Trincomalee and San
p. 11, Thomé. 'To the seven (remaining ships) they had also added the
l. 25. little yacht the *Ruby* of Mr. Sjearsey [Jearsey], seizing it as it
p. 12. attempted to pass their fleet without commission, and notwithstanding several protests of the English Governor (Sir) William Langhorne, have retained possession of it. Whether this is done with the knowledge of the Viceroy La Haye or not, or only according to the pleasure of Director-General Caron or others, we cannot tell.' One of the seven ships sailed three or four weeks ago to an unknown destination, and on the 3rd instant five more, namely three war ships, one other, and the little yacht *Ruby*, were sent to the southward (two French ships still remaining before San Thomé), some say to Tranquebar, others to Goa, but nothing further is known, as Monsieur La Haye is very secret in his business. The few French (about twenty) living at Masulipatnam, after the taking of San Thomé went aboard a ' Moor ' ship lying in the roadstead there, and have bought a little
p. 13. vessel from Mr. ' Cleedwood ' [Fleetwood] for 400 pagodas, to which they have transferred themselves and perhaps will return on it to San Thomé with the coming monsoon or a favourable wind.

It is thought that the French base their chief grounds for the seizure of San Thomé on the unfounded powers given them two years ago at Masulipatam by the Muhammadan Governor in the business of their servant Marhara, details of which were given to Your Honours.

A Portuguese yacht from Goa has recently anchored near Madraspatnam with miscellaneous goods, from which the French have bought all the wine. . . . This vessel came very opportunely, as it is said that no more than 400 men besides a few topazes and peons remain in the town with Mr. La Haye to garrison it, and that Monsr. Caron is with the fleet.

pp. 14, 15. Superintendent van der Goens went up the coast from 8th August to 1st September with 9 men-of-war. . . . Movements of Dutch ships.
p. 15, l. 17. It is also owing to want of time that it has not been possible to load any flagstones in these ships at Sadraspatnam. Several dozen have been ready for some time, as for their better provision we rented the village ' Arrialsery ', where the stone workers live, for five years from Heer Fattamia for 85 ' pards ' yearly.

Movements of ships and reasons for alterations of previous arrangements. ' On the 1st instant the *Buyksloot* followed the other ships to Masulipatam (whither they had been sent to assist in loading) with the merchants' cash and other things which could not be sent sooner, as the pagodas had first to be coined and the greater part of the yacht's lading was changed. . . .'

If it were possible to enter into the whole details of the commission of Chief Merchant Sir Pieter Smith concerning the Company at the
p. 18. Court of Golconda, at Masulipatnam and elsewhere in the Muhammadan kingdom it would require a quire of paper. We therefore rather beg to refer to our Journal, which gives a fully detailed account

up to August, and especially to our Resolutions of the 12th September, in which may be seen the motives of our letter of that date sent to Golconda recalling His Honour from there. The affair of complimenting the present King and his two chief Ministers, the Lord 'Miersinda Seydnived Sjaffer' and the Lord 'Chanchanna Superselaer Moffenchan' had not yet been initiated at the time of despatching this, it being necessary to leave all that, as well as the attempts necessary on behalf of the Hon. Company, to the chiefs of the factory at Golconda, the Chief Merchant Sir Willem Hartsinck, and the Merchant Sir Jan van Neyendael. For the 'Mierzamela zeyd'

p. 19. continues well pleased with them, and is willing to enlist the favour of the King towards the Hon. Company; but he will have nothing to do with the Commissary on account of that which occurred at his house on the last day of the past year, which resulted in mutual heavy losses, as Your Honours have already been informed.

l. 8.   Amongst the forementioned papers, to which we respectfully beg to refer you, we would mention particularly the following matters : That the former King Sultan Abdullah Qutb Shah was given a present to the value of pagodas 6453. 5½ and 'Chia Miersa', our now late patron was presented with pagodas 1937.3 six days later.   That the old general 'Nichnanchan' died on the 9th of April, leaving the King a treasure of 6,000,000 old pagodas. . . .   That eight days later the foresaid 'Mossenchan' was appointed to succeed him in his post.

p. 20. That the old king (before he could fulfil his promise to give a *farman* to the Company, owing to the loss of his sight) died in the night of the 1st-2nd May.   That the night following the younger of his two sons-in-law, Mirza Abdul Hassan, was placed upon the throne, by the two forementioned lords 'Miersumella and Chanchanna'.   That the new King then deprived 'Chia Miersia' of all his estates and fortune, and that our people, with the Lord 'Maersumela' for our patron, were present at the audience.   That he afterwards appointed the same lord once more to the Government of Masulipatnam, Kondapille, 'Vlaer and Ragiemandaren', having deprived Ja'far Beg of the same on the 24th August because he failed to bring in his dues.   That the same malicious person . . . since then, on partly frivolous pretexts of farming 'Paliacol', will not be satisfied with the sums paid to his predecessor, 'Mameth Beech', but insists upon a new system of

p. 21. imposing custom on the outgoing merchandise for Golconda, and further on tolls upon the piece-goods entering Masulipatnam.

The Company's trade has been obstructed in the northern quarters everywhere, from 10th March to about the middle of May, he having prevented the bringing of any provisions to the Masulipatnam factory on several occasions, through his 'habeldaer Miersja Momyn', adding severe threats of intending to surprise and kill our people there, and exhibiting such preparations thereto that the factors were obliged, for the preservation of their lives and the Company's property, to have a few of the guns of the *Moven* brought from the banksall to the factory, so that it might appear that it was intended to use them. . . .

p. 22.   Further, [we beg to mention] how Lord Abdul 'Naby' has once more been sent as 'Serlaskier' to Orixa [Orissa], which gives rather more hope than before of obtaining thence, some time or other, the belated 260 loads of rice.   That the subordinate governments of Ellore and 'Ragie mandaron' are given to Hussain Beg, and that of

Masulipatnam and its appurtenances to a certain Malik 'Soil', both favourites of Mir Jumla, with whom Abdul 'Naby' is also greatly in favour.

Many other matters are contained in the Journal. From the extracts communicated Their Honours will be able to judge that the presents to the late King and the deposed 'Chia Miersa' have been in p. 23. vain ; but how could this have been foreseen ? It once more appears (as far as the King and our patron are concerned) that it will be necessary to compliment and present a gift to the ruling prince and his two chief courtiers, on whom he allows everything to depend (being personally chiefly engaged at present in watching the fights of wild beasts and the dancing of tame dogs, so it is said).

The English had the good fortune shortly before the Nabob's death to obtain a *farman* for the farming of Madraspatnam for 1,200 pagodas a year.

A Mr. Richard Cohan, an Englishman, formerly in the service of their Company, and late gunfounder to the King of Golconda, arrived p. 24. here on the 15th September as great 'habeldaer' [havildar] of Attipatam, Waloer, the Sienket Koor, Dygoraetpatnam, Kotapatnam, Poneer, the seven Meganes, and Palliacat, they being the lands farmed to him by the Lord 'Chanchanna' for the period of five years for the sum of 38,938 pagodas a year, an amount which it is not considered possible to obtain from them ; and in that case his rule will be but of short duration ; which time will show.   On his arrival he arrayed the Governor in a Muhammadan raiment in the name of his Lord and Master, at the same time presenting him with a letter from His Highness containing nothing but a recommendation to live in good friendship with his forementioned havildar and to be helpful to him in those matters in which he might need the King's assistance in serving the Company.

Salutations. In the Castle of Geldria at Palliacat. 8 October, 1672. Signed : Pavilioen, P. Montenach, Roelant de Carpentier, Ducher, J. B. Sonhius, Johannes Huysman, J. Hervendonck.

(Dutch, 24 pp.)

No. 787 B.   9 Oct., 1672.   Jacob van der Meerse and Council at Negapatnam to the Governor-General Joan Maetsuyker and Council at Batavia.

By the hooker, the *Pagadeth* [? *Bagadeth*], sent to the Governor of the Coromandel Coast, they had heard of the safe arrival of their letter of the 14th March sent by the flute *Starmeer* to Their Honours at Batavia: the said hooker being here with the Fleet of Defence before the town. . . .

p. 2.   The French with a considerable naval force had arrived at Trincomalee and had fortified the inner part of South Bay, sending two ships, the *Phénix* and the *Europe*, to this coast for victuals.   These two ships on their return were seized by our people, the rest of the French naval force being thereby constrained to go out of Trincomalee Bay to seek provisions, leaving in the said bay a large ship, the *St. Jean Baptiste*, and about eighty whites and a few Singhalese, with thirty pieces of cannon to garrison the island lying in the entrance [of the bay].   Departing on the 9th July, the said p. 3.   fleet passed two days later before Negapatnam and arrived at Tranquebar.   Not being able to obtain sufficient provisions from the Danes, they passed on to San Thomé, which place they seized from the King of Golconda on August 5th with but little resistance and bloodshed, and they still hold it.   Their fleet lies about 1½ miles out to sea, before San Thomé, which they have since fortified and provided with many guns, and therefore it will not be so easily taken as it was lost.   The 'Moors' have invested it by land, but as they cannot cut their enemies off by sea, it is wasted trouble, since the besieged can obtain almost everything they need for money from Madraspatnam.

The French meanwhile seize all vessels without respect to owner-ship, and only a few days ago took possession of a Portuguese yacht

p. 4.   coming from Goa for Madraspatnam, because it flew too many flags and did not strike them betimes (so the story goes); but it may be a pretence, and the seizure may have been purposely arranged in order to give assistance to the French, without giving offence [? to us].   . . . We shall soon see where Viceroy De La Haye intends to winter with the King's fleet, since the northern monsoon is 'at the door'. . . .

Brief mention of Admiral van Goens' attack upon the French at Trincomalee, and increase of Dutch strength there; thirteen of the Dutch East India Co.'s ships arrived thence shortly after, ten of which were armed for war, principally to make a demonstration and to refresh the crew. . . .   On Sept. 2nd they directed their course to Punta dos Pedras under the orders of the Admiral.   Having been there, they passed by here again, fourteen strong, on the 12th of the same month, Captain Jan Fredericx being in command, with the merchant, Pieter Montenacq, as vice-commander, having instructions

p. 6.   not to go beyond Sadraspatnam, whence they were ordered to proceed to Pulicat by the Governor Anthonie Pavilioen, and they duly arrived there.   There they still lie, with the ships which have been ordered to Masulipatnam to remove the cargoes. . . .

Signed: Jacob van der Meerse, Isack Welsingh, J. Corbisier, Mattys Adams, Thomas van Ree.   (Dutch, 5½ pp.)

No. 785. p. 1.   11 December, 1762.   Joan Maetsuyker and Council at Batavia.   Extract of General Letter.

Bouton.   English attempt there and their enquiries about spices. Refusal of the King to admit them.

p. 2, l. 23.   Ceylon.   4 October [1672] arrived from Malacca the pinnace *Eendracht*, sent expressly by Governor Bort to carry letters and papers of Superintendent Ryckloff van Goens, dated 26th July, from Trincomalee Bay: and sent by the captured French flute *Europa*. 'The said flute arrived in the road here [Batavia] on October 12th, bringing one hundred Frenchmen, amongst them two mendicant friars named Frère Maurice and Bonnet, whereby it more clearly appeared how matters had gone after the departure of the flute *Claverskerck* from the roadstead there on the 10th of June, between His Honour and the French Viceroy De La Haye.   The latter was finally obliged by absolute want of sufficient provisions to leave the Bay of Trincomalee . . . on the 9th July with eight ships for Coromandel for refreshment and revictualling, leaving the island— by them called the Sun, and by us Dwars in den wegh—partly fortified, with the French ship *St. Jean* belonging to their Company, near by, with the well-appointed flute the '*Indiane*' [? *Indienne*.] Whereupon Heer van Goens and the Dutch fleet, coming into the

p. 4.   Bay and approaching the said island, first overcame the said *St. Jean*

on the 18th of the same month, and on the day following the island
was surrendered by capitulation, with thirty guns (mostly iron two-
pounders). The Lord be praised! This troublesome thorn is
removed, and no more than two Frenchmen and one of their blacks
were killed, but none of ours.'

On the island and in the ships *St. Jean, Europe, Phénix* and the
Indiane were found and came into the Dutch Company's hands,
according to inventory, 112 pieces of iron cannon, a large quantity of
powder, shot, hand grenades, a few gun-carriages, quantities of iron,
lead, etc. . . . 150 loads of rice, 24 loads of gram, wines and brandes,
indicating once again that their designs must have been great ; the
greater part of the French also declaring unanimously that these
p. 5. [ships] had been [intended] for Ceylon or for Banca, and that the
Viceroy's absolute orders were, according to several testimonies, that
they should settle as many posts as they thought fit on the island or
in other places . . . but just beyond cannon shot of Their Honours'
forts and fortifications. He had given the High Command over the
island to the monk Maurice aforementioned under the title of
' Intendant ', in whose name the agreement was made for the restitution of the captured ships and people (about three hundred and fifty
men) referred by us to our Sovereign Lords.

Heer van Goens and his Council on deliberation had felt unable to
release them, lest with the assistance they so surely expected, their
power should be still more increased. He promised, however, that in
accordance with the Third Article of the Capitulation, they should be
sent to Holland via Batavia, by the first opportunity, to be
transported from thence according to the pleasure of our Sovereign
Lords. And His Honour in residence here, not feeling able to decide
what [? might] happen respecting their expected recruits, it was for
the present resolved . . . on the 19th of the same month, to delay
a few days longer the [?] principal decisions (' *dispositie ten princi-
pale* '). Whereupon there arrived here the hooker, the *Lyster,* which
had been sent for them, bringing the unpleasant news of so great a
war against both mighty princes, and some fear that the Crown of
Portugal (if it had not already declared it) would soon join in, it being
as much to the latter's interest to come to an agreement, especially in
India.

p. 7. Your Honours may perceive from the three letters sent via England,
that we in India have been as far as possible upon our guard against
the French [at the same time not trusting the Portuguese] and in
some fear of the English, their King's disinclination to us being
only too well known. Upon receipt of the above news, the
monk Maurice and his people were put under safe guard, and the
papers etc., of this impertinent and no less crafty priest were seized
(all being carefully registered), it being considered that the subjects
of that nation could no longer be looked upon as only under arrest
upon articles of capitulation, but rather as actual prisoners, bereft of
the benefits of agreed privileges. Although Your Honours, with your
usual care and foresight, had ordered the flute *Saxenburgh,* and the
hookers *Posthoorn, Louwy,* and *Bulchesteyn,* to be sent out in haste
p. 8. to give warning of these affairs, both at Surat and in Ceylon, and also
here, we have still thought it our duty, as stated at the beginning of
this letter, to despatch the *Meercat* on the 3rd of November with
express advice for Malacca, Ceylon, Bengal, Coromandel, etc. . . .
We hope her voyage may be a short and safe one. . . .

There arrived on the 3rd instant [December] the hooker, the *Vlieger*, bringing us news from the Superintendent, and from Colombo, with one from Commander Cornelis van Quaelbergen in Trincomalee of the 3rd October, from whom we had also received another letter of the 15th September via Coromandel, reporting his safe arrival with the
p. 9. recruit which sailed under his command. We were not only surprised but troubled that Your Honours' advice ship had not yet been heard of there, by or before the 19th November, and that they still remained in ignorance of the actual tidings of war, which the last ship from England brought out on 26th April without doubt, but kept secret, as has already been noted in the Coromandel business.

So far His Honour has not felt justified in taking action therein, so long as we are not attacked by them; since it appears from all external circumstances, that the French also have not been informed by [the English]. Otherwise they [the French] would not have acted as it is alleged (if it be indeed true), viz: that the Viceroy De La Haye had not only dared to seize a certain little English ship the *Ruby*, belonging to Mr Sjerzey (Jearsey), but also refused restitution on its
p. 10. being claimed. The Viceroy with his eight ships sailed from Trincomalee direct for the Coromandel Coast, passing the town of Negapatnam and in full sight of Tranquebar, where, as well as at Porto Novo, not being able to obtain their great requirements they continued along the Coast. . . . On the 21st of the same month they were before San Thomé, belonging to the King of Golconda. There his officers, who were sent on shore for the needs of the fleet, were put off by the Commander until he could send word thereof to his superior officer some miles inland. De La Haye was so angered by this, that on the 23rd he first ordered the town to be bombarded from the ships, and afterwards to be attacked in force by land. It was then stormed (the garrison being without any suspicion thereof) and strongly held.

p. 11. Governor Pavilioen's letter from Pulicat to Batavia, dated 8th October, contained the above news in detail, and added that the 'Moors' had beleaguered the city with [10,000 men on foot and 500 horsemen. But during the] month which had elapsed the French had had sufficient opportunity to provide supplies for a year from the interior, apparently intending to remain in possession, for which purpose they still sought to strengthen themselves as much as possible, taking into their service a few Portuguese topazes of Tranquebar, Porto Novo and thereabouts, and endeavouring meanwhile to lay in as many provisions as could be obtained, also improving the fortifications as far as they could; so that they consider that unless the Moors bring up heavy guns for the siege they
p. 12. would besiege the town in vain, 'being a folk which is afraid of heavy shot.'

But had it pleased God to grant Your Honours' advices and instructions a speedy voyage to Ceylon beforehand, then in all probability not only would Your Honours' ship not have failed but the town itself could perhaps have been restored again to its lord. According to letters from Heer van Goens, the French were in a position to retain both the town and the ships. His Honour had received news that whenever he, with the main body of the fleet, was off Negapatnam, sailing before the wind, the French, who always employed their people on land by day, brought them back on board ship at night, for fear of being attacked and surprised by our people, complaining greatly of the uncertain state of things, which had prevented their getting the marked advantage which otherwise must have resulted.

Nevertheless the small flute the *Louys* [*Louis*] has also fallen
p. 13. into his hands . . . and their great ship the *Triomphe* (mentioned in ours of July 31st) they had beached and broken up, not being able to keep her afloat any longer before San Thomé.

No further sure advices can be given Your Honours, the reports being various. The last letters of the 9th and 12th September from Negapatnam seem to establish from Danish reports that Director Caron had sailed for Europe on the English ship *Ruby*. Heer van Goens in his last considers Caron's departure certain, but he believes that it was on the *Julius*, and that the ships *Navarre* and *Breton* . . . were to retire to Atche [Achin] or Tenasserim. . . . Time will show the truth thereof. In open roadsteads for such great ships there is a want of facilities for repairs ; and if we were certain of their withdrawal to those parts, we ought not to delay, if it were at all possible to make an attempt on them. It is sufficiently proved by this account that the redoubtable might of Viceroy La Haye is at any rate greatly reduced, and almost come to nought, the French having (according to the reports of prisoners to Heer van Goens) buried quite 500 of their men on land at Trincomalee, over 350 being in our power, while 300 are said to have deserted in Surat and almost as many escaped to Canara and other places ; 200 had been left in Fort Dauphin in Madagascar, besides almost 400 slain there in an expedition on land ; and although 4,300 men were said by them to have been brought out from France, from these accounts scarcely 2,000 can be left. It therefore appears to His Excellency to be certain that at the most 800 men had come with the ships to San Thomé. It may be however that their hopes of a great reinforcement were not quite vain, and that which the English and Danes have reported in Coromandel may also be true, i.e., that the first had seen anchored at 'Asnany' island five war-ships of forty to fifty guns, and the others had spoken with a still greater ship at sea, both asserting that they were followed by greater forces. At the same time the Resident in Vingurla, by letter dated the 5th September, to the Commandant in Malabar, reports that in Goa they expect a French fleet of twenty ships, but we hope it will not be so large, and that the time will soon show where the foresaid six ships may have appeared, so that we also may again be prepared against them.

p. 16, l. 25. Although the outbreak of the war between France and the United Provinces may make it difficult to settle the Trincomalee
p. 18. disputes and demonstrate the justice of the Dutch East India Company's procedure, they have, nevertheless, sent instructions to Ceylon to collect all irrefragable evidence towards the justification of the Company, and send it to Batavia, so that it may be forwarded also from hence if at any time it should be of use to Their Honours. The captured French ships and goods to be dealt with (on receipt of Inventory) by the Pact of Justice, awaiting Their Excellencies' orders. . . .

p. 19. On the 16th July the fleet before Trincomalee had been successively joined by the *Beurs* from Persia and the *Meerman* from Surat, and on the 28th the flute *Osdorp* returned from Negapatnam

20

(whither it had been sent to place 118 Frenchmen in safe keeping) with the news that La Haye had retired to Coromandel. His Excellency (van Goens) hastened to send out, to follow him there, besides the garrrisons on land to secure the bay, the yachts *Beurs, Durgerdam, t'Wapen van Batavia*, the French *Phênix* and *St. Jean*, sparsely manned but advantageously equipped, to make a great attempt between two land batteries. He sailed in person with the *Tulpenburgh, Damiatha, Bredenvoode, Noordioycq, Amersfoort*,

p. 20. *t'Wapen van der Gouw, Rysende Zonne, Meerman, Rammekens*, the flutes *t'Wapen van der Weer, Ysselstein, Papenburgh* and the *Osdorp*, first to 'Puncta de Pedras', where Alphen passed on his way to Persia, then both together on 8th August to Negapatnam, and on the 20th to Tegenepatnam. . . .

Meanwhile His Excellency took the opportunity of thoroughly refreshing the men, who were in great need of it, and sailed again on the 27th August with sound and cheerful crews for Negapatnam, having sent the flutes *Isselsteyn* and *Osdorp* to Bengal. . . .

p. 21. On the 9th, the yachts *Outhoorn, Buycksloot, t'Wapen van Batavia, Durgendam* and the *Beurs* joined them, from which main body (so as to supply us with merchantmen to bring over the Coromandel 'retours') there will at the first opportunity be despatched the *Alphen, Buycksloot, Beurs van Amsterdam, t'Wapen van Batavia, Durgendam, Papenburgh, t'Wapen van der Veer*, convoyed by the men-of-war *Outhoorn, Damiata, Bresdenroode, Noortuyck, Rysende Son, t'Wapen van der Gouw, Meerman* and *Rammekens*, under the flag of the Vice Admiral Jan Fredericxen. These have express orders in passing before San Thomé not to make the slightest acknowledgment of the French flag. It has not been thought desir-

p. 22. able that his Excellency should go in person, as they were still unable to make any attempt upon the place, and it was thought more necessary for him to remain in Ceylon, all the more so since Heer Paviloen was present there to give the necessary orders in the fleet's concerns. . . .

It appears from His Excellency's last letter of 19th November, that the whole fleet of Coromandel and the Bay of Trincomalee are united there under his command, making together a total of fifteen ships

p. 23. and yachts.   [Here follow the names of the ships.]

We hope that soon after it may have been possible to add from Coromandel the flutes *Ysselsteyn* and *Osdorp*, the yacht the *Cogge*, and perhaps also the *Laren* from Bengal. . . .

Finally it is, of course, understood that much is required for so many ships, especially as they may be necessarily detained there, to keep off all arriving enemies. Therefore, that they may not be in difficulties, we have sent by the yacht *Ougly* and the hookers *Bagdet* and *Lyster* via Malacca, [provisions] . . . to the amount of f. 88,947 : 10 : 11, with the promise to do our utmost if the home ships arrived in time, to send another ship this month from Sumatra.

In the meantime we are still expecting thence the hooker the *Swemmer* laden with cinnamon, which was to leave eight days after the *Vlieger*, by which we hope to receive without fail the acknowledgment of Your Honours' 'advice', and also to hear whether Heer Volger, who sailed on September 2nd with the armed yachts *Poelo-*

p. 25. *run* and *Nieuwenhove* for Surat, and was on October 8th in the inner bay of Madura before Wierandepatnam, has sailed for Cochin, or has returned to Ceylon. He had received certain reports as to the safety of the route for the continuation of his voyage, which must otherwise have caused us great anxiety, for there is no reckoning whether the four French ships forementioned and the five English of which Your Honours wrote (which had left in March last for Surat), have all now arrived near Goa, Bombay or Surat, undoubtedly not without knowing of the war there. The two ships with such costly cargoes could do little against them, and would otherwise rather add to the strength of the Ceylon fleet for in this state of affairs we must be content to place the needs of the war before those of trade, and must be pleased if those of the latter can be carried on seasonably and without noteworthy danger. It is greatly to be hoped that God will grant the two rich ships deliverance from our enemies; for if they arrived safely at Surat the Directors there could easily arrange to furnish some capital for Malabar and Ceylon, which is not at all convenient for us to do from here, yet both places nevertheless require it.

Time will show whether the six English ships mentioned in the headings of Coromandel and Bengal will really sail for England at the usual time, as asserted, whatever the others in Surat may order. In p. 27. that case it should set us much more at ease, than if they were to settle near each other somewhere on one or other of the coasts, or come to meet to the east of Ceylon, in which case so formidable a body would be brought together that we dare not at present even give definite advice, and respectfully beg your High Mightinesses to give the matter the consideration its importance demands, especially as regards the supply of the greatly needed recruits.

Meanwhile we think that a certain English ship, which put into the Bay of Gall when the *Vlieger* called, should not fail to fall into your Lordships' hands ; the advice-boat having followed soon after, it is not improbable that Heer van Goens has held it up upon some pretext, news of which we hope to receive by the *Swemmer*.

At Muscat the Sind envoy had made a present to the chief merchant Padbrugge to provide a troop of hired soldiers to be p. 28. employed in the Company's service where required, it having been recommended by us in our last letters to the respective Directors of Surat and Persia, to support them about the Rajah. . . .

Monsieur Martin having appeared distressed at being compelled to fight against his own nation, had been discharged by Heer van Goens and given leave to come to Batavia. . . . Owing, however, to the actual declaration of war by the Kings of both France and England against our State, he is still without present employment, p. 29. there being no military appointment vacant here, and he does not seem inclined to accept occupation on the Council of Justice.

' Raja Singa'. It has been evident that the Singhalese have admitted and openly assisted the French, whilst they have been unfriendly towards us, not only in the districts of Battacala and Trincomalee, but also at Gall and Colombo. In the first case it is proved that it was by the Rajah's direct and personal instructions, as appears in the papers, especially those relating to Colombo, and in olas, several of which have fallen into our hands. But in the Heer Superintendent's last despatch of 19th November, this appears again doubtful, His Honour reporting that the last courier sent about a year ago is now finely arrayed by His Majesty and daily honoured with new garments, whilst the French envoy remaining there at Court has been placed under guard in a house apart, as hostage. We have recommended in our last two letters to hold him innocent of any such prejudice, and to attribute all the harm done to evil councillors or bad courtiers, without however trusting him now. . . .

LIST OF SEVENTEENTH CENTURY
MANUSCRIPTS RELATING TO BRITISH INDIA
IN THE GUILDHALL LIBRARY, LONDON

LIST OF SEVENTEENTH CENTURY MANUSCRIPTS RELATING TO BRITISH INDIA IN THE GUILDHALL LIBRARY, LONDON

1641. **Some breife notes taken out of Captaine William Myners his journall,** in the *Royal Mary*, bound for Bantam . . . began from Gravesend the 25 March, 1641.

MS. No. 1757.

1695-96. **Letter from Sir John Gayer, Governor of Bombay to Sir Stephen Evance,** Lombard Street, dated Bombay Castle, 19 March, 1695-96.

MS. No. 1525 (Box 12).

He gives an account of trade, with a note of sword blades sold and the balance paid to Captain Randolph Pye. He reports trouble at Surat caused by Pirates.

1699. **Letter from Sir John Gayer to Sir Stephen Evance,** dated Bombay Castle, 11 Dec., 1699.

MS. No. 1525 (Box 12).

News of investments for the Company. Diamonds 'extreme scarce and dear'—can only get bad ones at extravagant rates.

1709-10. **Letter from Sir John Gayer to Sir Stephen Evance,** dated 6 January, 1709-10.

MS. No. 1525 (Box 12).

He remarks on Mrs. Cornwall's estate and the 'ill character' of her brother, Mr. Annesley, who is guilty of a 'detestable falsehood' in denying that he holds Rs. 4,000 of said estate in his hands.

He comments on the business methods of the Old and New Companies. The Union is of no advantage to the Company's servants. Diamonds are bad and scarce—none were procured from Golconda last year.

MSS. RELATING TO THE EAST INDIES IN THE ARCHIEPISCOPAL LIBRARY AT LAMBETH PALACE

MSS. RELATING TO THE EAST INDIES IN THE
ARCHIEPISCOPAL LIBRARY AT LAMBETH PALACE

1619
(before
July).

Propositions of the English Commissioners [relating to the proposed Treaty for the Joint East India trade of the English and Dutch East India Cos.], beginning 'The Commerce and Trafficke in the East Indies shalbe free as well for the Company of England,' etc.

Gibson MSS. Vol. V,
MS. 933, No. 3;
also No. 5.

Twenty-five articles with marginal notes.   Undated copy.   3½ pp.

No. 5 is a duplicate of the above.

The Propositions differ in some respects from the Treaty of 7 July, 1619, as finally concluded and printed in Rymer's *Foedera*, the order of Articles 1 and 2 also being reversed.   The annotated Articles containing the chief points of difference and the relative marginal notes are as follows, the words underlined being thus marked in the copies of the ' Propositions '.

[Article 5.]   'And to avoid all jealousies indirect dealing and future difference which may happen: the principalls of each partie shall meet and confer together at Bantam and other places of the Indies and agree of a moderate price as shalbe thought meet to give for Pepper. And to that end certayne sufficient men shalbe appointed by consent of both parties to buy the same which being so bought shalbe *divided equally to each partie a moiety.*'

'5. Upon this article we breake for the Hollanders will not agree to a division, nor our merchants have it otherwise.'

[Article 6.]   'In the Isles of the Moluccas, Banda and Amboyna, the Companie shall by mutuall consent, be so ordered that the Company of England shall partake *an half portion* of all the trade as well in the Commodities to be brought together and those to be sold; as in the fruites and merchandize there to be bought and exported.   And those of the United Provinces shall have the other moiety.'

'In this we shalbe content with the 1/3 part.'

*   *   *   *   *

[Article 20.]   'And for the Forts and Garrisons to be continued and mayntayned, in the Isles of the Moluccas, Banda and Amboyna, serving for the common assurance of the Commerce, they and for so many of them shalbe appointed and continued as shalbe thought fitt and necessary by the Councell of Defence of both Companies. And the forts *on both sides shalbe divided* according to the respective proportions of the trade and . . . of *both* (each) Companies and shalbe accordingly holden and mayntayned.'

'In this we shall yield to the Hollanders to keepe their owne fortes.'

·

1619.   **Discours anent the Union of the**   *Gibson MSS. II, No.*
                E.I. traders of England and [the   *146.*
                Low Countries].[1]

Begins : 'The Directors of the companie of Lowe Contry marchants trading into the East Indies, having seene a certain writing which came from the English merchants tradinge into the said Indies . . . they undertake to further as followeth : "First that it is impossible and therefore not to bee gratified to make a common Capital : betweene the two Companyes,"' etc. (11 pp.)

c. 1625.   **[Remembrances] for Mr. Murray.[2]**   *Gibson MSS. Vol.*
                                             XIII, MS. 941,
                                             No. 99.

1. 'His Majesty wellwishing to the Duke of Savoy[3] his ambition to have been King of the Romans—falling in so unfortunate a conjuncture. Which by the surprisall of Comte Mansfels[4] papers at his defeate the freedom his Majesty used in confidence with the Marquis? Tornelli, and the suppositions of Sir Isaak Wake[5] his making Heydelberg his way to Turin may be well presumed to have taken winde, and indeed but the Spanish Ambassador and a servant of King Ferdinand's have not obscuredly signified so much to me.

2. 'His Majesties Princely, and our memorable labours in settling the East India trade between his subjects, and the States of the low Countryes, and underhand abhetting of the new erected Company for the West Indies as is conceyved in the world and I can assure you doth crampe the Spaniards at the heart.'

Endorsed : 'For Mr. Murray. The Spaniards exceptions against His Majesty.' (1 p.)

1645-46,   **E[dward Montagu, Earl of] Man-**   *Cod. Chart. in fol.*
20 March.   **chester, Speaker of the House of**   *MS. 711, No. 6*
                Peers pro tem, to Mr. [Walter]   *(p. 1).*
                Strickland, Resident [for the Parlia-
                ment] with the States General of the
                United Provinces.

'The Parliament of England having caused declaration to be made ordering that Justice be duly administered touching the restitution of two ships belonging to the States of the United Provinces and their merchants, and earnestly demanding that the States be mindful of the damages sustained by the Subjects of this Kingdom, as in particular by William Courten Esquire on account of the loss of his ship bearing the name of *Bon-Esperance*, of London, with his goods and merchandize amounting to a very considerable sum. And since the East India Company of the States of the United Provinces has

---

[1] The above description does not appear at the head of the original, but only in the Catalogue of 1812, the word Scotland being by an oversight or misprint, substituted for Low Countries.

[2] Probably Thos. Murray, Secretary to Charles I. when Prince. Cf. *Cal. S. P. Dom. Chas. I.,* [July] 1625, p. 78. 'Remembrances for Mr. Murray, being representations to be made by him to the King.'

[3] Charles-Emmanuel I (1562-1630).

[4] Ernest de Mansfeld (1585-1626).

[5] Ambassador to Savoy and Venice, 1615-30 : he was in Turin in 1624.

seized these, as appears by a declaration of the 15th of August, 1645, and afterwards by the care and diligence taken to advance a matter of this sort, which so greatly concerns the honour of the Nation, and the rights of its subjects ; so that I can in no wise doubt [the same]; and can do no less (after having considered the humble and earnest petition of the said Mr. Courten) than recommend to you by these words the just, but none the less rigorous condition, as it may be termed, and declare that you are to see to the progress thereof with the States, as being on the spot, and I rest entirely assured in the care you will take of the matter and the conduct thereof, in which this House also has full confidence : and not being commanded to inform you of aught else for the present.

'[I am]
' Your Good Friend
'*Signed* E. MANCHESTER,

' Speaker of the House of Peers or Lords of England, pro tem. London, 20 March 1645—'

(French, 2 pp.)

1647, 9 Oct.	**Copy of the King's Letter (dated from Hampton Court)** to the States General respecting the claims of William Courten for damage suffered in 1643 in the East Indies and Mauritius, for the *Bonne Esperance*, and *Henry Bon Adventure*.	*Cod. Chart. MS. 711, No. 6, p.* [2]-[4].

Not in *Court Minutes* or *English Factories*.   (Latin, 1½ pp.)

1647, 9 Oct.	**Copy of the King's Letter to William, Prince of Orange** (his son-in-law), requesting his support of William Courten's claim at the approaching Assembly of the Dutch E.I. Co. at Amsterdam.	*Ms. 711, No. 6,* [*p.* 4, 5].

Not in *Court Minutes* or *English Factories*.   (French, 1 p. and 2 lines.)

1647, 9 Oct.	**Copy of the King's Letter to Resident at Boswell, The Hague.** Relating to W. Courten's Claim touching the *Bonne Esperance* and *Henry Bon Adventure*.	*Ibid.* [*p.* 6-9].

Not in *Court Minutes* or *English Factories*.   (French, 3 pp. and 4 lines.)

1648, 1 Oct.	**Attachment by Jonas Abeel, as Attorney of Sir Paul Pindar, of the sum of £5,500** transferred to him by William Courten, being part of his claim relating to the *Bonne Esperance* and the *Henry Bonaventure*.	*Ibid.* [*p. 9*].

' Mr. Jonas Abeel in the quality of Attorney of Sir Paul Pindar, Knight of the City of London, who has an action and transfer from William Courten Esquire of London, attaches under the Directors of the East India Company whatsoever they shall be obliged to give to the forementioned William Courten either by Liquidation or by agreement to be made with him, on account of two vessels, the one named the *Bonne Esperance* and the other *Henry Bonaventure*, together with the merchandize wherewith the said ships were laden, and this for a sum of 5,500 pounds Sterling, so that the said sum may be paid to the claimant in the said quality, before any portion thereof be repaid to the said Courten or to any person on his behalf; And this by virtue of a transfer thereof which has been made and of the writ which has been issued to the said Directors.

'By me undersigned Notary 1st of October, 1645.

'*Signed* Goosen Daniellz Bode'

(Copy.)   (French, 1 p.)

1648, 18 Nov.	**Renewal of the above Attachment by Jonas Abeel** through Willem Janssen Bode of Amsterdam.	*Ibid.* [*p. 10*].

(French, 1 p.)

1660, 24 Sept.	**[Daniel] O'Neal, (Groom of the bedchamber), to King Charles II [from the Hague]**, reporting *inter alia* an interview with De Witt, his presentation of credentials and letters to Mons. Bererens, proposing a loan to the King and a request that the regicide refugees should be delivered to English justice. The Burgomaster of Amsterdam and Mr. de Witt express their readiness to further the loan and to serve the King.	*Tenison Coll. MS. 646, No. 1*

[Printed in Japikse, *De Verwikkelingen*, etc., App., p. II.] Cf. *S. P. Dom. Charles II*, 6 Sept., 1660, p. 259 : 'Mr. O'Neale is sent to the King for the Princess of Orange who is to come direct to England without taking France in her way.'

1693, 12 May [—5 Dec., 1693?]	**Journal[1] of Events at Fort St. George [relating to prisoners there, the actions of Agent Higginson** and the charges against Elihu Yale, etc.]. (42½ pp.)	*Gibson MSS. Vol. IX, MS. 937, No. 6* [*p. 1.*]

'Fort St. George, May 12th, 1693.

'And In whom there is noe guile as yet found, these gentlemen were President Higginson's Prisoners, who having used all his arts and Westindian measures to persuade or terryfye them to some confession and charge against President Yale, but in vaine, lay'd about to finde some crimes against the poore men to authorize his confineing them, but in [this] as the reast, his evill Genius has failed him: however mighty threats and perpetual confinement were the days cordiall sent them, which at [last] work't its designed effect,

---

[1] It is impossible to abstract this long involved document. A section has been copied verbatim in order to show the character of the whole.

which was a Petition and Piscash to him for their Release, and procured a Promise of suddaine Enlargment upon bails; but this could not be performed with that expediditon but that the watchful Judge by his argus ey'd emissarys had intelligence of it and wanting his fleece too was pleased to putt a stop to the proceeding, and by vertue of his power the poore mistaken men remaine still in limbo, and are given to understand if his purss has a wolfe int too, it must be fedd, and manque New Englands power, there they must lye (which greats not a little) least their liberty should inflame the government a Just and far [? fair] pre [? rogative] for imprisoning innocents.

'The next is Rango Chitty formerly spoken off, who ere the Judgment in the Cunnanwar cause was read had liberty on bails, p. 2. which cost him as it is credibly reported, 1000 pagodas, and to befriend him had only 20 pagodas mulct layd on him by Judgment, and that only to make their art seeme lawfull, when as there is not the least law or Justice of Equity int, the poorer be[ing] whole ignorant, nay the whole business and all concerned are termed defendants : evidently wronged and abused, there not being one word of truth in the whole evidence, the shamed wittnesses now sorrowfully repenting of action, being moste of them, now they are growne useless tooles, layde aside and discarded from serving as the Company's merchants. And poor honest Rango, notwithstanding his soe severely paying for his liberty is noe more than a Prisoner to his house and all oportunity watcht (a very visitt to his ould master President would doe it) to reafleece him or any else they know to have mony, and it is the mighty and Just business these worthy Commissioners are sent out to manage, all trade or indeed its very thoughts being layd aside for which they have a very convincing argument, this want of mony, and if their Shipps be laden home, it must be by means of their unjust exaction and heavy Customes added to their worse than Robberys (could I find a name fort) committed on the goods and Estates of their servants and free traders here, nay the ravenous beasts are not satisfied with seazing their estates, but inhumanely detaine their Persons from returning to their due allegiance.

' Ancoh, whome we have had occasion to mention formerly, being after Judgment remanded to Prison, paid the 500 pagodas bribe before mentioned in hopes to meet a large abatement of the Sum condemned in by Judgment of Court, but all the buoyant hopes and flattering promises of the Just distributor of the laws had raised in p. 3. him, vanished to attoms, it being the poore broken backt man (I mean broaken as to Estate) if now nothing remained towards the Judges purchasing of his freedome but a speedy dischard [sic] of what was awarded the Company and of which there would be no abatement, that the Judges cordiall advice to him was with all expedition to dispatch the affaire that he'd doe well, could he not raise the mony other ways, to pawne and sell his mother's house, his wife, his owne and child's jewells : and then, being freed, he on the word of a Judge and a gentleman, should meet noe further molestation or trouble.   The poor long Imprison'd wretch grew extreme mallancolly at the newse and heartily wished his bribe ungiven, and finding noe amending but payment or a Prison, followed the cunning advice about himself and family, being wholy reduced to begging by it, and pawnd all the remains and more than he and his could call his owne to advance the Sums, and as by the Judge directed, imployed Captain Metcalfe to owne [?] and deposit the money, which was noe sooner paid and the poore fellow returning from the payment as he thought to his longed for liberty, but was passing through the Court de garde, by a warrant granted Mr Frazer by his [? Junior] Defender: the Judge arested in an action of schandell against said Scotch beast, which Schandall was his declaring the truth on examination, and that the voluntary confession of Said Fraser's owne servant, being the account of severall cheats committed by him in his severall Imploys of the Godowne and Custome house, but his actions are not to be inquired into, the toole being yet of use to them, since upon occasion he [would] swear to he knows not what, being a thing (worse than brute) made a mere compound of ignorance, arrogance and Envy. Tis therefore his servant is frightened into a recantation and turnes

p. 4. the Poynt upon Coalligo [?] Chitty, an able reputable merchant; and Ancoh who after the ould strayne, declares they forst him to the confession; and that very word, bare as it is is sufficient evidence in any cause whatever; and tho' the fellow could not tell what manner of force, whether threates, imprisonment, etc., were used, yet force it must be, and his masters confining him 3 days in his own chamber within the Fort till he had terrified him to said Recantation was noe force at all, on which barefaced base [? pretence] the poore fellowes were, when their hopes were at height, remanded to prison and all bails refused by said Fraser.

'The Judge then tax't by Mr Metcalfe of breach of promise, warded that without abuse, declaring hee could not alter the course of Justice, and thus were [?] the poore deluded people battled [?] to their utter ruin, and we'll leave them in prison till a new collected Some and lusty bribe lifte them through or till Heaven's Justice frees them from this unf [? infamy] of persecution.

'Having omitted entring in its due place a most materiall and singular instance of the unparraled equity, Justice and Candour of the Comissary, his Councell and Company created Court of Admiralty, I shall begin a distance out of sight and beyond my owne certaine knowledg laying foundation, it being what account I could gett from the Captain of his Transactions till his arrivall here; wherefore to omitt the long Story of his well managed enga-[ge]ment with a brisk and powerfull enemy, I shall begin where we concluded, which was with his purchasing of the shipp and pawning his mate and purser for the payment, thereby saving the

p. 5. lives of his whole ship's company, the French having by consultation resolved, would he not give them the summe demanded for the disabled ship, and on that condition too (which were he should engage never to restore her to the Company or former proprietor) to sink her and men too with themselves, being to numerous a Company to take in 60 prisoners; which consideration obliged the Captain for securing their lives who had bravely [? deffended] their little world till she had lost her polesand [? motion] to agree to all their articles, and sent both purser and mate on board them, Comitting himself and Company in a wounded vessell mastless to the mercy of the boundless Ocean, having neither compass or other mathematical Instrument, but what was broake and disabled, and nothing left to direct them but Providence, which happily brought them safe to poynt de Gala on the Island of Zelone where he mett civill usage and had from Capat. Cento Coderden [?] an account of the Government withall its appendixes acahracto [?] I believe sufficient to have encouraged any man (but him who thought Renowne and Honor sufficient guarde) at that distance to have swept out of their clutches from them our man of war ; made the best of way to gaine the coast and fell in with Trincumbar the 18th March, whence he immediately dispatch't advices hither and he intended to be here himself with all expedition. But in the Interim his Ship[s] company, whether out of a wandring, lazy, vagabond fancy common to such builds of men, or from encoradgement received from hence the last I am [?] to give most credit too,they being immediately on their arrival taken into protection and declaration against their Captain greedily

p. 6. imbibed and believed, even to the height, if [? that] the man, his ship and all was in Resolution condemned ere soon on board ; having after the best manner he could, reman[n]d his ship, he put to Sea and arrived that port the 17th of Aprill, mett from the Generall a very could welcome, and was required to deliver the lead on board him, it being the Company's, as allsoe to render an account of what of it he had disposed off, which his runaway Sailors had informed off. He civilly answered it was true he had when left England a quantity [?] of lead on board him belonging to the Honourable Company, but that unfortunately near the Cape, mett a flagg man of France, who after 8 hours engagement, took and made prize of him and after having riffled her, taken and distroyed whatever they pleased, they obliged him to purchase her for his owne account. He had done soe and given hostages for the payment of their demand. For his owne account he had accordingly drawne bill for the amount on President of Suratt, and by letter advized him he would allow usuall Interest for the same, whereby he thought, and by the law of nations the shipp and what they pleased to leave on board her became a lawfull part of his Estate. This pleased not the ould gentileman who tould him the lead was the Company's and they must have it, and if spoake the Ship his he'd then declared him an Interloper and as such would seaze him. He tould him he might doe his pleasure but it was a Company's Ship on that side the Cape and was there taken.

'19th. When noe argument could work [on] Captain Freak for

p. 7. disowning his Ship *James* and lead, then they went to act the ould tricke over againe, layd an Attachment on the Ship and an Arrest on him, who gave as baile Mr John Pitt, and prepared for his defence.

'In this Juncture the Judge (who has noe great stomack to manage the cause) advised the Captain to draw up his proposalls to the Generall, etc., which accordingly did, offering to deliver up the lead to them at such a price, provided they'd give a bond to pay it in England if the law gave it to be his, and they would advance him so much mony at the usuall rates to reafitting his Shipp, if they would secure him his men and lade him home in January. But they wholly denyed the main article and would not part with more money than the Charterparty 600 dollars, not a fifth part enough to fitt him with guns and ammunition according to contract with Company, by which wile they intend wholly to disable him from proceeding and doe therefore the more easily agree to the other articles : but they broak off the designe and now for law.

21

'Severall Cour[t] days are past without any progress made to purpose in Captain Freak's affaire, and till the 13th of May noe part of the intended Judgment apeared, when after a nott short dispute, a preface to what was the consequence, a Judgment was produced and the Defendant by it cast, the lead being condemned to be the Company's, which occasioned the Captains dislike of Court's proceeding and apeald home, which putt the Judges upon his ould declaration that his judgment was immutable and admitted noe appeal to any court in Christendome, which occasioned the Captain saying he gave noe Credit to that; and he hoped at home to meet

p. 8.   with Justice and Equity. That [?] I presume, nettled his Honor, who on the Captain's making way to be gone, passionately declared the world was come to a fine pass when every pittyfull fellow took liberty to prate and censure, which the Captain overhearing, the Judge in some heat for answer that it was true Mr. Dolben had more power her[e], but in England he was every day in the week and every way as good a man as himself; for which his presumption he is immediately ordered to be disarmed, but would not deliver his sword unless to an officer. The Captain of the Guard, coming, he gave it to him, and was then with a file of men guarded to the Trunk, a prison for base criminalls, but on consideration, kept upon the Guard, and afterwards to a small goedowne in the Fort where he remaned till the [blank], when he gave a protest. And in conclusion, the Judge and he were to meet and forgive each other, which perform'd, the Captain was unwittingly persuaded to give order for delivering the lead, which should not have done till execution was served. Those their unjust severitys and overreaching fetches doe disturb the good Captain to the measure that am of opinion it will runne him into distemper which may eand in his death and gaine his enemys the poynt.

'May 4. Mr. Samuel Owen, an ingeniouse, industriouse gentleman, but because well and deservedly cahractarized by President Yale, must be noe favourite of the times [?]. These Directors, endeavouring by all Possible means to finde some flaw that may authorize them to

p. 9.   discard him the service or empty his purse have, since they cannot squeeze him on Portanovan account, found an extraordinary just pretence to doe it by the way of Vizagapatam where he was sent in [16]92, by order of President and Council, to take the goedowne into his charge and finish that factory's books, as allsoe to inspect into affaires, by advice but illy and deceitfully managed by Mr. Daniell Duboyes. Not long after his arrivall there, the disaffected Councill, by private letters [sought] to slight and neglect Mr Owen as one sent without their consents, which the little Sophistes, glad to have such an oportunity, immediately put to execution, Jelouse that his wicked action would be discovered (as indeed a great many of them were) by him, from the beginning grew such a fewd of Mr. Duboise, as pretended fearfull of his carcase, took occasion, when Mr. Owen was abroad, to secure his castile to himself, shutting the gates, and at the portcullis planting a great gunne to keep off or battile this his formidable enemy and experienced souldier like when had taken the town fell to plunder [? thereupon] felloniously breaking upon said Mr. Owen's lodgings, seasing his papers, goods and chattele, with all his owne and other people's cases entrusted with him, of which some part was never returned. The advice of this Allarumd Mr. Owen, who being kept out of the Factory, p. 10. was forst to make Mr. Ramsden's house his sanctuary. In a short time came the Second, Mr. Fockett, forst to it by Mr. Duboise, whose [? act] is unwarrantable and which were noe longer to be swallowed, and said Mr. Fockett gave under his hand many accusations too black and idious [hideous] for my relation; many and daily accusations came against him, of which Mr. Owen punctually advized hither and were as confidently denyed by the other, soe that Mr. Symon Houlcombe was ordered downe to inspect that business, where he not only found all to be true that Mr. Owen had advised of, but added abundantly to it. But now to instance their Justice for that gentileman's good services: it was from the time of his and Mr. Fockett being turned out of the factory to Mr. Houlcomb's arrival some 6 or 8 months, during which time for themselves, Peons, etc. were necessitated to be at monthly charge, which was repaid Mr. Owen by Mr. Houlcombe and Councell; but now those just men, because it was not actually expended at the factory, force said Mr. Owen and Fockquett to pay the money, the amount 500 rupees.

*   *   *   *   *

'25 May. Vinketty, a servant of the Judges, was remanded from his larger prison of Choultry . . .

p. 11. 'The case of Mrs Catherine Nicks [? and] Anne Poddans . . .

'28th. President Yale received advice from Mr. William How supercargo of the [*George*] that was fallen in with the shoare to the] North of Onore River . . . and was there stopt by them . . .

'29th. About 8 at night Mr. Thomas Yale had notice that Mr. James Wheeler had followed a Pacquett directed sealed to Mr. [Edward Fleetwood and obliged by Mr.] Rd. Heathfield to open it before him, when he found and [? handed] a Pacquett to President Yale and a letter to his Brother, which being contrary to law or justice, Mr. Thos. Yale supposing it the single envyouse act of Mr. Wheeler wrote him the following noat:

'"Monr. Wheeler.

'"I am informed that Corporall Self has bin pleased to seaze on a letter of myne, but by what prerogative you do or what law allows it is beyond my knowledge, therefore returne my advise as you found it or believe me I shall not dye in your debt.

'"Yours T. Y."

*   *   *   *   *

'30th [June]. [Remarks on] the Company's ship *Anapurra* [and her passengers].

*   *   *   *   *

'July. Sometime after my aforesaid Protest which has reference to the unjust action entered against me, the Judge ordered the following declaration to be made against me. . . .

*   *   *   *   *

'Saturday. Mr. Thomas Yale confined prisoner. . . .'

1695, **Dr. Humphrey Prideaux to Arch-** *Gibson MSS. Vol.*
27 March. **bishop Tenison at the House of** *V, MS. 933, No. 1.*
     Lords.

'My Lord, Having while in London on further information which I gott there of the present state of our Factorys and Plantations in the East Indys, corrected and enlarged the Paper I formerly put into your Graces hands concerning that matter, I doe here send it inclosed to you. When the business of Parliament is over, I hope your Grace will have time to consider it, and alsoe opportunity to doe therein what you shall in your wisdome think fittest. The Bishop of Salisbury acquainted me that he was the person who transacted for Mr. Boyle all that was attempted by him in this pious designe and he can best informe your Grace how far it then went and what made it to miscarry. I find the Company hath over lash'd in the amount they give of the number of their subjects in the Indies, but your Grace hath their own printed book and this makes the argument against them that having soe great a number of souls by their own confession under their Government they have done nothing to instruct them in the means whereby they may be saved.'

The remainder of the letter has no connection with East India. 1½pp. Enclosing *Gibson V. No. 2*, see *infra*.

1695,
March.

'**The English East India Company are possessed of in India** 1° The Fort St. George and the City of Madras adjoining thereto in the Golfe of Bengala in which are an hundred thousand Familys.

Gibson MSS. Vol. V, MS. 933, No. 2.

'2° The City and Island of Bombay in the Golfe of Cambaya in which are fifty thousand Familys.

'3° The Fort St. David on the coast of Coromandell which is said to be as populous as Bombay, and therefore must be reckoned alsoe to contain about Fifty thousand Familys, and this last beeing a place exceedingly well situated both for health and Trade as being accomodated with a navigable River and a very good Castle for the defence of the inhabitants is dayly a growing and like in a short time to become as popular as Madras soe that in those 3 places only besides the Forts which the Company have in the Islands for the Security of their pepper Trade are two hundred thousand familys which we may well compute at a Million of Souls allowing five to a family and all these are Subject to such Laws for Life and Goods as the Company by virtue of their Charter shall think fitt to impose upon them. All which (excepting what relates to Fort St. David which is a place lately bought by this Company) is acknowledged in their owne printed papers which at several times they have published in their defence 1st against the interlopers and after when questioned in Parliament.

'These Million of Souls under the Subjection of the English East India Company are either Jews Mahometans Portuguise or Gentues but the bulk of them are Gentues. (Soe our Merchants call the Heathen Indians.)

'The Mahometans have in these places their Mosques the Jews their Synagogues the Gentues their Pagodas or Temples for Heathen worship, but there is not as much as a Chappell for the true Religion of Jesus Christ in any of them except at Fort St. George (where lately a church hath been built for the factory by the care and piety of Mr. Mathers [Masters] then President without any help and Countenance from the Company in order thereto); in other places the Roome they eat in contains their congregation : or is there any the least care taken by the Company to propagate the Gospell among the Natives, although it be their secular interest as well as their spiritual to make as many of their Subjects as they can of their owne Religion that soe they may be the firmer united to them, but on the contrary they are soe carelesse and impiously unconcerned in this matter that they permitt the Popish priests to come into the familys of the English setled there and pervert their servants and slaves to their idolatrous superstition which is there practised in the grossest manner in the world.   The Gentues who make the bulk of the inhabitants of these 3 places above mentioned are an ingenious civilised polite people who know letters and are well skilled in many Arts as their Manufactures imported hither abundantly demonstrate and for the most part of good Moralls which their Religion the most refined piece of Heathenism ever yet in the world most strongly oblidgeth them unto and therefore they are thus far the better prepared to hearken to what reasons may [?]be offered to them for Christianity and the easyer disposed to imbrace it.

' The Dutch East India Company doe maintain in The Indys about 30 Ministers for the Converting of these poor Infidells under their Dominions and the further instructing of those already converted, to each of which they allow an assistant to help them in Catechising and other inferior offices of the Ministry by whose labours they have converted many hundred thousands to the true Christian faith, and for the better propagating of it had publick schools in most of their Towns, for the benefitt of the natives, and have lately erected a College or University in the Island of Ceylon in which one place only (which is not the tenth part of their Dominions in the Indys) they have about eighty thousand converted Indians upon the Roll that are Communicants and they are farther at the charge to print Bibles, Catechisms and many other books in the Indian languages, which they annually distribute among the Converted natives for their better instruction in the Christian Religion.   In all which particulars they expend near twenty thousand pound per annum.

p. 9.

' The Dutch East India Company doe further take care that all places where they have any factory and all ships which they send to India be provided with able Ministers well encouraged to preach the Gospel and administer the Sacraments.   But the English East India Company are so negligent herein that although they have on the Island of St. Helena a Fort and Towne in which are severall hundred of inhabitants all English, they allow them noe Minister and consequently there being no preaching of the word of God or administration of the Sacraments among them, for wont [sic] hereof those poor people are degenerated to that degree of barbarity as to be reckoned the vilest and most wicked of any of our shipping met within all their whole voyage to the Indys.   The English Company before their late War with the Mogull did indeed maintain Chaplains for their Factorys at Surat, Hugeley, Bombay and Fort St. George, and lately had one also at Fort St. David, but allowed them soe ill and treated them so badly that they could doe but little service under those discouragements, but at present they have noe Chaplain at all [in] many of their Towns or Factorys but at Fort St. George only, and he being under the

Checks and Frownes of a President lately sent thither who had his birth and education in New England and is deeply bigotted to the Religion of that Country, it is expected that it will not be long ere the Church of England Chaplain be found to yield up his church and pulpitt to the Independent preacher which the President carryed thither with him.   And as to their ships, although they carry most on end great number of men and are sometimes eight or ten months on the voyage, as well going as returning, are yet all that time for the most part without preaching prayers or sacraments, seldom ever having any chaplain on board unlesse accidentally such as are going to or returning from their Factory in the Indys.

'Its evident that the English East India Company have of late in a short time from great wealth and power faln to nothing while the Dutch East India Company grow and thrive and are now arrived to that power as seen to equall in strength riches and extent of Dominion the greatest potentates in those parts of the world scarce excepting the Mogul himselfe.

'If we will examine into the Cause why the blessing of God . . .'

[There follow 9 proposals for the establishments of Churches, Schools, etc., a Seminary to be erected in England, etc., and that the orders and regulations which the Dutch East India Company have made be procured from Holland.   Also that a Choice of wise men in London be made to direct and carry out the whole.]

? 17—   **Petition of the Merchants of Lon-**   *Gibson MSS. Vol.*
(not dated).   **don trading into the East Indies,**   *XIII, MS. 941,*
         to the House of Lords, touching the   *No. 136.*
         subscription of £2,000,000 and begging
         'to be heard by their Counsel at the
         Bar of this Hon. House against the
         said bill before any further proceeding'.

                    Signed: R. BLACKBOURNE, Secty.

        Reference is made to a General Court on the 20th inst.   (2¾ pp.)

? 1700.   **'A Memento to the East India**   *Gibson MSS. Vol.*
         Companies, or an Abstract of a   *X, MS. 938, No.*
         Remonstrance, Presented to the   *21.*
         House of Commons, by the East India
         Company, in the Year 1628.   With
         some few Animadversions thereon.'

        Printed in London, 1700, 25 pp. small 8vo. Cf. British Museum (Press mark) 1029, a. 31.

        The 'Animadversions' are criticisms of the 'Remonstrance', the chief points of which are abstracted seriatim, each group being followed by the critical Animadversion. The first 'Animadversion' may be taken as a summary of the whole : 'But our Traders now, instead of supplying Foreign Nations with these *India* Wares they furnish more especially our own Nation with them, to be consumed at Home, which must prove a quite contrary effect than in those days' to the great injury of English manufactures, the silk manufactures, and ultimately that of silk and increased unemployment.

1700.   **T. S.   The Profit and Loss of the**   *Ibid. No. 22.*

East India Trade, Stated ; and humbly offered to the Consideration of the present Parliament.

Printed pamphlet, 8vo, 24 pp.   Cf. British Museum, 100, n. 46.

The Arguments and Opinions are very similar to those of the Animadversions in No. 21.

---

c. 1705-12.   Chaplains to the East India Company.   *Gibson MSS. Vol. XIII, MS. 941, f. 95.*

'That the East India Chaplains have 200£ per annum salary, payable in India, and to commence from the Ships breaking ground in River, and to be continued till their returne to England or death.

'To have the same allowance of diet, etc., as the old Company formerly granted.

'Their passage free from payment to the Ship, or Commander. The Company to make them a present of 20£, as formerly for necessaries in their voyage.

'That according to the diversions in the late Charter, every Chaplaine to any Ship of 500 Tunn or upward, shall have 60£ a yeare Salary and enjoy equall priviledges with the chiefe Mate of the same Ship,

'That the Chaplaine residing in the Factories take place next to the second in Council of the superior Factories, and have the like treatment in their passage.'   (1 p.)

1712,   [? Bartholomew Ziegenbalg] from   *Gibson MSS. Vol.*
20 June.   Tranquebar giving an account   *V, MS. 933, fols.*
of the Danish Mission Church   *110-13.*
there.

Two languages were necessarily in use and consequently two churches, the ' Ecclesiola Dannulica, *vulgo* Malabarica ', and the ' Ecclesiola Lusitanica ', i.e. Portuguese Church. An account is given of the Missionary schools, and the teaching there.   (Latin, 4 pp.)

1712,   Bartholomew Ziegenbalg and Er-   *Ibid. fol. 114.*
23 Sept.   nest Grundler to [? the Society for
the Propagation of Christian Knowledge].

Thanks for letters received, and for printing presses and accessories, donations of money, and Library materials.   Statistics of Church members.   (Latin, 7 pp.)

1713,   Bartholomew Ziegenbalg and John   *Ibid. fol. 113.*
9 Jan.   Ernest Grundler to [S.P.C.K.]

News of the Church.   (Latin, 3½ pp.)

1712-13,   Unsigned letter to [not from] **Mr.**   *Ibid. No. 116.*
10 Jan.   Boehm, relating chiefly to China, with
a short mention of the Tranquebar
Mission.   (4 pp.)

1713,   **Bartholomew Ziegenbalg and John**   *Ibid. fol. 111.*
11 Jan.   **Ernest Grundler to E. Newman.**
'Translated from the Original in High
Dutch.'

Contains besides other matters relating to Tranquebar, Thermometrical Observations for the year 1712.   'The 28th of Dec. last, N.S., we had here early in the morning an Eclipse of the Sun.   It began about four and lasted till seven . . .'

On fol. 112 is inserted an old engraving of 'Tranquebar in Ostindien'.   (3 pp.)

1712[13],   **George Lewis (Fort St. George) to**   *Ibid. No. 115.*
1 Feb.   **Henry Newman.**

'I have in my last Acknowledged the Receipt of Several Letters from your hands this last year both by the *Marlborough* and the *Jane.*

'The Society for propagating of Christian Knowledge, whose pious undertakings I beseech God to prosper, have been at a Considerable Charge, I find, to send out Books and other Materials to carry on the end of their Institution.   What came on the *Marlborough* for the use of the Gentlemen Missionarys at Tranquebar and directed to Mr. Jennings and myself came safe, and were delivered to the persons they were designed for.   What came upon the *Jane* were part saved and part lost, as doubtless the Gentlemen of the Mission will inform you.   The Box of Books for a Library in this place and another for a Library in Bengall by the *Marlborough* were both received, And I return the worthy Society my humble thanks for their Charity.

'I have often wondered with my self that in so many Yeares that We have been possessed of large Plantations, Settlements etc., in the East and West Indies, that no such thing hath been set on foot, and I bless God that there hath at length appeared such a truly pious and publick spirit of Christianity in the Gentlemen of our Nation, and I give the Society my thanks for the Honour they have done me in choosing me one of their Corresponding Members.

'As to Converting the Natives in the Dominions of the Rajahs and the Great Mogul, I believe it may be done in either, without Notice

p. 2.   taken, provided we do not sound a Trumpet before us.   In the Mogull's Dominions I believe Eight parts in Ten in most of the Provinces are Gentios and he never troubles his head what opinions they embrace.   But to tamper with his Musslemen is not safe.

'But to give you my Sentiments in this matter, I think we ought to begin at home, for there are Thousands of People, I may say some hundreds of thousands, who live in the Settlements and under the Jurisdiction of the Rt. Honble. Company at Bombay, Fort St. Davids, Fort St. George, Callcutta in Bengall, on the West Coast, etc., who may be converted to Christianity without interfering with any Country Government whatsoever: and while We have so large a harest at home, Let us first gather in that and then it will be time enough to look abroad.

'The way to Effect it in my Opinion will be to sett up so many Schools and Hospitals, Specially the last, to bring up children in, as there can be found funds for that use.   By hospitals I mean such foundations where the Children are maintained wholly by the House, for the Poor in these parts are very numerous, and those so poor that in a time of scarcity (which often happens) they are forced to sell their children in great Numbers, and sometimes themselves ; and such Miscreants at such a time would be glad of a Hospitall to receive them. Besides, there are at all times numbers of poor people who will part with their Children to any one that will bring them up. And of those who are able to bring up their children at their own charge, there are many that, for the sake of having them taught for nothing, would send them into any good School, and those who are trained up in the Christian Religion from their Youth, it is to be hoped may prove good Christians in their Age. But for those, who are grown up in their Idolatry, I conceive that in the main no great good can be done upon them. For as to the Rich and Great there are so many obstructions to hinder them from changing of their Faith, and thereby loosing of their Cast, That it is easier for a Camell, etc., for the moment they loose their Cast they can no longer Converse, Eat or Drink with any of their Cast or Kindred ; nor indeed of any other Cast. So that such must in a true, Literal Sence forsake Wife, Children, houses, Lands, Friends, etc., which is a degree of Faith few or none of them ever could arrive to.

p. 3. 'And as to the poorer Sort, and such as have no Cast to value themselves upon, they are so vile a People, that for a little Rice they will be of any Religion and for as small a Consideration leave it again. And it is out of these that the Roman Priests chiefly make their Proselytes : Whereby it is come to pass that the Christians of these Countrys, I mean Natives, are the Scoundrell part of Mankind and perhaps hardly a viler Generation in the world : and a Man had better have to do with an Infidel, Heathen, Turk, or anything, than with them.

'I remember some yeares agoe Governor Pitt was pleased to ask me to give my opinion how this Garrison might be brought to Consist of all Protestants. I delivered him my opinion in writing, which he thought fit to Communicate to the Company ; and their Answer was they would Consider of it. The Substance of it in Short was this : That the Company should erect two large Hospitals or Nurserys, one for Boys, another for Girls, to bring them up in the Protestant Religion. And if such Schools or Nurserys were set up, then it would be of great use to have some Catechisms, Common Prayer Books and New Testaments, etc. printed in Portugueze, etc., for the use of those Nurserys : But untill that is done they can be but of little Benefitt in these parts. For who is there in all India that read and write Portugueze Except the Portugueze themselves, and they of the Politer sort. And I do declare that in all the time I lived in India, I do not remember ever to have known a Gentio, Mahometan, or one of any other persuasion, Except Christian, that pretended to write or read that Language. There is a kind of Lingua Franca or Jargon, call'd Portuguese, spoke in most of the Trading Towns on the sea coast, in which many of the Nations can so far Express themselves, as to be able to buy and Sell. But you must speak to them in their own Jargon, or you will not be understood.

'Thus Sir I have freely given you my Sentiments on this Important Affair. I beseech God to Bless the Venerable Society and to prosper them in all their pious undertakings, I am with a Sincere respect, Sir

'Fort St. George }
'February Imo 1712/13. }

'Your most humble Servant,
'Signed : GEORGE LEWIS.'

1713, 'Manuscripts à Tanequebar vec *Cod. Misc. 1026,*
3 Dec. **Tranquebar.'** Johann Berlin from *No. 7.*
Tranquebar, to Frau Manicken, Halle.

Account of his journey to India. (German, 2 pp.)

1713, **Johann Berlin from Tranquebar to** *Ibid. 953, No. 102.*
3 Dec. **H. Manicke.**

Account of natives, ' Gentues ' and Malabarese. (German, 1 p.)

1713, **John Chamberlayne to Archbishop**
21 Dec. **Tenison.**

Enclosing a letter from Mr. Newman about the Malabar Mission, which he hopes will appease his Grace's ' just Resentments of the Proceedings of the wel-meaning Men at Tranquebar, and suspend the Effects of it.' (1 p.)

1714, **Johann Berlin (Tranquebar) to Hr.**
12 Jan. **Elers.**

1713-14. **Letters from Tranquebar,** from Bar- *Ibid. 1099.*
tholomew Ziegenbalg, John Ernestus
Grundlar and other Missionaries chiefly
in German, and relating to the Mission
and personal matters.

(German, whole vol.)

RECORDS IN THE INDIAN RECORD OFFICES

BENGAL RECORD OFFICE

WE may merely note the unsuccessful attempts made from Agra in 1621 to start a factory or trading station in Patna, described in the *Indian Antiquary* for 1924, and Peter Mundee's Travels, Vol. 2, Hakluyt Society, as they did not concern Bengal primarily. The first regular English settlements were established in 1633, when factories were commenced at two points on the Orissa coast; at Hariharpur, near Cuttack, and at Balasore. The former was abandoned in 1662, but the latter was carried on until the port silted up in the eighteenth century. Early in 1651 a factory was started at Hugli, and some seven years later we find merchants stationed at Kasimbazar and Patna, while subsequently trade was extended to Dacca (about 1668) and Malda (1676). When the English were driven from Hugli by the Mughals in 1686 they attempted to find a new factory at Sutanuti (Calcutta) further down the river, but it was not until the conclusion of peace in 1690 that Job Charnoc was able to fix the English headquarters at that place, where the original Fort William was built a few years later.

Except for two brief periods of independence in 1650-61 and 1682-84, the Bengal factories remained an agency under the control of Madras down to 1700, when Sir Charles Eyre became the first President and Governor of Fort William. This continued to be the official style until the India Act of 1773 changed it into that of Governor-General of the Presidency of Fort William in Bengal.

Many letters to and from the Bengal factories during the seventeenth century will be found in the India Office Record Departments in (1) the *Original Correspondence Series*, (2) the *Company's Letter Books*, (3) also in the records relating to Madras. Some of the latter have recently been printed at Madras, *vide* the *Sundry Books, 1677-1788, 1680-81*, etc.

The separate factory records for Bengal relating to factories in the seventeenth century are as follows:

BALASORE

Diary and consultations, 1679-81; 1684-87 (1 vol.).

HUGLI

Diary and consultations: 1663-64; 1669-70; 1678-82 (3 vols.).
Copies of letters sent, 1672-75; 1677; 1678-82; 1684 (3 vols.).
Copies of letters received, 1671-72; 1677-80; 1682; 1686-87 (5 vols.).

KASIMBAZAR

Diary and consultations, 1676-80; 1681-85; 1701-33; 1736; 1737-46; 1748-59 (13 vols.).

DACCA

Diary and consultations, 1678; 1681-82; 1690-91; 1736-57; 1762-63 (5 vols.).

MALDA

Diary and consultations, 1680-82; 1684-85; 1690-93 (2 vols.).
The 1680-82 vol. has been published in the Journal of the Bengal Asiatic Society for 1918 (Vol. XIV, Nos. 1 and 2) under the editorship of Archdeacon Firmenger.

PATNA

Copies of letters sent, 1620-21.
Diary and consultations, 1680-81; 1683-85; 1744-47 (2 vols.).
Accounts and invoices, 1781-82 (1 vol.).
Narratives of the massacre in 1763 (1 vol.).

CALCUTTA

Diary and consultations, 1690-91; 1694-95; 1696-99; 1702-3; 1704-6; 1708 (4 vols.). The latter portion contains the proceedings of the Old Company's council only.
Copies of letters sent, 1690-91; 1692; 1693; 1695-98; 1699-1702; 1704-5 (4 vols.).
Copies of letters received, 1690; 1694-96; 1699-1701; 1702-4 (3 vols.).
With regard to the Bengal factories in general the following volumes in the Miscellaneous section of the Factory Records should be borne in mind :
Vol. 3.   Extracts from letters and consultations from the Coast and Bay, 1664-73, with three letters of 1680-81.
Vol. 3A.   Abstracts of letters from the Coast and Bay, 1676-1708.
Vol. 6.   Abstracts of letters received by the New Company from Surat, Masulipatam, Bengal, etc., 1699-1707.
Vol. 7.   Extracts from letters from Bombay, Madras, Bengal, etc., 1716-23.
Vol. 7A.   Abstracts of correspondence with Bengal, Madras, Bombay, St. Helena, Bencoolen, Mokha, and Aujengo, 1711-41.
Vol. 9 contains an account of the revenues of Calcutta.
Vol. 13.   Charges by Thomas Stiles against the agent at Balasore, 1669.
Vol. 14.   Diary of Streynsham Master in his inspection of the Masulipatam and Bengal factories, 1675-77.
Vol. 15.   Journal of Agent Hedges, 1681-88.
Vol. 26 contains accounts of the trade at Hugli, Balasore, Dacca, etc. (1676).
Vol. 27.   Journal and ledger of Boalia Factory, 1833-34.
Abstracts of earlier documents in the Factories series will be found in the *English Factories in India* (see p. 11).

I have not thought it necessary to give a detailed account of all the records relating to all the factories found in Bengal in the seventeenth century, as that would have swelled the list unduly.

I searched for seventeenth century records in the Bengal Record Office and the Imperial Record Department. Unfortunately, the quantity of such records is small.

The Persian records, preserved in the Bengal Record Office, belonging to the seventeenth century are comprised in Volumes I-XVIII and XX in a series known as ' Persian Sanads and Parwanas ' which dates back to the year 1612-14. The documents are copies of firmans, sanads, petitions, sale deeds, security bonds, statements, qabuliyats, dustuks, relating to the grant or settlement of lands ; the appointment of revenue and judicial officers and the supply and payment of troops in various districts of Bengal relating to the years 1624-1791.

The Sanads, etc., usually begin with a statement to the following effect : Copy of Sanad with the seal of (name and authority) with effect from (date). Be it known to the Mutasaddies, Qanungoes, Faujdars, Raiyats, and cultivators etc. of the present and future that (subject matter of Sanad follows). They are issued by the following authorities : 1. Asif Khan, Vazirulmulk. 2. Mir Zumla (Moazzam Khan). 3. Asif-ud-doulah (Asad Khan). 4. Asif-Jah, Nizam-ul-mulk. 5. Kamruddin Hussain Khan. 6. Asif Jah Abul Mansur Khan. 7. Ala-ud-doulah, Nasir-Jung-Zafer Khan. Nusari, *alias* Murshid-Kuli-Khan. 8. Shujahud-doulah, Asad-jung, Shujah-ud-din Muhammad Khan. 9. Ala-ud-doulah, Sarfaraz Khan. 10. Mahabit Jung, Alivazdi Khan. 11. Sarafud-doulah. 12. Mir Muhammad Zafar Khan. 13. Mir Muhammad Qasim Khan. 14. Najim-ud-doulah. 15. Saif-ud-doulah. 16. Mubarak-ud-doulah. 17. Nabar Muzaffar Jung, *alias* Muhammad Reza Khan.

The revenue records of the Company's administration comprise Persian records which are included in the series known as 'Persian Sanads and Parwanas '. They deal with the eighteenth, but not with the seventeenth century. Besides these, there are mixed Persian and Bengali records which comprise Vol. 19 in the series known as 'Persian Sanads and Parwanas ' containing copies in Persian and Bengali, of sale certificates (Barnamas) of grants to the purchasers of land, relating to the years 1764-71 and of Sanads of land granted by zamindars for the maintenance of temples relating to the years 1753-54. Students may pick up bits of information on the seventeenth century in the Persian Sanads comprised in five volumes.

IMPERIAL RECORD OFFICE

There are only two documents of importance in the Imperial Record Department which throw light on the seventeenth century. One is headed ' Letters from Courts '. It contains various letters by the Directors of the East India Company to their servants in India. The originals of these despatches are to be found in the India Office Record Department. The following letters will be found interesting :

Letters from Courts

1. Director to Job Charnoc, dated 5 January, 1680.

' We do judge that you had not right done you in not being placed chief at Casimbazar. We do accordingly hereby constitute and confirm our chief of that factory and of all our affairs, managed therein; and we hereby require Mr. Edward Littleton and all persons of our Councill and all other persons in our services to yield you assistance and due obedience.

' Your experience is great in those countrys, our opinion you will see is great of you our expectations proportionate, which we doubt not but you will fully answer. Signed: William Thompson, Governor.'

2. Another letter dated 19 March, 1601. To Council at Fort St. George. Refers to Sir William Langhorne.

' Who contrary to our Rules and Practice took out cash before his coming out of the Fort, which he had undertaken to pay unto our youths, being three thousand two hundred and thirty-four pagodas, together with the usual interest of other countries.' The letter also refers to Mr. Edward Littleton who had ' sent home for his own account by the last shipping some quantities of Bengal taffeties, the same as ours '. The Directors say they had better opinion of Littleton.

.3. Dated, London, 22 April, 1681. To Chief and Council at the Bay.

' We would have you send us full quantities of every sort of raw silk.' The despatch deals mainly with goods made in India.

' It is not necessary we should give you the reason of our orders, but your duty is to obey them simply because they are ours, yet seeing our motives are of such a generous nature as must needs provoke the activity of any Englishman lodges in his breast the love of his country we shall tell you that our purpose is with God's assistance to increase our navigation as much as our trade that as our fleets grow yearly richer, may proportionately grow stronger.'

4. Chief of Council at Hugli, dated 22 July, 1681. Nothing of importance.

5. 18 Nov., 1681.

Extract only. Informs that Mr. Hedges ' one of your present Committee here ' has been despatched to India to subdue interlopers. Hopes that Mr. Hedges will behave himself gravely and with moderation. Commanders to forfeit £40 for any private goods they shall carry to the Bay and Matchlepatam. Signed by Josiah Child.

6. 15 Jan., 1681. London to Agent and Council, Bay of Bengal. Unimportant.

7. 25 Jan., 1681-82. The Agent and Council at Fort St. George.

Says that the 'Committee having found that Mr. Streynsham Master, late Agent at Fort St. George, having detained in his hands fourteen thousand Atlasses of the State of Mr. Methias Vincent, late chief in the Bay of Bengala, Willam Gifford, etc. are ordered to require him to pay the said money into the Company's cash.'

8. 10 March, 1681. To Agent and Council at Hugli.

The following paragraph will be found interesting: 'We are well informed that Mr. Pocock chief of Pattana is a creature of Mr. Vincents and that this last year he does wickedly abuse us in the sorting of our Romalls and other goods besides which information we find upon our owne view all our goods so abominably sorted from the Bay that (without such information) we should conclude those employed in that work there, unfaithfull to us and confederated with Vincent, wherefore we do hereby order you to discharge the said Mr. Pocock from our services and send him home, putting such person as you shall judge most trustie to us, and able to discharge the place into the chiefship of Pattana aforesaid.'

End of the volume.

Hugli Letters

This volume deals with letters written from Dec., 1680 to Nov., 1681. It is a most interesting collection of letters and throws light on the activities of that mysterious and elusive personality, Job Charnoc. The letters are signed by Mathias Vincent, Job Charnoc and Francis Ellis. Job Charnoc did not sign some of the letters as he left to join his chiefship. However, one long letter dated 4 June, 1681 is signed by Charnoc. There is an important despatch on pp. 118-27 signed by Edward Littleton, Francis Ellis and Richard Trenchfield. It is a fairly long letter and throws considerable light on Charnoc's quarrels with the Company's servants in Bengal. I have not seen a copy of the letter in any publication, and as it has not been noticed before I have reproduced it below. The Hugli letters deal with the minutiae of the Company's industries and commerce in Bengal. Most of the letters contain directions to captains of the ships, ordering them to lade on board the ships various articles of Indian manufactures. The following example will suffice: 'I have ordered Mr. Sowdon to lade on board your ship three bales of raw silk in the Honorable Company's tonnage, the freight therefore being made good here, and deliver him bills for them, they going per account of Mr. Thomas Lucas. Signed : Mathias Vincent.'

There are four letters dated 4 Dec., 1680. Most of them are signed by Mathias Vincent and Job Charnoc and contain the amount of silk and other stuff ordered from Hugli.

Other letters are addressed to Directors. The wretched Sowdon comes in for severe rebuke in some of the letters. ' Your brief letter we received and admire you should be so negligent as not to send copies of those receipts you took for the goods shipped on board the English ships out of the sloope *Ganges*; for want of them we are not now able to draw out the *Sampsons Invoyce* and we understand the sloope did not come thence in a day or two up to the date of your letter. These are things we shall not pass by, but strictly enjoin you to comply with your orders, and not to think off with foolish and idle excuses.' This is signed by Mathias Vincent and Francis Ellis.

In a letter dated 24 Feb., 1681, there is an interesting reference to Job Charnoc. The letter states, 'Wee are glad of Mr. Job Charnoc safe

22

arrivall to his station on Xmas day last, wishing good success in that chiefship ; Mr. Littleton arrived hither 12th ultimo, who brought the silver seals and weights of which wee having no other shall have yearly use.'

The following letter is reproduced from the Hugli Letters. It will be found interesting :

'Hugly, 29th June, 1681.

'MR. JOB CHARNOCK & CA.

'We have recd. yours of the 13th currtt. together with one pair of your bookes and your Diary for the last month.

'The saile of the 12 chests of treasure we note, and that Soocaun Nundsa & ca. refused to make the essaies at the mint of Rs. 93 or Rs. 91-3a the piece, which seems very unlikely since we know as well as themselves that the course silver is melted in such quantities and sometimes greater with Lead to be made Chaundree to pass the Gozansht, and then againe are weighed into Chuckatees of the aforesaid weight and only melted down to be fited to the stamp; had not silver been soe much demanded and Soocanno Gomosteh have proffered to take the silver on the consideration and essaies we advise you to, it had been more probable ; but these things being as above hinted makes us we know not what to think of it ; pray at yr. comeing out and agreeing on the essaies ; advise us how the plate comes out in conformity to the Invoice.

'Mr. Charnock haveing not signed to any bonds and indentures to the Hon'ble Compa. since he left their Service anno 1663 or 1664, and they having severale times pressed his doeing of saide, and have never hitherto reversed that order ; however, it has Lain dormant by the omission or forgettfullness of Mr. Walter Clavell deceased, the late Chiefe of Bengall. We haveing weighed the thing and do not finde it convenient that soe great a trust as Cossumbazar factory be reposed any longer in any one's hands (as Chiefe especially) who, contrary to the Saide Hon'ble Compa. practice with all their servants great and small, is under noe bonds or indentures to them ; we doe therefore herewith send you a blanck bond and indenture enordering him, in Psuance [? pursuance] to the Hon'ble Compa. Commands, immediately to sign and seal to them both, and to deliver them soe signed and sealed to Allen Catchpoole and John Thedder, who are of Councill of Cassimbazar factory, to be wittnessed by them, and that then he dispeed [? dispatch] them to us by two trusty expresses, and therewith send us a Govt. Letter the names of two persons in England he appoints for his security there that we may by the expected shipping accordingly advise our Hon'ble Employers, thereof.

'The Chiefe haveing Pused [? perused] your Diary for Last month, recd. here two daies since as above mentioned, findes himself confronted by Sevtt. notes therein, sly in their manner of bringing in and falce and injurious to him in their matter, as will appear by the due propension thereof.

'As for Mr. Charnocks saying he had prized the Compa. taffaties at their real and just value in his notes the 7th and 13th day, it appears as well by an accott. under his own hand (as what the Chiefe computed when there) to be falce, though even those acctt. (neither of them) come up to the worth of a piece of that November bund taffaties, when well made being well bought at one rupee more P. P. by the same calculation, and it held their due goodness in every respect they would well content the Hon'ble Compa. at said rate ; nor were these occasion could such be had of any Bazaur or shopkeeper of Muxadavad or Cassimbazar many competent quantity under Rup. 8 P. P. as the price of November bund sicke was at the time of the weavers buying thereof the last year. What the chief did herein he averse was to encourage the weavers to make

good wave and to stop their clamour which it had been much more easy
to him and more answerable to Mr. Charnock's cariage [? courage]
towards him to have let the business fallen on Mr. Charnock then to
have troubled himselfe therewith; but he had the Hon'ble Compa.
advantage without any by respects of his own before his eyes,
well knowing that something of content given the weavour produces
well made goods and alwais the contrary when they are too much, as here
they are, pinched and this was the present case according to the best of
his Judgment after securing the whole parcell of taffaties piece by piece;
and he hopes his experience in the business of Cassumbazar factory will
be allowed to over ballance Mr. Charnock's selfe conceit of his own
prompt partes and abilities as well as of those that assisted him herein
who are here under specified. For, where as Mr. Charnock saies in his
objections to the Consultation held about the time of the Chiefes
departure thence in Cassumbazar the ultimo that in prizing those taffaties
he tooke the opinion of severall others well experienced in the worth
thereof, it seems it was not of any of those appointed of the Councill of
the factory, they not careing or dareing to appear after a day or two, but
of John Naylor the Dyer there whose understanding in that or anything
else is taken nor to be over much and of Amutt Ram the Barber, who,
about the business of Juggoo Podaur's death, was by the Agent and
Councill orders publickly disgraced and turned away anno 1676 at
Cassumbazar—with a strickt exhibition of ever admitting him in on
any accott., Genl or Pticular, into that or any other place or factory in
Bengall or into any perticular man's service of the English nation;
and all this under the penalties (as inserted in Consultation in Cassumbazar of the 6 October 1676) as the Agent and Councll. should Judg
meet, and that such a villanies judgment should not only be taken but
alsoe thus by Mr. Charnock upheld against that of the Chiefs (who
has soe many years managed the business of that factory before him)
is a nonsensicall obstinate humor peculiar to the singular quallifications
and breeding of Mr. Charnock. But although Mr. Charnock would
take upon him to be a Little familliar in his resentments and Charrachter
of his Chiefe as to matter of the taffaties, yet he might (not to speak of
good manner) have been soe just as to have given a small hint in the
same Diary notes, where upon this concern he contents himself to pass
it over wholly in silence; it not it seemes sorting with his information
of Losse on the taffaties what the Chief (to made [sic] amends for the
taffaties rates) had saved the Hon'ble Compa. in prizing of the
raw silke, of what it seemes he himselfe would have given the Peicaurs
more than the Chiefe found it worth; though even here the Chiefe
gave a great allowance considering the vast difference between the goods
brought on and the Muster they were prized by, and it may seem justly
suspisable [sic] that Mr. Charnock was partly engaged to accommodate
some of those piecars in the prizing, but was hindred therefrom by the
Chiefe being present there at; and this his ghessanises from the heat of
Charnock thereupon and his since rateing the silke then thrown out by
the Chiefe and referred to him & ca. to prize at such under rates as it
deserved almost if not altogether as high as what was then taken at,
the Chiefe being there, as appears by the end of mo. of May's Diary
above mentioned; and this ghess must continue soe until time gives an
opportunity of a due serating [sic] to be made thereon upon the whole
matter. Should it be granted (as it no avails) is that upwards of rupees
1000 were lost by being allowed to the weavers, it may alsoe be saide
that sevll thousands were saved in the Chiefes nonallowance to the

Paicaurs by which the pretended accott. of Loss is very much over ballanced.

'And Lastly, Mr. Charnock sly reflection (on what tis saide he himselfe almost constantly practices) on the Chiefe drawing up the Consultation at his parting Last from Cossumbazar and giving Mr. Charnock noe time to consider on, or object against, till it was copied faire into the Consultation bookes remain to be spoken unto ; which, had it been soe as the case stood, could not have appeared so great a crime as it is hoped slyly it may seem, because the Chiefe and Mr. Charnock being the only persons then at Cassumbazar of the Gen. Councill of Bengall there could be no more then one drawer up of such a paper and but one to contradict ; and where any matters in the Compa. affaires stands on even votes, it has all long been the Custome and seems but reason that the Chiefe should cast it on his own side and supersede the other, which might without doubt have passed soe here, there being noe necessity of two such Diary notes as those of the 7th and 13th Last mo. thereon, especially since it is found Mr. Charnock is not soe exact to insert other things which might possibly deserve better consideration then this he has soe much puzled himselfe, in particularly what occurred in Cassumbazar and Muxadavad the 11 and 15 Last mo. But to come againe to matter, Mr. Charnock note here on is also falce, for he was called up by the Chiefe, and those two points concerning the Weavers and peicaurs were argued and disputed almost a whole morning between them ; but Mr. Charnock, though he could not say much in refuttation of the premises, yet alwaies takeing good heed to disallow of the conclusion, the Chiefe resolved to draw out the Consultation as he did, telling him that since we could not agree in our opinions he might sign with objections, to which there being a distinct answer laid down in our Consultation booke here, as well (as what materialls) spoken to in the foregoing discourse, the Chiefe thinks not worth his trouble to make any further reflection of those matters or expatiate thereon :

'We wonder you follow not the method of the Maddapollam Diary in the Keeping of yours ; for you may perceive that there in Consultation only, and not the Diary notes, are signed unto and accordingly we enorder you to keep yours not certainly knowing what the knack of all your previous after the Diary note of the 12 ultimo is, unless Mr. Charnock does slily intend the Compa. shall understand thereby that not only he but the rest of the Councill doe alsoe affirme to what he writes about the Taffaties in the notes of the 7th ultimo which those of Councill with you cannot doe, since it appears that neither Allen Catchpoole nor John Threder were present ; but as above declared, at Mr. Charnock and ca. prizing those goods, nor questionless have they since looked them over by which means only they could be capacitated to sign to the truth or falshood of what Mr. Charnock affirme concerning them.

'As soon as the raw silk of march bund is almost in, pray advise us thereof that in case no other business of import intervenes the Chiefe may come up to see whether the Peicaurs have complied with their contracts in that bund better then they did in that of the month of November Last 10th is all but present from

' Your loving friends,

'The contents of the 3d and 4th paragraphs is the Chief's concern.

' F. ELLIS.

' MATTHIAS VINCENT,
' EDWARD LITTLETON,
' FRANCIS ELLIS,
' RI. TRENCHFIELD.'

MADRAS RECORD OFFICE

The earliest British factories in Madras were established in 1611 at Masulipatam, and Petapoli (now Nizampatam), both of them ports of the then kingdom of Golconda. Ten years later, the East India Company servants were admitted to the Dutch settlement of Pulicat under an agreement that the trade should be shared equally by the two nations. This led to wranglings, and the British factors withdrew in 1623. In 1626, another settlement was made at Armgaon, now called Durgarayapatnam, situated about 40 miles north of Pulicat; and the factors removed in 1640 to Madraspatam, then a village. Here, on a strip of ground rented from a representative of the old Vijayanagar dynasty, was erected Fort St. George, and this became the headquarters of the Company. During the latter part of the seventeenth century other factories were established. Madras was definitely constituted a Presidency in 1684. Throughout the seventeenth century the British possessions in the Presidency were restricted to Fort St. David, and the district round Madras.

DOCUMENTS IN THE INDIA OFFICE

The documents relating to the seventeenth century are to be found principally in the Original Correspondence Series, in the Letter Books; and in the separate sections of the Factory Records, all preserved in the India Office Record Office. The most important records dealing with the seventeenth century are summarized below.

MASULIPATAM

Consultations, 1670-71, 1675-82,[1] 1684-85 (4 vols.).
Copies of letters sent, 1638, 1640, 1666, 1670-73, 1675-77, 1682-86 (4 vols.).
Copies of letters received, 1622-23, 1666, 1670-73, 1675-78 (with gaps), 1682, 1685 (3 vols.).
Diary of William Puckle, 1675-76 (1 vol.).
Proceedings of the New Company's representatives, 1699-1700 (1 vol.).

FORT ST. GEORGE

Diaries and consultations, 1655, 1662, 1672-73, 1675-76, 1677-78, 1680-81, 1683-85, 1686-90, 1693-99 (with gaps), 1701-4 (13 vols.).
Copies of letters sent, 1661-65 (with gaps), 1668-71 (with gaps), 1673-77, 1679, 1681, 1687-88, 1692-94, 1696-1700, 1704 (12 vols.).
Copies of letters received, 1669-77, 1680-81, 1687-88, 1692-94, 1696-97, 1700, 1703-4 (10 vols.).

---

[1] The Madras Government published in 1916 the Masulipatam Consultations from 14 Aug., 1682 to the end of 1683.

FORT ST. GEORGE (*contd.*)

Papers of Richard Mohun, 1676-79 (1 vol.).
Letterbook of Thomas Lucas, 1683 (1 vol.).
Proceedings in the Court of Judicature, 1678 and 1693-94 (1 vol.).
Correspondence with the country powers, 1703-5 (1 vol.).

MADAPOLLAM

Consultations, 1684-86 (1 vol.).
Copies of letters sent, 1676-77, 1681-84 (1 vol.).
Copies of letters received, 1676-77, 1681-82, 1683-85 (1 vol.).
Some records relating to this factory are included in the Masulipatam series.

CUDDALORE AND PORTO NOVO

Diary and consultations, 1683, 1685-87. Also a commission of 1681 (2 vols.).
Copies of letters sent or received, 1684-86 (1 vol.).
The Fort St. David records should be consulted for later references.

PETAPOLI

Consultations, 1683-87 (with gaps) (1 vol.).
Copies of letters sent, 1682-87 (1 vol.).
Copies of letters received, 1685-87 (1 vol.).

CONIMERE

Consultations, 1682-85 (1 vol.).
Copies of letters sent, 1684-85 (1 vol.).
Copies of letters received, 1684 (1 vol.).

VIZAGAPATAM

Diary and consultations, 1684, 1692-95 (1 vol.).

FORT ST. DAVID

Consultations, 1690, 1696-1712, 1723-51,[1] 1752-56 (8 vols.).
Correspondence, 1692-1759 (3 vols.).
It will be noticed that these papers cover the period (1746-52) during which Fort St. David was the seat of government, owing to the capture of Madras by the French.

MISCELLANEOUS

Vol. 1. Abstracts of letters received from Masulipatam, etc., 1617-32.
Vol. 3. Extracts from letters and consultations, Coast and Bay, 1664-73 and 1680-81.
Vol. 3A. Abstracts of letters from Coast and Bay, 1676-1708.
Vol. 6. Abstracts of letters received by the New Company from India, 1699-1707.
Vol. 7. Extracts from letters from various factories, 1716-23.
Vol. 7A. Ditto, 1711-41.
Vol. 9. Copies of records relating to Tanjore (1624), Armagon (1626), Petapoli (1625-31), Masulipatam (1628-38), Fort St. George (1658), and Triplicane (1681), with an account of the origin of Fort St. George, etc.

---

[1] Selections from the Fort St. David consultations for 1740 and 1741 were published at Madras in 1916.

Vol. 14. Diary of Streynsham Master, 1675-77.
Vol. 18. The mission of Francis Bowyear to Pegu and Cochin China, 1695-97.
Vol. 26. Contains a description of the Golconda Diamond Mines (1677), some letters from the Coromandel Coast, 1711-15, and a description of Divi Island, 1717.

For details, see the *List of Factory Records*, which, however, has been considerably amended since publication (corrected copies may be consulted in the India Office Library or Record Department). The earlier documents are included in *The English Factories*.

In addition to the *Press Lists*, the Madras Government has for some years been engaged in publishing its early records, which date from 1670. As far back as 1871 appeared a volume of extracts from those dating between 1670 and 1680, and in 1893-95 the consultations at Fort St. George for the years 1681-85 were printed in five volumes, under the editorship of Mr. A. T. Pringle, those for 1681 being selections, while those for the succeeding years were given in full. Since then the following have been published *in extenso*, under the care of Mr. H. Dodwell:

Consultations, 1672-81, 1686-94.
Despatches from England, 1670-77, 1680-86.
Despatches to England, 1694-96.
Letters from Fort St. George to subordinate factories, 1679, 1688, 1689, 1697.
Letters to Fort St. George from ditto, 1681-82, 1684-85, 1686-87, 1688.
Sundry books for 1677-78 (Madras letters sent); 1680-81 (Hugli Letters Sent); 1686 (Affairs in Bengal).

The COLIN MACKENZIE MSS. in the India Office Library include copies of some of the Fort St. George consultations between 1673 and 1694 missing from the India Office Record Department files.

DOCUMENTS IN THE MADRAS RECORD OFFICE

The Madras Consultation Books begin in 1672 and in that year John Nicks was Secretary with a gratuity of ten pounds a year in addition to the twenty pounds which he was to receive later on as a merchant. The despatches from the Court begin with the year 1670, and were preserved by being pasted into paste-books; these to the Court were copied into volumes, like the rest of the records, and date only from 1694. As a rule the despatches were in early times sent once a year from London, and twice a year from Madras. The Company generally sent out its shipping in January. It was designed to catch the south-west monsoon in the Indian Ocean and arrive at Madras in June or July. From Madras, shipping was normally sent to England twice a year. As pointed out by Dodwell, 'every January cargoes were despatched, and along with them the Madras Government sent its annual accounts, its annual record volumes, lists of the garrison inhabitants, and so on. These were regularly accompanied by a despatch reviewing the course of events in the previous year.' The annual letters sent from Court are remarkable for their solid common-sense, shrewdness, and homely idiom. The tone adopted by the Directors is not by any means friendly, and very few despatches are free from criticism. This applies especially to the despatches written during the time of Sir Josiah Child's supremacy. No one who has compared his letters in the Bodleian Library with the despatches written during the period can help being struck with the resemblance in style which they exhibit.   The reader is referred for a detailed examination of the despatches to my work on the *East India Trade in the XVIIth Century*; copies of despatches sent to Bombay during the period 1660-75, will be found in my *Anglo-Portuguese Negotiations Relating to Bombay, 1667-1673*.   Mr. Dodwell's statement that 'about the year 1700 there sprang up a practice of arranging our advices under several heads' is not quite correct.   The long and elaborate despatches sent by the Directors to Bombay at a period anterior to 1700 are divided into various headings, and deal with various items in a methodical manner.   Nor is it quite correct to assume that all the despatches were divided into six heads.   This is probably true of the despatches written in the year 1702, as pointed out by Dodwell. But this was not a fixed rule and in some despatches the number of heads is smaller while in others it is larger.   The first head dealt with ' our shipping gone out and returned and goods sent hence '.   The second dealt with the investment, for the English market, 'and wherein deficient or blameworthy, if soe '.   The third was concerned with trade in general and the country powers ; the fourth with revenues and fortifications ; the fifth with the Company's civil and military servants, and their accounts ; and the sixth with the New Company, ' our late competitors '.

Into the Despatch volumes not only were despatches pasted, but also the miscellaneous documents that were contained in the packets.   Hence a despatch to Madras might also contain despatches to other Company's settlements, besides a list of investments to be provided on the Coromandel Coast ; and accounts of coral and silver shipped to India.   The last item is, in my opinion, most important, for by calculating the amount of silver in these lists and the amount in other places, we are enabled to form an approximate estimate of the amount of silver exported to Madras in one year.   If we add together the amount exported to Bengal and Bombay in the same year, we arrive at a fairly reliable estimate of the total amount of silver exported to the country.   This, as I have pointed out, will serve as an excellent means of testing the volume of English trade with India. Again, it will also help us in analysing the various pamphlets and other works that were published in defence of, or against, the East India Trade. For further details the reader is referred to my work on *The East India Trade*.

The Early Despatches to England

For the history of Madras these despatches are indispensable.   Like the despatches from England, those from Fort St. George were divided into heads.   There are, besides, miscellaneous papers similar to those which exist in the Despatch volumes from Madras.   They consist chiefly of volumes of accounts and records sent to England ; sailing orders addressed to captains of the homeward bound ships ; registers of bills drawn on the Company, and of diamonds shipped from the coast.   There are also letters to the Governor of St. Helena, notifying him of the supply of necessaries that were regularly sent there.   This account of despatches is restricted to those sent in the seventeenth century.   I have not deemed it necessary to trace the later development.

1. 12 December, 1694 to 21 December, 1696.   This is the only volume of Despatches to England series that deals with the seventeenth century.

Despatches from England

The following despatches from England dealing with the seventeenth century are preserved in the Madras Record Office :

1. 29 December, 1670 to 20 December, 1677.
2. 19 March, 1679-80 to 26 May, 1682.
3. 4 January, 1680-81 to 30 April, 1683.
4. 25 March, 1682 to 24 October, 1684.
5. 31 May, 1683 to 24 October, 1684.
6. 29 February, 1683-84 to 20 April, 1686.
7. 13 February, 1684-85 to 26 June, 1686.
8. 29 April, 1686 to 11 April, 1688.
9. 6 February, 1687-88 to 15 February, 1688-89
10. 11 September, 1689 to 29 February, 1691-92.
11. 8 December, 1696 to 20 January, 1698-99.
12. 12 January, 1701-2 to 25 January, 1703-4.

LETTERS FROM FORT ST. GEORGE

1. 6 January, 1678-79 to 18 December, 1679.
2. 21 February, 1687-88 to 12 December, 1688.
3. 2 January, 1688-89 to 20 December, 1689.
4. 13 May, 1693 to 23 January, 1693-94 (pages 21-70 missing).
5. 14 March, to 9 April, 1695 (pages 1-16 missing).
6. 2 October, 1696 to 25 January, 1697.
7. 9 September to 28 December, 1697.
8. 3 January, 1697 to 28 December, 1698.
9. 3 January, 1698 to 27 June, 1699.
10. 4 January, 1700 to 29 December, 1701.
11. 1 July to 5 December, 1702.

LETTERS TO FORT ST. GEORGE

1. July, 1681 to January, 1682 (pages 92-113 missing).
2. January to December, 1682.
3. 7 December, 1684 to December, 1685.
4. 29 October, 1686 to 27 July, 1687.
5. 18 May, 1693 to 6 January, 1694.
6. April and May, 1699.
7. December, 1699 to December, 1700 (pages 1-16 and 309-28 missing).

CONSULTATIONS

The Consultation volumes are divided into two parts, the Diary and the Consultations proper. The Diary was supposed to be written day by day. Streynsham Master's Diaries show that the system of transacting business under Sir William Langhorne was very unsystematic, and when Master became Governor, he drew up rules for the Secretary's guidance. He was to 'summon the Council every Monday and Thursday morning at 8 o'clock; to enter all the consultations in the book appointed for that purpose; to take care that two copy books of the letters received and sent be duly and fairly written by the factors and writers appointed thereto'; and to have marginal notes and alphabets made both to the Consultations and the Letter Books (see Sir Richard Temple's edition of Master's Diaries). Some interesting references are to be found in the diaries kept, and there is unconscious humour in the bare record of the doings of the worthy factors and writers who celebrated the Guy Fawkes Day with a great bonfire, and a fine supper, and the Boxing Day when the pious Governor—worthy old man—extended invitations to all the English of most note, both men and women. The arrival and departure of shipping is regularly entered until 1812; the arrival of important persons at the settlement is entered, as also the departure of the Company servants for Europe and elsewhere. It also contains entries respecting the Court of Justice set up by Streynsham Master, notices of comets, of unseasonable weather, of discussions between the agents of the country powers and the Governor or persons authorised by him. There are also regular notes of the letters that were received and sent. In the eighteenth century, however, the quaint elements disappear. The letters, accounts and proceedings are entered in a more formal and official style.

The minutes of Consultations were supposed to be signed by the members of Council, and the volumes of Consultations contain the autographs of all the important men who take part in that memorable struggle, from the time of Sir William Langhorne to the time of Warren Hastings, and even much later.

As pointed out by Dodwell the early Consultations are meagre, and we get no glimpse of the details that must have taken place at some meetings of the stormy Council. At a later period the custom of writing minutes of dissent was developed, and was fully utilised by the members. It was not till the baneful connection of the Nawab of Arcot, the robbery in which some of the Company's chief servants were implicated, that the minutes of dissent became as plentiful as blackberries in September. The Consultations dealing with the seventeenth century contain the decisions at which the Government had arrived. In some cases, abstracts of letters submitted to the Council were entered, while reports and accounts were also frequently entered. The growth of these records may be measured by the fact that up to 1750 the Consultations and Diary formed one volume a year; in 1800 they formed thirty-five volumes; and in 1850 one hundred and twenty-five.

Besides the Despatches and the Consultations there are subsidiary volumes. The greater number of these consists of letter books which really belong to the Consultations.

The earliest volume of the ' Country Correspondence Series ' preserved in Madras is that of 1740. Letters to Fort St. George date from 1681, and Letters from Fort St. George from 1678. The early volumes of the two later series, and all the volumes of the Country Correspondence Series are extremely valuable and full in many details which the Consultations do not show.

The subsidiary volumes also contain reports of committees appointed to investigate some special matter; such, for example, as misdoings of a servant. The seventeenth century records published by Messrs. Hudgleston and Pringle throw light on some of the common and quaint details of seventeenth century administration. The Letter Books still await publication. There are several letters to ' our braminy Vira Raghaviah ' under date 1679, and to the famous François Martin, dated 1688, who was then busy at Pondicherry. In 1681 there are letters from Longapah and in 1686 there are communications from that desperate adventurer, Constantine Falcon, the Greek desperado, who became Chief Minister at the Siamese Court.

With the beginning of the eighteenth century, however, these records, like the Consultations, lost their quaint character, and became formal and stiff in style.

The Madras Record Office contains the following volumes of Consultations dealing with the seventeenth century :

1.   19 January, 1671-72 to 26 January, 1677-78.

2. 27 January, 1677-78 to 7 January, 1678-79 (with index).
3. 9 January, 1678-79 to 25 January, 1679-80 (with index).
4. 26 January, 1679-80 to 10 January, 1680-81.
5. 11 January, 1680-81 to June, 1681.
6. July to December, 1681.
7. January, 1681-82 to December, 1682.
8. 1 January, 1682-83 to January, 1683-84.
9. 16 January 1683-84 to 24 January, 1684-85.
10. January, 1684-85 to February, 1685-86.
11. February, 1685-86 to February, 1686-87.
12. February, 1686-87 to July, 1687.
13. July, 1687 to February, 1687-88.
14. February, 1687-88 to December, 1688.
15. January, 1688-89 to December, 1689.
16. January, 1689-90 to December, 1690.
17. January, 1690-91 to December, 1691.
18. January, 1691-92 to October, 1692.
19. December, 1692 to May, 1693.
20. June, 1693 to January, 1693-94.
21. February, 1693-94 to December, 1694.
22. February, 1694-95 to December, 1695 (some pages at the end missing).
23. January, 1695-96 to September, 1696.
24. October, 1696 to January, 1696-97.
25. February, 1696-97 to September, 1697.
26. September, 1697 to January, 1697-98.
27. January, 1697-98 to December, 1698.
28. January, 1698-99 to December, 1699.
29. January, 1699-1700 to December, 1700.
30. January, 1700-1 to December, 1701.

SUNDRIES

1. Letters sent to subordinate factories—15 August, 1677 to 30 November, 1678.
1A. Copy of register of letters sent to subordinate factories—December, 1680 to November, 1681.
2. Expedition to Bengal: July to November, 1686. Interesting.
3. Letters from subordinate factories, 1687 to 1688 (pages 1-20 missing).
4. Elliott's Standing Orders with index, 1664 to 1784 (No. 4 wanting).

DUTCH RECORDS

i. COCHIN RECORDS

1. Roman Catholic missal, 1657.
2. Mercantile suits, declarations, conditions of lease, 1664 to 1699.
3. Title-deeds, etc., 1665 to 1679.
4. Sundry resolutions, 1666 to 1735.
5. Mercantile, 1674.
6. Mercantile (illegible), 1676 to 1678.
7. Memoir, 1677 (printed in Dutch Records No. 14 of selections from the records).
8. Original letters from Batavia, 1679 to 1689.
9. Letters to Batavia, 1680.
10. Orders, 1680.

11. Letters to Quilon, 1680.
12. Reports, 1680 and 1681.
13. Fragment, 1680 to 1690.
14. Letters to Batavia, 1681.
15. Report, 1681.
16. Judicial records, 1681 and 1682.
17. Sales, 1681 to 1685.
18. Judicial records, 1682 to 1714.
19. Leases, 1684 to 1703.
20. Letters to Balasore, 1686.
21. Jurisprudence, 1686.
22. Letters from Batavia, 1686 and 1687.
23. Orders extracted from Resolutions, 1687 to 1735.
24. Diary, 1688.
25. Letters to Quilon, 1688.
26. Reports, 1688.
27. Diary, 1689.
28. Letters to Batavia, 1690.
29. Letters from Commissioners, 1690.
30. Letters from Commissioner-General H. A. Van Reade, 1690.
31. Letters from Commissioners, 1690 and 1691.
32. Letters from Cranganore to Cochin, 1691.
33. Letters from Kolamooky, 1691 and 1692.
34. Letters from Cayencoolam, 1692.
35. Letters to Cayencoolam, 1692.
36. Secret letters to and from sub-factories, 1692 and 1693.
37. Foreign correspondence, 1692 to 1705.
38. Resolutions, 1693.
39. Original letters from Batavia, 1693.
40. Law book, 1693.
41. Inventories, 1694.
42. Letters to Batavia, 1694 and 1695.
43. Letters to Coromandel, 1694 and 1695.
44. Orders, 1694 to 1779.
45. Correspondence with the English, 1695 and 1696.
46. Judicial records, 1695 to 1699.
47. Title-deeds, 1695 to 1706.
48. Book of contracts, 1695 to 1752.
49. Letters to Batavia, 1696.
50. Instructions, 1697.
51. Letters to Cochin, 1698.
52. Memoir on the condition of Malabar, 1698.
53. Original letters from Batavia, 1699 and 1700.
54. Letters from Malacca, 1699 to 1703.
55. Letters to Holland, 1699 to 1708.
56. Original letters from Batavia, 1700 and 1701.
57. Legal records, 1700 to 1705.
58. Law suits, accounts, 1700 to 1709.
59. Original letters from Batavia, 1701 and 1702.
60. Resolutions, 1701.
61. Miscellaneous, 1701 to 1708.

The above records deal with the seventeenth century. I have not included here a list of eighteenth century records. It is a voluminous one.

ii. Coromandel Records

1634. Memoirs of L. Pit, 1663.
1635. Memoirs of Speelman, 1665.
1636. Memoirs of D. Van Ghoen 1730 (1-126).
1636A. Memoir of A. Pla, 1730 (127-136).
1637. Memoir of Elias Guillot, 1738.
1638. Memoir of Mossel, 1744.
1639. Memoir of Mersen, 1748.
1640. Memoir of Vermont, 1748.
1641. Memoir of Haksteen, 1659.
1642. Negapatam political consultations, 1755-56.

Nos. 1634 to 1641 are copies supplied by the courtesy of the Dutch Government at Batavia.

Among the Danish records presented in the Madras Record Office, there are few or none dealing with seventeenth century history.

BOMBAY RECORD OFFICE

The first English vessel reached Surat in August, 1608, and from 1613 onwards the list of English chiefs at that place, called at first Agents and then Presidents, is continuous until the transfer of the headquarters to Bombay. From Surat, factories were quickly planted at Agra, Ajmer, Ahmedabad and Broach; and later on others were established at various ports down the coast of India, as well as in Sind and Persia, and the Arabian ports of the Red Sea. For the history of Bombay in the latter half of the seventeenth century, see my *Anglo-Portuguese Negotiations, 1666-1673*. In 1687 it became the headquarters of the Presidency in the place of Surat. The India Office Record Department contains various series from factories in the Bombay Presidency.

> For Surat, there are Consultations beginning with 1620-36, and ending 1724-1800. There are, besides, Commercial Diary and Consultations, 1800-4. There are also Copies of letters sent, from 1616-17 to 1690-1708 (altogether 19 vols.); and copies of letters received 1621-23 to 1724-26 (altogether 19 vols.).
>
> Rajapur. Copies of letters sent, 1659-60.
>
> Karwar. Miscellaneous, 1666-1717.
>
> Bombay. Consultations, etc., 1669-70 to 1702-4 (5 vols.).
>
> Copies of letters sent, 1670 to 1708-10 (14 vols.).
>
> Copies of letters received, 1670 to 1702-4 (12 vols.).
>
> Tellicherry. Copies of letters received by the Company, 1716-56.

The ORME MSS. in the India Office Library contain a number of records relating to Tellicherry and Calicut. There are some in the Madras Record Office.

In the documents entitled 'Miscellaneous' there are some very important records, e.g.

> 1. Abstracts of letters for Persia, Surat, etc., 1617-32.
>
> 2. Extracts from letters and consultations from Persia, Surat, Gombaroon, etc., 1633-72.
>
> Vol. 4, 5. Abstracts of letters received by the East India Company from Surat, etc., 1699-1707.
>
> Vol. 8. Copies of letters, etc., regarding Surat, 1608-24.
>
> Vol. 11. Charges against Boothby, 1629.
>
> Vol. 12. Letter book of Edward Knipe, 1642-44.
>
> Vol. 16. Correspondence regarding interlopers, 1682-83.
>
> Vol. 17. Correspondence of Sir John Golsborough, 1693.
>
> Vols. 19, 20. Letter books of Sir William Norris, ambassador to the Great Mogul, 1699-1702.

The contents of the Bombay Record Office consist mainly of the records of the proceedings of the governing body of the

Western Presidency, orginally the President in Council at Surat, now the Governor of Bombay in Council, and of the correspondence, documents and books received by that body.

The subsidiary records in the office are as follows:

A. Records of Factories and Residencies of the East India Company in (*a*) what is now the Bombay Presidency; (*b*) Bantam (Java) and certain places outside India subordinate to the Bombay Presidency.

B. Records of subordinate offices, past or still existing, located with few exceptions at Bombay.

C. Miscellaneous Records consisting principally of the proceedings of numerous political missions, committees appointed for administrative matters, records of obsolete institutions and a few miscellaneous registers and returns.

Records of Factories and Residencies. (*a*) In Western India.

(i) north of Bombay, the factories of Surat, and Broach, and the 'Commercial Residency Northward', a term which covered Surat, Broach, Cambay, and Kathiawar;

(ii) in the neighbourhood of Bombay, the factories of Caranja, Belapur and Tanna (Thana);

(iii) inland, the Kalyan and Poona residencies;

(iv) on the coast south of Bombay, the residencies of Raree and of Fort Victoria, at Bankot and the factory of Bankot, all in what is now the Ratnagiri District; the factory of Karwar in North Kanara and the Malabar Commercial Residency;

(v) the Sind factory, the letters of which are sometimes dated from Tatta, sometimes from Shahbandar.

The earliest of these records are those of the Surat factory, of which the first date from 1630. The remainder commence much later, the earliest records being those of Bankot factory commencing in 1756 and the latest those of Commercial Residency Northward which extend up to 1835.

The more important of the Company's settlements in the Bombay Presidency are thus all represented in the Record Office. It is noticeable that there are no records from Rajapur (Ratnagiri District) although there is a volume of letters despatched from Rajapur, 1659-60, in the India Office. The factory at Rajapur was, however, comparatively short-lived, being abandoned either in, or shortly after, 1661.

Besides the English records of Surat there are records in Dutch of 1768 and thereabouts, presumably seized from the Dutch factory.

Major T. Candy's preliminary report on the Bombay records submitted in 1864 shows that at that time records of certain factories and residencies on the Malabar Coast, viz. Tellicherry, the Malabar Residency, Calicut, Cochin and Aujengo, were in the Bombay Record Office. These were transferred in 1877 to the office of the Collector of Malabar, from which they were forwarded in 1913 to the Madras Record Office. It does not appear that there were at Bombay in Major Candy's time any records of the Company's settlements further inland, such as those at Agra, Ajmere, Baroda or Burhanpur.

(*b*) Outside India.

These comprise the Residencies and Factories at Mocha, on the Arabian Coast of the Red Sea, Basra, Bushire, Gombroon, now better known as

Bandar Abbas, Diego Garcia Island which lies in the Indian Ocean far south of Bombay, and Bantam in Java.

The earliest of these records is a letter book from Bantam, 1679-83. The latest are those of the Mocha Residency, 1821-28. Almost all the rest belong to the eighteenth century. In August, 1682, Bantam was taken by the Dutch and the Company's establishment at that port were forced to withdraw to Batavia whence in August, 1683, they retired to Surat; doubtless as being the Company's principal station in India, although Fort St. George (Madras) had by this time been constituted a Presidency. They must be presumed to have brought with them their current Inward Letter Book (1679-83) which is the only record of Bantam found in the Bombay office. A few years later (in 1677) when the factory had been sacked by the Javanese at the instigation of the Dutch, the factory books are stated to have been closed and brought to the Court of Directors. This explains the absence of the earlier Bantam records from Bombay. The Diego Garcia Diary records little more than the taking possession of that island, not then in the possession of any European nation, in 1786. The Mocha Factory records proper last for two years, 1722 to 1723 only, but the Diaries of Supercargoes and Commissaries continue, with gaps, from 1725 to 1795.

The records of the factories and residencies, it should be understood, are not mere records made at Surat or Bombay of correspondence carried on with the out-stations, but are records made at the factories and residencies themselves. They consist mainly of diaries with a few inward and outward letter books and other records. The records of the Commercial Residency Northward consist mainly of books of accounts. The series are in almost all cases exceedingly incomplete. Many of the factories were founded long before the dates of their extant records, and there are numerous gaps in the series.

For an understanding of the Surat and Bombay records it is necessary first to refer to the principal dates in the early history of these settlements. The student is referred to my work on Anglo-Portuguese Negotiations, and to *Calendars of Court Minutes* and *English Factories in India.*

The Factory of Surat was established in 1612 and was made the seat of a Presidency, with subordinate agencies at Gogo, Ahmedabad, and Cambay and subsequently at Gombroon (Bandar Abbas), Basrah and Broach.

Bombay was ceded in 1661 and actually delivered in 1665 and transferred to the E.I. Co. in 1669. The seat of the Western Presidency was transferred from Surat to Bombay in 1685-87. The Surat records continue for more than a century thereafter, but merely as the records of a factory. From the earliest times down to the year 1820, when a system differing little from the present day system of records was introduced, we find the most important form of record in Surat, Bombay, and the larger factories, to consist of what are known as diaries. The nature of these varied to some extent at different periods, their history being as follows:

The Diaries

In 1661 the London E.I. Co. when appointing Sir George Oxenden to be president at Surat, directed him to send them yearly 'a diary of all actions and passages remarkable that shall happen from time to time . . . with your Books of Consultations, Copies of Records, Letters, etc.'

By consultation is meant the meeting of the President and his Council. The word was also used to denote the minutes of such meetings.

The Surat 'Diaries' extant in Bombay commence in 1660. In the period previous to the transfer of the administration to Bombay, they consist almost exclusively of records of consultations. These set forth the matters arising at a meeting of the Council, with the decisions taken thereupon and in some cases a careful statement of reasons for the decisions. The proceedings purport to be signed by the President and members of his Council. In addition there are outward letters and a few other documents.

In the early eighteenth century, however, the Surat consultations are found to have assumed to some extent the form of diaries. Two or more dates with the events or proceedings belonging to each are found in the same Consultation, the whole being contained between a single heading of the names of those 'present' and a single set of signatures. At the same time the Consultations become to a greater extent a chronicle of events with copies of correspondence received and issued. Such correspondence is usually interpolated in the midst of a so-called 'consultation'. The Surat Diaries have in fact changed from minutes of Council meetings to what is, in the main, a station log-book and correspondence book, although discussions and resolutions passed in consultation between the Chief and his Council are still found here and there.

The Bombay Castle Diaries preserved in Bombay commence in 1720 only. They have at first much in common with the early eighteenth century Surat Diaries. Between the dates of the consultations which at that time were usually held weekly, events of interest were chronicled, and papers received were briefly summarised. The consultations purport to have been signed regularly. Letters dealt with and accounts passed at the meetings are often transcribed in full after the record of the consultation. In later years the chronicling of events in the settlement ceased, correspondence increased and the practice of interpolating long reports into the record of a consultation prevailed.

From the year 1755 the business of the Presidency was divided between two departments—the Secret and Political and the Public Department. From 1799 onwards other Departments appear in rapid succession. Each Department kept separate Diaries. The result was that on many occasions the proceedings at a particular Consultation of the Governor and his Council could not be recorded all together as was done in the early Diaries. The Diary of each Department continued, however, to keep up in form the pretence of being a Minute Book of Consultations. Letters issued were entered with the heading, 'The following letter was forwarded'; letters received were headed, 'Read the following letter' with a definite date of reading; and the decisions of the Government were occasionally prefaced by the words 'ordered that'. The Diaries from 1731 onwards, with a few exceptions, contain annual alphabetical indexes compiled contemporaneously. The indexes to the earlier of the Diaries are somewhat defective, often giving only the places from which the letters are received, such as, 'Surat, letter from thence'. But more usually they state the subjects of the documents contained in the Diaries.

23

A system under which all the proceedings and correspondence of Government had to be forced into the shape of minutes of imaginary meetings was an essentially artificial one, and in 1820 the Diary system was dropped, and a different system introduced.

OTHER FORMS OF RECORD

These are

1. Minute Books.
2. Despatches from the Court of Directors (known as the ' Honourable Court's Inwards ').
3. Despatches to the Court of Directors (known as the ' Honourable Court's Outwards ').
4. Inward or Letter Books.
5. Outward or Order Books.

The originals of the contents of later Diaries are to be found in a series of Minute Books, of which there is a very defective series in the Record Office commencing from 1756. These contain the same matter as the Diaries without, however, actual copies of correspondence, which was copied into the Diaries. The place where a letter or other document was intended to be copied is marked by the word ' Enter ', preceded by the necessary reference to the Document. The Minute Books bear the actual signatures of the Governor and his Council. But it is clear from their form that they were not written during a meeting. They are in the same formal shape as the Diaries and must have required time for their preparation after the meeting (if any), at which the orders embodied in them were passed.

An Inward or ' Letter ' Book contains copies of such letters, memoranda, etc. received as are not copied in full in the Diary. From 1786 letters are systematically in full in the Diaries, and the Inward Letter Books are discontinued. The Secretariat-General Outward Letter Books similarly disappear after 1787 ; but the Outward Letter Books of the several departments commencing in 1766 continue to a much later date. It appears that letters to out-stations were not usually entered in the latter till after 1787 when the Secretariat-General Outward Letter Books were discontinued.

The systematic preservation of records at Bombay would appear to have commenced about 1730. Both the Surat and Bombay records prior to that date are in a fragmentary state.

The earliest of all records preserved in the Record Office is the Outward Letter Book of the Surat Factory, then the principal seat of the East India Company's trade in India, for the year 1630. A gap of fifteen years then occurs, after which the Surat Inward and Outward Letter Books are extant from 1646 to 1701 and 1720 respectively. The Surat Diaries extend from 1600 to 1809. The rest of the old Surat records have been long since lost or destroyed. The dates of the earliest records—1630 and 1646— appear to be purely fortuitous. In the Surat records in the India Office there occur gaps similar to but not contemporaneous with those in the records extant at Bombay, Surat Diaries being found for the period 1660-66, after which there is a further gap of three years.

The Bombay records prior to 1720 consist of Outward and Inward Letter Books, despatches from the Court of Directors, correspondence and judicial records in Portuguese (classed under Foreign Idioms) and certain ' MS. Selections '. Diaries are not forthcoming, although there is in the India Office a long series of Bombay Diaries from 1670 onwards. Between

1720, which is the date of the first Bombay Diary here preserved, and 1733 there are only three years' Diaries in the Record Office. From the latter date, however, till 1820 there is a complete series.

Other records of this period deserving of notice are the Foreign Idioms Record, i.e., records in foreign European languages, and 'Foreign Powers', i.e., selections from correspondence and treaties with foreign states, Indian and European, but principally Indian.

PRESS LISTS

'Press lists' of the oldest records in Bombay Record Office have been drawn up in pursuance of instructions received in 1891 from the Secretary of State. This was in conformity with the treatment of records in the English Record Office which consisted in the preparation of :

(i) A press list giving a complete list of documents with some indication of their dates and contents.

(ii) A calendar giving a précis of nearly every document of importance or a reference to some publication where it might be found.

Four Press Lists have been issued containing entries of documents of the following years :

1. 1646-1700.	3. 1720-40.
2. 1701-19.	4. 1741-60.

The preparation of press lists has, however, now been discontinued under the orders of the Government of India who observed that the progress made in India had not been satisfactory and that the system of press-listing and calendering had been characterized as defective by the Royal Commission on the Public Records of England and Wales, press lists being considered too meagre and calendering a process too slow and elaborate for application to modern State Papers. The preparation of descriptive handbooks of all Record Offices was at the same time decided upon.

THE BOMBAY PRESIDENCY RECORDS, DOWN TO 1820.

I. Secretariat (All Departments)

OUTWARDS OR ORDER BOOKS

Twenty-five volumes (Nos 4-28), 1677-1787. No. 4 opens with 1676-77. Then comes a gap to 1686. And from April, 1687 there is a gap till May, 1694. The contents from 15 July, 1686 to 28 April, 1687 are given twice. No. 5 (1694-96) is partly a diary of proceedings and partly a letter book. It contains some inward as well as many outward letters. The outward letters are mostly to the Chief and Council at Surat. There are in this volume copies of letters from the Honourable Court of Directors addressed to 'our Lieutenant General President and Council of Surat', 'our Agent and Council in Persia'. These are of 1693-94. In No. 6 (1697-99) there seems to be confusion in the dates of some letters in 1699.

No. 7 (1699-1704) contains letters to the Honourable Court from Sir J. Gayer and Council (1699-1700), also letters from the Deputy Governor and Council at Bombay to Sir J. Gayer and Council at Surat, and various letters and orders by the Deputy Governor and Council.

Here comes a gap till 1738. There is another gap from December, 1741 to November, 1743.

No. 10 (1746) is much injured.

INWARDS OR LETTER BOOKS

Thirty-seven volumes (Nos. 1-37), 1646-1786. The letters to Government are not distributed in departments as the outward letters are, but are collected together under the head of Secretariat Letter Books.

These volumes contain letters from different factories and stations to the Government of Bombay and occasional letters from Fort William and Fort St. George. There are also copies of letters to the Honourable Court of Directors from different factories, etc., sent through the Government of Bombay. There are a good many gaps in the years embraced by these volumes. There are gaps from 11 October, 1647 to November, 1656; from 2 October, 1657 to August, 1696; from 4 February, 1697 to December, 1700; from 16 July, 1701 to January, 1740.

The first half of No. 1 belongs rather to Surat than to the Bombay Secretariat. It opens with a letter from the celebrated Mr. Gabriel Boughton and consists mainly of letters to the Chief and Council at Surat from different factories and stations, as Ahmedabad, Gombroon, Matchlepatam, Acheen, Mocha, Agra, Fort St. George, etc.

The latter half contains a letter to the Governor (then at Bombay) from the Council at Surat, letters to the Governor in Council from various stations, and letters to the Deputy Governor in Council at Bombay (the Worshipful John Burmston), from different stations and also from the Governor, Sir John Gayer, then at Surat.

This volume is illegible in many parts.

No. 6 is composed, in part, of translations of native letters.

No. 8 consists, in parts, of letters to 'the Agent for Persia in Council'.

This part does not belong to the Bombay Secretariat.

MINUTE BOOKS

Seven volumes (Nos. 1-7) 1756-91. There are no Minute Books for 1757, 1758, 1760-64, 1766, and 1769-76.

No. 1 (1756-68) is on bad paper, is ill written, much injured, and can scarcely be made out. No. 2 is nearly illegible.

HONOURABLE COURT'S INWARDS

Twenty-two volumes (Nos. 1-22) of the enclosures to the letters from the Court in all the departments from the beginning to the end of 1827, bound separate as arranged according to subjects by Major Candy.

HONOURABLE COURT'S OUTWARDS

Two volumes (Nos. 1 and 2) 1796, 1802. There are letters from the Honourable Mr. J. Duncan, Governor of Bombay, to the Court of Directors.

II. Public or General Department

The Public Department became the General Department from the end of 1820, before which all the other Departments had been separated from it.

DIARIES

Four hundred and forty-nine volumes (Nos. 1-439; Nos. 28, 29, 31, 66, 77, 185, 194, 259, 281, and 423 being double), from January, 1720 to December, 1820.

The Diaries for 1721-23, 1725-27, 1729, 1730, 1732 are wanting.   There is no index to some of the early numbers.   No. 1 has some leaves wanting.

No. 6 is an exceptional volume.   It is the record of the proceedings (June to October, 1733) of a committee appointed to procure for the Honourable Company the Suddies Tanka, i.e., a Jaghire for protecting the trade of Surat and this coast.

OUTWARD OR ORDER BOOKS

One hundred and ninety-two volumes (Nos. 1-187;   No. 8 being triple and Nos. 14, 78, and 137 double), 1766 to end of 1820.

It appears that as there was a series of Secretariat Letter Books up to 1787, the letters to out-stations were not usually entered in the Order Books, but from that date they were so entered.

MINUTE BOOKS

Fifty-five volumes (Nos. 1-55), 1790 to end of 1820.

HONOURABLE COURT'S INWARDS

Or Despatches from the Honourable Court to Government

Twenty-four volumes (Nos. 1-24), 1681 to end of 1820.   There is a gap from June, 1685 to December, 1742.   A general index by Major Candy of all the letters from the Court of Directors received in all Departments is with these volumes.

HONOURABLE COURT'S DUPLICATE INWARDS

Or Duplicate copies of Despatches from the Honourable Court

Twenty volumes (Nos. 1-20), 1743-1821.

HONOURABLE COURT'S OUTWARDS

Or Despatches from Government to the Honourable Court

Forty-four volumes (Nos. 1-44), 1746-1820.   There are no letters for 1782.

HONOURABLE COURT'S ROUGH OUTWARDS

Or Drafts of Despatches from Government to the Honourable Court

There are no duplicates for 1799, 1804 and 1819.   I have left out records that deal mainly with the eighteenth and nineteenth centuries, such as Political and Secret Department Diaries, etc.

EXTERNAL AND INTERNAL COMMERCE

Twenty volumes (Nos. 1-19 and 2 double), 1802 to end of 1820.   These volumes are exclusive of Honourable Company's investments.   They contain general abstract statements of the value of merchandise, prices current, rates of freight, etc.

No. 7 of 1806-7, a duplicate of No. 6, was lent to the Secretary of State in 1906.

No. 17 of 1817-18 is not forthcoming.

EXTERNAL COMMERCE

Six volumes (Nos. 1-6), 1816-22.

ABSTRACTS OF PAY AND ALLOWANCES OF THE SECRETARIAT

Eight volumes (Nos. 1-8), 1801-20.

Records in Portuguese

Six volumes (Nos. 1-6), 1717-41.   Filed under ' Foreign Idioms '.

No. 1 (1717-23) contains original letters in Portuguese and translations into that language of letters addressed to rajahs, chiefs and other persons.

No. 2 (1729-41) is of the same character.

No. 3 (1722-41) contains letters to and from the authorities at Goa and Bombay, and other places.

No. 4 (1714-17) contains a register of cases in a court, with the decisions.

No. 5 (1722) contains a register of lands and taxes.

No. 6 (1819) contains an avocation of judicial proceedings held at Goa regarding a claim against Capt. Cameron, Master of a brig.

For records in Dutch see under Surat records, p. 361.

Foreign Powers

Extracted selections of proceedings connected with foreign powers and copies of treaties.   Fifty-nine volumes (Nos. 1-53, and Nos. 1, 44, 47 and 50 being double, and No. 19 triple).

Nos. 5, 8, 9, 24, 32, 40, 42 and 51 have been sent to Malabar.

No. 15 is an incomplete copy of No. 14.

No. 19 is a mere duplicate of No. 18.

No. 19A is a detailed narrative of various affairs concerning the Sunsthan of Kuree.   The narrative is by Mulhar Row Guicowal, but in a parallel column are observations by Colonel Walker, the Resident at Baroda.

No. 19B is a mere duplicate of No. 19A.

No. 44 contains, besides the translation of an extract of a Persian manuscript regarding the origin of the tribes of the Hindoos etc., a paper on Berar affairs by Mr. Colebrook ; a paper on the Southern Mahratta Sudars by Sir John Malcolm ; a translation of a Marathi manuscript history of Balaji Baji Rao and his successors ; an account of Shahji and Sivaji ; and other papers.

No. 53 is a duplicate of No. 52 and contains more matter, having an appendix which is wanting in No. 52.

Selections

There is a large collection of volumes upon a great variety of subjects. Some of the volumes are compilations, i.e., the original papers of subjects brought before Government.   The number of volumes is 184.

No. 33A is a duplicate of No. 33 (Mr. Elphinstone's Report on the Deccan).

No. 38 is a duplicate of No. 37 (Mr. Duncan's Minute on the revision and reduction of Civil Establishments), with the Court's resolution on it.

No. 54A is a duplicate of No. 54 (Mr. Warden's Report on the land tenures of Bombay).

No. 61 contains all the papers on the subject from the beginning, viz., the complaint which led to the commission for the investigation of charges preferred by Zamorin Rajah, through the Sevade Karrigar Shamnath, against Messrs. Stevens, Senior and Agnew at Malabar ; the report of the commissioners ; and the minutes of Government on the report.   From this volume Nos. 52 and 53 of ' Foreign Powers ' are extracts.   No. 52 contains the report without its appendix and No. 53 contains the report with the appendix.

Mr. Warden's Selections

This is a series of selections called, *Schedules compiled by Mr. Warden* chiefly from the diaries of the Secret and Political Departments. Nineteen volumes (Nos. 1-19), 1754-1821.

There are three other sets of volumes:

1. 'Extracts of Inward and Outward correspondence of Government with subordinate settlements, etc.' Three volumes, 1768-80.
2. 'Schedules compiled by Mr. Duncan from the Diaries etc.' Three volumes, 1603-10.
3. 'Extracts from the Surat Records regarding commercial concerns.' One volume, 1787-93.

FACTORY AND RESIDENCY RECORDS

Surat Presidency and Factory

Diaries

Under the head of ' Diaries ' there is a great mass of records connected with Surat. Some are entered in one book and some in another; but they are here brought together. They consist of:

(*a*) Diaries of the Proceedings of the Chief in Council ;
(*b*) Diaries of Judicial and Juridical proceedings ;
(*c*) Diaries of the Commercial Board ;
(*d*) Letty (i.e., Customs) Records.

Diaries of the Chief in Council

Of these there are two sets, viz., 48 volumes (1-48) from 1659 to end of 1809 ; 98 volumes (611-708) from 1719 to 1799.

In the years covered by the first set there are many gaps, some of which are supplied by Diaries in the second set. Most of the other volumes of the second set are duplicates of volumes in the first set. There is also a good deal of repetition in different volumes, i.e., the same matter has been entered twice. Nos. 1 to 4 (1659-1704) are interesting volumes. Nos. 1 and 2 are nearly illegible in several places and are incomplete.

No. 1 (1659-96) is the Diary of Surat when supreme. The letters copied into it were copied very irregularly as regards their dates.

No. 2 (1699-1707) is a volume of the New (and rival) Company's affairs. There is a good deal in it of the disputes of the two companies and of the seizure and imprisonment of Sir John and Lady Gayer. The last complete letter in it is from Sir N. Waite, protesting his poverty and integrity and asking to be allowed to retire as Governor.

No. 3 (1701-4) is a volume of the Old Company's affairs.

No. 4 (1702-4) belongs to the New Company, Sir N. Waite being ' Public Minister and Consul General '. This volume, too, is incomplete.

After No. 4 there is a great gap in the years, but it is partly supplied by volumes of the second set. No. 5 (1740-42) is under quite a different order of things. It is the Diary of the Chief and his Council as subordinate to the Governor and Council at Bombay.

In No. 6 the Diary of 1742-44 is twice entered.

In No. 7 the Diary for six months of 1744-45 is given twice and that of the other six months given three times. The Diary of August and September, 1745 is given twice.

In No. 8 the Diary of August-December, 1746, is given twice. The Diary of 1747-48 is wanting here, but is No. 637. In this volume is a proclamation of the Dutch prohibiting other nations from trading within certain limits of the East Coast.

The Diary of 1749-50 is wanting.

No. 9 (1751-52) contains first a Diary of the Chief in Council. Then the Factory was suspended, a Committee appointed, a Diary of whose proceedings is given. The Committee having settled affairs, the Factory was re-opened, and its Diary follows. In December, 1751 the Committee engaged in a fight with a ' Moratta vessel thinking it to belong to Tolajee Angria '. They request the Bombay Government to ' reconcile this unfortunate mistake with the Moratta Government, who certainly may thank themselves for it '.

No. 11 is a duplicate of No. 10.

In No. 13 (1756-57) some parts of the Diary are given twice.

Of No. 14 some leaves at the beginning are wanting. No. 15 (1759-61) records the appointment of the Chief to be Governor of the Moguls' Castle and Fleet. The Governor of Bombay is styled ' President of the Coast of India, Persia and Arabia, Governor and Commander in Chief of His Majesty's Castle and Island of Bombay '. In No. 16 (1761-63) the style of the Chief is altered. He is styled ' Chief of all affairs of the British Nation ' (instead of ' the Honourable East India Company '), etc., etc.

No Diary from 31 July, 1768 to 31 December, 1771.

No Diary from January, 1778 to 31 December, 1779.

No. 22 (1781) records the taking of the Dutch Factory.

No. 31 (1793-94) records a dispute among the Bamans about an idol.

No. 32 (1795) records a riot in Surat on 6 September and an investigation of it.

No. 36 records a good deal of matter relative to the dispute about the idol between Maharanee Wowjee and Gokulnathjee. Governor Duncan proposes to the Maharanee that she should empower him to decide the matter and sends her a deed to that effect to sign.

No. 39 (1800) is a Diary of the Governor, Mr Duncan's, proceedings at Surat.

No. 40 (21 June to 10 July, 1800). From 15 May the English assumed the government of Surat. The Chiefship was abolished on 2 July and the Chief made Lieutenant-Governor. The treaty with the Nawab was dated 13 May.

No Diary for 1801.

No. 42 (1 February to 9 September, 1803) contains two Diaries ; (1) of the Lieutenant-Governor, (2) of the Agent to Government.

In consequence of arrangements proposed by General Wellesley, the office of Lieutenant Governor was abolished, and the head civilian was made Agent to Government.

No. 45 (1805). The Diary in this from 1 January to 29 September, is the ' Diary of the Agent to Government ', but from that date, it is the ' Diary of the Chief ' as formerly.

The other sets of Diaries have been left out, as they deal with a considerably later period.

OUTWARDS OR ORDER BOOKS

Four volumes (Nos. 1, 1A, 2, 3), 1630-1700. These volumes contain but few letters compared with the number of years they cover. The gaps are many and long.

Many of the letters are illegible or nearly so. In some places the letters have been copied without any regard to the order of their dates.

INWARDS OR LETTER BOOKS

One volume (No. 39), 1646-1701. This volume is illegible in several parts. Several of the letters in it are addressed to Bombay. In one letter from Fort William (Calcutta) Sir John Gayer is thus addressed: ' To His Excellency Sir John Gayer, Knight, Commissary General and Chief Governor of India for affairs of the Honorable English East India Company, and Council.'

RECORDS IN DUTCH

Thirty volumes (Nos. 1-30), filed under ' Foreign Idioms '. Volumes 1-29 contain miscellaneous formal deeds of the Dutch at Surat, with a few petitions and letters.

Volume 30 contains a long memorandum written by Seuff, the Dutch Governor at Surat, from 1763 to 1768, for the information of his successor. It describes the events during his governorship and the political and commercial situation at Surat. The volume also contains papers of a law suit at Cochin.

These volumes were examined at Madras in 1895-98 at the request of the Government of the Netherlands (G.D. vols. 117 of 1895, and 85 of 1898). A summary in English of their contents is given at p. 169 of G.D. vol. 115 of 1907. The numbering of the volumes in the summary is different from that which the volumes now bear. Vol. 19 in the summary is No. 30.

Nos. 1-29 were received by the Record Office from Surat in 1907. No. 30 was already in the Record Office when the Inventory was prepared in 1833.

There is also a volume of ' extracts from the Surat records regarding commercial concerns', 1787-93, among the Bombay Records.

Broach Factory

DIARIES

Fourteen volumes (Nos. 257-270) from 1772 to 1783.

No. 257 is a Diary of the expedition against Broach in 1772.

No. 258 (Nov., 1772 to Feb., 1773) is a Diary of the Military and Marine Commanders appointed as a committee to settle affairs after the capture of the place, which committee was afterwards enlarged.

No. 259 begins the regular Diary of the Resident and Factors (afterwards styled Chief and Factors) subordinate to the Chief and Council at Surat.

In No. 261 is entered the Diary of a committee sent from Bombay to enquire into the charges against the Chief ; after which comes the usual Diary.

No. 262 contains a duplicate of the Diary of the above committee.

No. 263 is the Diary of another committee.

No. 268 is a duplicate of No. 267 (Diary of 1781). See also No. 662 under Surat, Diaries of the Chief in Council.

Commercial Residency Northward

DIARIES

The Records of the Northern Factories and Residencies (Surat, Broach, Cambay and Kathiawar), entered under the head of Diaries, consist of 132 volumes (Nos. 457-587, No. 581 being double), ranging from 1774 to 1835. Gaps of several years occur in these records.

Ledgers, two volumes (Nos. 470, 471) from 1774 to 1819.

Diaries of the Commercial Board, seventeen volumes (Nos. 472-488), from 1795 to 1818.

Outward Letter Books, twenty-one volumes (Nos. 489-509) from 1724 to 1829; and four volumes (Nos. 588-591), from 1830 to 1835.

Inward Letter Books, twenty-one volumes (Nos. 510-530), from 1797 to 1830; three volumes (Nos. 592-594), from 1831 to 1835. Cash Accounts, eight volumes (Nos. 531-538), from 1802 to 1835. Besides these there are Cashbooks, two volumes (Nos. 595 and 596), from 1826 to 1831.

Warehouse Accounts and Investment Books, six volumes (Nos. 539-544) from 1763 to 1821.

Invoice Books, three volumes (Nos. 545, 546, 547), from 1764 to 1832.

Accounts Current, three volumes (Nos. 548, 549, 550) from 1724 to 1829.

Receipt and Expenditure of Cash, ten volumes (Nos. 551-560), from 1791 to 1819.

Warehouse Report Books, six volumes (Nos. 564-569), from 1796 to 1834.

Estimate Books (of probable receipts and issues), one volume (No. 576) from 1803 to 1820.

Annual Accounts, one volume (No. 571), from 1827 to 1834. Waste Book or Daily Deliveries, one volume (No. 572) from 1804 to 1810.

Abstracts of Pay or Pension and Bill Books, two volumes (Nos. 573 and 574), from 1810 to 1833.

In No. 578 Consignment Books of cotton are bound up with Minute Books of the Commercial Board.

In No. 580 extracts from despatches from the Honourable Court of Directors are bound up with a register of the daily attendance of the Establishment and with a register of the receipts of cloth.

No. 579 contains Order or Outward Letter Books from 1785 to 1804.

Nos. 584, 585, 586, 587 are entitled 'Loose sheets of several kinds of books'. They are not so well arranged. Some belong to various heads that have already occurred, and should be put with them.

In No. 457, the Journal of 1774-75 is given twice.

In Nos. 474, 475, 476, the Diaries of 1797, 1798, 1799, 1800 and 1801 are repeated, in an abbreviated way, i.e., the letters are only referred to, not entered.

In No. 478 the Diary of 1804 from 1 January to 11 April is given twice.

In No. 480 the Diary of 1806 is given twice.

In No. 481 the Diary of 1807 is given twice.

No. 484 contains a duplicate of No. 482, and a duplicate in an abbreviated form of a part of No. 485, the Diary of 1809.

In No. 486 a Letter Book of 1806 is bound up with the Diary.
Some of the Outward Letter Books contain Inward Letters as well.

Caranja Residency

DIARIES

Twenty-eight volumes (Nos. 767-794), from 1775 to 1802.   Nos. 771, 772 and 781 are not forthcoming.

Bellapore Factory

DIARIES

One volume (No. 285) from October, 1780 to December, 1781.

Tanna Factory

DIARIES

Proceedings of Chief and Council

Fifty-seven volumes (Nos. 710-766) from 1776 to 1817.   No Diary for 1788, 1789, 1790.
No. 710 is imperfect.
No. 711 is a duplicate of 710, and being perfect should be kept instead of it.
No. 714 is a duplicate of 713 (Diary of 1781), and is in better order than it.
No. 717 is a duplicate of No. 716 (Diary of 1783), and is better than it.
No. 720 is a duplicate of No. 719 (Diary of 1786).
No. 722 is a duplicate of No. 721 (Diary of 1787).
Nos. 723, 724, 729, are Letter Books.
Nos. 733 and 734 are Consultation Volumes for 1799-1800.
Nos. 735-750 are Inward Diaries or Letter Books for 1801-17.
Nos. 751-766 are Outward Diaries or Letter Books for 1801-17.

Proceedings of Court of Sessions

One volume (No. 308), 1801 and 1802.

OUTWARDS OR ORDER BOOKS

One volume (No. 32) 1780-82 and 1793-98.   There is a gap of ten years from 1782-1793.   Some of the Tanna 'Diaries' are Outward Letter Books.

INWARDS OR LETTER BOOKS

One volume (No. 12), 1781-92.

Callian Residency

DIARIES

One volume (No. 286) from 23 February to 27 December, 1781.

Poona Residency

OUTWARDS OR ORDER BOOKS

Thirty-four volumes (Nos. 39-69), from 1798 to 1819.   These volumes contain the correspondence of Colonel Close and the Honourable Mountstuart Elphinstone, Residents at the Court of the Peshwa at Poona ; the latter was subsequently Sole Commissioner of the Deccan.   The contents are both letters to them and letters from them.   The collection is usually called Poona Correspondence.

INWARDS OR ORDER BOOKS

Sixty-one volumes (Nos. 44, 104), from 1812 to 1819.   This collection consists partly of letters addressed directly by various high officials to the Honourable Mountstuart Elphinstone and partly of copies of despatches by high officials to high officials communicated to Mr. Elphinstone by the writers or by the Governors-General.   These high officials comprehend the Governor-General, the Residents at Hyderabad and Lucknow, Sir John Malcolm, Sir Thomas Munro, General Doveton, etc., etc.   It is an important collection.

Raree Residency

Subordinate to Fort Augustus

DIARIES

One volume (No. 213), 29 April to 4 October, 1766.   This is a record of operations against a 'Kam Savant Bouneello' (Khem Sawant Bhonsla).

Below are given brief extracts from some of the above records :

ARABIA

Bombay Secretariat.
Outward Letters,
1699-1702.

Letter from Mr. John Gayer giving an account of a battle between the Arabs and the Portuguese.

BANTAM

Bantam Factory In-
ward Letter Book,
1677.

Letter from George White, Company's agent at Siam, to Robert Parker, Company's agent at Bantam, giving an account of the coins and products of the country and the state of affairs there.

Bantam Factory In-
ward Letter Book,
I, 1680.

Letter from the Company's agent at Siam to the Company's agent at Bantam stating that the presents sent to the King of Siam by the Company were received in a damaged condition, and therefore were not approved of by the King and requesting that certain curiosities should speedily be sent as presents for the King in order that he may be kindly disposed towards the Honourable Company's affairs.

*Bantam Factory In-
ward Letter Book,
1, 1681.*

Letter from the Company's agent at Tonquin to the agent at Bantam, giving an account of the state of affairs there and stating that the Company has suffered a great loss on account of a fight between the Moors and the King of that place ; an account of the fight.

*Bantam Factory In-
ward Letter Book,
1, 1682.*

Letter from the Company's agent at Siam to the Company's agent at Bantam stating that the Company's factory is burnt down and that they have sustained a great loss, adding that the King of the place showed a great sympathy towards the Company at their misfortune and had ordered men to rebuild the factory.

GOVERNORS

*Surat Factory
Diary, 1, 1667.*

Lucas, Gervase, President and Governor : His estimate of the total revenue of Bombay for the year 1667.

*Surat Factory
Diary, 1667.*

Garey, Henry, President and Governor : Writes to Mr. Gerald Aungier to say that he should not give any more passes to anyone for the secure navigation of Jounks, but that he should direct to him all persons desiring such passes. A merchant of Calicut, offering to bring the Company's goods therefrom to Surat as they were exposed to the danger of falling into the hands of the Zamorin or the Dutch, the Hon'ble Captain Henry Garey accepts his offer.

*Surat Factory
Diary, 1668.*

His letter to the President at Surat stating that 1000 Rupees should be sent to supply the King's garrison; letter to him from the President at Surat giving information of the receipt of a Royal Charter from England for taking the Island of Bombay in the possession of the Hon'ble East India Company.

*Surat Factory
Diary, 1, 1671.*

Aungier, Gerald, President and Governor : Letter to him from Sir Thomas Rolt, Agent at Persia regarding the success which attended him in the Persian court; he makes certain important proposals regarding the improvement of the Island of Bombay in respect to its commerce, military, navy, etc., his letter regarding Sergeant Adderton's success against the Mallahars ; further letter from him stating the amount of salary to be given for the place of a judge; his letter to the Chief and Council at

Bombay stating that they should show the Dutch only usual civilities and that they must not be informed of the true strength and force of the island ; he and his Council make it a standing order that whatever thieves are condemned in court shall be kept in chains and at constant work in Bombay.   He receives a letter confirming the news of the death of Shivaji ; he sends some proposals for retrenching great expenses of the Island of Bombay and of the garrison thereof ; his letter to the Chief and Council at Bombay advising them not to allow the Siddi's fleet to winter in Bombay or in the neighbourhood thereof ; letter from him stating that Shivaji's army under Moro Pandi took Pindoli from the Raja of Ramnagar ; his letter to the Company stating that the news of the death of Shivaji is much doubted although some say that he was poisoned by his barber ; that a bold bravado was made by the Portuguese against the English ; he further writes to the Company that Shivaji has given a passport for the security of the English factory at Dangone and that he thinks it good to re-settle the factory ; he insists upon a retrenchment of the Company's militia ; his letter to the Chief and Council at Bombay, stating that Shivaji's attacks upon Surat are becoming more and more frequent ; news of his death from Surat.

Surat   Factory
Diary, 1695-96.

Gayer, John, President and Governor : writes a letter stating that the Portuguese are preparing for some great design against Muscat and that Muttahar is threatening them with war.

Surat   Factory
Diary, 1699.

He writes to the Company that the Island of Bombay is capable of having docks and makes suggestions for the great trade that can be enjoyed there.

INDEX

24

25